War *Like The* Thunderbolt

Atlanta, Georgia
View from Confederate fort, east of Peachtree street

War Like The ThunderBOLT

The Battle and Burning of Atlanta

Russell S. Bonds

WESTHOLME
Yardley

Frontispiece: View from a Confederate fort, east of Peachtree Street, looking towards Atlanta, Georgia. Photograph by George N. Barnard. (*Library of Congress*)

First Westholme Paperback September 2010

Copyright © 2009 Russell S. Bonds
Maps © 2009 Westholme Publishing, LLC
Maps by Russell S. Bonds and Tracy Dungan

All rights reserved under International and Pan-American Copyright Conventions. No part of this book may be reproduced in any form or by any electronic or mechanical means, including information storage and retrieval systems, without permission in writing from the publisher, except by a reviewer who may quote brief passages in a review.

Westholme Publishing, LLC
904 Edgewood Road
Yardley, Pennsylvania 19067
Visit our Web site at www.westholmepublishing.com

First Printing
10 9 8 7 6 5 4 3 2 1

ISBN: 978-1-59416-127-8

Also available as an e-Book.

Printed in the United States of America.

for *Jill*,
with all my heart

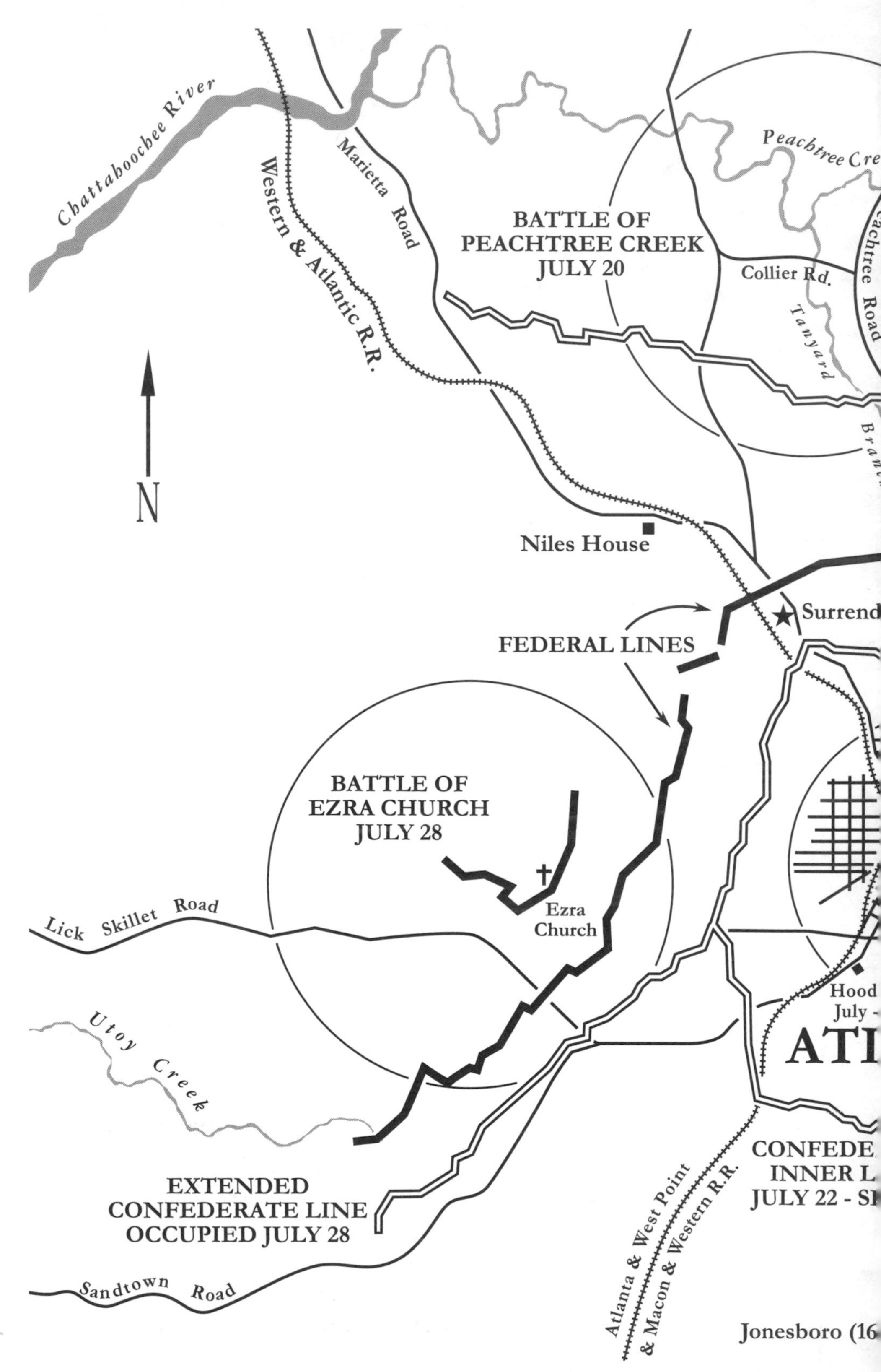
Chattahoochee River
Western & Atlantic R.R.
Marietta Road
BATTLE OF
PEACHTREE CREEK
JULY 20
Collier Rd.
Tanyard
N
Niles House
FEDERAL LINES
BATTLE OF
EZRA CHURCH
JULY 28
Ezra
Church
Lick Skillet Road
Utoy Creek
EXTENDED
CONFEDERATE LINE
OCCUPIED JULY 28
Sandtown Road
Atlanta & West Point
& Macon & Western R.R.

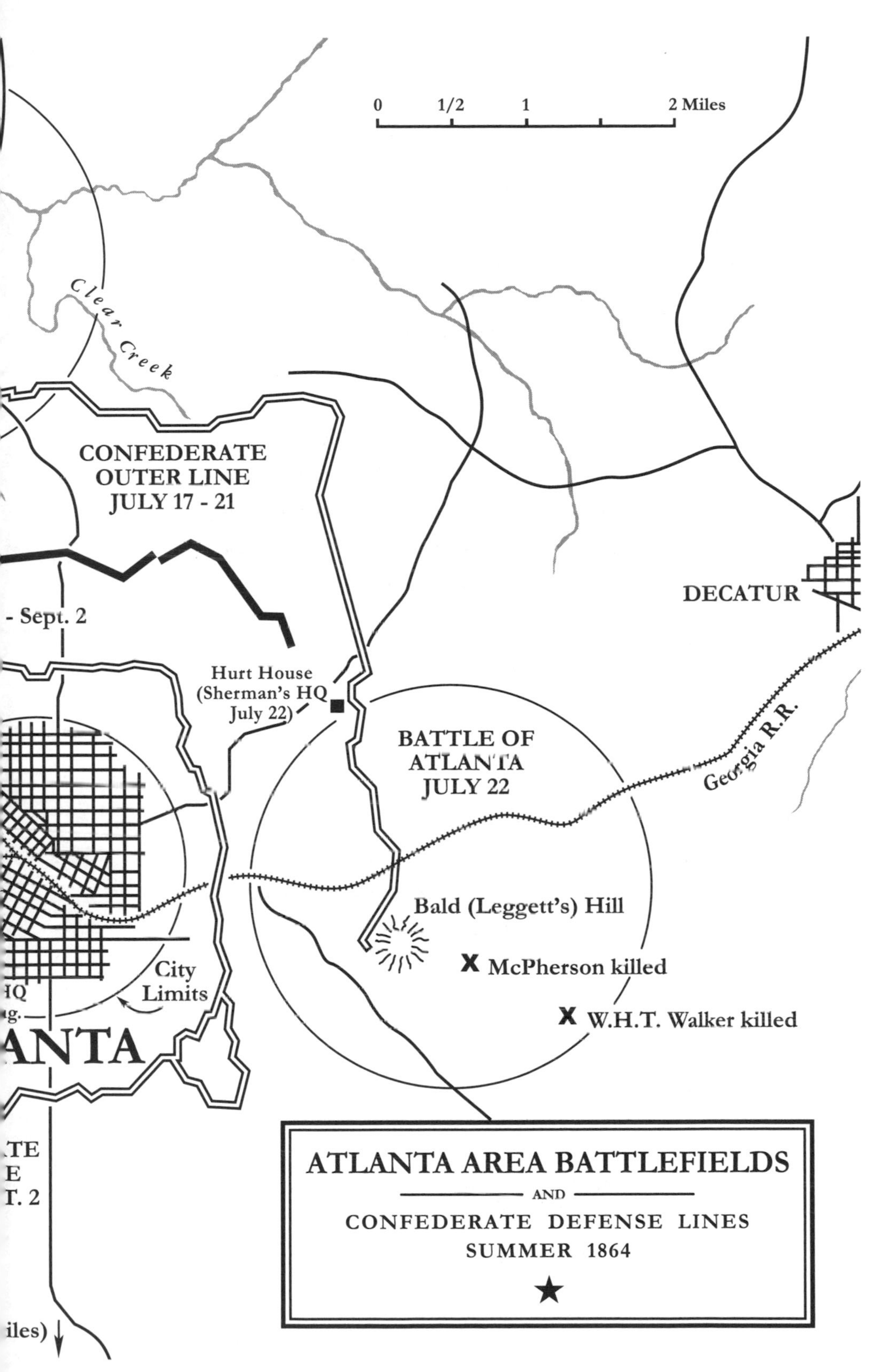

ATLANTA AREA BATTLEFIELDS
AND
CONFEDERATE DEFENSE LINES
SUMMER 1864
★

In Peace, there is a beautiful harmony in all the departments of Life—they all fit together like the Chinese puzzle: but in war, all is ajar. Nothing fits and it is the struggle between the Stronger & Weaker, and the latter, however it may appear to the better feelings of our nation, must kick the beam.

To make war we must & will harden our hearts.

Therefore when Preachers clamor, & the Sanitaries wail, don't give in, but Know that war, like the thunderbolt follows its laws, and turns not aside even if the beautiful, the virtuous and charitable stand in its path.

—Major General William Tecumseh Sherman
Letter to Charles A. Dana, Assistant Secretary of War, April 21, 1864

C'est un principe de guerre, que lorsqu'on peut se servir de la foudre, il la faut préférer au canon. ("It is a principle of war that when you can use the thunderbolt, you must prefer it to the cannon"; sometimes translated as: "Use the thunderbolt when you can.")

—Napoleon

Contents

Maps

A publicity still of the filming of the burning of Atlanta scene from the motion picture *Gone with the Wind*, Culver City, California, December 10, 1938. (*Author*)

PREFACE

"The Greatest Event of the War"

On the evening of December 10, 1938, the city of Atlanta burned again, this time on a studio backlot in Culver City, California. Twice before had the town gone up in flames, set afire first by evacuating Confederates and then by conquering Yankees in the bloody autumn of 1864. Now, seventy-four years later, the Gate City of the South would again be purged by fire, not for its secessionist sins or its military importance, but for the entertainment of the moviegoing public. The contrived inferno marked the start of filming of the epic motion picture *Gone with the Wind*—now regarded as a classic but then considered a risky proposition indeed.

For producer David O. Selznick—only thirty-six, and already a near legend for a slate of films that included *Anna Karenina*, *The Adventures of Tom Sawyer*, *Little Lord Fauntleroy*, and *A Star Is Born*—the road to principal photography had been long and treacherous, both from a technical and a financial perspective. In July 1936 he had paid $50,000, an unprecedented sum in those days, for the rights to Margaret Mitchell's Pulitzer Prize-winning novel and had since been widely criticized in the entertainment press and among the Hollywood elite. Not only had he overpaid, they said, but he had acquired a property that many considered unfilmable, and one that would have little appeal to modern audiences in any event. "Forget it, Louis," rival producer Irving Thalberg told studio boss Louis B. Mayer as MGM dropped out of the bidding war over the book. "No Civil War picture ever made a nickel."[1]

In the two and a half years since, "Selznick's Folly," as the project came to be known, increasingly seemed like a bad investment well on its way to becoming a box-office disaster. Foremost among the producer's burdens was that of expectation. Mitchell's novel had sold no less than a million copies in its first month in print and quickly developed a huge and outspoken following that persists even today. The enthusiasm for the story and its characters made *Gone with the Wind* one of the most anticipated pictures ever—a Gallup poll in May 1939 reported that no less than 56,500,000 people, or 65 percent of the moviegoing public, wanted to see the film—resulting in tremendous pressure on the filmmakers, who faced a sea of troubles. For one thing, editing the 1,037-page book down to a workable script was a monstrous challenge, and casting of the fifty speaking roles and 2,400 extras was an even greater chore. Although there was a groundswell of popular support for Clark Gable to play the part of the dashing blockade runner Rhett Butler, the lead role of Scarlett O'Hara had not yet been cast, despite a two-year worldwide search and more than ninety individual screen tests of actresses from Joan Crawford to Jean Arthur to Lana Turner. The casting controversy was the most visible of the almost insurmountable difficulties on the project, from financing problems to contractual snags with rival studios to endless script revisions by a parade of unsatisfied and unsatisfying writers. As filming was set to begin, Selznick sent a note to the film's then-director George Cukor reporting the latest bad news: "I am informed by MGM that Clark Gable refuses under any circumstances to have any kind of a Southern accent."[2]

Despite his woes and worries, here Selznick was at last, bundled against the chill and standing atop a twenty-foot platform that had been erected for him to watch with family and friends the filming of what he hoped would be the movie's greatest scene. Some among the production team had pushed for the pivotal scene of the burning of Atlanta to be filmed in miniature, using model buildings and railroad cars, but production manager Raymond Klune had the inspired idea of instead setting fire to old sets on the backlot of the RKO Studios. Some thirty acres of sets from other films, including the massive jungle gates from *King Kong* and the temple of Jerusalem from *King of Kings*, were to be burned, simulating the conflagration in Atlanta while clearing the way for other sets—including the mansion at Tara and Atlanta's streets, storefronts, and railroad depot—to be built for subsequent filming. The old sets wore period costumes, their false fronts themselves given false fronts to look like wartime factories and warehouses, the railyard before them littered with wagons and boxcars—the latter meticulously painted with appropriate acronyms ("W&ARR," "A&WPRR") to portray the rolling stock of the doomed city's hometown railroad companies. An ingenious system of piping was designed and constructed to distribute kerosene, coal oil, and water behind the facades to ignite or suppress the fire, as need be, while backlit stunt doubles for Rhett and Scarlett raced to and fro in a buckboard wagon. The setup was, as one Hollywood scribe later put it, "an arsonist's dream." Firefighters from several local departments leaned against their engines, smoking and waiting for the faux-apocalypse to begin. Seven three-strip Technicolor cameras—every Technicolor camera in the world at the time—had been placed in carefully determined positions and were ready to roll. The camera crews had rehearsed shooting the scene for most of the previous week, for retakes were not an option.

As it turned out, none were needed. The flames shot hundreds of feet into the air, illuminating the sky for miles around, and the massive wooden sets collapsed magnificently, right on cue, pulled down by an out-of-sight tractor when the moment was right. Selznick, the firelight reflecting brightly in the lenses of his round-rimmed glasses, had a look of unmistakable satisfaction on his face. He turned to Klune and offered an apology for ever doubting his plan for firing the old sets. Indeed, the fire was so terrifying and authentic that worried Angelenos living nearby—who were, after all, just five weeks removed from another scare brought on by CBS Radio's October broadcast of Orson Welles' radio play *The War of the Worlds*—jammed the phone lines, thinking the city itself was being consumed by fire. A number of skittish residents of Culver City rushed to their Hudsons and Packards and Oldsmobiles and quite literally took to the hills.

Selznick, much to his amusement, would hear a few days later of this local hysteria he had brought about; but for now, he shared his own reaction to the scene: "You have missed a great thrill," he wired later that night to John Hay "Jock" Whitney, his chief investor and chairman of the board of Selznick International Productions. "Gone with the Wind has been started. Shot key fire scenes at eight-twenty tonight, and judging by how they looked to the eye they are going to be sensational." Sensational they were indeed, so much so that moviegoers late the following year would push back in their dark cardinal plush seats, flinching from the flames and swearing to one another that they could feel the heat on their faces. But on this night, the pyrotechnics were mere prologue, and the evening's most legendary moment was still to come.[3]

As the sets crackled and crumbled to ashes and the firemen, unleashed with their hoses at last, amused themselves by shooting down embers rising like luminous quail flushed from the inferno, Selznick's brother Myron—late as usual and tipsy to boot—arrived on the lot with his dinner guests in tow. A journalist would describe Myron, accurately if a bit uncharitably, as "dumpy and belligerent," being "several inches shorter, three years older, and much richer" than his brother David. He had, by a combination of personal affability and financial ruthlessness—and one particularly advantageous family relation—established himself as the premier agent in Hollywood, with an inherited contempt for small sums of money. "'Peanuts' to Myron is anything under $5,000 a week," the reporter said. What was more, Myron knew the business and the value of a well-staged scene, in front of or behind the camera, and he had carefully planned his entrance. All heads turned when the agent called out to his kid brother, "Hey, genius—here's your Scarlett O'Hara." Selznick faced about and met for the first time twenty-five-year-old Vivien Leigh, escorted by her paramour and future husband Laurence Olivier, then in town to play Heathcliff in *Wuthering Heights*. She wore a mink coat that fell open to reveal her mannequin-slender waist, and her green eyes glittered brightly in the failing firelight. The producer later wrote that he knew at a glance that Leigh was perfect to play Scarlett, appearance-wise, and she would later prove, as he said, that she could "act the part right down to the ground" as well. Indeed, she reportedly auditioned that same night, reading Scarlett's lines until nearly midnight as the future Sir Laurence read the parts of Rhett, Ashley Wilkes, and even Mammy. Asked if she was too tired to read lines at such a late hour, Leigh replied, so the story goes: "Darling, I'm *never* tired."[4]

And the rest, as they say, is history, though *Gone with the Wind* would soon be—and is still today—much criticized for the history it depicts. Although Margaret Mitchell researched her novel meticulously, and both the book and (less so) the film weave the true-life military progress of the Civil War's Atlanta Campaign with the fictional events of the story, *Gone with the Wind* was chastised by historical nitpickers and, as time passed, blasted for its moonlight-and-magnolias portrayal of a society built on the blood and sweat of African slavery. W. E. B. Du Bois, for one, sought to give the epic the back of his hand, dismissing it as "conventional provincialism about which Negroes need not get excited." Later commentators were starker in their criticism—columnist Leonard Pitts, Jr., for example, referred to *Gone with the Wind* as "a romance set in Auschwitz." But neither crystal hindsight nor the retrospective prism of latter-day racial sensibilities were required to carp about the film and its subject matter. Complaints and protests rolled in from the outset and continued throughout all stages of production, worrying over perceived slights and insults in a film that had not yet been released. Southerners fretted that their heroes would be miscast, or the glory of the Old South unfairly portrayed; while Northerners complained of a story where the Yankees were rampaging villains.

David Selznick was certainly aware of the widespread grousing about sectional bias and historical inaccuracies, but decided in the end that he frankly didn't give a damn. "Most of the complaints that have come to us from various patriotic organizations are based on an alleged distortion of history by us to the detriment of the Northern troops," Selznick wrote in a memo to Jock Whitney. "We have not only followed Miss Mitchell, but we have also been careful to have each of our historical facts checked thoroughly by a historian," he wrote. "Further, we have actually toned down considerably Miss Mitchell's portrait of the depredations of the invaders." Selznick directed his historical consultant, the well-regarded artist and Atlanta historian Wilbur G. Kurtz, to compile a detailed response to the various charges of inaccuracy, which was never mailed or published. In the end, Selznick thought that the best way to deal with these criticisms was to "simply ignore them." And so he did.[5]

Gone with the Wind premiered at Loew's Grand Theatre on Peachtree Street in Atlanta almost exactly one year later, on December 15, 1939. The film had cost $4.25 million to make, the most expensive picture ever at that time, including one apocryphal line item: a rumored $5,000 fine reportedly paid to Hays Office censors for the climactic use of the word "damn." For the opening, which Jimmy Carter would later recall as "the biggest event to happen in the South in my lifetime," the city of Atlanta staged a grand three-day festival, which was glorious and well-attended yet not without controversy. Hattie McDaniel, who would win an Academy Award for her portrayal of Mammy, was informed by civic leaders that she would not be able to participate in the festivities or attend the premiere itself—unless she sat in the "Colored" section of the theater. Attempting to avoid an embarrassing scene, she sent a letter to Selznick declining to attend. Clark Gable was reportedly furious at this and threatened to boycott the premiere, though Ms. McDaniel later convinced him to go. The Old South prejudices depicted in the film were sadly being played out in fact, more than seventy-five years after Emancipation. Still, hidden among the glitz and chaos of the weekend were signs of progress for Atlanta, and for America. In honor of the occasion, a sixty-voice choir from Ebenezer Baptist Church, dressed as slaves and standing on choral risers made up to look like the front steps of Tara, performed several Negro spirituals for the all-white audience. Among the singers was a round-faced boy, son of the church's minister, whom family and friends called "M.L."—ten-year-old Martin Luther King, Jr.[6]

After its premiere, *Gone with the Wind* became a worldwide smash and in time a beloved classic, its success mirroring that of the novel—which has sold more than 30 million copies—more than any other book in history, it was once said, except the Holy Bible. Selznick's Folly went on to win eight Academy Awards, including Best Picture, and in the decades that followed would be seen by more than 300 million people. And the central, iconic scene of this most popular of all American movies was the first scene filmed—that of the destruction of the city of Atlanta.

Gone with the Wind "almost certainly has been the single most powerful influence on American perceptions of the Civil War," historian Gary Gallagher recently wrote. In studying the impact of film and art on the memory and historiography of the war, Gallagher concludes that "more people have formed perceptions about the Civil War from watching

Gone with the Wind than from reading all the books written by historians since Selznick's blockbuster debuted in 1939." For a new book on the capture of Atlanta, then, *Gone with the Wind* seems like a sensible, or perhaps even an essential, place to start. "The siege of Atlanta was splendid and the fire that followed magnificently pyrotechnic," critic Frank Nugent wrote in his December 1939 review of the film in the *New York Times*, but "we felt cheated, so ungrateful are we, when the battles outside Atlanta were dismissed in a subtitle and Sherman's march to the sea was summed up in a montage shot."

This book, though admittedly lacking in Southern belles and Twelve Oaks barbecues, aspires to provide a history of the battles Selznick "dismissed in a subtitle"—the true story of the struggle for Atlanta, and the fate that then befell the city and its citizens. The book's title is taken from a letter that Union commander William Tecumseh Sherman wrote in April 1864, on the eve of his campaign into north Georgia. "Know that war, like the thunderbolt follows its laws," he said, "and turns not aside even if the beautiful, the virtuous and charitable stand in its path." The volatile Ohioan would deploy the same meteorological metaphor again in the months to come, one that seemed to capture both the fury and the inevitability of the fate in store for the deep South and her citizens. "War is cruelty, and you cannot refine it," he would write later that year in what would become perhaps his most famous letter, in which he told the mayor of Atlanta: "You might as well appeal against the thunder-storm as against these terrible hardships of war. They are inevitable, and the only way the people of Atlanta can hope once more to live in peace and quiet at home, is to stop the war, which can only be done by admitting that it began in error and is perpetuated in pride."

Although the book's subtitle refers to "the battle" of Atlanta—a name that would come to identify the July 22 engagement around Bald Hill, east of the city—the surrender of the city was in fact preceded by a series of battles during the midsummer of 1864, from Peachtree Creek in mid-July through Jonesboro at the end of August, clashes which historian Bruce Catton would call "as desperate and at times as costly as any battles which American armies have ever fought." Similarly, there was more than one burning of Atlanta: one in early September 1864, when the Confederates blew up railroad cars and ammunition stores before fleeing the city—it is this "burning" that is depicted in *Gone with the Wind*—and a second, more infamous conflagration set by the Federals in November, as Sherman's forces departed to the east and south on his famous March to the Sea.

Other works have covered this ground, historically speaking—though none recently and none in the manner I propose. Most daunting is Albert Castel's 1992 book *Decision in the West: The Atlanta Campaign of 1864*, which won the Lincoln Prize and is widely and rightly considered one of the best books ever written on any Civil War campaign. Perhaps because of Castel's fine volume—a "category-killer," one reader called it—there has been comparatively little written on the Atlanta Campaign in the two decades since, though both Stephen Davis and Richard McMurry have published excellent books focused on the strategy and command relationships, and they and other scholars have contributed biographies, articles, dissertations, and other valuable studies to the literature. Despite this body of work, the story of the capture of Atlanta is in many ways yet to be told. For example, not a single modern book-length narrative or military analysis exists on the Battles of Peachtree Creek, Ezra Church, or Jonesboro—or on the Battle of Atlanta itself, for that matter.

Likewise, the burning of Atlanta, though seared in the national (or at least the Southern) consciousness and dramatized on film and in print from *Gone with the Wind* to E. L. Doctorow's recent novel *The March*, is in many Civil War histories either an afterthought or a prologue—presented briefly as the inevitable dénouement of Union occupation, or as the natural kickoff for the subsequent March to the Sea. Though "the burning of Atlanta" is frequently used as a historical or literary reference, appearing in modern culture everywhere from sports pages to country, folk, bluegrass, and heavy metal lyrics, there has been little serious consideration of the city's ordeal—the five-week artillery bombardment, the expulsion of its civilian population, and the devastating fire that followed. Eyewitness accounts and later analyses, such as they are, disagree widely about the extent of the devastation—from "the whole city" destroyed to "only" one-third or one-fifth of the homes and buildings, or "only" the central business district. Few historians have attempted to unravel these disparities.[7]

War Like the Thunderbolt presents the story of the battles for and the fall of the city of Atlanta—the culmination of a campaign that secured the reelection of Abraham Lincoln, sealed the fate of the Southern Confederacy, and set a precedent for military campaigns and war on civilian infrastructure that endures today. The book focuses on the fighting at the gates of Atlanta in the summer and fall of 1864—roughly, the last ten miles of Sherman's hundred-mile campaign. It is not intended as a tactical study, a campaign analysis, or a command critique, though there may be bits of each in its pages. The roster of battles herein includes the major engagements around the city: Peachtree Creek, Bald Hill, Ezra Church, and Jonesboro. But it is not just a book about battles, but about the officers and men who fought, and the people and the land caught in the maelstrom. I have endeavored to include a wide variety of first-hand perspectives, not only military (from generals to privates) but also civilian: politicians, merchants, reporters, local militia, refugees, and residents of Atlanta—free and slave, black and white, men, women, and children. Along the way, inevitably, the book will touch on and attempt to shed light on a number of enduring controversies: the firing of Confederate General Joseph Johnston in favor of the younger and more aggressive General John Bell Hood; the propriety of Sherman's thirty-seven-day artillery bombardment of Atlanta and his subsequent deportation of its residents; and the cause and extent of the destruction of the city by fire.

"The Atlanta Campaign was one of the most dramatic and decisive episodes of the Civil War," Castel wrote, "comprising military operations carried out on a grand scale across a spectacular landscape, pitting some of the war's best (and worst) generals against one another, involving multitudes of civilians as well as soldiers, and producing results that if they did not constitute a critical event in the struggle between the North and the South, definitely assured that this struggle would turn out as it did." Indeed, Northerners viewed the fall of the Gate City as a pivotal moment, both politically and militarily. New York lawyer George Templeton Strong, recording the glorious news in his diary, called the capture of Atlanta "the greatest event of the war." For if the Battle of Gettysburg in July 1863 had been the South's "High Water Mark," then Atlanta was, in many ways, its last chance. "The capture of

Atlanta was the first great death-blow to the rebel cause," a *New York Herald* correspondent wrote. "Thenceforward, they began to lose hope, and consequently became disintegrated."

This grim reality, and the fiery end to the campaign and the city itself, would for many Southerners in the after-years give the story an air of tragedy and romance of what might have been, and what was gone forever. Among these impressionable minds was a young Atlanta newspaper scribbler named "Peggy" Mitchell, who listened to tall tales from grizzled Confederate veterans as a girl, and was ten years old before she realized that the South had lost the war.

In the end, like Mitchell's novel, the saga of 1864 Atlanta is a portrait of a clash of civilizations—not just of the Union and the Confederacy, but the death throes of the Old South, and the birth of the thriving New.[8]

War *Like The* Thunderbolt

William Tecumseh Sherman. "Uncle Billy," or, sometimes, "Crazy Bill." (*David Wynn Vaughan*)

CHAPTER ONE

Crazy Bill

The Banks of the Chattahoochee, July 1864

For once, Major General William Tecumseh Sherman was not only relaxed, he was enjoying himself capitally. His uniform strewn on the bank nearby, the perpetually high-strung forty-four-year-old Ohioan stood chest-deep in the Chattahoochee River near Vinings Station, just eight miles north of the city of Atlanta. Around him, for miles up and downstream, Federal soldiers by the hundreds thronged the shallows like congregants at a revival baptism. The river was far from sparkling, its waters full of silted clay washed from the fortifications dug along its banks, its color that of forgotten coffee left to sit with too much cream—but no one seemed to mind. The Northerners splashed and whooped, rinsed their dusty uniforms, or scrubbed off ticks and chiggers, grateful for the respite from sixty days of constant campaigning and the wet flannel heat of a Georgia July. Along the banks, soldiers rested in the shade, playing cards and gathering green apples, blackberries, and "everything that ever was eaten by anti-cannibals." An Illinois lieutenant had good luck with the fishing rod, catching "46 fish and a turtle" in a single afternoon. Those out of sight from their officers at times arranged an informal armistice with Confederate pickets across the way, wading to the middle to talk with the Rebels and trade newspapers, pocketknives, canteens, and tobacco.

For his part, Sherman smoked and soaked, chatting amiably with a teamster who sat astride a mule on the red clay bank, basking in the sun and no doubt the satisfaction of having brought his army safely across the river. His thatch of wet hair was spiked and darkened from auburn to chestnut, his face coppered and worn like an old penny, his body—"tall and slender," according to a reporter, with "good muscle added to absolute leanness, not thinness"—almost scar-white. Intractable as always and reluctant to admit any weakness, Sherman refused to acknowledge, despite the teamster's needling, that the water was the least bit cold.

Up on the bank, an Illinois drummer boy admired the red-headed commander. "Gosh," he said to a comrade, "I'd follow Sherman to hell."

His companion was cynical and unimpressed. "We may have to before it's over," he said.[1]

Its name derived from a Creek Indian word meaning "painted rock," the Chattahoochee ribbons across the state on a northeast-to-southwest diagonal, draped like a wrinkled sash from Georgia's shoulder to her hip, winding from its trickling headwaters high in the Blue Ridge Mountains to the fall line at Columbus and the Alabama border. The Federals, whose armies were named for the nation's great rivers—the Potomac, the Ohio, the Cumberland, the Tennessee—were unimpressed by the "small and muddy" southern stream now bubbling around their ankles. The Chattahoochee "floats no wealth on its bosom; it rolls not amid enchanting and unbroken loveliness, or overwhelming sublimity," an Ohio correspondent wrote. "It is distinguished by nothing magnificent, either in itself or the scenery amid which it wanders." The crossing, too, seemed somewhat lacking, come to think of it—no battle had been fought along the riverside in recent days, and not a single Federal soldier had been lost in gaining the southeastern bank. Sherman's languorous dip in the Chattahoochee would pale in comparison to the martial glory of the other famous river crossings in the annals of military history—Caesar at the Rubicon, say, or Washington crossing the Delaware, or the Rhine River crossing at Remagen during World War II.

But the lack of picturesque scenery and military drama at the river crossing did not diminish its significance in the course of the campaign. The Chattahoochee, whether a grand, thundering river or modest Indian creek, was the last major geographic barrier between the Federal army and the city of Atlanta. Unable to defend the fords and ferries, upstream and down, the Confederate Army of Tennessee had pulled back across the river on July 9, burning the wagon road bridges and the railroad span behind them. Sherman had dispatched his cavalry in pursuit, and while he awaited their return, he accumulated supplies, ordered that additional crossings be set at fords and pontoons, and allowed his men some much-needed rest. In nine weeks, Sherman's army had advanced almost ninety miles from his jumpoff point in the north Georgia mountains near Dalton, and now stood at the gates of the Gate City. Finishing his cigar, he sloshed out of the dishwater river and got back to work, spreading his maps and reports to plan the final phase of what arguably had become the most important campaign of the American Civil War.[2]

The series of battles and marches that would come to be known as the Atlanta Campaign had opened in early May, far to the north, as Sherman's 100,000-man army stepped off on the advance from the vicinity of Chattanooga, hoping to flush and then destroy the Confederate Army of Tennessee, then 54,000 strong, under the command of General Joseph E. Johnston. Sherman's instructions, received from his friend and superior Lieutenant General U. S. Grant the month before, were "to move against Johnston's army, to break it up, and to get into the interior of the enemy's country as far as you can, inflicting all the damage you can against their war resources." The campaign that ensued was primarily one of maneuver rather than a direct clash of arms, so much so that writers down the years would consider the contest almost balletic, as Sherman repeatedly shifted westward to flank Johnston out of formidable defensive positions, only to have him reintrench and prepare to meet another attack. "The ball has opened," the *Memphis Appeal*'s correspondent wired to his newspaper's office in Atlanta on May 8.[3]

Sherman's Military Division of the Mississippi included three veteran Union armies of unequal size, each led by a distinguished commander and each boasting a distinct military reputation. The Army of the

Cumberland, 60,000 strong, was commanded by Virginia-born Major General George H. Thomas, famous by now as the "Rock of Chickamauga," though his admiring soldiers called him "Old Pap." He was, like his army, slow but powerful, over six feet tall and 220 pounds—a solid mass who, as one soldier said, "gradually expands upon you, as a mountain which you approach." The 25,000-man Army of the Tennessee, formerly Sherman's own command, was led by Major General James B. McPherson, a 35-year-old West Point graduate and a personal favorite of Grant and Sherman's. "I expected something to happen to Grant and me," Sherman later wrote, "either the Rebels or the newspapers would kill us both, and I looked to McPherson as the man to follow us and finish the war." McPherson had started out as a lieutenant colonel, Grant's chief engineer back at Fort Henry in February 1862, and his army's regimental flags were crowded with the stitched names of victories from Fort Donelson to Vicksburg to Meridian. Last and in Sherman's eyes least was the Army of the Ohio, in reality a 13,000-man corps, commanded by Major General John M. Schofield, a New Yorker and former professor of natural philosophy (known today as physics), balding, pudgy and wrinkled at age 33, who nonetheless had somehow managed to avoid a derisive nickname. Sherman didn't think much of the bookish Schofield, but he and his undersized force would prove their worth in the weeks to come.

In all, Sherman's veteran soldiers, most of them rough-edged Midwestern farmers back home, made up what one prominent military historian would call with breathless overstatement "quite literally the most impressive and deadly body in the history of armed conflict." Firsthand witnesses applied different and more realistic superlatives. A surgeon in Mississippi the year before, for example, had described Sherman's army as "the noisiest crowd of profane-swearing, dram-drinking, card-playing, song-singing, reckless, impudent daredevils in the world."[4]

In order to advance, the massive Federal army had to march against a skilled adversary through a region tailor-made for the defensive. If the rocky heights of the battlefield at Gettysburg, laid out on the map, famously conformed to the shape of a fishhook, then the north Georgia wilderness resembled the contents of a tackle box spilled entire across

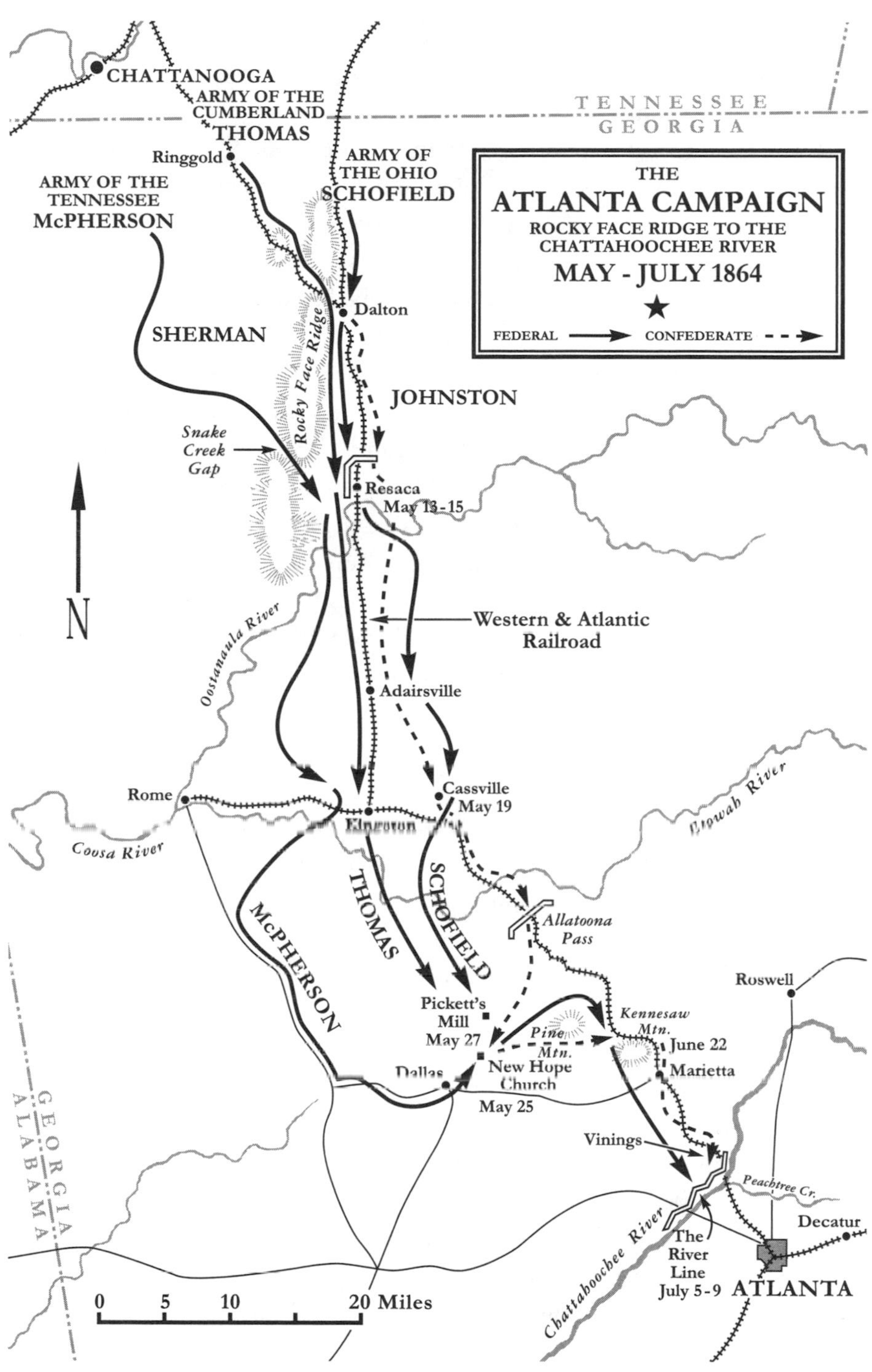
THE
ATLANTA CAMPAIGN
ROCKY FACE RIDGE TO THE
CHATTAHOOCHEE RIVER
MAY - JULY 1864
FEDERAL
CONFEDERATE
CHATTANOOGA
ARMY OF THE
CUMBERLAND
THOMAS
TENNESSEE
GEORGIA
Ringgold
ARMY OF THE OHIO
SCHOFIELD
ARMY OF THE
TENNESSEE
McPHERSON
SHERMAN
Dalton
Rocky Face Ridge
JOHNSTON
Snake
Creek
Gap
Resaca
May 13-15
N
Western & Atlantic
Railroad
Oostanaula River
Adairsville
Rome
Cassville
May 19
Etowah River
Coosa River
McPHERSON
THOMAS
SCHOFIELD
Allatoona
Pass
Roswell
Pickett's
Mill
May 27
Kennesaw
Mtn.
June 22
Pine
Mtn.
New Hope
Church
May 25
Marietta
Vinings
Peachtree Cr.
Decatur
GEORGIA
ALABAMA
0 5 10 20 Miles
Chattahoochee River
The
River
Line
July 5-9
ATLANTA

the landscape—weights and knots, hooks and knolls, mountains, gaps, and gorges, snarled with underbrush and scarred by twisted lines of uncharted creeks and runs. "I think God Almighty might have made the world in four days if he had not ruffed it up so," an Illinois soldier wrote. The strategic maps of the region, unrolled and spread on camp tables in headquarters tents across north Georgia, seemed entirely insufficient to capture the terrain, limited as they were in two dimensions and uncluttered by the briar-choked woods that blanketed the northern half of this state that was in many ways still Indian country. Red dirt roads wound through the pines and poplars along ancient Cherokee trails, and the Western & Atlantic Railroad from Chattanooga to Atlanta twisted like a moccasin past place names like Red Bud and Pumpkin Vine Creek and Laughing Gal.[5]

Similar maps were reproduced in miniature above the fold on the front pages of Northern newspapers, pored over by anxious readers as they followed the progress of the early summer campaign. Yet these were inadequate as well to tell the story of the weeks of fighting in the Georgia wilderness which, for the soldiers involved, seemed far from the romantic "minuet" some historians would later describe. "A look at the map will give you a little idea of the country we are passing through," Major James Connelly wrote to his wife, "though it will fail to point out to you the fields that are being reddened by the blood of our soldiers, and the hundreds of little mounds that are rising by the wayside day by day, as if to mark the footprints of the God of War as he stalks along through this beautiful country." Brigadier General Alpheus Williams, a kind-hearted officer who at times snuck out from the lines to collect Georgia wildflowers to enclose in his letters home, described the "hard and wearisome campaign" to his daughters. "For more than a month we have been day and night literally under fire, and day and night the din of war has ceaselessly gone on. From our crossing of the Etowah, the Rebs have entrenched themselves every five miles. Driven from one line, they would fall back to another and each one seemed stronger than the last." A "big Indian war," Sherman called the scattered maneuvering and near-constant sniping and skirmishing. "One can't say it is getting monotonous, but it is certainly getting continuous," a lieutenant wrote of being under fire.[6]

Johnston, on the defensive with an outnumbered army and pressed repeatedly by an experienced and aggressive opponent, had in the eyes of some observers done quite well. He had given up ground deliberately, lengthening the Federals' tenuous supply line and trying to lure his impatient adversary into attacking him in prepared positions. Though Sherman for the most part avoided this by his repeated flanking maneuvers, as spring turned to summer Johnston inflicted more casualties than he suffered, providing tangible validation for his Fabian strategy. In May and June, Sherman lost 17,000 men killed, wounded, and missing; while Johnston's losses would amount to just over 14,000. Meanwhile, Johnston received substantial reinforcements when the Army of Mississippi—three divisions of infantry and one of cavalry under General Leonidas Polk—joined him and increased his aggregate strength to nearly 70,000 officers and men. Johnston was still outnumbered, to be sure, but the additions to his force gave him the largest standing army in the Confederacy, larger even than Robert E. Lee's Army of Northern Virginia—which was at the time holding firm in Virginia and inflicting casualties on Grant and Meade at a rate of nearly 2,000 killed and wounded per day.

Yet despite these additions and the advantage of the terrain, Johnston seemed to be doing little to halt the unstoppable blue flood southward. He had kept his army intact in the face of a superior foe—no small accomplishment—and he had bloodied and evaded Sherman, yes—but he had not stopped him, nor had he fought a single major battle to do so. Whatever the brilliance of individual tactical moves and however impressive his sidles were logistically, the fact remained that what Johnston had done since May 12 was retreat. His campaign to defend Georgia and destroy the Yankee invaders in fact seemed more like a regular southbound schedule on the state railroad, the catalog of minor engagements and abandoned earthworks stretching from Dalton to Resaca to Calhoun to Kingston to Cassville to Allatoona Pass. He pulled back first across the Oostanaula and then the Etowah River, without fighting a battle or contesting the Union crossing at either place. Southern journalists reporting the progress—or regress—of Johnston's campaign were reluctant to describe the gray commander's movements as a retreat. The backward steps of the Confederates were "retrograde movements," they insisted, or a sensible counter to the enemy's maneuvers, "improperly called a retreat by those who do not comprehend them." At Allatoona, Johnston dug in athwart the railroad and again hoped to lure his opponent into an ill-advised attack against a formidable natural position.[7]

Sherman knew better. Having been stationed in the Etowah region as a young lieutenant twenty years before, he was familiar with the forbidding terrain at Allatoona Pass and had no intention of having his infantry ground up in the steep walls of the 180-foot railroad cut. Carrying twenty days' rations in their haversacks, Sherman's troops gave up the southbound railroad and plunged into a wooded region one reporter called "the midnight corner of Georgia," breaking the rhythm of the "red clay minuet" in an effort to swing wide around Johnston's left. And it was here, in the briar-choked woods of Cherokee country, that the dancing metaphors failed and horrific clashes ensued at places like Pickett's Mill, Dallas, and New Hope Church, which soldiers called the "Hell Hole." But despite the tactical blundering and seventeen straight days of rain to open the month of June, the Federals kept coming. The bloody foray to New Hope and Dallas succeeded in turning Allatoona Pass, and Johnston again retreated south to a line anchored by the 800-foot camel hump of Kennesaw Mountain. "Johnston can fight or fall back as he pleases," Sherman complained. "The future is uncertain, but I will do all I can."

In mid-June, Sherman returned to his railroad supply line north of Marietta and then made what would in retrospect be considered his greatest blunder of the campaign. Bogged down by the June rains and frustrated by what he perceived as a lack of aggressive spirit among his subordinate commanders, Sherman ordered a direct assault on Rebel trenches just south of Kennesaw Mountain. The attack failed miserably and the Federals suffered 3,000 casualties, compared to just over 1,000 for the Confederates. Sherman was undaunted by the setback and apparently indifferent to the suffering of the soldiers in his charge. "I begin to regard the death and mangling of a couple of thousand men as a small affair, a kind of morning dash, and it may be well that we become so hardened," he wrote to his wife three days after Kennesaw. What was more, Sherman characteristically refused to admit any error.

"The assault I made was no mistake. I had to do it," he wrote to Washington. "The enemy, and our own army and officers, had settled down into the conviction that the assault of lines formed no part of my game, and the moment the enemy was found behind anything like a parapet, why everybody would deploy, throw up counter-works, and take it easy, leaving it to the 'Old Man' to turn the position." Despite the failure of the attack, he claimed that Johnston "has been much more cautious since, and gave ground more freely." And give ground the Southern commander did, retreating from the Kennesaw heights on the evening of July 2.[8]

"This campaign is coming down to a question of muscle and nerve," an Illinois soldier wrote on July 1, and though he was exhausted, he took quiet comfort in the thought that the Rebels were "a good deal worse off." Muscle the Confederates may have had, but nerve again seemed lacking, as Johnston pulled back into prepared fortifications with his back to the Chattahoochee River. This river line was the brainchild of Brigadier General Francis A. Shoup, who had the month before secured permission from Johnston to use impressed slave labor to construct a six-mile interconnected system of log redoubts. The thirty-six arrowhead-shaped forts, soon to be called "Shoupades," boasted clay-packed walls ten to twelve feet high and twelve feet thick, spaced at regular intervals and crowned with a parapet. Each fort covered its neighbor and could sweep the spaces before and between them with converging fields of artillery and rifle fire. Shoup's idea was that a single infantry corps, perhaps even a lone division, could hold this line, freeing the remainder of Johnston's army to sweep around and crush the flank of the advancing Union host. But the brigadier misjudged Johnston in thinking he would be so daring, and seemed blind to the possibility that the Confederates would be cooped up in their fortifications while Sherman swung wide to cross the Chattahoochee elsewhere and thus clear the last geographical hurdle before Atlanta.

On July 5, Sherman climbed a hill near Vinings Station to reconnoiter the Rebel position and saw for the first time the spires and smoking chimneys of Atlanta a few miles to the south. "Mine eyes have beheld the promised land!" a staff officer with him wrote home to his wife. "The 'domes and minarets and spires' of Atlanta are glittering in the sunlight before us, and only eight miles distant." As word spread through the ranks that the city was in sight, "such a cheer went up as must have been heard even in the entrenchments of the doomed city itself." An aide would remember Sherman "stepping nervously about, his eyes sparkling and his face aglow—casting a single glance at Atlanta, another at the River, and a dozen at the surrounding valley to see where he could best cross the River, how he best could flank them." The elation at seeing the city near at hand was tempered somewhat by the recognition that more stood between the Federals and Atlanta than mere distance. "*Geographically* speaking it is only 8 miles from us, but *militarily* it may be much further," General John W. Geary wrote to his wife back home in Pennsylvania. Even so, "the sight of Jerusalem could not have a more inspiring effect on the devoted pilgrim than the sight of Atlanta had on our troops," another officer would recall. "It seemed the long-wished-for goal, and all were eager to rush on."[9]

Curiously, the city of Atlanta itself had been neither Sherman's assignment nor his goal, at least not at first. There had been in his original instructions—to "move against Johnston's army, break it up"—something of an echo of the strategy in the war's Eastern Theater, where for three years Abraham Lincoln had insisted that his commanders consider General Lee's army, not the Confederate capital at Richmond, their true objective. Yet over the course of the campaign, Sherman had been frustrated with his inability to bring the cautious Johnston to bay for a decisive battle, and now that the city was in sight, he began to shift his focus from the destruction of the Confederate army to the isolation, reduction, and capture of Atlanta. "Formerly the Gate City had been no more than the anvil on which he intended to hammer the insurgent force to pieces," Shelby Foote wrote of Sherman's change of goals. "Now it became the end-all objective of his campaign. He would simply pound the anvil." This poetic description of the shift in Sherman's target is appealing enough, but it is also somewhat unfair. A great anvil the city may have been, at least at first, but there was and is no question that Atlanta was much more than that, both militarily and politically. Atlanta was the Gate City of the South, the railroad intersection and turntable of the Confederacy, home to arsenals and warehouses and hospitals and reinforcements, as well as the connecting point to men and matériel from all points of the Deep South. Its capture would seriously cripple the Confederate war effort from home front to front lines. "This place," Governor Joseph Brown lectured Jefferson Davis from Atlanta in late June, "is to the Confederacy almost as important as the heart is to the human body. We must hold it."[10]

But it was more than that, too. Sherman understood, in a way that his opponent Joe Johnston never did, the importance of the stronghold of Atlanta as a symbol of continued Confederate strength and resistance. Battles were risky and confusing, their outcomes often indecisive or misreported in the newspapers, and fighting itself held no romantic sway on the practical Sherman—"its glory is all moonshine," he would say later. But the fall of a key Southern city would be an undeniable and tangible sign of Federal progress. Atlanta's capture would signal to Northern voters, as they approached the 1864 presidential election, that the years of toil and campaigning and battles and bloodshed were continuing to pay off, and that the doom of the Confederacy was not a matter of if, but of simply how and when.

How and when was the question now, as well, as Sherman considered how to dislodge Johnston from his fortifications along the river. An assault was out of the question—Sherman had learned his lesson at Kennesaw—so he had Thomas's army hold its position in Johnston's front while Schofield and McPherson searched, upstream and down, for a suitable crossing. Having repeatedly outflanked the Confederate left, Sherman now planned to feign in that direction but swing around Johnston's right flank to cross the river far upstream—not unlike a boxer who uses a series of right jabs to set up a roundhouse left. On July 7, the underappreciated Schofield reported finding "a pretty good crossing"—a submerged fish dam near where Sope Creek emptied into the Chattahoochee. The next day, using the ruined dam and an improvised armada of pontoon boats, elements of Schofield's XXIII (23rd) Corps* crossed the rain-swollen river and scattered the surprised Confederates

*Federal Corps were identified by Roman numeral designations. For clarity and readability here, I will refer to these units initially by both their Roman and Arabic numeral designations (XXIII [23rd] Corps), and thereafter will use Arabic numerals only (23rd Corps).

on the opposite bank. At another point downstream on July 9, a detail of dismounted cavalrymen stripped naked except for their cartridge belts to wade across and charge through the briars to secure another lodgment on the far bank. "I'll be durned if this ain't baring our breasts to the foe for a fact," one soldier griped. Union cavalry crossed the river in force at Roswell that same day, and Sherman ordered reinforcements to take advantage of the bridges now being constructed at several points. With the Federals across the river and positioned on his flank, Johnston ordered an immediate withdrawal from the river line to a position south of Peachtree Creek, just four miles from Atlanta.[11]

Supplying more ammunition to the critics of his generalship, Johnston had again pulled back across a major river barrier without giving battle, and in doing so abandoned what Sherman called "the best line of field intrenchments I have ever seen." Perhaps with those fortifications in mind, the Northern commander later recorded his surprise at his opponent's inaction. "I have always thought Johnston neglected his opportunity there," he wrote, "for he had lain comparatively idle while we got control of both banks of the river above him." Despite this rare criticism, Sherman still had nothing but respect for the Southern commander. "No officer or soldier who ever served under me will question the generalship of Joseph E. Johnston," he said—and then proceeded to unravel the compliment entirely by adding: "His retreats were timely, in good order, and he left nothing behind." Others thought it much more than a missed opportunity. Looking back across the years and the eroding ruins of his unused forts, a despondent Francis Shoup would later write that the abandonment of the Chattahoochee River works "was, in my opinion, the final turning point in the fate of the Confederacy."[12]

"All is well," Sherman reported to General Henry W. Halleck in Washington on July 6. "I have now accumulated stores at Allatoona and Marietta both fortified and Garrisoned points. Have also three points at which to cross the Chattahoochie in my possession, and only await Genl. Stonemans return from a trip down the river to cross the army in force and move on Atlanta." His soldiers, too, were confident. "This army is so situated now as to prevent a junction of the armies of Lee and *Johnston*, and they must fight it out separately," one officer wrote. "If Grant can whip Lee, we can whip Johnston, and then Jeff Davis might as well 'shut up shop.' We are now out of the mountains, we have pushed the rebel army from its last mountain stronghold and it must now rely on good luck alone."[13]

The Confederates' luck seemed to be running out, and some predicted dark days for the city on the horizon. "We expect to have a hard fite at Atlanty for they are fortified strong there," a New York corporal wrote in a letter to his wife. "It is said to be a nice city, but it wont be when we get through with it." General Sherman couldn't have said it better himself.[14]

One wartime observer claimed he never laid eyes on W. T. Sherman without thinking of the risen Lazarus, a fitting comparison not only because of the general's ragged, cadaverous appearance—"angular and spare," a staff officer described him, "as if his superabundant energy had consumed his flesh"—but also for his recent biography, which told the tale of a man back from the dead. Perhaps no commander on the national scene had enjoyed a more dramatic resurrection of his reputation during the course of the war than Sherman. During his prewar career, he had referred to himself as a "dead cock in the pit," and the description again seemed apt in the fall of 1861, when he was relieved from his first command after suffering what modern observers would call a nervous breakdown. At a time when public opinion held that the rebellion would be crushed in a matter of weeks, Sherman, then a recently promoted and unproven brigadier, had insisted that 60,000 men would be needed to hold Kentucky and no less than 200,000 required to move southward into Tennessee. He had "no doubt," he said, that the Confederates planned "a simultaneous attack on St. Louis, Louisville, and Cincinnati." He seemed frightened, depressed, entirely overwhelmed. He rarely slept or ate, chain-smoked cigars, berated subordinates, and on one occasion threatened to hang a reporter as a spy. His penmanship—which was at its best a challenge to the reader—deteriorated to the point that his letters were almost illegible. In November, he was sent home to Lancaster, Ohio, in the care of his wife, dishonored and despondent to the point of contemplating suicide.[15]

"General William T. Sherman Insane," the headlines cried. The *Cincinnati Commercial* falsely reported that Sherman was "stark mad," that he issued nonsensical orders and urged retreat northward into Indiana, that he was having hallucinations. The paper later published a refutation from Sherman's foster brother Philemon Ewing and would eventually retract its accusations, but the damage was done. Newspapers across the country reprinted the *Commercial* report, and the libel spawned poisonous gossip in the lobbies and barrooms of Washington. Officials up to and including Secretary of War Simon Cameron pronounced Sherman "luny," "stampeded," "unbalanced," "gone in the head." Those who had seen him in person were troubled by his rattled demeanor and "broken down appearance," but most unsettling were his dire predictions of what would be required to subdue the Rebels. "The conclusion was irresistible," one Washington insider wrote, "that either Sherman was crazy or that we were up against a war of whose magnitude we had just no conception whatever." True or not, fair or not, the charges of mental imbalance seemed to be a professional blow from which no military man could recover.[16]

The harsh treatment he received from the newspapers prompted a vigorous counteroffensive from his well-connected family and friends, chief among them his brother, Senator John Sherman, his foster father, former Secretary of the Treasury and Senator Thomas Ewing, and his wife, Ellen Ewing Sherman—who lobbied President Abraham Lincoln personally on her husband's behalf. Sherman, though despairing at the ignominy he had brought upon his family, acknowledged his error in overestimating the enemy's strength in Kentucky and expressed no confidence in his ability to prove himself. "I do not think that I can again be entrusted with a command," he admitted in a letter to John. He seemed strangely nonplussed by the substance of the charges themselves—after all, as he wrote to Ewing, "In these times tis hard to Say who are sane and who insane." Sherman was returned to duty in a matter of weeks, if somewhat carefully: he was first sent west to an innocuous post supervising a camp of instruction near St. Louis and then given a new, out-of-the-way command in February 1862 at Paducah, in western Kentucky. There, presumably, he would languish under an undistinguished department commander by the name of Grant, who was dogged by rumors of drunkenness and seemed to have a future as dubious as his reputation.[17]

Instead, Sherman joined Ulysses S. Grant just in time to bask in the reflected glow of his recent success in securing the unconditional surrenders that made him famous, first at Fort Henry and then at nearby Fort Donelson. Two months later came Shiloh, the bloodiest battle in American history to that point, and there Sherman's resurrection began. Though surprised by the Rebel attack on the morning of April 6, 1862, Sherman held fast during the fight and led his men with jittery aplomb, suffering a minor wound in the left hand and having three horses shot out from under him. Helping to avert disaster on the first day of the battle, Sherman's division took part in the counterattack on the second day that drove the Confederates from the field. Amidst exploding shells and whizzing bullets, Sherman at last seemed calm—so indifferent to the dangers of enemy fire that one biographer would discern "a suicidal element" to his behavior. "All around him were excited orderlies and officers," an aide would recall, "but though his face was besmeared with powder and blood, battle seemed to have cooled his unusually hot nerves."[18]

"It is the unanimous opinion here that Brig. Gen. W. T. Sherman saved the fortune of the day on the 6th instant, and contributed largely to the glorious victory on the 7th," Major General Henry W. Halleck wrote after arriving on the field. Sherman's performance under fire earned him a promotion to major general of volunteers and a chorus of praise from newspapers which, four months before, had branded him a lunatic. Sherman still hated reporters but now developed a fondness for headlines, instructing Ellen henceforth to "clip out all good articles and paste them in the Scrap book." What was more, the Confederate attack and the horrific casualties suffered on both sides served to validate his "crazy" predictions of the year before. "That single battle had given me new life," he wrote in his memoirs, "and now I was in high feather."[19]

Over the next eighteen months, the Union Army of the Tennessee won a string of triumphs, and along the way Sherman emerged as Grant's most trusted lieutenant. Chief among these successes was the capture of Vicksburg in July 1863—a victory that for Sherman would soon be clouded by personal tragedy. In the weeks after the capture of the Mississippi stronghold, Sherman invited his family to join him in camp along the Big Black River. Ellen arrived in August with the four oldest of their six children—Minnie, Lizzie, Tommy, and nine-year-old Willy, the general's namesake, pride and joy, whom he called the "child on whose future I had based all the Ambition I ever had." A precocious, fearless lad fascinated with his father's profession, Willy was a favorite of the soldiers in camp, who fitted him with an undersized sergeant's uniform and armed him, somewhat clumsily, with a double-barreled shotgun. But on the steamboat trip back northward to Ohio, the boy grew pale and sick, showing unmistakable signs of typhoid fever. He was taken ashore at Memphis, but the finest doctors in the city could do nothing for him. Within twenty-four hours, he was dead.

Sherman was devastated. "Sleeping—waking—everywheres I see poor little Willy," he wrote to Ellen, who had resumed the journey homeward with the other children. "His face & form are as deeply imprinted on my memory as were deepseated the hopes I had in his Future." Sherman blamed himself for the boy's death, deploring his "want of judgment in taking my family to so fatal a climate at so critical a period of the year." Some would later suggest that it was Willy's death that drove Sherman crazy, causing him to become unhinged and cruel and resulting in two years of vengeful depredations across the South. There is no evidence for this—Sherman had been considered unstable long before that time, and in point of fact seemed just as angry and heartless while his son yet lived. On the contrary, Sherman upon losing his son resolved to make himself a better man. "I will try and make Poor Willys memory the cure for the defects which have sullied my character," he told Ellen. But there could be no question but that he was wounded deeply by the loss. "I will go on to the End," he said, "but feel the Chief Stay to my faltering Heart is now gone."[20]

In the spring of 1864, Grant ascended to the rank of lieutenant general in command of all the United States armies, and Sherman took his former chief's place at the head of the armies in the west, a department whose rather administrative-sounding name—"the Military Division of the Mississippi"—hardly conveyed its breadth and its importance. Every Federal officer and soldier between the Appalachian Mountains and the Mississippi River now took orders from Sherman. So recently sitting at home in disgrace, the high-strung Ohioan now led the second largest military force on the continent, and the earlier statement that had provided the central evidence of raving madness now seemed nothing more than a sensible appreciation of the magnitude of the work ahead. "Subsequent events confirmed the wisdom and vindicated the calculation of General Sherman," a subordinate later wrote. "In view of the evil winds that blew upon him through the daily press from one end of the country to the other, Sherman might say with Hamlet: 'I am but mad, North, Northwest, when the wind is Southerly, I know a hawk from a hand-saw.'"[21]

Historians and biographers, even doctors and psychiatrists—not satisfied with a fellow general's assessment that Sherman was "a splendid piece of machinery with all of the screws a little loose"—have at various times attempted to get inside Sherman's head to diagnose his condition. The verdicts rendered by these experts range from clinical depression and "a mild anxiety state" to bipolar, manic depressive, and narcissistic personality disorders. This myriad of mental defects retroactively attributed to Sherman showed the exercise to be not only one in futility—a quest to scrutinize the inscrutable—but of staring at inkblots, where an observer merely sees what he wants to see. "Historians who try to apply psychiatric findings to this great General do not help us in our understanding of him or his contribution," Stephen Ambrose wrote, concluding: "Sherman was not manic depressive. He was Sherman, unique unto himself."[22]

He was unique in appearance as well and made an indelible impression on those who saw and sought to describe him. Sherman was by this point in the war an icon, one of the most famous men in America, and all who met him sought to take his measure and compare reality against rumor and reputation. The general was striking in aspect but careless in presentation—"tall and lank, not very erect, with hair like thatch, which he rubs up with his hands," an aide recorded, with "a rusty beard trimmed close, a wrinkled face, sharp, prominent red nose, small, bright eyes, coarse red hands; black felt hat slouched over the eyes—he says when he wears anything else the soldiers cry out, as he rides along, 'Hallo, the old man has got a new hat'—dirty dickey with the points wilted down, black, old-fashioned stock, brown field officer's coat with high collar and no shoulder straps, muddy trowsers and one spur." An underwhelmed Illinois soldier recorded in his journal that Sherman "certainly don't look like one endowed with anything more than the ordinary modicum of common sense, and certainly like he was Commander of one half of the government forces."[23]

Sherman was a moving target, never still, always pacing, stalking, muttering, hands either thrust deep in his pockets or fumbling with a cigar. He smoked incessantly, almost angrily, "a steam engine in britches," as one historian put it. W. F. G. Shanks of the *New York Tribune* ranked him as "fully as great a smoker as Grant," though Sherman burned through his cigars "with an energy which it would be supposed would deprive him of all the pleasure of smoking . . . as if it were a duty to be finished in the shortest imaginable time." He left a litter of half-smoked stumps behind him—"Sherman's old soldiers," hotel porters and camp orderlies called them. He shared the meager diet of his men, bacon and hardtack and black coffee. He slept four hours a night and looked like he slept less. "At night, by candlelight, the men could see him through the windows, pacing, pacing, pacing, head back, bristly bearded chin thrust stubbornly forward, hands plunged in his pockets," a soldier wrote. "'When Uncle Billy can't march by day, he marches all night,' they told each other."[24]

And then there was his talking. Sherman was a conversational machine gun among smoothbore muskets, a man "boiling over with ideas, crammed full of feeling, discussing every subject and pronouncing on all." One witness, exhausted by a morning spent with the general, struggled to record his impressions: "If I were to write a dozen pages I could not tell you a tenth part of what he said," he wrote, "indeed it would be easier to say what he did *not* talk about than what he did." Another complained that Sherman "*must* talk, quick, sharp, and yet not harshly, all the time making his odd gestures, which, no less than the intonation of his voice, serve to emphasize his language. He can not bear a clog upon his thoughts nor an interruption to his language. He admits of no opposition. He overrides every thing. He never hesitates at interrupting any one, but cannot bear to be interrupted himself." When riled, which he often was, Sherman would repeat phrases for emphasis, as in the spring, when he warned a sluggish quartermaster: "I am going to move on Joe Johnston the day General Grant telegraphs me he is going to hit Bobby Lee; and if you don't have my army supplied, and keep it supplied, we'll eat your mules up, sir—*eat your mules up!*" On another occasion, Sherman confronted an unlucky civilian who bumbled in his path in the midst of a battle. "My name is Lovejoy," the man protested, "and I'm a member of Congress."

"What are you doing here?" Sherman barked as he shooed away the politician. "Get out of my lines, sir! *Get out of my lines!*"

Sherman knew he had a short fuse but was unrepentant. "He is very well aware, and candidly admits that his temper is uncommonly bad, and, what is worse, he makes no attempt to control or correct it," a journalist wrote. A reporter for the *Cincinnati Gazette*, who thought the general's foul mood and bad manners nothing less than savage, compared him to a Pawnee Indian. A rival newspaper promptly demanded that the reporter apologize to the Pawnees.[25]

All this—the angry countenance, the indifference to dress, the rapid-fire talking, the chain smoking, the wiry, vigorous figure—combined to create "a very remarkable-looking man, such as could not be grown out of America: the concentrated quintessence of Yankeedom." Walt Whitman found him "seamy, sinewy, in style—a bit of stern open air made up in the image of a man." Another less poetic observer put it more simply. Sherman was, to him, "the most American looking man I ever saw."[26]

Southern eyes, not surprisingly, beheld Sherman quite differently by this stage of the war. "Vigorous war means universal destruction," he had told Admiral David Dixon Porter in 1862, and though at times he had exerted what he called "hard handling" to rein in the excesses of his troops, the veteran Midwesterners under his direction had shown themselves all too willing to take the war to the Southern people. And so it was that the same man who was hailed in Northern newspapers as a brilliant leader was to Southern correspondents a coward, a monster, and an "intolerable wretch." Reporters not only credited all the earlier rumors of insanity and incompetence, but they delved deeply into their own reservoirs of classical, Biblical and literary references in an effort to convey their distaste and disgust with the Ohio commander. "Of all the Yankee Generals he is the poorest, the vainest, the meanest. He is without honor as a man, or conscience as a human being," a correspondent for the *Augusta Daily Constitutionalist* would write that summer. "His wit, by which he sets great store, is that of a Dutch dissenting class leader, his wisdom that of a circus clown, his temper that of Meg

Merriles, his honesty that of Ananias and Sapphira, and his appearance and manners those of Uriah Heep," the reporter continued, warming to the task. "His fate will be upon the earth wreck and ruin, the exposure of his littleness and puppiness, the disgrace of his military pretensions and the discomfiture of all his schemes; in the world to come—though I judge not lest I be judged—you can imagine what awards will be assigned to a villain, who not content with insulting the purity of womanhood and assailing the innocence of children, points his blasphemous tongue like a hissing adder in the face of his Maker." Sherman was nothing less than "a paltry villain, a currish knave, the very Fawkes of society, a dull sharper, a cheat and shame upon the name of soldier, the very embodiment of an ill-begotten, ill-bred and destined caterpillar, clinging only to sloth and mildew, climbing no higher than the scum of a rank and putrid atmosphere." On July 4, the Atlanta *Intelligencer* derided him as a "brute," an "inhuman monster," a "butcher," and—somewhat to the contrary—"a merciless avenging angel of the Lord."[27]

Sherman was no more distracted by name-calling by Rebel newspapers than he was bothered anymore by the earlier mud that had been flung in his direction. Once timid, he was now profoundly self-confident. He no longer overestimated enemy strength, or worried over reinforcements, or counseled retreat, but instead spoke of pressing his advantage, of "keeping the ball rolling," of remaining at all times on the offensive. He was and always would be jittery in his manner, but the fearfulness that once seemed to bedevil him was gone. He was *restlessly* nervous, one soldier recalled, not timidly so—more like a mastiff, fenced and snarling, than the skittish housecat he had been in Kentucky. Mannerisms previously thought to be disturbing signs of instability were now considered emblematic of his vigor and determination. Wild-eyed raving had become "electric alertness"; insomnia was evidence not of nervousness, but vigilance. "He still slept little and talked endlessly," a recent biographer wrote, "but now words were of personal power and military conquest, and instead of a crazy loser, he now appeared to others as a somewhat quirky conquering genius."

His family called him "Tecumseh" or, more commonly, "Cump;" his wife addressed her letters to "My Dear Cumpy." His men, fond of him despite his prickliness and appreciative of the way he shared their hardships in camp and on the march, usually referred to him as "Uncle Billy." But soldiers on both sides sometimes called him "Crazy Bill"—the Rebels invoking the name with a mixture of derision and respect, and the Yanks considering it not an insult but a compliment. The veterans in the blue ranks not only accepted the quirks of their commander, they took pride in his record, his rhetoric, and his sharp edges. "We all have great Confidence in Sherman," one officer wrote. "Although he was pronounced Crazy at one time, I wish all Generals were afflicted as he is." An Illinois soldier wrote to his mother, "The boys all call him 'crazy Billy,' but there seems to be some 'method in his madness.'"[28]

Method there was in spades, as shown by the logistical and strategic accomplishment of bringing a massive force southward across rugged terrain to within ten miles of its objective. Now that he had reached the Chattahoochee, Sherman spent most of the week seeing to his uncertain supply line—remarkably, his engineers would reconstruct the nine-hundred-foot railroad bridge in only four days—and catching up on his correspondence, official and unofficial. Always wound tight, he was even more anxious this week, mostly because of a lack of news from home. His wife Ellen had borne him a son three weeks before, and not only did he not yet know the child's name, he had heard nothing directly from Ellen herself, which made him fear for her well-being. He also learned of the death on July 10 of his alcoholic older brother James, a loss which the general seemed to accept in sadness and in stride. "Poor James," he would close a letter later that month. "He was a good fellow, but John Barleycorn was too much for him." Still haunted by Willy's death, he now grieved for his brother and worried for his wife and the newborn son he had never seen. But he also boiled at being made to worry. He was distracted, and he resented the distraction. "I should not thus be kept uneasy whilst charged with so high responsibilities," he complained.[29]

Sherman also took the opportunity to recap for his family his view of the campaign thus far, emphasizing the hurdles he had cleared and bristling that his achievement was insufficiently appreciated. "I have brought one hundred thousand men from Chattanooga 120 miles and drive a well commanded & well organized army of 60,000, from the fortified positions at Dalton, Resacca, Cassville, Alatoona, Kenesaw,

Smyrna and the Chattahoochee," he wrote to his foster brother Philemon Ewing from his camp along the Chattahoochee. "We had sixty days of continual combat, with several pretty smart battles interspersed. I dont believe there are ten men in the United States other than those here who appreciate & measure the vast labor of mind & body consumed in accomplishing these results." He expressed confidence in ultimate success—and in any case, he said, "you Know I never turn back." Yet he had no illusions about the hard work still ahead, and noted that success would require not only grand strategy but hard fighting.[30]

"Shallow People have been taught to believe the war is over," Sherman had written to Ellen in late June, "& you will see troubles enough to convince you I was right in my view of the case from the first." And so he was. Distrusted, despised, derided as a paranoid and a kook, Sherman in the end was proven right about the rebellion and what it would take to subdue it. He knew a hawk from a handsaw, indeed, and he said so in his letters home.

"The worst of the war," he warned, "is not yet begun."[31]

A visitor to Atlanta in the early days of the war might have been forgiven for wondering what it was that made the place worth having. Part railroad yard, part dusty frontier town, the city's population according to the 1860 census was less than 10,000, slaves included—making Atlanta considerably less than half the size of the port city of Savannah, one-third the size of Nashville, and one-fourth the size of Charleston. The town boasted no navigable river, no significant forts or major military installations—nor was it the state capital, a distinction that went to the unimpressive town of Milledgeville, eighty miles to the southeast. But Atlanta, though small and grubby and far from historic, was the indisputable linchpin of the Confederacy's transportation system. The city sat at the center of a snarl of railroad arteries that led to disparate points of the compass, splotched on the map like a knot at the middle of the Southern knitting, or a widow sitting center-web. Four major lines spun out from Atlanta: the state-owned Western & Atlantic Railroad, winding north to Chattanooga and in mid-1864 serving for most of its 138-mile distance as Sherman's supply line; the Georgia Railroad, running east to Augusta and then branching on to Charleston and Wilmington; the Atlanta & West Point Railroad, leading southwest to the state line and thence to Montgomery and Mobile; and the Macon & Western Railroad, which branched off the Atlanta & West Point to run through Macon and on to the Georgia coast. These lines stitched together the patchwork of the Confederate States, and their interruption would do much to rend the whole.

Atlanta's importance to the Confederate war effort also had grown by a process of military elimination. Vicksburg, Mississippi, the so-called "Gibraltar of the West," had surrendered to Grant the summer before, and though some referred to Atlanta thereafter as "the Gibraltar of the Rebellion," there was no question but that the South was running out of Gibraltars. Nashville and Memphis, New Orleans and Jackson, Knoxville and Chattanooga all had fallen and were occupied by Union forces. As one Georgia matron put it, "The Confederacy was being narrowed down." One newspaper editor argued that Atlanta was not so much a last Gibraltar as a second Richmond: "The Richmond in Virginia is the political Richmond; but the Richmond of Georgia is Atlanta, which to the Confederacy is a more important point than the capital of the Old Dominion," he wrote. Another warned that Atlanta's fall "would open the way for the Federal Army to the Gulf on the one hand, and to Charleston on the other, and close up those rich granaries from which Lee's armies are supplied. It would give them control of our network of railways and thus paralyze our efforts." Richmond, after all, was on the South's periphery, while Atlanta was at its heart. "To lose the one would be as the loss of a limb; should we be driven from the other, it will be a terrible blow at our most vital point."[32]

The locals took some measure of pride in their newfound national prominence and in Atlanta's status as "the Crossroads of the Confederacy" and the "Gate City of the South," though outsiders forced to traverse the muddy streets and crowded hotels and sooty railroad yards seemed to resent the necessity of passing through. Foreshadowing the complaints of generations of latter-day travelers, *London Times* correspondent Charles Francis Lawley noted that "no one goes anywhere without passing through Atlanta." Another reporter called the city a "great railroad whirlpool and auction mart" with "side-walks paved with goober shells and apple peelings," and the place to be if one "wished to invest in dust, heat, and noise, and get so cuffed about and beplucked as to wonder if you ain't some other man." Atlanta not only relied upon but defined itself around the railroad—so much so that the limits of incorporation were laid out in a circle, two miles in diameter, with its center at the railroad station.[33]

No such place existed thirty years before. The site that would one day become Georgia's largest city was as recently as the 1830s a "howling wilderness," not far removed from Creek Indian days. The never-closed Gate City had started out as a dead end, marked in 1836 as the designated southern endpoint of the new state railroad and initially named "Terminus," which hardly seemed promising. The chief engineer charged with laying out the Western & Atlantic had selected the terminating point carefully, no doubt, though the placement of the Zero Mile Post miles from any navigable watercourse or other natural feature seemed almost random—as one historian put it, it was "as if one surveyor stuck his rod in the ground while he tied his shoe and another immediately made it the point of reference for laying off the city limits." The town fathers renamed their would-be metropolis twice: briefly calling it "Marthasville," after the governor's daughter, and then settling on "Atlanta," a made-up word meant to suggest both a certain mythological grandeur and the more practical connection from the West to the Atlantic Ocean that the early railroad bosses hoped to achieve.[34]

"Atlanta exhibits more signs of life than any city in Georgia," a Confederate lieutenant wrote as he passed through the place in the summer of 1862, describing to his father the merits of the growing railroad town. "Great improvements are constantly progressing," he wrote. "Fine stores with iron and granite fronts. Neat residences meet the eye on every hand. But a few years since, Atlanta had been regarded as the home of only speculators, railroad hands, businessmen, demireps, and rowdies; but the tall spires of newly erected churches, frequent schoolhouses, and the increasing comforts of private residences, and the permanency of stores and public buildings give ample token that the rude infancy of this busy place has been superseded by an age of quiet, mature civilization." But the quiet, such as it was, did not last. The progress of

The Union Passenger Depot "Car Shed," constructed in 1853, left, the Trout House hotel, center background, and the Masonic Hall, dominated the heart of Civil War-era Atlanta. (*Library of Congress*)

the war and the armies' insatiable appetite for men and matériel had transformed Atlanta from an up-and-coming whistle stop to a vital hub for the young Confederate nation and a significant arsenal and storehouse in its own right. The city's population more than doubled as workers streamed in to man the city's booming industries and work on the railroads, which by 1864 were running nearly around the clock, Sundays included. Rolling mills and foundries turned out iron rails, cannons, and armor plate for Confederate ironclads, tanneries produced saddles, harnesses, and other leather goods, and a textile factory "manned" by more than two thousand women sewed woolens and socks and gray uniforms. Along the railroad tracks, freight depots and warehouses brimmed with ordnance, dry goods, and other supplies, as heavy-laden boxcars carried supplies and reinforcements to the front.[35]

At the center of the whirlwind of citizens and commerce was the Union Passenger Depot, a cavernous, three-hundred-foot-long brick station known to the locals as the Car Shed. Just to the north was the State Square—once a tree-lined park but now a clearing station for arriving wounded soldiers, and to the west was a collision of dirt streets known as Five Points—the intersection of Whitehall, Marietta, Decatur, Peachtree, and Line Streets (now Edgewood Avenue), the heart of the city's commercial district. Two diagonal blocks to the south was the City Hall and Fulton County Court House, in an oak-studded neighborhood of churches and homes of some of Atlanta's most prominent families—the Lyons, the Neals, the Calhouns, the Claytons. A number of fine hotels were just steps from the Car Shed—Washington Hall, the Atlanta Hotel, and the four-story Trout House, the city's largest hostelry, from which a visitor could view the city's "spacious streets, its magnificent warehouses of brick, its rising cupolas and steeples, the substantial edifices, staunch hotels, airy parks and thrifty avenues," as well as the granite hump of Stone Mountain, sixteen miles away. Atlantans still enjoyed their summer picnics and garden parties, but concerts, plays, and other entertainment had for the most part come to an end. In February, the mayor had ordered closed the Athenaeum on Decatur Street, depriving residents of the theater's myriad of spectacles that ranged from snake charmers to Shakespeare; thereafter, the stage was employed as an auction house. The nearby Concert Hall likewise held no performances, having been taken over as a Confederate hospital some months before.[36]

Trains arriving from the north brought throngs of refugees into the city. For eight weeks, the dueling armies had scoured clear the fields and woods and villages above Atlanta like a locust plague of old. "We have devoured the land," Sherman told Ellen in late June. "All the people retire before us and desolation is behind. To realize what war is one should follow in our tracks." North Georgia was swept of its resources and its residents as if by a great push-broom, and southbound roads were choked with what one officer called a "hegira of poor, forlorn refugees," a parade of "human sufferings that might appall the angels." An Illinoisan wrote home to his birdwatching wife: "I have been looking out for that mocking bird for you but have not seen one since you wrote me about it. Johnston, in his retreat, appears to have swept along with him not only his army, but all the white men, white women and mocking birds, leaving us nothing but scorpions, wood ticks and worn out Africans." Despite the destruction, a retreating Georgia soldier told his mother of the "relics of departed bloodshed and carnage. We will leave walls of stone and earth which will be gazed upon by generations to come, as the earth which protected father and grandfather," he wrote. "Tread lightly, this is sacred ground, made so from the many gallons of Southern blood it has drunk and the many mangled bodies it contains."[37]

North Georgia residents dislodged by the fighting and the sweep of the armies southward streamed into Atlanta by the hundreds. "If Mr. Shakspeere were correct when he writ that 'sweet are the juices of adversity,' then it are resunabul to suppose that me and my foaks and many others must have some sweetnin to spare," the downhome Georgia columnist "Bill Arp"—pseudonym of "country philosopher" Charles Henry Smith—wrote of his experience as a "runagee" after abandoning his north Georgia home. "When a man is aroused in the ded of night, and smells the approach of the fowl invader; when he feels constrained to change his base and bekum a runagee from his home; when he begins a dignified retreat, but soon is konstrained to leave the dignity behind, and git away without regard to the order of his going—if there is any sweet juice in the like of that, I havent been able to see it." Arriving in the city, weary travelers found the overpriced hotels sold out and the city park already filled with hospital tents. Refugees slept in hallways and sheds and dooryards. "Everything and everybody seemed to have concentrated in Atlanta until the town was immense," a refugee remembered. "People were crowded like sardines in a box." Many without a place to stay in the city continued on further south or east or west in search of what they hoped would be a safe haven, somewhere. The mournful diaspora of fleeing civilians brought to mind for one observer nothing less than "a Confederate edition of *Les Misérables*."[38]

Even more miserable were the throngs of sick and wounded men. In early 1862, chief surgeon Samuel H. Stout had designated Atlanta as a center for general hospitals for the Army of Tennessee, ideally suited because of its railroad connections, its medical college, and its central location. The city's prominence as a medical center grew as the war in the Western Theater progressed and casualties mounted, and the city obtained another honorary title: "the Hospital of the South." Immediately following the Battle of Chickamauga in September 1863, Atlanta's hospitals, with a capacity of approximately 1,800, were flooded with more than ten thousand casualties. Six months later, still nursing hundreds of convalescing soldiers from earlier fights, the hospitals struggled to handle the many thousands wounded in the spring campaign or stricken with measles, dysentery, or typhoid fever. The city's overflowing infirmaries by now included improvised facilities at the Gate City Hotel, the Atlanta Female Institute, and the Atlanta Hotel, whose halls and yard were said to be so grisly that residents would detour for several blocks to avoid its sights and its stench. In early June, state officials took over City Hall itself to serve as a hospital for wounded Georgia soldiers, naming the facility for the state's staunch wartime governor Joseph E. Brown. A local gravedigger regularly trolled the wards of Brown Hospital in search of new customers. "Anybody dead here?" he cried. "Anybody about to die?"[39]

The hospitals were staffed with overwhelmed doctors and nurses, slaves and occasional free black orderlies, along with priests, pastors, and local women volunteers. Nineteen-year-old Sallie Conley Clayton visited the hospital frequently with a family slave in tow to carry a tray of food, though she and her other unmarried adult sisters were not permitted to venture into the wards themselves. Her fearless younger sister, fifteen-year-old Augusta "Gussie" Clayton, spent hours that spring and summer working in the hospital rooms, helping doctors change dressings caked with blood and holding cool cloths to the foreheads of men blazing with fever. Thirty-three-year-old Father Thomas O'Reilly, the Irish-born pastor of the Catholic Church of Immaculate Conception near City Hall, had been commissioned a Confederate chaplain back in March, but spent most of his time ministering to the wounded and preparing the dying for their journey home.[40]

Kate Cumming, a thirty-six-year-old nurse visiting from nearby Newnan, met an arriving train of wounded soldiers at the Car Shed during the campaign. "O, what a sight we beheld!" she wrote in her journal. "No less than three long trains filled, outside and in, with wounded." Ladies at the depot met the cars with baskets "filled with edibles of all kinds, and buckets of milk, coffee, and lemonade." Kate, who had tended to the wounded since Shiloh, noticed that most of the men were wounded in the head or upper limbs—the result of fighting behind chest-high breastworks. She worked well into the night at the Gate City Hospital, helping a surgeon dress shattered arms, disabled hands, missing eyes, and others far more grievously wounded. Exhausted, she stepped from the converted hotel into bright moonlight to find injured men "lying all over the platform of the depot." Seven or eight hundred men had been brought in that day, she was told—only one day among dozens like it that summer.

She looked back on the morning as "one of the gloomiest I ever passed. It was damp and cheerless; and, look which way I would, the prospect was dreary. Hundreds of wounded men, dirty, bloody, and weary, were all around us. And when I thought of the many more which were expected, I was filled with despair, and felt like humbling myself in the dust, and praying more earnestly than ever before, that God would send us peace."[41]

By the summer of 1864, these human accretions—factory workers, transplants, refugees, runaways, sick and wounded soldiers—had brought Atlanta's population to nearly three times its prewar total. Among Southern cities still in Confederate hands, Atlanta was second in size only to the capital at Richmond. No less than seven newspapers were in circulation in the city—prominent among them the *Daily Intelligencer* and the *Southern Confederacy*, and refugee papers displaced from Union-occupied Tennessee: the *Memphis Appeal*, the *Chattanooga Rebel*, and the *Knoxville Register*. The papers reported the increasing chaos in the city, but editorials preached a childlike faith in the Confederate defenders that bordered on insensible bluster. "There is an invincible host still between Atlanta and our ruthless foe, which, like a wall of fire, will resist his advance into it," the *Intelligencer* insisted on July 6. The next day, the paper expressed "the utmost confidence that if battle is made before the city, we will scatter the enemy like leaves before an autumnal frost."

A "wall of fire." An "autumnal frost." But then the editor posed the question: "If battle is not made, what then?"[42]

What then, indeed? Word of Johnston's retreat across the river on the night of July 9 quickly made its way into the town, and the residents' uneasiness, intangible but undeniable since the sound of distant guns to the north were first heard at the end of May, soon changed to outright alarm. The soldiers who were supposed to stop the Yankees three months ago a hundred miles to the north were now manning fortifications within view of the city or even straggling through its streets in search of whiskey and tobacco. So recently filled to overflowing with the wayward and the wounded, Atlanta suddenly began to empty out.

"I can give you no idea of the excitement in Atlanta," the *Mobile Register*'s correspondent wrote on July 9. "Everybody seems to be hurrying off, and especially the women. Wagons loaded with household furniture and everything else that can be packed upon them crowd every street, and women, old and young children innumerable, are hurrying to and fro, leading pet lambs, deer, and other household objects of affection, as though they intended to save all they could. Every train of cars is loaded to their utmost capacity, and there is no grumbling about seats, for even the fair ones are glad to get even a standing place in a box car. The excitement beats anything I ever saw, and I hope I may never witness such again." The newspapers continued to urge the citizens to show a little backbone, even as they crated their presses and packed their suitcases for parts south. The editor of the *Southern Confederacy* encouraged his worried readers to exercise "a little philosophy and reason," insisting that "the chances are that in many instances that removal may not be necessary at all." He then promptly fled the city aboard a southbound train.[43]

The excitement swung briefly toward elation, as a rumor swept the city's barrooms and hotel lobbies in early July: General Sherman had been captured after wandering into a Confederate outpost along the Chattahoochee. Alas, the news seemed too good to be true, and it was. A Federal officer by the name of Sherman had been captured, indeed, but he was the entirely unimpressive Colonel Frank Sherman from Chicago, a member of General O. O. Howard's staff and no kin to the red-headed Ohio commander.[44]

The order came to evacuate the city's hospitals, including the medical college, the commandeered hotels, and the great receiving hospital located on the city fairgrounds. Convalescent furloughs were given to the walking wounded as more serious patients were prepared for the arduous train journey southward. One soldier charged with helping to transport these patients had difficulty putting the experience into words. "The battle field is a mear Trifal compared to it," he wrote to his wife. In the meantime, what had passed for normalcy over the past few weeks was giving way to disorder. The mayor's and the superior court, both overwhelmed in recent days with arrests, did not meet after July 1; and the police force, according to one historian, was made up of "greybeards, cripples, and riffraff." The *Intelligencer* wrote, with a mixture of levity and sorrow, that "any one who desired to get murdered with the certainty that the murderer will escape, let them come to Atlanta, and they will be gratified." As one historian noted, "the mood typified the eve of destruction whereby it was every man and woman for himself."

For many residents, the evacuation of the hospitals was the last straw. "My dear Cousin," Mary S. Mallard wrote after fleeing the city with her two young children, "You have doubtless heard that we have left Atlanta—at least for the present—and are now numbered among the numerous throngs of refugees. We had hoped to have remained longer in Atlanta, but when the order came to move all hospitals in a few hours and the enemy were reported crossing the river within six miles of us, we thought we better move our furniture while we could get transportation." Samuel P. Richards, owner of a stationery shop in Atlanta, recorded his apprehension in his diary. "This has been a sad day in our city, for it has been quite evident for some days past that there is a great probability of Atlanta falling into the hands of the enemy and the city has been in a complete swarm all day and for several days," Richards wrote on July 10. "All the Govt. stores and Hospitals are ordered away and of course the citizens are alarmed and many have left and others are leaving." Richards had been among the small congregation to hear Rev. William Brantley preach at the Second Baptist Church that Sunday morning, and only a handful had stayed for the afternoon communion. The pastor was "so affected that he could hardly speak" as Richards took home the pulpit Bible and hymn book for safekeeping—after all, "it seemed almost certain that it would not be again needed there for the present."[45]

Amid the exodus—churches and hospitals closing, trains departing, roads south crowded with wagons and footsore refugees—families across Atlanta resolved to stay, some resolute, some frozen with fear, some tied to the city by ill or infirm loved ones. "If there is any danger, we will go immediately to Augusta," young Gussie Clayton had written to a friend a few weeks before, "tho' I sincerely hope we will not have to leave our homes, as I should not think the life of a refugee very pleasant." But Gussie had since fallen ill with typhoid fever, no doubt contracted in the course of her long hours at the hospital. Her older sisters departed the city for Montgomery, Alabama, but her anguished parents, William and Caroline Clayton, would stay and tend to their now-failing daughter, "happen what may." Father Thomas O'Reilly had no intention of leaving his church and parsonage or, more important, his regular rounds in the city's hospitals. A contractor named Maxwell R. Berry, who lived near the Claytons at the corner of Walton and Fairlee Streets, had five children under the age of ten with his wife Harriet, who was pregnant with their sixth. They, too, seemed to have no choice but to remain. The Berrys' eldest daughter, nine-year-old Carrie, helped with household chores and tended to her younger siblings, fretting as the Yankees approached. Her father would soon come home with a package for her tucked under his arm—a small diary, in which the young girl would record with unblinking clarity the coming siege. Bookseller and stationer Sam Richards talked with his wife, and they decided to see the thing through. "Sallie and I have about decided to stay at home, Yankees or no Yankees," he recorded in his diary. "We hear and read terrible tales of them, but I don't think they are as bad as they are said to be."[46]

Meanwhile, members of Atlanta's black community, both free and slave, waited and watched the crumbling social order and the two great armies moving ever closer. Back in November 1863, the city tax collector had counted 2,523 slaves and only 11 free blacks in the city—though both numbers were surely low by the following summer. The Emancipation Proclamation, which was by its terms effective January 1, 1863, had abolished slavery in areas beyond the reach of Federal authority, and thus had little practical effect across much of the South eighteen months later. Although the grim reality of life for slaves in Atlanta had been altered somewhat by the approaching military storm, the South's "peculiar institution" at its core remained unchanged. Partly because of the convenient flow of railroad transportation into the city from Savannah and other Eastern ports and then out to plantations across the South, Atlanta's business district had a number of well-established slave markets and depots. The city's newspapers advertised Robert Clarke's "Slave Yard," on Whitehall Street—"a commodious, well arranged Yard, with every convenience for the health and comfort of slaves." Clarke's rival Robert Crawford bragged of "the most extensive Negro depot in the Confederacy, clean, healthy, safe and comfortable," offering a "constantly replenished stock" of cooks, washers, blacksmiths, carpenters, field hands, shoemakers, plow boys and girls, waiters, drivers or entire families—all for "speedy and satisfactory" sale on Peachtree Street.

By 1864, however, the ancient prison-house that was Southern slavery had begun to show its cracks in Atlanta. Though Messrs. Clarke and Crawford struggled to continue in their "trading" business, squeezed by soaring costs, limited supply, and plummeting demand, other slavers began to close their doors. With growing frequency, advertisements began to appear in the city's several newspapers seeking to hire black men and women for salaried jobs. "Wanted," one ad said. "E. McDonald, surgeon in charge of the Lumpkin hospital . . . wishes to hire, by the month or year, thirty negroes, at $25 per month." And though large numbers of slaves still worked in and around the city—many of them impressed black workers brought in to toil in factories, construct fortifications, or staff the fly-swarmed hospitals—uncounted numbers of free black refugees arrived in the city, along with former slave escapees shaken loose by the havoc created by the blue army's advance through northwest Georgia.[47]

City ordinances carefully restricted the activities of blacks in the city, free or slave. By order of the provost marshal, no slave or "free person of color" was permitted to walk the streets past nine P.M., except in the presence of his owner. The city code prohibited any slave or free black from hiring horses or carriages; from hawking "beer cake, fruit, or confectionary;" from walking with a cane, club, or stick (unless blind or infirm); from smoking a pipe or cigar in any street, lane, alley, or square. The typical punishment for violations of these ordinances was whipping, "not to exceed thirty-nine lashes."[48]

The handful of free black men in the city struggled, as they always had, to build a life and a business under these restrictions and the generations-old tendency among whites to view a dark-skinned man as a natural inferior. One notable citizen among Atlanta's freedmen was a former slave named Robert Yancey—his surname taken from his former master Benjamin C. Yancey—and though city directories listed him under that name, as a free man he preferred to be called Robert Webster. Benjamin Yancey had moved to Atlanta in the 1850s and allowed his servant Robert to open a barbershop and work toward purchasing his freedom. Robert Webster proved to be not only a talented barber but a brilliant, natural businessman who soon owned two barbershops with nine employees and then expanded to other fields, prospering as a produce seller and loan shark. He lived in a comfortable four-bedroom house and made substantial monthly payments to Yancey to "buy his time." Throughout his life, the extremely light-skinned Robert Yancey/Webster claimed, remarkably but not implausibly, to be the illegitimate son of legendary orator and statesman Daniel Webster. What was more, the mulatto barber was a well-known Unionist who was briefly detained under suspicion that he had helped a group of Federal prisoners who had escaped from the county jail. He would have a substantial role to play in the drama still unfolding on the Atlanta stage.

Other free blacks included Roderick D. Badger, a young mulatto who had learned dental work as an assistant to his former master, Dr. J. B. Badger of nearby DeKalb County. He had purchased his freedom and overcame prejudiced opposition to his practice: "We feel aggrieved, as Southern citizens, that your honorable body tolerates a negro dentist in our midst, and in justice to ourselves and the community it ought to be abated," a group of citizens had complained to the city council, which rejected the petition. Roderick Badger would persist and become the favorite dentist of many prominent Atlantans, black and white, practicing at 37 1/2 Peachtree Street until his death in 1891. Another favorite of the locals was a free black barber by the name of Solomon Luckie, who ran a barbershop and bathing salon at the Atlanta Hotel on Alabama Street, right across the tracks from the Car Shed. Already popular before the war, Luckie's razor and shears could hardly keep up with the demands of army officers and workers with newfound funds. "Sol" Luckie worked hard and marveled at his good fortune—not knowing that it was about to run out.[49]

Perhaps the least fortunate among Atlantans, or at least the least enviable under the deteriorating circumstances, was the city's well-regarded mayor, whom fate had placed in the position of defending his city in a conflict he had opposed from the outset. South Carolina-born lawyer

James M. Calhoun—his father was a cousin to the former vice president and fellow Carolinian, the late John C. Calhoun—was, according to his youngest son Patrick, an "old-line Whig" who believed the Union should be preserved. "He acknowledged the right to secede, but doubted its wisdom," Patrick remembered. Back in the uncertain days of 1860–61, Calhoun had been a delegate designated to vote for "cooperation" with neighboring states to settle the looming controversy; that is, opposing the ordinance of secession. The following year, Calhoun ran for mayor and was elected to the first of his one-year terms. Despite his prewar opposition to the ordinance of secession, "when the war came, there was no better Confederate than he," his son insisted—though after the war, Calhoun would claim he had been Union-loyal all along. His older sons served in the Confederate Army, including a future Atlanta mayor Captain William Lowndes Calhoun, who fought at Vicksburg and in the Atlanta Campaign before being shot in the hip at Resaca in May 1864.[50]

Twice reelected, Calhoun had shown himself to be conscientious and steady, if not steadfast, as those who knew him might have expected. Having served as a captain against the Creeks as a young man, Calhoun was a vigorous defender of his city from enemies foreign and domestic. He bristled at interference by Confederate authorities and attempted to either inspire or shame Atlanta residents into fighting to defend their city. "I require all the male citizens of Atlanta, capable of bearing arms, without regard to occupation, who are not in the Confederate or State service, to report by 12 M. on Thursday, the 26th inst. to O. H. Jones, marshal of the city, to be organized into companies and armed," he had written in May. "And all male citizens who are not willing to defend their homes and families are requested to leave the city at their earliest convenience, as their presence only embarrasses the authorities and tends to the demoralization of others." The mayor's military bluster and confidence in deliverance from the foe was undermined somewhat by his own actions. The *Montgomery Advertiser*, noting those "weak kneed" folks of "little faith" in the city, included in their numbers the mayor—who despite his ringing proclamations and appeals to Southern manhood had demonstrated his lack of faith in the result by sending his own family out of Atlanta and thus from harm's way.[51]

The war had aged the mayor beyond his fifty-three years, and though his hair resisted gray, his thin shoulders were slumped by his earthly burdens and his eyebrows arched and knitted to a worried frown. Throughout the campaign, Calhoun presided over a city government that was crumbling and a community overrun with transients and sick and wounded soldiers. On July 2, the Atlanta Aid Association appealed to the city council for $3,000 for the relief of the destitute refugees, but the council refused—there was no money in the treasury for such an effort and no way to administer and distribute the aid in any event. The wolf was growling at Atlanta's door, and the mayor and aldermen focused their efforts on last-minute measures to deal with the emergency.

On July 18, the Atlanta City Council pulled together a quorum and held what would turn out to be their last meeting for months to come. The agenda focused mostly on contingency planning and emergency evacuations—the week before, the assembled councilmen had sent the city's mules away for safekeeping and authorized Mayor Calhoun to do the same with city records. The last item for consideration was the fire department.

Four companies defended the city against fire—the Atlanta Fire Company No. 1, the Mechanics Fire Company No. 2, the Tallulah Fire Company No. 3, and the Atlanta Hook & Ladder Company No. 1—all established the previous decade, and all of them volunteer. The companies had come a long way from their bucket brigade days in the 1850s, though it had taken a deadly fire in 1858 in a two-story building on Whitehall Street to inspire the city to equip them with ladders; and they still relied on hand-drawn, hand-pumped engines. One of the newer companies had temporary quarters in a livery stable on Walton Street, though another boasted a two-story station on Pryor Street, complete with seasoned hickory poles for the firemen to slide down. A point of pride was the department's natty uniforms—helmets and oilcloth capes stenciled with the name and number of the company. The alarm bell sounded shortly after one company received its uniforms, but "the men refused to budge until they had put on their new regalia," a local historian wrote. "By that time, the building had burned to the ground, and the firemen were no longer needed for that particular job. At any rate, they hung around the smoking embers until everybody had seen and admired the new uniforms to their complete satisfaction."

The department was undermanned and understandably distracted, as a large number of its volunteers were serving in the Confederate ranks. Two members had been killed at Fredericksburg; another at Second Manassas. Those still in Atlanta split their time between firefighting and militia duty—one company, in fact, had been recently converted into a makeshift cavalry squad.

At issue before the city council that day was the well-being of certain firefighting equipment, especially the companies' two best hand-pumped fire engines. After discussion, the council decided to send the precious engines and other valuable equipment out of the city "in case of Atlanta's being occupied for a time by the enemy."

Whatever perils might be ahead for the city of Atlanta, surely there would be no need for fire engines.[52]

Joseph E. Johnston. "The Gamecock," or, more commonly, "Old Joe." (*Library of Congress*)

CHAPTER TWO

The Gamecock

Confederate Headquarters, Atlanta, July 17

The commander of the Confederate Army of Tennessee, General Joseph E. Johnston, was the diametric opposite of his adversary Tecumseh Sherman, not only in manner and military philosophy, but also in appearance. Whereas Sherman was a rumpled officer once mistaken by his troops as a drunk passed out by the side of the road, the fifty-seven-year-old Johnston looked at all times like a distinguished portrait hanging above the mantel. "In face, figure, and character, General Johnston was thoroughly the soldier," an aide wrote. "Above the medium height, with an erect figure, in a close-fitting uniform buttoned to the chin; with a ruddy face, decorated with close-cut gray side-whiskers, mustache, and tuft on the chin; reserved in manner, brief in speech, without impulses of any description, it seemed, General Johnston's appearance and bearing were military to stiffness; and he was popularly compared to 'a gamecock,' ready for battle at any moment."

Ready for battle he may have been, but by this point in the war, Joe Johnston was primarily known for his apparent unwillingness to expose his soldiers to the perils of combat. What was more, his demeanor, while kind and gracious to subordinates, was disdainful, even hostile, to superiors. One historian, noting this contrast, described the charming Johnston as an ideal dinner guest, but warned that the prideful Virginian "could also be pedantic, quarrelsome, bitter and even paranoiac." He struck another acquaintance as "tempermentally an aristocrat," though also "as dry as the remainder biscuit after a voyage, and technical to the dotting of an i." Each one of these faults had revealed itself in the course of the eleven-week campaign, and would soon do so again.[1]

Johnston came from soldiers' stock. Son of a Revolutionary War cavalryman and grand-nephew of Patrick Henry, he was educated at the United States Military Academy, where fellow cadets called him "the Colonel"—a reference, equal parts respectful and snide, to his by-the-book devotion to his studies and his fondness for military spit and polish. After graduating a respectable thirteenth in the West Point class of 1829, eleven places below his classmate and fellow Virginian Robert E. Lee, Johnston received his commission in the artillery and embarked upon a stellar thirty-year career in the United States Army. He served with distinction in the Seminole and Mexican Wars, where he was twice brevetted for gallantry and twice wounded. By the time the Civil War began, Johnston had ascended to the top of the American military pantheon, serving as quartermaster general of the army and thus becoming the highest-ranking general officer to resign and join the Confederacy.

His Civil War debut was an auspicious one. On July 21, 1861, displaying a boldness and celerity that would seem entirely absent in later engagements, Johnston brought his 9,000-man force to the aid of the outnumbered General P. G. T. Beauregard at Manassas, Virginia. Thanks in large part to Johnston's nick-of-time reinforcements, the upstart Rebels swept the field in the war's curtain-raising battle, known in the North as Bull Run and by Southern wags as "Yankee Run." Crowned with this golden triumph at the outset, Johnston seemed destined for greatness—but he soon ran afoul of the Confederate president, Jefferson Davis. In August, Davis promoted five Confederate officers to the rank of full general, placing Johnston fourth on the hierarchical list, below Adjutant General Samuel Cooper, General Albert Sidney Johnston, and General Robert E. Lee. Johnston, who had outranked all three in the old army, considered Davis's list a professional demotion and a personal slap in the face. He fired off a lengthy, blistering letter to Davis, accusing him of seeking "to tarnish my fair fame as a soldier and a man, earned by more than thirty years of laborious and perilous service." Unmoved, the president in two icy sentences gave Johnston's rant the back of his hand. "Sir: I have just received and read your letter of the 12th instant," he wrote. "Its language is, as you say, unusual; its arguments and statements utterly one sided, and its insinuations as unfounded as they are unbecoming. I am, &c. Jeff'n Davis." In the end, both men felt insulted, each believed himself entirely in the right, and neither would ever forget or forgive.[2]

Despite this clash of correspondence with the commander-in-chief, Johnston was placed in command of the Confederacy's largest army, standing between 100,000 Federals under Major General George B. McClellan and the Confederate capital at Richmond. Facing McClellan on the York-James Peninsula in the spring of 1862, Johnston—in a harbinger of things to come—fell back repeatedly as he moved closer and closer to the city he was charged with protecting. Finally, on May 31, Johnston attacked McClellan south of the Chickahominy River, near a crossroads hamlet called Seven Pines. Proudly wearing his father's Revolutionary War sword, Johnston was issuing orders astride his horse when a musket ball smacked his shoulder and fragments from a bursting shell tore through his thigh and chest. The Virginian was carried from the field, thereby opening the door to history. The next day, Robert E. Lee replaced the injured Johnston in command of the Army of Northern Virginia, and would in the weeks that followed execute a daring counteroffensive to drive back the Army of the Potomac. With uncharacteristic self-deprecation, Johnston told a friend, "The shot that struck me down was the best ever fired for the Southern Confederacy, for I possessed in no degree the confidence of the Government, and now a man who does enjoy it will succeed me."[3]

Johnston spent six months convalescing from his Seven Pines wounds, and by then there was no chance that he would displace General Lee at the head of the Army of Northern Virginia. He went instead to a command in the West, which encompassed the Army of Tennessee under General Braxton Bragg and the Army of Mississippi under Lieutenant General John C. Pemberton. In the spring and summer of 1863, as the Federal noose tightened around Pemberton's garrison at Vicksburg, Johnston was charged with bringing a newly assembled force against Grant to raise the siege. But Johnston dawdled for weeks and in the end claimed that he could not assemble enough men to distract or dislodge the blue-clad besiegers. Cut off and starving, the Vicksburg defenders surrendered to Grant on July 4, 1863, a loss Davis would attribute to a "want of provisions inside, and a general outside who wouldn't fight." For a time, it seemed that Jefferson Davis would never again trust Johnston with an important command.

In September 1863, the Army of Tennessee under Bragg won a heartening Confederate victory at Chickamauga. But two months later, the irascible Bragg—who was arguably despised more intensely by his own soldiers and subordinate officers than any general on either side—suffered a crushing defeat at Missionary Ridge that was not only a tactical debacle, but also changed the strategic situation, unlocking the gates to an invasion south from Chattanooga into North Georgia. Lieutenant General James Longstreet, on detached service from Lee's army, had warned Secretary of War James A. Seddon some weeks earlier that "nothing but the hand of God can save us or help us as long as we have our present commander." Then came the Missionary Ridge fiasco, and Davis felt he had no choice but to accept Bragg's resignation—but who would replace him? Davis offered the command to Robert E. Lee, who firmly declined—leaving Southerners to dream of what might have been, had the Confederacy's greatest general been deployed to deal with the erratic W. T. Sherman. Davis brought Bragg to Richmond to serve as his military advisor and, despite his qualms, and in the absence of other candidates, placed Joseph Johnston in command of the Army of Tennessee.[4]

Johnston arrived at Dalton, Georgia, in late December 1863 to find his new command not only outnumbered and poorly supplied, but disorganized and demoralized. He brought in double rations, ordered a regular distribution of tobacco and whiskey, and improved uniforms, shoes, and tents. He granted furloughs to veterans in the ranks and amnesty to those absent without leave, encouraging their return. "A new era had dawned; a new epoch had been dated," a Tennessee soldier remembered. "He passed through the ranks of the common soldiers, shaking hands with every one he met. He restored the soldier's pride; he brought the manhood back to the private's bosom. . . . He was loved, respected, admired; yea, almost worshipped by his troops." The newspapers called him a gamecock, but most of his men rejected that puffed-up description—they considered him a father figure, and they called him "Old Joe." Even through the subsequent weeks of profitless battles and the ninety miles of backtracking, most officers and men retained their confidence in Johnston, believing that he knew best, that he was simply waiting for the right moment to spring the trap and cripple Sherman, and that he would not needlessly or carelessly sacrifice their lives. Even so, included in one soldier's catalog of Johnston's admirable qualities was one telling compliment: "He could fall back right in the face of the foe as quietly and orderly as if on dress parade."[5]

Old Joe, though heavily outnumbered, enjoyed a number of advantages: the favorable defensive terrain, Sherman's vulnerable and ever-lengthening railroad supply line, and a cadre of capable and experienced subordinate commanders. Foremost among these was Georgia-born Lieutenant General William J. Hardee, who had quite literally written the book on military operations. In 1855, at the request of then-U.S. Secretary of War Jefferson Davis, Hardee had written a manual entitled *Rifle and Light Infantry Tactics for the Exercise and Manoeuvres of Troops When Acting as Light Infantry or Riflemen*, known thereafter as *Hardee's Tactics* and used as the military bible by Confederates and Federals alike. Wounded at Shiloh, Hardee had fought in all the Army of Tennessee's battles except Chickamauga. Now fifty years old, Hardee was a handsome, graying widower and a "great admirer of the fair sex." "During the Kentucky campaign last year," a distinguished foreign observer wrote, "he was in the habit of availing himself of the privilege of his rank and years, and insisting upon kissing the wives and daughters of all the Kentuckian farmers." To veterans in the ranks, Hardee was such a known quantity that while the nicknames of other Civil War generals were simple endearments (Old Joe, Old Pap, Uncle Billy) or based upon personal quirks (Prince John, Shanks, or Old Clubby), Hardee's was an undiluted compliment: "Old Reliable."[6]

Hardee's younger colleague Lieutenant General John Bell Hood was likewise a man who could be counted on in a crisis, though he had shown himself throughout the war to be a blunt instrument, more war hammer than rapier. Aggressive and unpredictable, Hood had always attacked when his instructions permitted, and sometimes when they did not—most recently at Kolb's Farm on June 22, where he had charged a

Union division without orders and suffered 1,000 casualties. A Kentuckian by birth and a Texan by virtue of his many years of cavalry service in the Lone Star state, Hood was only thirty-three but was one of the South's most famous heroes, formerly a star brigade and division commander under Robert E. Lee and, with the exception of Chancellorsville, a veteran of all the Army of Northern Virginia's battles from Seven Pines through Gettysburg.

The difference in Hood's and Johnston's respective mindsets had been established very early in the war. In May 1862, in the course of Johnston's withdrawal from his fortified position at Yorktown, Virginia, he had directed Hood's brigade to "feel the enemy and fall back" near a Pamunkey River plantation called Eltham's Landing. Hood's Texans, later said to be "sp'iling for a fight," instead charged the Union position headlong, driving the bluecoats back toward the river and inflicting nearly two hundred casualties while suffering only forty-eight. Johnston was at the same time pleased and miffed, summoning Hood and demanding that he repeat the orders he had been given.

"General Hood, have you given an illustration of the Texas idea of feeling an enemy gently and falling back?" Johnston asked by way of cross-examination. "What would your Texans have done, sir, if I had ordered them to charge and drive back the enemy?"

"I suppose, General, they would have driven them into the river, and tried to swim out and capture the gun-boats," Hood replied.

Johnston allowed himself a smile, though he hardly seemed amused. "Teach your Texans that the first duty of a soldier is literally to obey orders," he said.[7]

He was "Sam" Hood to his friends, a nickname that got its start at West Point—possibly a reference within the corps of cadets to British Admiral Samuel Hood, colleague of Lord Nelson and hero of the Nile. Southerners hailed the young general as "the Gallant Hood of Texas," and observers then and later likened him to a knight, a crusader for the Confederate cause. Along the way, Hood had paid a heavy personal price for his aggressiveness and bravery, suffering a serious wound in the left arm at Gettysburg and then losing his right leg to amputation after a grievous injury at Chickamauga. "Hood tells his troops that it is safest always to be near to the enemies' guns," Richmond diarist Mary

Chesnut wrote. "Hood is a splendid proof to the contrary—shot to pieces as he is."[8]

Lieutenant General Alexander P. Stewart, Johnston's newest corps commander, was a one-time Whig and a former Tennessee militia officer who had until recently led a division under the late Episcopal bishop and Lieutenant General Leonidas Polk. In late June, just days after Bishop Polk was killed—nearly torn in half by a shell at Pine Mountain, near Kennesaw—Stewart was promoted to lieutenant general and placed at the head of Polk's old corps. Freckled and fair-haired, with a mustache and neatly barbered chin-beard, Stewart was forty-two, a by-the-Book Presbyterian with a professorial air still lingering from his days as an instructor of mathematics and natural and experimental philosophy, first at West Point and later at Cumberland University back home in middle Tennessee. His men called him "Old Straight," a reference to his devotion to clarity and precision—Stewart was a man who expected things to run like clockwork—though a fellow officer would suggest that the nickname also embodied "the straightforward simplicity of his character." But this bookishness and simplicity, perceived at first glance, was somewhat misleading. Stewart had shown himself to be a courageous fighter, most recently at the Hell Hole of New Hope Church, where, when implored by his soldiers to move to a place of safety, he told them calmly, sitting his horse among the whizzing bullets, that he was there to die with them. Despite this evidence of past staunchness, his reputation as a brigade and division commander had been solid, but not stellar. Whether Old Straight could handle his new and greater responsibilities remained to be seen.[9]

The casualties of the previous ten weeks, as the campaign progressed from Dalton down to the banks of the Chattahoochee, had reduced the Army of Tennessee to approximately 50,000 effectives—a little more than half the 90,000 Federals across the way—but for the most part, the soldiers in the ranks had remained undaunted during the long retreat. "Some Say we will retreat again in a day or Two & in the event will give up Atlanta but I do not beleav it," Sergeant John W. Hagan of the 29th Georgia Regiment wrote to his wife. "Gen Johnston well Knows he has but few men & no whear to get more when they are Killed up so he will make his fight a successful fight when he dose fight. We have given up a large country but when the grate fight is fought & his plans Known the country will be Satisfid & give him credit for he is as Shur to whip them as he fights them." The Southern papers, too, kept their spirits up. The editor of the *Richmond Whig* insisted, apparently with a straight face, that Johnston's lofty reputation had "grown with every backward step." A war correspondent for the *Memphis Appeal* summed up the prevailing mood on the Fourth of July, snug in Johnston's riverbank entrenchments. "The army is satisfied with the situation," he wired. "Let the people rest easy, and in the meantime, send forward their surplus vegetables; and then, like we do, trust to Providence and Gen. Johnston."[10]

And yet, how sorely one's faith is often tested. By the second week of July, as the Confederates pulled back across the Chattahoochee, even the most optimistic Southern soldier had cause to fret. "Well, it looks like we are gone up the spout," Private William Adams of the 30th Georgia Regiment wrote to his sister. "I am worse out of hart than ever." The early July diary entries of Private Robert Patrick of the 4th Louisiana—who back in May had written that Johnston was "the best General in the Confederacy, not even excepting Robt. E. Lee"—reflected the erosion of confidence in the butternut ranks:

> *Sunday, July 3*: Another fall back. I must acknowledge that it begins to look a little squally for our side.
>
> *Tuesday, July 5*: It has been nothing but a run from Dalton down and there must be a stop somewhere, or we had just as well not have an army in front of Sherman. . . . Our army is in good spirits however, and have an abiding faith in Johnston.
>
> *Wednesday, July 6*: It's a devilish gloomy looking time for us certain, and I feel despondent. One more retreat and the fate of Atlanta is irrevocably pronounced. It is "now or never."
>
> *Sunday, July 10*: We can't run much further, for we will soon be down to the Gulf of Mexico. I can't see into it.[11]

Hundreds of others in the butternut ranks apparently couldn't see into it either, and they began to desert in increasing numbers. Union soldiers recorded in their diaries and letters handfuls of Johnnie Rebs creeping through the lines after dark to surrender. "The men is all out of heart and say that Georgia will soon have to go under and they are going to the Yankees by the tens and twenties and hundreds a most every night," Private Celathiel Helms of the 63rd Georgia wrote to his wife in early July. "Johnson's army is very much demoralized as much as an army ever gets to be for all the news papers say that Johnson's army is in fine spirits but the papers has told nothing but lies since the war commenced. I see that the Officers is down in the mouth and their faces looks very long and some of them say that they are fearful that all their men will go to the Yankees." Those going over were often greeted and treated warmly by their captors. "Without a single exception, I have seen these men always kindly and hospitably received by our soldiers," a Massachusetts officer wrote home. "It is always, 'How are you, Johnny? We're glad to see you; sit down and have some coffee, and tell us the news." In response, one Rebel deserter gave his captors a sense of the mindset in the Southern ranks. "Our boys say General Sherman never makes but one speech," he told a Union lieutenant. "When ready for a movement, he says: 'Now boys, let's get ready to go;' and they get ready—on both sides."[12]

Few soldiers were as conscious of the desperate need to protect Atlanta as twenty-seven-year-old Lieutenant Andrew Jackson Neal of the Marion Light Artillery, whose family and home were there in the city, just a few miles behind the Confederate entrenchments. Originally from Zebulon, Georgia, Neal's family had moved to Atlanta in 1856 and lived in a house at the corner of Washington and Mitchell Streets, directly across from City Hall. "I am in fine spirits & confident that God will bless our arms with a signal victory over our cruel and unchristian enemies," young Neal had written back on May 15. But two months later, his spirits had fallen and his confidence was gone. "I do pray we may never march with our face turned southward again," he wrote on July 17. "There was not an officer or man in this Army who ever dreamed of Johnston falling back this far or ever doubted he would attack when the time came. But I think he has been wofully outgeneralled & though he has inflicted loss on the enemy only precedented by Grant's losses in Va he has made a loosing bargain."[13]

Though time and space appeared to be running out for the embattled Confederates, there were anecdotal indications that ample portions of Southern pluck remained. "Remember Moscow and Napoleon's splendid advance and miserable retreat," commissary officer Benedict J. Semmes wrote to his wife, assuring her, "we are all in fine spirits." Despite substantial evidence to the contrary, Lieutenant Robert M. Gill told his wife in Mississippi that "Sherman is much worse off than if he had never left Chattanooga, his whole campaign a failure."

Around the same time, Sherman himself received a letter penned by an anonymous Southern soldier on the Fourth of July. "Dear Mr. Sherman," it read. "Come on! Yours with anxiety, a Rebel."

"P.S.—We intend to give you a whipping."[14]

Having come this far by way of maneuver and the leverage afforded by his larger force, Sherman had no intention whatever of attacking the Confederates in their trenches south of Peachtree Creek, and certainly had no thought of being whipped. For one thing, though he would never say so, he had learned his lesson from the disastrous headlong charge at Kennesaw Mountain. Correspondent Whitelaw Reid of the *Cincinnati Gazette* later said of Sherman, "He never acknowledged an error, and never repeated it." What was more, an all-out assault on the Atlanta defenses was unappealing because it was entirely unnecessary. Johnston was a dangerous adversary leading a veteran army with a sizable force dug in a well-prepared defensive position. But Sherman had superior numbers, ample supplies, and freedom of movement to the east or west of the city. Knowing full well that Atlanta's primary worth was its value as a railroad hub, he reasoned that destroying those three remaining railroad lines leading to the city would not only render the place entirely useless, but it would also cut off and strand the Army of Tennessee, should they choose to remain. "Instead of attacking Atlanta direct, or any of its forts," Sherman had written to Halleck on July 6, "I propose to make a circuit, destroying all its railroads." If he was not yet able to stab the Confederacy's industrial heart, then he would sever its major veins and arteries, one by one.

Although he would be criticized by academics and armchair generals for various missteps and missed chances over the course of the campaign, Sherman's detractors would be forced to acknowledge not only the campaign's results thus far, but also the general's well-documented foresight. In point of fact, Sherman was not only at the gates of Atlanta with his army well-supplied and intact, but the campaign had also played out just as he had envisioned back in the early spring. Discussing his assignment with Grant back on April 10, Sherman had written, "Should Johnston fall behind Chattahoochee I would feign to the Right but pass to the Left and act on Atlanta or its Eastern communication according to developed facts." Having said as much, three months later, he would do exactly that—pass to the left and send Thomas and Schofield directly toward Atlanta and McPherson swinging wide to "act . . . on its Eastern communication"—the Georgia Railroad to Augusta. Grant and Halleck had warned earlier that week of the possibility that General Lee might detach some portion of his army in Virginia and send it by rail to Johnston's assistance. Despite their inferior rail system and industries, the Confederates had shown themselves adept at executing tactical and even strategic movements of forces by rail, most recently at Chickamauga the previous autumn. Sherman was far from panicked at this suggestion—"I do not fear Johnston with re-enforcements of 20,000 if he will take the offensive," he said—but he passed the intelligence along to his subordinate commanders, closing with the obvious: "It behooves us, therefore, to hurry."[15]

"We now commence the real game for Atlanta, and I expect pretty sharp practice," he wired Halleck on July 11, "but I think we have the advantage, and propose to keep it." How he would do so was first spelled out in detail in a warning order issued on July 14. Now that he was across the Chattahoochee River, Sherman's plan was to break from his normal pattern of flanking Johnston to the west and instead throw the bulk of his army around to the east of the city in a grand movement he called "a general right wheel." Farthest out, General McPherson's Army of the Tennessee would swing wide toward Stone Mountain and press south to break the Georgia Railroad beyond the town of Decatur. Schofield's Army of the Ohio was to move southeast toward Decatur itself, maintaining close contact with McPherson. Meanwhile, the largest portion of the army, Thomas's Army of the Cumberland, serving as the axle for the grand wheel, would cross the river at Pace's and Power's Ferries and advance directly toward Atlanta, moving past a country tavern and grocery known as Buck Head and then to the valley of Peachtree Creek.[16] "A week's work after crossing the Chattahoochee should determine the first object aimed at; viz., the possession of the Atlanta and Augusta road east of Decatur, Ga., or of Atlanta itself," the order closed.[17]

The blue army stepped off on this latest phase of the campaign under clear skies on the morning of July 17. By late the following afternoon, McPherson's veteran foot soldiers were tearing up track, burning depots and wood stations, and wrecking water tanks along the railroad toward Augusta. A "week's work" might have seemed like an optimistic timetable to execute a complicated maneuver of three armies moving through wooded terrain deep in enemy territory; but in fact the movement was completed just two days after the river crossing and was executed with ease and with little opposition. "No resistance was met anywhere I can hear of," General John A. Logan reported on July 18. "The loss in the whole command, so far as I can learn, is 1 horse with pains in his belly from eating green corn."[18]

Sherman was pleased, but not yet satisfied. "To-morrow I want a bold push for Atlanta and have made my orders, which, I think, will put us in Atlanta or very close to it," he wrote to General Thomas near Buck Head later that afternoon. He had his doubts as to whether "Johnston will give up Atlanta without a fight," but given the meager response to his operations since crossing the Chattahoochee, Sherman began to hope and even believe that the Virginian may well do just that. "Let us develop the truth," he said. But the truth was that in executing his change of steps, so to speak, from an allemande left to a right-hand do-si-do, Sherman had committed the military sin of dividing his force in the face of the enemy. Substantially dividing it, in fact: Thomas's force moving south through Buck Head was separated by more than two miles from Schofield to the east, a considerable chink in the Federal armor. The blue armies' spread-eagled deployment may have resulted from overconfidence or indifference to enemy intentions—after all, Johnston had let go of every other position he had held before in the campaign, and he would no doubt leave this one too. Sherman apparently had no thought that the outnumbered Confederates might lunge out of their works and attack.[19]

Even as he positioned his knights and rooks on the board and reported his progress to the War Department, Sherman kept up frequent correspondence with General Grant in Virginia. "I have now fulfilled the first part of the grand plan," Sherman had written to his friend as he prepared to cross the river. Admitting that his progress had been slower than expected, the redheaded Ohioan attributed any delay to the June rains and "the peculiar sub-mountainous character of the country from the Etowah to the Chattahoochee. But we have overcome all opposition and whipped Johnston in every fight where we were on anything like fair terms, and I think the army feels that way—that we can whip the enemy in anything like a fair fight." Now with all three armies over the river and again on the move, Sherman had indeed, as he told Halleck, commenced the real game for Atlanta. "Let us persevere and trust to the fortunes of war," Sherman closed, "leaving statesmen to work out the solution."[20]

In Washington, a friend visiting President Abraham Lincoln the second week of July found the careworn commander in chief more depressed than he had ever seen him, "indeed quite paralyzed and wilted down." As well he might be. The war was now in the dog days of its fourth bloody summer with the conflict far from over, and for the North, far from won. A struggle that most Americans had thought would be resolved in three months had dragged on for more than three full years. The Union's stirring twin victories at Gettysburg and Vicksburg the summer before—thought at the time to be the beginning of the end for the Confederacy—now seemed like distant memories as Lee's army continued its bloody resistance in the East. The bright optimism born with the opening of Grant's and Sherman's spring campaigns had been clouded over by months of largely profitless battles, horrific casualties, and outright defeats. On July 9, a Rebel force under Lieutenant General Jubal Early routed Federal forces under Major General Lew Wallace at Monocacy, Maryland, before continuing their raid toward Washington itself. Early's men pressed on and came within sight of the Capitol dome before pulling back, causing no small degree of panic among residents of the District. "In the memory of men who lived in Washington during the months of July and August, 1864, those days will appear to be the darkest of the many dark days through which passed the friends and lovers of the Federal Union," reporter Noah Brooks would remember. "No joyful tidings came from the army now; a deadly calm prevailed where so recently resounded the shouts of victory. In every department of the Government there was a manifest feeling of discouragement. In the field of national politics, confusion reigned."[21]

Even the United States Congress seemed to be reduced to praying for deliverance, adopting in early July a resolution "worthy of the Hebrews of the Old Testament or the Puritans of the English Civil War." The measure requested that the president appoint a day for national humiliation and prayer, so that the people may "confess and repent of their manifold sins, implore the compassion and forgiveness of the Almighty, that, if consistent with his will, the existing rebellion may be speedily suppressed," and, more desperately, "implore him as the supreme ruler of the world not to destroy us as a people." Old Abe was not a churchgoing man—indeed, his acceptance of Christian doctrine is debated even today—but he firmly believed in God and wanted Him on the Union side. Lincoln, "concurring . . . in the penitential and pious sentiments expressed," duly appointed the first Friday of August for the national observance.[22]

Lincoln needed all the help he could get. Victory in the great campaigns in Georgia and Virginia, and in the war as a whole, would depend not so much on the power of prayer or even on short-term military successes, but on political resolve—a quality many believed that only one man could provide. Abraham Lincoln approached his 1864 quest for reelection with his administration fractured and faltering, the war effort stalled, saddled with the criticism of his opponents and the doubts of his friends. The month of June brought the nomination of Lincoln and his running mate, Tennessee senator, fellow lawyer, and former tailor Andrew Johnson, but there was hardly an ovation of national acclaim at the news. "The age of statesmen is gone," railed the *New York World.* "The age of railsplitters and tailors, of buffoons, boors and fanatics has succeeded. . . . In a crisis of the most appalling magnitude requiring statesmanship of the highest order, the country is asked to consider the claims of two ignorant, boorish, third-rate backwoods lawyers for the highest stations in the Government. Such nominations, in such a conjecture, are an insult to the common sense of the people. God save the Republic!" Hoping to do just that, Lincoln would face in the fall an election that would serve as a national referendum not only on him personally or his administration, but on the war itself—its conduct and its cost. Approaching this test at the polls, Lincoln was battling uphill not only against recent military failures and a surging antiwar movement, but established American political history. No president had been reelected since Andrew Jackson, and the parties and the public had grown accustomed to a tradition, almost a gentleman's agreement, of the chief executive serving a single term. "Running again had become the thing not to do," one political historian said of the period.[23]

Assaults against the commander in chief as to his personal character and his allegedly woeful conduct of the war came from all quarters. Lincoln was called "a Presidential pigmy," a "buffoon and a gawk, disgracefully unfit for high office," a "mole-eyed" monster with a "soul of leather," derided as "an orangutan," or, for those who prefer a different animal metaphor, "the present turtle at the head of Government." Meanwhile, Northern peace Democrats known as Copperheads—so called because of their resemblance to the venomous and unpredictable viper, though they soon embraced the name and wore pennies as a sort of badge of honor on the lapels of their suitcoats—thundered on the floor of the House of Representatives, demanding an end to hostilities. Newspaper editors and White House delegations begged the president to open a dialogue with the South for a negotiated resolution to the conflict, presumably on terms of a status quo antebellum, with slavery remaining intact. "Our bleeding, bankrupt, almost dying country longs for peace—shudders at the prospect of fresh conscriptions, of further wholesale devastations, and of new rivers of human blood," prominent Republican and *New York Tribune* editor Horace Greeley wrote to Lincoln on July 7, imploring him to "submit overtures for pacification to the Southern insurgents." Even Lincoln's friends and political allies thought him sure to lose in November, and many discussed openly the possibility of replacing him with a candidate of greater promise. It was enough to make a man lose confidence in himself.[24]

The Democrats had originally scheduled their convention for July 4, but postponed the gathering until the end of August, the better to reconcile differences over the party's platform and perhaps take further advantage of the prevailing war weariness, which seemed to be growing stronger by the day. The frontrunner for the Democratic nomination was Major General George B. McClellan, former general-in-chief of the Union armies, whom Lincoln had dismissed as commander of the Army of the Potomac in late 1862 after he allowed Lee's army to escape in the aftermath of the Battle of Antietam, or Sharpsburg. The dashing young McClellan, hailed in early days as "the Young Napoleon" and still only thirty-seven years old, had been extremely popular in the Union ranks and would presumably attract the soldier vote—though hardline Copperheads insisted that they would accept no candidate with the "smell of war on his garments." Still, the former general seemed to give the party its best chance to appease both the peace wing of the party and the more moderate war Democrats—and of course, for McClellan personally, "rarely would a fired employee have such a spectacular and public opportunity to get back at the boss who sacked him." Wrangling over the party's platform would continue throughout the summer, but it was clear that a prominent plank—if not the joists and underpinnings of the entire platform—would be this: that the Republican Party's war was an abject failure that must be brought to an end.[25]

Lincoln's greatest burden in preparing to respond to this charge, apart from the slow and costly progress of the campaigns in Georgia and Virginia, was the appalling Union casualties. "A Confederacy that had seemed on the ropes at the end of 1863 had come back fighting and appeared likely to survive after a season of slaughter whose toll eclipsed even that of the terrible summers of '62 and '63," historian James M. McPherson wrote. Sherman had by now lost nearly 20,000 men in Georgia, a heartbreaking number, yet one that paled in comparison to the butcher's bill in Virginia. The Army of the Potomac's stumbling if dogged campaign from the Wilderness to Cold Harbor in May and June resembled a great funeral procession. In just over two months, more than 65,000 Union soldiers had been killed, wounded, or were missing.

General Grant, so recently the idol of the North, was scorned as a butcher and again (mis)cast as a bumbling drunk. Casualty lists, sometimes grimly headed "The Dead," filled column after column in the Northern papers. As Lincoln said, the terrible war had "carried mourning to almost every home, until it can almost be said that 'the heavens are hung in black.'"

But if the resolve of the nation wavered, Abraham Lincoln's held firm. Speaking at a sanitary fair in Philadelphia, Lincoln addressed head-on the question of when the war was to end. "We accepted this war for an object, a worthy object, and the war will end when that object is attained. Under God, I hope it never will until that time," he said. Then, referencing Grant's widely quoted comment that he would continue along the same line "if it takes all summer," Lincoln asserted, "The war has taken three years; it was begun or accepted upon the line of restoring the national authority over the whole national domain, and for the American people, as far as my knowledge enables me to speak, I say we are going through on this line if it takes three years more."

The president's determination was reflected among the Union forces pressing toward Atlanta. "I long as earnestly as you do, for such a change in public affairs, as will permit the sun browned defenders of the Nations life to return to their homes," wrote Colonel Emerson Opdycke from the Army of the Cumberland's camps within sight of Atlanta on July 17, "but it will hardly come this year: perhaps not for many long and weary months; *we must go on with the war, until the final triumph of our cause is secure*. To fail now, would result in anarchy and savage feuds for a generation; so we must fight on. Our choice is plain; we must elect Mr Lincoln and joy and joke along to the bitter end." The next day, Lincoln reinforced his intention to see the thing through by issuing a call for an astounding 500,000 additional volunteers for military service. Even if it took "fresh conscriptions, wholesale devastations, or even new rivers of human blood," as the mercurial Greeley put it, Lincoln would win the war or be thrown out of office for trying his damndest to do so. But he needed a victory badly, and soon.[26]

The prevailing gloom at the Executive Mansion in Washington by no means suggested a countervailing air of optimism at the White House of the Confederacy, an imposing columned edifice on Clay Street in Richmond, ironically Federal in style and as pale and severe as its present occupant. President Jefferson Davis faced no campaign for reelection, being only five months past the halfway point of the single six-year term prescribed in the Confederate constitution, but he had his own woes to contend with. For one thing, the South, too, had seen her sons die in ever-increasing numbers, and Davis was in no position to fill the places of the fallen by issuing a call for hundreds of thousands of new recruits to flock to the Southern banner. "Affairs look to me more and more critical," Brigadier General Josiah Gorgas, the Confederacy's chief of ordnance and a confidant of Davis's, wrote in June. "I cannot see where further re-enforcements are to come from." Then there were the battles and campaigns lost in the previous year, from Gettysburg to Missionary Ridge, and with them a commensurate diminution in southern morale, resources, and territory. Still, though the young republic had indeed suffered grievous setbacks in recent months, the widespread popular and political discontent in the North was no secret, and Southerners knew that impatience and war weariness on the one hand could result in victory on the other. Even now, from a strategic perspective, the South retained its inherent but substantial advantage of merely having to hold what it had, to continue to exist until the bloodshed and the cost caused the North to sue for peace. By contrast, Union forces—led by the "skittish" Sherman and the "thickheaded" Grant, as Southern papers portrayed them—would have to beat the Confederacy's two mightiest veteran armies, led by its two best generals, fighting on Southern ground in defense of their homes. At this point, all indications were that the people of the United States lacked the political and popular will and the military wherewithal to see such a war of conquest through to its end.

So Davis had believed as the campaign opened. But within days, he found himself wrestling with the same intractable problem he had faced back in 1861 in eastern Virginia and again in 1863 in central Mississippi—how to get Joe Johnston to put up a fight. As spring warmed to summer, Davis spent long hours in his office at the Confederate Executive Mansion—his only companion a cat named Maryland, appropriately gray and presumably neutral—worrying over Johnston's retreats and puzzling over his intentions. Unlike General Lee, who not only fought like the Devil but regularly reported his movements and plans to Richmond in good times and in bad, Johnston's messages from Georgia were infrequent and his plans usually opaque. Davis had grown accustomed to the Virginian's tendency to play his cards close to the vest, but he never accepted nor could he understand Johnston's reluctance to ever push his chips forward and take a risk. At the time he appointed Johnston to command, Davis had in mind an aggressive, longshot plan for the Army of Tennessee to drive into eastern and middle Tennessee, thereby obliging Sherman to pull out of Chattanooga to meet the threat and perhaps recovering lost territory all the way to Nashville. Even if such an offensive had been wise and practicable, it soon became clear that Johnston was hardly the man to carry it out. After Johnston pulled back from Dalton and Calhoun, then across the Oostanaula and the Etowah, Richmond was in turmoil, and the Confederate high command found its strategic worries reduced to a simple question—would General Johnston ever fight? "Johnston verifies all our predictions of him," Josiah Gorgas wrote in his diary in late May. "He is falling back just as fast as his legs can carry him. . . . Where he will stop heaven only knows."[27]

"I thought it our policy to stand on the defensive," Johnston later wrote. In sum, his campaign strategy was founded upon an earnest hope that his adversary would blunder and order an attack against the Confederates in their prepared positions. When Sherman declined to oblige and instead used his superior force to keep Johnston's lines under pressure while repeatedly moving around his flanks, the Southern general's only response was to keep retreating, and keep hoping. Along the way, Old Joe pleaded for reinforcements and help from other quarters—especially cavalry, which he believed could be used to break the Federal supply line in Tennessee. Leaving aside the question of whether a temporary break in a railroad line would be enough to convince the stubborn Union commander to throw up his hands and withdraw from Georgia, Johnston had but feeble excuses as to why he could not employ his own cavalry under Major General Joseph Wheeler to accomplish such a valuable object.

Meanwhile, Johnston took his editorial pen to the ledger, manipulating the numbers on the rolls to make his force seem insufficient while grossly inflating Sherman's headcount. Johnston only counted enlisted men armed and on the front lines as "effectives," while adding every orderly, cook, staff officer, and teamster west of the Appalachians to the Federal total—hence the oft-repeated canard that the Yankees had him outnumbered by more than two or even three to one. By way of example, on June 10—at the same time he was pleading for cavalry from another department to attack Sherman's supply line—Johnston reported that he had 27,256 "aggregate present" in his cavalry force, yet he listed only 10,903 horsemen as "effectives." In short, Johnston's reports compared apples to oranges—Confederate "effectives" versus Union "aggregate present"—and then compounded the problem by undercounting the apples and overcounting the oranges.[28]

There was in Richmond a glimmer of hope in June, as Johnston held his position on the Kennesaw lines for several weeks and then inflicted a bloody repulse on Sherman at Kennesaw Mountain—but then word arrived that Johnston had ordered hospitals evacuated and munitions and other valuable army stores removed from Atlanta, and had then pulled back to the Chattahoochee—news which sparked first confusion, then consternation and ultimately condemnation in the Confederate government. Davis needed to know firsthand what General Johnston planned to do to defend the city. On July 9, he dispatched his military adviser, Johnston's predecessor and enemy General Braxton Bragg, to Atlanta to meet with Johnston.

While Bragg was *en* roundabout *route* to Atlanta, Johnston continued to undermine the confidence of the Richmond authorities. On July 10, he gave up his Shoupade-anchored line and completed his withdrawal across the Chattahoochee. The next day, he wired without explanation or elaboration a one-sentence message: "I strongly recommend the distribution of the U.S. prisoners, now at Andersonville, immediately." The suggestion that the soon-to-be-notorious Confederate prison camp be evacuated was beyond prudent or even overcautious—it was downright alarming. Andersonville was near Americus in south-central Georgia—more than a hundred miles south of Atlanta.[29]

Davis's adviser Braxton Bragg—a bird of ill omen, to be sure—stepped off a train in the Atlanta Car Shed on the morning of July 13. The air was thick with boiler smoke, and the smell of horses clashed with the rotting stench of gangrene from the Distributing Hospital across the tracks. All around him, cars were being loaded with ammunition, supplies, and sick and wounded soldiers, as doctors and quartermasters argued on the platform and battled for boxcar space. The day was already hot and the dirt streets dry and dusty, which was just as well, as the locals knew that even a modest shower would turn the red clay of the Whitehall railroad crossing into a sea of mud. Bragg climbed into a coach for the ride out the Marietta road to Johnston's headquarters. He wasted no time in reporting to Davis, getting off a wire confirming the withdrawal across the Chattahoochee and noting that "indications seem to favor an entire evacuation of this place." Later the same day, he reported from Johnston's headquarters that the army was "sadly depleted. . . . I find but little encouraging."

After two full days in Atlanta, Bragg reported to Davis that he had been received "courteously and kindly," but he still had little idea of what Old Joe had in mind. "He has not sought my advice, and it was not volunteered," he wrote. "I cannot learn that he has any more plan for the future than he has had in the past." (Johnston would later insist that Bragg had represented that the visit was "unofficial," and that he never revealed his plans because the chief military adviser had never asked—which causes one to wonder what on earth the two generals spent two full days talking about.) With that being the case, Davis decided that he himself would give Johnston one final chance to reveal his intentions. On July 16, he sent a blunt telegram that he believed would surely light a fire under Johnston. Referring to reports of Federal movement from the river toward the railroad to Augusta, east of the city, the president inquired: "I wish to hear from you as to present situation, and your plan of operations so specifically as will enable me to anticipate events."

Johnston, as always, was untroubled, and he wrote a noncommittal reply that sealed his fate. "As the enemy has double our number, we must be on the defensive," he said. "My plan of operations must, therefore, depend on that of the enemy. It is mainly to watch for an opportunity to fight to advantage. We are trying to put Atlanta in condition to be held for a day or two by the Georgia militia, that army movements may be freer and wider." In other words, he had no plan at all, and would continue to watch from his trenches and evacuate his supplies, while Sherman moved wherever and did whatever he pleased with his superior force.[30]

There was much to worry about in this dispatch: the lack of details and initiative, the overestimation of enemy strength, the suggestion of holding the town "a day or two"—but most appalling was Johnston's reference to the Georgia militia. As historian Richard McMurry notes, General Johnston (wrongly) claimed that Sherman had twice his number, or nearly 120,000 men. Yet central to Johnston's plan was the idea that the ten-mile ring of fortifications around the city—which a Confederate engineer estimated would require 55,000 men to hold—could be defended by 5,000 Georgia militiamen. Governor Joseph Brown's state militia, a ragtag force of men too old and boys too young to fall within the broad ambit of Confederate conscription laws, contained a number of brave men. But they would be no match for Union regulars and were widely mocked by observers as "Joe Brown's pets." One Confederate veteran, seeing the militia on the march, thought it "a fitting burlesque to tragic scenes," and "the richest picture of an army I ever saw."

> Every one was dressed in citizen's clothes, and the very best they had at that time. A few had double-barreled shotguns, but the majority had umbrellas and walking sticks and nearly every one had on a duster, a flat-bosomed 'biled' shirt, and a plug hat; and, to make the thing more ridiculous, the dwarf and the giant were marching side by side; the knock-kneed by the side of the bow-legged; the driven-in by the side of the drawn-out; the pale and sallow dyspeptic, who looked like Alex. Stephens, and who seemed to have been just taken out of chimney that smoked very badly, and whose diet was goobers and sweet potatoes, was placed beside the three-hundred pounder, who was dressed up to kill, and whose looks seemed to say, "I've got a substitute in the army, and twenty negroes at home besides—h-a-a-m, h-a-a-m."

The central role of such a rabble—who would be charged with defending the city against the Union host while Johnston made "freer and wider" movements—rendered Johnston's plan, to the extent he had a plan, almost laughable. After all, except for the Kennesaw Mountain line, Johnston himself had yet to hold any position against Sherman with ten times that number of hardened Confederate infantry and artillery.[31]

Johnston would later insist not only that he had a plan all along to save Atlanta, but maintained that he would have held the city "forever."

Having retreated a hundred miles into Georgia and with his back to the wall, Old Joe would contend that he had Sherman just where he wanted him. Sympathetic biographers and Lost Cause apologists down the years would maintain that Johnston had his "sword figuratively torn from his grasp" just as he was about to give orders to crush the advancing Yankees. The crux of his supposed strategy was an ingenious plan to strike the divided Union force just as it moved across Peachtree Creek (the same movement his successor would attempt three days later). But he made no mention of such a plan, or of any plan of operations at all, in response to a pointed inquiry from the commander in chief. Instead, he suggested blandly that he would have to wait to see what Sherman did, and that he could hold the place "a day or two," with the help of the militia.

Jefferson Davis had his flaws—"ambitious as Lucifer, and cold as a lizard," Sam Houston would famously say of the Mississippian—and he had without question made certain command decisions during the war on the basis of personal relationships, grudges, and animosities rather than supporting the best man for the job. But he was a thoroughgoing military man—West Point graduate, Mexican War veteran, former United States Secretary of War—and he knew the undesirability of removing an army commander not only during an active campaign, but in the presence of an advancing enemy almost on the eve of battle. He had for weeks resisted calls from newspapers, citizens, army officers, and his own cabinet to sack Johnston and replace him with a general who would put up a fight for Atlanta. Now he felt he had no choice.

As the ordnance officer Gorgas put it, "Everybody has at last come to the conclusion that Johnston has retreated far enough." On the morning of July 17, Jefferson Davis met with his cabinet—all of whom wanted to fire Johnston weeks earlier—and made his decision.

General Johnston had to go.[32]

Old Joe had established his headquarters on the Marietta wagon road, just three miles northwest from the center of Atlanta, in a white frame house owned by a Massachusetts-born slave trader named Dexter Niles. The transplanted Bay State businessman had purchased the pioneer homestead two years before and "turned it into a slave plantation, or maybe it was a wholesale slave market," neighbor Sarah Huff, then a girl of nine, would remember. But with the armies approaching, Confederate money declining in value, and the "peculiar institution" under threat, Niles, no doubt conscious of the uncomfortable situation in which he might find himself in the event of Yankee occupation, sold out and went back to Boston. The house was a perfect command post—spacious, convenient to the railroad across the way, and facing the primary wagon road from Marietta to Atlanta, which was crowded most hours of the day and night with marching soldiers and rolling caissons and shovel-wielding slaves.

If there was among the high command of the Army of Tennessee any consternation owing to the latest backward movement and the pressing of gray-clad backs against the figurative, if not the literal, walls of Atlanta, it was hardly apparent to outside observers. Neighbors just up the road from the Niles place enjoyed nightly concerts from a military band, which serenaded the officers and local residents with "Dixie," "The Homespun Dress," and "The Bonnie Blue Flag." General Johnston's wife, Lydia, arrived at headquarters on July 10 to spend time with her husband in celebration of their wedding anniversary. (Years later, Johnston would cite the presence of his family in Atlanta as proof that he intended to hold the place.) A Federal spy named J. C. Moore, sent through the lines to gather information on Confederate positions south of the river, observed the house and grounds of the Niles residence early one evening. "Moore says he saw Mrs. Johnston and other ladies at General Johnston's headquarters yesterday," the spy's contact reported. "They seemed to be having a jollification."[33]

Another party was apparently in progress on Sunday night, July 17, with a gaggle of crinolined ladies chatting in the yard and the regimental bands again playing softly. Nine-year-old Sarah Huff, standing with her mother on the porch next door, would never forget the scene. "I have always thought of that night whenever I hear music on a lovely evening," she wrote years later. "As is usual with army people, even if comes a Waterloo tomorrow, 'There is a sound of revelry by night.'" Rows of cannon stood parked in an orchard nearby among ranks of orange trees planted in sunken tubs. The early evening moon was bright and full, illuminating the scene that for generations of Southerners would thereafter be known as "the Removal" or "the Transfer."

Across the Marietta road from the picket-fenced Niles house stood a wooden building, hard by the tracks of the Western & Atlantic Railroad, which for the past six days had housed the telegraph office, manned by a handful of telegraphers under the direction of Major Charles W. Hubner. Born in Baltimore, Hubner had as a boy of fourteen been one of a handful of witnesses at the funeral of Edgar Allan Poe. Inspired, perhaps, by this indelible brush with literary greatness, Hubner became a poet himself, who would in the course of his ninety-four years write and publish numerous volumes of memorial odes, Confederate campfire songs, and other acclaimed poetry and prose. Later praised as the "Poet Laureate of the South," Hubner would himself be awarded the Poe Memorial Medal by the University of Virginia in 1909. His present assignment was more prosaic, requiring him to oversee the Telegraph Corps of the Army of Tennessee. Johnston had appointed the twenty-nine-year-old Marylander to the post back in February—either unaware of or indifferent to the fact that Hubner could not operate a telegraph himself and could neither send nor read Morse code.[34]

Major Hubner had a good eye for separating the transcribed telegraphic wheat from the chaff and was well attuned to personalities and military protocol, so his eyes must have widened that night as he read the transcription of a message—an order—from the War Department in Richmond. No courier could deliver this message; Hubner would walk it over to headquarters himself. He stepped from the office and strode across the Marietta road and up the steps into the front parlor of the Niles house. There he found General Johnston bent over a map of the Atlanta defenses, conferring with his chief engineer, Colonel Stephen Presstman. It was nine o'clock. Hubner apologized for the intrusion and handed the deciphered message to Johnston. It read:

> RICHMOND, July 17, 1864
> General J. E. Johnston:
> Lieutenant-General J. B. Hood has been commissioned to the temporary rank of general under the late law of Congress. I am directed by the Secretary of War to inform you that as you have failed to arrest the advance of the enemy to the vicinity of

> Atlanta, far in the interior of Georgia, and express no confidence that you can defeat or repel him, you are hereby relieved from command of the Army and Department of Tennessee which you will immediately turn over to General Hood.
> S. Cooper,
> Adjutant and Inspector General.

No one present recorded Johnston's immediate reaction to the receipt of the order, though considering the months of prodding from above, the pointed inquiries as to his plans, and the recent visit of the president's military adviser, he could hardly have been shocked. Whatever emotion he felt was reserved for the future, when he would write a scathing memoir in defense of his actions, and for his troops, whom he addressed in an affectionate farewell order composed that same night, in which he praised the army's "soldierly virtue, endurance of toil, obedience to orders, brilliant courage." He also wrote a stinging reply to the adjutant general in Richmond. "Your dispatch of yesterday received and obeyed," it began, and proceeded to state a brief but plainly flawed case that Johnston's campaign had in fact been more effective than Lee's against Grant in Virginia. Always fiercer in correspondence than in combat, Johnston closed with a barb directed at his aggressive young replacement: "Confident language by a military commander is not usually regarded as evidence of competency."[35]

A disturbing rumor began spreading up and down the Confederate line south of Peachtree Creek: that General Johnston had been relieved from command. "It is dismissed in a moment; scoffed at, laughed down; it is absurd," a Louisiana officer recalled. "But it keeps coming, and with steady sad, convincing reiteration. Uneasiness seizes all of us; men gather in groups; they cannot, will not believe." Then comes Johnston's own announcement and farewell. Soldiers recalled the news as "a clap of thunder from a clear sky"—for even if their frustration and worry had increased in recent weeks, most saw their recent withdrawals as the only option in the face of superior numbers, and their admiration for Johnston was undiminished. "Great stalwart, sun-burnt soldiers by the thousands would be seen falling out of line, squatting down by a tree or in a fence corner, weeping like children," a Tennessean remembered. "This act of the War Department threw a damper over this army from which it never recovered, for 'Old Joe,' as we called him, was our idol. Whatever 'Old Joe' said was right; if he said, 'fall back,' it was right; if he said, 'Boys, halt, and let's give them battle,' it was right. If we were ragged, barefooted, and half fed, the boys would say, 'Old Joe is doing the best he can,' and you heard no complaint."[36]

Soldiers passing by the Niles house on the march lifted their hats in silent tribute, as Johnston stood watching on the porch. "There was no cheering!" one among the marchers remembered. "We simply passed silently, with heads uncovered. Some among the officers broke ranks and grasped his hand, as the tears poured down their cheeks." Others were more conspicuous in their lamentations. "For the first time, we hear men openly talk about going home, by tens (10) and by fifties (50). They refuse to stand guard, or do any other camp duty, and talk open rebellion against all Military authority," a Texas captain recorded in his diary. "All over camp, (not only among Texas troops) can be seen this demoralization—and at all hours in the afternoon can be heard Hurrah for Joe Johnston and God D— n Jeff Davis." A staff officer thought there was imminent danger of a mutiny. "I believe that a word from any Col. of good standing, would have induced the army to stack arms then and there unless their old Gen. was restored." In the end, however, this talk ended up being just talk, and there were no reports of widespread desertions immediately after the change of commanders. After all, many had been dissatisfied with the retreats and impatient for a fight; others, perhaps, were soothed by the rumors that Hood had done his best to forestall the switch and had lobbied to keep Johnston in place. It wasn't that they did not like Hood—many expressed respect for his bravery and his record—but he did not inspire the sort of affection that Johnston had a talent for sparking. "Genl. Hood the present commander of this army is a fighting man and no doubt a fine officer and under him we will gain the victory," a Georgia lieutenant wrote home to his mother, "but he is not Genl Johnston."[37]

John Bell Hood received word of his new appointment as army commander about eleven P.M., and later pronounced himself "astounded" by the order and "overwhelmed" with his new responsibilities—though this was somewhat disingenuous, as he had done his part in recent weeks to undermine Johnston. Later accused of being a dullard, Hood was in fact very clever, even conniving, with respect to positioning himself for promotion to a higher post. During his convalescence in Richmond, he curried favor with President Davis and other Confederate luminaries, and he had since engaged in fairly regular correspondence, disregarding the chain of command, with the War Department and with the president himself. On July 14, he submitted a letter to Bragg, then visiting the army at Atlanta, which a Georgia historian would call "a classic of military intrigue," a missive "packed with half-truths and damaging insinuations, and addressed over the head of the commander of the Army of Tennessee." Hood claimed in the letter that he had repeatedly urged Johnston to stand and fight, that the army had had numerous opportunities "to strike the enemy a decisive blow," and that it had failed to take advantage. "I have, general, so often urged that we should force the enemy to give us battle as to almost be regarded as reckless by officers high in rank in this army, since their views have been so directly opposite," Hood claimed. "I regard it a great misfortune to our country that we failed to give battle to the enemy many miles north of our present position. Please say to the President that I shall continue to do my duty cheerfully and faithfully, and strive to do what I think is best for our country, as my constant prayer is for our success." And now, three days later, with his burning ambitions answered (if not his prayers), Hood claimed, both to his compatriots and to the historical record, to be surprised.

The War Department order that placed him in command made General Hood the eighth and the youngest Confederate commander to hold the rank of full general. He would also be the last. As if to emphasize the burden now resting upon the young Kentuckian, Secretary of War James A. Seddon sent along a separate message, worthy in tone of a commission for a sacred quest. "You are charged with a great trust," it read. "You will, I know, test to the utmost your capacities to discharge it. Be wary no less than bold. . . . God be with you."

The next morning, July 18, Hood joined the other corps commanders, Hardee and Stewart, at Johnston's headquarters at the Niles house, shortly after daybreak. The trio spent most of the day trying to convince Jefferson Davis to reconsider or at least postpone the change of commanders, or to persuade Johnston himself to—as General Hood put it—"pocket that dispatch, leave me in command of my corps, and fight the battle for Atlanta." Both requests were summarily rejected by Davis and Johnston, both proud and stubborn men. "A change of commanders, under existing circumstances, was regarded as so objectionable that I only accepted it as the alternative of continuing a policy which had proved so disastrous," the president wrote in a telegram to Hood, Hardee, and Stewart, and closed: "The order has been executed, and I cannot suspend it without making the case worse than it was before the order was issued."[38]

For his part, Johnston had no intention of ignoring or resisting the decision to relieve him. Echoing almost word-for-word the statement he made to Hood at Eltham's Landing back in early '62, Johnston told the assembled generals, "Gentlemen, I am a soldier. A soldier's first duty is to obey—I turn over the command of the army tonight!" Hood, who knew nothing of Johnston's plans (if any) and claimed not even to know where the other two corps were posted, spoke with Johnston privately to plead for his help. Years later, Hood would assert that Johnston, with tears brimming in his eyes—promised that after a brief ride into the city, he would return and help all he could. Johnston never spoke of any such promise—and if he made it, he broke it. Boarding a carriage for the ride into Atlanta, he remained in town only long enough to gather his wife and his baggage, and then, "without a word of explanation or apology," as Hood alleged, "left that evening for Macon, Georgia." The two generals would never meet again.

Of course, there may have been something more to Johnston's reluctance to remain in command—and his hasty departure for Macon—than an old soldier's obedience to orders. As one historian put it: Johnston was off the hook, and he intended to stay off. "Things are so bad out there. They cannot be worse, you know," Hood's love Sally "Buck" Preston lamented up in Richmond, referring to the general by his nickname: "And so they have saved Johnston from the responsibility of his own blunders—and put Sam in. Poor Sam!"[39]

The splash created by Hood's appointment rippled throughout the Army of Tennessee. In addition to the shock to the morale of the troops and the impending change in strategy, Hood's appointment resulted in changes and inevitable tensions in the army's command structure. To succeed to the command of his old corps, Hood appointed Major General Benjamin Franklin Cheatham—a hard-drinking forty-four-year-old Tennessean and former California gold miner described by one witness as a "stout, rather rough-looking man with the reputation of 'a great fighter.'" He had built this reputation on battlefields from Shiloh to Kennesaw, where the site of the most vicious fighting, remembered by veterans as the Dead Angle or the Devil's Elbow—would be known ever after as Cheatham Hill. Though some journalists tried to dub him "Bulldog Cheatham," his men had no use for glorious nicknames for their unpretentious leader—they just called him "Frank." Cheatham dressed like a farmer and swore like a sailor, said to be the best (or, depending on your perspective, the worst) swearer in the army—a considerable distinction indeed, given the level of foulmouthed competition in the ranks. "It is said that he does all the necessary swearing in the 1st *corps d'armee*, which General Polk's clerical character incapacitates him from performing," a British observer wrote of the Tennessee general. One soldier thought him "one of the wickedest men I ever heard speak," and "Give 'em hell, boys!" was about as mild as Cheatham ever got. After the war, Cheatham would trade his military fame for a fitting role endorsing Jack Daniel's Tennessee Whiskey, but for the moment he would direct Hood's former corps, now placed at the eastern end of the Confederate position, standing between McPherson's advancing force and Atlanta.[40]

Not only would the Confederates march into battle under a new army commander, but with Alexander Stewart—just given permanent command of Polk's old corps—and the newly promoted Frank Cheatham, two of the Army of Tennessee's three corps would be led by generals new to corps command. The third would have its own command issues to deal with, perhaps less tangible but more emotional. In receiving the appointment to command, Hood had been promoted over the heads of other commanders senior to him in rank, most notably William J. Hardee. Old Reliable, though he made no official protest, was plainly miffed at being passed over by a man not only seventeen years his junior, but also a transplant from the Eastern theater who had been with the Army of Tennessee for less than six months. Jefferson Davis had seriously considered Hardee for the command—Hardee was more experienced than Hood, and R. E. Lee had all but recommended him outright in recent telegraphic exchanges with the president—but he had turned down command of the army when he was considered for it the previous winter, and he appeared to be supportive of Johnston's Fabian strategy. For now, the disgruntled Hardee would not only stay on at the head of his corps, but he would play a key role in executing Hood's plans in the days to come.

From the generals down to the privates, the Confederates had no illusions about the reasons for and the immediate implications of the replacement of Joe Johnston with John Bell Hood. "I was handed early this morning before I got out of blanket (I won't say bed) an order of Genl. Johnston turning over the command of the army to Lt. Genl. Hood," one of the army's most colorful characters, Major General William H. T. Walker of Georgia, wrote in a letter to his wife, noting his disapproval of Johnston's falling back and his lack of surprise at the change of command. "Hood has 'gone up like a rocket.' It is to be hoped that 'he will not come down like the stick.' He is brave. Whether he has the capacity to command armies (for it requires a high order of talent) time will develop. I will express no opinion." As for the future, Walker predicted, "A fight now is obliged to come off for if Johnston has been relieved for falling back (as I take it for granted he was), it is as much to say to Hood, don't you try the same game." A Louisiana private summed up the new Southern commander in his diary: "Hood is a fighting man," he wrote, something rarely said about the revered General Johnston. Other Rebels sensed that the time had come for goodbyes. "Hood in command I fear the result," a Mississippi lieutenant wrote to his wife. "I bid you fare well," he closed, and added a prediction: "there will be a slaughter here in a few days."[41]

With the steeples of the city in sight and intelligence reports coming in that Sherman had swept to the east and broken the railroad line to Augusta, there was a sense in the ranks that the preliminaries—the flanking maneuvers, the campsite rumors, the political squabbling, the informal river-line truces with enemy pickets—were a thing of the past. "I now beleave the grate storm is gathering," Sergeant John Hagan wrote home to his wife that same day, July 18.[42]

And indeed it was.

John Bell Hood. "The Gallant Hood," or "Old Pegleg," or sometimes, "Old Woodenhead." (*Library of Congress*)

CHAPTER THREE

Old Woodenhead

Hood Takes Command

"*In revolutionary times*, there are no Sundays," Daniel Webster once said in emergency session on the floor of the U.S. Senate, and by all appearances, Sherman would have agreed. Never one to notice much less defer to religious pretensions, the Yankee commander had put his army in motion on its clockwise lunge around Atlanta that same Sunday, July 17, even as his Confederate opponents were in the process of their midstream swap of commanders. A sporadic cannonade near the railroad bridge that afternoon, crashing and rumbling in the distance like a muffled accompaniment from the percussion section, signaled the movement and drew the ire of the devout. "Sherman has no regard for the Fourth Commandment," Major General Samuel French, commanding a Confederate division under Stewart, complained in his journal. "I wish a Bible society would send him a prayer book, instead of shipping them all to the more remote heathen: but it would be the same in either case. The one is wicked by nature; the other, I fear, is becoming so from habit. Perhaps 'Tecumseh' has something to do with it. There is much in a name."

The Union commander was not alone in this respect, however—there was habitual wickedness on the Southern side as well, tattered clothes and small vices. A Texas lieutenant frankly admitted that on that bright Sunday, "the boys, instead of all going to hear preaching, had their blankets spread and were playing draw-poker or shaking dice." Gambling would give way to gossip in the hours to come, however, as news of the change in commanders spread through the ranks. "The boys threw down their cards and collected in little groups discussing the new move," the Texan recalled. "They were all dissatisfied, but soon dismissed the whole with the remark: 'Hell will break loose in Georgia sure enough now.'"[1]

By Monday evening, word of Hood's ascension to the command of the Army of Tennessee likewise made its way around the streets and remaining households of Atlanta. Stationer Samuel Richards, just home from singing in the dwindling choir at the Second Baptist Church, recorded the news in his diary. "All of a sudden Gen Johnston has been *relieved* of the command of the Army and Gen Hood or 'Old Pegleg' as the soldiers style him placed in command," he wrote, "so that there is thought to be a prospect for a fight before Atlanta is given up, as Hood is said to be a fighting man, if he *has* only one leg."[2]

A fighting man he certainly was, and one that, as W. H. T. Walker said, had "gone up like the rocket." John Bell Hood had risen from low expectations and modest means, militarily speaking. As a cadet at the United States Military Academy, he had struggled in almost every subject, from natural philosophy to French to artillery to infantry tactics, and was far from exemplary in his conduct. He was caught sneaking to Benny Haven's tavern—a frequent sin among members of the corps of cadets—but was also cited for other minor instances of Kentucky hell-raisin', infractions ranging from chewing tobacco and being late for chapel to "making unnecessary noise and dancing on the piazza" and "visiting the commandant's tent with a segar in his hat." In September 1852, Robert E. Lee took over as commandant of the Academy, and as the year proceeded, whether by cause or by coincidence, Hood seemed to settle down. He accumulated not a single demerit in his last five months at the Academy, ending up with the precarious total of 196, just four short of the amount that mandated expulsion. He graduated from West Point in 1853, ranking forty-fourth in a class of fifty-two.

After an unremarkable fourteen-month stint in the Fourth Infantry in California—and, in the autumn of 1855, a passing encounter with a nervous bank manager in San Francisco named W. T. Sherman—he was reassigned to the Second U.S. Cavalry under Albert Sidney Johnston. There, he was reunited with Lee, then the lieutenant colonel of the regiment, and served with then-majors George Thomas and William Hardee. For the next six years, Hood rode with the famous cavalry unit and stood watch at posts from Missouri to the Texas frontier, developing along the way a strong affection for the Lone Star State. In early 1861, with his native state of Kentucky reluctant to secede, Hood entered the Confederate service from his adopted home of Texas. Still just a lieutenant, having not yet turned thirty, Hood rose within a year to brigadier general and established himself as one of the best and bravest fighters of the war.

His record in Lee's Army of Northern Virginia during 1862 and 1863 was filled with hard-fought honors, including the battles of Gaines' Mill, where his Texas Brigade lost nearly half its men but played a central part in breaking the enemy's triple line; Second Manassas, where his men led the charge that overwhelmed the Union position and swept the field; and Sharpsburg, or Antietam, as the Yankees called it, where his division's charge through the corn field near the Dunker Church became the stuff of legend. As the cannon-smoke cleared, an officer found Hood off by himself, eating an apple, and asked him where his division was. "Dead on the field," Hood replied.[3]

Hood's costly misjudgments in the closing months of the Civil War, along with decades of postwar criticism, would so eclipse his once-bright reputation that it is easy to overlook how highly he was regarded during most of the conflict. No less an authority than Stonewall Jackson praised the young Texan's "ability and zeal" and thought him "one of the most promising officers of the army." ("Oh! He is a soldier!" Stonewall once exclaimed to a staff officer who had mentioned Hood.) Newspapers lauded Hood for his "courage and genius," and singled out his Texas Brigade for not only its fighting capabilities but also its admirable discipline. James Longstreet, in recommending Hood for promotion to lieutenant general after Chickamauga, wrote that the young general had "handled his troops with the coolness and ability that I have rarely known by any officer on any field." An aide to General Longstreet, echoing Jackson, called Hood "one of the finest young officers I ever saw," and thought "had we had many more of the like sort at Sharpsburg, we would have whipped the Yankees worse than they were ever whipped before."[4]

He was an imposing figure—six feet two inches tall, with blond hair and a tawny shovel of a beard that reached to his sternum and framed what an acquaintance called a "sad Quixote face," his blue eyes hound-dog tired except in battle, when they glittered Jackson-like with martial fervor. But by 1864, after the mangling of his left arm at Gettysburg and the loss of a leg at Chickamauga, Hood was something close to half the man he used to be. He wore his left arm in a sling and had only the one good arm to help him scratch around on his crutches. Fitted with a prosthetic leg, made of cork and intended more for balance than support, he required three orderlies to hoist him up onto his mount and strap him into the saddle. The stump of his right thigh, which was so short that it was difficult to fit with an artificial leg, frequently became irritated and caused him pain. Postwar critics would level the speculative charge—unsupported by any evidence whatever—that he spent much of his time heavily drugged by laudanum, opium, or other narcotics—an accusation, interestingly, that has never been made against other well-known and active amputee commanders like O. O. Howard or Richard Ewell.[5]

Some might argue, to the contrary, that Hood's wounds and amputation were not a sign of weakness, but testament to the general's constitution and resolve. The operation that took Hood's leg—disarticulated amputation at the hip—was the most dangerous surgery widely performed during the war, with a mortality rate of 83.3 percent. Yet Hood not only survived the ordeal, but returned to active and grueling duty in the field—campaigning for weeks at a time in the Georgia wilderness, out in the elements, sleeping in tents, and spending long hours on horseback, guiding his mount one-handed with his crutch strapped to the saddle behind him. "I have been riding all over the country with Gen. Johnston," Hood had written to a friend that spring, "and have been in the saddle every day enough to have fought two or three battles, without feeling any inconvenience whatever from it. I ride with perfect comfort to myself, and expect to walk with a cane before long." Hood never felt sorry for himself—he barely mentions his amputation in his memoirs—and apparently never considered retiring from the fight. "As long as I have a leg or an arm, and I can ride a horse, and command such men as I do," he told a hospital chaplain, "I will fight those Yankees."[6]

No one could deny that Hood was determined, then, or that he was brave. But by this point of the war, courage was to many men an expected, unremarkable commodity. Veterans, after all, had been under fire by the hundreds of thousands. A commander's fearlessness under fire was taken for granted—hence the reaction in the ranks that Hood was nothing more or less than "a brave, hard fighter." As one historian wrote, "in courage's depreciating currency, the ultimate accolade had fallen to faint praise." A Union soldier, speaking of the "good pluck" expected of generals, summed it up. "You hear people say, 'Oh, everyone is brave enough,'" he said. "'It is the head that is needed.'"[7]

Which brings us to another common slander, again repeated more after the war than during—that John Bell Hood was stupid. Critics begin by pointing to his relatively undistinguished record at West Point—though other officers with lackluster Academy records, from James Longstreet (fifty-fourth out of fifty-six in the class of 1842) to George Armstrong Custer (dead last in the class of 1861), seemed never to face similar questions about their intelligence. Undeterred, Civil War historians have given Hood a nickname, suggesting that his men called him "Old Woodenhead"—though there is no evidence that any such derisive label was applied by the soldiers in the ranks. Instead, veterans simply referred to the big, blond Texan as "Hood" or "the Sergeant" (a nod to his commanding demeanor and booming voice) or "Old Pegleg" (all generals were "Old," it seems, even those who were just thirty-three). Aspersions as to Hood's intelligence appear to be retrospective, a campaign led by postwar Lost Cause historians and pro-Johnston partisans like E. A. Pollard, who described Hood as having "a lion's heart and a wooden head."[8]

No one who served with him or under him complained—at least not at the time—of any intellectual failings. True, Hood was young—twenty-four years younger than his predecessor—and he lacked the experience of a Bragg or Johnston or Hardee, but he was hardly empty between the ears. His correspondence and records reveal an officer who spoke, wrote, and gave orders clearly, and his plans in the days to come, as we will see, would be praised by contemporaneous observers and later critics as well thought-out and militarily sound, though hardly foolproof. In short, Hood was neither brilliant nor dense—the truth was probably somewhere in between. The Texan's chief shortcoming was not a lack of intelligence, but a lack of nuance, caution, discretion, attention to detail. Hood was, as historian Bruce Catton would put it, "uncomplicated." He was, as the saying goes, all lion, none of the fox.

What was more, Hood's considerable military achievements had been scored as a subordinate executing the orders of some of the greatest generals of the war—Robert E. Lee, Stonewall Jackson, James Longstreet, and most recently Joseph Johnston. Now he was the top man, and he was on his own. Even those who thought highly of Hood's battlefield leadership and prior record had concerns about whether he was capable of heading the Army of Tennessee. General Lee, whom Davis had consulted a week before as to Hood's fitness for the post, had tempered his praise with reservations. "Hood is a bold fighter," Lee had written, "very industrious on the battlefield, careless off, and I have had no opportunity of judging his action, when the whole responsibility rested upon him." Promoted to the lofty perch of army commander, Hood may well turn out to be—to borrow a phrase from Davy Crockett—a huckleberry over his persimmon.[9]

Throughout the summer of 1864, from the firesides of the army to the parlors of Charleston and Richmond, Southerners debated the Johnston-Hood controversy. Some believed that Hood had been placed in a thankless, no-win situation. "If Hood fights & is victorious there will be plenty who will say 'behold the fruits of Johnston's strategy,'" Josiah Gorgas wrote from his office in Richmond, "while if he is defeated these people will cry 'see the fruits of the removal of Johnston!'" Others chewed over the contrast between the two Confederate heroes. Johnston was said to be every inch a general, while Hood was a soldier. Johnston was a planner and master logistician, supposedly "brave as Caesar" but cautious to a fault; Hood full of "dash and fire," a battlefield leader and a commander unafraid to shoulder great risk in search of great rewards.[10]

The distinction was embodied in two hearsay stories about the respective commanders that made their way along the grapevine and then on into diaries and memoirs—rumors that had the air of legend and the ring of truth. It seemed that Joe Johnston, at the time a U.S. Army colonel, had once gone on a bird shoot with Wade Hampton and Hamilton Boykin. "We all liked him," Boykin recalled, "but as to hunting, there he made a dead failure." This was not due to any lack of marksmanship—Johnston was by all accounts a "capital shot"—but conditions were never right to pull the trigger. "The bird flew too high or too low—the dogs were too far or too near—things never did suit exactly. He was too fussy, too hard to please, too cautious, too much afraid to miss and risk his fine reputation for a crack shot." Hampton and Boykin fired away, "happy-go-lucky," and each ended the day with a bagful of birds, but Johnston came home empty-handed, having never fired a shot. The outing was emblematic of the distinguished Virginian, who one acquaintance would note "could solve on paper any military problem," but was not a man of action.

Hood, though perhaps not one to be trusted with pen-and-paper calculations, was the subject of secondhand stories as well. The most famous tale was related around the campfire by a Kentucky colonel who claimed to have witnessed the young commander at the poker table in old army days.

"I seed Hood bet twenty-five hundred dollars," he said, "with nary a pa'r in his hand."[11]

Sherman was riding with General Schofield towards Decatur on Tuesday morning, July 19, when he learned of the change in Southern commanders. The news of Old Joe's displacement and the appointment of John Bell Hood came by way of a smuggled copy of the previous afternoon's *Memphis Appeal*, the only paper still being printed in the city, brought through the lines by a Union sympathizer and then passed back from Schofield's advance guard. The Ohioan had never crossed paths with Hood himself (unless he remembered the Kentuckian's bank draft in San Francisco nine years before), but he knew that an accurate assessment of the new Confederate commander would not be difficult to come by. Not only had Schofield and McPherson been classmates of Hood at West Point—the latter graduating as top man in the class of

1853—but Thomas had been an instructor in artillery tactics at the Academy during the same period. "Schofield, do you know Hood?" Sherman asked over the folded newspaper. "What sort of a fellow is he?"

"Yes, I know him well," replied Schofield, who had been Hood's roommate and had spent long hours tutoring him in mathematics. "I will tell you what sort of man he is. He'll hit you like hell, now, before you know it." The normally mild-mannered Oliver Otis Howard, one of Thomas's corps commanders, was even harsher in private criticism expressed in a letter to his wife. Hood, he said, was "a stupid fellow, but a hard fighter—does very unexpected things." Sherman, who had always admired and respected Johnston, was delighted with the change. When Major General Grenville M. Dodge of the XVI (16th) Corps rode up just after Sherman's exchange with Schofield, Sherman cried, "Dodge! Dodge! Glorious news. Joe Johnston is relieved and Hood is in command, and we will butt his brains out before tomorrow morning." He reiterated his delight at Hood's appointment years later, along with his conclusion that Hood was "bold even to rashness, and courageous in the extreme."[12]

With cool, cautious Johnston gone and the hotheaded Hood in his place, Sherman did more than plan for battle—he earnestly hoped for one. "I inferred that the change of commanders meant 'fight,'" Sherman wrote in his memoirs. "This was just what we wanted, viz., to fight in open ground, on anything like equal terms, instead of being forced to run up against prepared intrenchments." Later that afternoon, Sherman sat down on a stump by the side of the road and began drafting orders for his three subordinates. "The whole army will move on Atlanta by the most direct roads to-morrow, July 20, beginning at 5 A.M.," the order began. Thomas would move south from Buck Head, McPherson would march west from Decatur, and Schofield would converge on the city between the two. "Each army commander will accept battle on anything like fair terms, but if the army should reach within cannon-range of the city without receiving artillery or musketry fire he will halt, form a strong line, with batteries in position, and await orders," Sherman directed, and already he showed himself willing to employ a hard hand in dealing with local civilians. "If fired on from the forts or buildings of Atlanta no consideration must be paid to the fact that they are occupied by families, but the place must be cannonaded without the formality of a demand."[13]

Everyone—the Northern command, the Southern rank and file, the local population and the press—now predicted that Hood would give battle, and true to form, he would not disappoint. Johnston had waited seventy-three days for conditions to be exactly right for him to launch an attack against the blue invaders. Hood, less than forty-eight hours after the midnight order placing him in command, had not only resolved to go over to the offensive but convened a council of war to explain to his subordinate commanders the specifics of his plan of attack. "I feel the weight of the responsibility so suddenly and unexpectedly devolved upon me by this position," he had told his troops in an address issued as he took command, "and I shall bend all my energies and employ all my skill to meet its requirements."

In his memoirs, Hood would declare himself an "ardent advocate of the Lee and Jackson school"—a declaration that was both a statement of his beliefs and an attempt to recapture past glories. Hood had witnessed General Lee's campaigns, including a number of victories scored against more numerous foes—the Peninsula Campaign, where Lee had used repeated attacks and maneuvers to drive back a superior force from the gates of Richmond; and Second Manassas, where the Gray Fox launched a surprise attack against an overconfident opponent. The young general would now attempt to take elements of each of these and craft them into a battle plan that would throw back Sherman from Atlanta. Once a pupil under Lee and Old Jack, now it would be up to the supposedly woodenheaded Hood to take advantage of the brilliant Northern commander's tactical carelessness and momentary disregard of military principles and teach him a bloody, decisive lesson.[14]

On July 19, the day after he took command, intelligence reports informed Hood that Sherman was moving on the Georgia Railroad out past Decatur and that Thomas's army was approaching the crossings of Peachtree Creek, four miles north of the city. Hood discerned from this that the wings of the blue army were widely separated—Decatur was seven miles from the bridges and fords of the creek—and immediately decided that this was the time to strike one of the two. He quickly settled on a plan to attack the Federals just after they crossed Peachtree

Creek. Both Hardee's and Stewart's corps were already in position south of the creek and could launch an unexpected attack before Thomas's men had the chance to entrench. Hood's instructions, as he recalled them, were "to drive the enemy back to the creek, and then towards the river, into the narrow space formed by the river and the creek; everything on our side of the creek to be taken at all hazards, and to follow up as our success might permit." In other words, Hood planned to catch the bluecoats in the open and sweep the field from right to left, corralling the Army of the Cumberland as if into a dustpan—after which Hardee and Stewart could either turn and assist Cheatham in crushing the isolated wing under McPherson; or could pitch into Sherman's rear, severing his supply line and forcing him to let go of Atlanta once and for all.

All this was explained in person to each of the three corps commanders, along with G. W. Smith, commander of the Georgia state militia, in a council of war held late on the night of July 19. Hood wanted no mistakes and no misunderstandings. "I was very careful in this respect," he later wrote, "inasmuch as I had learned from long experience that no measure is more important, upon the eve of battle, than to make certain, in the presence of the commanders, that each thoroughly comprehends his orders." The attack was to be launched promptly at 1:00 P.M. the next day, July 20, which would give ample time for getting set without allowing the advancing Federals a chance to brace for what was coming.[15]

Hood's plan—a surprise attack against a divided force, presumably exposed and unfortified, with a water barrier in its rear—was not only militarily sound, it also was conceived in a way that would bring a total of seven Confederate divisions onto the field of battle against only four Union divisions. For the first time in the campaign, the Rebels would have the advantage of superior numbers—at least in the area where the trap was to be sprung. But the plan, if sound in its conception, would face considerable obstacles in execution. The first was that if Sherman was strung out, then unavoidably, so was Hood. In all, his own curving line covering the city from the Chattahoochee to the northwest to the Georgia Railroad out to the east would be nearly six miles long—and circumstances would soon require him to make it even longer.[16]

The second was Hood's choice of where his attack would be made—or not so much where, but against what, and whom. In choosing to strike north of the city, the Rebel attack would be aimed at a portion of the Army of the Cumberland—not only Sherman's largest force, but also the one commanded by George H. Thomas, the Rock of Chickamauga and arguably the best defensive fighter in the Western Theater. Phlegmatic and imperturbable, Old Pap seemed to one witness like a figure "hewn out of a large square block of the best-tempered material that men are made of, not scrimped anywhere, and square everywhere: square face, square shoulders, square step; blue eyes, with depths in them, withdrawn beneath a pent-house of a brow, features with legible writing on them, and the whole giving the idea of massive solidity, of the right kind of a man to 'tie to.'" There was no shortage of previous examples of Thomas's unwillingness to be budged, even under the most alarming of circumstances—from the council of war considering a withdrawal at the Battle of Stones River, where Thomas said simply, "This army cannot retreat," then covered himself with his blanket and went to sleep; to being besieged in Chattanooga, when he assured General Grant, "We will hold the town until we starve." He was like that—unflappable, self-assured, given to matter-of-fact pronouncements that seemed to put an end to debate and to foreclose even the possibility of defeat.[17]

Even as Hood pieced together his plans for a strike against Thomas north of the city, the Federals were bearing down on the city from the east. With the arrival of McPherson's army astride the Georgia Railroad and Schofield's advance units approaching Decatur, local citizens were getting their first close-quarter view of the Yankees and their first taste of what was in store. Thomas Maguire, who owned a plantation near Stone Mountain he called the Promised Land, recorded the progress of events in his diary:

> *July 18*: Yankees at Stone Mountain—water station burned—part of track torn up—great excitement.
>
> *July 19*: Fighting at Atlanta—Yankees at the Mountain—folks badly scared in this settlement.
>
> *July 20*: We are now cut off and in the enemy's lines . . .

> *July 21*: At 12 or 1 o'clock at night the Yankees came here in force. Knocked us up. The house was soon filled with the thieving Yankees—robbed us nearly everything they could carry off. Broke open all our trunks, drawers, etc. & carried off the keys. They must have practiced roguery from their childhood up, so well they appeared to know the art.

Meanwhile, in nearby Decatur, thirty-five-year-old Mary Gay and her elderly, twice-widowed mother found herself at the mercy of Schofield's soldiers. "Advance guards, composed of every species of criminals ever incarcerated in the prisons of the Northern States of America, swooped down upon us, and every species of deviltry followed in their footsteps," she remembered. "My poor mother, frightened and trembling, and myself, having locked the doors of the house, took our stand with the servants in the yard, and witnessed the grand *entre* of the menagerie." Soldiers were undeterred by the locked door—they broke in and ransacked the house, breaking china and crockery, rifling drawers and chests, and stealing "everything of value they could get their hands upon," while committing other "outrages and indignities" Miss Mary would later find "too revolting to mention." Outside, the Federals slaughtered hogs, cows, and chickens for their campfires and cookpots and commenced pitching their tents in the yard. "One of the beasts got down upon his all-fours and pawed up the dust and bellowed like an infuriated bull," Mary wrote. Another teased the lady of the house and asked if she did not expect to see the Yankee devils with hooves and horns. "No," she replied, "I had expected to see some gentlemen among them, and was sorry I should be disappointed."

The tension in Atlanta was palpable. The streets were increasingly deserted, scattered with garbage and the discarded belongings of fleeing residents. The gaslights were out and had been for weeks. Army skulkers and rear-echelon troublemakers prowled the darkness, as the remaining citizens hunkered down and waited for news. "Suspense, the most depressing of human senses, holds possession of the popular mind, and anxious care is written in every line of the popular countenance," an *Augusta Constitutionalist* correspondent wrote from the city that evening. "There is not a sound but startles the expectant ear. The roll of distant carriage wheels is mistaken for artillery, and the clatter of wagons over the stones of the street for the rattle of musketry. The fall of any heavy body, as a bale or a box, often startles one as though it is a shell fallen in that part of the town." And all were starved for information. "You rise in the morning very early, and you find the town up before you," the reporter wrote. "People are eager to be a stir and to hear the news, which comes in shoals of falsehood, barley sprinkled with fact. Not an hour in the day but additions are made to the lies of the dawn, and you lie down at night to dream of loud alarums, and neighing steed and bursting rockets and guns. Such a city is Atlanta."[18]

Wednesday, July 20, 1864, opened with the "The Star-Spangled Banner," played with commendable verve early that morning by a regimental band in the XVII (17th) Corps, as McPherson's men took up the march westward along the Georgia Railroad leading toward Atlanta, six miles away. Daybreak revealed a cloudy sky, and the heavy warmth of the early morning warned of a stifling day ahead. It was here, on the east side of the city, where Sherman expected Hood to strike—against the Army of the Tennessee, a force half the size of Thomas's, farthest from its base of supply and advancing out in the open. In point of fact, however, there was no meaningful Rebel threat to McPherson or Schofield. On the contrary, Hood was massing two-thirds of his army north of the city for a blow against Thomas, and nothing stood between McPherson and Atlanta but Wheeler's dismounted cavalry and a handful of "Joe Brown's Pets" from the Georgia militia.

At noon, John Bell Hood stood quietly in the doorway of his headquarters, "arrayed in full uniform, leaning on his crutch and stick." Reporter Felix De Fontaine, who wrote for the *Savannah Republican* under the pen name "Personne," saw in his eyes "a strange, indescribable light, which gloams in them only in the hour of battle." De Fontaine was a familiar face around headquarters, and Hood shook his hand and greeted him warmly. "At once I attack the enemy," he said. "He has pressed our lines until he is a short distance of Atlanta and I must fight or evacuate. I am going to fight." The big blond Kentucky-born Texan, though plainly resolute, seemed to have no illusions about the Rebels' chances. "The odds are against us," he said, "but I leave the issue with the God of battles." As the appointed hour of the attack drew near, Hood and his staff mounted up and rode off toward General Stewart's headquarters along the Howell Mill Road. The correspondent De Fontaine remained behind to scribble a few "hurried words anticipatory of the battle":

> The moments are slipping by, as anxious moments always do, tediously and yet not without a sensation of near agony that is utterly depressing. One more hour and the mettle of an army opposed by double its numbers, fighting behind breastworks, with diabolic incentive, the spires of Atlanta in view, and its booty in prospect, will be undergoing an ordeal by fire. One hour more and hundreds of dead friends, whose merry laugh you have answered around their camp fires, may be weltering in their blood at these strange hillsides, or gone forever to their long homes. One hour more and thousands will become widows and orphans, and weary heart cries will ascend to Heaven over the new sacrifice which the cruel struggle demands.[19]

Though George Thomas would hold the overall command, the bulk of the Union forces on the field that day were three divisions of the Federal XX (20th) Corps under forty-nine-year-old Major General Joseph Hooker, known far and wide by this stage of the war as "Fighting Joe." Like many others in the present dramatis personae, the Atlanta Campaign was Act II for Hooker, who had reached and fallen from his apogee the year before. In January 1863, he had been placed in command of the Army of the Potomac, the first army of the Republic, and had welcomed his ascension by announcing, immodestly but characteristically, "My plans are perfect. May God have mercy on General Lee, for I will have none." Marse Robert was unimpressed, however, and soon taught the man he contemptuously referred to as "Mr. F. J. Hooker" a very bloody lesson at the Battle of Chancellorsville, a signal victory to Confederate arms referred to ever after as "Lee's Masterpiece." President Lincoln soon relieved Hooker of command and thereafter he was sent west with two divisions from the Army of the Potomac to reinforce the Federals under siege in Chattanooga. He now led a corps in

Sherman's army and was determined to make a good showing in his new assignment—but there was no question but that the demotion rankled, especially when he looked around and saw former "juniors" like McPherson in command of an army while Hooker was himself subordinate to both Thomas and Sherman.

Major General Joseph "Fighting Joe" Hooker. (*Library of Congress*)

What was more, Hooker and Sherman despised each other, each for his own reasons. Sherman's dislike for Hooker dated back to his banking days in California, when, it was said, Hooker had speculated in land, ran up gambling debts, and never repaid a significant sum he had borrowed from Sherman. For his part, Hooker thought Sherman unstable and overrated, pointing to his various tactical defeats like Kennesaw Mountain and complaining to Secretary of the Treasury Salmon Chase in out-of-channels correspondence that Sherman "will never be successful." The rivalry and animosity between the two men had revealed itself earlier in the campaign. At Resaca, the two generals and their aides found themselves in an exposed position and came under Rebel fire. Staff officers and subordinate commanders scattered in all directions, but Hooker and Sherman stood fast, glaring at one another as the bullets zipped past them, each silently daring the other to be the first to wilt and seek cover. Aides soon intervened and tugged the two generals to safety, but the episode made plain that neither general intended to back down from the other, then or later.

The men in Hooker's corps admired him deeply—more than one soldier, in diaries and letters home, likened their commander to George Washington—but no one held Joe Hooker in higher esteem than did Joe Hooker. "You must know," he had written to a friend in the spring, "that I am regarded with more jealousy in this my new sphere of operation than I ever was in the East. It is not without reason for it is as certain as any future event can be that I shall be regarded as the best soldier in this Army if I am not now, provided we have a few opportunities to establish our relative merits." And though he did not yet know it, he was about to have just such an opportunity.[20]

Federal engineers and pioneer details had been hard at work since the day before, completing the construction of bridges at several points. Peachtree Creek was a "difficult stream," according to a Northern correspondent—difficult not only for its unpredictable depth, breadth and current, each of which varied significantly depending on recent rainfall, but also for its steep banks and uneven, rocky bottom. The stream took its name not from any nearby orchard but from an ancient Creek Indian settlement known as "Standing Pitch Tree." Settlers corrupted "pitch" to "peach" and thus the name of the stream, and with it one of Atlanta's iconic place names and thoroughfares, was imperfectly born. (The city of Atlanta today has more than seventy streets and avenues with "Peachtree" in the name.) Twisting like a rattlesnake, the watershed flowed east to west, passing roughly four miles north of Atlanta as it wound its way to its confluence with the Chattahoochee River. Smaller tributaries fed into the stream, most notably Clear Creek—which was to form the eastern edge of the two-mile-wide battlefield—and Tanyard Branch (or Tanyard Creek), which dangled south on the map like a loose thread. The branch was named for an antebellum tannery down in the city, whose discharges often turned the waters of the stream black.[21]

Sherman's order had implied the need for haste—a movement on Atlanta beginning at 5 A.M. by the most direct roads possible—but now that the Army of the Cumberland had moved south of Peachtree Creek, there was more a sense of lethargy rather than urgency, perhaps owing to the oppressive July heat. In the center, the 20th Corps completed its crossing, then halted and stacked arms for a midday meal. Generals Hooker and Williams, along with staff and escorts, gathered in the shade while men started small fires and began frying pork and boiling coffee. Some soldiers moved back to the creek to fill canteens; others crept forward into the brush in search of blackberries. "It was a bright day, though hot; after we had our meal we made ourselves as comfortable as we could," Sergeant Rice C. Bull of the 123rd New York Infantry recalled. Some men read novels, or wrote letters; others slept; while "a good many were having a friendly game of cards using the greasy pack that always was handy when we halted." A rumor spread up and down the line that the Confederates were on the retreat and that the Federals would enter Atlanta the next day without opposition.

"There had been so far no sign of the enemy, not a warlike sound broke the stillness; and were it not for the distant sound of cannonading far to our left, we might have felt we were on a pleasure trip in the most peaceful of lands," Bull remembered. Whatever the expectations of the blue army's senior commanders, no one had warned the rank and file of the likelihood of an attack. "Johnston, by his caution, had made us careless," one Union officer later admitted. But Hood intended to "fight, and fight at once, and all the time."[22]

North of the city, Confederate units spent the morning hours moving into position for the attack. Soldiers left behind their knapsacks and extra gear and were ordered to load muskets and prepare for the advance. "Every movement pointed with the unerring finger of certainty to the fact that somebody was going to get badly hurt, and that in short order," a Texas lieutenant later wrote. At ten o'clock, Hood received a dispatch from his cavalry commander General Joseph Wheeler reporting that not only was McPherson advancing toward Atlanta from the east, but that the force overlapped considerably, and therefore could outflank Cheatham's corps. If this was so, Hood would have no choice but to shift his entire line southward to cover the city's eastern approaches, lest McPherson march in and take the city almost unopposed. He sent orders for Cheatham to shift half a division front to the south, and directed Hardee and Stewart to conform. The minor adjustment caused major confusion, however, as Cheatham moved too far—shifting southward nearly a mile—and then Hardee wavered indecisively as to whether to maintain contact with Cheatham or to stop the time-consuming movement and begin the attack. One P.M., the time Hood had directed the action to begin, came and went. Then two P.M. passed, and then three. And so it was that more than two hours past the hour of attack, some 20,000 Confederates found themselves not charging the enemy but sidestepping to take up new positions, their stop-and-go-and-stop movement as awkward as a dinner party scooting down chairs to make way for an unexpected guest.

The righthand shift of the Army of Tennessee and the resulting postponement of the Rebel attack would provide a ready explanation for the battle's result. Civil War tradition afterward held that the three-hour delay gave the bluecoats time to intrench after crossing Peachtree Creek and therefore doomed the Rebel attack—but this was not really the case. Almost all the Federal units had crossed the creek by one P.M., the original jump-off time, in any event; but only a few of these had even begun to construct entrenchments almost three hours later when the attack opened. Not only were the Yankees not dug in, but the various division commanders had called a halt at differing points south of the creek, so that the Union force did not even form a continuous line of battle, east to west.[23]

What was more, the substantial delay did nothing to lessen the surprise Hood had hoped for, thanks to the screening woods and rumpled terrain that served to disguise his movements. Readers of Northern newspapers may have had the impression that the land south of the Chattahoochee River was level, open ground—but it was nothing of the sort. "Atlanta being a city of considerable size, no one is likely to have, before visiting it, a conception of the rough character of the approaches to it," General Howard would later write. "There are no plains about it. The country is rolling and thickly wooded. The undergrowth is dense, with a few openings for cultivation. The creeks cut deep and run crooked. It is just the country to bring on a rough-and-tumble fight between hostile forces, where neither commander can anticipate precisely the place or the time of the conflict." For all the Rebels' sidling and repositioning, their preparations for the attack went unobserved by the bluecoats to the north.

Around 3:30 P.M., there was a commotion in the woods to the south, in Thomas's front, and presently the blackberry pickers came scurrying back toward the main line. Hard on their heels came the blue skirmishers, stumbling out of the brush like hares flushed from a thicket. "Here they come, boys!" one skedaddling picket cried. "By god, a million of 'em!"[24]

CHAPTER FOUR

Hood's First Sortie

The Battle of Peachtree Creek, July 20

The charging Rebels were far from a million, of course, but they presented quite a spectacle nonetheless as they cleared the treeline to the south and rushed toward the Federal lines in the dappled sunlight. It was "a beautiful sight," Lieutenant Stephen Pierson, adjutant of the 33rd New Jersey, would recall. "Down through the great, open fields they were coming, thousands of them, men in gray, by Brigade front, flags flying. Hood was making his first general assault, and it was against Thomas that he was making it. I stopped but a few moments to take it all in, and then rode back to report." Brigadier General John W. Geary found the view of the approaching enemy "magnificent" along the line just west of the trickle of Tanyard Creek. "Pouring out from the woods they advanced in immense brown and gray masses (not lines), with flags and banners, many of them new and beautiful, while their general and staff officers were in plain view, with drawn sabers flashing in the light, galloping here and there as they urged their troops on to the charge." The prevailing reaction to the sight of thousands of screaming Rebels rushing at them was not so much fear as excitement at the potential shooting gallery now laid out before them. "O God, boys, they are out of their works!" men exclaimed. "We've got 'em now!"[1]

Hood had directed that the attack proceed *en echelon*, east to west, but his textbook plans went awry almost immediately. The first to charge would be the division of Major General William B. Bate, a native and future governor of Tennessee known in the ranks as "Old Grits," posted on the extreme right of Hardee's line and therefore expected to start the chain-reaction charge like the first of a row of dominoes. Not only would Bate's three brigades do no such thing, however; they would ultimately fail to strike the Union line at all. Having sidled to the right nearly a mile, Bate's Division charged blind through the heavy woods, not only into the yawning gap between Thomas and Schofield, but also into the deep valley of Clear Creek (south of Brighton Road, in today's Brookwood Hills neighborhood). There, Bate's three brigades would flounder for the next two hours, trying in vain to find some Yankees to stab or shoot at and removing themselves from the actual fight as effectively as if they had stayed back in their camps. Just to the west, the adjoining brigade of Major General W. H. T. Walker's Division—the next domino in line, as it were—likewise charged into a vine-choked miasma of Georgia forest. "Our own division advanced over very difficult ground," Colonel Charles Olmstead wrote, "first through a thick wood, then across a boggy valley through which a small water course meandered tortuously. It turned and twisted so much that we had to wade it two or three times in pressing forward. Indeed we never got fairly into action as the attack had failed in other parts of the field and the Division was withdrawn before it reached a close touch with the enemy." The Rebel force that was to strike and crush the Union left flank had missed it altogether.[2]

The beginning of the attack was scarcely more auspicious to the west. There, Walker's other two brigades, under the direction of Brigadier Generals Clement Hoffman Stevens and the splendidly named States Rights Gist, advanced along and just west of the Peachtree Road, beginning their uphill charge toward the Union left. Stevens, a strict disciplinarian who by his "iron nerves" and "splendid physique" had earned the nickname "Rock," was urging his men forward up the road when his horse tumbled over, a bullet in its breast. As he disentangled himself from the stirrups and stepped free from his mount, Stevens suddenly dropped like a puppet snipped from its strings, never to know what hit him. A minié ball, perhaps fired by the same Federal marksman who had taken down Stevens's horse, had struck him in the side of the head—as if to demonstrate at the outset that no man, whatever his rank or reputation—not even a general named "Rock"—would be immune from slaughter here at the gates of Atlanta.[3]

Brigadier General States Rights Gist. (*Library of Congress*)

The position up ahead, the far left of the Union line, was defended by the division of Major General John Newton, a Virginia-born West Pointer, like his chief George Thomas, and a veteran of eastern battles from Gaines' Mill to Gettysburg. Newton's Division, on detached service from O. O. Howard's IV (4th) Corps, had crossed the creek that morning and advanced a half mile south along the Peachtree Road to take a position at the crest of a hill, with a four-gun battery of artillery in support. Something didn't feel right to Newton, and he reported to Thomas that the situation had an "ugly look." Concerned that his division was exposed, with nothing but forest to his left and the adjoining division not yet "up" on his right, Newton had his men begin constructing log barricades and had curled his lines back at either end—part of the reason why the wayward Bate had expected to strike the Union flank and instead struck nothing at all.

Despite the mortal wounding of their commander, Stevens's Georgians continued their attack with a fury, "charging with great confidence," one Federal officer would report, "with a rapidity and an absence of confusion I have never seen equaled." Newton ordered his troops to fire steady and low, and the eruption of fire that followed sounded to one of his cannoneers "like the heavens and earth had suddenly come together." Above the roar of cannon and the clatter of musketry, the Northerners could hear "from a host of voices" the bloodcurdling wail of the Rebel yell—"a fearful yell, not easily described," as one defender wrote years later, "but once heard never to be forgotten!" The

Federals stood along the crest of the hill, taking cover behind their hastily constructed fortifications, while the graybacks came screaming toward them without protection. "They were cut down like grass before the scythe," Howard wrote.[4]

Thomas's headquarters, such as they were, were within sight of Newton's lines, and he had watched the Confederate attack from the outset. Even as the Rebels began their advance, an ordnance sergeant, sent to the rear to gather ammunition, saw Old Pap sitting on a pile of fence rails a short distance south of the creek beside the Peachtree Road, "his elbows resting on his knees which were drawn well toward his body, and field binoculars in his hands" directed toward the smoky treeline up ahead. A courier clattered up and saluted. "General Thomas," he said breathlessly, "Major McGraw presents his compliments and says to inform you that the enemy is moving on him en masse, and it will be impossible to hold his position."

Thomas, as usual, seemed unconcerned. "Orderly, return to Major McGraw, give him my compliments and tell him to hold his position. I will attend to those fellows as soon as they get out from behind the woods." No sooner had the courier galloped off when "the first rebel line appeared, followed by another and another." The rebel column moved toward the Union flank at the quick step, and the force seemed to the watching sergeant to be unstoppable.

Just then Thomas, ready to "attend to those fellows" at last, turned his head and said to a nearby officer, "Now you may give it to them, captain."

With that, more than a dozen cannon, partly hidden 'til then in the roadside undergrowth, thundered to life, sending "charges of shot, shell and canister tearing straight down the enemy's lines. Load after load as fast as the artillerymen could handle their pieces followed—a continuous shower of murderous iron. No troops on earth could stand that long, for they were taken at a disadvantage, could not reply and were in an open field at point-blank range." The attackers made "a heroic effort" to maintain their lines, but "in a minute or less it was apparent that they would go to pieces under the unmerciful pounding of artillery." Go to pieces they did, falling dead or wounded among the briars or scattering back to the cover of the trees behind. Almost as quickly as it had developed, the threat to Newton's flank had been dispelled. "All this transpired in less time that it takes me to tell it," the ordnance sergeant closed his description of the scene. Thomas's orders had been given "as deliberately and pleasantly as he might request his orderly to bring him a drink of water; but their execution was the breaking of an overwhelming cyclone. Nothing could withstand it; confusion, destruction, death and defeat to the enemy marked its pathway."[5]

Major General George H. Thomas, the "Rock of Chickamauga." (*Library of Congress*)

The Union left would hold, thanks to the diligence of John Newton, the strong hilltop position and the temporary breastworks his division had constructed, and the timely artillery support, directed personally by General Thomas. But other portions of the line were less prepared to receive attack, and no such natural advantages would aid the blue defenders in the center, where the long, east-west ridge running past Collier's Mill gradually lost elevation and dipped to a shallow valley around Tanyard Branch.

Next in Hood's planned east-to-west attack was the division of Brigadier General George Maney, still known as "Cheatham's Division" after its former commander. Maney's force could and should be considered the heart of Hardee's attack— four brigades, perhaps 4,500 men, every one a Tennessean like their commander, ordered to drive toward the unsuspecting Union left center. Maney had been a brigadier since early '62 and had led a brigade at Perryville and Chickamauga before being wounded at Chattanooga—a solid commander leading a formidable collection of veterans into battle. But rather than striking the hardest blow along the line that day, Maney's Division crept forward and barely fought at all. The Tenneseeans stepped off on the advance but soon encountered thick, screening woods to their front. Unwilling to fight blind, not knowing what was in front of them, Maney's front line called a halt and sent out skirmishers to see what was ahead as the afternoon wore on and the daylight failed. No one really knows why Maney's men appeared to flinch and failed to press their attack, and the contrast between their timid advance and the ferocious charges by the Confederates to the right and left of them is striking. Hood would eventually blame Hardee, in overall command of the attack, while neither Maney nor any of his four brigade commanders would submit an official report on the battle to explain themselves. Whatever the reason, what should have been the strongest portion of the Confederate assault came to nothing.[6]

No such lack of backbone afflicted the next division in line. Bearing down on the Union center were two brigades from the division of Major General W. W. "Old Blizzards" Loring under former Mississippi lawyer and antebellum congressman Winfield Scott Featherston and Georgia-born Thomas Moore Scott, who had left his farm in Claiborne Parish, Louisiana, to join a local regiment there in 1861. Their brigades—a total of about 2,700 men from Alabama, Mississippi and Louisiana—found the going tough as they pressed forward on a shallow diagonal toward the low ridge up ahead. Their advance—first through woods and then breaking into a field some 800 yards from the Union line—would initially be slow and uncertain, especially since the field itself was divided by the thorn-choked trickle of Tanyard Branch. "Owing to the rough and broken ground, the ravines, the small streams with their overhanging and exuberant growth of vines and brambles, and fences covered with briers so dense as to form an almost impenetrable jungle, it was found exceedingly difficult, and, in fact, impossible, to advance in good order," a Mississippi major would record in his report of the battle. Despite the difficulties of the landscape, the two brigades surged toward the waiting Federals and almost immediately broke through the advance line of skirmishers. What had looked like fortifications were in fact just the tracks and banks of a red dirt road running east to west near Collier's Mill, with makeshift bulwarks in the form of fence rails that had been piled hastily to provide some semblance of cover for the defenders. These last now pulled back to a ridgeline just to the rear, while Featherston's men waited for support to help exploit their breakthrough and struggled to hold what they had. This would soon prove impossible.[7]

At dead center of the Union line (Third Division, 20th Corps) to their front was the brigade of Brigadier General William Thomas Ward,

Brigadier General George Maney. (*Battles and Leaders*)

a pear-shaped rumple of a man whom an Indiana soldier would call, with ample cause, "the poorest excuse for a Genl I ever saw." The fifty-five-year-old Ward was a Virginia-born Louisville lawyer, a former U.S. Congressman, and, as one soldier put it, "a regular old Falstaff," with a frequently displayed fondness for the bottle and a knack for leading his troops down the wrong road. He had conjured up a respectable military career out of a brew of hometown prominence and political influence and had avoided disaster to this point almost in spite of himself. Most of his subordinates, from the colonels on down, seemed to have a story of their commander's ineptness and lack of fortitude. Earlier that spring, Ward had lost his way twice in two days among the mountain passes near Wauhatchie, Tennessee. When confronted, the befuddled general insisted that he had not been drinking, claiming instead that "the road was so crooked it had made him drunk." On another occasion, spying an enemy force ahead, Ward had halted his column in alarm and started his men frantically throwing up breastworks, only to find that the foe was in fact a friend—the Federal XXIII (23rd) Corps, which had taken a different route and passed him by. His troops called him Grandfather Ward, with more disdain than affection, and his tipsy bumbling was apparently tolerated by Hooker in part because Fighting Joe had been known to take a drink or three himself.[8]

The thing that had saved Ward in the past and would soon save him again was his capable, experienced subordinates, including two colonels, both of them Indianans, and both with something to prove. Colonel John Coburn was a thirty-eight-year-old attorney and judge of the court of common pleas back home who had suffered the indignity of having to surrender his troops a year before, after being surrounded by Confederate cavalry under Nathan Bedford Forrest at Thompson's Station in middle Tennessee. Imprisoned in Richmond and later

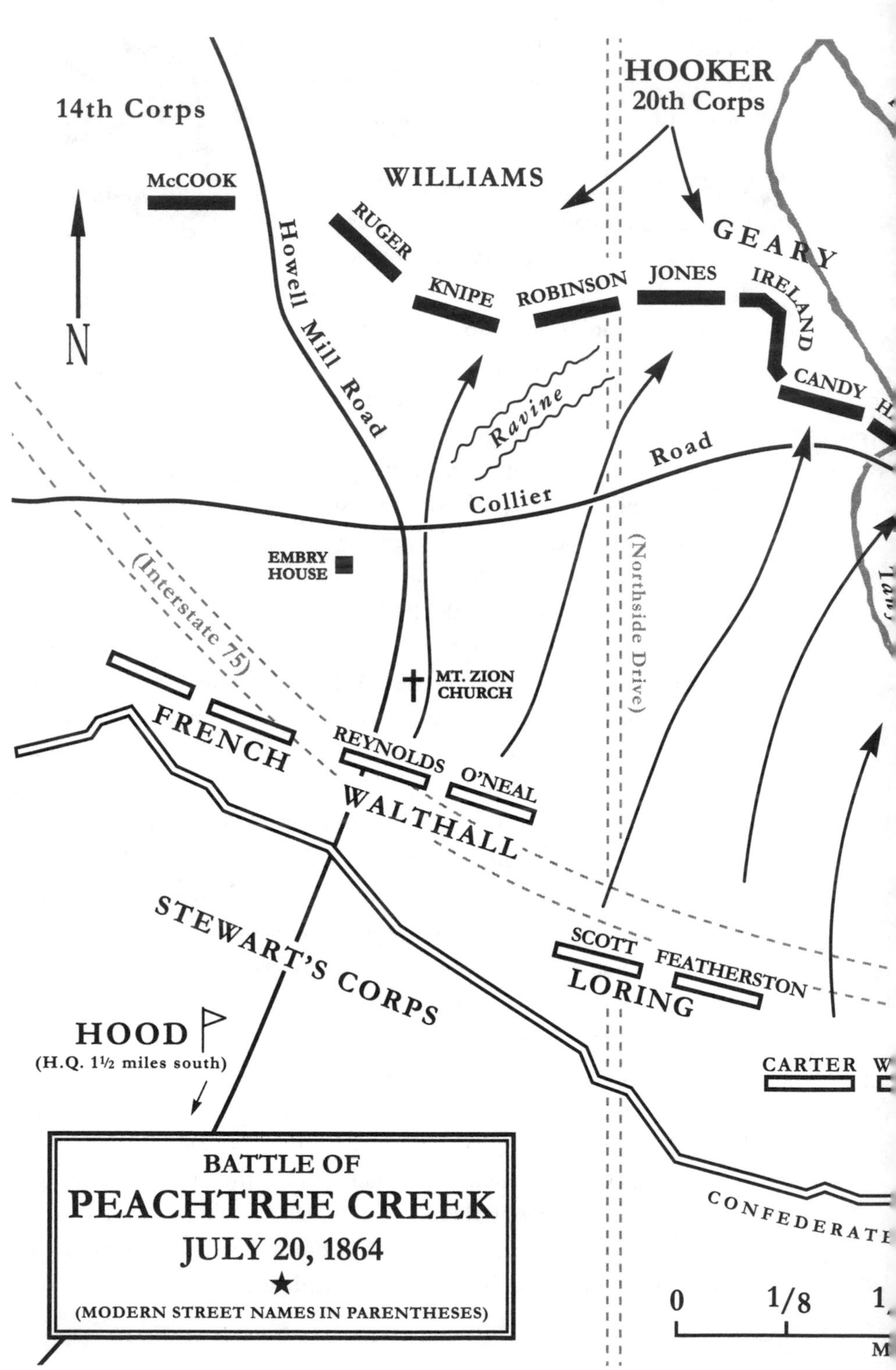
14th Corps
McCOOK
HOOKER
20th Corps
WILLIAMS
RUGER
KNIPE
ROBINSON
JONES
GEARY
IRELAND
CANDY
N
Howell Mill Road
Ravine
Collier Road
EMBRY HOUSE
(Interstate 75)
(Northside Drive)
MT. ZION CHURCH
FRENCH
REYNOLDS
O'NEAL
WALTHALL
STEWART'S CORPS
SCOTT
FEATHERSTON
LORING
HOOD
(H.Q. 1½ miles south)
CARTER
BATTLE OF
PEACHTREE CREEK
JULY 20, 1864
(MODERN STREET NAMES IN PARENTHESES)
0
1/8

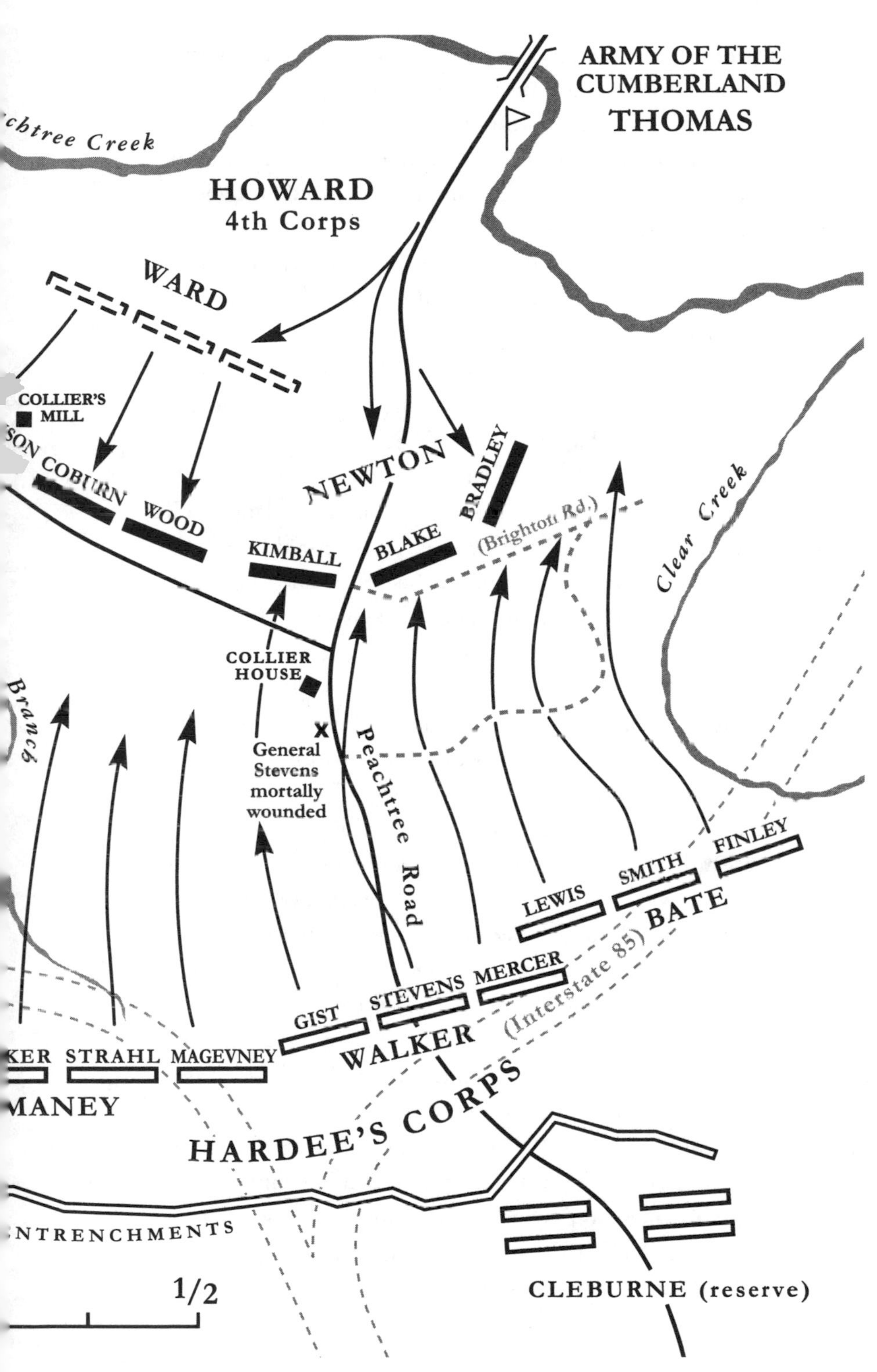

ARMY OF THE CUMBERLAND
THOMAS
chtree Creek
HOWARD
4th Corps
WARD
COLLIER'S MILL
SON
COBURN
WOOD
NEWTON
BRADLEY
KIMBALL
BLAKE
(Brighton Rd.)
Clear Creek
COLLIER HOUSE
Branch
General Stevens mortally wounded
Peachtree Road
FINLEY
SMITH
LEWIS
BATE
MERCER
STEVENS
GIST
(Interstate 85)
WALKER
KER
STRAHL
MAGEVNEY
MANEY
HARDEE'S CORPS
NTRENCHMENTS
1/2
CLEBURNE (reserve)

released in a prisoner exchange, Coburn had been posted to garrison duty for months before being returned to the field. Every man in the brigade, from the commander down to the youngest drummer boy, was eager to have an opportunity to retrieve their reputation and write a new chapter in their regimental histories beyond the story of their inglorious capture sixteen months earlier.[9]

Colonel Benjamin Harrison, by contrast, had his own reputational battles to fight, laboring under the burden of his family name and heroic military and political lineage. Born in Ohio and raised in a household of politics and Presbyterianism, Harrison was an Indianapolis lawyer and grandson of William Henry Harrison, the ninth President of the United States and before that the bane of Tecumseh and the hero of Tippecanoe. A witness would remember him, still a full month short of his thirty-first birthday, as "a slim-waisted, quick-moving, dapper, affectionate little officer" with "smiling blue eyes, a brown-red beard sometimes trimmed with a fine military mustache, fair blond skin, a clear commanding voice, and a ton of dignity. He wore clothes like a manikin, was particular about the amenities of his colonelcy, and a slave to his men."

After joining the army as a lieutenant in 1861, Harrison had raised and then led the 70th Indiana Regiment on fields from Kentucky to Georgia before being promoted to brigade command in June. Along the way, the boyish officer had refuted suggestions of any unseemly ambition or nepotism by his stalwart work ethic and forthright demeanor. "He went at tactics with the brain of a scholar, the heart of a gentleman, and the energy of an ambitious little beaver," one admirer would recall. The soldiers in his charge were extremely fond of their commander, and would fill their postwar remembrances with stories—some no doubt true, others possibly apocryphal—of Little Ben's strength and many kindnesses: bringing hot coffee on a winter night to pickets along the skirmish line (a good deed either commonly performed or commonly attributed to a number of Civil War officers); dismounting during a long day's march to let a sick soldier ride for a while; leading church services in the chaplain's absence and praying above all for the safety of his men. He had been in the thick of the fight at Resaca and more recently at Gilgal Church, which the bluecoats ominously called Golgotha. There,

Colonel Benjamin "Little Ben" Harrison. (*Battles and Leaders*)

finding a shortage of surgeons at the field hospital, Harrison had rolled up his sleeves and wielded bandages and bonesaws himself. He had suffered in recent weeks a severe, almost debilitating, case of poison ivy, which so badly afflicted his hands that he would in the future habitually wear gloves to protect them—a precaution that would lead years later to unfair accusations that he was a kid-glove politician out of touch with the concerns of the working man. Cartoonists would later jibe that the diminutive Hoosier lawyer was too small to wear his grandfather's hat; though a more immediate question was whether he could fill Old Tippecanoe's shoes, militarily speaking.[10]

Coburn and Harrison were friends and fellow members of the bar back home, and both had been concerned by their position after crossing the Peachtree Creek. Ward had halted the brigade in a cornfield south of the stream, with a ridgeline visible up ahead. Both General Newton, to the left, and General John Geary, to the right, had advanced their divisions to the high ground—but not Ward, who merely sent a line of skirmishers forward to the ridge. Neither Coburn nor Harrison were professional soldiers, but to their credit, both men saw, as surely as any West Pointer would, the need to fill the gap ahead, move up to form a solid line with Newton and Geary left and hold the high ground in their front. The two Hoosier officers reported to General Ward their belief that the enemy was advancing and would occupy the ridge ahead. Ward was unmoved, insisting that Hooker had ordered him to remain where he was in the cornfield and advance only skirmishers. But if Grandfather Ward was willing to ignore the yawning gap and the dominant ground in their front, his colonels certainly were not.[11]

Harrison brought his men around him and issued their orders to move forward even as the Rebel attack opened up ahead and the skirmishers came tumbling back. "Come on, boys, we've never been licked yet, and we won't begin now," he was to have said. "We haven't much ammunition, but if necessary we can give them the cold steel, and before we get licked we will club them down; so, come on." As long-winded battlefield pronouncements go, it was not quite *Henry V*, but Little Ben probably didn't say exactly these "unlikely words" (as a sympathetic biographer called them) in any event. In point of fact, some witnesses on the field reported that the roar of cannon and the clatter of musketry were so loud that officers could not make themselves heard at all and had to direct the movements of their men by signals and gestures. Other postwar accounts would assert that Harrison had made one simple pronouncement of his intentions to hold his ground. "Here we shall stay," he said. Whatever his rallying cry, Harrison led his men forward to the ridge ahead and blunted the Rebel attack, with Coburn's brigade, along with that of Colonel James Wood, moving up beside him to link up with Newton to the east. "The rebels were losing heavily, and began to halt, waver, kink up, and finally break to the rear," a witness wrote. "Our advance, though desperately resisted by the enemy, was steady and unfaltering," Harrison would later report. "The fighting was hand to hand, and step by step; the enemy was pushed back over the crest in our front and the key point of the battle won."[12]

The Confederate attack on the center was repulsed, and the gray soldiers were torn mercilessly by shot and shell as they made their way back toward the cover of the woods and the safety of their own lines. "As our adversaries hastened down the hill and through a wide field in the direction of Atlanta," one among the defenders recalled, "volley after volley was poured after them, dotting the field with the dead and the dying." To the rear, Brigadier General Ward, apparently sober, sat on his horse and watched in delight as his soldiers blocked and then pushed back the Rebels, perhaps realizing that he was likely to receive the credit for a stirring victory he had had little part in bringing about. "See my brigade! See my brigade!" he cried, smiling in wonderment and clapping his hands like a child delighted by a magic trick. "Meeting my line of battle seemed to completely addle their brains," he would soon brag in his report.[13]

Even as the Rebel attack faltered on the Union left and center, the fighting continued desperately on the right, as two of Stewart's brigades drove along and west of the Howell Mill Road to strike two blue divisions under Alpheus Williams and John W. Geary. Both were experienced and capable commanders, especially Geary, who was arguably one of the most impressive officers in the Federal army, both for his physical stature and his past accomplishments. He was a Goliath in those days, standing nearly six feet six inches tall and weighing some 260 pounds, and fellow officers would compare him to Napoleon's Marshal Ney "in size, deportment and vigor." A veteran of the Mexican War, he had served as the governor of the Territory of Kansas during the bloody period before the war, and before that had been the last *alcalde* and first mayor of the city of San Francisco. (The future would hold more positions of authority for the towering Geary, who would later serve two terms as governor of Pennsylvania.)

The surprise was considerably lessened on this end of the Union position, as the bluecoats heard the attack to the east and then watched as it rolled closer to them along the gently curving line. The problem here was the terrain, thickly wooded and cut with deep ravines, in contrast to the mostly open fields in the left and center. Geary had taken a position on the western end of the Collier ridge and ordered a single regiment, the 33rd New Jersey, to advance to a small hill three hundred yards to his front to keep a lookout as he waited for Ward to come up on his left.

The Rebel charge—Scott's Alabamians and Louisianians—boiled out of the woods ahead and quickly overwhelmed the exposed New Jerseyans, who lost their regimental flag along with seventy-one men killed and wounded. The survivors came stumbling back into Geary's line, where a blast of musketry slowed the charging Confederates. A series of bloody charges and countercharges followed, soldiers on both sides firing blind through the underbrush and the smoke. "The enemy made five charges on our line, coming at times within a hundred feet," the New Yorker Sergeant Bull recalled, "yet I did not see a single Johnnie." Geary bent his line sharply backward to connect his lead and reserve units and block the Rebels from advancing down a ravine, wrenching nearly into a Z-shape on the map. In the confusion, Fighting Joe Hooker himself rode forward to rally Geary's troops, "magnificent in appearance, mounted on a splendid horse, looking, as he was, the beau ideal of a soldier of the olden type," the 33rd New Jersey's adjutant

Stephen Pierson recalled. "Boys, I guess we will stop here," Hooker said—"and stop there we did," Pierson wrote.[14]

The fighting became hand-to-hand at some points along the line, and the firing almost constant. "The gunbarrels would get so hot we could scarcely hold them and I saw many guns discharge as the powder from the cartridge was being placed in the barrel," Sergeant Bull remembered. "One of the boys near me, after biting off the top of the cartridge, had placed it in the barrel and was ramming it down, when the powder exploded and the bullet and ramrod went together. He looked a good deal surprised, and shaking his fist in the direction of the Johnnies yelled, 'Take that you —— and see how you like it!'"[15]

"For three hours the fury of the battle along our entire line could not be surpassed," General Geary would write in his report. His command, he said, especially the Pennsylvania and New York brigades in the center of the zigzag position, "stood firm as a rock and mowed down column after column of that vast, struggling mass that charged them from three sides." John Geary had seen much of what he called "the stern realities of war"—wounded at Cedar Mountain, he had fought at Chancellorsville, Gettysburg, Lookout Mountain, and Wauhatchie, where his eighteen-year-old son Edward had died in his arms. But for him, the fighting at Peachtree Creek would stand out. "It is with a feeling of unusual admiration for the troops under my command that I record the history of their part in the battle of Peach Tree Creek," he reported. "I have never seen more heroic fighting."[16]

In the end, despite the initial rout of the exposed New Jersey regiment and the awkward contortions of the Federal line, the Rebel attack was no more successful here than on the Union left. Geary and Williams, though they would suffer the greatest portion of the Federal casualties that day, finally drove back the three Confederate brigades to their front. Around seven o'clock, the firing sputtered out, and by eight, all was quiet save for the mewling of the wounded and the cries of dying men pleading for water. "As twilight crept slowly over the scene, the hideous clamor of battle ceased, and a wondrous quiet took possession of the hillside," an Indiana officer wrote in a letter home. "Men in low tones inquired of the wounded and spoke of the dead. In every heart was a strange conflict, exultation over the victory and grief over the fallen."

Those alive and unhurt were exhausted, uniforms soaked through, hands and faces stained "blue as indigo" from smoke and powder, ears ringing from the roar of cannon. "For two days our hearing was almost gone; it was several days before it was again normal," a Union sergeant recalled.

Local legend would hold that Peachtree Creek ran red with blood that day, and though this might not have been literally true, there was no question but that the bloodshed had been great on both sides. "I never have seen the dead rebels lie so thickly strewn upon the ground, since the battle of Shiloh," an Illinois colonel wrote home. An Ohio lieutenant found the field "a harrowing, pitiful sight," and thought that "the dead did not have that angry look which we ascribe to men fighting for their lives, but rather a sorrowful, frightful one of death by violence." Another veteran, blessed with long life but haunted by what he saw that day, wrote to a state historian sixty-three years later, "I was in many fights, but I never saw more dead and wounded than I saw at Peach Tree Creek." Bodies sprawled across the field before them, the blood around them spattered and dried to black in the red dirt of the Collier Road. Burial details would scour the field the next day, seeing to the interment of corpses, blue and gray, before the summer sun made the nauseating labor even worse than it was already. The gravediggers, kerchiefs tied around their faces against the stench, occasionally rifled the pockets and pouches of the fallen, a benefit that compensated somewhat for the grisly duty. "My captures," an Indiana soldier proudly reported in a letter home, "are one Captain's sword marked C.S.A., Reb canteen (cedar), haversack &c." The dead were piled into mass graves, hastily dug and sporadically marked—one with a crackerboard sign that read: "Col. Drake, 33 Miss., and 34 men."[17]

For the wounded, the tale, as one among the unfortunates put it, was "no longer a story of weary marches, sleepless nights, battle, danger and death, but on the contrary a triumphal march to the rear, where the surgeons held court supreme." Union commissary sergeant Rufus Mead wrote to his family in Connecticut that the fighting that day was "the worst battle our regt was ever in except Cedar Mountain and I dont know but full as disastrous as that. But the most sickening sight of all was at the Hospital where we lay with the team. It was more than seeing killed to . . . the suffering and dying conditions of the poor fellows that lay there wounded in every part of the body, some crazy & raving and other suffering all that mortals can. Doctors were busy cutting off limbs which were piled up in heaps to be carried off and buried, while the stench even then was horrible. Flies were flying around in swarms and maggots were crawling in wounds before the Drs could get time to dress them. But enough of this now. Suffice it is to say that the 20th of July 1864 was the saddest day I ever saw, I think I never saw half of the suffering before in one day." Ambulances rattled south into Atlanta, carrying wounded men to City Hall, which "had been turned into a carving pen," the doctors having "more subjects than they had table room."[18]

Some among the Confederates marveled at their escape. "I thought I would certainly see my 'Valhalla' that day," remembered Colonel James Nisbet of the 66th Georgia, who had lost one-fourth of his officers and men in their charge up the Peachtree Road with the mortally wounded Rock Stevens. A Rebel private named Angus McDermid wrote of the battle in a letter to his father. "I hav bin spared to live this long and fought the yanks twice," he said. "Well we saw a hot time yesterday you may be shore. I was in a nother Battle yesterday. We charged the yankes and we whiped them but I think that we got the most men killed." On this, the young Georgia farmboy was right. The Federals had suffered approximately 1,900 killed, wounded, and missing—a literal "decimation" of the ranks, in that the casualties amounted to approximately 10 percent of the forces engaged. But the Confederate losses were considerably worse—more than 2,500 killed and wounded. For years to come, historians cast Hood's defeat at Peachtree Creek as even more lopsided than it was, largely because most chose to credit Sherman's own inflated estimate of 4,796 Confederate casualties. And though these numbers were decidedly smaller than the horrific western battles like Shiloh and Chickamauga, they were nonetheless appalling, especially considering the limited numbers engaged and the short duration of the battle—only, and almost exactly, three hours long.[19]

The casualties were unevenly distributed, particularly among the attacking Confederates. The four brigades of Maney's (Cheatham's) Division suffered only 277 men killed and wounded, while two brigades of Loring's Division (Featherston and Scott) suffered almost five times as many: 1,062 killed, wounded, and missing in the battle. Featherston's brigade suffered 616 casualties—almost precisely half of the soldiers he had engaged—and all but one of his regimental commanders were killed or wounded. One regiment in the brigade, the 31st Mississippi, reported an appalling casualty rate of 76 percent—of the 215 men who had made the charge against the Union center along Tanyard Branch, 164 had fallen.[20]

News of the Union victory was warmly received across the North, though the celebration was tempered somewhat by the harsh realization that under General Hood, the Confederates would put up a fight for Atlanta after all. One exuberant correspondent, eager for a scoop, erroneously reported in the wake of the battle that Atlanta itself had been occupied and the Stars and Stripes raised over City Hall. Newspapers gave the credit to Fighting Joe Hooker and Grandfather Ward—"Terrible Repulse of the Enemy by Gen. Hooker," the *New York Times* headline read—and an illustration of Hooker riding his lines in triumph soon graced the cover of *Harper's Weekly*. Ward was all too willing to bask in the undeserved praise, inflating and misrepresenting his role in the battle in his official report and, the following spring, posing in the studio of Mathew Brady for a photograph with Harrison and Coburn that would come to be captioned "Hero-Trio of Peach Tree Creek." The result would also be attributed to the initiative and pluck of subordinate commanders like Coburn and Harrison and Geary and Newton, and to the hard fighting of the Union forces engaged. Five Union soldiers would be awarded the Medal of Honor for various acts of gallantry during the battle. Harrison modestly accepted the laurels bestowed upon him by the public and the press, but insisted to his wife in a letter home on his thirty-first birthday, "I am not a Julius Ceasar, nor a Napoleon, but a plain Hoosier colonel, with no more relish for a fight than a good breakfast & *hardly* so much." Over time, most of all, history would give the credit to the imperturbable, redoubtable Thomas, who had directed the defense of the Federal left in person and who, "as usual, refused to be budged or flustered." In choosing the point of assault for his first battle as an army commander, Hood had launched a surprise attack against the one Union general who seemed entirely incapable of being surprised.[21]

The reverse of the coin of Northern pride and acclaim was, of course, the distribution of blame on the Confederate side for the failure of the attack. The tactical reasons were many: the three-hour delay in launching the attack; the misadventure of "Old Grits" Bate, who got lost in the Georgia woods and missed the opportunity to strike the Federals on their unguarded left flank; the curious hesitancy of Maney's four brigades in the center—all of which combined to negate Hood's planned-for numerical advantage, causing portions of only four divisions, rather than seven, to strike the Union line. Moreover, despite having two days to prepare a reception for the advancing Yankees in the valley of Peachtree Creek, the Confederates made almost no use of artillery, relying instead on muskets and bayonets against the stalwart defenders. In contrast, Union batteries, though few had time to deploy, played a critical role in breaking the Rebel charge on both the right and the left, where General Thomas himself helped to direct the enfilading fire of a masked battery. The echelon attack, so beautiful when drawn up on the map or practiced on the drill field, was a stumbling lurch through the Georgia pines and briars and creeks. The textbook maneuver broke down from the outset, leading to an uncoordinated, piecemeal assault and depriving later-advancing units of the advantage of surprise. A Kentucky soldier would later sum up the fight at Peachtree Creek as "a straggling, haphazard kind of hide and seek affair, magnified into a battle."

Of course, the Confederates could point with pride to certain achievements of the day. They had inflicted grievous injury on the defenders, especially in the center and left of the Union line; had captured a number of enemy colors; and some units, such as Featherston's, Scott's, and Stevens's brigades, fought fiercely and with admirable valor. As Geary reported, the Rebels to his front "seemed to rush forward with more than customary nerve and heartiness in their attack." But others, for whatever reason, seemed to have faltered, most notably Maney's Tennesseans—who by all appearances merely halted, sent out skirmishers, and watched the show. As a prominent historian concluded, "where the Confederates had the advantage in strength; they did not fight well; and where they fought well, they were too weak. And because they did not fight well enough where they were strong enough, they lost."[22]

As for blame at the command level, some would later credit General Johnston's somewhat dubious claim that the plan to attack the Federals at Peachtree Creek had been his, and that Hood, having inherited a brilliantly conceived plan from Old Joe, had bumbled and botched it. "A man of only moderate intellectual power, suddenly called to execute the plans of a military genius, with an army of disappointed discontented men without confidence in their leader, under changed conditions from those upon which those plans were based, was not the one to command success," one disgruntled Rebel colonel later wrote. Others, including General Stewart, later blamed the delay in the Rebel attack and the lack of coordination on Hood, complaining that he remained a mile to the rear and had failed to direct the assault in person. (The criticism of Hood's absence from the battlefield rings particularly hollow coming from Stewart, as Hood had spent the duration of the Battle of Peachtree Creek at Stewart's own headquarters.)[23]

Active front-line participation by an army commander, as with Thomas along Peachtree Road, was the exception and not the rule in Civil War battles. Hood was in fact trying to emulate his idol, Robert E. Lee, who told a Prussian observer after Gettysburg that it would "do more harm than good" for him to interfere once a battle was under way, adding: "It would be a bad thing if I could not rely on my brigade and division commanders." Hood did just that on July 20, depending not only on subordinates but, as he said, on "the God of battles," who must have seemed far from merciful that day.[24]

Hood was irked and perplexed by the failure of the attack. "I was at the time unable to discover a satisfactory reason for which an united attack by two corps d'armee, at even 4 o'clock in the day, should have failed to destroy Thomas's Army, which was protected by only slight entrenchments and was situated within a pocket formed by two streams difficult of passage," he wrote in his memoirs. His solution was to blame General Hardee. "Unfortunately," he wrote years later, "the corps on Stewart's right"—Hardee's corps—"although composed of the best troops in the army, virtually accomplished nothing. In lieu of moving promptly, attacking as ordered, and supporting Stewart's gallant assault, the troops of Hardee—as their losses on that day indicate—did nothing more than skirmish with the enemy."

Hardee would angrily reject this criticism in his own report of the action, leading to considerable debate in the months and years ahead. But as the battle smoke cleared on the evening of July 20, the recriminations and fingerpointing were yet to come. For now, Hardee would again be entrusted with the main effort against the Federals two days hence—whereby the seeds of failure and discontent were sown for the next battle to come.[25]

The Battle of Peachtree Creek, or Peach Tree Ridge, or Hood's First Sortie, as it would variously come to be called, would in many ways become a forgotten battle, overshadowed by the larger-scale engagements for Atlanta that would soon follow. Although more men fell there than at Kennesaw Mountain the month before, no land would be marked off and preserved for a national battlefield park, no visitor center constructed. No books have been written on the battle. Few memorials have been erected to mark the fighting or commemorate the fallen—just a few state historical markers hidden along oak-lined streets and parking lots, along with an overlooked, magnolia-shaded granite monument on the front lawn of an Atlanta hospital. The lovely woods just south of the winding creek would soon be divided into residential lots for Atlanta neighborhoods—Peachtree Hills, Collier Hills, Loring Heights (named for "Old Blizzards")—where generations of Atlantans have driven the streets and lingered on their porches and mowed their lawns, perhaps without realizing that Americans by the hundreds fought and bled and died right there in their yards. Roughly along the line of the Confederate jump-off point, twentieth-century interstates would carve and alter the landscape and make the Rebel attack difficult to map and follow.

But the battle would have its lasting effects—some military, and others political. The military message was clear—Hood, as all expected, was a fighter. The cost of demonstrating his willingness to put up a fight for Atlanta and his adherence to the doctrines of the "Lee and Jackson school," however, was considerable. "The long list of casualties in this regiment in the engagement of the 20th instant will be sufficient evidence of its deep devotion to the cause of Southern liberty and independence," an Alabama captain would write with pride in his report. "Though we lament the fall of our best and bravest," General Loring reported, "yet

The battleground of Peachtree Creek photographed by George N. Barnard, showing the mixture of open fields, ridges, and thick forest. (*Library of Congress*)

it is pleasing to know that the records of the enemy's dead and wounded bear witness not only to the courage and patriotism of the division, but that our honored dead have not been unavenged." Still, these fruits—demonstrated patriotism, evidence of devotion, and the grim satisfaction of vengeance exacted upon the foe—were hardly the tangible results that had been hoped for. From a strategic perspective, nothing whatsoever had been achieved. Hood had thrown two corps at the Rock of Chickamauga, and the gray wave had crested, broken, and receded, with the situation much as it was before. As one forlorn Texas private wrote, "We fought hard, lost heavily and accomplished nothing."[26]

As for political echoes from the fighting, the staunchness displayed by the diminutive, self-described "plain Hoosier colonel" at the center of the Union line would provide a ready narrative for the Northern press and for political campaigns to come. Benjamin Harrison's leadership was first recognized by General Hooker, who came upon the young officer the morning after the battle and bestowed his congratulations in the form of a commitment. "By God, Harrison," Fighting Joe said, "I'll make you a brigadier general for this fight." Hooker would do his best to make good on the promise weeks later, when he wrote a letter to Secretary of War Edwin M. Stanton calling for Harrison's promotion. "In the achievements of the Twentieth Corps in that campaign, Colonel Harrison bore a conspicuous part," he wrote. "At Resaca and Peach-Tree Creek the conduct of himself and command was especially distinguished. Colonel Harrison is an officer of superior abilities and of great personal and professional worth."[27]

His talents, however, were soon needed elsewhere, and he was redeployed and sent north in service of the Union, or at least the Republican, cause. Granted leave to enable him to stump for the Republicans in the fall campaign, Benjamin Harrison would depart from Georgia and arrive home in Indiana on September 20, just three weeks after his thirty-first birthday. His return trip northward aboard a steamer on the Ohio River would provide yet another flattering portrait of the little Indianapolis lawyer who folks were now calling the Hero of Peach Tree Creek. Rounding a bend in the Ohio, the riverboat came under fire from bushwhackers on the banks, and passengers cowered under tables as bullets shattered glass and whistled through the dining room. But a witness peering from the cabin spied Colonel Harrison standing on the hurricane deck, all five feet six inches of him, with "a revolver in each hand . . . blazing away with great enthusiasm and vigor at the people on the shore." He won his race in the November election—reelected to the humble post of reporter for the state supreme court—but was plainly destined for higher office.

Harrison would twice be defeated as a candidate for governor of Indiana before being elected to the U.S. Senate in 1880. Finally, in 1888, his campaign biography laden with stories of his heroics in Georgia, Little Ben was elected the twenty-third President of the United States. Three years later, in the course of a presidential visit to Atlanta in the spring of 1891, he asked to be taken to the field of battle where he had fought—but he never got there, his delegation led by an inept guide to the banks of the wrong creek.[28]

CHAPTER FIVE

Night March

Skirmishing and First Shots, July 21–22

Sherman had no part in the fighting north of Atlanta on July 20—in fact, for a time, he had no idea that a battle had even taken place. He had spent the day at his headquarters, some three miles to the northeast of the Peachtree Creek battlefield. Owing to the humidity and the thickly wooded terrain, Sherman heard nothing of the thundering clam or of battle, and throughout the afternoon sent impatient dispatches urging General Thomas, his line still just south of Peachtree Creek, to march his men southward toward the city. Sherman still believed that the bulk of Hood's force was out to the east, in front of McPherson. "All your troops should push hard for Atlanta, sweeping everything before them," he told Thomas in a dispatch headed 3:15 P.M. Three hours later, he sent another note to Thomas suggesting (incorrectly) that the enemy was so strong in front of McPherson and Schofield that "I was in hopes none were left for you. . . . We cannot pass Atlanta without reducing it, and the more time we give them the harder it will be to carry." And again, in another message two hours after that: "I think you will have no difficulty in pushing your line up close to Atlanta," he wrote.[1]

This incessant prodding of Thomas—which had to be annoying to the Union-loyal Virginian, the stream of dispatches received even as he was fighting the largest and bloodiest battle of the campaign to date—

was the product of Sherman's natural impatience and his settled perception that Thomas was too slow on the advance. Though his men called him "Old Pap" or "Old Tom," outside of his own army Thomas was at times derided as "Old Slow Trot." After all, everything about the man seemed to support this characterization: his heavyset build, his always deliberate manner, his tendency to fall asleep at the drop of a hat, and even his sprawling headquarters, a veritable metropolis of Sibley tents and wagons and orderlies and equipment that Sherman derisively referred to as "Thomastown." Over the years, some historians and friendly biographers would take exception to this depiction of Thomas as a military tortoise, but even his friends and admirers provided corroboration. "It's the God of Mighty's truth he *was* slow," his chief of staff later said. But he certainly wasn't slow at Peachtree Creek—urging battery horses forward, directing the fire at Hardee's advancing line, and even quite uncharacteristically flinging his hat and crying "Hurrah!" as the Rebel attack was repulsed. The slowness that day was at the other end of the seven-mile Union line, with the supposedly more aggressive McPherson and his Army of the Tennessee.

It was nearly midnight when Sherman received a message from the beleaguered Thomas, sent nearly six hours before, that revealed the truth. "General," Old Pap reported, "The enemy attacked me in full force about 4 P.M., and has persisted until now, attacking very fiercely, but he was repulsed handsomely by the troops all along my line. Our loss has been heavy, but the loss inflicted upon the enemy has been very severe. We have taken many prisoners, and General Ward reports having taken 2 stand of colors. I cannot make at present more than this general report, but will send you details as soon as I can get them from my corps commanders."[2]

With that, the scales fell from Sherman's eyes, and he saw that the opportunity for a quick drive into Atlanta that day was not with Thomas, but instead was with his own protégé McPherson, and had been all along. His three corps had started their march westward toward the city the morning of the 20th, even as Thomas's troops were crossing Peachtree Creek, and by just after noon were only two and a half miles east of Atlanta. There, Major General John A. Logan, in command of the XV (15th) Corps, brought forward an Illinois battery of 20-pound

Parrott rifled guns commanded by twenty-three-year-old Capt. Francis DeGress, who announced the Federals' arrival by firing three rounds into the streets of the city in plain view just ahead.

According to local legend, the first shot fell on Atlanta at the corner of Ellis and Ivy Streets downtown, where it exploded and supposedly killed a little girl. No contemporaneous eyewitness accounts support this heartbreaking story, however, and the newspapers made no mention of any such tragedy. (In fact, the first appearance of the tale of the unfortunate child was in newspaperman Wallace Reed's *History of Atlanta*, published twenty-four years after the war.) Instead, diarists and newspaper articles reported that shells had fallen in the City Hall square, at the Female Institute, at the Car Shed, and several other locations—raising the possibility that the Federals fired off considerably more than three long-range shots on the 20th of July. This seemed another in the series of plagues visited upon the people of Atlanta—first the rumble of cannon and the boil of battle smoke on the horizon, then wounded men by the thousands, and now 20-pound shells exploding in the streets. The effect was predictable panic. "We found the city in a wild state of excitement," a Confederate captain passing through the town would remember. "Citizens were running in every direction. Terror-stricken women and children went screaming about its streets seeking some avenue of escape from the hissing, bursting shells, as they sped on their mission of death and destruction. Perfect pandemonium reigned near the union depot."[3]

But then, with the city spread before him and his artillery rattling the windows and scattering the helpless, hapless civilians of Atlanta, McPherson pulled up short and his advance faltered. Lacking the blustery self-assurance of his chief, Mac inched forward carefully, perhaps a bit intimidated by an undersized brigade of rapid-firing Rebel troopers who made up in spirit what they lacked in numbers. McPherson's XVII (17th) Corps under Major General Francis P. Blair, Jr., ran into determined Confederate resistance on the left, south of the railroad, where a small force of dismounted gray horsemen occupied a prominent knoll, cleared of timber and known to local folks as Bald Hill. Blair told his subordinate Brigadier General Walter Gresham to push his division forward, insisting that there was nothing before him but scattered cavalry. Gresham did so and promptly got himself shot, a bullet from a butternut marksman tearing through his lower leg as he attempted to reconnoiter the ground to his front. The stepped-up firing, the almost intolerable July heat, and the severe wounding of a division commander all seemed to counsel increased caution on the part of the advancing Federals.

Deployed to the right of the wounded Gresham was the Third Division of Brigadier General Mortimer Leggett, forty-four, a law professor and school superintendent before the war, whose troops emerged from the woods to find themselves facing Bald Hill, its shadow outlined clearly as the sun slipped down the sky behind it. Leggett was a well-traveled veteran but to this point had done little to distinguish himself—except, if photographs are any indication, for boasting perhaps the wildest head of hair in the Federal service—wiry and brown, mashed flat across the crown of his head before erupting left and right into an asymmetrical snarl of curls. His moment had nearly arrived, however, and the hill that loomed before him would by sundown the day after tomorrow bear his name. With perhaps an hour of daylight remaining, Leggett inquired of the army commander whether he was to charge the Rebels on the high ground ahead. "General McPherson decided that it was too late to assault the hill that night," Leggett recalled, "but directed that we do so in the morning, unless we got orders to the contrary."[4]

Shortly after nightfall, McPherson reported to Sherman his new position and halting progress—including a dubious claim that there was a substantial line of breastworks to his front—and all but admitted outright that his advance toward Atlanta that day had been slowed by minimal opposition. "We have had some pretty lively skirmishing and have driven the enemy from several pretty strong positions, though I do not think there has been much of anything but cavalry in front of us," he reported, adding somewhat lamely, by way of excuse, "But they have had four pieces of artillery and are armed with short Enfield rifles, making it difficult at times to dislodge them." Whatever the proffered explanation, the fact was that a single battery of artillery and some 2,500 dismounted troopers had succeeded in dissuading what one historian called a "twenty-five thousand man juggernaut" from bowling over them or going around them and marching straight into Atlanta. Nor had the Rebels constructed meaningful fortifications—no breastworks at all, in

Brigadier General Mortimer Leggett. (*Library of Congress*)

fact, but shallow rifle pits to provide some semblance of cover for the overmatched defenders. "From the line of works occupied by my troops they could see masses of the enemy, fully 20,000 strong, all aligned and ready to attack," the Confederate cavalry commander Major General Joseph Wheeler later reported. "I felt that any respectable effort on their part could easily dislodge my force and leave nothing between McPherson and the interior works which had been erected for the final defense of Atlanta."[5]

It was the second time in the three-month-long campaign that McPherson's caution had cost Sherman a chance to swing behind his unsuspecting Southern foes and bring an early end to the contest. Back in May, in the very first week of the campaign, Sherman had sent the Army of the Tennessee sweeping wide around General Johnston's flank and through a mountain pass called Snake Creek Gap. McPherson's two corps made the march without incident, and he reported to Sherman on May 9 that he was in position, deep in the Confederate rear, with the town of Resaca and the Western & Atlantic Railroad bridge in view just ahead. "I've got Joe Johnston *dead!*" Sherman had cried, knowing that once McPherson destroyed the railroad, Old Joe would be cut off and caught as if in a vise between Thomas and Schofield to his front and McPherson directly in his rear.

But McPherson had hesitated. Coming under fire from a small but vigilant force of about 4,000 recently arrived Rebels in his front, he declined to push for the railroad and instead pulled his 25,000 men back into the protective cover of Snake Creek Gap. Johnston soon retreated to Resaca and then slipped out of the Union snare. "Well, Mac, you have missed the opportunity of a lifetime," Sherman had said.[6]

Now it had happened again. A staff captain watched as McPherson stalled that afternoon, then waited for support, then waited still longer for a better alignment of his troops, and finally declined to attack altogether. "The precious time passed swiftly away and Oh! the golden opportunity to take the ridge commanding the City glided by all unused because forsooth, some one who had the power, had not the nerve, the *spirit & dash* to order *forward-march!*" the captain wrote, crying to heaven in exasperation. "How long o Lord! will our leaders continue to let such opportunities slip through their fingers & afterwards sacrifice hundreds of lives in vain efforts to take the same position they let the enemy fortify & occupy under their very noses?"[7]

Sherman saw this too; though again he chastised his favorite subordinate rather gently. "I was in hopes you could have made a closer approach to Atlanta yesterday," he wrote in the small hours of the morning of July 21, warning McPherson that he would now have to deal with a larger force and stronger defenses in his front come daylight. Seemingly untroubled, however, Sherman expressed his intention to tighten his stranglehold on Atlanta—"contract our lines by diminishing the circle," as he put it—and instructed McPherson to "gain ground so that your artillery can reach the town easily."

Still, there could be no doubt of the chance that had been lost. Ten weeks after he missed "the opportunity of his life" at Resaca, McPherson had gotten a *second* once-in-a-lifetime opportunity—and he missed it again. And as for the necessary sacrifice that would result—no one would have cause to regret the coming battle for the city ahead more than James B. McPherson.

"*I think our only chance of entering Atlanta* by a quick move if possible is lost," Sherman wrote on the evening of July 20, and he was correct in thinking so. By midnight, McPherson faced on the high ground before him not only Wheeler's frazzled cavalrymen and a handful of Georgia militia, but perhaps the finest infantry division in the Confederate army. North of the city, Hardee had held one gray division in reserve during the attack at Peachtree Creek, prepared to commit them in the later rounds of the fight to complete the Confederate triumph. The reserve division was that of Major General Patrick Cleburne, composed of three veteran brigades of Arkansans, Mississippians, Alabamians, Tennesseans, and Texans, some 4,000 officers and men in all. Cleburne's veterans had bloodied Tecumseh Sherman in the past, from Missionary Ridge to Pickett's Mill to Kennesaw Mountain, and they relished the opportunity to do so again.[8]

A Charleston newspaperman would describe their commander Patrick Ronayne Cleburne as a man "as Irish as Sir Patrick O'Plenipo," and in point of fact, the young general could hardly have been more Irish, born as he was in County Cork on St. Patrick's Day, 1828. As a youth, Pat Cleburne had fallen short in his early efforts to follow in the footsteps of his doctor father and so enlisted as a Redcoat private in Her Majesty's Forty-first Regiment of Foot. After three years of honorable but arduous service in the British army, Cleburne emigrated to the United States and made his way to Helena, Arkansas, in 1849. There he worked as a clerk and later a part owner of a drugstore before reading and practicing law in the small community. Though he was born overseas and owned no slaves, Cleburne felt an abiding loyalty to his adopted home. "I am with the South in life or death, in victory or defeat," he wrote in a letter to his brother in 1861. "I never owned a negro and care nothing for them, but these people have been my friends and have stood by me on all occasions."[9]

Cleburne enlisted as a private in a local volunteer regiment, the 15th Arkansas, and was presently elected captain and later colonel of his regiment. By March 1862, he was promoted to brigadier general, and would soon prove his merit and build a reputation as one of the best fighting commanders in the Southern army. A Northern correspondent who saw Cleburne after Kennesaw considered the thirty-six-year-old general "the fit type of a lean Cassius"—a shade under six feet tall, with brown hair, high cheekbones, and clear gray eyes. Men thought him plain-looking or worse in light of an ugly scar on his face, the result of being shot through the left cheek at Richmond, Kentucky, two years before (the bullet "emerging through his mouth, which fortunately happened to be open," an adjutant wrote), though women perhaps saw him differently. A young lady who had met Cleburne at Tullahoma the year before remembered him as "slender, with small dreamy hazel eyes, a little awkward but very agreeable, and cultured in conversation. . . . Gen'l

Cleburne won the hearts of all who knew him, he was so kind and considerate of others."[10]

An Episcopal vestryman back home, Cleburne never swore and abstained from tobacco and alcohol. (A glass of wine, he found, unsteadied his gun hand and clouded his judgment at the chessboard.) He was a strict disciplinarian, an awkward horseman, and an exceptional marksman. An acquaintance recalled that shortly after Cleburne first came to Arkansas, he was invited to try his hand at target shooting with a revolver. "The result was a laughable failure," the witness remembered—the recent immigrant had never used a pistol in Her Majesty's army. But a few weeks later, "he was present at another trial of skill and, to the astonishment of all, he beat the entire party with the greatest ease."

More recently, a friend had recounted Cleburne's irritation with a mouse he spotted in his room at the Commercial Hotel in Helena. Cleburne retrieved his pistol and vowed to kill "the little rascal," whereupon he settled into a chair, sighted his gun onto the hole in the wooden floor where the vermin had appeared, and waited. His friend protested against the effort, which he maintained would almost certainly be futile, but Cleburne didn't move. His companion checked back a half hour later and found him still in the same position, "his gaze riveted on the rat-hole." At one A.M., returning from an evening on the town, the friend noticed the light still on in Cleburne's room, and peered in the door to find him "in exactly the same posture, statuesque as if he had been made of stone." Retiring for the night, Cleburne's friend had his sleep disturbed at two by the sharp crack of a pistol shot. Cleburne came down the stairs to breakfast in the morning and revealed the remains of the mouse, its head shot cleanly off.[11]

Such was the extraordinary focus, determination, and ruthlessness of the man who had been prepared to lead his veteran troops against Thomas's solid but shaken line near Peachtree Creek late in the afternoon of July 20. A charge by Cleburne's Division at that time and place could have altered the course and perhaps the outcome of the battle—but it was not to be. General Hardee had summoned Cleburne and was about to give the order for him to advance when a staff officer galloped up with a dispatch from Hood, directing Hardee to send Cleburne's Division south "with all haste" to aid in blocking McPherson's advance

Major General Patrick R. Cleburne. (*Library of Congress*)

east of Atlanta. "Five minutes more would have been too late, and would have found this command heavily engaged," Cleburne's adjutant Irving Buck recalled. Cleburne's men promptly withdrew and began their march southward, arriving well after nightfall to replace Joe Wheeler's weary, scattered troopers. "It was extremely dark, and the cavalry line so slight that there was great difficulty in tracing it," one among the arriving soldiers would remember. Confederate officers crept through the darkness, placing their regiments and companies as best they could and whispering orders to avoid drawing the fire of the Federals.

As the sky to the east began to lighten toward dawn, sporadic firing began, and sunrise revealed the Confederate position for what it was: "weak, ill protected, commanded by higher ground in front, and badly enfiladed by the enemy's artillery on the left," Buck wrote. Cleburne's Division held a tenuous line running south from the Georgia Railroad, with a bled-down brigade of Wheeler's cavalry under Brigadier General Samuel Ferguson occupying Bald Hill to their right. Federal cannoneers opened on the exposed position at around seven A.M., and witnesses would record scenes of "dreadful havoc" in the ranks of the butternut soldiers suffering under the murderous enfilading fire. The Union artillery "are killing our men very fast," a Texas captain scratched in his diary that night. "One company just to my left after finishing their works sat down to rest in a little ditch they had dug, when a shell came and took them at one end and killed and crippled every man in the ditch. Knocked one man in a hundred pieces—one hand and arm went over the works and his cartridge box was ten feet up in a tree."

"I have never before witnessed such accurate and destructive cannonading," Brigadier General James Argyle Smith later wrote, reporting forty men killed and over one hundred wounded in a matter of minutes. "In the Eighteenth Texas Cavalry (dismounted), 17 out of 18 men composing one company were placed *hors de combat* by one shot alone."[12]

With the Rebel line riddled with cannon fire, General Leggett directed his largest brigade, that of the admirably named Brigadier General Manning Ferguson Force, to carry Bald Hill. Force, a thirty-nine-year-old Cincinnatian and a graduate of Harvard Law School, would later in life become a judge but for now was a strict taskmaster whose manner matched his name—"a spare grave man with an eye that penetrated to the spine of a culprit," one of his soldiers remembered. "All who knew him then would agree," a fellow officer wrote years later, "that a better commander for the undertaking before us could not have been found in the Army of the Tennessee, in Sherman's army, or, as I believe, in any army that ever marched." Force had formed his skirmishers for attack in a screening strip of woods and had them creep forward under cover of darkness, moving so near to the Rebel line that they could see by dawn's early light the curling campfire smoke of the defenders. A Yankee lieutenant would remember General Force as a commander who, when he spoke, "made every man feel that his day of reckoning had come." His soldiers must have felt just so at about 8:30, when his voice rang out: "Right shoulder shift arms! *Forward, March!*"[13]

The Rebel defenders, their breastworks still unfinished as the attack began, watched the Yankee attackers as they charged, the morning sun bright in the sky behind them. "Line after line of the enemy came into sight and as the blue columns advanced towards us in perfect formation with flags flying and bayonets flashing in the sunshine, they made a splendid appearance," a Texas private named Jim Turner would recall. "Our brigade and regimental officers passed along the line and calling our attention to the advancing columns told us that we must drive them back or die—the safety of Atlanta and of the Confederate Army depended upon us alone."[14]

Force's five regiments of Illinois and Wisconsin soldiers, most of them farm boys back home, rushed up the steep slope. "Our men fell in bunches," a Northern officer recalled, yet "still came the charging column on; faster and faster it pressed forward." Within minutes the Yankees poured over the sparsely defended crest of Bald Hill—"handsomely, eagerly, and well aligned," as one among the attackers remembered. "Then began our firing and our fun." The ragged gray troopers who had held the position scattered to the rear, moving through the

Brigadier General Manning Ferguson Force. (*National Archives*)

gunsmoke toward the city just a mile and a half away.

Force was so elated with the quick capture of his assigned objective that he asked to be permitted to continue and take the next ridge as well. Leggett refused to unleash him, and instead took the opportunity to place a high-sighted battery on the hill and throw long-range shells into the city ahead. He sent a messenger to report the capture of the position to the commander of the adjoining Fourth Division, Brigadier General Giles A. Smith, who had just taken over command from the wounded Gresham. Upon hearing the report, Smith thought Leggett's courier was joking, as it "seemed doubtful to him that such an important point had been won so quickly."[15]

Holding the position so handsomely won might well be another matter, and the defending Confederates had by no means thrown in the sponge elsewhere along the line. Just to the north, Cleburne's men suffered grievously under the early morning artillery fire but then held fast against the blue flood to their front. In contrast to the double-quick charge by Leggett's Third Division on Bald Hill, Smith's Fourth Division advancing against Cleburne's line would find it hard going, meeting "a murderous fire of musketry," as Smith would later report. "Not one of our men wavered, but on the face of everyone was written a determination to drive them back or die," the young Texan Jim Turner proudly wrote. "When they came within range of our rifles the order to fire was given and a sheet of flame ran along our line. They made charge after charge and after each repulse would form and charge again. After many attempts to drive us they fell sullenly back leaving the ground strewn with their dead and wounded."[16]

The late July heat was all but unbearable, the day almost endless—"it truly seemed that a modern Joshua had appeared and commanded the sun to stand still," a Rebel captain wrote. On both sides, men succumbed to sunstroke and exhaustion, uniforms soaked with sweat and lips blackened with powder-grime from biting cartridges. The drifting smoke gave way to thickening clouds, and a passing shower rolled across the landscape late in the afternoon. In response to a request from Cleburne, Hood directed Hardee to send George Maney's Division of Tennesseans south from Peachtree Creek to aid in blocking McPherson. Despite this welcome assistance, it became clear that with the defeat of the dismounted gray cavalrymen on Bald Hill and the failure of a series of counterattacks attempting to retake the dominant height, Cleburne's Division would have no choice but to withdraw.[17]

The bloody fighting that day, July 21, would be considered by historians to be little more than skirmishing, mere friction between the two great armies as they jostled for position between the great battles of Peachtree Creek and Atlanta. Hood would provide a cursory initial report of the engagement to Richmond, along with the questionable claim that the enemy was "handsomely repulsed," but would disregard it entirely in his official report and his memoirs. Likewise, the Federal telegrapher reported to Washington that evening: "Skirmishing sharp and lively all day, but no general engagement." The soldiers involved would hardly have agreed with this assessment, for they had no such detached view of the matter. Union casualties were far from light—728 officers and men killed, wounded, or missing in the 17th Corps, with the losses fairly equally divided between the Third Division (charging and holding Bald Hill) and the Fourth (facing Cleburne's Division). The number of Confederate casualties in the daylong "skirmish" is uncertain, though Cleburne later told General Hardee that the fighting that day was "the bitterest of his life"—a remarkable statement, in light of the sanguinary battles he had endured at Shiloh, Perryville, Murfreesboro, Chickamauga, Pickett's Mill, and Kennesaw.[18]

"It was a terrible day and the loss in our brigade was great," the Lone Star private Jim Turner concluded, "but we remained there until darkness set in, and . . . crawled silently away in the dark on our hands and knees leaving the empty trenches to the enemy's force that was trying to envelop us from the left and right." As dusk fell, Private W. W. Royall of the 5th Texas was knocked down by the shattered head of his comrade Bill Sims, who had survived the daylong struggle only to be struck and killed by a cannonball just as he was about to fall back. "In the evening when we left our breastworks," Royall wrote years later, "our clothes were sprinkled with blood and men's brains and the bottom of the breastworks was nearly half covered with blood."[19]

At his headquarters in Atlanta, John Bell Hood had in mind yet more bitter fighting, immediately resolving "to make another effort to defeat the Federal army." Even as Cleburne and Wheeler fought to hold off McPherson's advance to the east and Atlanta's surgeons continued their grisly work on the wounded from Peachtree Creek, Hood was stooped over his maps, drawing up a new plan to bring about Sherman's demise. Disappointed though he was by the failure of his assault north of the city the day before, the big Texan was no less determined to drive back the Yankee hordes now clawing at the gates of Atlanta. McPherson was now within easy cannon range, able to reach not only the city's outer defenses, but also its factories, stores, homes, and churches. For the past two days, his army had torn up the railroad to Augusta at will. With the rail lines to the north and east in Yankee hands, McPherson might try to move by his left, lunging around to the south in an effort to cut the Macon railroad and surround the city entirely. Hood's attack at Peachtree Creek had slowed Thomas for the moment; clearly, now, he had to do something about McPherson if he was to have any hope of holding Atlanta.

As he searched for a way to accomplish his West Point classmate's destruction, Hood had, on the night of the 20th and during the day on the 21st, received two pieces of welcome intelligence. First, reports confirmed that—notwithstanding the bloody reminder the Confederates had given Sherman of the danger inherent in dividing his forces—the wings of the Union army were still widely separated. Hardee may not have succeeded in destroying Thomas, but he certainly had stopped him from tightening the noose and quickly reuniting with the remainder of the Federal army. South of Peachtree Creek, Thomas's men spent the daylight hours of July 21 improving their fortifications, bracing for another attack rather than continuing their advance toward the city.

Other intelligence indicated that McPherson's supply train—hundreds of horses and wagons heavy laden with ammunition and matériel—was unguarded and vulnerable, parked in and around the town square in Decatur.

Second, although McPherson had succeeded in dislodging Wheeler and Cleburne and moving his line within two miles of Atlanta, the south end of that line—his left—was entirely unprotected, or "in the air," as military men would put it. Again disdainful of Hood's intentions, Sherman had sent Brigadier General Kenner Garrard's division of cavalry—the troopers who would normally be assigned to cover the Union flank and warn of any approaching force—on a four-day raid to further destroy the Georgia Railroad as far as Covington, some thirty miles east-southeast of Decatur. Having dismissed such a move as too risky when McPherson first proposed it a week before, Sherman now told Garrard that the importance of his objective would "justify the loss of quarter of your command." His judgment here was questionable. Despite the battle and maneuver of the past two days, he was sending Garrard and his horsemen galloping off on a raid to break a railroad that was already broken, and in doing so removing them entirely from useful service in opposing the aggressive Hood.[20]

Partly blinded though he was, McPherson was a bright and experienced officer, by no means oblivious to the danger to his unprotected left. "McPherson was confident our army would be attacked," one of his aides later wrote, "and said repeatedly that the attack would come, in his judgment, upon his left front." Nor was he convinced, as Sherman seemed to believe, that the bulk of Hood's army was still entrenched in front of Thomas before Peachtree Creek. The crescendo of Confederate resistance throughout the day suggested that Hood was shoring up his line to the east of Atlanta, and Leggett could see from the top of his hard-earned hill long lines of gray-clad marchers—"at least ten regiments" were moving southward through the city, he reported.[21]

McPherson did all he could to address this touchy tactical situation, and one could detect a tone of resentful complaint between the lines of a dispatch he sent to Sherman late that afternoon to report the successful repulse of Confederate counterattacks on Bald Hill. "Since that time, the enemy has been moving troops in the direction of our left,"

McPherson wrote. "I have strengthened that portion of the line with all the available troops I have got, and will simply remark in closing, that I have no cavalry as a body of observation on my flank, and that the whole Rebel army, except Georgia militia, is not in front of the Army of the Cumberland." In other words, Hood was no longer threatening Thomas, nor was he gone, nor was he idle—and Sherman himself had sent away the cavalry force that would otherwise have been protecting McPherson's southern flank.[22]

Thus was presented to John Bell Hood another opportunity, a chance to emulate his hero Robert E. Lee, by re-creating his famous plan for victory at the Battle of Chancellorsville in May 1863. There, an overconfident Fighting Joe Hooker had similarly left a flank in the air, unfortified and unprotected. Lee had sent Stonewall Jackson's corps on a roundabout march to strike the Union army on its flank and sweep the field. Hood had been on a detached assignment at the time and to his eternal regret had missed Chancellorsville, but he knew its plans and its principles, and he intended to duplicate them here in the piney woods tomorrow. "I determined to make all necessary preparations for a renewed assault; to attack the extreme left of the Federals in rear and flank, and endeavor to bring the entire Confederate Army in united action," Hood recalled.[23]

The young general convened another council of war to explain in detail his plan to his lieutenants: Joseph Wheeler, the cavalry commander; Hardee, Cheatham, and Stewart, the commanders of the three infantry corps; and G. W. Smith, leader of the Georgia militia. Hood would begin by pulling back his forces to the interior defenses of Atlanta. There, Stewart's and Cheatham's Corps, along with the militia, would defend the city while Hardee's Corps marched south, then southeast, then back northeast all the way to Decatur before turning back due west and striking McPherson's rear. Wheeler's cavalry would accompany Hardee and destroy the enemy's wagon train. The march would be made that very night, and the attack was to be launched at dawn.[24]

Hood's flank march plan was daring and well-conceived—sound in its military concepts and a thing of beauty on the uncluttered map. Historians down the years would pronounce the Texan's scheme "bold," "brilliant in its conception," and "Lee-like in its boldness and sweep."

And yet the annals of military history are replete with examples of brilliantly conceived battle plans that melt away like so many candles before the flame of reality and execution. Others detected a certain irony in Hood's proposal, which had a faint echo of the unrealistic plan that had gotten his predecessor Johnston sacked—to hold the city with a skeleton force while using the remainder of the army to make "freer and wider movements." But such a comparison, suggested by some latter-day critics of Hood's generalship, is far from apt. Johnston had proposed to leave only 5,000 Georgia militia in the Atlanta defenses; whereas Hood planned to hold them with two entire corps, using only Hardee's force for the curving whiplash strike around and against McPherson's flank.[25]

Hood seemed to know that he was asking a great deal of the army and its commanders. "To transfer after dark our entire line from the immediate presence of the enemy to another line around Atlanta, and to throw Hardee, the same night, entirely to the rear and flank of McPherson—as Jackson was thrown, in a similar movement, at Chancellorsville and Second Manassas—and to initiate the offensive at daylight, required no small effort upon the part of the men and officers," he later wrote. And yet he would try it nonetheless. "No time was to be lost in taking advantage of this second unexpected opportunity to achieve victory and relieve Atlanta," he wrote years later. As the troops began their movement, Hood mounted up to move to an observation point where he could monitor the fighting, earnestly hoping, as he said, "that the assault would result not only in a general battle, but in a signal victory to our arms."[26]

Whether he was aware of it or not, Hood had given Hardee and his men an assignment that was a damn sight more difficult than the challenging flank march Stonewall Jackson had led through the Virginia wilderness fourteen months earlier. For one thing, there was the distance. The initial plan to march all the way to Decatur was abandoned in favor of allowing Hardee discretion to attack not in the rear but on the Union left flank—Wheeler's cavalry would peel off from the infantry column and raid the Federal supply base in Decatur. Yet even with these modified orders, a march of no less than fifteen miles would be required to arrive at their assigned positions for the attack the next day, three miles longer than Jackson's movement at Chancellorsville. What was more, the redoubtable Stonewall had marched by day, led by a trusted guide, and he had reliable intelligence as to the exact position of the enemy. Hardee would have to make his march by night, through the thick woods and even thicker summer heat, uncertain of McPherson's deployment east of Atlanta and, thanks to questionable roads and inadequate maps, unsure of how to get there.

Lieutenant General William J. Hardee. (*Library of Congress*)

Most of the butternut marchers refilled their cartridge boxes and set out on the road that Wednesday evening without knowing where they were headed, which perhaps was just as well given their current state of mind. "Well! My opinion is that if Hood follows up the policy inaugurated yesterday, we will either drive the enemy back or we will go up the spout ourselves," a Louisiana private recorded in his diary. "There seems to be general dissatisfaction among the men on account of the headlong way in which they were put in yesterday, and they think that 'it costs more than it comes to.' They say Hood cares no more for the loss of his men, than Grant does of his in Virginia." But despite the isolated grumbling, their spirits lifted once they were on the move. At eight P.M., Walker's and Bate's Divisions, which would form the lead elements of the Rebel flanking column, left their entrenchments south of Peachtree Creek and started off due south, down Peachtree Street. As they passed through the city, Cleburne and Maney were to leave their fortifications, head west, and join the march.[27]

"Orders came to march and we soon found ourselves going rapidly through the city," one gray soldier recalled. "Odd, such a movement seemed, but we welcomed it. Anything was better than the aimless going here and there under the new leadership. There seemed to be a purpose in this new movement. We soon found ourselves part of a large, swiftly marching column of men, and with a swinging gait in a short while reached Atlanta." Hardee's men tramped south down Peachtree Street and through the darkened buildings of the city. As the long gray columns passed through the city streets, discipline broke down among Wheeler's free-swinging cavalrymen, and some troopers broke from the ranks to engage in indiscriminate looting of downtown shops and other businesses. One witness described the scene in his diary as nothing less than "a raid upon the principal stores in the city," the offenders making off with everything from clothing to rations, with whiskey and tobacco prized above all. "Next morning," the soldier wrote, "every man in the Army had a cigar stuck in his mouth and any amount of rations could be purchased from the soldiers at more reasonable prices than we had known for many a day." The gray horsemen were less practical in their appropriations, jingling along on their mounts with baubles and trophies of every description. "All along the army to-day can be seen fancy ornaments, brass and porcelain door knobs, call bells and other items decorating the harness of the horses and mules."[28]

Their passage southward through the dark cavern of Peachtree Street sparked a rumor that the Confederates were evacuating the city—a reasonable supposition, given the battle and bombardment over the two days just past and now the plundering of local shops and storehouses. This, in turn, inspired yet another panicked, midnight civilian exodus. "The citizens became alarmed . . . and hurriedly packed up such things as they could carry and began to leave the city in every direction—every available means of transportation was called into service," a Rebel lieutenant wrote in his diary, recalling throngs of refugees crowding the roads south in the wake of the marching gray columns. "Everybody thought the army was running and everybody wanted to run, too—and they did."[29]

"A glorious night," one among the marchers recalled, moonlight spilling through the tattered clouds and painting the soldiers a ghostly white. A battery of cannoneers began singing "Anne Darling," and then "Annie Laurie," the infantrymen soon joining in the lilting verses.

Her brow is like the snow drift,
Her throat is like the swan,
Her face is the fairest

THE NIGHT MARCH
HARDEE'S FLANK MOVEMENT
JULY 21 - 22
CONFEDERATE POSITION
south of Peachtree Creek
Hardee's Corps
begins march here
Peachtree Road
Decatur
ARMY OF THE
TENNESSEE
McPherson
(present day
North Ave.)
ATLANTA
Georgia Railroad
15th Corps
17th
Corps
16th Corps
Battle of Atlanta
begins here
Wheeler's
cavalry raid
to Decatur
Fair St.
(present day
Memorial Drive)
MANEY
CLEBURNE
WALKER
BATE
Cleburne's
division
joins here
Mill
Pond
Fayetteville Road
Terry's
Mill
Flat Shoals Rd.
Intrenchment Creek
N
McDonough Road
Cobb's
Mill
0
1
2
Miles
Sugar Creek
South River
(Adapted from Wilbur G. Kurtz - 1937)

That ever the sun shone on,
That ever the sun shone on.
And dark blue eyes,
And for bonnie Annie Laurie,
I'd lay me down and die.

The column moved from the commercial district and past well-kept gardens surrounding brick and wood-frame houses on the southeastern part of town. The dwellings remained dark, "as close and silent as convents," the remaining residents of Atlanta peering through curtained windows at the swinging, singing lines of men. (The singing, though spontaneous and good for the army's morale, was perhaps not the best idea: a Union lieutenant colonel, across the way on Leggett's Hill, reported hearing "considerable noise" to his front.)[30]

And so the march started well enough, with hours remaining 'til daylight and the men in high spirits with their songs and cigars, glad to be on the move—but soon things began to go awry. Cleburne, instructed to quietly withdraw from his position and join the tail end of the column, found himself too close to the enemy's line east of the city to pull back undetected. His men were finally able to creep out of their entrenchments, leaving behind a line of screening skirmishers to the front, but it was long past midnight before they began their movement, and nearly three A.M.—seven hours after the march began—when the last man stepped onto the road south. The designated route would take them down Peachtree Street, then southeast down the Atlanta-McDonough Road well past the extreme left of the Federal lines, then turning back to the northeast up the Fayetteville Road, and then finally due north into the Union flank and left rear.

Clearing the city, the songs and chatter died and the winding gray column fell quiet as the tired soldiers "bent forward silently to the all night march before us." They made slow progress, stumbling in the darkness and having to clear the road from time to time to make way for couriers or cavalry, the foot soldiers grumbling as they sidestepped into the weeds and brush to let Wheeler's horsemen clatter past. So clean and precise when depicted as an arrow on the map, in practice the movement was, as an Atlanta historian described it, "a confused mass of milling men, artillery and cavalry."[31]

Then circumstances grew still worse. Some of the obstacles encountered in the night march were perhaps to be expected—the difficulty in disengaging with the enemy, the clots of foot- and horse-traffic on the narrow road, the steaming late July heat. But what Hood had failed to consider, most of all, was the frailty of human flesh and bone and muscle. Hardee's attack was made up of four divisions, all of which had spent the last two days in battle to varying degrees. Even when not under fire, the soldiers had been busy day and night with picks and shovels, working to improve their meager breastworks. Walker's men had suffered grievously in the fight at Peachtree Creek two days before—indeed, Hardee referred to the division in his report as "Walker's beaten troops"—and Cleburne's men had fought from before dawn until dusk holding back McPherson's advance toward the city. Now, added to the exhaustion resulting from their exertions in battle over the past two days was the bone-deep weariness that all men experience after a sleepless night of strenuous physical exertion. "Halts came, the men jamming up against each other each time (for they were sleepy) just like cars on a freight train," a soldier remembered. Men fell out by the roadside by ones and twos and then dozens, collapsing footsore and exhausted.[32]

The fleeting shower at sundown had barely dampened the red clay roads. The moisture soon steamed off and thousands of shuffling men kicked up a choking, oppressive dust, hanging like a funereal pall in the humid air over the marchers. "When morning came we looked like the imaginary Adam 'of the earth earthy,' so completely were we encased in dust," one of the marching soldiers recalled, their initial enthusiasm for the movement by now a thing of the past. "The most tedious and harassing night march I ever experienced," Hardee's disgruntled adjutant T. B. Roy would later complain, while another went even beyond that: "It was to me the most ill-conceived and unsatisfactory executed plan of the whole war in which I participated."[33]

Hood's plan had called for an assault at dawn on the Union flank and rear, but it was soon plain to all—with the marchers weary, the eastern sky graying toward dawn, and the column strung out for miles along the Fayetteville Road—that Hardee was again going to be late in launching the attack. At about five A.M., Hardee, Cleburne, and Walker arrived at the residence of a man named William Cobb, who operated a grist mill along nearby Intrenchment Creek. Hardee judged that he was still three miles from his objective. A halt was called to distribute another twenty rounds of ammunition and allow the men to fill their canteens and get some badly needed rest. Cobb, along with an elderly millworker by the name of Case Turner, were brought before the commanders and soon volunteered—or were "volunteered"—to serve as guides. The two locals "gave every indication of being frightened," according to one account of the meeting, somehow suspecting "that the job was not disassociated with danger." Cobb was appointed to accompany Cleburne, while Turner mounted up on an old gray mule like a backwoods Sancho Panza, charged with conducting the column of the irascible Major General William Henry Talbot Walker through the forest. "The whole country through which we passed was one vast densely-set thicket," another gray officer recalled, noting that "a line of battle could not be seen 50 yards."[34]

Hardee was increasingly agitated, certainly aware that he was already hours behind schedule and nowhere near the point of attack. Wheeler left the Cobb place and led his troopers on up the Fayetteville Road toward his assigned objective at Decatur. "We knew we were in rear of General McPherson's line," the cavalryman wrote years later, adding, as if still unsure of the Confederate position, "at least in rear of his left . . ."[35]

"*July 22, 1864, dawned in calmness and beauty*, presaging a perfect summer day," a Union artilleryman remembered, "but as the sun rose upon the horizon, an angry red flushed his broad disk, which seemed to presage one of the very fiercest battles ever fought, and to reflect what would ere nightfall be the blood-drenched ground of the battlefield of Atlanta."[36] After a delay of more than two hours, Walker and Cleburne at last got the men to their feet and continued the plodding advance, north up the Fayetteville Road past the homesteads of Dr. Thrash and Grandma Akers and thence to a fork in the road. Here, in the thick mid-summer woods, the column would split: Cleburne and Maney would take the left fork, moving up the Flat Shoals Road to approach Leggett's Hill from the southeast; while Bate and Walker would take the right, toward Decatur, preceded by Wheeler's cavalry, off on their mission to destroy McPherson's wagon train. Bate was a capable commander, but as his floundering during the Battle of Peachtree Creek had suggested, perhaps not the man whose sense of direction should be trusted to conduct the column through unfamiliar country far from the rest of the army. But all was not lost: the column had its recently acquired civilian guide, the old man Case Turner, and it had General Walker—a dauntless veteran of three wars and perhaps the orneriest officer in the Confederate army.

William Henry Talbot Walker was born and raised in Augusta, the son of the town's mayor Freeman Walker, later a United States senator. Known to his family as "Willie," young Walker attended West Point but was a far-below-average cadet, a member of the so-called "Immortal Section"—always late, reckless and rowdy, not the wheat of the storied institution but the chaff. He graduated a not-so-respectable 46th out of 59 in the class of 1837. Commissioned a second lieutenant and dispatched to Florida to fight the Seminoles, he was severely wounded on Christmas Day, 1837—"literally shot to pieces," one witness said—struck in the neck, shoulder, leg, left arm, and chest. Stretcher bearers were carrying the unconscious Walker back to camp for burial when to their astonishment, he revived. Surgeons considered his case hopeless, doing their best to make him comfortable and sending him to Tampa to die. Instead, he made a full recovery—just "to spite the doctors," he was fond of saying, though others suggested that perhaps he had encountered the healing waters of the Fountain of Youth. A decade later, he fought in the Mexican War and was wounded twice, first at the Battle of Churubusco and then severely at the Battle of Molino del Rey, where he was shot through the body and left on the field for dead. (His unsightly wounds probably saved him from being stabbed to death by the Mexicans, who ranged across the field bayoneting the wounded.) He was bedridden in Mexico for ten months, too seriously injured to be moved, but finally healed enough to return home to Augusta.

Walker spent much of the next decade on sick leave, though from 1854 to 1856 he served as the commandant of West Point—a considerable irony given his undistinguished record, though he was eminently qualified to teach his assigned topic: military tactics. Walker was a

Southern firebrand and resigned his commission from the United States Army on the same day that South Carolina seceded from the Union, becoming the first officer of the Old Army to do so. Because of his various injuries by shot and shell, not all of which had been removed by doctors, the seemingly indestructible hero—easy to hit, but hard to kill—was given the nickname "Shot Pouch." It seemed he might be "immortal," indeed.

But far from invincible. Now forty-seven, the crotchety Georgian suffered chronic pain from his wounds and the significant quantities of lead and fragments still embedded in his body. He was afflicted with terrible asthma, which forced him to sleep in a sitting position. As a result, he was often hurting and usually exhausted, which only served to further inflame his already volcanic temper.[37]

One fellow general would recall that battle "always brought to his eyes an unusual glitter"—not unlike his chief Hood—and thought him "the bravest man he had ever known." But the general's odd appearance and his stormy temperament inspired other superlatives as well. General Richard Taylor, who had served with Walker earlier in the war, thought him the strangest character he had ever met; while George Cary Eggleston pronounced him "the queerest of all the military men I met or saw during the war." He was, Eggleston said, a "peculiarly belligerent man," always in search of a battle—and because "certain periods of inaction are necessary in all wars, however, General Walker was forced to maintain a state of hostility to all those above and around him." He had started the war by refusing the colonelcy he was offered, demanding a higher rank. Commissioned a brigadier, he feuded with General Braxton Bragg, with Secretary of War Judah Benjamin, with Jefferson Davis himself; he complained about strategy; he carried on ugly, high-profile arguments with the War Department in the Richmond newspapers; he exchanged angry words with prominent men at dinner parties. In the fall of 1862 he resigned his commission, only to return a year later to an out-of-the-way post in Savannah. Bored and irritated, he was reassigned to Mississippi and finally to the Army of Tennessee. In late June, he had hoped to fill the vacancy created by the death of Leonidas Polk at Pine Mountain, but command of the corps went to Alexander P. Stewart instead.[38]

Major General William H. T. Walker, "Old Shot Pouch." (*Battles and Leaders*)

"I shall calmly tread the path of duty," Walker told his daughter, "feeling that my position is above the shafts of malice and revenge." Other letters revealed the depth of his contempt for the enemy. He encouraged his children "to grow up hating the Yankee nation more & more every day" and instructed his wife to leave the country if the South were to lose the war.[39]

Walker was predictably irate as the sun climbed higher and his men struggled forward toward their assigned position. Running late and eager to begin the attack, Hardee deployed his soldiers for battle too far from the Union position, changing from the marching column to a line of battle stretching off right and left into the trees as they stepped off the Fayetteville Road near Sugar Creek. Considerable time was expended in forming the line, the growth so thick that it was impossible in places for each brigade to see the flank of its neighbor. A cannoneer posted behind the infantry watched the ragged gray foot soldiers as they set off through the trees. "Soon, 'Forward march' went along the infantry line in quiet tones, and off they went, our comrades of the musketry, a long brown dirt colored line, deeper and deeper into the forest until swallowed up by the trees."[40]

The straggling advance moved slowly through the woods to the northwest, thousands of exhausted armed men on a hike without a trail. "The advance line soon seemed to have had much difficulty in keeping the proper direction, soon moved by the right flank, then forward, then by the right flank again, then forward, then by the left flank," Brigadier General Mark Lowrey later reported. "The difficulty of following the movements in such dense woods can scarcely be imagined." The men started forward well enough, then disappeared—companies and brigades, then entire divisions tripping through heavy brush and becoming disconnected from one another. "I marched in line for two miles through a dense forest," Hardee later wrote. "Of course it was impossible to keep up an alignment."[41]

As the infantry divisions began their advance, one of Walker's aides observed in front of one of his regiments a seemingly impenetrable expanse of briars. Walker rode over to Hardee and asked that his men be allowed to skirt the obstacle, but Old Reliable was irritated at the many delays and touchy as a blister. "No, sir!" he snapped at Walker. "This movement has been delayed too long already. Go and obey my orders!" Walker reddened and rode away, furious at the undeserved reprimand and the implication that he would ever do anything less than follow his orders. "I shall make him remember this insult," he vowed to the staff officer riding with him. "If I survive this battle, he shall answer me for it." The aide remained convinced that Walker intended to challenge Hardee to a duel to reclaim his honor, if he ever got the chance.[42]

The Confederate line picked through heavy trees and underbrush, moving northwest along the banks of the trickling creek. It was nearly 11 o'clock when Walker emerged from the woods to see before him the expanse of the Terry's Mill Pond, brimming full in the creek valley like a bowl of muddy soup. Guides or no guides, the Confederates would now pay the price for attempting a night march through unfamiliar ground without first conducting a proper reconnaissance. The roughly diamond-shaped pond was nearly a half mile wide and branched off toward the west, so that any effort to skirt around it would further disrupt the already fragmented Rebel alignment. The shoreline was tangled with brush, and the water stood ten feet deep in some places, more lake than pond. Horses floundered in the soft mire along the banks, and the infantry slogged through mud and reeds amid the frogs and dragonflies, their objective now reduced to "anywhere on the other side of that damnable sheet of water called a 'mill pond'." They struggled through a swamp "filled with logs, stumps, brush and what-not in water and mire knee-deep, the men in many instances being compelled to extricate their comrades by pulling them onto logs and other footings before we could pass the obstruction," a Kentucky soldier would remember. "Out of dust ankle deep into water and mire knee-deep was too much for the nerves and patience of the strongest man and most patient Christian."[43]

And certainly too much for the angry and just-insulted General Walker. Shot Pouch and his staff were nearly around the left side of the pond in a cluster of willows when Walker's horse bogged down in the muck. This was altogether more than the seething general could take, and he directed his fury at the civilian guide whom he now believed had deliberately led him astray. Walker drew his revolver, whirled in the saddle, and took aim at the startled Case Turner, who froze in terror on his mule.

Walker's aide Major Joseph B. Cumming intervened, reminding the general that Turner had warned them about the obstruction when they first spoke back at the Cobb place. Thus dissuaded from violence against his befuddled, terrified guide, Walker took his place at the head of his troops and prepared to lead them forward. At last they reached the head of the millpond, and Walker steered his line back to the northeast to correct for any sidling disruption caused by their muddy detour. Around this time, a young private spotted the general and later described the scene:

> We passed close to Walker himself. "Fighting Billy," as he was called, a hero of the Mexican War. One of the thinnest men I ever saw. Imagine a fence rail, dressed in complete uniform, closely buttoned up as warm as it was, topped by a long pale face, almost hidden, however, by a bushy black beard, and above all a huge black felt hat with a big black feather curling around it. I saw him "full front" as we went by, and there seemed hardly space enough on his attenuated body for the double row of buttons of his general's uniform coat. Long and tall as he looked, as he sat on his horse, straight as a ram rod, evidently waiting with his staff around him to "go in."[44]

It was just after noon when Walker began the advance, stepping clear of the line of trees into the dappled sunlight. No doubt he was astonished by what he saw. Having marched all night and half a day to reach the Federal left rear, he found before him an entire corps of bluecoats in a triple line stretching across his front. He raised his binoculars to survey the line before him, when a bullet, apparently fired by a Union picket hidden somewhere in the trees, struck him in the breast.

Walker tumbled from his mount and fell heavily to the ground, field glasses still grasped tightly in his hands. His luck—if a man wounded over and over again in the course of a thirty-year, three-war military career could be said to be lucky—had finally run out, and he lay dead on the soil of his native state. Nearby, the badly frightened guide Case Turner, deciding that this startling turn of events signaled an end to his brief tenure as a military scout, fled the scene as fast as his braying mule could carry him.

W. H. T. Walker had been shot down before the engagement was even fairly under way. The single musket shot "not only toppled Walker from his saddle," as one historian would later suggest, "but began the battle of Atlanta." His soliders pressed forward to the front, even as the general's wiry corpse was taken off the field, a handkerchief tied around his face. His body was carried by wagon back to Atlanta and would eventually return by train to his hometown Augusta (though not for a while, as the Federals had broken the railroad in that direction). Upon its arrival, a long funeral cortège of horsemen and black carriages rolled from the depot to the Walker cemetery on Arsenal Avenue, where he was laid to rest. Thus Old Shot Pouch departed the war and this earth, never to retrieve his besmirched reputation and left defenseless against postwar slights in the memoirs of men who jumbled his initials or misspelled his name. His temper and his tactics were certainly subject to criticism, but no one could doubt his gallantry and his devotion. As one veteran would write, years later: "I am sure no battle soil on God's green earth in all the ages was ever stained by braver or by nobler blood than William Henry Walker's."[45]

But yet more noble blood was to be spilled that day.

CHAPTER SIX

"An Iliad of Woes"

Bald Hill, or The Battle of Atlanta July 22

By sunrise on Friday, July 22, General Sherman thought, or maybe just hoped, that the Rebels were gone. Once a pessimist, always fearing the worst, the red-haired Ohioan had evolved into a man who often seemed to believe what he wanted to believe. His supposition was founded upon a series of dispatches, starting about three o'clock in the morning, from various brigade and division commanders reporting that the Confederate lines to their immediate front were empty. Imprecision in the language of these reports, combined with a generous dash of wishful thinking on the part of the recipient, resulted in the conclusion that Hood had departed Atlanta entirely. "The enemy has evacuated his works in front of General Stanley," one dispatch read, headed 3:15 A.M.; and an hour later, another reported, "the lines in our front are also found to be evacuated." These and others like them soon led to more general statements: "The enemy has evacuated his works around Atlanta," one said, and finally there arrived a definitive and plainly erroneous generalization: "The enemy has evacuated Atlanta." Sherman was understandably delighted by this intelligence and began firing off orders pressing his subordinates to undertake "a vigorous pursuit" of the Rebels, who he presumed were scattered and disorganized on the roads south of town.[1]

"The enemy having evacuated their works in front of our lines, the supposition of Major-General Sherman is that they have given up Atlanta and are retreating in the direction of East Point," McPherson wrote in an order headed 6 A.M. But the chase was brought up short as he and Thomas, pressing forward, found the Confederates in possession of a heavily fortified line of works closer to the city. The Rebels had not gone, after all—or rather, it appeared that they had only gone about 1,200 yards.

Captain John C. Van Duzer, the army telegrapher with Sherman, clicked an update to the War Department in Washington later that day, apparently somewhat bemused at the morning's developments. "At daylight to-day it was found that the rebels had gone from the entire front, and General Sherman announced the occupation of Atlanta by Schofield, and ordered pursuit by Thomas and McPherson," Van Duzer wrote, and then continued dryly: "Vigorous pursuit was made, and the enemy was found in the fortifications of Atlanta, and not Schofield." Sherman soon corrected his misimpression and somehow managed to avoid the embarrassment of having widespread reports of the glorious occupation of Atlanta make their way into Northern newspapers, only to later prove false.[2]

Sherman rode with Schofield and arrived midmorning at the home of Augustus F. Hurt, a beautiful two-story white frame house surrounded by cotton fields and standing timber on a hill some two miles due east of Atlanta. Hurt had refugeed with his family some time before, and a local ne'er-do-well—a pig farmer and whiskey distiller by the name of Howard ("just Howard, and no more, as far as is recorded," a local historian wrote)—had occupied the home, apparently uninvited, since that time. For that reason, the reports and memoirs of Federal officers would refer to the structure, soon to be Sherman's headquarters, as "the Howard house." Gazing westward from the yard of the Hurt-Howard House, Sherman could see plainly between him and the buildings of the city "the rebel main line strongly manned, with guns in position at intervals." The Confederates were hard at work improving their parapets, digging trenches, placing headlogs, and dragging small trees and saplings up to serve as abatis. Having now seen with his own eyes that Hood had not left Atlanta and in fact appeared determined to hold it, Sherman sent a message to Thomas informing him that "we were mistaken in supposing the enemy gone," and directing him to "use artillery freely, converging in the town."[3]

McPherson had witnessed the same thing, having spent the early hours with Mortimer Leggett on the crest of Bald Hill. From there, the two generals could see "without the aid of a field-glass, large bodies of infantry moving about the city and in the interior line of intrenchments. The rifle-pits were full of men; and heavy guns, well manned, peered from embrasures all along the Rebel line." McPherson, whether due to military instinct or some shadow of foreboding, repeatedly predicted to his aides "that we were likely to have during that day the severest battle of the campaign." With that in mind, and unwilling to ignore the dark clouds of possible ruin that seemed to be gathering in the neighborhood of his southern flank, he rode over to visit Major General Grenville M. Dodge, commander of the XVI (16th) Corps. McPherson gave Dodge verbal orders to send the division of Brigadier General Thomas W. Sweeny south to cover the exposed left end of the XVII (17th) Corps. He also notified Sherman, who promptly disagreed with the order, perhaps believing that McPherson was again being overly cautious. "Instead of sending Dodge to your left, I wish you would put his whole corps at work destroying absolutely the railroad back to and including Decatur," Sherman wrote, apparently unmoved by the fact that the railroad was already broken and the knowledge that he had sent Garrard's cavalry out to Covington to break it further. "I want that road absolutely and completely destroyed," he said, "every tie burned and every rail twisted."[4]

This brought McPherson in person to Sherman's headquarters. He arrived along with his staff around eleven A.M. and requested that Sherman allow him to postpone the railroad destruction, leaving Dodge's relocated men to cover the exposed left until later in the day. Sherman agreed to the delay, and then sat for a spell on the steps of the Howard House, discussing "the chances of battle and Hood's general character" with the Rebel commander's former West Point classmates Schofield and McPherson. "We agreed," he later wrote, "that we ought to be unusually cautious and prepared at all times for sallies and for hard fighting, because Hood, though not deemed much of a scholar, or of great mental capacity, was undoubtedly a brave, determined and rash man."[5]

McPherson took his leave from Sherman and then rode along his lines for a time before meeting his corps commanders John Logan and Frank Blair in a grove of oaks just south of the Georgia Railroad. Looking back, an aide would recall McPherson's "fine appearance, seated on his horse in the sunshine of the summer morning."[6] The three generals and their aides dismounted and settled underneath the trees to enjoy a noontime meal. As they finished eating, a courier arrived with a handwritten note from Sherman headed 12 noon, directing McPherson to send one of Dodge's two divisions east to begin tearing up railroad track, as originally contemplated. By then, with no attack having been made and the Rebel force still clearly visible in their trenches before Atlanta, Sherman must have thought that the danger had passed.

McPherson took out a pencil and wrote out a dispatch forwarding Sherman's order to Dodge and instructing him to put his men to work burning the railroad east and west of Decatur. But despite the silence as the sun stood high and the heat spilled down hard and thick like rain, McPherson remained uneasy. "The men should take their arms along and stack them near where they are at work, so that they can be ready for any emergency," he warned.[7] Meanwhile, in the woods to the south, finally clear of Terry's Mill Pond and the worst of the vine-choked forest, some 12,000 Confederates formed for their attack.

The sun slipped past the overhead as the unsuspecting Union generals rested in the shade of the oak trees, chatting and smoking cigars. The day was very quiet. Almost peaceful.

The Rebel attack was to begin on the far right of the Confederate line with the division of Major General William B. Bate, who again would start the battle in confusion. In a way, Old Grits found himself wrestling with the opposite problem of the one he had faced two days earlier. At Peachtree Creek, he had stumbled through the forest and could not find the Federal line where he was supposed to; now, thinking he was about to plunge into the Union rear, he instead found a line of blue infantry where there wasn't supposed to be one. "I was ignorant of what was in my front but believed the enemy was without defenses," Bate later reported. "In this we were mistaken." With the tactical situation presented before him apparently not contemplated by his orders, he sent a courier off to Hardee seeking further direction, but never heard back. Around a quarter past twelve, his men stepped off on their assault—not on the Federal rear or even an unguarded flank, but against the fresh, experienced veterans of Dodge's 16th Corps, who would not spend the day tearing up railroad track in Decatur after all.[8]

Grenville M. Dodge was a slump-shouldered thirty-three-year-old, a New Englander by birth and an Iowan by choice, and according to the cursory evaluation of one witness, "a small and very ordinary man." He was actually not that small—a shade over five feet eight inches, about average for the times—and he was also far from ordinary. After the war, he would become chief engineer of the Union Pacific Railroad and one of the great builders of the transcontinental railroad, such an icon of the Old West that the famous cattle town of Dodge City would be named for him. "Level Eye," the Indians would call him, and he brought the same keen perception and judgment to his task as a corps commander. Dodge had arrived with Sweeny's Division from the far end of the Union line just before noon, and two of Sweeny's three brigades, resting in a column of fours along the road, were now directly across the Rebel line of advance. Just to the west, another brigade from Brigadier General John W. Fuller's Division was positioned near Sugar Creek, just opposite Walker's Division.[9]

What should have been an open lane to the Federal rear was now blocked, and all Dodge had to do was get his men on their feet and face them toward the advancing Confederates to meet the attack. Put another way, McPherson's flank was no longer "in the air" at all—now, in military terms, the flank had been "refused," the left end of the line bent back in an L-shape to cover against just such an attack as the Confederates were in the process of launching. "So Walker and Bate, moving north and northwest, instead of delivering a surprise attack in rear of the 15th and 17th Corps, marched right into a compact line of Federals, who could not have been better placed had Hardee served advance notice of his intentions," one analyst of the movement wrote. No doubt there was some luck involved in this perfect placement—though there was credit due, as well. "Thanks in part to McPherson's foresight," historian Steven Woodworth wrote, "the Sixteenth had been in exactly the right place at the right time to ward off the opening blow of Hood's ambitious offensive." Counting his blessings, the grateful 17th Corps commander Frank Blair thought someone else deserved the credit. "The Lord put Dodge in the right place to-day," he said.[10]

Or the wrong place, depending on your perspective. Federal skirmishers had just felt their way forward to the timber line across the way when they met a long line of butternut soldiers rushing toward them out of the forest. Bate's men broke into the sunlight and charged down an open slope, across a boggy mire, and then up toward Sweeny's waiting line. Dodge, "cutting red tape," as a staff officer would suggest, made dispositions in the heat of battle by giving orders not only to Sweeny but directly to his regimental commanders. ("This act afterwards caused trouble," an aide noted.) On the extreme left of the Union line, Brigadier General Elliott Rice watched the Confederates charging toward his line of Midwesterners "in truly magnificent style," with "their battle-flags proudly flaunting in the breeze." The Iowa, Illinois and Indiana boys sighted down their barrels "with cool and deadly aim," and smoke and flame boiled up from the line as they opened on the charging Rebels. The volley staggered the advancing line, and mixed with the Rebel yell came the higher, piercing screams of the wounded. "Still on came the charging columns, more desperate than ever, those in front urged up by those in rear," Rice wrote, proudly reporting: "Yet still my thin line stood like a fence of iron, not a man deserting his colors, which were all the time being proudly and defiantly waved in the very teeth of the enemy."[11]

Next to Rice, the brigade of German-born Colonel August Mersy, once a Prussian army officer and more recently an Illinois bank clerk, stood against the center of Bate's charge. The Confederates, an Ohio major later wrote, "came tearing wildly through the woods with the yells of demons," repeatedly renewing their assaults "until the sight of dead and wounded lying in their way, as they charged again and again to break our lines, must have appalled the stoutest hearts." Rebel bravery and musketry was no match for the well-positioned Federals, who were supported by two batteries of artillery—an Ohio battery of six 3-inch ordnance rifles and a Missouri battery of Napoleons. The cannon put down "a sweeping and deadly fire" that "mowed great swaths in the advancing columns," a Union witness would write. What was more, a number of the defenders were armed with what firearms curator Joseph Bilby called "the fastest shooting firearm used in the Civil War": the .44 caliber Henry repeating rifle, which carried one round in the chamber and another fifteen in a spring-loaded magazine. Henrys were rare and expensive, but the 66th Illinois Regiment of Mersy's brigade was armed with more Henrys than any other unit in Sherman's army. Private Prosper Bowe of the 66th recalled aiming at the Rebels as they broke into the open. "We started our sixteen-shooters to work, and the first column in front of us nearly all fell at the first two or three volleys," he said. Bowe reloaded five times and thus fired "ninety rounds without stoping."

The combination of blasts of artillery tearing at the flanks and rapid rifle fire from the front was more than the stoutest Rebel charge could bear. The Confederates "showed great steadiness, closed up the gaps, and preserved their alignments," a Federal observer remembered, "but the iron and leaden hail that was fairly poured upon them was too much for flesh and blood to stand." Stumbling over the bodies of fallen comrades in the smoke and confusion, Bate's Division faltered and then fell back.[12]

To the west, the adjoining Rebel division of the dead General Walker, now led by Brigadier General Hugh W. Mercer, fared little better. The change of commanders no doubt caused some delay, as did the tardy emergence from the woods of Walker's leftmost brigade, that of States Rights Gist, which had been slowed and discombobulated by briars and brush. The attack was poorly coordinated, the brigades of George A. Smith and then Gist advancing alone across a marshy stream and then up the hill toward Fuller's troops, where they were riddled with shot and shell and then repulsed. Both Smith and Gist were wounded in the charge, and Smith's successor Colonel James C. Nisbet was captured. Mercer's own brigade was held in reserve under Colonel Charles H. Olmstead, but presently he too was wounded, struck in the head by a shell fragment and carried from the field. His replacement, Colonel William Barkuloo, a New Yorker who had moved south to marry a Georgia girl and therefore chose to wear gray, took the brigade forward as far as the swampy little branch, and looked up the slope at what he faced across several hundred yards of open ground. "We found the enemy drawn up in three lines of battle on the crest of the hill and supported by two batteries," he later reported, with the Federal lines "outflanking ours both to the right and left." Barkuloo knew a hopeless task when he saw one, and immediately gave orders for a withdrawal. (Ordered to lead the brigade back into the fight shortly thereafter, Barkuloo would instead turn over the command to a subordinate and retire to the brigade hospital, explaining rather lamely that he had recently returned from a sickbed and was "exhausted by the fatigues of the day." Whether a failure of health or of nerve, this act effectively ended his military career.)[13]

In the course of the exhausting night march, Walker and Bate had made the deepest penetration around the flank and toward the Federal rear and perhaps had the best chance to create havoc behind the Union line. Now Walker was dead, and Bate's and Mercer's attacks had been stymied by the 16th Corps in a stand-up engagement one witness would call "one of the fiercest of the war." Fierce, but futile. "Pickett's famed charge could not have been braver or more desperate, and I may add more signally repulsed," an Illinois captain wrote. Six Rebel brigades had charged courageously against three Union brigades, but their attack had not lasted an hour, and they had never gotten closer than a hundred yards from the Federal lines. Hood's flank attack, it seemed, might come to nothing.[14]

But next in line was the hard-driving division of Patrick Cleburne, and if the placement of Dodge's corps had been fortuitous for the Yankees, so was the disposition of Cleburne's Division a lucky break for the Confederates. The Irishman's route along the Flat Shoals Road had not only brought his three brigades up close to the Federal position without substantial hindrances like the millpond Walker had faced to the west—though the men had struggled through a vast expanse of blackberry bushes, leading them to remember the attack as "the Blackberry Charge"—it also placed him right across from a gap between Blair's 17th Corps and Dodge's newly arrived 16th. Moving forward, Cleburne's veterans would strike a weak point at the intersection or hinge of the L-shaped Union line.

Cleburne gave the order to go forward at about 12:45, and his division charged against the Old Iowa Brigade of Colonel William Hall,

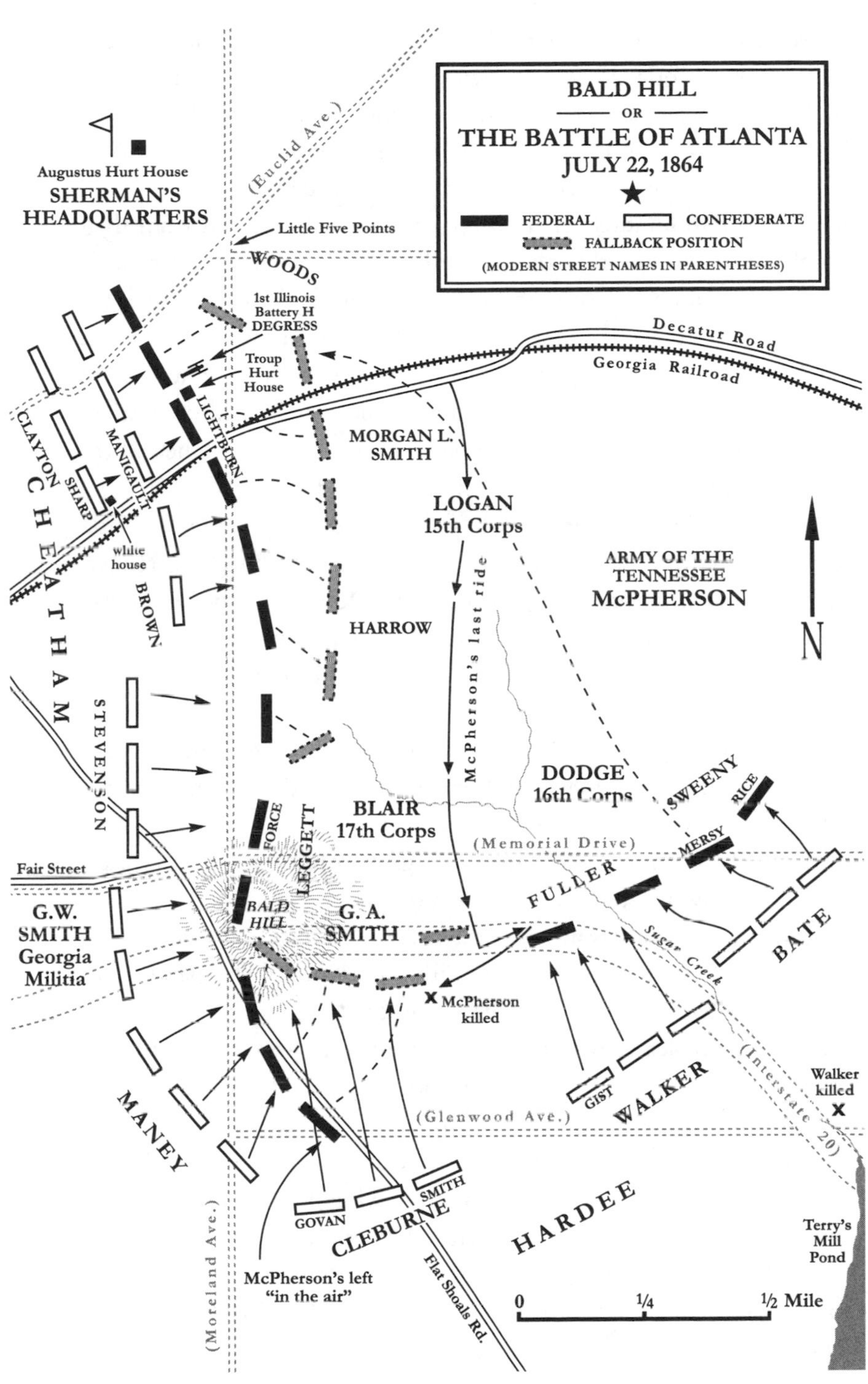
BALD HILL
OR
THE BATTLE OF ATLANTA
JULY 22, 1864
FEDERAL
CONFEDERATE
FALLBACK POSITION
(MODERN STREET NAMES IN PARENTHESES)
Augustus Hurt House
SHERMAN'S HEADQUARTERS
(Euclid Ave.)
Little Five Points
WOODS
1st Illinois Battery H DEGRESS
Troup Hurt House
Decatur Road
Georgia Railroad
CLAYTON
MANIGAULT
SHARP
LIGHTBURN
MORGAN L. SMITH
CHEATHAM
white house
BROWN
LOGAN 15th Corps
ARMY OF THE TENNESSEE McPHERSON
HARROW
McPherson's last ride
N
STEVENSON
DODGE 16th Corps
SWEENY
RICE
BLAIR 17th Corps
FORCE
LEGGETT
(Memorial Drive)
MERSY
Fair Street
FULLER
G.W. SMITH Georgia Militia
BALD HILL
G. A. SMITH
Sugar Creek
BATE
McPherson killed
(Interstate 20)
Walker killed
GIST
WALKER
MANEY
(Glenwood Ave.)
SMITH
GOVAN
CLEBURNE
HARDEE
Terry's Mill Pond
(Moreland Ave.)
McPherson's left "in the air"
Flat Shoals Rd.
0
1/4
1/2 Mile

posted at the left end of Frank Blair's 17th Corps. Brigadier General Daniel Govan's brigade of Arkansans, though "much wearied," struck the Union line with such ferocity that a number of the defenders surrendered at the outset. But Govan's two lead regiments, the 2nd and 24th Arkansas, their ranks depleted by the fighting the day before, numbered only about two hundred men. When the Iowans recovered from their initial shock and saw that they actually outnumbered their attackers, they picked up their muskets and resumed fighting, demanding that the Arkansans give themselves up and their officers turn over their swords. But Govan's other two regiments then hit the Iowans' flank and again obtained the surrender of the defending Yankees, who laid down their arms a second time and meekly handed back over to the colonels of the 2nd and 24th Arkansas their recently surrendered swords.

Watching the confusion, with fighting taking place before and behind the Federal breastworks and the two sides alternately surrendering and demanding surrender, an Arkansas soldier and a nearby Iowan stood next to each other and tried to make sense of the ruckus. "Which side is surrendering?" the Iowa soldier asked. "I'll be damned if I know," the Arkansan said with a laugh.[15]

On Govan's right, Brigadier General James A. Smith's Texas Brigade swept aside "feeble resistance" and poured through the gap between the 16th and 17th Corps, splitting the Federal position like firewood. With blue soldiers retreating before them "in great confusion," the attackers made their way into the rear of the Union line. Advancing with almost "ungovernable enthusiasm," the Texans soon found themselves among quartermaster tents, wagons loaded with shovels and picks, parked batteries of artillery, and even "a table set ready for dinner for 4 men." A few scavengers, pleased with their good fortune, stopped to pick through the tents and look for spoils while others pursued the skedaddling Yankees northward. Feeling their way forward through "woods very thick consisting of Oak Chestnut poplar and undergrowth," clots of Rebel skirmishers continued to advance, moving deeper into the woods toward a fateful collision with General McPherson.[16]

McPherson, the young commander of the Army of the Tennessee, was "in his prime," as Sherman would note—only thirty-five, tall and dark, with twinkling eyes, elfin features and a curling mustache and beard lightly peppered with gray. "A very handsome man in every way," Sherman would remember; the man he called "Mac" was "universally liked, and had many noble qualities." McPherson's prowess as an engineer was well-known—he graduated as the top man in the West Point class of 1853 and then served as an engineering instructor at the Academy before working on forts and installations literally from sea to shining sea, from New York Harbor to San Francisco Bay. He had distinguished himself as chief engineer under Grant and Sherman and had proven a capable fighter during his term of service. Indeed, some army wags contended that a bullet through McPherson's head would knock out Sherman's brains.

Yet despite his stellar academic record and his engineering achievements, he was not at all quiet and bookish, but outgoing and sociable; his mind not merely practical but often inclined toward romance. After the fall of Vicksburg, for example, he had joined brother officers in walking the streets in the evening and serenading the ladies of the town with lovelorn ballads and songs of home. He was warm in manner and kind to subordinates, down to the corporals and privates, and was popular with the rank and file. Other generals, for example, were known to gallop right through a marching column, sending the men scrambling off the road, but McPherson would often steer his horse off into dense underbrush to give way to the common footsoldier. "I do not think I ever saw General McPherson without a smile on his face," one acquaintance would recall. "He was very vivacious in conversation and very bright."[17]

In recent months, McPherson's fondest wish had been to secure a leave so that he could travel to Baltimore and marry his fiancée Emily Hoffman, whom he had met some years before while posted in San Francisco to supervise the building of fortifications on Alcatraz Island. Sherman had refused to let him go on the eve of the campaign, considering his presence essential as the army prepared to advance into north Georgia. "Mac, it wrings my heart, but you can't go now," Sherman had told him back in March. Now it was almost August, and McPherson saw on the horizon not only the city of Atlanta but his ticket to a furlough and a long-awaited wedding.[18]

He was still relaxing after his luncheon with Logan and Blair near the railroad when the party was startled by the sound of a single gunshot somewhere in the trees off to the south, echoing like the bang of a hymnal dropped in church. (One scholar would later suggest that perhaps this was the opening shot that had claimed the life of Shot Pouch Walker.) The bark and clatter of small arms fire soon thickened as Hardee's surprise attack exploded against McPherson's left. Orderlies scrambled to fetch the generals their horses, and Logan and Blair soon pounded off to join their respective corps. McPherson mounted and rode south with his adjutant Lieutenant Colonel William E. Strong and an orderly, Andrew Jackson "Jack" Thompson, to a hill on the right of Dodge's position, where he watched the repulse of Bate and Walker's Divisions in the valley of Sugar Creek below. Strong found the scene "grand and impressive," with the Rebel officers bravely mounted and riding at the front of the first line of battle as "regimental colors waved and fluttered in advance of the lines." Satisfied with the work being done there, McPherson dispatched Strong with orders directing General Logan to send a brigade to help fill the gap between the 16th and 17th Corps, and then rode off down a narrow wagon road running behind the line. An aide would later note that McPherson had ridden safely down that same road not ten minutes before.[19]

According to the most commonly told version of the events of the next few minutes, McPherson was riding alone with his orderly down the narrow path; but in fact, some evidence suggests that a number of people were with him, or at least were close by. Witnesses would later describe "a considerable staff," perhaps even a bodyguard, accompanying the general as he rode. His orderly Thompson was riding with him, with a gaggle of signal corps officers trailing some distance behind. As McPherson started off, Colonel Robert K. Scott rode near the party as well, on his way to retrieve an Ohio regiment that had been posted in reserve.

"Just as this moment," Thompson remembered, "the shrubbery became fairly alive with gray uniforms, and more than 100 muskets were leveled upon McPherson and myself." Captain Richard Beard of the 3rd Confederate Regiment,[20] Govan's Brigade, raised his sword in a demand for surrender, just yards away from McPherson. Startled by the sudden appearance of the cluster of Rebels, McPherson checked his horse so sharply it almost slid on its haunches as the Confederates shouted for the

Major General James B. McPherson (*Library of Congress*)

Yankee officers to halt. McPherson wheeled his horse to the right, tipped his hat and bowed—"as politely as if he was saluting a lady," the Rebel captain recalled with amazement—and then gave his horse the spurs, sending it lunging forward through the trees. A chorus of voices cried, "Shoot him!" and the woods echoed with the sound of gunfire. A bullet struck McPherson in the back, lifting him from the saddle and hurling him to the ground. His frightened horse was also hit and disappeared into the forest. McPherson's orderly Thompson tried to make his escape but was swept from the saddle by an overhanging bough. The same volley killed the horse of Colonel Scott, who tumbled to the earth as well. Farther back down the road, one of the signal corps officers, Lieutenant William Sherfy, struck a tree as he fled, breaking his pocket watch. The stopped hands showed the time as 2:02 P.M.

Dazed from the hard fall he had taken, Jack Thompson crawled over to the general, who was lying with his hand pressed to his breast. Thompson looked down at McPherson and saw that "with every breath he drew, the blood flowed in streams between his fingers."

"General, are you hurt?" Thompson asked.

McPherson could barely speak. "Oh, orderly, I am," he said.

Just then, Thompson was yanked back by his belt and spoken to harshly by the advancing Johnnies. "Git to the rear, you Yankee son of a bitch," one snarled, starting the young orderly on a journey that would end with a nine-month hitch in the Confederate prison at Andersonville. But Captain Beard had no interest in the orderly. He was focused instead on the handsome officer lying on the ground, resplendent in sash and gauntlets with gold stars on his collar. He turned to the lightly wounded Colonel Scott, sitting nearby, whom he took to be an adjutant or inspector-general.

"Who is this man lying here?" Beard asked.

"Sir, it is General McPherson," Scott replied, his voice trembling and his eyes brimming with tears. "You have killed the best man in our army."[21]

Sherman was anxious, almost rattled, like the Sherman of old. Hearing the gunfire off to the southeast in increasing volume—"too far to our left rear to be explained by known facts," he later said—he spent the early afternoon pacing back and forth on the wide porch of his headquarters as he waited for news. It was not long in coming. Shortly after two o'clock, McPherson's adjutant Lieutenant Colonel William T. Clark rode up on a lathered horse and reported that McPherson had been killed or was a prisoner. The general's horse had limped out of the brush, bleeding and riderless, minutes before, and soldiers had been dispatched into the woods to try to find him. "McPherson dead," Sherman said in disbelief. "Can it be?" Another courier soon arrived to confirm the news.[22]

A counterattack reclaimed the ground where McPherson had fallen and captured a number of Confederate skirmishers, including Captain Beard. The general's body was quickly recovered and brought in a slow-rolling ambulance to Sherman's headquarters. The Confederates had taken McPherson's watch, hat, field glasses, and sword belt (he carried no sword), though they neglected a wallet stuffed with cash and a diamond ring on his left hand. A surgeon examined the fatal wound and found that the ball had struck in the lower back and "ranged diagonally forward, coming out at the left breast and passing near the heart." McPherson could have survived no more than a few minutes with such an injury. A door was taken from its hinges to serve as an improvised catafalque, and McPherson's body was laid out, "still and beautiful in death," and covered with an American flag. Sherman, weeping openly at the sight of his friend, told Schofield that "the whole of the Confederacy could not atone for the sacrifice of one such life." He arranged for transportation to take the body to Marietta in preparation for passage back north to McPherson's hometown of Clyde, Ohio. "Better start at once and drive carefully," he said, his voice cracking and tears trickling into his beard.[23]

One of George Barnard's photographs of the spot where General McPherson fell, near Atlanta, Georgia, July 22, 1864. (*Library of Congress*)

Then he turned back to the task at hand. Sherman immediately ordered that the senior corps commander John A. Logan should take temporary command of the Army of the Tennessee. He directed that Logan be told "that he has both the ability and the men that can stay Hood where he is, and I expect him to do it." Some time later, perhaps considering his initial orders not emphatic enough, he added: "Tell Logan to fight 'em! Fight 'em! Fight 'em like hell!"[24]

With the chain of command thus temporarily repaired, Sherman then sought to fortify himself. "Gen'l Sherman was not much addicted to drinking, but he always carried an extra large pair of saddle bags behind him on his saddle, and in one of these he had an extra large canteen made to fit the pocket," an officer present at headquarters recorded. "This canteen contained the best the Country or Medical Stores afforded and was always supposed to be well filled." After dispatching the courier with orders for Logan, Sherman "went to his saddle bags, took out his big canteen and swallowed a full allopathic dose."[25]

By that time, Cleburne's attack had carried three lines of works and swept northward, driving hundreds of fleeing blue soldiers back toward the linchpin of the Federal position: the high ground of Bald Hill. With

Smith's Texans advancing along and in rear of the Union works and George Maney's Division moving toward its front from the Flat Shoals Road, Leggett's division was now threatened from both sides. Seeing the Rebels rushing toward the line from the south, the Yankees scrambled to take cover. An Ohio colonel ordered his men to get into the breastworks, only to be asked urgently which side of the works they should occupy, east or west. "I don't care which side, but get into the works!" the colonel answered. "Get in we did," a bluecoat private remembered, "but it was a puzzle to us to know which side would be the safest as the attack came from front and flank, which compelled us to fight first on one side of a barricade of rails and dirt, and then on the other." For weeks the Federals had seen their gray adversaries standing between them and Atlanta—now they jumped over to the west side of their red clay parapets and fought with their own backs to the city. There was irony, too, for the Confederates, as Cleburne's Division now attacked from the south and east the same hill they had been defending yesterday.

Hardee would later describe the engagement on July 22 as "one of the most desperate and bloody of the war," and nowhere was it worse than on the slopes of Bald Hill, where there was vicious, close-quarters fighting. As Leggett would write years later, "For vindictive desperation, this encounter was probably never exceeded." Hand-to-hand combat was actually a rare thing in Civil War battles, in part because, as Henry Dwight of the 20th Ohio explained, "When men can kill one another at six hundred yards they generally would prefer to do it at that distance than to come down to two paces." But the fighting on the slopes of Bald Hill was the exception to the rule. "Men were bayoneted, knocked down with the butts of muskets, and even fists were used in default of better weapons in that deadly strife," Dwight wrote. "Officers used their dress swords, which they had hitherto considered as mere playthings for the parade, to hack down a troublesome enemy." Those with guns in their hands fired and loaded and fired and loaded until their shoulders were bruised from the recoil and droplets of sweat sizzled as they dripped on the gun barrels. "Men begged for more cartridges as they would for bread, and made every one count," Dwight remembered.[26]

Hard pressed atop Leggett's Hill was the Illinois and Wisconsin brigade of Brigadier General Manning Force, who had so bravely captured the height the day before. Amid the smoke and yelling and confusion, Force screamed for someone to bring him a flag, hoping to rally his embattled troops and signify to other Union brigades that U.S. forces still held the critical knoll. A terrified lieutenant misunderstood the request. Seeing the flood of advancing gray soldiers on all sides and thinking the time had come to surrender, he scrambled around the trenches looking for a white shirt or handkerchief. Force's blood was up, and he was outraged at the suggestion.

"*Damn* you, sir!" he roared above the thunder of battle. "I don't want a flag of *truce*! I want the *American* flag!" thereby heartening his troops and startling those who had never heard him utter an oath. "If he did say it," a subordinate recorded, doubtful of the story given the general's reputation as a fine Christian gentleman, "we are sure that, as in Uncle Toby's case, 'The accusing spirit which flew up to Heaven's chancery with the oath blushed as he gave it in; and the recording angel, as he wrote it down, dropped a tear upon the word and blotted it out forever.'" Force got his flag and planted it on top of the works, making clear to all that the Federals still occupied the hill. Minutes later, he was shot in the face, the bullet entering below his left eye and shattering his palate before exiting on the right side of his head. Blood poured from his eyes, nose, and mouth. Remarkably, Force survived the terrible wound and after the war would be awarded the Medal of Honor in recognition of his valor. His superior Mortimer Leggett had high praise for the gallant Force, writing years later that the bald knoll east of Atlanta that his men had named after him "ought to have been christened 'Force's Hill.'"[27]

But General Smith's Texans were too weary—"much worn and exhausted," their commander would report—and they were too few.[28] The fearsome attack began to lose its vigor, and Smith's calls for reinforcements went unanswered. His men had penetrated so far from any adjoining Confederate forces that they found themselves almost completely unsupported. Finally, a Federal brigade under Brigadier General Charles Walcutt struck them on their flank, breaking the Rebel charge and capturing most of two Texas regiments. Smith gave the order to retreat just before being wounded and taken from the field.

South of the Bald Hill, however, the Confederates continued to roll up the Yankee line. Govan's Brigade, along with the adjoining division of George Maney's Tennesseans, began to advance into and along the Federal entrenchments. "The enemy commenced retreating up their works as soon as we charged them and we having an enfilating fire upon them and they being in great confusion and huddling together we mowed them down with awful havoc," a Tennessee captain recorded in his diary.[29]

In the 1st Tennessee, Private Sam Watkins described the ensuing charge of Maney's Division:

> We rushed forward up the steep hill sides, the seething fires from ten thousand muskets and small arms, and forty pieces of cannon hurled right into our very faces, scorching and burning our clothes, and hands, and faces from their rapid discharges, and piling the ground with our dead and wounded almost in heaps. It seemed that the hot flames of hell were turned loose in all their mad fury, while the demons of damnation were laughing in the flames, like seething serpents hissing out their rage.
>
> We gave one long, loud cheer, and commenced the charge. As we approached their lines, like a mighty inundation of the river Acheron in the infernal regions, Confederate and Federal meet. Officers with drawn swords meet officers with drawn swords, and man to man meets man to man with bayonets and loaded guns. The continued roar of battle sounded like unbottled thunder. Blood covered the ground, and the dense smoke filled our eyes, and ears, and faces. The groans of the wounded and dying rose above the thunder of battle.[30]

The fighting on and south of Bald Hill became a confused melee, and the participants struggled to make sense of the action, then and later. "The exact sequence of events that afternoon I cannot give; nor do I believe any man can, or ever could, do so," a Michigan cannoneer wrote. Smoke obscured the field, so thick in the almost windless air that "though a July sun was shining, there was the appearance of a dense fog." Regiments, even brigades, lost their organization as officers fell and adjoining units overlapped and jumbled together. The defending bluecoats faced their gray attackers from different directions, and some units jumped back and forth as many as four times as they fought on alternating sides of their breastworks. "Thus they fought," a witness wrote, "looking for all the world like a long line of these toy-monkeys you see which jump over the end of a stick." Soldiers went to the rear to replenish ammunition, only to become captives as the rearward line had been occupied by the enemy. On both sides, men stripped off their uniform coats and tunics, blue or butternut or gray, and fought in shirtsleeves, making it almost impossible in the fury and the smoke to distinguish Johnny Reb from Billy Yank.[31]

All along the line, acts of heroism were mixed with bloody scenes depicting the horrors of war. In the 33rd Alabama Regiment, soldiers were lying prone and firing uphill toward the Federals when they were startled to see a comrade standing upright. "One of the regiment wandered about among us with a minie ball in his forehead and a knot of brains as big as a hen's egg over the whole," a witness recalled. "Occasionally we would hear another ball strike him, which he did not appear to mind." The Alabama boys could do nothing for him and prayed silently for the walking corpse to fall, "thinking the sooner he died the better." Across the way in the Federal works, Private Robert Elliott of the 20th Ohio saw that his brother Mathias had been shot down while lunging for the regimental colors. "Oh, they have killed my brother," he cried, and he stood boldly in the hail of bullets, loading and firing until he, too, fell dead.[32]

The Confederate attacks slowly lost their power, as exhaustion overtook the soldiers of Hardee's corps, some of whom had been marching and fighting, with meager rations and almost no sleep, for the past two days. Despite the flank attack, the gap in the line, and the Rebel foray into the Federal rear, the Yankees held the line anchored on Bald Hill. Reflecting years later on the 16th Corps veterans, standing fast against Cleburne's relentless charges, an Ohio colonel was put in mind of a verse from the Book of Job: "Thus far shalt thou come, but no farther; and here shall your proud waves stop."[33]

In Decatur, six miles to the east, the Army of the Tennessee's wagon train was parked in and around the town square, and the morning had passed "without any immediate adventure." Miss Mary Gay would later recall Union officers holding a council of war in her parlor—"their parlor *pro tem*," she said bitterly—while outside, "the teamsters and army followers were lounging about promiscuously, cursing and swearing and playing cards, and seeming not to notice the approaching artillery until their attention was called to it, and then they contended that it was their men firing off blank cartridges." Toward Atlanta, Dodge fretted at the sound of firing so deep in the Union rear, and one soldier gave his assessment: "That's Wheeler after our hard tack."[34]

It was Wheeler, indeed, and his horsemen were not firing blanks. The Confederate cavalry commander was only twenty-seven years old, having graduated in 1859 near the bottom of his class at the United States Military Academy, where his worst subject had been cavalry tactics, and where fellow geometry-minded classmates called him "Point"—because, they said, "he had neither height, breadth, or thickness." Only five foot five and a hundred and twenty pounds with his boots on, he was a formidable officer nonetheless, in part because of his vigorous and apparently endless energy. Acquaintances described the Georgia-born cavalier as "surcharged with electricity" and "active as a cat," and one colleague suggested that Wheeler might just live forever, for "he never stays in one place long enough for God Almighty to put his finger on him."[35]

Beginning his wartime service as a lowly lieutenant in the Georgia militia, Wheeler went on to command an Alabama infantry regiment and then transferred to the cavalry, rising to major general in less than two years. A neighbor in Alabama called Wheeler "the gamest little banty I ever seen. He warn't afraid of nuthin' or nobody," and he had proved his fearlessless on battlefields from Shiloh to Chickamauga. Nobody made fun of his size anymore—now they called him "the little Hero," or "Fighting Joe."[36]

Wheeler's troopers, around 1,500 sabers in all, had peeled off from the infantry column at Cobb's Mill early that morning and approached Decatur shortly after noon. General Hardee had supposed that the town would be guarded only by Union cavalry, but a brief reconnaissance revealed instead what Wheeler would describe in his report as "a division of infantry, strongly intrenched." Wheeler ordered his men to dismount and deployed them for a charge on the Federal position, which was in fact manned not by a whole division, but a detached and undersized brigade of infantry under a forty-seven-year-old New Yorker named John W. Sprague.[37]

The gray cavalrymen came whooping forward and brushed aside two regiments of infantry before coming under a stout artillery fire. "Shot and shell flew in every direction, and the shingles of the roof were following suit, and the leaves, and the limbs, and the bark of the trees were descending in showers so heavy as almost to obscure the view of the contending forces," Mary Gay remembered. Seeing that his frontal assault was faltering, Wheeler quickly organized an attack on the right flank and then the rear of the position, and "with a triumphant shout the entire line of works was carried"—though not before Sprague retired to the north of town in good order, bringing off the overwhelming majority of the wagons and their teams.[38]

Mary Gay was thrilled by what she had witnessed. "I had seen a splendidly equipped army ignominiously flee from a little band of lean, lank, hungry, poorly-clad Confederate soldiers, and I doubted not an over-ruling Providence would lead us to final victory." But soon Wheeler himself was overruled—summoned by an urgent stream of dispatches from Hardee, who requested his immediate assistance in the fight just east of Atlanta. Wheeler would proudly claim credit for the (temporary) capture of Decatur, along with "some 225 prisoners, a large number of small-arms, 1 12-pounder gun, 1 forge, 1 battery wagon, 1 caisson, and 6 wagons and teams," as well as various "camp equipage, storage and hospitals." For his part, Sprague would gather laurels for decades for his gallant conduct and the "delaying action" he had fought in the so-called Battle of Decatur, culminating in an award of the Medal of Honor in 1894. Wheeler "won" the fight and drove the blue infantry from the field, but Sprague saved the Army of the Tennessee's wagon train and smothered the flare-up in the Union rear.[39]

Mounting up again, Wheeler galloped off to help Hardee in the main battle, and though Little Joe would report that his troopers "fought warmly" when they got there, they arrived too late to do any good.[40]

In Atlanta, the prevailing mood that day alternated between elation and terror. The artillery fire that had fallen on the town's buildings and streets the past two days had subsided for the most part, as the Federal artillery was presented with new targets in the course of the Rebel attack. Residents climbed onto rooftops to watch the progress of the fighting, and Union officers could see through their field glasses a group of young ladies atop the Female Institute, waving white handkerchiefs. With the battle raging less than two miles east of Five Points, the sound of small arms fire could be heard so distinctly that folks in town were "firmly convinced that the forces were butchering each other on Whitehall Street."

John Bell Hood had spent the morning and early afternoon hours near the Atlanta railroad depot, sending couriers and receiving dispatches from various parts of the field. A gaggle of citizens gathered nearby, "watching the iron face of the general in the vain hope of reading his thoughts." Couriers and officers raced through the streets on their horses, wearing a "bright, exultant" look as they hollered exciting, dubious reports from the front—"We've got 'em!" "We're whipping them like hell!" In the early afternoon, surgeons arrived and set up long rows of tables in the city park next to the station, their sleeves rolled up and instruments at the ready. "It was not long before ambulances and wagons rolled into the park by the dozen, and the wounded were hastily taken out and placed upon the tables," a journalist wrote. "After that it was cut and slash, for the work had to be done in a hurry. The green grass took on a blood-red hue, and as the surgeon's saw crunched through the bones of the unfortunates, hundreds of gory arms and legs were thrown into the baskets prepared to receive them." The arrival of the bloody, fly-blown caravan and the ensuing surgery served to break up the crowd of citizens. "One by one they disappeared, and soon the park was given up to the surgeons and their patients, the grim general meanwhile awaiting the returns a few yards away."[41]

One Atlanta family cared nothing about the progress of the battle going on two miles away. For several days, Caroline and William Clayton had kept vigil at the bedside of their daughter Augusta, hoping against hope, though all could see that she was fading, day by day, stricken by the disease she had contracted in the sickrooms of the city's hospitals. Finally, she could hold on no longer. Gussie Clayton died at her home around 2 P.M., about the same time Rebel skirmishers shot McPherson off his horse. That was just the beginning of the trials for the

Clayton family, who quickly learned that they could not take their daughter to the city cemetery for burial, as it was too close to the fighting. A kindly neighbor rode through the streets and was able to locate a modest casket, but the family was at a loss as to what to do to lay their poor daughter to rest—"it was a bad day for funerals," a local journalist would write. "To think of getting to the cemetery was out of the question and there was nothing else to do but to make a place of burial of the garden," Gussie's older sister Sallie wrote, "and even that was dangerous for all who were there, as shells from the battlefield fell not many feet from them before the services were ended." And so the Claytons buried young Gussie in her mother's flower garden, close by the corner of Walton and Spring Streets.[42]

Around two o'clock, Hood mounted and rode about a mile east to a rise at the eastern edge of the Atlanta Graveyard or City Burial Place, later to be known as Oakland Cemetery. There he watched the struggle for Bald Hill from the second story of a house. Hood would later write that he was alarmed to receive reports that the attack was being stopped because of "contact with different lines of entrenchments," suggesting to him that Hardee had failed to carry out his orders to make his assault in rear of the Union position. (In fact, Hardee's soldiers were by then attacking the bluecoats in front, flank, *and* rear.) But soon, more welcome intelligence arrived, reporting Cleburne's and Maney's partial success in rolling up the Union flank south of Bald Hill. Perhaps the fight could still be won.[43]

The battle was nearly four hours old when Hood ordered Frank Cheatham to take his corps forward from their trenches and make a frontal assault on the Union line. Having struck the Army of the Tennessee a body blow with a roundhouse right, Hood would now follow with a straight left.

Way back in November 1861, Benjamin Franklin Cheatham had participated in the Battle of Belmont, Missouri—a minor, indecisive engagement on the banks of the Mississippi famous as Ulysses S. Grant's first battle—and just afterward met to discuss a prisoner exchange with a then-long-bearded Grant, with whom he shared a fondness for horseracing (and for the whiskey bottle, some would say). Since that time, the unprepossessing Cheatham, whom the lowliest drummer boy addressed as "Frank," had fought in virtually every major battle of the Confederate Army of Tennessee, from Shiloh to Perryville to Chickamauga to Kennesaw Mountain. Though perhaps not as flashy as the younger Cleburne, with his lean figure and his Irish brogue, the red-faced, thick-set Cheatham had a record of success and a reputation as a tough, stand-up fighter, especially on the defensive. Now his three divisions, nearly 15,000 men, would make their charge on Logan's 15th Corps, now commanded by Major General Morgan L. Smith, occupying trenches that had been abandoned by the Confederates the day before.

The blow was to fall on Smith's old division, now led by Brigadier General Joseph Andrew Jackson Lightburn, a thirty-nine-year-old Baptist minister known later as "the Fighting Parson." Lightburn's three brigades occupied a line of parapets running north and south of the Georgia Railroad about two miles east of Atlanta, which had its vulnerabilities. The Union position was pierced by the east-west line of the railroad tracks, passing through the low ridgeline in an open and apparently unguarded railroad cut nearly twenty feet deep. Next to the railroad, the red-dirt wagon road running out to Decatur also cut through the line and was likewise "open and unoccupied by works or troops." Nearby were two large houses: in front of the line, a two-story white wooden house (referred to in some accounts as the Widow Pope House) with scattered outbuildings; and a short distance to the rear, an unfinished but formidable brick house owned by Troup Hurt (the brother of Augustus Hurt, the absentee owner of the house now serving as Sherman's headquarters). Certain officers had recommended to Lightburn that these houses be destroyed and the railroad cut barricaded to patch up the gap in the line, gaping like the hole left by a missing tooth. Lightburn spurned the proposal, thinking at the time that the Rebels were retreating and that he would be having dinner in Atlanta that same night.[44]

Cheatham's men came rushing toward the entrenched soldiers of the 15th Corps at around 4 P.M., and a Union major found their assault a

Major General Benjamin Franklin Cheatham. (*Library of Congress*)

grand sight to behold, despite his being on the receiving end of it. "How well they moved, how perfectly and how grandly did the first line advance with the beautiful 'battle flags' waving in the breeze, and not an unsteady step nor a waver was perceptible in it."[45] Still, the charge seemed destined, as frontal attacks often were in this war, for a quick repulse. On the right, Major General Carter Stevenson's division advanced south of the Georgia Railroad and attacked the Federals just north of Bald Hill from the west. But for whatever reason, the charge had little spirit, and firing from the high ground of the hill quickly threw the attackers into confusion and then retreat. On Stevenson's right, the Georgia Militia, "Joe Brown's Pets," advanced tentatively—just long enough to add fifty men to the casualty list—but soon pulled back after seeing Stevenson retreat.

So far, not so good. But along and north of the railroad, the Confederates soon began to make headway in rather dramatic fashion. In the center, "Hindman's Division," now under Tennessee lawyer and Brigadier General John C. Brown, moved forward in neatly dressed lines astride the line of the railroad. Leading the charge along the railroad itself was the brigade of Brigadier General Arthur Middleton Manigault, a Charleston-born businessman and plantation owner, followed by another brigade under Colonel Jacob Sharp. Manigault's Alabamans and South Carolinians had moved into position for the attack completely blind as to what was in front of them and unaware of the result of the fighting thus far, as the field was entirely obscured by smoke. Then, the order to advance was given and the scene cleared to reveal the Yankees in their entrenchments, just two hundred and fifty yards away, with their flags "fluttering lazily" in the newly awakened summer breeze. "I saw and noticed all this only for a moment, and thought it looked very pretty," Manigault recalled, "but in the next instant the whole scene was shut out, everything enveloped in smoke. A deafening roar smote upon the ear, and a storm of bullets and cannister tore through our ranks and around us."[46]

The attack stalled for a time; but then, as historian Albert Castel put it, "suddenly and spectacularly, the course of the fighting changes." Manigault's men took advantage of the two-story white house near the railroad, taking cover in the yard and then sending sharpshooters to occupy the upper floor of the house and fire down into the Yankee lines. With these advantages now at hand and support in the form of Sharp's Brigade moving up from behind, Manigault's men dashed forward and over the works, as two Ohio regiments before them broke and ran. "Our major ordered us to 'git,' and such 'gitting' you never saw before, unless you were at Bull Run," a Buckeye private remembered. Those still in the trenches quickly surrendered. One bluecoat, cowering in the works, asked a Rebel sergeant, "Are you going to kill all of us?" The sergeant nonchalantly replied, "That's our calculation. We came out for that purpose."[47]

"I regret to say that the command did not behave as on former occasions," Lightburn later reported, admitting that his men "became panic-stricken and fell back in disorder"—though the pastor-general might have been ashamed of himself as well. Even as colonels and staff officers attempted to rally the fugitives and form a new line, Lightburn was spotted heading for the rear at a dead run.[48]

At the same time, a number of regiments from Sharp's Brigade took advantage of the other point of Federal neglect, and the defenders saw "a great stream of grey pouring through the railroad cut," which provided a covered approach to the Union rear. Those Yankees not killed or captured were obliged to fall back in a hurry, and the Confederates occupied a quarter-mile-wide section of the Federal breastworks. The captured line included sixteen pieces of artillery, including Captain Francis DeGress's Illinois battery of Parrott guns, which had fired the first shots on Atlanta two days before. Some of the whooping Rebels gathered abandoned knapsacks, blankets, and canteens, while others took pot-shots at the skedaddling Ohioans. "I picked up loaded guns and fired in a hurry," Lieutenant Robert Gill of the 41st Mississippi recalled. "I never enjoyed a thing better in my life. We had the pleasure of shooting at Yankees as they ran without being shot at much."[49]

The success of Cheatham's frontal assault on the lines of the 15th Corps was startling. As historian Steven Woodworth observed, "The Army of the Tennessee had survived an afternoon of hammering at its flanks and rear, only to have a hole the size of a two-division front ripped in its right center by a head-on assault." And unlike the fighting earlier in the day in the pine and oak woods to the south, this break in the Union line, just half a mile south of army headquarters, was plainly visible to General Sherman.[50]

Notwithstanding Sherman's initial assessment that the newly elevated Black Jack Logan had the men to "stay Hood where he is," other officers offering their counsel at headquarters thought the situation, if not an outright emergency, at least offered a substantial opportunity. The struggle on McPherson's flank made clear that a large portion of Hood's army was out of their fortifications and had attacked at a point some miles distant from their original position and the remainder of the army; and now Cheatham's frontal assault had exposed that portion of the Rebel force as well. Although the Army of the Tennessee was hotly engaged, Schofield's Army of the Ohio was in a position to wade in and crush the now-vulnerable Confederates. Schofield proposed that both his army and O. O. Howard's 4th Corps go directly to Logan's assistance, or better yet launch a counterattack, strike Cheatham's flank from the north, and sweep the Rebels from the field. But Sherman was unconvinced. Years later, he would argue—preposterously, in the judgment of most historians—that McPherson's army, which used to be Sherman's own, could take care of itself, and that "if any assistance were rendered by either of the other armies, the Army of the Tennessee would be jealous." Schofield was disappointed by this decision, and other blue officers were downright appalled. "During the whole of this day's battle—the most serious, threatening, and hotly contested of the campaign—over 50,000 soldiers of Sherman's army stood idle auditors and spectators of the doubtful conflict, almost within gunshot of the scene, anxiously waiting for some order from the Commanding General to aid in the work," one of Thomas's staff officers wrote. "Such order never came." Notwithstanding the after-the-fact second-guessing of his judgment, Sherman was unwavering in his orders at the time. Howard recalled that Sherman's face "now relaxed into a pleasant mood," and he said confidently, "Let the Army of the Tennessee fight it out."[51]

But that was before he saw a swarm of Rebels break through the center of the Union line, rounding up prisoners and attempting to turn the captured guns against the scrambling bluecoats. "I had never till then seen Sherman with such a look on his face," Howard recalled. "His eyes flashed. He did not speak. He only watched the front. There appeared not only in his face, but in his whole pose, a concentrated fierceness." Though he still stopped short of sending Schofield's infantry into the fray, Sherman quickly ordered that Schofield bring all his available artillery to the dominant height just south of the Augustus Hurt house. He also sent word to Logan directing that he gather reinforcements, counterattack against the Rebels, and restore the broken line "at any cost." This done, he oversaw the placement of Schofield's guns and personally directed an enfilading barrage against Manigault's and Sharp's Brigades in the recently abandoned Federal works to the south. "The artillery practice of the enemy was splendid," Manigault later wrote, "and that of a battery on our left under the supervision of General Sherman was accurate in the extreme." Schofield later had high praise for his chief's "splendid conduct as a simple soldier." Sherman, he said, "led the batteries in person to some high, open ground *in front of our line* near the Howard House, placed them in position, and directed their fire. . . . With the aid of that terrible raking fire, the division of Union troops very quickly regained the intrenchments they had lost."[52]

Just as the Federals were forming for their countercharge, "a well-known form came galloping furiously up the Decatur road on a coal-black charger streaked with foam, hatless, his long black hair flying, his eyes flashing with wrath—a human hurricane on horseback." It was Black Jack Logan. He had been over on the left, helping see to the gap between Blair and Dodge, when he heard the roar of the Cheatham's attack. He detached one brigade that had thrown back Bate's earlier charge—Mersy's rapid-firing Illinois and Ohio boys—and led them cross-country toward the threatened Union right. The thirty-eight-year-old former Illinois congressman had a rare combination of steel and panache that seemed to be lacking from most political generals, and both were on full display as he rode back and forth, rallying the troops by appealing to the memory of their dead chief. "Boys! McPherson and revenge!" Logan roared. "It made my blood run both hot and cold," one soldier later wrote, and the men began to chant his name—"Black Jack! Black Jack! Black Jack!"—as they moved forward to take back their breastworks.[53]

With Logan's countercharge bearing down on them, and lacking support on the right and left, Manigault and Sharp were ordered to retire. "There was nothing left for us to do but obey," Manigault recalled, "and I never saw men obey an order more unwillingly." They did their best to take with them the prizes of their gallant charge, but the lack of artillery horses limited their ability to bring off the captured Union cannon. They took with them eight artillery pieces, though not Francis DeGress's Parrott guns, which were left behind. In the gathering dusk, the 15th Corps reclaimed their abandoned fortifications, firing somewhat halfheartedly after the retiring Confederates but, as Manigault said, "not daring to follow."

No one was happier with the recapture of the Federal works than young Capt. DeGress, who "was so rejoiced to get his battery back again that he put his arms around the guns and cried for joy."[54]

To the south, the five-hour fight at Bald Hill had continued into early evening, as Maney's and Cleburne's men renewed their assault on the dug-in Federals. "The enemy has become quiet," General Blair reported to Sherman at 4:30, after Leggett's soldiers fended off repeated assaults on the beleaguered position—but the quiet didn't last. In the dying afternoon, the Confederates "made a determined and resolute attack, advancing up to our breast-works on the crest of the hill, planted their flags side by side with ours, and fought hand-to-hand until it grew so dark that nothing could be seen but the flash of the guns," General Blair reported. The firing lessened and then stopped, as the defenders fell exhausted or simply ran out of targets to shoot at, and the sound of battle gave way to the cries of wounded men, pleading for help or for water. The Rebels withdrew from the slope, slowly and stubbornly, taking advantage of the darkness to remove a number of their wounded, along with "the dead bodies of many officers." The soldiers of Hardee's Corps returned during the night to a position near their jumpoff point along

Intrenchment Creek, still on the southern flank, but were pulled back the next day to the main line of defense around Atlanta.[55]

So ended the largest engagement of the campaign, one that would therefore be dubbed "the Battle of Atlanta" by historians and participants alike, later to be known as "Hood's Second Sortie," once it was established that the Confederate commander intended to make these occasional sallies a habit. Others would refer to the fight as "the Battle of Bald Hill," therefore overshadowing the contest fought the day before for the same knoll. It was a terrible, bloody, confusing battle, but it was also far from decisive. "Brave men on both sides fought as only Americans can fight," a Michigan lieutenant wrote—and yet the struggle for Atlanta would continue.[56]

The day after the battle dawned cool, though the mild weather may have seemed the only blessing that morning. Sherman rode over the shell-torn ground and later wrote that "it bore the marks of a bloody conflict." The once summer-green landscape east of Atlanta was shredded and torn, with red clay scars across the ground and small fires burning here and there. Trees were splintered, branches gone, and trunks blasted. Alongside the railroad, the walls and roof of the Troup Hurt house were riddled with bullets and shell fragments. No one would ever live there; in fact, the house would be burned on Schofield's orders two days hence. The swollen, stinking corpses of hundreds of dead horses littered the ground—DeGress's battery alone lost thirty-nine horses; a neighboring battery commander reported "55 horses killed and captured, mostly killed." But worst of all, of course, were the hundreds of dead men, blue and gray.[57]

A truce was called midmorning to allow for the burial of the dead. Dr. A. W. Reese, a surgeon with the 31st Missouri, ventured out over the battlefield to survey the human cost. He saw the mangled corpses of "mere boys" lying "in windrows and piles," in "ghastly, sickening, repulsive heaps" before the Union lines. He went on to describe the "*horrible* faces of the *dead*":

> Some had fallen forward and laid flat upon their faces, with their white hands clutched full of dust—some seemed to have

> sunk down dead at once, and remained in a sort of "doubled up" posture—others lay stretched out upon their sides with faces turned to the ground—but the major part had fallen on their backs, or had perhaps, struggled, in the last death agony, into that position—and so still laid, their white and bloodless hands, with fingers spread apart, thrown wildly up into the air above them, and their glassy, open eyes staring with their expressionless balls, straight up toward the pitiless sky.[58]

"This war has demonstrated that earth-works can be rendered nearly impregnable against direct assault," Lt. Henry O. Dwight, a war correspondent and soldier in the 20th Ohio, wrote in an article for *Harper's Magazine*. "An attack on fortified lines must cost a fearful price, and should be well weighed whether the cost exceed not the gain." As if to provide evidence in support, Dwight sketched that morning a group of forty-five dead Confederates lying in a tangled heap before a log breastwork. One body was propped so it was partly upright, as if it were trying to struggle free from Death's downward pull. In the background of the picture, a Union soldier sits atop the log fortification—legs dangling down casually, pipe in hand—quietly looking out over the appalling carnage. "This, then, is what an assault means," Dwight wrote. "A slaughter pen, a charnel house, and an army of weeping mothers and sisters at home."[59]

By now, many soldiers had grown indifferent to the slaughter. "All quiet this morning, after a terrible day yesterday all along the lines," Texas Captain Samuel T. Foster wrote. "Our men are getting boots hats &c watches knives off of the dead Yanks near us in the woods—lots of them. . . . Our dead have all been buried, and the Yanks will be as soon as they can do so. We cook and eat, talk and laugh with the enemys dead lying all about us as though they were so many logs." A soldier from the 45th Alabama Regiment would recall the solemn interment of a pair of comrades. "Two men out of our mess had been killed late in the evening," he wrote, "and I, with three other men who were brothers and one a brother-in-law to the two dead men, carried their bodies off the battlefield and buried them, making the graves with the aid of our tin pans and bayonets, and wrapping them in their own worn out blankets. There was hardly a half dozen words uttered during the time."[60]

Such horrible scenes gave some inkling as to the extent of the numerical losses, which were severe on both sides. General Logan would report that the Army of the Tennessee lost 3,722 men killed, wounded, and missing in the course of the eight-hour battle. (Sherman's other two armies, of course, were idle and suffered no losses in the battle at all.) Confederate casualties, though difficult to establish from the spotty official reports, were significantly greater. Logan would overestimate Rebel losses, placing them at over 10,000; Sherman would, with a characteristic lack of any doubt, peg Confederate casualties at "an aggregate loss of full 8,000." An emerging consensus among modern historians, however, places the figure at a more realistic 5,500.[61]

Although he had suffered more grievous losses and failed to either destroy McPherson's army or dislodge it from its position, Hood's report to Richmond made it sound as if he had won the battle. "General Hardee, with his corps, made a night march and attacked the enemy's extreme left at 1 o'clock today; drove him from his works, capturing 16 pieces of artillery and 5 stand of colors," Hood reported to Secretary of War James A. Seddon in Richmond. "Major-General Cheatham attacked the enemy at 4 p.m. with a portion of his command; drove the enemy, capturing 6 pieces of artillery. During the engagements we captured about 2,000 prisoners, but loss not fully ascertained. . . . Our men fought with great gallantry."[62]

Despite the arguable sins of omission in his report, Hood and his army had much to be proud of. Hardee had struck and partly rolled up the Union flank; Wheeler and his horsemen had caused temporary chaos deep in the Federal rear; the center had been broken and artillery captured; and the commander of the Army of the Tennessee had been shot dead. Both Hardee's and Cheatham's Corps had fought fiercely and lost heavily. "The battle of Atlanta was a warfare of giants," a Union historian wrote just after the war. "In the impetuosity, splendid *abandon*, and reckless disregard of danger with which the Rebel masses rushed against our line of fire, of iron and cold steel, there has been no parallel during the war, not even before the fortunate death of Stonewall Jackson."[63]

What was more, were it not for the fortuitous arrival of Dodge's corps on the Union left, Sherman may well have suffered an outright disaster. "The movement of General Hood was a very bold and a very brilliant one, and it was very near being successful," 17th Corps commander Frank Blair would write after the war. "If my command had been driven from its position at the time that the Fifteenth Corps was forced back from its entrenchments, there must have been a general rout of all the troops of the Army of the Tennessee . . . and, possibly, the panic might have been communicated to the balance of the army." Had McPherson not placed Dodge where he was, as an Ohio major wrote, "there would have been absolutely nothing but hospital tents and wagon trains to stop Hardee's command from falling unheralded directly upon the rear of the Fifteenth and Seventeenth Corps in line." Such were the "might have beens" of the Battle of Atlanta. And yet, as Hood would admit by way of understatement, "the grand results desired were not accomplished."[64]

There were a number of reasons for the failure of the Rebel attack, in addition to luck and solid leadership by men like Dodge and Logan and Force. Hood expressed a desire to "endeavor to bring the entire Confederate Army into united action," but for a variety of reasons, many of them not at all his fault—he had accomplished no such thing. The attack had started six hours late, the troops exhausted and the units scattered and disrupted by natural obstacles. Then the various divisions and brigades had advanced in piecemeal fashion. Cleburne's attack did not open until Walker's and Bate's had been largely repulsed; then Cleburne fought alone for forty-five minutes before Maney joined the fray. Finally, Cheatham's Corps did not go forward until more than three hours after the battle had opened, perhaps missing an opportunity to slice up McPherson's army as if between the blades of a pair of shears. Sherman, for one, afterward regarded the uncoordinated nature of the Rebel attacks as a good thing, indeed: "fortunately their attacks were not simultaneous," he wrote in his report.

Again there had been little use of the Confederate artillery. Although Cleburne attempted to bring up guns in support of his charge, most batteries were kept from the field by the difficulties of terrain (one missed a turn and ended up almost in Decatur). A Rebel cannoneer summed up the battle as "an infantry fight, pure and simple," and more harshly: "Another fiasco." Union guns had played a larger part, not only in being captured and recaptured, but in the terrible storm of shot and shell that had beaten back Rebel attacks, first on the left, where Bate and Walker were repulsed, and then on the right, where Sherman helped to sight the guns against Manigault's and Sharp's Brigades and Clayton's Division.[65]

"Notwithstanding the non-fulfullment of the brilliant result anticipated, the partial success of that day was productive of much benefit to the army," Hood would later argue. "It greatly improved the *morale* of the troops, infused new life and fresh hopes, arrested desertions, which hitherto had been numerous, defeated the movement of McPherson and Schofield upon our communications, in that direction, and demonstrated to the foe our determination to abandon no more territory without, at least, a manful effort to retain it." A manful effort it had certainly been, though others viewed the result in a different light. By some estimates, Hood had lost as many men in three days as Johnston had lost in ten weeks. "Hood's accession to command was the beginning of an Iliad of woes," Cleburne's adjutant Irving Buck wrote, while a Union private judged the Gallant Hood another way: "If he keeps on chargeing as he has dun for the last 3 days, he will soon have no army to charge with."[66]

Illinois adjutant F. Y. Hedley summed up the battle for both sides. "July 22d was a day of disaster and sorrow," he wrote. "The disaster was retrieved. The sorrow will endure as long as patriotism and heroism are honored."[67]

In the North, no loss was felt more deeply than that of the fallen McPherson. No less a poet than Herman Melville composed a dirge for the Northern patriot: "*Pass the ropes the coffin round, and let descend; Prayer and volley—let it sound McPherson's end*," he wrote. "Genl. McPherson fell in Battle, booted and spured as the Gallant Knight and Gentleman should wish," Sherman said in reporting the sad news to the adjutant general in Washington. "His public enemies, even the men who directed the fatal shot, never spoke or wrote of him without expressions of marked respect, those whom he commanded loved him even to idolatry, and I his associate and Commander fail in words adequate to express my opinion of his great worth." Soldiers recorded in their diaries scenes of hardened veterans weeping like children at the news of their leader's death. Up in Virginia, General Grant, too, was reportedly brought to tears at the news. "The country has lost one of its best soldiers," he was to have said, "and I have lost my best friend." Even McPherson's foe John Bell Hood would later make special mention of his old schoolmate and friend. "Neither the lapse of years, nor the difference of sentiment which led us to range ourselves on opposite sides in the late war, had lessened my friendship," he wrote in his memoirs, adding: "No soldier fell in the enemy's ranks, whose loss caused me equal regret."[68]

Word of McPherson's death arrived in Baltimore by wire the next day. The telegraph operator with Sherman's forces, a conscientious fellow, directed the message to Miss Emily Hoffman's mother, no doubt hoping to blunt the force if not the nature of the blow. And yet, how fate is often cruel: "Emily, there is a telegram, and I don't have my glasses," Mrs. Hoffman said. "Would you read it to me?" And so the message was handed to General McPherson's fiancée, who read:

> Near Atlanta July 23 1864
> To Mrs Saml Hoffman Franklin St
> Genl Barry desires me to say that Genl McPherson was killed in battle yesterday His remains were sent to his home last evening in charge of his staff
> JC Van Duzer
> Capt & Asst Supr

Emily dropped the telegram and retreated to her room, and there she would remain for the next year. Her meals were left on a tray by the door, and no one was admitted save for her sister Dora, who crept in from time to time to read to Emily by the dim light that seeped in through the drawn curtains. Eventually, Emily emerged from her room, but never from mourning.

In August, a letter arrived from General Sherman, offering her his condolences. "My Dear Young Lady," the general began, offering heartfelt sympathy to Miss Hoffman while claiming a considerable share of grief for himself. "I yield to no one on Earth but yourself the right to excel me in lamentations for your Dead hero," he said, and went on to describe the circumstances that led to McPherson's death. "I see him now, So handsome, so smiling, on his fine black horse, booted & spurred, with his easy seat, the impersonation of the Gallant Knight," Sherman recalled. "Though the Cannon booms now, and the angry rattle of musketry tells me that I also will likely pay the same penalty," he closed, "yet while Life lasts I will delight in the memory of that bright particular star which has gone before to prepare the way for us more hardened Sinners who must struggle on to the End."[69]

After the war, Miss Hoffman championed the remembrance of her "bright particular star," her family financing in part the grand equestrian statue placed by the Society of the Army of the Tennnessee in Washington, dedicated in 1876 in a city park known thereafter as McPherson Square. In her twilight years, she would periodically take the train from Baltimore to the capital and sit alone in the park, a frail, solitary figure dressed in mourning black and gazing up at the gallant figure of her dead hero. "Better the Bride of McPherson dead, than the wife of the richest Merchant of Baltimore," Sherman had told her—and she apparently agreed.[70]

Emily Hoffman never married, and would die alone at age fifty-seven in 1891. Never married, and a widow nonetheless.

CHAPTER SEVEN

The Battle of the Poor House

Ezra Church, July 28

"*Light breaks from the only dark point in our lines,*" the *Richmond Enquirer* exulted on July 25. "Atlanta is now felt to be safe, and Georgia will soon be free from the foe. The central army of the Confederacy has recovered its prestige and defeated the exultant enemy." The Virginia paper acknowledged the limits of its information—"Of the completeness of this victory, at the time of this writing nothing is known," the editors said of the recent battle—but nevertheless pronounced that "a new policy had successfully inaugurated, that may lead to recovery of all that has been lost, and eventually carry our victorious banners into the territory of our enemy." After all, "The attack was made, not received; the enemy was driven, not repulsed." Other Southern newspapers joined the chorus. "Glorious Success of Our Arms. Capture of Artillery, Prisoners, &c." the headlines read. "Fighting in Atlanta. Yankees Driven From Their Entrenchments. Capture of Prisoners and Guns. . . . Gen. Hardee in Sherman's Rear." The *Savannah Republican* printed a letter from a Georgia lieutenant describing the spoils of the victory and boasting of "the skill of our Generals and the impetuous valor of subordinate officers and men." The army, the young officer wrote, is "large-spirited, determined, well-appointed, and fond of their new and great Commander-in-chief (Hood). Under him, the pride of Texans and the hope of Georgians, they expect to be led to new fields of imperishable glory and renown."[1]

Soon word came that General McPherson had been killed, and the perception of a great Southern triumph grew even stronger. Robert E. Lee, then under siege up in Virginia, was heartened by news of "the glorious victory at Atlanta." Should it prove true, he wrote to Jefferson Davis, "it will again open to us Alabama and East Mississippi, and remove a part of the great weight pressing upon us." Davis's military adviser Braxton Bragg confirmed the preliminary reports of the battle in a wire sent to the Confederate president on July 25: the Federals had been "badly defeated," he claimed. "The moral effect of our brilliant affair of the 22d has been admirable on our troops," he wrote, "and I am happy to say our loss was small in comparison to the enemy's."[2]

For his part, Hood went so far as to issue that same day a motivational if not an outright congratulatory order. "Soldiers," he wrote, "Experience has proved to you that safety in time of battle consists in getting into close quarters with your enemy. Guns and colors are the only unerring indications of victory. The valor of troops is easily estimated, too, by the number of these secured. If your enemy be allowed to continue the operation of flanking you out of position, our cause is in great peril. Your recent brilliant success proves the ability to prevent it. You have but to will it, and God will it, and God will grant us the victory your commander and your country expect."[3]

The country and the commander had indeed come to expect victory at Atlanta. But these initial indications that Southern prospects in the campaign had somehow brightened would only serve to make the truth more painful when it came. As one despondent Confederate veteran would put it, "Although heralded at first as a victory throughout the South, when the facts became known, the people turned away sick at heart."[4]

Surely the soldiers on both sides were heartsick, too, along the fortified lines and in the bivouacs around the city of Atlanta, as they mourned fallen friends and spent their days either improving their breastworks or burying the dead. Majors and colonels wrote letters of condolence to loved ones left behind. "He retained his reason to the last moment, but sobbed bitterly as he directed me to take your likeness from his breast pocket," read a letter of sympathy sent to the grieving fiancée of a fallen Michigan lieutenant. "He said that he was betrothed to you, that though it was sad to die, he was prepared to meet his God."[5]

Some companies and regiments assembled and tried their best to account for the quick and the dead. "Few scenes in a soldier's life are touched with sadder interest than the first roll call after a battle," a Rebel orderly sergeant wrote. The corporals and privates lined up in noticeably thinned ranks, standing with eyes downcast as the silence drew out after certain names were called. The roll calls were particularly grim in the Confederate ranks, where in some units as many as one in three had fallen. In the fighting on July 21 and 22, General Cleburne had lost 40 percent of his men and more than half of his officers. Walker's Division, with its regiments badly mauled and its commander dead, was broken up and its three brigades reassigned to the other divisions of Hardee's Corps.[6]

Apart from the occasional rumble of cannon as the Federals continued lobbing shells into the streets of the town, the days following the Battle of Atlanta were quiet, though one Union officer found it "that kind of quietness that the tiger or the cat uses before springing on its prey." The break must have been especially welcome for some among the Confederates, such as the veteran's of Cleburne's Division, who had gone without sleep for almost three full days. "The boys enjoyed a freedom, rest and relief from the severe tension such as they had not experienced since May," a Kentuckian wrote. Soldiers on both sides took advantage of the relative calm to sleep and write letters home. Lieutenant Robert Gill composed two letters to his wife, Bettie, back home in Okolona, Mississippi. "After getting into a fight there is something grand about it—it is magnificent," he wrote. "I feel elated as if borne along with the tide of battle." But he also made a confession. "I must tell you some truths which you will be very sorry to hear. . . . During the fight I done some heavy swearing I am told." He went on to describe his transgressions, including the vile insult he had hurled at a squad of surrendering Yankees ("I called them 'damned miscegenators,'" he confessed). But he vowed in future battles to hold his tongue. "I try to do right but it seems impossible for me to keep from cursing when I get under fire. I hope I will do better hereafter. I do not wish to die with an oath on my lips."[7]

Others gave family members back home boiled-down assessments of the strategic situation. "The rivers are all crossed and the mountains all scaled, and nothing now remains between us and the doomed city but the ridges of red clay thrown up by the rebel army," a Union major wrote to his wife in Illinois. "The rebels have been more vigorous since we crossed the river than they were before, but it is only the vigor of desperation, and the more frequently they assault us, the sooner their army will be destroyed, for they *can't whip* this army; we are like the big boy, 'too big to be whipped.'"

The city of Atlanta by now was a shambles, ravaged over the previous three days and nights by Union shells and scattered looting, though even some Southerners felt there was a certain justice in the devastation. "I rode over to Atlanta yesterday, and it really made me sad to witness the ruin and destruction of the place," Confederate Lieutenant Andrew Jackson Neal wrote to his mother. "If Sodom deserved the fate that befell it, Atlanta will not be unjustly punished, for since this war commenced it has grown to be the great capital place of corruption in official and private circles. While I regret the loss of Atlanta on account of its great value to the country as a military base and its incalculable value on account of its arsenals, foundries, manufacturies and railroad connections, I can scarcely regret that the nest of speculators and thieves, &c. is broken up. The constant and glorious patriotism and self-sacrificing devotion to our cause displayed by the women of Atlanta is the only redeeming virtue of the place."[8]

Perhaps not, however, as other Atlantans demonstrated their virtue as well. James Dunning, part owner of an Atlanta foundry, came across a number of wounded Federal soldiers in a city park, apparently taken there during the battle and since left untreated, their wounds open and festering, some "almost rotting with gangrene." Apparently the city's residents had been afraid to help the suffering Northern boys, fearing retaliation from Confederate authorities. But Dunning, a staunch Unionist, found their sufferings "intolerable." He went to the free black barber Robert Webster for assistance, and in him the poor Yankees found their Samaritan. "Webster took charge of the whole matter himself, hired other colored people to help him and paid them for their services," an admiring witness said. He not only tended to their wounds and provided food and water, but saw that they were taken to a local hospital for treatment.[9]

Meanwhile, the long-range Federal cannonade, which had lessened somewhat while the battle was fought the day before, had now resumed. "We have had a considerable taste of the beauties of bombardment today," bookseller and stationer Samuel Richards recorded in his diary on July 23. "The enemy have thrown a great many shells into the city and scared the women and children and *some* of the *men* pretty badly. . . . This seems to me a very barbarous mode of carrying on war, throwing shells upon women and children." For Richards, the day after the battle was notable for another reason—the city authorities required him to do "police duty." That night, the kindly London-born proprietor of J. J. & S. P. Richards' Book, Music and Fancy Store stood as a sentry on McDonough Street and, for the first time in his life, held a gun in his hands. As for the bombardment, neither Richards nor anyone else had any idea how bad it was going to get.[10]

At his headquarters outside the city, Sherman had a number of matters to attend to in the days after the Battle of Atlanta. First and foremost was the question of who would take the place of McPherson in command of the Army of the Tennessee—a post that had been filled temporarily by Black Jack Logan. The new appointment should have been a straightforward decision, but Sherman instead found it to be a "delicate and difficult task." Seniority, army tradition, and experience all weighed strongly in favor of Joseph Hooker, the senior corps commander in the whole of Sherman's department, the Military Division of the Mississippi. Not only had he performed well in the recent fight at Peachtree Creek—just ask him and he would surely tell you—but he also previously led both the Army of the Potomac and what one historian called the "fightingest corps" in Sherman's army. For all these reasons, elevating Hooker to lead McPherson's army would seem not only sensible but also a case of merely giving Fighting Joe the post that was due him, commensurate with his rank and experience. But Hooker, with his "fine martial presence and his princely air," had an indelible black mark against him, one that neither capability nor charisma could erase: Sherman could not stand him.[11]

The other obvious choice, if an alternate to Hooker was needed, was John Logan. Black Jack had taken temporary command of the army literally in the heat of battle on July 22, and he not only had performed admirably but had secured his place in history by virtue of his inspiring leadership. Logan had been with the Army of the Tennessee throughout the war from 1861 on and had come up through the ranks to command a brigade, a division, and a corps. Sherman was inclined to give the command to Logan and be done with it—but then he had second thoughts, largely provoked by General Thomas. Logan, Old Tom pointed out, was a nonprofessional—a *politician*, for God's sake—and though he was, according to Sherman, a "whole-souled fellow," brave as Julius Caesar, with a knack for rousing battlefield oratory, he was somewhat lacking in the administrative and logistical work required for army command and hardly seemed a stickler for tactical details.

Accordingly, Thomas proposed another candidate. "You cannot do better than put Howard in command of that army," he told his chief. "He is tractable, and we can get along with him."[12]

The officer thus damned with Thomas's faint praise was Major General Oliver Otis Howard, then in command of the 4th Corps in Thomas's Army of the Cumberland. Folks then and later were of two minds about Howard. On the one hand, he was extremely intelligent, having obtained a degree from Bowdoin College before attending West Point, where he graduated fourth in his class. He was disciplined, a pious officer known throughout the army as "the Christian General," or by the men as "Old Prayer Book." He was experienced, having served as a colonel, a brigadier, and then a major general in the Army of the Potomac for two years. And he was brave, as shown by his conduct at the Battle of Fair Oaks (or Seven Pines) in 1862, a battle which had cost him an arm and later earned him the Medal of Honor. Even when things had not gone well, Howard was known to struggle fiercely and lead from the front, as at the Battle of Chancellorsville, where he had held an American flag under the stump of his amputated right arm and tried desperately to rally his routed troops. Indeed, Howard was said by one witness to be "the only man in his command that was not running at that moment."[13]

Major General John A. "Black Jack" Logan. (*Library of Congress*)

On the other hand, despite his smarts and his indisputable courage, some thought the young Maine-born general incompetent, snakebit, or both. During his time with the Army of the Potomac, his command, the XI (11th) Corps, a force largely composed of German immigrants, was mocked as "Howard's Cowards" and "the Flying Dutchmen." Howard himself was famous—and arguably is still most famous today—for presiding over two Union near-catastrophes, first at Chancellorsville, where Stonewall Jackson crushed his flank and sent his men running for their lives, and second, on the first day of the Battle of Gettysburg, where he tried desperately to halt a similar stampede by his corps. Opinions differ as to whether Howard was responsible for these misadventures, or whether he was just unlucky—a general always in the wrong place at the wrong time. Either way, wags in the ranks played on his unusual initials, calling him not "O. O." but "Uh-Oh" Howard. More recently, during the Battle of Pickett's Mill in May, he had terribly misjudged the position and strength of his Rebel adversary, reporting to Thomas: "I am now turning the enemy's flank, *I think*," and then finding before him instead Patrick Cleburne's veterans, with predictable results. And so, the man who was arguably responsible for the inglorious skedaddle at Chancellorsville and the so-called "crime at Pickett's Mill" would now take command of Sherman's favorite army—based largely upon a prediction that he would be, well, "tractable."[14]

Howard's appointment was sent to Washington for approval, and the appointment was promptly announced—whereupon there was considerable outrage. Logan was understandably upset and referred to Sherman as "an infernal *brute*" in private letters to his wife, but—thinking either of his duty or of his future aspirations for higher political office—he kept his disappointment to himself and returned to command of the 15th Corps. But Howard's elevation was altogether more than the proud peacock Joe Hooker could abide. Howard was sixteen years younger than Hooker and his junior by far in rank and service. "I have just learned that Major General Howard my junior, has been assigned to the command of the Army of the Tennessee," an indignant Hooker wrote to his immediate superior George Thomas. "If this is the case I request that I may be relieved from duty with this army. Justice and self-respect alike require my removal from an army in which rank and service are ignored."

Thomas forwarded Hooker's resignation to Sherman and "*heartily*" recommended that it be accepted—which it promptly was. Hooker is "envious, impervious, and a braggart," Sherman wrote to his wife, Ellen. "This ought to damn him, showing that he is selfish & not patriotic." Adding insult to injury, Major General Henry W. Slocum, another enemy of Hooker's (he had lots of enemies) was summoned from Vicksburg to replace Hooker at the head of the 20th Corps. As it turned out, this would be Hooker's last field command; according to his biographer, "he realized his sun had set." He would serve out the war in command of the Northern Department, headquartered in Chicago and then Cincinnati—about as far from the fighting as Fighting Joe would get. "Yet he had played a not undistinguished part in the greatest drama of American history," the *Atlantic Monthly* wrote by way of a eulogy to his career, "and with all his faults there was something about him of the true heroic stamp, something of the boyish, prating, blustering, panic-harboring, death-defying heroes of the Iliad."[15]

The Sherman-Hooker-Howard controversy, while certainly emotional and by far the most significant in its impact on the army, was relatively tame compared to other conflicts at Union headquarters. On July 25, the fiery Irish general Thomas Sweeny confronted his fellow brigadier, the English-born John W. Fuller, and a swirling pot of professional criticism and historic animosity (seasoned, perhaps, with a shot or two of whiskey) soon came to a boil. Sweeny accused Fuller's division of breaking and running in the fight on the left flank on July 22, thereby exposing Sweeny's own division to possible destruction. Hearing the argument, Major General Grenville Dodge, both men's superior, intervened and sided with Fuller—whereupon the hot-tempered Irishman's fuse was lit.

Sweeny, who had lost his right arm in the Mexican War and was said to express himself in three languages—"English, Irish-English, and profane"—redirected his fire at Dodge, who had angered him during the battle by ignoring the chain of command and issuing orders to Sweeny's subordinate commanders. Erupting in a blistering tirade, he called Dodge "a god damned liar," an "inefficient son of a bitch," a "god damned political general," and "a god damned cowardly son of a bitch"—and then, reverting to military form, he added contemptuously: "*sir.*" Finally, Dodge had all of this he could take, and he slapped the insubordinate Irishman full and hard across the face. Sweeny—who would live up to his nickname "Fighting Tom" that day—swung with his left arm and punched the commanding general of the 16th Corps square in the nose, sending blood pouring; then he grabbed Fuller and wrestled him to the ground. Nearby officers separated the high-ranking combatants, and Dodge—whose greatest injury was to his pride, having been decked by a one-armed man—placed Sweeny under arrest. He was relieved from duty but ultimately acquitted of the court-martial charges.[16]

As the soldiers rested and the generals fought among themselves, Sherman got back to the task of working out how best to fight his opponent. "It was a great game of chess," a Union officer later wrote of the contest around Atlanta. "Hood had castled, and Sherman moved to checkmate him." Metaphors about the game of chess certainly have their place in the telling of military history, but the comparison here is hardly appropriate. Hood had hardly "castled" and retreated to his corner—rather, he had tried a desperate gambit, or even jostled the board and knocked the pawns and knights and rooks off the squares entirely with an angry sweep of the hand. But at this point—with the Confederates hunkered in their trenches and the Federal armies free to maneuver—the move was Sherman's.[17]

"We have Atlanta close aboard as the Sailors say but it is a hard nut to handle," Sherman wrote to Ellen. "These fellows fight like Devils and Indians combined." His infantry pressed up close to the ring of defensive works around Atlanta and found them to be formidable indeed. The fortifications "consisted of a system of batteries open to the rear and connected by infantry parapet, with complete abatis, in some places three and four rows, with rows of pointed stakes, and long lines of chevaux-de-frise," Sherman's chief engineer Captain Orlando Poe reported. "In many places rows of palisading were planted along the foot of the exterior slope of the infantry parapet with sufficient opening between the timbers to permit the infantry fire, if carefully delivered, to pass freely through. . . . The ground in front of these palisades or stockades was always completely swept by the fire of the adjacent batteries, which enabled a very small force to hold them." Poe talked with Sherman the day after the Battle of Atlanta, and found that his chief had already decided that "no assault would be made at present; neither did he desire anything like regular siege operations." Instead, he would continue his efforts to circle the city and snip the threads of railroad that both supplied Atlanta and justified its existence. Two of these roads were already in his hands—the Western & Atlantic Railroad down from Chattanooga had supplied his army for weeks, and the Georgia Railroad to Augusta was now torn up for nearly fifty miles.

That left the two lines running to points south of the city, the Macon & Western Railroad and the Atlanta & West Point Railroad, which shared a single track for the first six miles before splitting into two lines at the junction town of East Point. (East Point, though positioned southwest of Atlanta, was so named because it was originally the eastern terminus of the Atlanta & West Point Railroad.) Sherman's next move was to aim at this junction, cutting Hood's last railroad connection and thus rendering the Gate City a dead end. Despite the recent fighting, Sherman reported the army "in good condition in all respects." On July 24, he wrote to General Henry Halleck in Washington and outlined his intentions. "As soon as my cavalry rests, I propose to swing the Army of the Tennessee round by the right rapidly and interpose between Atlanta and Macon, the only line open to the enemy," he said. His plan was to send Howard's army from the extreme left of the Federal position, east of Atlanta, around to the extreme right. Two days later, he was ready. "To-morrow we begin the move against Atlanta," he wired Halleck. "I move the whole Army of the Tennessee to the right, extending the line south, threatening East Point, and forcing, as I think, Hood to abandon Atlanta."

The counterclockwise movement around the city would be directed by the newly appointed General Howard. Although Hooker had been

Major General Oliver Otis Howard. (*Library of Congress*)

popular with the rank and file, no one seemed to miss him much once he was gone, and the soldiers quickly warmed to Howard, who had accepted the command with a general order to the troops. "I assure the gallant soldiers of this renowned army that I fully realize the delicate nature of my responsibility," he wrote. "Your late beloved commander was my personal friend, and while I unite with you in profound sympathy and regret for our irreparable loss, it shall by my constant aim to emulate his noble example."[18]

That was Howard—determined and serious, loyal and sincere. The thirty-three-year-old father of three was dignified and slender, pale as a truce flag, with earnest dark blue eyes and a "profusion of flowing moustache and beard." He looked young, not a hint of gray in his thick brown hair, though the lines of care around his eyes hinted at what he had been through. His right sleeve, pinned and empty, was a constant reminder of his courage and sacrifice, and men respected him for that, if nothing else. Although some found him irritatingly, ostentatiously pious—"he told us all about himself and his little family and the Ten Commandments," one soldier said—others saw the Christian General as evidence that God was on their side. "The promotion of General Howard suits the rank and file," an Illinois soldier wrote. "He is known to be a Christian gentleman and somehow the hardest swearer in the ranks feels that Howard's prayers will help win the battle." Soldiers found it comforting to pass Howard's headquarters on Sunday and see the sign posted on his tent admonishing them to REMEMBER THE SABBATH DAY. "Instinctively we raise our caps and say, 'Thank God for one Christian soldier.'"[19]

The Army of the Tennessee—which once had been Grant's army, then Sherman's, then McPherson's, then (briefly) Logan's, and now Howard's—began its roundabout march as scheduled on the morning of

July 27th, a shift of three entire Federal corps (Logan's 15th, Dodge's 16th, and Blair's 17th) from their trenches on the extreme left of the horseshoe-shaped Union line, east of Atlanta, all the way around to the extreme right, southwest of the city. "Thus was the Army of the Tennessee transferred for the *fifth* time from one flank to the other," a *Cincinnati Gazette* correspondent wrote. "The boys say that Gen. Sherman styles this army his corkscrew, by which he draws out the obstinate cork out of the Rebel position." The column headed north, then west, passing behind the lines of George Thomas's massive Army of the Cumberland, still posted to the north of the city. "Look! There, I see a soldier!" an Ohio captain said drolly, pointing toward Thomas's camps. "We could see forty thousand men stretching for miles before us, their blue figures standing out in relief on the glimmering horizon," his companion said. "It gave us a feeling of confidence and strength to look upon such a mighty host."[20]

Howard was riding with Grenville Dodge at the head of the column, and Sherman joined them as they passed by his new "meager headquarters" hard by the Peachtree Road. The generals continued to the west and then south, and then Sherman pointed out a ridge west of the city that would conduct the army southward toward the Macon railroad. Winding off ahead into the woods was a road running southwest toward an intersection with the Lick Skillet Road, near a country chapel known as Ezra Church. Howard expressed concern that Hood would attack him before he could get into position, and proposed that he move up carefully, "so that each successive division would protect the flank of the preceding." Sherman didn't seem to care one way or the other how Howard chose to deploy his troops, and he hardly shared the younger man's concern as the day of tiresome marching drew to a close.

"I don't think Hood will trouble you," Sherman said, and he rode away.[21]

Hood's newest corps commander Lieutenant General Stephen D. Lee was no relation to Robert E. Lee, the iconic Confederate hero considered by many to be the greatest general of the age. This must have bothered the

Lieutenant General Stephen D. Lee, no relation to the more famous Robert E. Lee. (*Battles and Leaders*)

young general, at least a little. As a handsome, brown-bearded officer named Lee wearing a crisp gray gold-buttoned uniform, he surely was asked all the time whether he was kin to Marse Robert, and perhaps, under the circumstances of the present conflict, it pained him to answer no. He had much to be proud of, being by far the youngest lieutenant general in the Confederacy. But he was and always would be General Lee—but not *the* General Lee, as he would presently demonstrate.

Lee was only thirty, and he had played a prominent role in the war from the time of the opening curtain. On April 11, 1861, Lee, then a twenty-seven-year-old aide-de-camp to General Pierre Gustave Toutant Beauregard, had delivered to Major Robert Anderson, commanding U.S. forces at Fort Sumter, a demand for the garrison's surrender—which had of course been denied. Since that time, Lee had seen distinguished service in all three branches of the Confederate Army: the artillery, where he started with a battery and ended up commanding a battalion in the Army of Northern Virginia; the cavalry, serving briefly as a colonel in the 4th Virginia; and finally the infantry, where he had commanded a division and, at Chickasaw Bayou, Mississippi, had fought Tecumseh Sherman to a standstill. Captured at Vicksburg on July 4, 1863, he was paroled, promoted to major general, and returned to command of the Department of Alabama and East Louisiana. By 1864, Lee had had so many assignments that Rebel soldiers had taken to calling him not something solid like "Old Straight" or "Old Reliable"—but "Old Temporary."

His latest posting was a position of great responsibility and opportunity. In June, he had been promoted to the rank of lieutenant general—the youngest man to hold that grade in the entire Confederate Army, east or west—and in July was brought from Mississippi to take command of Hood's old corps. Frank Cheatham, who had led the corps on an interim basis in the ten days since Hood's ascension to command, would return to head up his old division. Lee arrived on July 26 and was "most favorably received," no doubt eager to make his mark and justify his appointment.[22]

That same day, Hood received a cavalry report that the enemy were pushing around to the west of the city and "seemed desirous of extending their line down the river"—that is, moving down the near bank of the Chattahoochee toward East Point. By the early morning hours of July 27, General Hood was warning his subordinates that "indications are that the enemy will attack our left," and that all should hold fast and be on the lookout. It appeared that, yet again, Sherman was separating the wings of his armies and sending a portion some distance away from the remainder of his force, exposing it to potential destruction—so Hood drew up yet another plan to attack the isolated column and destroy it in detail.

On the evening of July 27—not long after Sherman predicted to Howard that Hood wouldn't bother him—the Kentucky-born Texan convened another council of war to explain his plan. This time, Hardee's Corps would hold the Atlanta defenses, while Hood's own former corps, now under the newly arrived Stephen Lee, would march out to form a defensive line and block the southward advance of the Federal column. With the bluecoats stalled and in the open, Stewart's Corps would then swing around behind Lee and attack Howard's right flank on the 29th—a maneuver, needless to say, that Howard had not responded to well in battles past. It was another good plan, though somewhat complicated. "Hood was still dreaming of Stonewall Jackson," as one historian wrote.[23]

The next day, July 28, was clear and hot. In the woods northwest of Atlanta, Howard was up early and got his three corps in motion, flushing out occasional cavalry scouts and Rebel pickets as they moved southward. Howard was riding with Sherman around midmorning, approaching the east-west wagon track called the Lick Skillet Road when a spatter of what Howard took to be grapeshot clipped through the trees overhead. "General," Howard said, turning to his chief, "Hood will attack me here." Sherman thought the notion preposterous. "I guess not," he snorted. "He will hardly try it again." But the crackle of firing only increased, and Sherman rode off to the east toward Atlanta to summon reinforcements from Thomas should Howard need them. But whether because of past (bad) experience or excessive caution, being less than two days in command, Howard was unwilling to ignore the threat that Sherman scoffed at. He had been a year behind John Bell Hood at West Point, and he knew him to be "indomitable." With that in mind, Howard took up a strong position on a stretch of high ground facing south, the line of the 15th and 17th Corps drawn like a crooked smile on the map, and had his men prepare to receive an attack.

Along this gently curving stretch of the road running out from Atlanta to a country village bearing what a Union brigadier would call "the cacophonous name of Lickskillet," two institutions stood on what was about to become the battlefield. To the east was a tiny Methodist log chapel known as Ezra Church, north of the road and near the intersection of the Marietta Pike. A half mile to the west was a cluster of modest wooden buildings that between them made up the Fulton County Poor House, established in 1860 and dedicated to the high moral purpose of providing food and shelter for the county's unfortunates. (These unfortunates, fortunately, had been "refugeed away," and only the empty buildings were in danger.)[24]

Lee's instructions were to block the Federals from reaching the Lick Skillet Road, but when he arrived that morning, coming up from the southeast, he found that the blue skirmishers had already reached the road. What to do? The normally aggressive Hood had directed Lee to take up a defensive position and forestall Howard's advance, going so far as to warn his young subordinate that he was "not to attack unless the enemy exposes himself in attacking us." For whatever reason, Lee either forgot these instructions or disregarded them entirely. Thinking perhaps that his opponent was just arriving and would not be prepared for an attack, he issued orders "to attack and drive the enemy to Ezra Church." In short, whether sloppy, incompetent, or overeager to prove his mettle, Lee was about to do everything wrong. He would attack, not defend, as Hood had instructed; he would launch the assault against Howard's front, not his flank; and he would send his men into the battle piecemeal as they came up—like feeding ax-split kindling into a furnace, one stick at a time.

What was more, the Federals were by no means taken off guard—their wary new commander had seen to that. "It was too late for intrenchment," Howard later recalled, but his bluecoats scrambled to pile fence rails and dirt into a meager parapet, while those near Ezra Church dragged the wooden pews out from the chapel and piled up knapsacks to shore up their own makeshift fortifications. By the time the attack opened, the defenders along most sections of the line had only managed to construct a rickety, knee-high barrier, but it would have to do—and it would be more cover than the Rebels would have.[25]

The butternut attackers charged through the woods "with a terrifying yell," so that the Federals heard the approaching Rebels before they saw them. "When the fearful Confederate shouts, so strong and confident, reached our ears," Howard wrote, "every man along the exposed front line carefully knelt behind their slight defenses, or lay prone upon the ground with rifle in hand, gazing steadily through the forest toward the ominous sound." Officers ranged up and down the line, barking well-drilled reminders to the riflemen at their feet. "Take steady aim and fire low at the word!" they said. Soon the Rebels appeared from the underbrush ahead, rushing northward across three hundred yards of open ground, and the blue-clad marksmen sighted down their barrels. Unlike the battles last week, there would be no confusion, no fighting on both sides of the breastworks, no scavenging graybacks loose in the rear. This was going to be a target shoot.[26]

Sherman, two miles away, heard the unmistakable drumroll-sound of musketry as it "swelled louder and louder into the full chorus of battle." A courier arrived and breathlessly reported that the Confederates had launched an attack on Logan's corps. Sherman was pleased, jabbering away and echoing himself, as he was prone to do when excited. "Good, fine," he said, "that's just what I wanted, just what I wanted; tell Howard to invite them to attack, it will save us trouble, save us trouble; they'll only beat their own brains out, beat their own brains out."

"And so, in this confident tone our chieftain talked on gaily, while his boys in blue were reaping the terrible harvest of death," a major present at headquarters wrote. "He understood his own strategy, he saw it was working as he designed, and he was satisfied."[27]

The first Confederate unit to charge was Brigadier General John C. Brown's Division, advancing toward the Federal right from the neigh-

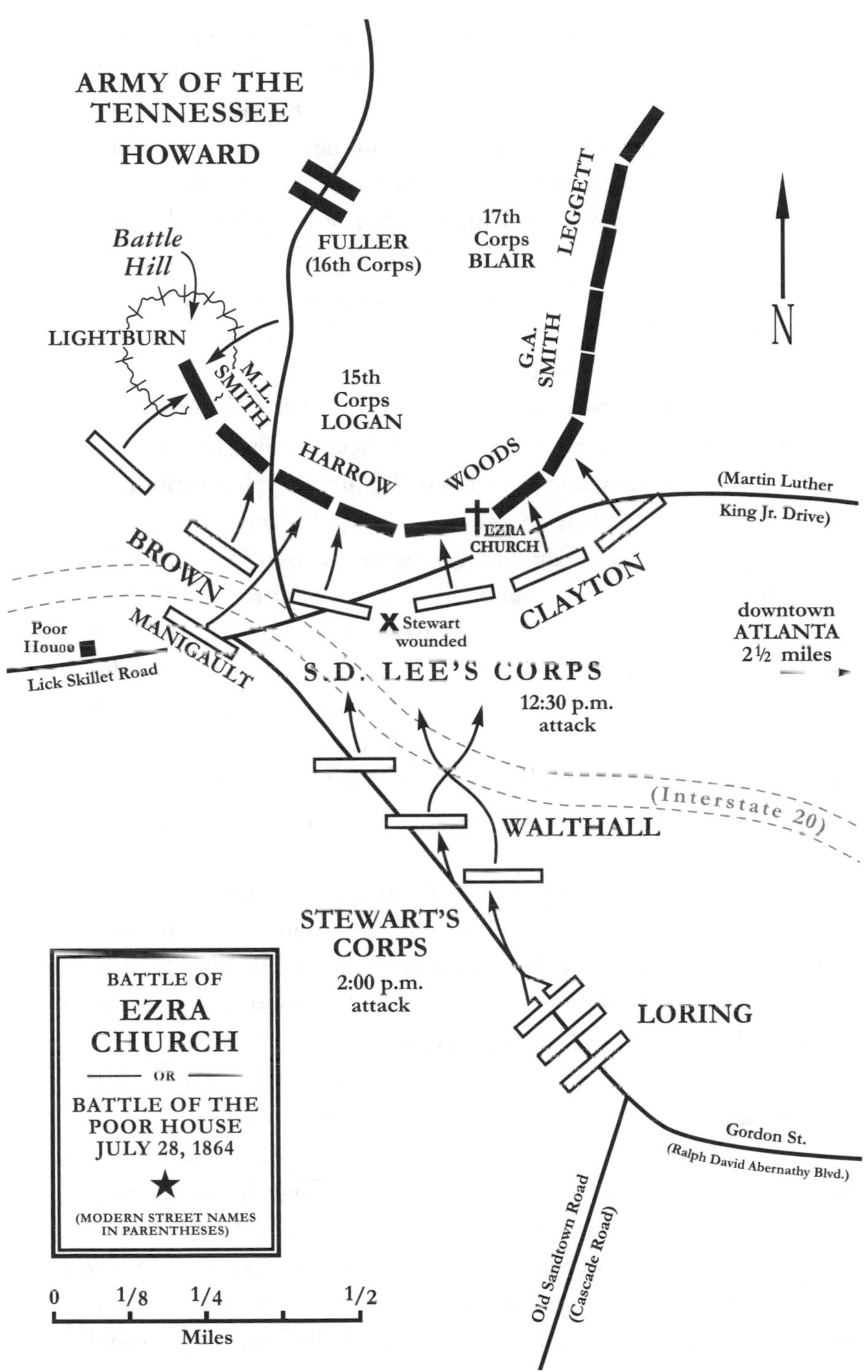
ARMY OF THE TENNESSEE
HOWARD
Battle Hill
LIGHTBURN
M.L. SMITH
FULLER (16th Corps)
17th Corps BLAIR
LEGGETT
G.A. SMITH
15th Corps LOGAN
HARROW
WOODS
EZRA CHURCH
(Martin Luther King Jr. Drive)
BROWN
MANIGAULT
CLAYTON
Poor House
Lick Skillet Road
Stewart wounded
S.D. LEE'S CORPS
12:30 p.m. attack
downtown ATLANTA 2½ miles
(Interstate 20)
WALTHALL
STEWART'S CORPS
2:00 p.m. attack
LORING
N
Gordon St.
(Ralph David Abernathy Blvd.)
Old Sandtown Road
(Cascade Road)
BATTLE OF EZRA CHURCH
OR
BATTLE OF THE POOR HOUSE
JULY 28, 1864
(MODERN STREET NAMES IN PARENTHESES)
0
1/8
1/4
1/2
Miles

borhood of the deserted almshouse. A brigade of Mississippians made some initial headway against the far-right Union brigade—that of the "Fighting Parson" J. A. J. Lightburn, now back in brigade command—but they were soon pushed back under a murderous fire as reinforcements came up. As the storm broke, Lightburn directed a fifteen-year-old orderly and drummer boy named Robinson Murphy to bring up reserve troops to shore up the wobbly flank. The young boy from Oswego Township, Illinois, did just that, personally leading two blue regiments to the front, and was later awarded the Medal of Honor for his actions.

Black Jack Logan was there as well, ranging back and forth behind the threatened line—"we'll hold it till hell freezes over," he reportedly said—urging his men to stand fast and thwacking stragglers with the flat of his sword. "The enemy re-enforced so rapidly and with such an immensely superior force, that my troops were driven in great slaughter," Brown later reported. Coming up in support of the initial charge was the brigade of Brigadier General Arthur Manigault, who was given orders to carry the highest portion of the ridge some three hundred yards ahead, and was further advised, either foolishly or disingenuously, that "the enemy were not in force, and held it with a few light troops." This was the Rebel brigade that had torn through the Yankee line at the Troup Hurt House two days earlier—but there would be no repetition of that feat today.

Manigault's Brigade charged alone across the field, with the defenders ahead pouring a galling fire from the front and into both flanks. Companies at either end of the brigade gave way, and the Rebel line fell into disarray, crumbling toward the middle. "The rest was flight and confusion," the South Carolina brigadier remembered, "until we reached the ground from which we had started to make the assault." The brigade reformed in good order and went forward again, "with diminished numbers, against an enemy fully as strong as he was before"—and again suffered a bloody repulse. Manigault had just withdrawn his surviving men to the shelter of a nearby hillside, when twenty minutes later came a repetition of the same order: his brigade was to charge the Federal line *again*—as he said, "unsupported, after two failures, with the command reduced to seven hundred men." Manigault was certainly no coward, but he thought the order absurd. "I could scarcely credit my senses," he said. He rode over to his superior General Brown, who said that the order to renew the assault had come from Lee, not from him; but before Manigault got back to his brigade, Brown countermanded the order. (Brown would contend in his report of the fight that Manigault's brigade was so demoralized that "it could not be made effective").[28]

Next, the division of Brigadier General Henry D. Clayton—an Alabama lawyer and no relation to the Atlanta Claytons—was sent into the fray. The three gray brigades advanced toward the center and left of the Federal line near the church, and were, as their commander reported, "driven back with great loss." An Illinois soldier described the progress of the attack: "the well-known yell; the pop-popping of the preliminary shots; the magnificent on-coming of proud lines from behind the opposite ridge, with flag-bearers seeming to dance defiantly in their front; the crash of the volleyed musketry; the hopeless struggle, growing confusion, slaughter, and helpless rout." A Missouri private named Tom Coleman described the repeated Confederate assaults in a letter to his sister Lizzie. "They tried it five times, but with no better success," he wrote. "The boys took delibrat aime and nearly every shot fetched a man."

None of this was particularly surprising: Lee had sent forward two divisions in disjointed fashion against two entire army corps posted "in strong works and upon ground well chosen." Behind those works, Howard rode along his line, encouraging the troops. In between Rebel charges, the thirty-three-year-old veteran of fights from Bull Run to Antietam to Gettysburg to Chattanooga looked out over the smoky field. "Well, boys, I thought I had seen fighting before," he said, "but I never saw anything like this." A reporter watching the battle thought the scene unprecedented as well. "I have frequently heard of the murderous fire poured forth from the heights of Bunker Hill or from the cotton bales of New Orleans," he wrote, "but how feeble those compared with the destroying volley which swept in a single instant hundreds of men to eternity and laid thousands upon the earth maimed, many of them for life, on the plains before Atlanta."[29]

General Alexander P. Stewart soon arrived on the field with his corps, having been directed by Hood to give Lee his full support. Lee—who a

The Battle of Ezra Church, July 28, 1864. Beginning their attack on the right side of the Federal line, three Confederate divisions under Lieutenant General Stephen D. Lee were repulsed with heavy casualties by the well-entrenched bluecoats. (*Harper's Weekly*)

nearby lieutenant thought "looked like the God of War"—immediately requested that Stewart send his corps forward into the maelstrom as well. "The enemy was still within easy range of the Lick Skillet road, and I believed he would yield before a vigorous attack," Lee later insisted. Stewart's two divisions, under W. W. Loring and Edward C. Walthall, immediately formed for the attack shortly after 2 P.M., more than an hour after Brown had charged and failed. Walthall's Division went forward in a "bold and bloody assault," stumbling over the dead and wounded left from Brown's earlier charge. Arthur Manigault watched this charge from behind a large tree, curious to see whether three brigades could accomplish what his one could not. The fresh troops advanced "in a style much to be admired," but soon where thrown back in "utter confusion and rout" under "a storm of bullets that scattered death and destruction on all sides." Manigault stood behind his tree and shuddered as he thought of his escape from the same danger a short time before.[30]

Walthall's Division, though the last to charge, suffered worse than either Brown or Clayton, losing 152 officers and 1,000 men under a

Major General Edward C. Walthall. (*Battles and Leaders*)

"murderous volley of musketry which made the very heavens ring." Walthall's own personal escape from injury seemed nothing short of miraculous. The thirty three-year-old major general, a district attorney back home in Mississippi, led his men through a tempest of whizzing bullets, saber drawn, mounted on a "fiery, dappled gray horse," and both horse and rider must have been charmed. "Three times he led that grand veteran column, as it were into the jaws of death, to charge upon our works and three times they were repulsed—it seemed as if half the army were firing at the General," an admiring Iowa colonel across the way remembered. "I took seven shots at him myself as fast as a musket could be loaded for me. It is not strange that I did not hit him, but I have often wondered how he escaped, as I learn he and his horse also did, with all those sharpshooters after his scalp."[31]

The battle was brutal, and simple. "They done the charging and our men the shooting," an Illinois colonel recorded in his diary. Lee's men, and then Stewart's, charged forward repeatedly—in some places as many as seven times—but never was there a coordinated attack on the Federal position from end to end. Instead, the attacks continued, division by division, as the Confederates essentially took turns advancing and getting themselves shot. In between charges, Private Albert B. Crummel of the 30th Ohio Regiment crept forward from the Federal line to search the fallen Rebels for tobacco. "No sooner were their backs turned than I would be out among the dead and explore their knapsacks for the precious weed," he said.[32]

An Indiana regimental historian pronounced the battle "a most terrific affair," recording that Morgan L. Smith's division of the 15th Corps "fired 34,300 rounds of cartridges in the fight." As the Rebel assault subsided, General Stewart rode forward into an open field, concerned about the possibility of a Union counterattack, when a nearly spent bullet, perhaps a ricochet, struck him in the forehead. Although the wound was not severe, the ball knocked Old Straight senseless and put him out of action for two weeks—and carved a peculiar V-shaped scar in his forehead. Loring, too, was wounded and toppled from his horse as he was about to bring his division to Walthall's support. "The Yankees had us like sittin' ducks on a pond, in the open, and we could only see the smoke from their guns and muskets," a Mississippi soldier would remember.[33]

Lee's order to attack and drive the enemy had asked the impossible of his men. "If it had been possible for the daring of officers and the desperate fighting of the men to have overcome such odds in numbers and strength of position as we encountered that day all along my whole line, the enemy must have been beaten," Walthall later reported, "but double the force could not have accomplished what my division was ordered to undertake."[34]

Perhaps the person most surprised by Lee's surprise attack was his superior General Hood. Although he would later praise his newest subordinate—he "promptly obeyed orders," Hood wrote in his memoirs—in fact it appears that Lee did nothing of the kind. Hood's true reaction to Lee's conduct that day was shown more by what he did than by what he later said. Receiving word of the struggle, which by all accounts seemed to be going very badly, Hood took the extraordinary step of summoning General Hardee and directing him "to proceed to the field, and, if necessary, to assume command of the troops engaged." Old Reliable promptly mounted up and rode the three miles out toward Ezra Church. "Upon my arrival on the field the fighting had nearly ceased, and I found it unnecessary to take command," Hardee recalled.[35]

Hood sent news of the engagement to Richmond later that evening. "About 1:30 o'clock a sharp engagement ensued with no decided advantage to either side," he wired—a dispatch that historian Stephen Davis notes displayed "a rather shameful insensitivity to the truth"—though Hood may have lacked full intelligence as to extent of the disaster at that point, and no doubt felt that, whatever had happened out on the Lick Skillet Road, it was contrary to his instructions and not his fault.

But disingenuous reports could not gloss over this defeat. Peachtree Creek had been a hard-fought loss for Hood; and Bald Hill had cost him dearly, though it allowed him to claim a "partial success." Hood's Third

Sortie, however, had been an outright debacle—in the words of a Louisiana private, "a perfect slaughter." Historians would call the battle fruitless, uncoordinated, botched, and, for the Federals, a relatively easy victory. The only remotely positive thing that could be said, from a Confederate perspective, is that the attack had stalled, at least for the moment, Howard's southward advance toward the railroad at East Point. The Federal line, with its fence-rail and church-pew fortifications, had held from end to end. Logan had again performed magnificently. Both Ezra Church and the scattered buildings of the Poor House were subsequently destroyed, nothing but the chimneys left standing.[36]

And Uh-Oh Howard had finally, and decisively, won a battle. As dusk fell, he rode slowly along his lines, and the soldiers cheered.

Hood had vowed to fight the Yankee invaders, and now he had fought them so much and so often that folks around the nation had trouble telling one "battle of Atlanta" from another. Herman Melville, for example, following reports of the clashes down in Georgia from his home in New York City, seemed to have no idea of how to refer to the most recent battle. "It is significant of the scale on which the war was waged, that the engagement thus written of goes solely (so far as can be learned) under the vague designation of one of the battles before Atlanta," he wrote. Indeed, no one seemed to know what to call this latest fight, whether because of the multiplicity of recent battles or the obscure Georgia geography. The contest would come to be called, most often, the Battle of Ezra Church, although historians and military students would consider it "Hood's Third Sortie," and some locals called it the Battle of the Poor House, while others preferred the Battle of Lick Skillet Road. The newspapers, and many soldiers in the ranks, just called it the Battle of July 28.[37]

Whatever the name, "the battle of the 28th" was perhaps more devastating to Hood and his Army of Tennessee than even the larger-scale engagements at Peachtree Creek and Bald Hill. Final judgment was pronounced by General Hardee, who had arrived on the field too late to affect the battle but in time to witness the results. "So great was the loss in men, organization, and morale in that engagement that no action of the campaign probably did so much to demoralize and dishearten the troops engaged in it," he said. Lieutenant John W. Lavender of the 4th Arkansas agreed with Hardee. "This Battle Discouraged our men Badly as they could never understand why they Should have been Sent in to such a Death Trap to be Butchered up with no hope of gaining any thing," he wrote.[38]

In the aftermath of the battle, again there was no shortage of heartbreaking scenes. A reporter for the *Cincinnati Commercial* ventured across the field and found the dead "scattered where they had fallen, in all the attitudes of fierce despair, of agony, or placid repose. . . . All along a little rivulet of muddy water the poor wretches had crawled down into it, in their dying agony, to quench their thirst, and made its banks bloody from their wounds." An Ohio chaplain came across a rebel soldier with a broken leg with a Federal surgeon lying across his feet—both were dead. "The surgeon was evidently dressing his wound when he received his death shot, for there is the bandage wound twice around the limb, the other end of which is still in the dead surgeon's hand," the chaplain recalled.[39]

Atlantan W. P. Archer met Brigadier General Randall Gibson's brigade of Louisianans—"or what was left of it"—as it returned from the battle. "It was one of the most pitiful sights I witnessed during the war," Archer recalled. "Their litters were as bloody as if hogs had been stuck on them; their flagstaffs were shot to pieces; their colors were shot into ribbons, and not more than one-half of that fine brigade that left that morning returned." And it wasn't just the flags that were shot to ribbons, but the men carrying them—the 44th Mississippi, for example, lost five successive color bearers killed or wounded in the attack.[40]

A Union private looking out over the bloody field said with grim satisfaction, "This pays for Kennesaw." And it did, almost exactly. At the Battle of Kennesaw Mountain, one month before, Sherman had lost 3,000 men in his assault; here along the Lick Skillet Road, Hood—or Lee, rather, for Hood really had little to do with it—lost 3,000 men killed, wounded, and missing as well. Howard estimated Confederate losses at more than twice that number, and also reported the capture of 200 prisoners, 1,500 muskets, and five battle flags. Even so, the kind-hearted general mourned even for his enemy. "Poor fellows," he said of the Rebel wounded in a letter to his wife, "they were rushed into the fight without mercy." Federal losses were only 642, with perhaps as few as 100 killed.[41]

"I felt satisfied that the rebels would fight to the bitter end for Atlanta, after we should cross the river, but did not expect them to manifest such senseless desperation," Illinois Major James Connelly wrote to his wife after Ezra Church. "Why it was a perfect murder. We slaughter them by the thousands, but Hood continues to hurl his broken, bleeding battalions against our immovable lines, with all the fury of a maniac. Reason seems dethroned, and Despair alone seems to rule the counsels within the walls of Atlanta."

The state of affairs after the Battle of Ezra Church was summed up in an old army story, widely reported in memoirs and regimental histories, of an exchange between opposing soldiers posted on the skirmish line. "Hey, Johnny," a Yankee called out from his rifle pit as darkness fell. "How many of you are left?"

"Oh, about enough for another killing," the Rebel replied. And so it was.[42]

Despite the lopsided victory at Ezra Church, his numerical superiority, and his ability to maneuver and do as he pleased, not all of Sherman's schemes had turned out well. One such plan—an effort to use a mounted force in a belt-and-suspenders attempt to destroy the Macon & Western Railroad, the same line that had been Howard's goal—was inspired by two recent cavalry successes. First, Brigadier General Kenner Garrard's troopers had recently returned from their three-day raid along the Georgia Railroad toward Covington, having severed the line to Augusta, perhaps for good. Around the same time, Major General Lovell Rousseau reported from Alabama that he had captured and destroyed a thirty-mile stretch of the Atlanta & West Point Railroad near Opelika. These twin horseback exploits meant that the Macon railroad was now the only trunk line running to Atlanta that was still in operation from end to end; and they also seemed to demonstrate that mounted raiders could be used to accomplish its destruction.

Sherman therefore had ordered a two-pronged strike, designed to break the railroad far south of Atlanta, that would come to be known as the Great Cavalry Raid—a puzzling, ironic name, given the ultimate result. No less than three divisions of Federal cavalry—around 10,000 sabers in all—were to converge in separate columns on Lovejoy's Station, a whistle stop on the Macon & Western some twenty-five miles south of Atlanta. Brigadier General Edward M. McCook's division would cross the Chattahoochee west of Atlanta and swing toward Lovejoy from that direction; while Major General George Stoneman's division would approach from the northeast, joined by Garrard's division, now rested from their foray to Covington. From there, the blue raiders were to unite and push southward all the way to Macon, dismounting from time to time to tear up track along the Macon railroad as they went. This would put out of commission some 74 miles of the 108-mile line between Atlanta and Macon, and would leave Hood no choice but to give up the Gate City.

All this seemed simple enough—but Stoneman had, he thought, a better idea. George Stoneman, Jr., was forty-two, a native New Yorker and a career army man who had shared a room at West Point with Stonewall Jackson. Like many of Sherman's officers, Stoneman was a transfer—or, put less charitably, a castoff—from the Army of the Potomac, where he had served as George McClellan's chief of cavalry before being forced to take medical leave for a vicious case of hemorrhoids, the nightmare affliction of every cavalryman. Hard-driving and ambitious, Stoneman requested that he be allowed to continue on past Macon into southwestern Georgia on a mission to liberate the 30,000 Union prisoners in the notorious prisoner-of-war camp at Andersonville. "I would like to try it, and am willing to run any risks, and I can vouch for my little command," he assured his chief. Sherman agreed that Stoneman could make the attempt—"after having fulfilled my present orders," he stipulated—and he told the headline-seeking cavalry commander: "If you can bring to the army any and all of those prisoners of war, it will be an achievement that will entitle you and the men of your command to the love and admiration of the whole country." Stoneman immediately focused on Sherman's latter point and neglected the former, whereupon he immediately disregarded the initial plan and instead resolved to bypass Lovejoy and ride first to the prisons

Major General George Stoneman, left, and Major General Joseph Wheeler, right, opposing cavalry leaders. (*David Wynn Vaughan*; *Library of Congress*)

at Macon and Andersonville. The idea of a rescue mission appealed to Sherman, though curiously, he authorized the effort even as he expressed doubts in official correspondence that it would be successful.[43]

The joint cavalry operation opened on schedule on July 27, as McCook crossed the Chattahoochee a few miles south of Campbellton and began moving east toward the rendezvous at Lovejoy's Station. The blue horsemen found it easy going, though the country was unfamiliar and the strangers far from helpful. ("Bub, where does this road go?" an Indiana sergeant inquired of a young cuss sitting on a fence rail. "It don't go anywhere, and never has went anywhere since I've been here," the boy replied.) The column tore up track in Palmetto on the Atlanta & West Point road and then wrecked a Confederate wagon train near Fayetteville, burning five hundred wagons and killing with pistols and sabers the horses and mules while they were still in harness. "It may be said that this was cruel," a cavalryman wrote. "Admitted. No one denies that it was cruel. But it was war, and war is cruel."

It was about to become cruel, indeed, for the Union cavaliers. The Confederate cavalry commander, the redoubtable Joseph Wheeler, received reports of the Federal raid on the morning of July 27th, learning first of Garrard's advance south from Decatur and then receiving word of McCook's force near Lovejoy and Stoneman's column heading for Macon. Fighting Joe was heavily outnumbered, having a total of about 6,000 sabers as compared to the enemy's 10,000—but he nevertheless resolved to attack each of the invading columns and destroy them in turn before they could unite. The buglers sounded "Boots and Saddles" and the gray horsemen mounted up, eager for the hunt, having become sick and tired of the muddy, bloody fighting as dismounted riflemen in the trenches around Atlanta. "We entered into the chase like schoolboys in a game of baseball," one Southern trooper remembered.[44]

Within twenty-four hours, Wheeler had overtaken, swamped, and surrounded the closest Federal column, that of the often underwhelming Kenner Garrard. Wheeler sent a blindfolded emissary through the lines to demand the Yankee general's surrender. Garrard angrily refused. "Tell your general that as soon as I get ready I will walk out of here," he huffed. He did get out, though hardly at a walk—it was more of a stampede, the blue riders frantically cutting their way through the Rebel cordon and skittering pell-mell for Decatur and the safety of their own lines. Satisfied with this as a beginning, Wheeler left a single brigade there to bottle up Garrard's force, then led three brigades to deal with McCook, while sending three brigades under Georgia-born Brigadier General Alfred Iverson, Jr., in pursuit of Stoneman.

McCook, whose men pronounced the raid "a picnic" at first, had reached the agreed rendezvous point at Lovejoy's Station on July 29, and there his troopers promptly burned the depot and outbuildings, cut the telegraph wires, tore up a stretch of track—and waited for Stoneman and Garrard, who strangely and somewhat ominously failed to show. Then Wheeler's whooping horsemen descended upon them, sending McCook's panicky column racing for the Chattahoochee River. Little Joe Wheeler, who was said to have fought in more than six hundred battles and skirmishes and had five horses shot out from under him in the course of the war, mounted an attack on the Federal column at Newnan, forty miles southwest of Atlanta, and inflicted almost 1,000 casualties on McCook, who finally got safely across the river on July 30.[45]

Thus had Wheeler's horsemen battered two of the three Yankee columns and sent them, staggering and bloody, back to their corner. But that was nothing compared to what was in store for the glory-hound George Stoneman—who as it turned out would not make it to Andersonville, though he would see the inside of a Confederate prison soon enough. His high-spirited cavalrymen had enjoyed the initial joyride as well, moving without opposition east to Covington and then heading south toward Macon, stopping to loot roadside homesteads along the way. In the little village of Clinton, the rampaging troopers reportedly "stripped ladies of rings and pins, broke open drawers and trunks, and stole silver and plate of every description"—and, in one home, demanded that the mistress of the house surrender the wine from the cellar. Their saddlebags heavy-laden with trinkets and bottles, Stoneman's riders had arrived on the outskirts of Macon on July 30, but were stalled by a combination of the Ocmulgee River (an obstacle he seemed to have no plan for dealing with) and a surprisingly spirited band of local militia.

A false report that a large column of Rebel horsemen was approaching from the south sent Stoneman clopping back northward—where, to his surprise and regret, he ran smack into Iverson's three brigades of Confederate cavalry. Then followed two days of headlong pursuit mixed with occasional running battles along farm lanes and near tiny rural settlements with wonderful country names like Walnut Creek and Jug Tavern and Sunshine Church, where Iverson's troopers all but surrounded Stoneman's frazzled command, the mud-spattered blue riders exhausted and almost out of ammunition. The Northern general, seeing no alternative, ordered two brigades to make a break for it while a single brigade remained behind and did its best to hold off the gray riders. (Stoneman, in the finest "captain-goes-down-with-the-ship" tradition, stayed with the unfortunate contingent of seven hundred men chosen to make a last stand.) In short order, the remaining Federals were trapped and rounded up as prisoners, and one of the two escaping brigades was corralled and wrecked as well.

As his sword was taken from him and his horse led away, General Stoneman, so the story goes, sat down on a log and wept. The old dragoon's bid for glory and fame had come to nothing—instead, he now held the embarrassing distinction of being the highest-ranking Union prisoner captured during the entire war. "Without entering into particulars," he wrote to Sherman from his prison cell in Macon a few days later, "we were whipped." His nemesis Joe Wheeler would have agreed, justifiably gloating in his official report: "Thus ended in most ignominious defeat and destruction, the most stupendous cavalry operation of the war." Wheeler and his deputy Iverson had not only saved the Macon & Western Railroad from destruction, they had also crippled Sherman's cavalry and captured 3,200 troopers, including a major general and five brigade commanders, along with their horses and batteries. Sherman pronounced his own benediction on the raid in a dispatch to Washington that Shelby Foote would call "the prize understatement of the war."

"On the whole," Sherman reported, "the cavalry raid is not deemed a success."[46]

Sherman was understandably disappointed, if not completely disgusted, by Stoneman's disregard of his orders and the failure of the grand cavalry operation—commonly known thereafter as Stoneman's Raid, though it just as well could have been called Wheeler's Rodeo. But the Northern commander was perhaps even more frustrated by the events that would culminate in the halting, sputtering Federal infantry effort at the Battle of Utoy Creek. After the battle of the 28th, Hood had directed that a line be extended outward from the rough circle of defensive works around the city to cover the railroad line toward East Point. William Bate's division of Hardee's Corps was dispatched to occupy and improve this new line, which stretched out from the Atlanta entrenchments on a diagonal to the southwest like the tail of a kite. Meanwhile, Sherman was planning a second effort to lunge with a fresh body of troops for the Macon & Western, the last remaining supply line for Hood's army inside Atlanta.

There was no portion of the army that was fresher and thus better suited to make such a movement than John Schofield's Army of the Ohio. Apart from providing late-afternoon artillery support on July 22nd, Schofield's command had essentially remained on the sidelines during all three of the major battles fought over the previous two weeks. Accordingly, Sherman directed Schofield to advance his troops down the Sandtown Road, cross Utoy Creek, and break through the Rebel line toward East Point. Because Schofield's force was comparatively small—around 12,000 men—Sherman directed that the 14th Corps under Major General John M. Palmer be detached from General Thomas and join Schofield. This would give the bookish Schofield a total of around

Major General John Schofield, commander of the Army of the Ohio. (*Library of Congress*)

30,000 effectives, surely an ample force to sweep aside the thin-stretched Confederates and reach the Macon road. "Major-General Schofield with his own command and General Palmer's corps will move directly on the railroad which leads south out of Atlanta," Sherman ordered on August 4, "and will not stop until he has absolute control of that railroad." He also sent what should have been a noncontroversial dispatch to Palmer, directing him to obey the orders and instructions of General Schofield.

But Palmer, a prickly former Illinois judge and state senator and a delegate to the Republican convention of 1860 that had nominated Abraham Lincoln, took exception to the order. "I am General Schofield's senior," he insisted. "We may co-operate but I respectfully decline to report to or take orders from him." This was surprising and irritating, being flatly incorrect, but the message Palmer then sent to Schofield was almost outrageous: "I will not obey either General Sherman's order or yours, as they violate my self-respect," it read. A hurricane of official correspondence ensued, with Sherman, Thomas, Schofield, and Palmer exchanging almost three dozen dispatches over the next twenty-four hours, back and forth and back again, over the question of who ranks who. At 10:45 P.M. on August 4, Sherman reached a verdict, telling Palmer in no uncertain terms that Schofield "ranks you as major general"—and adding sharply that the railroad "must be gained tomorrow if it costs half your command." The army telegrapher summarized this bizarre command squabble in a dispatch to Washington, reporting: "Nothing accomplished today."[47]

Nor the next day, either. Schofield tried to order an advance, but Brigadier General Absalom Baird of Palmer's corps refused to take any orders from him. Finally receiving what he considered proper orders, Baird moved forward, scattering or capturing a handful of Rebel skirmishers and losing eighty-three men killed or wounded, but then all three divisions halted and—having been ordered by Sherman to reach the railroad if it cost half the command—instead settled down to conduct a "reconnaissance." Sherman, who had intended that the attack commence at 3 P.M. the day before, was incensed at the insubordinate Palmer and his slow-footed soldiers. "I would prefer to move a rock than move that corps," he complained in a dispatch to Thomas. "If an enemy can be seen by a spy-glass the whole corps is halted and intrenched for a siege." Meanwhile, Palmer continued his petty telegraphic argument over the niceties of seniority and the relative timing of various congressional confirmations, and ultimately decided to submit his resignation rather than to have to take orders from John Schofield. The bickering in the Union command and Palmer's apparent "manifest determination not to move toward the enemy" allowed Bate's Confederates an additional two days and nights to fell trees, dig trenches, and strengthen their works in preparation for the coming attack.

The next morning, Schofield—finally giving up on the possibility of any sincere cooperation from the 14th Corps—decided to send one of his own brigades forward against the Confederate position. At midmorning, Brigadier General James W. Reilly's brigade advanced against a stout line of fortifications, complete with thick brush entanglements, log emplacements, and branch-and-briar abatis that brought the advance to a standstill. A blast of musketry then sent the brigade reeling. Reilly's men were thrown back easily, renewed the charge, and were again repulsed. Denied reinforcements, Reilly broke down and cried as he watched his shattered regiments move to the rear.

Thus ended the comparatively minor engagement known as the Battle of Utoy Creek—"a noisy but not a bloody battle," Sherman called it, but a notable one in two respects, neither of them good from the Northern point of view. First, the casualties were perhaps the most lopsided of the campaign—Schofield suffered three hundred killed, wounded, and missing, while the reported Confederate loss was only fifteen to twenty—again confirming the futility of charging carefully prepared defensive works in an effort to gain Atlanta. Second, the little fight and the thorny extension of the Rebel works had halted in its tracks, for the second time, Sherman's attempt to extend the reach of his infantry to the right and gain the last railroad below Atlanta. He was going to have to try something else, and he sent a dispatch to Washington that indicated what he had in mind.[48]

Having failed to destroy Hood or to cut him off, Sherman now resolved to simply batter his adversary—or, at least, the city he defended—into submission. "We keep hammering away here all the time, and there is no peace inside or outside of Atlanta," Sherman reported to General Halleck that same night. "I do not deem it prudent to extend more to the right, but will push forward daily by parallels, and make the inside of Atlanta too hot to be endured." He had, he said, already ordered up large caliber guns to be sent down from Chattanooga, "with which," he bragged, "we can pick out almost any house in town."

"I am too impatient for a siege," Sherman added, and closed: "One thing is certain, whether we get inside of Atlanta or not, it will be a used-up community by the time we are done with it."[49]

Stripped and shelled houses alongside Confederate breastworks and chevaux-de-frise, north of Atlanta. Lumber from some of the houses was used to build the fortifications. (*Library of Congress*)

CHAPTER EIGHT

"A Used-Up Community"

The Bombardment of Atlanta

The bombardment of Atlanta had begun back on July 20, during the Battle of Peachtree Creek, when the young Captain Francis DeGress fired three rounds into the city from his Illinois battery of 20-pound Parrott guns. "The city seems to have a line all round it," Sherman reported to General Halleck in Washington the next day, "at an average distance from the center of the town of the mile a half, but our shot passing over this line will destroy the town, and I doubt if General Hood will stand a bombardment." In the days that followed, as Sherman probed to the right toward boggy Utoy Creek in an effort to break through and deprive Hood of his only remaining supply line, Federal gunners to the east, north, and then west of the town kept up a desultory, random fire, lobbing shells into the streets in their spare time, as it were. Historians would largely dismiss this initial off-and-on cannonade as mere "light shelling," but folks on the receiving end of it had no such perspective. Confederate prisoners taken by the Federals in the days after Peachtree Creek reported that the bombardment had produced "great consternation" among the people of Atlanta. For them, as a local historian wrote, the incessant shelling "was doubtless the nearest thing to hell on earth they ever experienced, before or later."[1]

An artillery bombardment upon defenseless civilians in their homes and shops and churches, sad to say, was not unprecedented in the Civil War. Vicksburg, Mississippi, had been shelled both from the landward side and by Union gunboats during the siege of the river stronghold during the early summer of 1863. Charleston, South Carolina, came under a two-day cannonade in August 1863 by a massive eight-inch Parrott rifle called the Swamp Angel, which launched 200-pound projectiles a range of 8,800 yards. "It would appear, sir," Charleston's defender General P. G. T. Beauregard wrote to the Federal commander, "that despairing of reducing these works, you now resort to the novel measure of turning your guns against the old men, the women and children, and the hospitals of a sleeping city, an act of inexcusable barbarity." And back in December 1862, Union shells had reduced homes to rubble in Fredericksburg, Virginia, in the hours before the great battle there. Robert E. Lee had been outraged. "Those people delight to destroy the weak and those who can make no defense," he fumed. "It just suits them."[2]

Such was the reaction of Generals Lee and Beauregard to bombardments that each lasted only a few hours. But Sherman—who would down the years be accused himself of being a man who delighted "to destroy the weak and those who can make no defense"—would now shell the city of Atlanta day and night for *thirty-six days*. Despite Sherman's postwar notoriety as the man who burned Atlanta and tore his way through the heart of Georgia on the March to the Sea, it is arguably this act that is his most callous and deliberate destruction of civilian life and property. Here, no one could argue that a fire spread unwittingly and got out of control, or that private soldiers had disobeyed their officers' orders or had gone too far in their foraging.

Nor could they credibly contend that the shelling of civilian Atlanta was the result of poor marksmanship, of wayward shots that had missed their targets. Sherman would later assert—lying to the face of no less a moral authority than the Right Reverend Henry C. Lay, Episcopal Bishop of Arkansas—that he had not intended to throw shot at private dwellings, insisting that any overshots were the fault of the Confederates, for putting their lines so close to Atlanta. This was ridiculous, and the reverend said so. The Rebel defensive works, after all, were well more than a mile outside the center of the city. "I reminded him that I was in Atlanta all through the siege, and the shells fell everywhere," Bishop Lay wrote of the meeting. "The hottest fire I had been in was at private houses, and shells struck St. Philip's church." Sherman also justified the bombardment on grounds that the town's inhabitants had fled—"Most of the people are gone & it is now simply a big fort," he wrote to Ellen—but this was untrue as well, and Sherman knew it. Spies and captured Rebels and even newspaper reports, North and South, made clear throughout the month of August that there were large numbers of civilians still in the town—those with civic or other duties; those caring for the wounded or sick or old or very young; those with businesses or property they wanted to protect; those too poor or too frightened to leave; those with Union feeling; those with nowhere else to go. Although thousands had fled the city over the past three months, there were still 2,000, and possibly as many as 5,000 civilians remaining in Atlanta.[3]

Sherman's own field orders and correspondence make plain his true intentions. "You may fire from ten to fifteen shots from every gun you have in position into Atlanta *that will reach any of its houses*," he told Thomas on August 1; and on August 7 directed Old Tom to have 30-pounder Parrott guns sent down from Chattanooga, then put them "into your best position, and *knock down the buildings of the town*." He gave specific direction to subordinates on the positions where batteries could best be placed to "make sad havoc in Atlanta," or, as he wrote in another dispatch, to "*reach the heart of Atlanta and reduce it to ruins*." On August 9, the heavy guns arrived from Chattanooga—three 4 1/2-inch rifled siege guns, not 30-pounder Parrotts, as it turned out—ready to add the weight of their metal to the shellstorm already under way from the 10- and 20-pound Parrott guns already in place. Sherman directed Thomas: "Get your guns well into position . . . let them open slowly, and with great precision, *making all parts of the town unsafe*." Indeed, Sherman specifically warned his artillerists not to be distracted by efforts by the Confederates to divert the Union batteries away from the city itself. "Hood is anxious to draw our fire from the town to their fort at White Hall, which is of no value to us," he wrote to General Howard, and then made sure he was absolutely clear. "Let us destroy Atlanta," he said, "and make it a desolation."[4]

Certain historians have noted, sensibly enough, that the bombardment was permissible under the laws and usages of war, as Atlanta was a "fortified and garrisoned" city that contained military personnel and stores. Other biographers and commentators would make excuses for Sherman, arguing that military targets were interspersed in civilian areas, so of course there was some "incidental" damage. But the military men and matériel of Atlanta escaped the brunt of the bombardment, as Confederate soldiers and their guns took refuge in thick-walled fortifications while the shells "passing over" the lines (as Sherman suggested to Halleck) rained down on Atlanta's unprotected residential and business districts. During the first two and a half weeks of the so-called "light" bombardment, shells struck the Trout House Hotel, the Atlanta Medical College, the Concert Hall, and the Female Institute—each of which housed wounded soldiers. Dozens of homes were struck with solid shot or shell fragments, many catching fire. A cannonball tore away the cornice of S. P. Richards's bookstore, and another entered the back door like an angry intruder and splintered the wooden floor. Also damaged was Bohnefield's Coffin Shop on Luckie Street, one of the few businesses that had been thriving in recent weeks. The Tallulah Fire Company's modest engine house was hit. Several shots struck the Car Shed, and about twenty hit the Western & Atlantic locomotive roundhouse. A large number of the city's churches were struck and suffered damage to varying degrees, including the First Presbyterian Church, the African Church, the Second Baptist Church, the Wesley Chapel—which quite literally had its bell rung by a solid shot—and St. Luke's Episcopal Church, where, as the tale was told, a Bible fell on a live shell "so as to apparently smother it and prevent it from exploding."[5]

Instructed to sight their guns slowly and deliberately, Union gunners aimed for the huge mass of the depot, or sighted on smokestacks or church steeples. There was a certain sport in aiming and firing, without the terror and frantic pressure of an ongoing battle, at stationary targets hundreds of yards away, and the cannonade was a sight to behold, especially at night. "It was an interesting spectacle to watch these fiery messengers sailing over the tops of the trees with their long, curved flight, terminating in a flash over Atlanta," an Ohio soldier remembered. At times, solid shots "failed to keep their equipois, went whirling end over

Sherman leaning on the breech of a gun at Federal Fort No. 7 on the outskirts of Atlanta. (*Library of Congress*)

end, producing a peculiar sound not unlike the puffing of a locomotive. This would bring about a shout from some of the boys, 'All aboard for Atlanta!'"[6]

Officers proudly reported the effect of their shells. "I have the honor to report that at least three houses, two frame and one brick, were destroyed by the fire in Atlanta," a signal officer reported one afternoon. "Our shells burst in the city right and left of brick stack." General Thomas sent a dispatch to Sherman noting that shells fired from the newly arrived 4 1/2-inch siege guns "burst beautifully" inside the city. Some batteries experimented with firing up temporary furnaces and heating up cannonballs in hopes of igniting fires. The effectiveness of these "hot shots" was uncertain, but whether from the red-hot projectiles or from mere explosions, fires started frequently at various points in the town.

Throughout the month of August, Atlanta's volunteer firefighters were kept dashing about the streets to deal with these shell-sparked blazes, large and small. There were devastating fires on Marietta, Alabama, and Loyd Streets; a cotton warehouse burned on Alabama Street; and houses caught fire almost daily. The companies were without their best pump engines, and the cisterns where they typically drew water were dangerously low. The ranks of the individual companies were likewise depleted, with some of their number in the Confederate ranks and others having fled the city with their families, but local citizens, including slaves and free blacks, helped to fight the flames. What was more, the fires, their locations marked by bright flames at night and columns of smoke during the day, made easy targets for Federal gunners. "The firemen found it about as dangerous to go to a fire as it was to go to the front," a reporter wrote. Despite these dangers, the volunteers extinguished the fires or struggled to keep them from spreading as best they could, and newspapers and local histories consistently report that not a single firefighter was killed.[7]

Amid the thunder of the guns, nine-year-old Carrie Berry, encouraged by her father, decided to record the terrible spectacle of the bombardment in the little blank journal he had given her. Carrie was a beautiful young girl who wore ribbon in her hair and a cross around her neck, and was devoted to her parents, her church, and her little sister Zuie. On August 1, she made her first entry in a diary that would provide a clear if sometimes wide-eyed account of the Federal cannonade. "Dear Diary," she began. "General Johnston fell back across the river on July 9, 1864, and up to this time we have had but few quiet days. We can hear the canons and muskets very plane, but the shells we dread. One has busted under the dining room which frightened us very much. One passed through the smoke-house and a piece hit the top of the house and fell through but we were at Auntie Markham's, so none of us were hurt. We stay very close in the cellar when they are shelling." Three days later, on August 3, she recorded a personal milestone. "This was my birthday," she wrote. "I was ten years old, But I did not have cake times were too hard so I celebrated with ironing. I hope by my next birthday we will have peace in our land so that I can have a nice dinner."[8]

But peace, and even a nice dinner, seemed far away in those oppressive late summer days, and the terror of the bombardment got considerably worse before it got better. The most terrible day of the five-week cannonade occurred on August 9, just after the three big long-range guns arrived from Chattanooga. Sherman sent the following message to all three of his army commanders, Thomas, Schofield, and Howard:

DOWNTOWN
ATLANTA
1864
SCALE
0 100 500
Feet
to Chattanooga (138 miles)
Western & Atlantic R.R.
W. & A.R.R. Freight Warehouse
Car Factory
Macon & Western R.R.
to Macon (104 miles)
Broad St. Bridge
Berry House
St. Luke's
Athenaeum
FIVE PTS.
Atlanta Hotel
Concert Hall
Trout House
Masonic Hall
Calico House (Poe's HQ)
African Methodist Church
State Square
Freight Depot
Car Shed
City Hotel
Loyd's Hotel (Washington Hall)
Atlanta Intelligencer
Gate City Hotel
Distributing Hospital (Wayside Inn)
Mayor Jas. M. Calhoun House
Engine House No. 2
Georgia R.R. Locomotive House
Georgia R.R.
to Augusta (171 miles)
Church of the Immaculate Conception
Father Thomas O'Reilly
St. Philip's Episcopal
Central Presbyterian Church
Second Baptist Church
City Hall and Fulton County Court House
John Neal House (Sherman's HQ)
Clayton House (Schofield's HQ)
Trinity M.E. Church
Jas. R. Crew House
Wm. Solomon House
HOUSTON STREET
WHEAT STREET
LINE STREET (NOW EDGEWOOD)
MARIETTA STREET
FAIRLIE
WALTON STREET
POPLAR STREET
LUCKIE ST.
PEACHTREE STREET
WADLEY ST.
MARKET (BROAD) ST.
ALABAMA STREET
HUNTER STREET
MITCHELL STREET
PETERS STREET
WHITEHALL STREET
PRYOR STREET
LOYD STREET
WASHINGTON
GILMER STREET
DECATUR STREET
COLLINS STREET
CALHOUN STREET
McDONOUGH STREET
FAIR STREET (NOW MEMORIAL DRIVE)
to Fair Grounds & City Cemetery
N

"Orders for to-morrow, August 9: All the batteries that can reach the buildings of Atlanta will fire steadily on the town to-morrow, using during the day about fifty rounds per gun, shell and solid shot." The Federal batteries opened in the morning and fired between 3,000 and 5,000 rounds into the streets and houses of the city, all day long. The days of "light shelling" were over. "We have had to stay in the cellar all day the shells have been falling so thick around the house," Carrie recorded in her diary. Reporter Wallace Reed remembered it as "that red day in August, when all the fires of hell, and all the thunders of the universe seemed to be blazing over Atlanta." Despite the sound and fury, the incessant one-sided artillery duel signified, or at least accomplished, absolutely nothing. "From a military standpoint there were no results worthy of mention," Reed wrote. "Nothing was gained by either side."[9]

The next morning, a newspaper correspondent ventured out and surveyed the damage. "The old burgh has fared roughly, and wears as wan and vailed an aspect as you'd see on a winter's day," he wrote, and went on to catalog the damage. "Mangled shade trees, distrought flower beds, topsy-turvy summer houses. Some of the handsomest residences are so altered that their own masters would not know them. Great slices cut out of cornice work; chimneys torn away; roofs gaping with ugly rents and broad seams; trim porticos, where vines and honeysuckles hung in rich festoons, broken and blackened by powder and soot; and gardens, which once glittered with 'lilly, pink and jessmin,' and were enclosed by pretty fencing, as shorn and wicketless as so many bits of waste common."

"The very streets stare at you mournfully and spectrally," the reporter continued. "The breezes . . . roam up and down the broad, bare avenues like unhappy ghosts. The sunshine pours its lonely rays on deserted pavements. . . . And at night the poor stars look feebly down on 'the rocket's red glare, and bombs bursting in air.'"[10]

The citizens pulled up mattresses and slept by their brick chimneys, and many families dug and constructed shelters or "bombproofs" or "gopher-holes" in yards and gardens to provide sanctuary from the deadly, daily storm. An Atlanta resident described these shelters as "holes dug in the earth eight or ten feet deep, and of a desirable width and length to suit the builder, covered overhead with heavy beams, which contained a covering of boards or tin to keep out the rain, and then covered with

Ten-year-old diarist Carrie Berry. (*Atlanta History Center*)

earth from three to five feet deep. The entrance to the small door was dug out in the shape of the letter L, and many persons' lives were preserved by using them as a shield." Both the ingenuity and the spirit of the city's residents made a strong impression on the Confederate commander. "It was painful, yet strange, to mark how expert grew the men, women and children in building their little underground forts," General Hood recalled. "Often mid the darkness of night were they constrained to seek refuge in these dungeons beneath the earth; albeit, I cannot recall one word from their lips expressive of dissatisfaction or willingness to surrender."[11]

Those without cellars or bombproofs made their way to neighbors' shelters, or the rock-walled basement of a flouring mill. "The more furious the firing the bigger the crowd in the basement," one Atlantan would remember. "There was no such thing as a stranger." The men and boys of the city puffed up to show their courage—young lads in the bombproofs tried not to flinch and teased each other when they did. Old women rocked and prayed for deliverance, whispering, "Lord, have mercy on us." But even the stalwart made a break for cover on occasion. "Sometimes dignified and courageous men who affected indifference to the iron hail in the daytime and scorned to join their families underground at night, would tumble precipitately into the family bomb-proof, minus their wearing apparel, when a shell struck uncomfortably close." Most nights the cannon fire was limited in duration, rumbling and then subsiding like so much thunder. "Like an electric storm going over, the shelling seldom lasted more than an hour or so," Sarah Huff remembered, "and the people then went home and put the children to bed."[12]

The Confederates fired back, of course, though not as often or as effectively. "Your sharpshooting is excellent," a captured bluecoat told General Bate, "but your artillery isn't worth a damn." Cannonballs fired from the Rebel works came howling over and sometimes bouncing through the Federal lines. Occasionally a solid shot would "ricochet and go bounding along, clear to the breastworks, knocking down trees in flight and jumping up like a dog who has lost sight of the rabbit he was chasing, and jumps up to get a sight of it again," Union Lieutenant Chesley Mosman wrote in his journal. Members of his regiment measured one of the Confederate shots and found "it was about a foot long and seven and a half inches in diameter and should be about a 64 pounder," he wrote in amazement—he had no idea that there was such a thing. The massive shells, fired from eight-inch guns, were "shaped very much like, and nearly as large, as the common water bucket," according to a reporter who saw one half-buried in the earth near General Thomas's tent. The boys called them anchors, tar buckets, flour barrels, camp kettles. "Look out for that cart-wheel!" they would cry as the shells came screaming in. "Look out for that blacksmith's shop!"[13]

Union regiments posted on the front line rotated out from time to time, though the rear echelon seemed to afford little comfort. "There was no safety or security," Brigadier General John M. Corse reported. "Cooks, grooms, clerks at work in their offices, were as subject to being hit by the random shell or shots as men in the extreme front." Like the Mississippi lieutenant Robert Gill, who worried to his wife about dying on the battlefield with an oath on his lips, men in blue likewise did their best to make themselves ready for what might happen at any moment. "I am trying to be prepared for any event that may happen to me, out here where there is so much danger and men are struck down dead around me every day without a moments warning," surgeon Samuel B. Crew wrote to his family back in Ohio. "I am not without hope and I feel that my Savior is precious to my soul and trust that I may meet him and my angel children in the 'Better Land' beyond old Jordan's stormy waves. I try to pray, but I fear not enough." Familiarity breeds contempt even for death itself, however, and in time, soldiers hardly looked up from their card games as a cannonball whistled overhead. "Try it again, Johnny, a little lower," they would say, and then calmly shuffle and deal another hand.[14]

The five-week cannonade killed and injured a substantial but unknown number of civilians inside Atlanta. Diaries, newspapers, and later history books were filled with hearsay stories or uncorroborated accounts of the sad demise of unnamed victims—"a mother and child have been killed"; "one white woman wounded, one negro man killed and another wounded"; "a lady ironing some clothes in a house on Pryor Street was struck by a shell and killed," and so on. Some deaths, however, were well-documented and widely reported, such as the horrible death of J. F. Warner and his six-year-old daughter, both killed by a direct hit on the bed where they were sleeping. The shell struck the child and killed her instantly—one witness said she lay dead "with a smile on her face"—and Warner himself had both legs severed. "I shall not live," he said quietly. "I shall soon be with Suzy in heaven." He survived only a few minutes, asking for paper to make out a meager will; then he called for a glass of water and slipped quietly away.

Another well-known victim of a Yankee shell was the popular free black barber Solomon Luckie, who was standing near the corner of Whitehall and Alabama Streets when a shell struck a nearby lamppost, ricocheted, and exploded. Passersby carried the severely injured Luckie to the Atlanta Medical College, where Dr. Noel D'Alvigny amputated his leg in hopes of saving him—but he had lost a lot of blood, "never rallied from the shock, and died in a few hours." Poor Sol Luckie was buried in an unmarked grave in the City Cemetery, its location lost to history.[15]

Estimates of the total casualties suffered by the people of the city vary widely. A reporter wrote that the total number was "601 wounded and 497 killed"—almost certainly an inaccurate and inflated number. No cemetery interment or hospital records exist, though two sources quote an Atlanta doctor who reported in mid-August that there had been 107 limbs amputated in the city during the course of the shelling. In a thorough analysis of news reports, diaries, and other primary sources, historian Stephen Davis concludes that "some twenty civilians were killed or mortally wounded, with an estimated one to two hundred more residents injured." This estimate, which may be rather conservative given the tens of thousands of solid and exploding shells fired into the city, squares with one given by bookseller S. P. Richards in his journal. "It is said that about twenty lives have been destroyed by these terrible missiles, since the enemy began to throw them into the city," he wrote on

August 21. "It is like living in the midst of a pestilence, no one can tell but he may be the next victim."

And still the thunder of the cannons continued. Henry Watterson, writing for the *Augusta Daily Constitutionalist*, reported the situation on August 24—the thirty-sixth day of the bombardment. "Meanwhile, affairs in the city remain in their usual condition," he wrote. "Shells all night, shells all day, shells for breakfast, dinner and tea, shells—'For all hours and all sort of weather.'" Then he turned to poetry, no doubt reflecting the mindset of all those trapped inside the beleaguered Georgia city:

> *Tell me ye winged winds,*
> *That round my pathway roar—*
> *Is there not*
> *Some favored spot*
> *Where Yankees shell no more.*[16]

As the shells arced overhead, day and night, and the citizens of Atlanta huddled in their bombproofs or went about their business as best they could, the soldiers in the trenches adapted as well. The war had changed, not just over the past three weeks but the past three years, from a spectacle of glorious, well-dressed charges, regimental colors flapping in the breeze, to a contest of endurance fought by men huddling in rifle pits and log-and-mud gun emplacements. In the war's early days, soldiers on both sides had complained that hiding behind breastworks was dishonorable, even cowardly, and that digging ditches and building fortifications was degrading work not fit for a soldier. Now they dug with a will, improving their works with picks and shovels, or sometimes using tin pans and bayonets to scratch deeper into red Georgia clay that somehow managed to be cowhide-tough when dry and slick as grease when wet. On August 7, a Wisconsin soldier wrote home that he had spent the past two days working on the twentieth set of fortifications his regiment had built since Snake Creek Gap—that is, twenty breastworks over seventy-five miles in less than ninety days. "We have been working our way nearer Atlanta, and hard work it is," he wrote.[17]

The ring of Confederate fortifications around Atlanta that had so impressed Sherman's engineer Orlando Poe had been a year in the making. In the summer of 1863, shortly after the fall of Vicksburg, the State of Georgia's chief engineer, a Maine-born former railroad builder named Lemuel P. Grant, had received a wire on the subject of possible fortifications for the city of Atlanta. He promptly replied with a plan to conduct a survey and construct a system of parapets and artillery emplacements ringing the city. Grant moved quickly to secure equipment, requesting one hundred picks, one hundred shovels, and fifty axes from the arsenal at Augusta, and to impress slave labor from surrounding farms and plantations—offering twenty-five dollars a month or one dollar per working day (paid to the owners, of course, not to the workers themselves). On August 4, 1863, less than three weeks after the summons to Grant, construction was under way on the Atlanta defenses.

The project was largely complete three months later, though adjustments and improvements would continue until the following summer. The finished fortifications crinkled in an erratic, ten-mile ring around the city, an average of one and a quarter miles from the Five Points intersection in the heart of Atlanta. The line of defenses consisted of seventeen carefully situated redoubts connected by lines of trenches and rifle pits. The works generally consisted of a revetted parapet with an open trench in front, the earth walls shored up by logs or lumber shipped from local sawmills or taken from torn-down houses that had stood in the way of the fortifications. Yankee besiegers attempting to storm Colonel Grant's carefully devised earthworks—which had been made even more impenetrable by the Confederates in late July—would have to make their way across several hundred yards of open ground cleared to create crisscrossing fields of fire before struggling through as many as four rows of abatis—an obstacle made up of felled trees with sharpened branches or stakes pointed toward the enemy—along with occasional rows of *chevaux-de-frise* or, as the soldiers called them, "sheep racks"—logs bristling like porcupines with sharpened stakes.[18]

The bluecoats dug their own trenches, at points no more than a couple of hundred yards from the Confederate works across the way, the ground in front honeycombed with shallow rifle pits perhaps fifty yards in advance of the main line. (One Federal soldier wrote in a letter home that he had been posted so close to an enemy vedette that he could hear the Reb blowing his nose.) The soldiers, blue and gray, settled in to wait and, from time to time, to kill each other. "We ride, walk, sit down, write, eat, sleep, and do everything else under fire," a *New York Tribune* reporter wrote. This was true on both sides of the lines, and a Rebel cannoneer described the month of August in the trenches:

> The "ping" and "spit" and "sputter" and "drop" of bullets about you, the shriek and gobble and flutter of shells, all became monotonous, mere matters of routine in which interest and excitement flag, and life becomes a bore. . . . There were no assaults on either side worth speaking of. We took their steady shelling philosophically and now and then returned it. We took the rain and sun and heat and mud and the short rations as old soldiers learn to do. No books, no newspapers, no writing material, only here and there a pack of cards or improvised checker board and checkers, the only steady diversion being the killing and wounding of a man now and then, or a visit to another part of the line, or very rarely a trip into town.[19]

The soldiers kept their heads down, of course—a hat raised above the parapet on a ramrod would quickly be shot full of holes—but they no longer flinched or dodged when a bullet came whistling or a shell whining into (or more often, beyond) the trenches. It seemed pointless to do so. "It was a common saying among the boys," a Confederate veteran would recall, "that a shell could hit you just as well where you wasn't as where you was." Despite this fatalist view, some who felt they had more to lose—those, for example, whose terms of service were about to expire—did cringe from time to time. One afternoon, as cannonballs from the Rebels were "crashing through the trees in such a way as to make nervous persons very uncomfortable," Union Brigadier General Richard W. Johnson rebuked a German-born captain on his staff who was dodging and ducking his head. "Mein Gott, Sheneral," the captain replied, "my time vil pe out in a veek, and I don't vount to pe kilt py acshident."[20]

Defiance and dull routine led to indifference to mortal danger, even carelessness at times. "We go right along about our duty or business in camp regardless of the bullets," an Illinois lieutenant wrote. "Its our duty and we can't afford to think of it. Still, when some fellow puts a hole in your hat or coat, or a shell knocks the frying pan out of your hand and scatters your campfire in every direction, one has to stop and think a little. At least he thinks whether he stops or not. But its no use moving for you might move right in the way." Such near misses made for good stories to pass the long hours. Chaplain George Pepper saw two soldiers sitting one on each side of a stump, upon which sat their can of hot coffee. Along came a shell and exploded, passing between the two without a fragment touching either and sending their coffeepot flying. "Their surprise and astonishment over, they began to curse the Rebs for spoiling their breakfast," Pepper said. An Ohio corporal told of the narrow escape of a soldier in his company. A ball came zipping over the works, through several tents before striking a man named Henry Shepherd on the chest. "We all thought the way he yelled that the ball had gone through him," the corporal wrote. "We ran to him and he was holding his hand on his breast, and still kept yelling. We got him to take his hand down and the flattened bullet dropped to the ground. It had not even penetrated his clothes."[21]

Countless others were not so fortunate. The Buckeye regimental surgeon Dr. Samuel Crew composed a letter late one evening, the paper resting on his operating table in the still hours near midnight as he wrote. "Still hours—Ah! no! we have no still hours here—for I hear the ring of guns on the skirmish line, and four wounded men have been brought in since dark. And so it has been day after day for more than three months. . . . I am tired of it—worn out and exhausted almost, and so are our men. . . . But when this cruel war will end the Lord only knows. I could give you many heartbreaking cases of deaths on the battlefield and in the Hospital if I had time and space in this letter. . . . What a sad, savage, unchristian and inhuman thing war is."[22]

There were examples daily all along the line of cruel injustice, not only of untimely Death, but of a cold-eyed, heartless Fate, which saw that previously lucky men who had emerged without a scratch from frontal assaults and bayonet charges and blasts of cannon fire were suddenly dropped by a shot they never heard while boiling coffee or playing cards or writing letters home. The killing was, of course, completely senseless, and made not a whit of difference one way or the other to the battle or the campaign or the war. "Picket firing in the war is in my opinion simply legalized murder," a Rebel orderly sergeant wrote. "The losses sustained in this way can never affect the final result. 'Only a picket or two now and then' does not count 'in the news of the battle,' but in some little cot on the mountain the shadow of lifelong grief falls just as heavily on the lonely wife or mother as if the victim had hallowed by his life blood a victory that changed the fate of a nation."[23]

Among those killed, though "not affecting the final result," was Lieutenant Andrew Jackson Neal of the Marion Light Artillery, whose home stood right across from the Atlanta City Hall. Word of the young man's death reached his family, then taking shelter forty-five miles away in Zebulon, a few days later. Others were wounded, including a significant number of men of lofty rank—"Parson" J. A. J. Lightburn, for example, and "Old Grits" Bate, hit in the knee by a minié ball, and Grenville Dodge, the Iowa banker and civil engineer who would later play a major role in the building of the transcontinental railroad. Dodge was struck by a bullet that glanced off his forehead, knocking him out cold and out of the campaign, though he would return to duty in December and would live a long life filled with accomplishments until his death in 1916.

Yet despite the heartbreak occasioned by these losses for family and friends, the soldiers in the ranks grew accustomed, even callous, to the periodic slaughter. "Mother," a young Rebel private confessed in a letter home, "I am a heep hearder hearted than I ought to be but I hav seen so many men killed and wounded till I dont care for it no more than if it was a chicken. I do want to go home so bad I cant rest well." An Illinois lieutenant recorded in his journal that during a duel with the a battery across the way, "one poor fellow 'lost his head'—that is, a solid shot struck his head and it totally disappeared. Someone said he had no further use for it anyway." A blue regiment passing by a graveyard saw a man sprawled on the ground, suffering from the August heat and apparently "gasping his last." A cold-hearted wit commented as they passed that the fellow was lucky "in getting sun struck so near good buryin' facilities."[24]

Soldiers reminisced over fallen comrades, speaking both good and ill of the dead. "If, as sometimes happened, a soldier had been killed near the skirmish-line while looking on, it was unanimously voted that he was 'a damned fool' and 'it served him right,'" an adjutant wrote; after all, "there were opportunities enough for a man to be killed while in the strict line of duty, without poking around where he had no business. Not that these men were heartless, but they regarded death as a necessary and familiar incident to soldiering, and they had grown into the habit of putting their best face upon their surroundings. It would have been a spiritless army if the troops had gone into mourning over every comrade lost."[25]

As the long, hot days of sharpshooting and shelling continued, Sherman spent his time studying maps, issuing orders, writing letters, and riding along the lines. "I regard the war as hardly begun," he told Ellen. Some days he accompanied General Thomas, stopping off at batteries or observation points to watch the effects of the long-range bombardment. He still felt his customary impatience, of course—after all, the tightly wound Ohioan could hardly sit still at the dinner table—but he kept up an uncharacteristic display of calm as the days of tactical inertia turned into weeks. A visiting lieutenant colonel who spent a day or two with the general that August found him to be "cool as a cucumber," notwithstanding the prevailing nervousness and apprehension among those who had expected to see the inside of Atlanta weeks ago. In due time, Sherman assured his companion, "Atlanta will fall into our hands like a ripe apple." And until that time, and despite the lack of any apparent result from the ceaseless sharpshooting and overarching cannon fire, Sherman had no intention of easing up on either the gray army or the city they defended.

"Let us give these southern fellows all the fighting they want and when they are tired we can tell them we are just warming to the work," he telegraphed to General Grant. "Any signs of a let up on our part is sure to be falsely construed and for this reason I always remind them that the siege of Troy lasted six years and Atlanta is a more valuable town than Troy. We must manifest the character of dogged courage & perseverance of our race."[26]

"*Amid the confusion and the destruction*, the loneliness and the weariness, there rises one inspiring figure," a Southern reporter wrote during what Sherman called the "quasi siege" of Atlanta. "Early or late, or by the branding camp-fire or the sun's first ray, may be seen a tall spare form, with a single arm and a single leg, a youthful face and a beaming eye in the line of the front. It is Hood."

Hunkered in his Atlanta entrenchments lo these many days, John Bell Hood hardly considered himself trapped, nor was he despondent. He had made no official complaint and indeed seemed to take little notice of the shelling of the city, though a large number of shots fell near his headquarters on Whitehall Street. (Some histories would later report, erroneously, that Hood sent a message to Sherman demanding that the bombardment be stopped, but in fact he did no such thing—saving his indignant protests for later, as we shall see.) Nor, though his army had not taken the offensive since Ezra Church, had he given up on his plans to defeat the Yankee hordes now clawing at the gates. Indeed, now that Joe Wheeler had whipped the bulk of Sherman's horsemen, he saw a new possibility to force Sherman to relinquish his stranglehold on the city.[27]

"Since our late success over the enemy's cavalry," Hood wired to Jefferson Davis, "I hope now to be able, by interrupting Sherman's communications, either to force him to fight me in position or to retreat." Davis agreed with the proposal, having tried for most of the spring and early summer to convince Johnston to make a similar strike with his cavalry upon the Federal supply line. (Johnston had wanted an attack to be made on Sherman's railroad line, but refused to deploy his own cavalry to do it.) Still, having placed Hood in command and having urged him to fight for Atlanta, Davis now fretted over the casualties that inevitably resulted from doing just that. "The loss consequent upon attacking him in his intrenchments requires you to avoid that if practicable," he told Hood. This backhand rebuke of Hood's tactics was arguably undeserved. In all three of his so-called "sorties" against Sherman, the sad-eyed Southern commander—despite his reputation as a man who would charge the gates of Hell—had carefully devised plans designed to attack the Federals while they were *not* in their entrenchments; but in each case circumstances (or, in the case of Ezra Church, a disregard of Hood's orders) had resulted in an assault on fortified lines.[28]

Now, instead, he would send Wheeler's cavalry on a mission to snip Sherman's all-weather supply line—the 138-mile-long Western & Atlantic Railroad running to Chattanooga—and thus deprive the Federal armies of vital stores and ammunition. Wheeler set out on August 10 with 4,500 troopers, about half of Hood's total mounted force, and they made quick progress, striking the railroad north of Marietta and tearing up track at Acworth and Tilton. Elsewhere, however, the Western & Atlantic proved to be considerably less vulnerable. Stoutly built fortifications and blockhouses protected important bridges and crossings, and garrisons of soldiers were posted at key points along the line.

On August 14, arriving outside the junction town of Dalton, where the East Tennessee & Virginia Railroad branched off the W&A to the northeast, Wheeler sent forward a message demanding the immediate surrender of the 400-man Federal garrison there. Their commander, a Missouri colonel by the name of Bernard Laiboldt, was unimpressed. "I have been placed here to defend the post, but not to surrender it," he tersely replied. Laiboldt's force fell back from the town and took refuge in a hilltop fortress prepared for just such an eventuality, and the colonel got off a wire to Chattanooga seeking assistance. Help for the defenders soon arrived in the form of 2,000 soldiers under Major General James B. Steedman, brought south from Chattanooga on freight and flatcars—including the 14th Regiment USCT, or United States Colored Troops.[29]

Sherman's massive army at the gates of Atlanta included no black troops, for the frivolous but determinative reason that the army commander lacked confidence in their soldierly qualities. "Is not a negro as good as a white man to stop a bullet?" Sherman was asked around this time, and he had answered: "Yes, and a sandbag is better; but can a negro do our skirmishing and picket duty? Can they improvise roads, bridges, sorties, flank movements, &c., like the white man? I say no." There were exceptions to the rule, he acknowledged, so he was thus willing to use black soldiers "as far as possible, but I object to fighting with 'paper' men." Units of black soldiers in Sherman's department, the Military Division of the Mississippi, were thus kept not only off the front lines—"in the rear with the gear," as the latter-day army saying goes—but very far from it, posed on garrison duty at various points along the railroad in north Georgia and Tennessee. But now, summoned from Chattanooga to deal with a mounted Confederate threat to the precious thread of iron that supplied the great blue armies a hundred miles to the south, the 14th Regiment not only found themselves in combat but acquitted themselves most nobly indeed.

Steedman got his force aligned—four regiments in all, including what the soldiers called the "14th Colored" on the left—and brought them forward shortly after dawn on August 15. Wheeler's troopers resisted the advance at first, but soon began to give under the pressure of the advancing infantry. Steedman, concerned about how his untried black regiment would respond under fire, sent a staff officer over to the left to "look after" the black soldiers. The aide returned minutes later. "General, you needn't have any fears," he reported, "they're holding a dress-parade over there under fire." Pushing forward through briars and small outbuildings under a steady fire from Wheeler's troopers, the men of the 14th flushed out the gray horsemen and maintained their alignment as if they were on the drillfield. "The fight was short, and not at all severe," their commander Colonel Thomas J. Morgan later wrote. Still, he said, "to us it was a great battle, and a glorious victory." As the Confederates withdrew and galloped off to the north, the soldiers of the 14th USCT—former slaves and cooks and field hands and teamsters and washermen—re-formed and marched through Dalton, and their white comrades in the 51st Indiana Regiment cheered them as they passed.[30]

Thus rebuffed at Dalton, Wheeler continued his ride northward, sending back to Hood flowery reports with inflated descriptions of his achievements. The Rebel horsemen rounded up 1,000 head of beef cattle to be driven south to feed the Atlanta defenders, and made several small breaks in the railroad, but did no damage that could not be repaired in a day or two. The Confederate raiders continued on past Chattanooga and Knoxville, where they crossed the Tennessee River and then turned west toward Nashville. Back in Atlanta, Sherman received reports of the sporadic attacks on the railroad and the raid's continuation northward into the mountains. He was heartily glad to see Wheeler go. The hardscrabble mountain country of East Tennessee, Sherman wrote in a dispatch to Washington, is "a good place for him to break down his horses, and a poor place to steal new ones." Hood had hoped and expected that Wheeler would wreck large portions of the railroad and be back in just a few days; instead, Fighting Joe did the line little harm and would not return to the Army of Tennessee until October.

Joe Wheeler's August raid was therefore at the same time a success and a failure—a sound military concept endorsed by the commanding general and the Confederate president and a terrible mistake. The cavalry, of course, not only supplied to the army mounted riflemen, lightning raids, and protection for vulnerable flanks and rear areas, but also provided critical intelligence-gathering capability—a general's "eyes and ears," as historians often note—and Hood, in sending Wheeler riding off northward, also sent him riding out of the Atlanta Campaign. With his army largely cooped up in the Atlanta fortifications and Sherman free to maneuver beyond the horizon, Hood had deprived himself of half his cavalry and the capable Wheeler at a time when he needed them most of all.[31]

With Wheeler gone with a large portion of Hood's mounted force, Sherman soon decided to take one last shot with his own cavalry at Hood's own supply line, the Macon & Western Railroad south of Atlanta. To lead this second mounted effort against the M&W, Sherman selected Brigadier General Judson Kilpatrick, a scraggly, bowlegged Jerseyman known inside and outside the ranks as a scoundrel and a crook. Having recently returned to active duty after being wounded in the thigh back in May, Kilpatrick was a detestable hypocrite who preached temperance but drank whiskey, an unapologetic rake widely known to keep company with mistresses and prostitutes even in camp (he was a recent widower but had carried on just the same while his wife was yet living). Major James Connolly called him "the most vain, conceited egotistical little popinjay I ever saw." He was, as another officer put it, "a frothy braggart, without brains and not overstocked with desire to die on the field"—yet he was known to be careless with the lives of his men, who disliked him intensely and had long ago dubbed him "Kill-Cavalry." Sherman was well aware of the cavalryman's peccadilloes and his overaggressive bluster—"I know Kilpatrick is a hell of a damned fool," he said—but it seemed to him that a general with more swagger than caution might be just the type to lead the attack.

With horses freshly shod and five days' rations in their saddlebags, Kilpatrick's troopers mounted up for their foray south on August 18, presenting what one witness called "their usual combination of Gypsy and Don Cossack." Before setting out, a rousing order from their commander was read to the men, "some parts of it written in the 'Thirty centuries are looking down upon you' style," an Ohio captain remembered—and thus inspired and instructed, off they went. Supplemented by two brigades from Garrard, the mounted force numbered 4,500 sabers, larger than any of the three columns that had come to grief in late July.[32]

Kilpatrick's troopers reached the town of Jonesboro, twenty-three railroad miles south of Atlanta, on the afternoon of August 19. "Damn the Southern Confederacy!" Kilpatrick crowed. "I can ride right through it!" His men set to work pulling up rails and burning the depot, but both the fire and the Federal troopers got out of hand. Roaming squads of cavalrymen torched the courthouse, the jail, a number of stores, and a handful of houses; others looted the hotel and several shops, making off with treasures ranging from silverware to tobacco to ladies' dresses. As night fell, the blue horsemen went into camp just east of town, cooking supper and lighting up newly appropriated cigars as the regimental band of the 92nd Illinois played "Yankee Doodle" and "Come Johnny Fill Up the Bowl." Just beyond, the little railroad town of Jonesboro, one among the raiders would remember, was "a sea of fire, and the heavens lurid with the flames of the burning buildings."

But the party wouldn't last. Before midnight, Kilpatrick was attacked by a substantial force of Rebel cavalry under Brigadier General W. H. "Red" Jackson and a brigade of Arkansas infantry under Brigadier General Dan Reynolds, who had been sent south by train that morning to help protect the railroad. Deploying his men in line of battle, Kilpatrick found himself assaulted in front and threatened on both flanks as a heavy summer thunderstorm rolled in and a hard rain began to fall. The Federals fell back and managed to slip out of the tightening Rebel cordon around the town. After a brief but sharp engagement at Lovejoy's Station the next day, Kilpatrick's column fled in a wide loop, riding east, then north, then back west to the Union lines at Decatur.[33]

Kilpatrick's cavaliers arrived back at their camp near Atlanta at 3 P.M. on August 22, all of them exhausted and most bareheaded, having

Brigadier General Judson Kilpatrick, "a hell of a damned fool." (*Library of Congress*)

slumped over asleep in the saddle and lost their hats. The column had made a complete circuit of Atlanta, covering 140 miles in eighty-seven hours—the past forty-eight of which were spent in fight or flight or both. Northern papers praised the raid and the raiders, who "fought with splendid pluck," had not an hour's sleep in three days and nights, and subsisted on nothing but coffee and hard bread. "The charge of Federal steel was irresistible," wrote a *Cincinnati Commercial* reporter whose hearsay account was based largely on the glory-stories of the returned horsemen. "The heads and limbs of some of the Rebels were actually severed from their bodies," he wrote, "the head of the rider falling on one side of the horse, the lifeless trunk upon the other." But the report acknowledged that "the results of the raid are not as complete as we would wish."[34]

Not as complete as Sherman would wish, either. Kilpatrick himself reported promptly and proudly that he had destroyed four miles of the Macon railroad at Jonesboro and another ten miles at intervals elsewhere, predicting that the line would remain out of commission for at least ten days. The welcome intelligence, however, proved to be the sort of baseless overstatement all too common in cavalry reports—especially Kilpatrick's vainglorious statements, which were said to be "great in the 'most glorious charges ever made,' 'sabering right and left,' and such stuff." The general had been criticized as having "consistently demonstrated an aversion to the unpleasant truth"—and so it was with this report of his raid on Jonesboro. The next morning, heavy-laden trains were seen chuffing into Atlanta from the south over the tracks of the supposedly wrecked Macon & Western, quite as if Kilpatrick had never been gone at all. Sherman was furious, but somehow not surprised, and no doubt would have agreed with a staff officer who said that the cavalry was "good for nothing but to run down horses and steal chickens."[35]

"I became more than ever convinced," Sherman later wrote, "that cavalry could not, *or would not*, work hard enough to disable a railroad properly, and therefore at once resolved to proceed to the execution of my original plan." That plan, which he had conceived the month before and had discussed in official correspondence for the past two weeks, was to leave the Atlanta trenches and make a broad sweep to the south to cut the Macon railroad—not with a small portion of his force, but with six of the seven army corps.[36]

The month of August had been a brutal, sweaty, bloody grind, but despite the bombardment and partial investment of the city and the series of cavalry attacks intended to bring about their discomfiture, the heavily outnumbered Confederates were holding. "Rest assured that all is well here," correspondent Henry Watterson wrote. "Pin your faith not only to Providence, but to the excellent condition of affairs. There is no demoralization, there is no want, there is no lack of ability to meet the enemy and defeat him. Look cheerily upon the campaign as it moves forward, and never cease to hope. We are resolved to conquer or die in these ditches."[37]

In 1864, as in other presidential election years before and since, perception was reality—and as the month of August wore on with no news of further progress, the perception was that Sherman's legions had been roughly handled by the "one armed, one legged, fighting devil" John Bell Hood and were now hopelessly bogged down, as if the Georgia clay were quicksand. "Sherman is checked before Atlanta," the *Chicago Tribune* reported in early August, one among a host of American and foreign papers that had reached a similar conclusion. "The world has never seen anything in war so slow and fatuous as Grant's recent movements, except it be those of Sherman," W. H. Russell wrote in the *London Gazette*. "Each is wriggling about like a snake in the presence of an ichneumon [an Egyptian mongoose]. They both work round and round, now on one flank and then on the other, and on each move meet the unwinking eye of the enemy, ready for his spring and bite." Nor did the British editor have any respect or hope for the bombardment. "As for shelling! Will they not learn from history? Then they will know that they cannot shell an army provided with as powerful artillery as their own out of a position."[38]

And so it seemed. Hood's outnumbered Army of Tennessee had suffered mightily in the three battles at the gates of Atlanta in late July, but they had also apparently stopped Sherman in his tracks. To most observers—many, admittedly, eager to find fault at this point with the increasingly unpopular president and his war policy—it seemed that Sherman was stymied, his grand strategy now reduced to making feeble, ineffectual railroad raids with his cavalry while petulantly shelling women and children cowering inside Atlanta. The newspapers focused on what Sherman's army had *not* accomplished instead of what it had. "Sherman has neither occupied the centre, the circumference, nor, indeed, any part of the defences of Atlanta," the pro-Southern weekly *London Index* insisted, asserting that the Northern commander had been "completely defeated by General Hood on July 22." The *Richmond Whig* gloated that "Sherman's whole army is 'sicklied o'er with the pale cast of thought,' in view of the dread alternative of a retreat or an attack upon the intrenched Army of Tennessee."[39]

The consequences of this apparent stalemate reached far beyond the trenches outside Atlanta and Petersburg. By early August, Northern anti-war sentiment, appalling casualty figures, and the gloomy military outlook in both Georgia and Virginia had combined to make the present administration's prospects for victory in the November election almost nonexistent. "Mr. Lincoln is already beaten," Horace Greeley, the influential editor of the *New York Tribune*, wrote on August 18. "He cannot be elected. And we must have another ticket to save us from utter overthrow." Other prominent political minds agreed, and said so to the president. "I told Mr. Lincoln that his re-election was an impossibility," New York political boss Thurlow Weed told Secretary of State William H. Seward, adding that "unless some prompt and bold step is taken, all is lost. The people are wild for peace." A number of Republican leaders considered asking Lincoln to withdraw in favor of another nominee—Grant, or Benjamin Butler, perhaps, or even Sherman—though others believed that such a midstream shift would be unwise, if not disastrous.

Everywhere there were doubters, even in the headquarters tents outside Atlanta. "There is a growing feeling in the army that McClellan will succeed Mr Lincoln," Ohio Colonel Emerson Opdycke wrote. "Many think Mr L unequal to the position. . . . Had he been a great leader the Country would have been delivered before now." Still, Opdycke had not lost hope. "My faith in God is strong that lasting good to the human race *must* result from such a terrible war. Such a sea of blood ought to regenerate any people."

There had been a flicker of light in early August from Alabama, of all places, where sixty-three-year-old Admiral David Farragut—lashed to the rigging of his flagship and crying "Damn the torpedoes! Full speed ahead!"—led a fleet of eighteen warships in a spectacular naval battle that resulted in the capture of Mobile Bay. But the glow of this small and distant triumph quickly faded, and the good news was quickly lost in the Northern papers amid grim reports from the battlefields of Virginia and column after column of casualty lists. "The tide is setting strongly against us," Henry J. Raymond of the *New York Times* warned Lincoln on August 22. "Nothing but the most resolute and decided action on the part of the Government and its friends can save the country from falling into hostile hands." Raymond predicted that New York, Pennsylvania, Indiana, and even Lincoln's home state of Illinois were likely to go Democratic, some of them by huge majorities. "You think I don't know I am going to be beaten," Lincoln told a friend around this time, "*but I do* and unless some great change takes place *badly beaten.*"[40]

On August 23, just after Weed and Raymond delivered their gloomy predictions, Lincoln drew out a sheet a paper from his desk and scrawled a note in his careful, gently sloping hand. "This morning, as for some days past, it seems exceedingly probable that this Administration will not be re-elected," he wrote. "Then it will be my duty to so co-operate with the President elect, as to save the Union between the election and the inauguration; as he will have secured his election on such ground that he can not possibly save it afterwards. A. LINCOLN." He folded and sealed the document and took it to the cabinet meeting that afternoon, where—in a curious procedure—he had each member of the cabinet place his signature on the back, though none knew what it said or why they were being asked to sign it.[41]

The Democrats were ebullient, smelling blood as they headed toward their convention, set to begin on August 29 in Chicago. The first order of business was the platform, prepared under the direction of former Ohio congressman and notorious Copperhead Clement L. Vallandigham. One of the resolutions—the so-called "peace plank"—declared, "as the sense of the American people, that after four years of failure to restore the Union by the experiment of war . . . justice, humanity, liberty, and the public welfare, demand that IMMEDIATE EFFORTS BE MADE FOR A CESSATION OF HOSTILITIES . . . to the end that at the earliest practicable moment peace may be restored on the basis of the Federal Union of the States." A problematic document, that. In addition to declaring the war a "failure" and deriding an epic three-year national effort fueled by the blood of thousands as a mere "experiment," this was political baby-splitting of the highest order—an effort to appease both the Peace Democrats who sought an immediate end to the conflict and the War Democrats who insisted that the Union be preserved, lest all the bloodshed be for nothing. (Notably absent from the statement of Democratic priorities was any mention of slavery or emancipation.) The party had given its opponents a ready campaign slogan, and Republicans, running under the banner of the National Union Party, promptly branded the Democratic platform "the Chicago Surrender." The Democrats had explicitly declared the war a failure—and what Lincoln needed more than anything was solid evidence to the contrary.

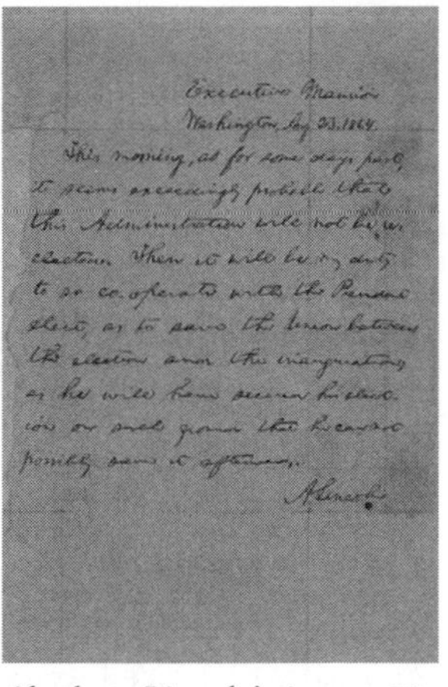

Executive Mansion
Washington, Aug. 23, 1864.
This morning, as for some days past, it seems exceedingly probable that this Administration will not be re-elected. Then it will be my duty to so co-operate with the President elect, as to save the Union between the election and the inauguration; as he will have secured his election on such ground that he can not possibly save it afterwards.
A. Lincoln

Abraham Lincoln's August 23, 1864 memorandum. (*Library of Congress*)

With the platform set, the convention moved to the next order of business—the nomination of the Democratic candidate. All indications were that the delegates would nominate Lincoln's former general-in-chief George B. McClellan, who would do his best to secure the soldier vote while running on a platform of reconciliation, if not capitulation. A brass band played patriotic airs in the huge "wigwam" erected for the proceedings, and though there was polite applause for "Yankee Doodle," the newspapers reported that the crowd went wild when the band played

"Dixie." Such were the stakes at the Chicago convention as it proceeded through floor debates in preparation for the nomination vote. The atmosphere was electric, with the party certain that they were about to put forward the man who would soon become the next president of the United States. As Sherman would later write, "Success to our arms at that instant was a political necessity; and it was all-important that something startling in our interest should occur before the election in November."[42]

In Washington, despite the clouds that hung over him, there were indications that, deep down, Abraham Lincoln still held out hope for victory, both personally and nationally, in the election and the war. On August 24, a Wednesday, his friend the reporter Noah Brooks, had called on the president to bid him farewell before traveling to Chicago to cover the Democratic convention.

"Good-by," Lincoln said, shaking the young man's hand. "Don't be discouraged. I don't believe God has forsaken us yet."[43]

CHAPTER NINE

"I Have Atlanta in My Hand"

The Battle of Jonesboro, August 31–September 1

"*The shelling still goes on,*" the *Augusta Daily Constitutionalist* reported on August 23.

> "The murder of the innocents" bids fair to be one of the most poignant tragedies of modern times—night and day it is unabated, one continuous explosion of forty pound spherical case balls. Can you imagine anything more brutal than the bombardment of a city, crowded with poor people, who are unable to get away, and are forced by their poverty to remain and suffer? Bear in mind that this bombardment is not pretended even by the enemy to bear upon the military situation one bullet's weight. There are no stores to destroy, the soldiers are all in the trenches, and the thousands of shells thrown into harmless dwellings cannot possibly effect the reduction of the city. The motive is one of petty spite, the spite of cowards, who dare not attack our lines and wreak their disappointment upon women and children.[1]

The Northern soldiers didn't see it that way, of course, regarding the shelling as a legitimate effort to shake loose a determined opponent, though they surely recognized the consternation among the city's residents. "The rebs stick like wax to the city, but they will have to git in the end," a New York corporal wrote to his wife. "Our corps has advanced our lines within three hundred yds of there forts and are shelling the city evry day with 20-pound Parrots. It must make the ladies of that city nervous, I should think."[2]

Carrie Berry's diary reflected the terrifying monotony of the continuing bombardment. "When I woke up this morning I thought the hole town would be torn up," she wrote on August 18. Almost every day that month, she made similar entries: "We had shells all night"; "We have had shells all day"; "We have ben frightened twice to day by fire"; and the like. One morning, Carrie and her baby sister were playing on a platform outside their house when a shell came whistling past. "It made a very large hole in the garden and threw the dirt all over the yard," Carrie wrote. "I never was so frightened in my life. Zuie was as pale as a corpse and I expect I was too. It did not take us long to fly to the cellar."[3]

The Federal cannonade continued into the last week of August, the exploding shells sparking a number of fires in town. "Within the past four and twenty hours as many as nine buildings have touched the ground, and are now visible only in smouldering walls and charred ruins," Henry Watterson reported as the destruction continued at various points around the city. A cannonball struck the Presbyterian Church and passed right through the pulpit. P. E. McDaniel's cotton warehouse caught fire and burned along with five hundred bales, a spectacular blaze, as did a wooden building near the State Road Machine Shop. "Not brave enough or strong enough to drive Hood from Atlanta, Sherman is trying to burn the city," an indignant Confederate captain wrote, though the scattered flames admittedly made for striking visual theater. "These conflagrations are very beautiful," Watterson acknowledged. "They mingle uniquely with the explosion of the shells."[4]

But then on August 25, after five weeks of hellish, deadly thunder, all of a sudden—it stopped. The next morning, the day broke clear and bright and the sun rose over a city as quiet as Monday chapel. Not even a rifle shot broke the stillness, and the air was free of powder-smell and battle smoke. The explanation for the silence appeared to be more than any Atlantan dared hope.

The heavily shell-damaged home of Ephraim Ponder, sometimes misidentified as the "Potter House." (*Library of Congress*)

The Yankees had not merely ceased firing. They were gone.

Rebel pickets crept forward and found the Federal trenches yawning empty, the camps beyond abandoned. Only northwest of town, covering the railroad bridge across the Chattahoochee River near Vinings Station, did it appear that the bluecoats were still present in force. Gun emplacements were vacant, with grooves in the red dirt where the cannon trails and wheels had been; and at some points, planks had been nailed, ladder-fashion, to tall pine trees to afford lookouts a view of the city. The Federal works, according to a Georgia captain, were found to be even heavier and stronger than the Rebel fortifications, though "badly policed and very filthy." Fly-swarmed refuse, discarded papers, broken chairs, ammunition boxes, blankets and whatall were strewn along the miles of abandoned breastworks, as were occasional sutler's stores of flour, bacon, and all manner of other foodstuffs—suggesting that Wheeler's cavalry had been somewhat less than perfectly successful in their effort to break the Western & Atlantic Railroad and choke off Sherman's supplies. Ragged bands of butternut soldiers marveled at the abandoned abundance and picked through the litter-strewn camps gathering trinkets and treasures, some of them worth having and some not worth a damn. "The boys had a merry time reading Yankee love letters which were left in their entrenchments," a Confederate correspondent wrote. "There were all kinds of letters from the friends, relatives, and sweet-hearts of the ceruleans, and I must confess I spent yesterday, while on picket, quite an interesting day, in learning the art of love-making."

Pickets returned from the deserted Union lines and reported discovering scraps of paper stuck up on trees with what one described as "all kinds of nonsense" scratched on them. "Don't follow us, if you do you will catch Hell," one such note read. "Goodbye Johnny Reb, we'll see you later," said another.[5]

Curious civilians ventured out into the streets, exchanging congratulations on their survival of the bombardment and the apparent departure of the Federals. "The feeling of relief experienced when it was ascertained beyond peradventure that the Yankees had entirely abandoned nearly all the works from which the city had been so mercilessly bombarded, exhibited itself on every countenance," the editor of the *Appeal* wrote. Some residents even made their way out to the Federal lines to take a look. "I had been hunting Yanks, but nary a Yank did I find," a young lady named Mollie Smith remembered years later. "Alas, they found me, to my sorrow."[6]

It was difficult to know what to make of the vacant fortifications across the way. Throughout the month of August, rumors, unreliable reports and outright lies had spread among civilians and Confederates in Atlanta. One resident recorded the existence of a new species of prevaricator in the embattled railroad town—the so-called "siege liar," who distributed information, the more farfetched the better, ever confident of its truth despite an absence of evidence. "Do you know that Sherman is going to open fire with three hundred cannon all at once?" one such rumormonger offered.

"Great heavens," another citizen said. "Is it possible? How do you know?"

"I don't know," came the reply, "but it seems to be well understood that it is a fact."

Every day, or even multiple times a day, such rumors were started: that there would be an armistice of sixty days; that James Longstreet or Richard Ewell or even Robert E. Lee himself was coming south from

Virginia with 30,000 reinforcements; that Sherman had demanded surrender by a certain hour or he would wipe the town out entirely; that Hood had given Sherman an ultimatum to withdraw his troops or face destruction. "Ten thousand rumors are current, and many believe them all," wrote Hardee's adjutant W. L. Trask. And now that the Yankee besiegers ringing the city had disappeared like a dove in a stage illusion, no one knew what to think. Henry Watterson recorded the various opinions on the night of August 26. "It is a plan of assault," he wrote. "It is a preparation for retreat. It is a flank. It is merely a pause. It means everything. It means nothing."[7]

Some assumed that the Federals, starved of supplies and short of ammunition, had thrown in the sponge and were retreating. This notion was "rather contrary to common sense, yet many believed it," an Arkansas private recalled. "The scales have turned in favor of the South, and the Abolitionists are moving to the rear toward their own homes," a bullish Rebel captain recorded in his diary. "Thank heaven for this and for the gallant soldiery who so nobly have fought against overpowering numbers." There were skeptics amid the optimists, however. "It was rumored that the enemy was retreating and it is now known that they have deserted their camps around the city and are going *some*where but what is there design it is hard to tell," Samuel Richards wrote in his journal. "I fear that we have not yet got rid of them finally, but that they have some other plan in view to molest and injure us." While some among the citizens and Confederates celebrated the Yankee withdrawal, Richards dug his bombproof an extra three feet deep and built a barricade of dirt-filled boxes.[8]

"Atlanta is again quiet," the *Constitutionalist* reported on Sunday, August 28. "After more than four weeks of constant bombardment, one can now walk the streets of the 'Gate City' without fear of death or bodily harm. Terrible has been the fiery ordeal through which she has passed, but the beautiful Sabbath morning she smiles even in her ruins. It is the smile of proud defiance, for no vandal footprint has yet marked her streets." In the ring of works outside the city, the gray soldiers relaxed, no longer under fire, and enjoyed the first real rest they had had in months. Major General Samuel French rode between the lines and marveled at the tangible evidence of the intensity of the rifle and shellfire. The dry grass and brush were clipped short, mowed like stubble in a freshly cut field, and he noticed trees, some three or four inches in diameter, that had been cut through by musket balls as if felled by an axe. In an open field between the opposing rifle pits, one brigade picked up five thousand pounds of lead balls and bullets. "The ground was literally covered with them—oxidized white like hailstones," French wrote.[9]

Those gray soldiers not on duty—and not scavenging, sleeping, or sinning—gathered that morning for church services. A Presbyterian preacher from New Orleans named Thomas Markham delivered the sermon to one of the pewless congregations, and a Mississippi sergeant would remember the lesson as one of the most eloquent he had ever heard. Markham was a brave, noble chaplain who had on one occasion during the late bombardment continued his preaching amid incoming shellfire, standing bolt upright even as his congregation of soldiers cowered and scattered.

This Sunday, at last, was quiet, and the pastor took as his text, Isaiah 53:3: "He is despised and rejected of men; a man of sorrows, and acquainted with grief."[10]

Sherman had not retreated, of course, nor was he truly gone. "A beautiful Sunday morning," Illinois Lieutenant Chesley Mosman wrote in his diary that same day. "Look out for Uncle Billy, Johnny, for its just like him to choose Sunday for some movement."[11] As the citizens of Atlanta gathered in their churches and rejoiced at, or continued to pray for, their deliverance from the foe, Sherman was in the midst of executing his best and boldest move of the campaign.

A "grand movement," the Ohio commander had called it, and it was one that he had been planning for some time. Back on August 10, he had wired General Grant of his intention to "leave a corps at the railroad bridge, well intrenched, and cut loose with the balance to make a circle of desolation around Atlanta." The intended target of this looping, right-hand swing was the railroad town of Jonesboro*—sixteen

*During the Civil War era, Jonesborough was properly spelled with "ugh" at the end; the name was shortened in 1893 to "Jonesboro."

miles due south of Atlanta as the crow flies, though twenty-three miles along the winding route of the Macon & Western Railroad. But just as Sherman was about to put this plan in motion, Hood had sent Wheeler's cavalry galloping off into north Georgia. Sherman therefore postponed the movement, deciding instead to give Kilpatrick's horsemen a chance to cut the road and save the infantry the trouble. Within a day of Kilpatrick's return from his futile raid and the resumption of rail traffic along the Macon & Western, however, Sherman had dusted off what he called "the former plan" and directed his chief subordinates to prepare for the movement. The Union army had come at Atlanta from the north, the east, and the west, resulting in major engagements being fought on three sides of the city; now they would complete the circle and thereby spark a battle to the south.[12]

This time, Sherman intended to leave no doubt as to the sufficiency of his force; this would be no pinprick railroad raid or wayward march of an undersized portion of the army. He would take with him six full army corps and two divisions of cavalry, "60,000 men, reduced to fighting trim," he said. Surplus baggage and heavy wagons were sent to the rear, along with any sick or lightly wounded men still in the ranks. The heavy guns that had pounded Atlanta were quietly rolled back under cover of darkness, their emplacements filled with limbs and brush. Staff officers and scouts gathered information on all available roads southwest and due south of Atlanta; maps were completed showing the country from Utoy to Red Oak to Fairburn to Fayetteville to Jonesboro. The telegraph wire was interrupted and gathered in; Sherman would keep in touch with the single corps left behind by means of mounted couriers. The commanding general first moved his headquarters near the Chattahoochee railroad bridge, where his engineer Captain Orlando Poe had been ordered to lay out a line covering the bridgehead, and then southward near Utoy Creek in preparation for the massive flank movement. Orders directed that the strictest secrecy be kept—conversation with enemy pickets, normally a common occurrence along the line, was now strictly forbidden.[13]

The "movement round Atlanta by the south" commenced on August 25 with the withdrawal of Slocum's 20th Corps to Poe's line along the Chattahoochee, covering the railroad bridge. The men of Thomas's

Army of the Cumberland, posted north of Atlanta, then crept back from their trenches that same night, followed by Howard's Army of the Tennessee, and then Schofield's Army of the Ohio, which hit the road next day. "All well thus far," Sherman reported to Halleck in Washington on August 26. "I have moved the Twentieth Corps to the Chattahoochee bridge, where it is intrenched, and with the balance of the army am moving for Jonesborough on the Macon road. If Hood attacks he must come out, which is all we ask."[14]

Spirits were high in the blue columns as the movement began, the Northern soldiers stepping out lively, glad to be out of the trenches and on the move. The long lines of marchers snaked out of the dense woods and into open country, moving west and then south of Atlanta, the rolling landscape with its late summer pastures, orchards, and cornfields a far cry from the north Georgia jungle they had cut their way through two months earlier. There were occasional culinary pleasures—corn for roasting, sweet potatoes in abundance—and various sights and curiosities along the way, including "several good looking women, and a negro with six toes," according to one regimental historian. With nine days' rations (including fresh beef) and a seemingly "unlimited amount of ammunition" in the wagons, the veteran soldiers traveled light, "stripped of everything except the clothes we wore," one bluecoat recalled. This wasn't exactly true, of course: spades and coffeepots (perhaps their two most precious possessions, apart from their guns and tobacco) dangled from knapsacks or belts and gave the column "a rather tinkerish aspect." And an occasional luxury item could be seen—a sergeant with a pipe clenched in his teeth; a corporal with a jar of molasses; a captain carrying slung over his shoulder a cane-bottom chair, which he sat on during rest-halts as if on a porch back home. "Every man seemed to know that a great crisis was approaching, and each nerved himself to do his particular best," one of the marchers remembered.[15]

Major James Connolly had recently written of the Federal army's high morale and the soldiers' remarkable blend of looseness and toughness. "A difference between this army now and a year ago is very perceptible," he observed. "A year ago, when our men were marching toward a heavy musketry fire, you could see that they felt nervous, and there would be a slight shade of anxiety on most faces; their looks would be turned toward where the fire was heaviest, as if to penetrate the dense forest and see what fate had in store for them; but now our columns move toward the heaviest fire, the men laughing, singing, whistling, making jocular remarks about the Johnnies, nobody straggling, no cheeks blanched; not that our men fear *death* less than they used to, but they have learned by experience that of the hundreds of thousands of bullets that are fired, but very few hit anybody." They hadn't been paid in weeks, he noted, but it was no matter: "we don't *need* money down here—don't need *anything* but men, muskets, ammunition, hard tack, bacon, and *letters from home*."[16]

Even so, the marchers took advantage of the passing country to supplement their needs and wants. "Our men are living high on the products of the land," an Ohio sergeant wrote. "Chickens, hogs, cattle, sheep, geese, turkeys, corn, flour, meal, potatoes and everything eatable are brought in by the quantity. Soldiers have consciences, but they make very little use of them." These hard-handed appropriations were troubling to some of the more straight-laced officers, including the pious general O. O. Howard and Sherman's chief engineer Captain Poe. "It is perfectly pitiable to witness the distress of the people through here, and I pray God it may never be my duty to see the like again," the latter wrote to his wife. "A great many of our soldiers are acting very badly, robbing and plundering." Poe did what he could to stop the looters and scroungers, but met with little success. "My attempts to stop this thing are but a small & feeble effort, when we regard the great number of those who either wink at it or openly encourage it." To him, it was hardly necessary to "lend this additional cruelty to a war already bloody and sanguinary without parallel."[17]

As they marched—an "endless river of men," according to one wide-eyed observer—Lieutenant Mosman pictured their red-haired commander somewhere in the lead. "I suppose 'Crazy William' is now out in front, watching his chances for an opening that he can take advantage of, or somewhere pacing back and forth with his hands under his coat tails and his eyes on the ground at his feet in deep cogitation over the next move," he said. "He don't care for anybody or anything for his but his Army, and nothing attracts his attention that has not some relation to it, or to the Rebels in front of it. He is long, lank, lean and hungry looking; wonderfully independent and self contained, asks no advice from nobody and keeps his own counsel."[18]

Indeed, a witness with him at the time would depict Uncle Billy much like the young lieutenant imagined him. Accompanying the great, glittering blue column, a reporter spotted Sherman riding with a small escort, though he almost overlooked the famous commander entirely. "The face is one I should never rest upon in a crowd, simply because to my eye there was nothing remarkable in it, save the nose, which organ was high, thin, and planted with a curve as vehement as the curl of a Malay cutlass," the newspaperman wrote. Other features caught the attention: the well-worn uniform, "bordering on a hazy mellowness of gloss"; the reddish hair and beard; the eye, "bounding like a ball from one object to another, neither piercing or brilliant"; and of course the hat, "a simple felt affair with a round crown and drooping brim." Again the often high-strung Sherman seemed to be without a care. "Though I looked for and expected to find them," the witness wrote, "no symptoms could I detect that the mind of the great leader was taxed by the infinite cares of a terribly hazardous military *coup de main*. Apparently it did not lie upon his mind the weight of a feather."[19]

Sherman was at ease, as well he might be, his advance opposed from time to time only by isolated handfuls of scattered and scattering gray cavalry. What was more, the weathervane seemed to be pointing North, so to speak. Apart from a brief shower on the 26th, which served to cool the marchers without miring the roads, the late August days were dry and clear—"hot but otherwise very pleasant," Sherman would recall. On a wide front moving south and then turning east like a gate, the three-pronged Federal advance arrived at the Atlanta & West Point Railroad, which ran southwest through West Point, across the Alabama line and then on to Montgomery, on August 28—the Army of the Ohio at the hinge, just a few miles south of East Point; the Army of the Cumberland in the center at Red Oak Station; and the Army of the Tennessee on the outside at Fairburn. Union cavalry had previously made minor breaks in this line, often referred to in these parts as the "Montgomery railroad," but Sherman wanted to make sure once and for all that its useful life was at an end. He gave detailed instructions for regiments to line up and dislodge the track rail by rail, burning the ties,

Sherman ordered the railroads to be destroyed around Atlanta by burning the ties and bending and twisting the rails. (*Library of Congress*)

heating the iron rails until they were soft and then twisting them into useless curlicues—"Sherman's neckties," or "Mrs. Lincoln's hairpins," the soldiers called them. "Let the destruction be so thorough that not a rail or tie can be used again," he told General Thomas.[20]

After-the-fact critics nitpicking Sherman's every decision would later suggest that this effort was unnecessary—after all, the Atlanta & West Point had been lightly used in recent months, with most supplies arriving in Atlanta on the Macon & Western; and besides, a single corps could have been left behind to do the work, allowing the remainder to keep moving. But too many times in recent weeks had Sherman been assured that a railroad line had been broken, only to hear the taunting whistle of a locomotive just days or even hours later. This time, there would be no doubt. On August 29, tens of thousands of Union soldiers labored to render Atlanta's rail connection to Alabama a complete ruin for a full twelve-and-a-half-mile stretch. "The railroad was utterly wrecked," an Ohio sergeant recalled. "Nothing was left, except the roadbed, and even that looked exceedingly disconsolate." The soldiers were looking rather ill-used themselves after their long, hot day in the demolition gangs. "Perspiring like old soakers, the boys used their blackened and rusty hands to brush the great drops of sweat from face and neck and breast until they were a sight to behold," all smeared a sooty black as if they had been embracing "unwashed camp-kettles and frying pans." They laughed at each other, then cleaned up as best they could and prepared for the resumption of the march the next morning. "Men in good spirits, expecting a fight or a foot race," an Illinois colonel recorded in his diary.[21]

An early reveille woke the bluecoats on August 30, and by seven o'clock they were again in line of march, bearing down in three separate columns on the Macon & Western Railroad, Hood's last remaining railroad supply line. Farthest south, Howard's Army of the Tennessee converged around midafternoon at Renfroe Place, a plantation about midway between Fairburn and Jonesboro—but the parched column found no creek or other water source nearby, so Howard ordered that they push on to the Flint River, another six miles ahead and just two miles short of Jonesboro. Resuming the march, the dry-throated soldiers arrived at the shallow Flint late in the day, with John Logan's 15th Corps in the lead. Fleeing Confederate horsemen attempted to slow the blue advance and fire the Flint River bridge behind them, but a detachment of Kilpatrick's cavalry dashed forward, shooed away the Rebels, and doused the flames. Using the bridge and other crossing points upstream and down, all three of Logan's divisions crossed to the eastern bank by sundown and deployed in the failing light along a low ridge west of Jonesboro. The bluecoats could just make out the somewhat charred railroad village before them, just a half mile distant, with the tracks of the M&W also in view, running on a north-south line through the town. An unknown number of Confederates manned a line of fortifications before them. The Federals took up a strong position and began digging entrenchments, preparing to meet the attack they were sure would come in the morning.

Sherman's engineer Captain Poe wrote to his wife Eleanor from his camp outside of Jonesboro on August 30. "We have not had any hard fighting yet," he said, "but fully expect to have a battle to-morrow, for the enemy will certainly contest our attempt to effect a lodgment on the Macon Road."

His chief General Sherman—though he, too, surely realized that a battle was imminent—was supremely confident in the ultimate result.

Approaching the Flint River that evening, Sherman turned to General Thomas, riding quietly next to him, and made a pronouncement that, if not yet true, was about to become so.

"I have Atlanta as certainly as if it were in my hand," he said.[22]

At his headquarters in a two-story mansion on Whitehall Street—actually, not *in* the big white house; the Confederate commander had given that over to his staff and pitched his tents in the yard—John Bell Hood had been gratified by the news of the empty Federal trenches, and he had reason to be optimistic. After all, his army had in the last thirty days stopped cold the Union advance at Utoy Creek, defeated four cavalry attacks—Stoneman's, McCook's, Garrard's, and Kilpatrick's—on the Macon & Western Railroad, held fast against a round-the-clock bombardment, and now Wheeler was sending reports from north Georgia that his cavalry had destroyed twenty-five miles of Sherman's rail supply line. For these reasons, Hood initially may have been hopeful that the departure of the Yankees signaled a change for the better—but he wasn't naïve, and he wasn't stupid.

Observers and critics down the years, perpetuating the "Old Woodenhead" tradition, would assert that Hood was downright giddy at the bluecoats' departure from their horseshoe-shaped lines around Atlanta, even putting words of foolish rejoicing in his mouth. ("Sherman is starved out! We have won!" one historian said in writing lines that Hood never spoke; another asserted that Hood reported a "great victory" to Richmond, when he did no such thing.) General Hardee, who by then detested Hood and had turned from reliable to resentful, claimed in his report that Hood "believed the enemy to be retreating for want of supplies." Other accounts would record that hoop-skirted ladies were brought up by rail from Macon to join in the victory celebration—though the source for that particular tall tale was Sherman himself. The fact is that once the initial elation of the empty Yankee trenches wore off, no one truly believed that the Federals were retreating. Within a couple of days, even the newspapers were carrying reports on possible enemy movements south of Atlanta. ("The latest reports yesterday afternoon were to the effect that the Yankees were advancing eastwardly from the West Point road, in two columns, by different roads, in the direction of Rough and Ready, on the Macon Railroad," the *Appeal* reported on August 29.)[23]

In reality, Hood responded quickly and cautiously to news of Sherman's disappearance. Receiving word of the empty trenches early on August 26, he ordered his remaining cavalry under Red Jackson to locate the missing blue columns and directed Pat Cleburne, holding the extended line of fortifications toward East Point, to "push out your scouts and ascertain what the enemy is doing." By the following afternoon, Hood had determined that the Federals, while gone from their lines west of the city, still held their position out toward East Point; and that an enemy column was advancing toward Fairburn, seventeen miles southwest of the city. Plainly, Sherman was not retreating, and Hood did not delude himself into thinking that he was. "From his preparations," he wrote to Braxton Bragg a few days later, "I was convinced that [Sherman] intended a movement in force upon my left or to my rear upon the Macon railroad."

Still, as the one-legged Southern commander tried to make sense of the scraps of information coming in from Jackson's undersized cavalry force, the fact remained that he had no idea of the strength of the enemy force, or of its destination. No one else knew, either—William Hardee and Stephen D. Lee, in fact, were likewise floundering about trying to determine the enemy's intentions. As historian Stephen Davis wrote in defending Hood's deliberate reaction to the Federal movement, "there is a vast difference between knowing where the enemy is and what he intends to do." Deprived of half his cavalry and charged with defending not only Atlanta but a twenty-five mile stretch of railroad to his south, Hood was doing his best—but his army was not large enough to protect Atlanta, East Point, Jonesboro, and all points in between. Under the circumstances, he would have no choice but to wait until he determined where Sherman was headed, and then try to meet him there. There were a number of possibilities: East Point, Rough and Ready, Jonesboro, Lovejoy's Station, or even a point farther south, like Griffin.

Hood began massing forces to his left, preparing them to move southward out of the city to head off the Union threat. Apart from that, he would have to wait. "To take the offensive I would have been compelled to have hazarded battle against a labyrinth of field-works over a very broken country, and in any event I could not have hoped for more than a partial success," he told Bragg. "I determined to await further developments." He would not have to wait long.[24]

On August 29, Hood's chief of staff, Brigadier General Francis A. Shoup—he of the abandoned "Shoupades" along the banks of the Chattahoochee—recorded in his journal that the enemy "appear to have a large force of cavalry, artillery, and infantry, moving in the direction of Jonesborough and Rough and Ready, on the Macon railroad. The general commanding, in his opinion, has taken all necessary precautions, and made such disposition of his forces as to prevent either of the above-named places from falling into the enemy's hands." Actually, not yet he hadn't. Hood had sent no additional troops to Jonesboro, and by his own admission underestimated the size of the force threatening the Macon road, supposing it to be two or perhaps three corps instead of six. Even on August 30, confusion reigned as to Sherman's target. Hardee, who would later claim that he warned Hood to prepare for a massive attack against Jonesboro, reported to Hood around 1 P.M. that the enemy was moving against him at Rough and Ready. Given discretion to move troops in that quarter however he thought best to cover East Point and Jonesboro, Hardee stayed put. For his part, Hood believed that there was no large force advancing on Jonesboro; though by midafternoon, he was convinced otherwise. He immediately summoned Generals Hardee and Stephen D. Lee to his headquarters in Atlanta for a council of war, instructing them to leave their commands under arms and ready to move at a moment's notice.[25]

The locomotive *N. C. Munroe* picked up the two Confederate corps commanders around sundown and brought them up to Hood's headquarters. At the council of war, Hood ordered Hardee to take two of the three army corps—Lee's, from East Point, and Hardee's own, from Rough and Ready—down to Jonesboro. There, as early as possible the next morning, they were to attack the Federals west of the town and "drive them, at all hazards," into the Flint River. Hood would remain in Atlanta with the corps of Alexander Stewart (who had by then recuperated from his slight wound at Ezra Church) and the Georgia militia, in case the movement south of the city was a diversion intended to cover for an attack on the city. The attack against the Federals at Jonesboro—one final "sortie"—would be, as Hood later said, "the last hope of holding on to Atlanta."[26]

Again it was General Hardee whom Hood would entrust with command of this critical operation, and some in the ranks, including Hardee himself, may have been surprised that he was still present to lead it. Having played a major part in the two fruitless assaults at Peachtree Creek and Bald Hill, and then having witnessed a third botched attack at Ezra Church, Old Reliable had decided back in early August that he had had enough and sent a wire to Richmond requesting to be relieved of command. "I rely upon your kindness to relieve me from an unpleasant position," he wrote to Jefferson Davis. The president responded promptly, expressing his regret and imploring Hardee to remain. "Your country needs every effort of all her sons," he wrote, adding: "You can most aid our cause in your present position." Hardee stood fast and renewed his request, whereupon Davis strengthened his appeal to the general's sense of duty. "I now ask, is this a time to weigh professional and personal pride against the needs of the country, or for an old soldier to withdraw the support he can give the public defense from the place it is most wanted?" Thus chastised by the chief executive a second time, Hardee decided to remain for the present—fate having in store for him yet another battlefield debacle.[27]

By the time Hardee boarded the engine in Atlanta for the clattering ride back south, the men of his corps, under the temporary command of Patrick Cleburne, were already on the march for Jonesboro. Initial hopes that the movement might be made by rail had been quickly dashed, as there were too few boxcars and flatcars to carry the troops. That meant yet another dozen-mile overnight movement for the gray soldiers, and it would prove to be, in the words of one Rebel general, an "exceedingly fatiguing march." The night was hot and humid, the men bone-tired and water scarce. Frequent halts had to be called, and soldiers dropped in their tracks and slept right in the dusty road. "The roads were bad and narrow, the horses of the guns and mule teams of the wagons, much reduced from the great scarcity of corn and forage, were scarcely able to carry their loads," General Arthur Manigault remembered.[28]

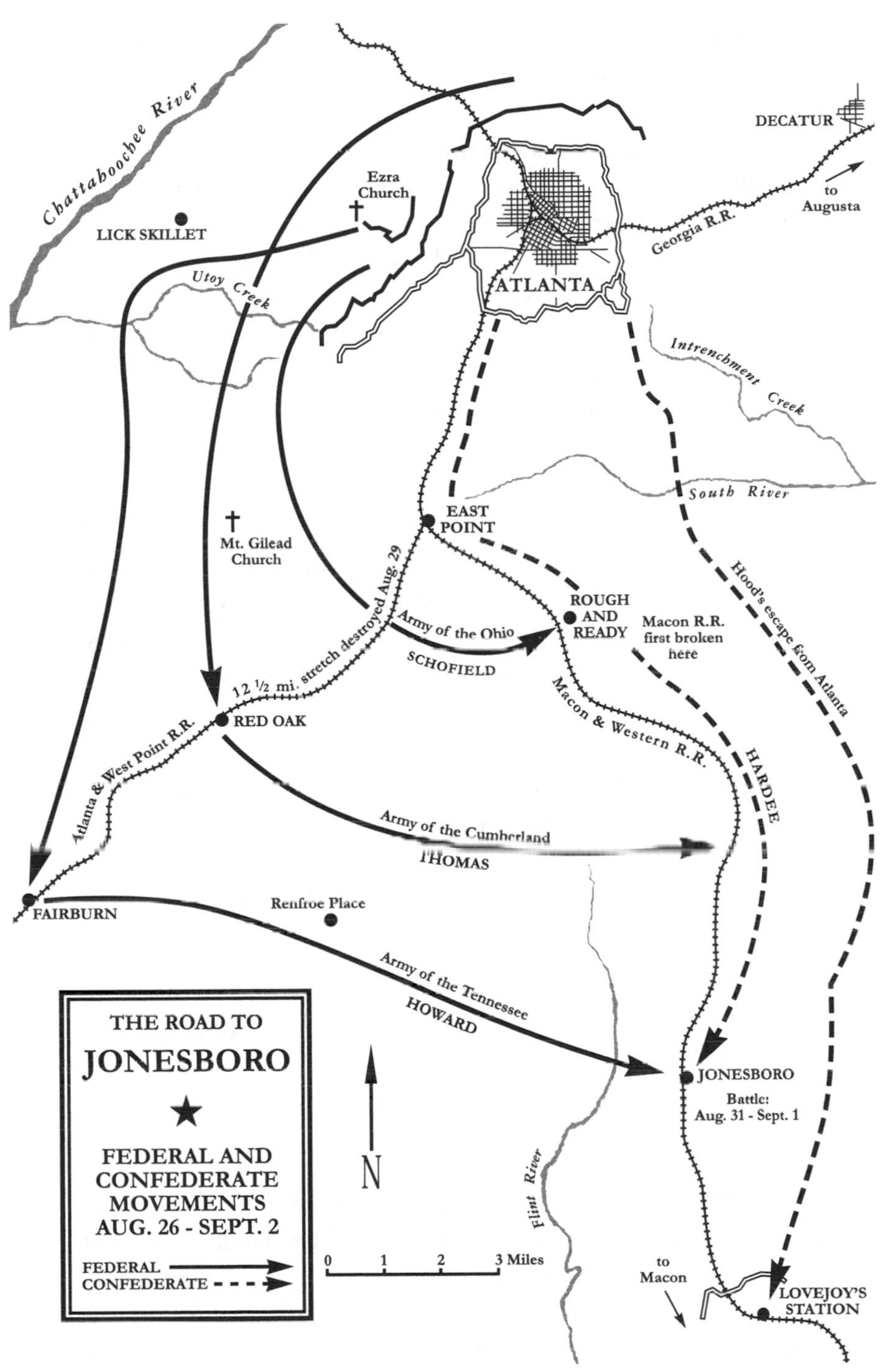
Chattahoochee River
LICK SKILLET
Ezra Church
Utoy Creek
ATLANTA
DECATUR
to Augusta
Georgia R.R.
Intrenchment Creek
South River
EAST POINT
Mt. Gilead Church
12 1/2 mi. stretch destroyed Aug. 29
Army of the Ohio
SCHOFIELD
ROUGH AND READY
Macon R.R. first broken here
Hood's escape from Atlanta
RED OAK
Atlanta & West Point R.R.
Macon & Western R.R.
HARDEE
Army of the Cumberland
THOMAS
FAIRBURN
Renfroe Place
Army of the Tennessee
HOWARD
THE ROAD TO
JONESBORO
FEDERAL AND CONFEDERATE MOVEMENTS AUG. 26 - SEPT. 2
FEDERAL
CONFEDERATE
N
0 1 2 3 Miles
Flint River
JONESBORO
Battle: Aug. 31 - Sept. 1
to Macon
LOVEJOY'S STATION

With the march already "most tedious and annoying," the relief column was delayed and the march extended when Cleburne discovered a body of Federals obstructing his planned route southward. Intended to arrive overnight in time for a dawn attack in the morning, Cleburne arrived with Hardee's Corps around 9 A.M. on the 31st, with Lee's Corps still trailing out somewhere behind. It was 1:30 P.M. before Lee's last three brigades filed into position. Late launching the attack at Peachtree Creek and late again after the night march that opened the Battle of Atlanta, it was plain that through no fault of his own, Hardee would be tardy yet again. At Jonesboro, Old Reliable would be launching his early morning attack in the middle of afternoon.

"The march during the night had been toilsome in the extreme to troops who had not been out of the trenches for thirty days, and daylight revealed a wearied and jaded column, with ranks considerably diminished by straggling during the night," Major General Patton Anderson later reported. "Although the most diligent exertions were made by the officers of all grades to prevent this evil, their efforts were but partially successful. The darkness of night, the dense woods through which was frequently marched without roads, the want of shoes by many, and the lack of recent exercise by all, contributed to induce a degree of straggling which I do not remember to have seen exceeded in any former march of the kind." A Louisiana soldier later wrote of barefooted soldiers leaving bloody footprints behind them, recalling that "fully half of them were straggling when we arrived at last on the battlefield."[29]

Such was the pitiful condition of the hobbling band of Southern scarecrows now expected to drive the well-fed, well-rested, dug-in Federals "at all hazards, into Flint River."

The little trackside town of Jonesboro, population 1,600, would later be made famous as the fictional land of Tara, the O'Hara family plantation imagined by Margaret Mitchell to be a rather rough five-mile wagon ride from the depot. Known as Leaksville in the quiet days before the railroad, the village was renamed for railroad pioneer Samuel G. Jones, who had helped to survey the route back in the late 1830s. Just like the quiet, peaceable residents of dozens of other sleepy hamlets across the nation, or both nations, the citizens of Jonesboro found that their hometown had by happenstance become a desirable strategic objective and therefore a target. The unfortunate whistle stop had suffered much in recent days, a majority of its buildings having been destroyed by gallivanting Union troopers ten days earlier. "It has been a very pretty town," one soldier observed as he passed through, "but there is a look of Desolation on it now that is pitiful." Now, as the four-month campaign for Atlanta drew to its close, it appeared that Jonesboro and its few remaining people would suffer again, the dot on the map now marking a decisive collision point between two armies struggling for a possession of a city miles to the north.[30]

As the sun rose on the last day of August, blotted by a silver curtain of mist, O. O. Howard expected the enemy to attack him at any moment. They *had* to attack him, he thought. His lead elements were now just a few hundred yards from the railroad, which he could reach with artillery and even rifle fire from that distance. "The enemy is shoving troops down here with great rapidity, and is preparing, I think, to attack Logan's position," he reported to Sherman in a dispatch headed 9:10 A.M. Howard was unsure what to do next, though he believed that the decision was about to be taken from him in any event. "If the enemy will attack, and I think he will," he told Sherman, "that will simplify the matter." The matter was certainly simple: if the Rebels intended to hold the town and the railroad, they would have to charge the bluecoats and drive them off.[31]

Hardee's orders from the army commander had been to do exactly that. "I impressed upon General Hardee," Hood later wrote, "that the fate of Atlanta rested upon his ability, with the aid of two corps, to drive the Federals across Flint river, at Jonesboro." Apparently fearing that he had not sufficiently stressed to General Hardee the importance of the fight that day, he followed the council of war with a string of inspiring (or perhaps merely irritating) dispatches. At 3 A.M., from chief of staff Shoup: "As soon as you can get your troops in position the general says you must attack and drive the enemy across the river." Then at 3:10, from Hood himself: "You must not fail to attack the enemy so soon as you can get your troops up. I trust that God will give us victory." Again, ten minutes later from Shoup: "General Hood desires you to say to your officers and men that the necessity is imperative. The enemy must be driven into and across the river." And later that morning, perhaps after a couple of hours of fitful sleep: "General Hood desires the men to go at the enemy with bayonets fixed, determined to drive everything they may come against."[32]

The damp, heavy air that morning muffled the sound of skirmish firing, a sporadic, dull knocking coming to the ears of the Confederates "as though an army of wood choppers was at work in the distance." Even as they awaited the signal to advance, some among the Southern officers felt that the attack was doomed to fail. It was plain to even the most inattentive brigadier or colonel or captain that the hangdog Rebel soldiers in their charge were exhausted and footsore, their canteens and stomachs empty. Arthur Manigault, whose men had charged repeatedly against the strong Federal position at Ezra Church, looked down the line and thought the condition of his troops by no means satisfactory. "I saw pretty plainly that there was not much fight in them," he wrote. "The troops were weary, dull, sluggish, and entirely without the spirit that had hitherto characterized them on all such occasions as the present. They had long since lost confidence in their leaders, and knew full well what was likely to be the consequence of an attack against superior numbers, protected by a complete set of field works."[33]

The bluecoats posted in those works were waiting, too. Black Jack Logan had deployed his corps on the high ground some six hundred yards to the west of the Rebel lines, forming a sort of parenthesis to anchor his flanks on the Flint River behind. Experienced division commanders were posted all along the gently curved line: John M. Corse, of the 16th Corps, on the far right, Peter Osterhaus and William Harrow, in the center, and William B. Hazen, on the left. Frank Blair's 17th Corps arrived and was posted in reserve, giving Howard in all around 20,000 men to oppose the expected Rebel assault—but it would be the 12,000 men in Logan's crescent in the center who would bear the brunt of the attack. Though the Federals had arrived in position after dark the night before, they had set right to work—"'Shovels' was the order of the night," one remembered—and by midmorning they had constructed "quite a respectable line of breastworks from right to left."

Riding along these lines in the lifting fog, Logan arrived at the division headquarters of Major General Osterhaus, forty-one, a fine Prussian-born officer who had enlisted as a thirty-seven-year-old private after Fort Sumter and rose within a year to brigadier general. A veteran of a roster of Western battles that included Wilson's Creek, Pea Ridge, and the Vicksburg and Chattanooga campaigns, Osterhaus was a solid tactician with a certain Old World panache, evidenced by his crisp uniform and fine indigo cape, often thrown back over his shoulder to reveal its red silk lining. He had been on sick leave and missed the three previous battles around Atlanta and no doubt looked forward to his opportunity today.

Logan interrupted Osterhaus at breakfast, the immigrant general resting on one knee with a handful of crackers in one hand and a cup of coffee in the other. He rose and saluted as his chief approached, holding the handle of his steaming cup in a crooked finger.

'Well, General, keep your eyes open," Logan said. "They may come at any moment."

"All right, General," Osterhaus replied. "Youst gif me time my goffee to drink, und I vill make 'em hell schmell!"[34]

Over to the east, General Hardee had stepped off onto the platform at the Jonesboro depot in the wee hours to find himself without any soldiers. He set up his headquarters in a vacant lot in the center of the burned-out village and waited for Cleburne and Lee to arrive, though the delay at least afforded him time to plan his assault and reconnoiter the Union position along the low hills to the west. When Cleburne got there late morning and Lee shortly after midday, Hardee gave them their orders. Cleburne's troops, posted on the left, would open the attack, swinging north in a wheeling movement against the southern end of the Federal position, posted along a swampy ravine. Once Lee heard Cleburne's guns open the attack, Lee was to charge due west with his corps against Logan's front. Thus assaulted first on the right flank and then in front, the Federal lines would hopefully crumble, their position having little depth and a river, however shallow, in its immediate rear.

Finally, around 3 P.M., the order to go forward was given, and the execution of the attack immediately deviated from its conception. Again, the assault had been launched hours later than planned; again, the

Federals had adequate time to prepare and entrench; and again, a complex tactical plan involving *en echelon* attacks and wheeling movements was fumbled by subordinate commanders. Cleburne's division under Brigadier General Mark Lowrey stepped off as ordered, about to make its clockwise turn toward the Union right, when a detachment of Kilpatrick's cavalry, armed, as one Rebel said, with "breeck loaders and SixShooters"—opened on the passing Rebels. (The "breeck loaders" were in fact seven-shot Spencer repeating carbines, which the bluecoats believed made a single Union trooper the equal of "any two Rebs in Dixie." One Federal officer said of the Spencers: "Our men adore them as the heathen do their idols.") Angered by the annoying and unexpected fire, Lowrey's men, led by Brigadier General Hiram B. Granbury's brigade of Texans, charged due west, whooping as they pushed the outnumbered blue troopers to and then across the babbling waters of the Flint. "They couldn't stand it and broke and ran like good fellows," one of Lowrey's men remembered, "they runing for life and we for fun."[35]

A debate would afterward ensue as to whether the impetuous charge against the dismounted cavalry had been contrary to Hardee's orders for the attack. Certainly it ruined the planned wheeling movement, though Granbury quite sensibly pointed out that his orders had been "to drive all opposing forces across Flint River." Either way, the distraction pulled Lowrey wide and opened a huge gap between his whooping soldiers and the adjacent division under John C. Brown (in for the wounded Bate), exposing that force to a terrible concentrated fire in front and flank. Next in line was George Maney, boosted to command of the division of Frank Cheatham, who was sick, and he did not like the look of things. With Lowrey veering off and Brown all shot to pieces, Maney called a halt and sent a courier to Cleburne while he decided what to do. In the end, he decided to do nothing. Having pulled up short at Peachtree Creek, Maney had again failed to advance, and later that night would be relieved of command.[36]

Lee's part of the attack was off to a bad start as well. The young South Carolinian sometimes known as "Old Temporary" was still only six weeks in command of his corps, and again he let his inexperience show. Ordered to begin his attack after Cleburne had struck the Federal right, Lee instead mistook the sporadic fire of Cleburne's skirmishers for a general assault and literally jumped the gun—sending his men forward too early and exposing them to the undistracted attentions of most of Logan's corps. An Illinois captain watched them as they came, advancing in triple line across the open field, "with their colors flying, and yelling like so many wild Indians." The bluecoats watched and waited, under orders from their officers not to fire until the Rebs came within easy range. The Confederates drove the blue skirmishers back toward the main line, but then the word was given, and, as one Federal major wrote, "a sheeted volume of fire and lead carrying confusion with it swept o'er them like a fierce monsoon." Having stepped off handsomely despite their weariness, the attackers rebounded back like "a ball hurled against a rock."[37]

The deadly volley by no means put an end to Lee's charge, though it may as well have. The Union line was so strongly placed and the Rebels so timid and exhausted that the Yankees actually mocked them as they advanced. "They charged," one of the defenders would recall, "but our boys held their ground, and kept them at bay, with so little effort that they laughed at the Johnnies—cheered, as they came up—talked with them when they charged our line—and halloed after them as they retired toward their position." As they aimed and fired at the tangle of gray, the bluecoats could hear each other shouting above the banshee screech of the Rebel yell and the crackle of gunfire: "Wake 'em up, Yanks!" and "Oh no you don't!" and "Try again, Johnny!" men cried. "The air was resonant with spirited huzzahs," an Illinois private wrote. "Every man felt as though he was a phalanx—every command seemed to partake of the animation, and seemed anxious for a fray in which to work off their super-abundant enthusiasm."[38]

In the center, Osterhaus and his men had made the Rebels "hell schmell," indeed, opening on the advancing gray lines first with solid shot and then with canister—ammunition that soldiers of a later generation would classify as "anti-personnel" ordnance. To soldiers in the Civil War, it was nothing less than "canned hell-fire," the wicked artillery round not unlike a coffee can filled with steel or iron balls that sprayed out and shredded an approaching foe like a giant shotgun shell. "The effect of our fire was immediate and terrible; the enemy's line, compact until now, broke and dispersed in all directions," Osterhaus would report. "A number came over into our lines; the masses, however, fell back into the timber on their right and rear to find protection from our fire. The enemy formed again several times under cover of this timber, and attacked again, though very feebly, showing their first repulse to have been a very severe and decided one." An Ohio sergeant saw Osterhaus ranging back and forth along the line in his shirtsleeves, his suspenders down "like a woodchopper at work," warning his riflemen not to fire too high. Nearby, the cannoneers worked their guns as fast as they could swab and load and ram and fire. "Sweating and black with powder, they looked like coal heavers on a river steamboat," the sergeant recalled.[39]

Logan also rode along his mile-long fingernail curve of line, in high spirits and quite possibly under the influence of spirits, if some of his soldiers are to be believed. He exhorted his troops to greater exertions, loudly damned the Rebels, and marveled at the "unerring and steady fire" of his troops, which he later pronounced the "most terrible and destructive fire I ever witnessed."[40]

Again the Confederates fell in heaps—something that was by now characteristic of the battles for Atlanta—and one Union soldier would later pronounce the fight "more like a butchery than a battle." A Louisiana private named John Kendall was advancing through what he would remember as "a perfect hurricane of shot," losing all sense of direction in the smoke and dust and bursting shells. When a comrade asked him where their company was, Kendall looked around him and found that it had simply disappeared. Father Emmeran Bliemel, chaplain of the Irish 10th Tennessee Regiment—the "Fighting Tenth"—was decapitated by a cannonball as he bent to administer last rites to the regiment's mortally wounded colonel. In the 4th Louisiana, a boy named Smith was struck in the leg and was in peril of bleeding to death. Two comrades improvised a tourniquet out of a handkerchief, and had just gotten the strap twisted and tight when a second bullet struck poor Smith right in the heart and ended the need for further treatment. Mississippi Lieutenant Robert Gill, who had promised his wife that he would try not to curse on the battlefield, was shot through the lung just twenty paces from the Federal works as he led his men in the charge. He would die in a field hospital two days later.

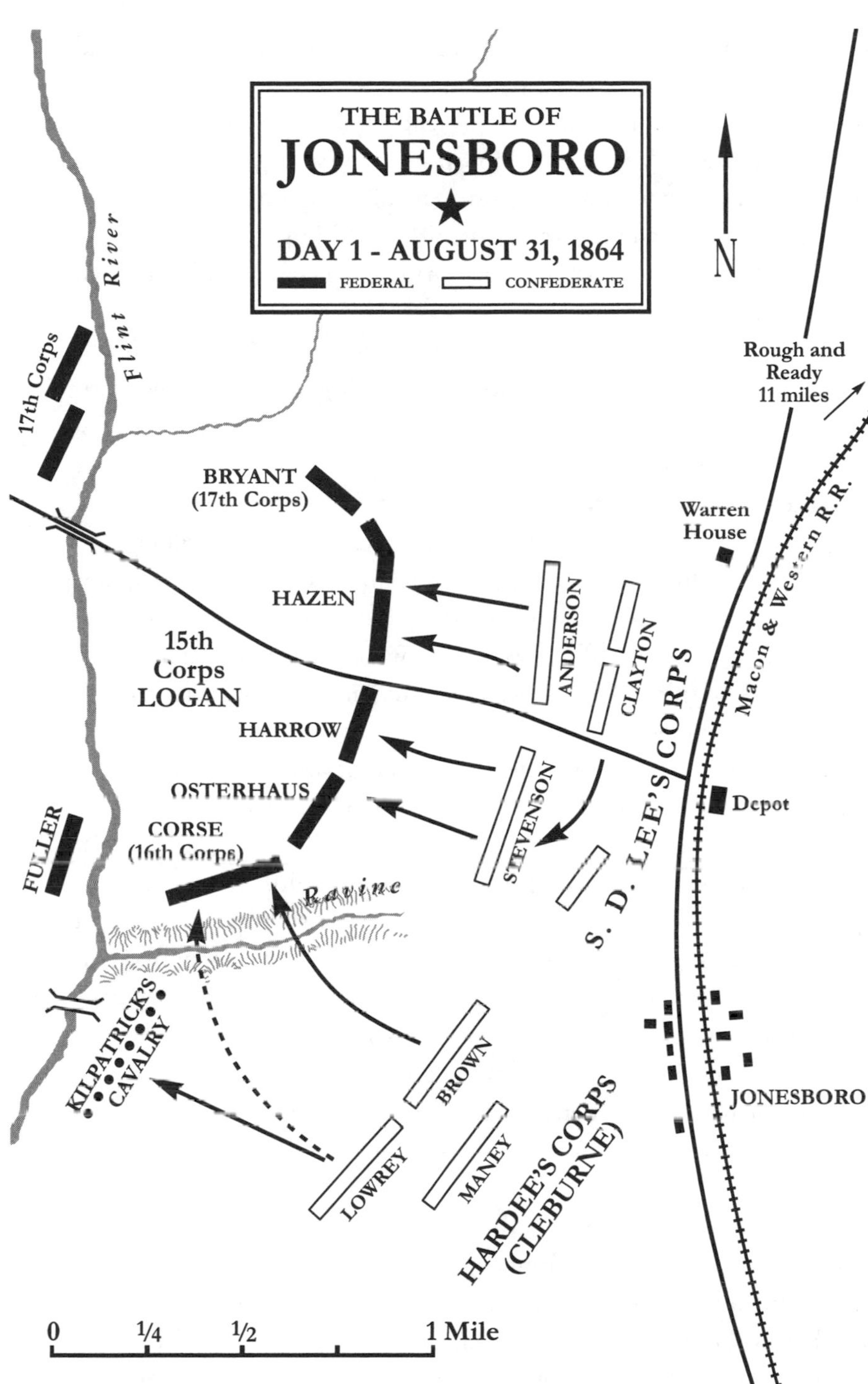
THE BATTLE OF
JONESBORO
DAY 1 - AUGUST 31, 1864
FEDERAL
CONFEDERATE
N
Flint River
17th Corps
BRYANT
(17th Corps)
HAZEN
15th
Corps
LOGAN
HARROW
OSTERHAUS
CORSE
(16th Corps)
FULLER
Ravine
KILPATRICK'S
CAVALRY
ANDERSON
CLAYTON
STEVENSON
S. D. LEE'S CORPS
Rough and
Ready
11 miles
Warren
House
Macon & Western R.R.
Depot
JONESBORO
BROWN
LOWREY
MANEY
HARDEE'S CORPS
(CLEBURNE)
0
1/4
1/2
1 Mile

Other Rebels had fallen, too, though not from wounds—some had dropped at the first volley and were hugging the ground, seeking shelter in rifle pits or behind furrows or fence rails. Prostrate men were crammed two and three deep in some places, "cursing, groaning, and firing as well as they were able." John Kendall spotted his colonel "lying flat on his face, in anything but a dignified position." At last the order to fall back was given, and the Rebels made for the rear, "without much order of any kind."[41]

The Confederate assault was, as S. D. Lee admitted, "a feeble one and a failure," badly planned and executed and disjointed from the start. Hood would later criticize the charge even more harshly—"a disgraceful effort," he reported, basing his judgment on an examination of Hardee and Lee's casualty figures, which he considered embarrassingly low for a major battle. These comments from the Gallant Hood—calling into question the valor of his exhausted soldiers by denigrating the amount of blood they had spilled—were unseemly and unfair, though numerous other official and unofficial accounts would likewise describe the notable lack of spirit in the Rebel attack that day. According to witnesses, blue and gray, Southern soldiers who had charged gallantly on other fields were for some reason cowed and timid at Jonesboro—something no one on either side in the campaign had ever seen before.

Ohio Major Thomas Taylor thought the Confederate attack "wholly disorganized" and "scarcely respectable"—in effect, little more than "colors advancing after stragglers with hardly a guard and the remainder of the line straggling after." Alabama Captain Bushrod Jones reported that the men in his brigade had moved up to the skirmish line and then halted without orders, seeking shelter behind a scattered pile of fence rails. "The men seemed possessed of some great horror of charging breastworks, which no power, persuasion, or example could dispel," he wrote. Patton Anderson, who was himself seriously wounded in the assault, witnessed a Louisiana color bearer trying in vain to rally the soldiers of his regiment to move forward. To the disgust of General Anderson and no doubt of the gallant flagman, neither the officers or the men responded. Elsewhere, these same men had acquitted themselves with the highest honors, but here, Anderson wrote, their fear and faltering brought "discredit upon a gallant regiment from as gallant a State as shines in the Southern constellation." One Federal officer suggested a simple explanation for scenes such as these—he thought that his adversaries had simply been worn down. "Besides losing a host of men in this campaign, the Rebel Army has lost a large measure of *vim*, which counts a good deal in soldiering," he wrote.[42]

Hardee spent the afternoon pacing to and fro in the empty lot in Jonesboro, waiting for dispatches on the progress of the battle and ignoring the occasional stray shell or bullet that came whizzing past. Presently, reports from the front described the disorganization on the left, the confusion of Maney in the center, and the repulse and demoralization of Lee's men on the right. Concerned that the Federals were massing for a counterattack against his weakened line in front of Jonesboro, Hardee canceled orders to renew the assault and instead ordered Cleburne and Lee to brace for the expected Union charge. "It is true that the attack could scarcely have been called a vigorous one," he would acknowledge in his report, "nor is it surprising that troops who had for two months been hurled against breast-works only to be repulsed or to gain dear-bought and fruitless victories, should now have moved against the enemy's works with reluctance and distrust."[43]

Despite the repeated orders to attack and drive the Federals into the river, and the persistent reminders from Hood that the attack must be pressed with the utmost vigor—"you must attack," "you must not fail," "the necessity is imperative"—the issue was never in doubt, and the Confederate assault was snuffed out in about an hour and a half. Federal losses would later be tabulated as a trifling 172 killed and wounded, while the Confederates counted more than ten times that many casualties, reports ranging from 1,800 to 2,200. The terrible suffering of the St. Helena Rifles, two severely depleted companies from the 4th Louisiana Regiment, was indicative of the slaughter. Lieutenant J. D. Killian brought twenty-one veteran soldiers against Logan's line that day, and nineteen were killed or wounded.

The fighting west of Jonesboro on August 31 was, according to historian Albert Castel, "perhaps the most one-sided slaughter of the war involving army-size opponents." But the battle was not yet ended. For Hardee and his men, tomorrow would bring a new ordeal.[44]

"*Our boys have been repulsed all along the line*," an Alabama private wrote in his diary, "and I see it requires no military man to tell that Atlanta is gone." Another Rebel soldier later recorded a simpler epitaph for the engagement. "The battle of Jonesborough," he wrote, "was the fall of Atlanta." This was both true and untrue—in point of fact, the last Confederate lifeline to Atlanta was severed not at Jonesboro, but nine miles to the northwest, near Rough and Ready. Even as O. O. Howard's Army of the Tennessee fought to reach the railroad at Jonesboro, John Schofield's Army of the Ohio had been closing in on the Macon & Western as well. At 3 P.M., just as the long gray lines started their attack at Jonesboro, elements of the 23rd Corps under Brigadier General Jacob Cox reached the M&W, roughly halfway between Atlanta and Jonesboro. As the bluecoats cut the telegraph wire and dug in to secure their position astride the railroad, a southbound locomotive chuffed into view from the direction of Atlanta. The engineer, who was no doubt startled to see several thousand blue-uniformed soldiers across his path, reversed his engine and sped his train back up the line toward East Point to spread the word that the Macon road was in Yankee hands.[45]

All day long in Atlanta, Hood had waited anxiously for reports on the determined Rebel assault he had expected to begin shortly after daybreak. "The arrival of no messenger from Hardee caused me to fear that the attack had not been made at an early hour, according to instructions," Hood later wrote. "This apprehension proved, unfortunately, but too well grounded." Then, around midafternoon, news started to arrive from points south, all of it bad. First the telegraph to Jonesboro went dead—hardly a good sign—and then came word that the enemy was at Rough and Ready "in considerable force."[46]

It seemed to General Hood that the noose was tightening on Atlanta. Still under the misimpression that only three Federal corps were moving on Jonesboro, with the remainder of Sherman's army still presumably lurking off to the west, Hood remained convinced that the Federal movement south of the city was not the main effort. At 6 P.M., acting on what Hardee would later call "a marvelous want of information," Hood ordered Old Reliable to send S. D. Lee's corps—which, unbeknownst to Hood, had just been repulsed at Jonesboro—back up toward Atlanta to help guard against such an attack. "There are indications," Hood informed his lieutenant, "that the enemy may make an attempt on Atlanta to-morrow." Hardee was directed to remain at Jonesboro with his single corps to "protect Macon and communications in rear." In retrospect, this order may have seemed foolish, pulling Lee's men out of line with the battle barely ended and leaving Hardee exposed in the face of a superior force at Jonesboro. But at the time he issued the order, Hood knew nothing of the fight at Jonesboro, and had received no request for reinforcements; indeed, no word at all, from Hardee.[47]

Then, after midnight, a courier arrived bringing word of the defeat at Jonesboro. "My God! It cannot be possible!" Hood supposedly exclaimed at the news. But this development, however unwelcome, served to dispel the fog of uncertainty and make clear the grim situation. The failure south of the city, as Hood later wrote, "gave to the Federal Army the control of the Macon Road, and thus necessitated the evacuation of Atlanta at the earliest hour possible." The fate of Atlanta was no longer in doubt. The only question now was whether the Confederate Army of Tennessee could survive and escape.[48]

Word reached Sherman's headquarters about 4 P.M. that Schofield had hold of the Macon & Western and was fortifying near the station at Rough and Ready. The red-bearded general was ecstatic at the news. "I have your dispatch and am rejoiced," he told Schofield late on the 31st. "I think we now have a good game." Now in possession of the railroad between Hardee at Jonesboro and Hood in Atlanta, Sherman planned to take care of both. "Don't get off the track; hold it fast," he told Schofield, directing him to move southward down the tracks toward a junction with Howard and Thomas. "We will get our whole army on the railroad as near Jonesborough as possible and push Hardee and Lee first, and then for Atlanta."

Sherman could not or would not wait for all his forces to arrive—he knew Hardee was alone and in trouble, and he wanted his subordinates to press the issue. "Impress upon these commanders that it is not so necessary to have united lines, but rather columns of attack," he told Thomas. "We are not on the defensive, but offensive, and must risk everything rather than dilly-dally about."[49]

"*September 1. A real autumn morning,*" an Illinois soldier recorded in his diary. "We were aroused at 3 a.m. and the air was then almost crisp. A breath of cold air is a luxury we can appreciate. A fresh, cool breeze is now stirring and I can almost hear the leaves falling." The Confederates had tried and failed to drive the Federals into the river; now, on the second day of the Battle of Jonesboro, the bluecoats would have their turn to attack in an attempt to destroy the outnumbered Rebels across the way.

In his lines in front of Jonesboro, Hardee had three divisions left, some 12,000 men in all—and approximately five times that number of Federals had been ordered to concentrate against him. His soldiers would man a two-mile line, stretched in a single rank with soldiers posted at some points "not quite touching elbows" and at some points six feet apart. Hardee had shifted Cleburne's Division from the extreme left of the position to the right to draw a diagonal line across the railroad and block Jonesboro from the north and west. On the map, Hardee's line bent back like an arrowhead pointing north, with Brigadier General Daniel Govan's brigade of Cleburne's Division manning the blunted point, near a white house owned by railroad agent Guy L. Warren, who had had his smokehouse plundered and his horse stolen by Kilpatrick's troopers two weeks before. This exposed northern end of the position formed a vulnerable salient, and it was here at the tip of the arrow that the Federal attack would concentrate. Hardee had done his best with what he had to work with, but the position, as one of Cleburne's officers noted, was "a sorry one."[50]

Bearing down from the north that morning was the Federal 14th Corps of the Army of the Cumberland, now under Brigadier General Jefferson C. Davis, who had replaced the recalcitrant, rank-obsessed John Palmer after the botched attack at Utoy Creek. Known throughout the army for his notorious name, Davis had been placed at the head of the corps at the specific request of Sherman, one of the few men willing to overlook Davis's terrible reputation and dastardly deeds. Back in September 1862 at the Galt Hotel in Louisville, three-hundred-pound Major General William "Bull" Nelson had insulted and then slapped his subordinate Davis, whereupon Davis retrieved a pistol, walked up to Nelson, and shot him dead. This in itself was scandalous enough, the crime being committed in a crowded hotel before a lobby full of witnesses including the governor of Kentucky—yet more remarkable was the fact that Davis was never convicted or even placed on trial for the crime. His only punishment, it seemed, was to deny him further promotion. He had begun the war as a lieutenant and rose quickly to brigadier before the Nelson killing, though he looked as if he was carved down by the effort—so thin that one could almost discern the skull beneath the skin of his face, with coarse brown hair, heavy beard, and ice-pale eyes, hard as flint with bloodhound bags underneath. Rounding out this rather unappealing ensemble, Davis possessed a volcanic temper and deep reservoirs of foul and creative language, being said to have "mastered the vocabulary of the 'Army in Flanders' more completely than any man of his rank."[51]

Davis took his time in getting set—indeed, there seemed to be no hurry. Receiving word that the railroad had been broken and that Hardee thus had no hope of reinforcements from the direction of Atlanta, General Howard later recalled that he had "decided to run no risk of a hasty advance," notwithstanding Sherman's earlier remonstrance against "dilly-dallying about." Because of the deliberate preparations and the hours spent railroad-wrecking off to the north, it was nearly 4 p.m. before Davis's corps was in position north of Jonesboro, its right connecting with Howard's left. Meanwhile, the Rebels continued to fortify their thin-stretched position throughout the day, hard at work with axes and shovels even as the bluecoats stepped off on their advance—"We cut & piled some logs & dug for dear life," one Confederate remembered.

An initial charge by the U.S. Regular Brigade swept aside the Rebel skirmishers in their front but then stalled after a volley of musketry from Dan Govan's Arkansas brigade and converging fire from two batteries of artillery. Reinforcements were called for, and Davis had plenty—the Third Division, two brigades of Midwesterners under Brigadier General Absalom Baird, was quickly brought forward to add its weight to the charge.

Baird was a Pennsylvanian and a West Pointer who had just turned forty, though he looked a good bit older—wrinkled and thin, with receding gray hair and an astounding mustache that swept out right and left under his nostrils like pair of squirrels' tails. Despite his having the facial hair of a frontiersman, one acquaintance would pronounce Baird "one of the most elegant officers of the army," personifying "the ideal of a gentleman and a soldier." He had distinguished himself on a number of fields and was about to write his name even higher today. General Baird had his horse shot from under him during the charge. He took over the mount of an orderly, but that horse, too, was felled with a bullet in the brain, sending the general sprawling and causing some of his soldiers to think him dead. But he bounced up almost immediately and led the assault on foot, "cheering the men with his voice and presence," one of his soldiers remembered. "Many acts of heroism was displayed on the field by officers and men," an Indianan wrote in his diary, "and none deserves more praise than Genl Baird in leading the charge in person." For his valor that day, Baird would later be awarded the Medal of Honor.[52]

"The Bugle sounded the charge and we went in on Double quick with fixed Bayonetts," Sergeant William Bluffton Miller of the 75th Indiana recalled. The Rebels held their fire until the swarm of bluecoats drew close. Then, as one of the Union attackers remembered, "they opened up on us and when they did our Boys melted like Snow under a Summer sun." But though these same Bunker Hill whites-of-their-eyes tactics had worked well the day before when the Federals swept away the weak Rebel charge—today, the Confederates waited too long to open fire. The charging Yankees were too close, too determined, and too many. A second charge was immediately sounded, and the bluecoats surged up and over the hastily built ramparts north of Jonesboro while many of the Confederates were still fumbling to reload. "Then a Slaughter commenced the like of which I never witnessed before and pray I may never see again," Miller wrote. "A great many of the Rebels threw away their arms and proposed to surrender but the next instant they were Shot down or received a Bayonett and the Bugle sounded to 'cease fireing' three times before our boys gave any quarter." An Ohio private concurred in his description. "For a few minutes it was simply awful," he recalled. "On both sides men acted like infuriated devils. They dashed each other's brains out with clubbed muskets; bayonets were driven into men's bodies up to the muzzle of the gun; officers ran

Brigadier Generals Jefferson C. Davis, left, and Absalom Baird, right. (*Library of Congress*)

their swords through their opponents; and revolvers, after being emptied into the faces of the rebels, were thrown with desperate force into the ranks."

At one point along the line, the struggle became one of brother against brother, where the Union 10th Kentucky Regiment of Col. George Este's brigade, "by the queerest luck in the world," found themselves up against the Confederate 9th Kentucky Regiment. "The commanders of the two regiments were brothers-in-law, and the men relatives, friends, acquaintances, and schoolmates," a witness wrote, "and they hated each other accordingly." Here the close-quarters fighting along the Rebel works was "more bitter, if possible, than anywhere else on the line." The melee was point-blank and hand-to-hand, the officers firing pistols and the soldiers swinging muskets and in places almost fencing with their bayonets. "On no occasion within my own knowledge has the use of the bayonet been so general or so well authenticated," General Baird wrote in his report of the battle. "Three brothers named Noe, of the Tenth Kentucky, went over the rebel parapet together, and two of them pinned their adversaries to the ground with the bayonet." Despite the prevalence of officers ordering bayonet charges in the Civil War, this sort of desperate thrusting and parrying in the trenches was exceedingly rare—indeed, an Ohio surgeon reported treating "the first bayonet wounds I have seen since the commencement of the war. I saw many a rebel wounded by the bayonet, which shows with what desperation they defended their works and how determined our boys were to capture them."[53]

Survivors in the trenches would later invoke all manner of metaphors to describe the massive attack against the salient manned by Cleburne's Division on the second day at Jonesboro. The Federals formed a massive blue wave—seven, ten, perhaps even twelve ranks deep, according to some witnesses—and came rolling across the field "like an avalanche" upon the Confederates. "The second assault was made in seven columns, with fixed bayonets, guns atrail," an Arkansas soldier who was taken prisoner recalled, "and without firing a gun, they ran over us like a drove of Texas beeves." The Union attack swamped Govan's Arkansans, spilling over the breastworks on the left and then swinging around behind the Rebels to cut them off. "The corps seemed to be in the center of a circle of hissing lead and hurtling iron," a captain later wrote, the position "so surrounded that there was literally no rear."[54]

The proud veterans of Govan's Brigade had never lost a position, but they would lose one here today at Jonesboro—though not for any lack of valor or determination. "We fought all day against seven corps of Yankees," a private in the 1st Arkansas would recall, far overstating the enemy's numbers but surely capturing the sentiments of the beleaguered Rebels. "We were surrounded and fought in front and fought in rear. Fought as General Cleburne always fought." Fought and refused to stop fighting, in fact, until many were shot or stabbed or had their muskets literally wrenched from their hands. More than six hundred Confederate soldiers, including General Govan himself, were captured in the rush and sent to the rear. But next in line was Hiram Granbury's Texas Brigade, and they moved at a double quick to form a new line and seal off the penetration. "As soon as the Yankees send their prisoners off, we go to shooting into them (for they are right here at us) and hold them there until night," one of the Texans wrote of the action.[55]

A few hundred yards to the west, Howard's position along the high ground afforded an excellent view of the fighting. "It was a grand sight to see the blaze of fire between the two contending lines," one observer wrote of the spectacle. Sherman sat his horse nearby watching the battle

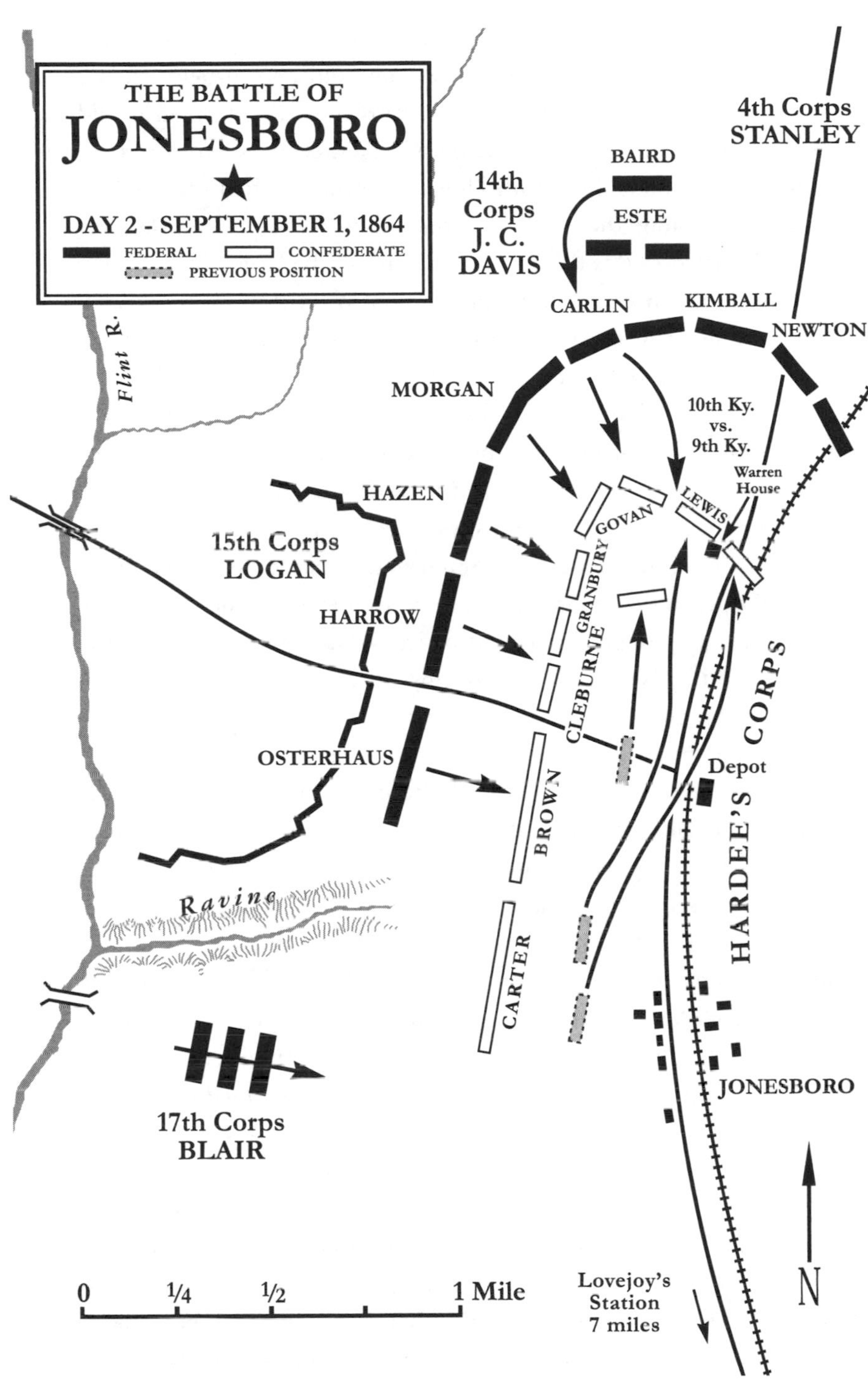
THE BATTLE OF
JONESBORO
DAY 2 - SEPTEMBER 1, 1864
FEDERAL
CONFEDERATE
PREVIOUS POSITION
4th Corps
STANLEY
BAIRD
14th
Corps
J. C.
DAVIS
ESTE
CARLIN
KIMBALL
NEWTON
Flint R.
MORGAN
10th Ky.
vs.
9th Ky.
Warren
House
HAZEN
LEWIS
GOVAN
15th Corps
LOGAN
GRANBURY
HARROW
CLEBURNE
HARDEE'S CORPS
OSTERHAUS
Depot
BROWN
Ravine
CARTER
JONESBORO
17th Corps
BLAIR
0
1/4
1/2
1 Mile
Lovejoy's
Station
7 miles
N

with O. O. Howard and George Thomas and was predictably delighted as Davis's attack "swept forward across some old cotton-fields in full view and went over the rebel parapet handsomely," as Sherman would recall the scene. "They're rolling them up like a sheet of paper!" he cried, rubbing his hands together. With Howard pressuring the front and Jeff C. Davis crumbling the flank, the only thing required to complete Hardee's destruction was to come down hard on the Confederate rear.[56]

Sherman had an entire corps in position to do it—Major General David S. Stanley's 4th Corps of the Army of the Cumberland, which had been moving down the east side of the railroad to close on Jonesboro and the Confederate right rear from the northeast. Davis had done his worst and torn up the enemy right; now Sherman, impatient as always, expected Stanley to drop the other shoe and stamp out the Rebels for good. But Stanley's corps was nowhere to be found. Sherman sent an aide to locate the wayward Stanley, then dispatched his engineer Captain Poe, then finally ordered Thomas to hurry him along. The big Union-loyal Virginian uncharacteristically scampered off on the errand—"and that is the only time during the campaign I can recall seeing General Thomas urge his horse into a gallop," Sherman recalled.[57]

Stanley's men, occupied late the night before and early that day in tearing up railroad track, had arrived late in the afternoon to find the ground before them tangled with underbrush and abatis and a line of breastworks frowning along what was supposed to be the Confederate rear. Hardee, sensing the danger, had stripped his left and sent Cheatham's division to shore up the threatened right. Hesitant to launch an attack in the failing light, Stanley ordered a halt and had his men dig in—though a strong advance may well have crushed the already shaky Rebel position. Darkness fell, and a number of Federal officers and men would say that another hour of daylight would have doomed the embattled Confederates. "Three hours more of daylight," a Union officer wrote, "and Hardee would have had no corps left."

All this would come later, of course, when there was time for the customary second-guessing and hand-wringing over missed chances, but for the present, the victorious Federals exulted in what they had achieved the past two days. "I could have lain down on that blood-stained grass, amid the dying and the dead and wept with excess of joy,"

Major James Connolly wrote to his wife. "I have no language to express the rapture one feels in the moment of victory, but I do know at such a moment one feels as if the joy were worth risking a hundred lives to attain it. Men at home will read of that battle and be glad of our success, but they can never feel as we felt, standing there quivering with excitement, amid the smoke and blood, and fresh horrors and grand trophies of that battle field."[58]

Brigadier General Daniel Govan. (*Battles and Leaders*)

Fresh horrors there were, both on the field, thick-strewn with the dead of both armies, and in the field hospitals, which some men considered far worse than the shell-torn fields themselves. Broken bodies, Reb and Yank, were brought to the surgeons' tents in great numbers, and one Yankee sergeant hurrying past found he could not escape the sounds of the "cries, groans, prayers, even cursings" of the men inside. Recently a headquarters, the Warren House near the Rebel salient was converted to a hospital, and its walls today still bear the signatures of wounded soldiers who convalesced there. A passing Federal officer found his eyes drawn to a nearby water well, where a number of soldiers had gathered around as if marveling at some carnival oddity. "The curbing was gone," he remembered, "and the well was literally filled up with legs and arms thrown there by surgeons' assistants who had no time to bury them. How deep the well was I do not know, but it was filled with the bloody limbs of southern soldiers and afterwards covered with earth to hide from the public gaze the hideous cruelties of war."[59]

Still, scenes like these, though they varied in their particulars, were by now all too familiar to the soliders on both sides, and though Union casualties the second day had balanced the bloody ledger somewhat—Federal losses totaling 1,274, while the Confederates lost an estimated 1,200 killed, wounded, and missing, almost 900 of those captured—the two-day battle was a devastating defeat for Hardee and for Hood. But it was also another missed opportunity for Sherman, who had been in position to annihilate Hardee's Corps or bag it entirely, but let it first survive and then slip away in the night. Hardee's battered corps crept out of the Federal cordon at Jonesboro as if through the open ends of a horseshoe and marched southward under cover of darkness down the railroad to Lovejoy's Station. There the Rebels formed a defensive line, took out their picks and shovels, and began to dig. "Our movements are very quiet," a Texan wrote, "and as we go we can hear Genl Hood evacuating Atlanta, or rather we can hear him burning up the ammunition that he can't carry away with him, now that all the RRs have been cut by the Yanks and the place nearly surrounded and we 20 miles from him with our backs to him. He is in a bad fix."[60]

Tramping southward in the darkness, a wrung-out Rebel soldier spoke to a friend plodding along beside him. "Hood's played 'ell, hasn't he?" he said, and though he meant the question rhetorically, he nonetheless drew a response.

"I should say he has," the comrade said.[61]

CHAPTER TEN

"A Day of Terror and a Night of Dread"

The Surrender of Atlanta, September 2

John Bell Hood had "played 'ell," sure enough—just six weeks in command, he had fought four major battles and lost them all—and now he was "in a bad fix" indeed. The three corps of his heavily outnumbered army were dispersed from Atlanta to Lovejoy's Station, a span of more than twenty miles, with no rail or telegraph connection and six high-spirited Federal corps interposed between them. A Union force of unknown strength was still posted just to the northwest, and Atlanta was now cut off for the foreseeable future from any hope of resupply. The great Southern railroad town, the so-called Turntable of the Confederacy, now had no railroads to speak of and seemingly nowhere to turn.

Hood's task, if daunting, was at least very simple: to evacuate the city with Stewart's Corps and the Georgia militia, to bring off such ordnance and provisions he could and destroy those he couldn't, and to reunite his divided army to fight another day. Atlanta would be lost, of course—nothing could be done about that—but it was the Southern army, and not the city, that was truly important from a military perspective. Orders went out to begin preparations for the evacuation in the early morning hours of September 1, with the movement to begin that afternoon.

Focused on destroying Hardee and on severing the railroads, Sherman had been slow to push troops southeast of the city—Schofield's Army of the Ohio, for example, which had been comparatively idle during the Battle of Jonesboro—to block the remaining wagon roads. Sherman had executed a brilliant maneuver over the past few days, but had failed to see it through to its conclusion, essentially leaving open the gate to—or, rather, out of—the Gate City. Hood would take advantage and make his escape southward as easily as a dog let out of the yard, marching out of the city along the McDonough Road toward a junction with Hardee and Lee at Lovejoy's Station.

All that day, Thursday, September 1, "unusual bustle and activity prevailed," with the city "in a state of near anarchy," a witness recalled. "This was a day of terror and a night of dread," Samuel Richards recorded in his diary. "About noon came the tidings of a severe fight on the Macon RR and that our forces were worsted and the city was to be evacuated at once." Carrie Berry's cousin Emma came by the house just after dinner with news that the city was to be evacuated and the Federals expected to arrive tomorrow. "It was not long till the hole town found it out," Carrie wrote, "and such excitement there was." Although many residents cowered behind closed doors, hundreds of fretful citizens milled about the streets, trying to learn what was happening, though the prevailing reaction was disbelief at the possibility that the place might be surrendered. "Then began a scramble among the inhabitants to get away—others to procure supplies of food for their families," Richards wrote. "If there had been any doubt of the fact that Atlanta was about to be given up it would have been removed when they saw the depots of Government grain and food thrown open and the contents distributed among the citizens free gratis by the sackful and the cartload." Citizens who had been struggling to feed their families, and soldiers who had seen their requisitions for additional food and equipment routinely denied, were appalled at the teeming storehouses—mountains of "sugar, bacon, coffee, whiskey, shoes and clothing of every description"—all of which had been rationed ungenerously if not refused outright to those who needed it most. Now it would all be destroyed.[1]

The Confederates began their withdrawal from the city at 5 P.M. Hood led the way, riding slowly out front with his staff, followed by

Stewart's Corps and then the Georgia militia, as the column trickled southward into the deepening gloom. "The troops filed through the streets with a steady tread, it is true, but nevertheless with sorrow depicted on their weather-beaten countenances," an *Augusta Sentinel* correspondent wrote of the scene. No regimental band played to boost the spirits of the marchers, and though some true Confederate women could be heard singing "Dixie" and "The Bonnie Blue Flag" as they rolled in wagons out of the city, the gray soldiers themselves gave voice to melancholy ballads and lonely songs normally reserved for homesick nights around the campfire. "*We loved each other then Lorena / More than we ever dared to tell.*"[2]

Major General Samuel G. French's division formed the rear guard for the retiring infantry and witnessed the growing chaos as the Confederates departed, leaving Atlanta without any governing authority. "There is confusion in the city, and some of the soldiers in the town are drunk," he recorded in his diary. "Common sense is wanted." At the tail end of the long column, undisciplined stragglers picked the city clean like a devouring plague as they left. Soldiers broke ranks to vault fences or push their way into gardens to strip them of "every green thing that could be eaten by man or beast." The forlorn locals stood silently, watching. No one made any objection.[3]

Hood had ordered removed all army stores and wagons, but realization came too late that parked out on the Georgia Railroad, just east of the city next to the Markham and Schofield Rolling Mill, was the army's massive reserve ordnance train, consisting of five fine steam locomotives and eighty-one cars filled with guns, ammunition, equipment, and provisions. Obviously, with all the railroads leading from the city now under Union control, there would be no way to bring off the rolling stock and precious cargo. Hood was predictably incensed at the oversight, laying the blame at the feet of the chief quartermaster, who was supposedly charged with seeing to the removal of the train some time before. (Hood would later charge the hapless quartermaster with drunkenness and dereliction of duty, and a court of inquiry would eventually be called to look into the matter—though by the time it convened in March 1865, the Southern Confederacy had far more serious problems that the loss of an ammunition train in Atlanta.) Whoever was responsible for this military sin, the course of action with respect to these cars and magazines was clear—they would have to be utterly destroyed to prevent them from falling into Federal hands.

Engineer troops and rear-guard cavalrymen set to work on the cache of guns and ammunition. Large cannon were spiked, warehouses and mills set afire, and boxes containing innumerable rounds of small arms ammunition dumped in ponds or wells close by the railroad. The trains were parked on the main line and a siding hard by the rolling mill before being abandoned by their frightened crews. Engineer Dave Young, instructed to knock out the cylinder heads of the famous engine *General*—hero of the so-called Great Locomotive Chase back in '62—could not bring himself to do it. He removed and pocketed an oval-framed tintype portrait from the cab and then simply walked away. Years later, memories would differ as to the method of destruction of the abandoned iron horses—some recalled them run backward at high speeds and smashed dramatically into lines of cars or other engines, while a Georgia militiaman claimed that he and his comrades poured barrels of tar over and into the engines, counting on fire to do the work. The rear guardsmen, torches in hand, ranged up and down the packed ammunition train touching off slow-burning matches in the boxcars. Then they turned and ran like hell.

Then followed what one scholar pronounced perhaps the greatest explosion of the American Civil War. "The flames shot up to a tremendous height, and the exploding missiles scattered their red hot fragments right and left," reporter Wallace Reed wrote. "The very earth trembled as if in the throes of a mighty earthquake. The houses rocked like cradles, and on every hand was heard the shattering of window glass and the fall of plastering and loose bricks." Residents who lived near the rolling mill and the railyards east of town had been ordered away from the area—good thing, too, as "every building for a quarter of a mile around was either torn to pieces or perforated with hundreds of holes by fragments of the shells"—though those farther away mounted rooftops and balconies and gazed slack-jawed at the volcanic spectacle. "The Heavens were in a perfect glow, while the atmosphere seemed full of flaming rockets," sixteen-year-old Mary Rawson, daughter of city councilman E. E. Rawson, wrote in her diary. "Crash follows crash and the

The remains of the reserve ordnance train that was blown up on Hood's orders as the Confederate forces abandoned Atlanta. The massive explosion lit up the night sky and set surrounding buildings and stores on fire, as recreated in the film *Gone with the Wind*. (*National Archives*)

swift moving locomotives were rent in pieces and the never tiring metallic horse lay powerless while the sparks filled the air with innumerable spangles." The noise was "perfectly deafening," the explosions heard plainly thirty miles away, and the smoke-filled sky over the city glowed an angry orange for most of the night. The inferno was so tremendous that it would cause the common misconception that it was the Confederates, and not Sherman, who had burned Atlanta in 1864—and two generations later, millions of Americans would watch the scene recreated on screens in playhouses and odeon theaters around the country.[4]

The loss in matériel, especially to an army in need of every gun and bullet available, was grievous: six 6-pounder and one three-inch rifled cannon, three 12-pounder howitzers, dozens of caissons, limbers, and carriages, 14,000 artillery rounds, 5,000 "splendid Enfield or Tower muskets, entirely new, with all their equipments," and countless numbers of other small arms and ammunition—all of it up in smoke, and all in addition to the eight rifled and five smooth 32-pounder heavy siege guns that had been spiked and abandoned in their emplacements along the Rebel breastworks. Six million dollars worth of ordnance, "which we so much needed," as a Confederate captain wrote, had literally gone up in smoke—not to mention boxcars full of bridles, saddles, canteens, horseshoes, swords, axes, shovels, and other hardware and implements of war.[5]

In the thundering confusion, soldiers became separated from their squads and wandered in the darkness as the light of the flames died away, the streets crowded with "men, horses, and a little of everything," as one said, with "a perfect babel of voices in every direction." In time the city cleared out, the army retreating and the citizens retiring, the streets largely deserted as the noise died away. After the violent thunderclap of the exploding magazines, the early morning quiet seemed almost eerie. "It was very dark and I could hear no sound whatsoever," a departing Rebel private wrote. "The silence was so profound that it seemed to me I could feel it. It caused a painful, uneasy sensation."[6]

Also ill at ease were the members of the sparse rear guard strung out at various points across the city, who were left not only without clear orders or commanding officers but without comrades as well. Lonely sentries stood nervously in doorways and on street corners and wondered how long they should stay. An Alabama private named John Green kept watch at Five Points and years later would remember the once-bustling downtown intersection as "the most dismal place I was ever in." Not knowing who was posted next to him or when if ever he would be relieved, he remained at his post until around four in the morning and then hustled down the road to catch up with his departing brigade.[7]

One group of Confederate officers passed through the empty streets, "not a human being visible, or a light to be seen in any direction," as one remembered. "All was as dark and silent as the grave." Turning a corner, the gray riders saw a light and then a young lady appearing at a window. "Gentlemen," she asked, "it is true that General Hood is about to abandon Atlanta?" They confirmed that the news was all too true, and that the army in fact had already gone. "She was very pale and we could see by the dim light that the tears were coursing down her cheeks," the officer recalled. "I shall never forget that look, nor that pale and haggard face. It seemed an unuttered prophecy of the fate of those we left behind."[8]

By then it was nearly dawn. The rattled, bleary-eyed citizens of Atlanta emerged from their houses to face the new day and with it the arrival of their long-awaited conquerors. "The sun rose as it had set the evening before, a blood-red ball, magnified by clouds and mists that were the handiwork of man," reporter Wallace Reed would recall. "In the dread silence of that memorable morning, ten thousand helpless people looked into each others' faces for some faint sign of hope and encouragement, but found none." The appropriations yesterday from the abandoned army stores gave way this morning to outright looting, as desperate citizens broke through doors and windows and plundered downtown shops. "Every one has been trying to get all they could before the Federals come in the morning," Carrie Berry wrote. "They have ben running with saques of meal, salt and tobacco. They did act rediculous breaking open stores and robbing them." Samuel Richards arrived at his Book, Music and Fancy Store to find a host of plunderers, black and white, men, women, and children, "crowded into the store each one scrambling to get something to carry away, regardless, apparently, whether it was any thing they needed, and still more heedless of the fact that they were stealing!"[9]

The duty to take charge amid the disorder fell to the city's mayor, the Honorable James M. Calhoun. The mayor, said to be a "gentle, truthful and courteous" man, "without the tinsel of attractive display in company possessed by some," had performed few official duties in the seven weeks since the city council last met and presumably spent his time during the bombardment hunkered down like his constituents. His efforts were spent, he later asserted, in furnishing food and medicine to the sick and wounded soldiers in town, some of whom he took into his home, and in providing what comfort he could to families suffering in the absence of a loved one serving in the army. Now, with Hood gone, he was determined to do what he could to save the city. Early on the morning of September 2, he called on Brigadier General Samuel Ferguson, commander of a detachment of cavalry that appeared to be the last remaining Confederate force in the town, and asked that they withdraw and make no further resistance. At 11 A.M., Ferguson sent word that he would comply with the mayor's request.

Shortly thereafter, the last Confederate soldier rode out of Atlanta. In the absence of any remaining military presence, Mayor Calhoun made preparations to surrender the city to the United States forces.[10]

The Union XX (20th) Corps—formerly that of the angrily departed Joe Hooker but now under the command of the newly arrived Major General Henry W. Slocum, who had come to Georgia from Vicksburg at Sherman's specific request—had been left behind in the trenches northwest of Atlanta during the grand Federal movement south of the city. This might have been considered the most perilous assignment—a single corps left alone with their backs to the Chattahoochee River, separated from the rest of the army—but the men in fact found their post guarding the bridges "a soft thing" indeed. With their breastworks for the most part complete, the bluecoats devoted their energies to making themselves comfortable, clearing the dense woods to create what one soldier called "a most helpful camp with charming shade trees." They cut pinewood poles and fashioned them into something approximating real beds, and, as an Illinois soldier wrote home, "you can hardly imagine how happy all the boys are at being so comfortably camped after our long weary campaign." When not on duty, they swam and fished in the Chattahoochee, or pitched horseshoes, or even ventured out to nearby farms and homesteads to barter or buy green corn or sweet potatoes or new beans from the locals. Writing home on August 29, the same day Howard's and Thomas's men were laying waste to a dozen miles of the Atlanta & West Point Railroad, an Ohio corporal noted that yesterday had been the first since May 14 that they had not heard artillery or musketry or both.

The late summer days continued hot but the nights were clear and cool. They passed the starry evenings around their campfires, listening as the bands played and talking politics. "We are all anxious to hear who will be the nominee of the Chicago Convention," a Wisconsin soldier wrote. "Two months more and we will know who will be our roolers for the next four years. I hope it will be our present incumbent." They also speculated as to what had become of Sherman, having heard nothing for several days after the movement toward the Macon railroad began. No one seemed worried at the silence, however. "As to General Sherman's latest movements we don't know much," an Ohioan recorded, "but we have all confidence in his ability to perform whatever he undertakes."[11]

On August 31, after the first day of the battle of Jonesboro, Sherman sent orders to Slocum to feel down toward Atlanta, but a brief reconnaissance revealed the Confederates still manning their formidable works. But around midnight the next night, Slocum, too, heard the series of explosions from the south—"the ground trembled under us," one of his soldiers said—and ordered each of his three divisions to press forward at first light. They did so, moving southeast toward the city, a dark blanket of smoke spread across the spires and steeples before them. The cool morning was still and quiet, and it soon became clear that the Rebel intrenchments were empty, left almost completely undisturbed except for a few discarded belongings and the occasional spiked heavy gun. Captain Henry M. Scott of the 70th Indiana was riding with a small detachment of cavalry when he spotted coming up the road toward them a group of about a dozen civilians, all on horseback, one of them carrying a white flag.[12]

With Atlanta in a fiery tumult since the night before, Mayor Calhoun had determined that the best way to ensure the safety of the city and its residents was to facilitate an early and peaceful occupation by the Union army. Accordingly, early that morning he had assembled a delegation of sorts to ride out to meet the arriving Federals and to effect a formal surrender of the city. The group included one city councilman, E. E. Rawson, and a number of prominent citizens apparently selected for their Northern birth, their Union sentiment, or both: including the aforementioned Rawson, a native of Vermont; Connecticut-born businessman and former mayor William Markham, whose still-smoking rolling mill had been destroyed the night before; Julius Hayden, also from Connecticut, who had presided over antisecessionist meetings in Atlanta; Thomas G. Crusselle, a stonemason and contractor originally from Washington, D.C.; and, somewhat remarkably, the free black entrepreneur and staunch Union man Robert Webster.

All agreed with the plan to venture out toward the lines in an effort to locate the Federal authorities and inform them of the departure of the Confederate army. There was a considerable fuss, however, over whether the contingent should go armed. Mayor Calhoun protested that this would never do and may cause "serious trouble," being inherently inconsistent with the truce flag they would carry—while others quaked at the prospect of riding out among the Yankee devils without so much as a pistol for reference. The mayor prevailed, insisting that the party must rely on the protection of their white flag and otherwise take their chances. Thus instructed, though perhaps not entirely convinced, the delegates emptied their holsters and left their guns in the care of friends—including one member who opened his coat to reveal four six-shooters. With that settled, the now-unarmed peace party improvised a white flag and rode slowly out Marietta Street, Calhoun leading the way astride a splendid white horse. They passed the deserted earthworks, nosing their horses carefully through considerable amounts of rubble, and soon thereafter—completing a ride of well under two miles—came upon a group of blue horsemen led by Captain Scott.

With a deferential bow, Mayor Calhoun introduced himself and asked Scott if he was the officer in command. Scott said that he was not and politely asked Calhoun to remain where he was while he fetched his superior. He returned promptly with Colonel John Coburn, the one-time Indianapolis lawyer who along with Benjamin Harrison had so staunchly held the Federal center at Peachtree Creek. Coburn had come a long way from his inglorious capture at Thompson's Station a year earlier—this time he would play the role of the victorious conqueror, accepting the formal surrender of one of the great prizes of the war. Again introductions were made all around, and then Mayor Calhoun began. "Colonel Coburn," he said, "the fortune of war has placed Atlanta in your hands. As mayor of the city, I came to ask protection for non-combatants, and for private property."

"We did not come to make war upon non-combatants, or on private property," Coburn replied. "Both shall be protected and respected by us."

Considerably gratified by this response and the sentiment expressed, Calhoun then advised the Indiana colonel that the last remaining Rebel cavalry had departed the city, that he could go in and take possession, and that no resistance would be made. The next day, Coburn would ask that Mayor Calhoun reduce to writing the words used in the surrender. Calhoun did so—but "not seeing the importance of it at the time," he failed to ask Coburn to likewise put in writing his own explicitly stated promise of protection for the citizens of Atlanta and their property.

Mayor James M. Calhoun. (*Atlanta History Center*)

The mayor would regret this oversight for the rest of his life.[13]

In any event, what was done was done, and thus fell the city of Atlanta. "About noon today the Yankees came in sure enough a party of five or six came riding by our house," Sam Richards wrote. "The Stars and Stripes were soon floating aloft over the city." A detachment from the 111th Pennsylvania Infantry won the footrace to City Hall, raising their regimental colors over the building and sparking a bitter debate with Coburn's 70th Indiana as to which regiment could rightly claim to be the first to move into Atlanta. For a long moment, the flag hung lifeless against the staff, but presently a stiff breeze sent it rippling outward, drawing a hearty cheer from the fast accumulating bluecoats in the streets below.[14]

The long blue columns bore down on the center of town, provoking various reactions among the town's residents. One group of young local boys, scrounging for food near the depot like a scurry of squirrels, heard it announced that the Federals were already in the city. "The boys cast their eyes in that direction and discovered that the announcement was only too true," a witness wrote, "for they could plainly discern the bluecoats in the distance, who were rapidly moving toward them, which sent a thrill of terror to their young hearts; and then, as it seemed to them, their race for life began, and with a swiftness almost equal to that of a deer they sped to their homes in hopes of safety." For weeks, the lads had sat wide-eyed listening to scary fireside tales depicting the Yankees as "beastly and bloodthirsty monsters, whose delight it was to catch men, women and innocent children for no other purpose than to murder them." One of the trembling youngsters concealed himself under his grandmother's bed, "and it took considerable persuasion under promise of protection to get him out." Another more sensible boy went to see the Yanks for himself, and "upon closer investigation found that they had neither hoofs nor horns, and were just like the Johnnie Rebs, only that they wore blue and our boys gray."[15]

Terror was the exception, however, not the rule; and the prevailing feeling among the citizenry seemed to be simple curiosity. Residents stood at their front gates and along the sidewalks to watch the Northern army marching in. "They expected no doubt to see a huge set of beings," a New Yorker wrote, "but I rather think they came to the conclusion that we were human, in appearance at least." This they did, though a Cincinnati reporter would presently overhear one old lady express surprise at being able to understand the Yankee tongue. Here and there the soldiers saw signs of Union feeling—an occasional cry of "welcome," a gaggle of ladies fluttering handkerchiefs, a sign in a window that read "United We Stand—Divided We Fall." Scores of blacks lined the streets as well. "The negroes, black, yellow, and white, hailed our men as their deliverers sent of God," a Massachusetts colonel wrote. "'Bress de Lord,' they shouted, 'de Yanks am come, yah! yah! yah!'"[16]

For their part, the arriving bluecoats could hardly have been happier. "The boys was in the best possible good humor," a Wisconsin soldier remembered, men all along the column "full of fun and talk." They marched with a spring in their step, the bands playing "Yankee Doodle" and "The Red, White and Blue," or the men offering up a rousing impromptu chorus of "We will hang Jeff Davis from a sour apple tree." Passing by a downtown hotel, the members of one blue regiment called out to a group of spectators gathered out front, asking them what they had to eat lately. "20-pound Parrott shells," a man hollered in reply.[17]

"It is strange to go about Atlanta now and see only Yankee uniforms," Sam Richards observed the next day, noting that City Hall had been made headquarters for the provost guard. "The enemy behave themselves pretty well except in the scramble for tobacco and liquor during which every store in town nearly was broken into." Carrie Berry, who had passed the uncertain hours by knitting a new pair of stockings, also watched the Union soldiers moving into town. "We were afraid they were going to treat us badly," but instead they "were orderly and behaved themselves very well," she recorded in her diary.

So far, the surrender of the city had not been nearly so bad as the struggle that preceded it. "I think I shall like the Yankees very well," Carrie wrote.[18]

Sherman had trouble sleeping on the night of September 1–2, and though this was hardly unusual, the Ohio general's fitful rest at his bivouac near Jonesboro was further disturbed after midnight by the kettle-drum rumble of what sounded like a cannonade off to the north. Curious and perhaps a bit worried—he had, after all, left only a single corps near Atlanta, and though a night attack seemed highly unlikely, the indomitable Hood could very well have launched yet another sortie to swamp General Slocum. Sherman made his way to a nearby farmhouse, where his staff roused the owner to speak with the Union commander. The farmer confirmed that he had lived there for many years and that the thunder to the north was what it had sounded like when there was a battle raging near Atlanta. Even at a distance, the sound was tremendous. "At times the roar would rise step by step to almost deafening volume, and then subside into silence," a Federal officer posted nearby remembered. "Again it would break forth as if the earth itself were being torn into atoms."[19]

Along around four o'clock, the distant booming thundered to a crescendo yet again before falling away into an ominous silence. Dawn showed Hardee gone from his Jonesboro entrenchments, and Sherman moved southward down the railroad to find the Rebels holding a stoutly defended line at Lovejoy. David Stanley's 4th Corps pushed forward to test the Confederate works but was easily brushed back. "I have never seen the enemy take a stronger position or one of a more difficult approach," Stanley reported. The Confederates, however dire their situation, were apparently still full of fight, and Sherman was inclined to leave it at that while he endeavored to learn the "exact truth" from Atlanta. With couriers deployed and rumors swirling, he told Howard, "we don't care about pushing the enemy any farther at this time. Had we prevented his making intrenchments it would have been well, but as he has a strong line, I do not wish to waste lives by an assault."[20]

Sherman spent the day reconnoitering the Rebel position and exchanging messages with his subordinates theorizing over the cause of last night's commotion. "Very large fires were visible in the direction of Atlanta," Schofield reported. "Brilliant flashes followed at regular intervals by loud explosions, far too loud for any artillery, and then by very rapid explosions of shell." It seemed to Schofield that these circumstances all suggested the burning of Rebel magazines in Atlanta. "I cannot explain the phenomena of last night in any other way," he wrote. "No battle I have ever witnessed would begin to account for it." Shortly thereafter, a former slave was brought to Schofield's tent with a harrowing tale (and quite an accurate one, as it turned out) that the Confederates had abandoned Atlanta and retired down the McDonough Road "in great confusion and disorder," and that "houses were burned, magazines blown up, and a wagon train of ammunition burned." Schofield passed this heartening rumor on to Sherman, but it was far from official confirmation.[21]

Finally, late that afternoon, a staff captain from Garrard's cavalry brought news to Sherman, who was at the time with General Thomas, that Hood had indeed abandoned Atlanta. Once the young officer confirmed that, yes, he had seen the inside of the Rebel works with his own eyes, the two generals "gave extravagant vent to the joy of the announcement." Sherman—normally high-strung and fretful—and Thomas—usually calm and stoic—both "let loose and actually danced and flung up their hats, and embraced each other," while the bemused captain "bore the brunt of hand-shaking that made my arms sore." The news, Sherman would recall, seemed almost too good to be true.[22]

But it was not only true, it was fast becoming old news. The 20th Corps's new commander Henry W. Slocum had sent word of the victory to Washington even before it had reached General Sherman. Slocum was, according to an admirer, not only "one of the most persevering and indefatigable men I ever knew," but also seemed to be a decidedly lucky fellow—and so it was at Atlanta, where the New York-born West Pointer had arrived just in time to have his corps claim the distinction of capturing the city. ("Hooker was a fool," Sherman would later write. "Had he staid a couple of weeks he could have marched into Atlanta and claimed all the honors.") Not necessarily handsome but always elegantly dressed, with dark, wavy hair, brown eyes and a bootbrush mustache, Slocum was only thirty-six, but he was an Old Army man, and it showed. Although his chief Sherman had at the time of the surrender been twenty miles away and had no idea what was happening, his newest subordinate knew very well the proper way to transmit news of the fall of the city.[23]

"General Sherman has taken Atlanta," Slocum wired directly to Secretary of War Edwin M. Stanton on the evening of September 2. "The Twentieth Corps occupies the city. The main army is on the Macon road, near East Point. A battle was fought near that point, in which General Sherman was successful. Particulars not known."[24]

Sherman followed this the next day with a rambling dispatch to General Halleck reporting the results of his southward swing over the past three days—the break in the West Point railroad, the movement on Jonesboro, the battle there, Hardee's retreat toward Lovejoy, and the explosions inside Atlanta. The message ran 325 words and would in later years be largely ignored—except for a single statement buried therein, abbreviated by newspapers and historians alike to make the long-winded Sherman seem far more straightforward and pithy than he was in fact: "Atlanta is ours, and fairly won," the excerpt read. Then, perhaps thinking of Hood and Hardee's strong defensive position bristling in his front at Lovejoy's Station, Sherman added: "I shall not push much further on this raid, but in a day or two will move to Atlanta and give my men some rest."[25]

Sherman's six electrifying words—"Atlanta is ours, and fairly won"—confirmed straight from the horse's mouth Slocum's wire of the night before and touched off an eruption of rejoicing not only in Washington but all across the North. "All Yankeedoodledom is clapping hands, and huzzaing and flinging up caps, as though there were no longer a 'live rebel' in all America," one newspaper wrote. Church bells rang in towns around the country. One hundred-gun salutes were fired in Philadelphia, in Trenton, in New York, and on Boston Common. "Thank God! Atlanta has fallen; and victory at Atlanta means success everywhere," a Federal supply officer wrote to his family from Nashville. "The star of the Republic is once more in the ascendant; and the friends of Freedom should take heart and rejoice! Our flags are out, our bells are ringing; and from Capitol Hill a hundred guns are thundering on the air the great Union victory!" With the heart of the Confederacy now pierced at Atlanta, and the "bulldog Grant" (though Sherman thought him more of a Scottish terrier) lunging for its throat in Virginia, many in the North now believed that the end of the rebellion was at hand.[26]

The press, which two and a half years earlier had dismissed Sherman as crazy and just days before had pronounced him hopelessly stalemated, now compared him favorably with Napoleon and Wellington and Washington. "Hood Hoodwinked," was the predictable headline in the *New York Herald*, while its rival the *Times* pronounced the victory "so great in itself, of such wide scope, such far-reaching result, such indisputable importance, that the country will receive the news of it with unbounded exultation. . . . The rebel military force in the Southwest can now find no point in all their territory of anything like [Atlanta's] strength or value, and their army must soon break up in small and predatory hordes, which will in due time be exterminated."[27]

Most papers chose not to eat crow in print, and instead dealt with the inconsistency posed by their earlier critiques of General Sherman by simply pretending that they never happened. W. H. Russell of the *London Gazette*, for example, who two weeks before had declared Sherman's "slow and fatuous" campaign to be a failure, now wrote without blushing that "General Sherman has fully justified his reputation as an able and daring soldier." An occasional newspaper took note of—though none apologized for—past coverage of the Ohio commander. "Even those who called General Sherman 'crazy' must at least acknowledge 'there is method in his madness,'" the *Jersey City Standard* said.[28]

What was more, the political impact of the fall of Atlanta was undeniable. "Glorious news this morning—*Atlanta taken at last!!!*" New York diarist George Templeton Strong wrote on September 3. "If it be true, it is (coming at this political crisis) the greatest event of the war."

Indeed, the city had fallen to Sherman's forces just two days after the Democrats nominated George McClellan for president. Breathless, bold-type reports of the stunning triumph in Georgia ran side-by-side in the columns of Northern newspapers with details of the newly adopted and suddenly discordant Democratic platform declaring the war a failure. The *New York Times* called the news nothing less than "a Thunderbolt for Copperheads," and the capture of Atlanta, especially when paired with the recent victory achieved by Admiral Farragut at Mobile Bay, seemed to be the death-blow to the Confederate cause. "Sherman and Farragut have knocked the bottom out of the Chicago platform," Secretary of State William Seward exulted. "The sunlight is again shining," the *Cleveland Leader* wrote, "and the Republic is sure to triumph."[29]

Official congratulations rolled in as well, prominent men adding their voices to the chorus of praise in the newspapers. "The national thanks are tendered by the President to Major-General William T. Sherman and the gallant officers and soldiers of his command before Atlanta for the distinguished ability, courage, and perseverance displayed in the campaign in Georgia, which, under divine favor, has resulted in the capture of the city of Atlanta," President Lincoln wrote in an executive order issued on September 3. "The marches, battles, sieges, and other military operations that have signalized this campaign must render it famous in the annals of war, and have entitled those who have participated therein to the applause and thanks of the nation." Army chief of staff General Henry W. Halleck, who had tormented subordinate commanders in the field and complained about lost opportunities and half-won victories for three years now, offered his own personal ovation. "I have watched your movements most attentively and critically," he told Sherman, "and I do not hesitate to say that your campaign has been the most brilliant of the war." And in Virginia, General Grant, after ordering that a hundred-gun salute be fired "with shotted guns from every battery bearing upon the enemy," sent a follow-on letter with his heartfelt congratulations as well. "In conclusion, it is hardly necessary for me to say that I feel you have accomplished the most gigantic undertaking given to any general in this war, and with a skill and ability that will be acknowledged in history as unsurpassed, if not unequaled," he said.[30]

Certain admirers went so far as to propose General Sherman as a potential presidential nominee, the one particular compliment that irritated him to no end. "Some fool seems to have used my name," Sherman said of the polticial brouhaha. "If forced to choose between the penitentiary and the White House," he wrote, "I would say the penitentiary, thank you, sir. If any committee would approach me for political preferment, I doubt if I could have patience or prudence enough to preserve a decent restraint on myself, but would insult the nation in the reply."[31]

Still, Sherman plainly reveled in the host of accolades coming in from friends and former foes alike, even as he patted himself on the back in his own correspondence. "My part," he told Halleck in reviewing the campaign, "was skillful and well executed." Describing his "quick" and "well-executed" recent movement to a friend in Louisville, he tallied up the results: "The rebels have lost, besides the important city of Atlanta, immense stores, at least 500 dead, 2,500 wounded, and 3,000 prisoners, whereas our aggregate [loss] will not foot up 1,500. If that is not success, I don't know what is." And to his wife Ellen, he pronounced his campaign for Atlanta "the best, cleanest and most satisfactory of the war."

But he wasn't satisfied, and as he made clear to Ellen, he wasn't finished. "I have received the most fulsome praise of all from the President down, but I fear the world will jump to the wrong conclusion that because I am in Atlanta the work is done," he wrote. "Far from it."[32]

Sherman was right. The war was far from over and the last battle in Georgia not yet fought, in part because he had chosen to focus his efforts not on the destruction of Hood's army, but on the capture of Atlanta. Northern newspapers made occasional mention of "Hood's escape," doing their best to portray the survival and regrouping of the Southern army as an inglorious skedaddle, but for the most part that minor detail was lost in the national acclaim for the army and its commander for their glorious achievement. Sherman himself was aware of the potential for criticism and was defensive about what he had and had not accomplished. "The town of Atlanta, after all, was the prize I fought for," he told Halleck, though he admitted, "I ought to have reaped larger fruits of victory." In time, Sherman would be harshly criticized by historians for letting the Army of Tennessee get away—"Sherman's Failure at Atlanta," one article was provocatively titled.[33]

Now that Sherman had succeeded in the campaign—at least, succeeded in reducing Atlanta—a number of officers and men in his army believed that the war should be at an end. "No sane person could have hoped for any possible advantage to be gained by further prosecution of the bloody war," one Federal officer wrote, "but there were no signs of surrender on the part of the Confederates."[34]

Southern newspapers acknowledged the loss of Atlanta as a regrettable development, or merely an ample helping of sorry luck, but insisted that the damage to the Confederacy itself was slight, or at least not fatal. "We regard the evacuation by our troops as a misfortune only in so far as it will have the effect of consolidating all parties in the North in favor of a continued prosecution of the war. In itself it is no misfortune whatever," the *Richmond Dispatch* editorialized on September 5—protesting too much, methinks. The editors considered the fall of Atlanta to be completely unsurprising—after all, "The Yankee papers have been telling us for many weeks past that Sherman could enter and take possession any day he pleased." In any event, the column concluded, "We do not regard these operations as by any means decisive of any question whatever. Hood's army still exists, and its spirit is still unbroken. Every step that Sherman takes in advance increases the difficulty of retreat in case of disaster, and that disaster will eventually come is among the probabilities, at least, of the future."[35]

The *Richmond Whig* agreed. "The situation is very grave," the editors wrote, "but it is not so dangerous as many would suppose. The troops, though very much humiliated at the necessity of abandoning Atlanta, are still in good spirits, and are as defiant as ever." Closer to the present seat of war, the *Columbus (Ga.) Times* scoffed at the triumphal chest-beating to the north and the embarrassing hand-wringing to the south. "Whoever heard of such a fuss being made over the fall of a twenty-year-old town, three hundred miles in the interior of the state, as we and the Yankees are making over the *evacuation* of Atlanta," the paper huffed.[36]

Official Richmond likewise rejected any talk of coffin nails, insisting not only that the fall of Atlanta was not decisive, but that no loss anywhere would be decisive either. "There are no vital points on the preservation of which the continued existence of the Confederacy depends," Jefferson Davis presently told the legislature. "There is no military success of the enemy which can accomplish its destruction. Not the fall of Richmond, nor Wilmington, nor Charleston, nor Savannah, nor Mobile, nor of all combined, can save the enemy from the constant drain of blood and treasure which must continue until he shall discover that no peace is attainable unless based upon the recognition of our indefeasible rights."[37]

But whatever state of denial prevailed among the Confederate press and politicians, Southern civilians and soldiers alike were heartbroken by the news of the fall of the Gate City. Hood regretted the loss of Atlanta not so much for its strategic importance but for its effect on morale. "I was not so much pained by the fall of Atlanta as by the *recurrence* of retreat, which I knew would further demoralize the army and renew desertions," he said—and the blow to Southern morale extended all the way to Richmond. A correspondent wrote to the *Mobile Register* that the surrender of Atlanta had caused a more "painful expression" in the Confederate capital than either the fall of Vicksburg or the loss at the Battle of Gettysburg the year before. Civilians, too, mourned the city's loss like death in the family. "Atlanta gone," diarist Mary Chesnut wrote. "Well—that agony is over. Like David when the child was dead, I will get up from my knees, will wash my face and comb my hair. No hope. We will try to have no fear."[38]

The same grim perseverance seemed to endure in the Army of Tennessee, reunited with the arrival of Hood and Stewart and Lee at Lovejoy's Station on September 4. "The army is now safely together again, and though beaten and outgeneraled, we are still beligerent and rebellious," General Hardee's adjutant W. L. Trask wrote. "Most of our boys say, 'Well, we'll get 'em after awhile.'" As for himself, Trask reported: "My present condition is rather Barbarish, particularly as regards my apparel—my hat is without a crown—my pants of which I have but one pair, show a 'flag of truce' at the rear (if I had a flag)—my shoes have no soles on them and my socks have only the legs left, but they served to keep up appearances anyway. I have had but one pair of socks in the last four months and I have never taken them off my feet except to wash them. The feet have long since disappeared and altogether my general appearance is rather dilapidated and decidedly unpleasant."[39]

So, too, with the general appearance and condition of the Confederate Army of Tennessee. The men had suffered greatly in recent days, especially Hardee's Corps, bloodied at Jonesboro, and Lee's, which had marched from East Point to Jonesboro, fought there, then were recalled to Atlanta by Hood, arriving just in time to take part in the long march down to Lovejoy's Station—in all, six days and nights of intermittent and demoralizing marching, countermarching, and retreating. Hundreds of soldiers were unaccounted for; those present were footsore, bedraggled, and hungry. "Shoes and clothing are very much needed," Hood told Richmond, though he insisted that the army was "not discouraged." If not discouraged, they were certainly disheveled and depressed. "Everybody was thoroughly broken down," a cannoneer would remember. "Although not broken in spirit, our state of mind had no spring of faith or hope in it. We had simply arrived at a state of indifference. We knew not what was before us and cared less."

The Rebel soldiers recovered from their exertions as best they could, though no one could raise his head above the breastworks, as Lovejoy brought a replication in deadly miniature of the murderous picket firing along the Atlanta fortifications. "The situation was decidedly hot and vicious," a soldier wrote, "one long fierce incessant skirmish not merely between the rifle pits but between the main lines." All indications were that the Federals would soon renew their attack, and Hood and Hardee braced to receive it, both wiring Richmond with desperate requests for help. "To prevent this country from being overrun re-enforcements are absolutely necessary," Hood wrote to Braxton Bragg on September 3. A day later, Hardee portrayed the Army of Tennessee's situation as even more dire. "Unless this army is speedily and heavily re-enforced Georgia and Alabama will be overrun," he wired directly to the president. "I see no other means to avert this calamity. Never in my opinion was our liberty in such danger. What can you do for us?"[40]

Jefferson Davis responded promptly that every available reserve had already been forwarded. "No other resource remains," he said. Even so, remarkably, Hood was determined not only to continue to resist, but to look for opportunities to go on the offensive, reinforcements or no reinforcements. "Whatever forces are sent, I shall use them in the best manner possible to defeat our enemy," he told Bragg. "It is necessary for me to give battle should the enemy continue to advance."[41]

But then on the morning of September 6, much to the astonishment and no doubt the relief of the still-overmatched Confederates, daylight showed the bluecoats gone from their immediate front. "No shooting of us, everything as quiet as a meetinghouse," a Texan wrote. Scouts soon confirmed the Federals' departure back northward—"The Yanks have gone back to Atlanta surenough."[42]

"Upon that date it may be justly considered that the operations round Atlanta ceased," Hood wrote in his memoirs, and he would go on to make his case for what the Rebels had accomplished. "We had maintained a defence, of an untenable position, and had battled almost incessantly, day and night, with a force of about forty-five thousand (45,000) against and Army of one hundred and six thousand (106,000) effectives, flushed with victory upon victory from Dalton to Atlanta." Noting the "splendid material" that composed the Army of Tennessee, Hood insisted that none of his countrymen could "hesitate to accord them the highest praise for the patriotic and noble work performed by them during the siege of Atlanta."[43]

Others would hardly sum up the campaign that way, however, including some of Hood's own countrymen—indeed, his own soldiers. "From the time Hood assumed command of our army," an Arkansas private wrote, "five great battles had been fought, a siege of a month or so endured, the town we were defending torn to pieces by bombardment and finally abandoned. The cost was the destruction or desertion of an immense mass of government stores, precious to us at that stage of the war and of an amount unprecedented in all the previous history of the Confederate misfortunes, the loss of 14,000 of his best men, killed, wounded or captured, and worst of all, the absolute loss of his army's trust and confidence."[44]

Such reviews and recriminations were still to come, however; for the present, Hood and his army had to assess and respond to Sherman's next move. A Mississippi regiment captured a solitary Federal straggler near the lines outside of Lovejoy. The prisoner, brought to headquarters and interrogated about the enemy's movements, seemed no less proud of the Union army despite his unenviable circumstances.

The Federals, he said with a smirk, were "going back to Atlanta to elect a President."[45]

At 10 A.M. on September 3, just hours after sending his "fairly won" telegram to Washington, Sherman issued a special order to the troops. "The general commanding announces with great pleasure that he has official information that our troops under Major-General Slocum occupied Atlanta yesterday at 11 A.M.," the order read, "the enemy having evacuated the night before, destroyed vast magazines of stores, and blowing up, among other things, eighty car-loads of ammunition, which accounts for the sounds heard by us on the night of the 1st instant. Our present task is, therefore, well done, and all work of destruction on the railroad will cease." The order was read at the head of each regiment, as one colonel recalled, "amid cheers for 'Crazy' Sherman."

This welcome news and the pronouncement that the object of the campaign had been achieved ended any real thought of further pursuit of—and certainly of any Kennesaw-style frontal assault against—the entrenched Rebels at Lovejoy's Station. Whether his Confederate opponent remained intact or not, Sherman considered him defeated. After all, to his way of thinking, Sherman had beaten Hood at every turn, had wrested Atlanta from him, and now had him huddled in his entrenchments pleading for reinforcements thirty miles south of the city. As far as Sherman was concerned, the Atlanta Campaign was over, the victory won. "All the corps, regiments, and batteries composing this army may, without further orders, inscribe 'ATLANTA' on their colors," he ordered on September 4.[46]

Meanwhile, inside Atlanta, soldiers of the 20th Corps were getting their first close-up inspection of what one would call "the Golden Apple." Officers and men wandered the streets of the city and took its measure, giving descriptions and drawing comparisons to communities back home in an attempt to give a sense of the dusty, down-home metropolis. "The city is a very pretty place, built much in northern taste and stile," the six-foot-six-inch Pennsylvania Brigadier General John Geary wrote to his wife—somewhat comparable to Harrisburg, he thought. An Illinois captain accurately judged the railroad town "not over half as large as Nashville," while an Indiana doctor estimated it to be "about the size of Evansville." Sherman's engineer Captain Orlando Poe pronounced Atlanta "quite a town—about the size of Dayton, Ohio. It has something of the tumbledown look of all Southern towns, but still there are some fine residences, and more evidences of thrift than are usually met with south of Mason & Dixon's line."[47]

Some observers thought the Gate City had the feel of a budding frontier community. "Atlanta looks more like a new, thriving Western city than any place I have seen in the South," Major Connolly wrote. "It has none of that built-up, finished, moss grown, venerable, aristocratic air, so noticeable in Southern cities; and in days of peace, I have no doubt Atlanta throbbed with the pulsations of that kind of enterprise that is converting our Western prairies into gardens, and dotting them with cities that rise up with the magic and suddenness of coral isles." The inhabitants of the city seemed a little rough, however, especially the women. "The ladies are better looking in general than they ware at Bridgeport, but that ain't saying much," an underwhelmed New York corporal wrote in a letter home. "They are tall, sparse, thin, tawny, starved looking objects to pity. You could not finde a young lady with rosy cheeks, full faced, hansomly formed if you were to travel for six months. Theyr general looks are as if they had bin hauled through a knothole and beat round the room with a safron bag. If all men admired them as I doe, they will always be plenty of unmarried ladies in the southern states."[48]

On the positive side of the ledger, the blue soldiers were pleasantly surprised by the amount of Union feeling apparent in the city. Atlanta, then as now, was filled with transplanted Northerners who had moved south with their families, mostly for business opportunites, in the years leading up to the war. "The most of the inhabitance has left," one soldier wrote, "but what did stay was glad to see us come in." In fact, the true Union families, who had for the most part laid low over the past several years, now found themselves with new station among their neighbors. And large numbers of residents now claimed to be for Uncle Sam, first, last and always. As one officer put it, "all pretend to be loyal now."[49]

One Federal commissary sergeant pitched his tents in the dooryard of a loyal Union family. "I have made the acquaintance of the whole family even to the dog, who now lies in one corner of the tent as contented as he can be, in fact he is a thorough going Union dog. The children are playing around as happy as any children can be, while the

The Masonic Hall and Trout House hotel along Decatur Street soon after the Federal occupation in September 1864. (*Library of Congress*)

whole family appear as cheerful as any family I have seen, quite a contrast to the generality of the citizens we have met hitherto."[50]

Whether patrolling or merely sightseeing, soldiers toured other notable points around the city—the passenger depot or Car Shed, for example, which had held up remarkably well and seemed little damaged despite the bombardment; the foundries, machine shops, mills, and factories; and the city cemetery—"almost a wonder," Geary wrote, "it contains nearly 10,000 newly made graves filled principally by rebel losses in the late battles." For the most part, they avoided the battlefields on the outskirts of the city to the north and east and west, where there was little to see apart from the treeless, shell-torn landscape and the not-yet-decayed corpses of poor boys who had been washed from their shallow resting places by the late summer rains as if trying to claw their way from the grave.

Perhaps the greatest marvel, and the one most commonly remarked upon in soldiers' correspondence, was the damage done by the Federal artillery over the past several weeks—"the ravages of war illustrated," one private wrote. "I have been around the city somewhat and the destruction in the northern & eastern portions is astonishing," another said. "I know our batteries threw over enormous quantity of shells but I couldn't think they were so effective. . . . Shade trees a foot through are cut off, fences broken down in short every kind of mischief is done by those iron missiles. I don't see how any one ever ventured to live there yet some did and escaped too." Soldiers peered into the bombproofs or gopher holes hidden in gardens and basements and backyards, some of them dug fifteen feet deep, others furnished with carpet and chairs and tables and other comforts of home.[51]

The torn-up buildings and the caves where women and children had huddled amid the shellfire elicited sympathy from many of the officers and men, and gave them a measure of understanding of the ferocity of the opposition they had faced. "I had often heard of the terrors of a bombardment of a crowded city but I had never realized it before," Indiana surgeon James Patten wrote. "Houses were shattered and torn in every shape that can be imagined, some utterly destroyed and some but little injured. Some had shell through the doors, some places the shell had burst inside a house and torn it all to pieces. After seeing the destruction I no longer wondered at the insane fury with which they charged our works, rushing on as they often did with their hats pulled down over their eyes so that they could not see the certain destruction that awaited them."[52]

"The city, in some localities has been a good deal injured by our shot, and I learn that several women & children were killed," Orlando Poe wrote in a letter to his wife. "You know I was opposed to shelling the place for it did no good at all, and only brought harm to unoffending people." The destruction made no sense to the practical and by-the-book young engineer, both because it rendered useless certain structures that could have been useful to the Federals as depots or warehouses, and because it had no real military effect. "I venture to say that all the shelling we did did not get us into the town a *single second* sooner than we would have got in anyhow," he asserted. "It was the movement of our army around to their rear that drove the rebels out, and not the burning & destruction of a few houses occupied by non-combatants instead of rebel soldiers who were safely and snugly stowed away in the forts."[53]

Far more astonishing than the shell-riddled buildings was the apocalyptic scene along the Georgia Railroad where Hood's reserve ordnance train had been destroyed. "Got there, and such a sight I never saw," a Wisconsin soldier wrote of his visit to the railyards. "There stood 4 large trains of cars and 5 locomotive in ashes, except the iron." Another witness described the varieties of ammunition strewn about, including "unexploded shell, solid shot, grape, canister, and bullets," some of it melted into frozen globs of metal by the searing heat. A pond nearby was nearly filled to overflowing with drowned boxes of ammunition. Along the rails themselves, stretching for hundreds of yards along the remains of the east-west line, were dozens and dozens of paired wheels, buried in dirt and ash up to the axels. The still-smoking rolling mill had disappeared entirely except for its stacks, standing like weathered columns in an ancient ruin, with the scattered bones of industry strewn among them—"steam boilers, fly wheels, great piles of iron in various stages of manufacture."[54]

Despite the ramshackle appearance of the town and the somewhat anticlimactic denouement of the grand campaign—with the Rebel army gone in the night, the general commanding absent from the scene, and six-sevenths of the Union army still posted two dozen miles away—the fall of the war-torn city had an epic feel to it, and put men in mind of stories of cities and civilizations and wars long past. "Here amidst the glories of victories which God has vouchsafed to give us, is the best place to witness the horrors of war," General Geary wrote. "The wounded and the dying—the starving, ruined people . . . mope around the corners as if some unearthly catastrophe had occurred, and it brings to my mind a vivified scene of the times when it was said, 'Babylon is fallen.'"[55]

Whether in official reports over the next several weeks or in memoirs written down the years, veterans of the grand campaign would take stock of what had been accomplished, along with the terrible price that had been paid. The campaign for Atlanta from May to September had covered more than a hundred miles as the crow flies, and far more as the flanking and fighting soldier marches (an Illinois sergeant would tally the distance covered at no less than four hundred miles), 128 days of marching and fighting in the Georgia heat, ten major battles, and countless smaller fights and skirmishes. One soldier estimated that his regiment dug, over the course of the campaign, trenches amounting to sixty times the length of its line—not including the grim hours of gravedigging along the way. Official tabulations would show that over the course of the campaign, Sherman's army fired 149,670 rounds of artillery ammunition and more than 22 million rounds of small-arms ammunition—roughly 173,000 per day, or an average of 120 shots fired for every minute of the four-month struggle.

Concluding his own official report, John Geary would pronounce the campaign "unequaled in the present war for glorious victory over almost insurmountable difficulties, and unsurpassed in modern history," and one "which shall stand forever a monument of the valor, the endurance, the patriotism of the American soldier." In a letter to his wife, he would sum up the contest more briefly. "It was indeed but one grand battle," he wrote, "one grand victory from beginning to its end."[56]

And so it may have been, from the Northern perspective, with a few notable exceptions like Pickett's Mill and Kennesaw Mountain and Utoy Creek and the various cavalry fiascoes. But the cost in bloodshed on both sides—though casualties would pale in comparison to the murderous contest in Virginia—was grievous indeed. "Our rejoicing is tempered, as it always must be, by the soldier's sorrow at the loss of his companions-in-arms," O. O. Howard wrote in a congratulatory order to the Army of the Tennessee. "On every hillside, in every valley throughout your long and circuitous route, from Dalton to Jonesboro, you have buried them." Federal losses in the four-month campaign, from May through August, would come to 34,514—4,988 killed, 24,773 wounded, and 4,708 missing. Notable losses included James B. McPherson killed and George Stoneman captured; while Grenville Dodge, Manning Force, Walter Gresham, and the Fighting Parson Joseph Lightburn were wounded. (Departing the campaign in less mournful circumstances were Benjamin Harrison, who left to campaign in Indiana; John Palmer, who refused to take orders from Schofield; Tom Sweeny, who was court-martialed after his fistfight with Dodge; and Joe Hooker, who departed in a huff.) And thousands of men were lost not to bullets or bombs or even sickness, but by the simple expiration of terms of service, which cost Sherman 9,917 men in the month of August alone.

Confederate losses are very difficult to ascertain, due to incomplete or outright false reporting, though one meticulous scholar of the campaign estimates Southern casualties at 35,000 killed, wounded, and missing—the losses roughly evenly divided between Johnston, who had commanded the army for ten and a half weeks, and Hood, who had commanded it for six and a half. Among men of high rank, Leonidas Polk, W. H. T. Walker, and Rock Stevens had been killed; Daniel Govan captured at Jonesboro; and States Rights Gist, Alexander Stewart, Patton Anderson, W. W. Loring, James A. Smith, and William Bate were among the wounded. "Atlanta had fallen, and our loss in men and stores could never be replaced," a Kentucky lieutenant wrote, "but I will not permit myself to indulge in criticism of any one on this great disaster to the Confederacy. No doubt it was our fate, but it was none the less bitter."[57]

Yet bitter fate had crueler things in store. Sadly, for the Army of Tennessee, the worst of its horrors was yet to come.

Armed Federal guards and a supply wagon train along Alabama Street. The buildings on the right include a furniture warehouse and the Franklin Printing House and Book Bindery. (*Library of Congress*)

CHAPTER ELEVEN

Yankee Town

Occupation and Expulsion, September–October

Sherman rode into Atlanta on September 7, five days after the surrender, apparently with little fuss or fanfare. "His entry was without parade or ostentation," staff captain and newspaper correspondent David Conyngham wrote, "no beating of drums, no flaunting of colors, no firing of salutes, to humble the pride of the conquered." Again, curious residents ventured out to catch a glimpse of the red-bearded Union commander, who was pointed out along the way to a group of black men gathered on a corner. Ohio captain George Pepper recounted their reaction. "Lord, massa, is dat General Sherman?" one of the old men exclaimed in disbelief. "Why, bless your soul, they tell us he had long whiskers, way down to his knees! Dey told us he had big eyes and ears, and had horns! . . . Why, all of us used to run when dey holler Sherman. Why, all de white folks run. Lord, it made old Johnston run to hear of dat man. . . . I'se glad I'se seen him," he said with satisfaction as the general and his staff rode on past. "I just wanted to see de man what made my old massa run."[1]

Sherman established his headquarters directly across from City Hall in the former home of John Neal, now resident in Zebulon, whose son Lieutenant Andrew Neal had been killed in August by a Union sharpshooter in the trenches outside Atlanta. Three days earlier, the Ohio commander had written to General Henry W. Halleck in Washington to give an update on the military situation. The 20th Corps occupied Atlanta, he said, with the remainder of the army still posted south of Jonesboro, facing the Rebel lines down near Lovejoy's Station. Sherman explained that the enemy was well entrenched and could be neither attacked in front nor turned in his present position. While he determined how best to deal with Hood, Sherman planned to rest and refit his troops while bringing forward his base of supply and converting Atlanta to a military post. Accordingly, he wrote, "I propose to remove all the inhabitants of Atlanta, sending those committed to our cause to the rear, and the rebel families to the front. I will allow no trade, manufactories nor any citizens there at all, so that we will have the entire use of railroad back, as also such corn and forage as may be reached by our troops."

"If the people raise a howl against my barbarity and cruelty I will answer that war is war, and not popularity-seeking," he closed. "If they want peace they and their relatives must stop the war."[2]

Sherman had practical reasons for wanting to move out Atlanta's civilian population. He was well aware of the problems Federal commanders had encountered in dealing with civilians following the capture and occupation of other Southern cities, from Nashville to New Orleans. By removing the population of Atlanta, he would not only avoid having to feed them—Hood had been supplying up to 1,500 rations per day to the city's poor during the month of August—but would also remove thousands of potential sympathizers, smugglers, and spies from the midst of what was now the largest Union outpost in what Sherman considered "the so-called Southern Confederacy." Besides these fairly matter-of-fact reasons, others would suggest that the stern Ohio commander meant to send a message—one Unionist opined that the order was "nothing more than a clever ruse to provide 15,000 Missionaries to scatter through the State to beseech their fellow Citizens to lay down their arms." Indeed, Sherman admitted as much years later. "I knew that the people of the South would read in this measure two important conclusions," he wrote in his memoirs, "one, that we were in earnest; and the other, if they were sincere in their common and popular clamor 'to die in the last ditch,' that the opportunity would soon come."[3]

And though some historians would pronounce Sherman's deportation order "virtually without precedent in the war," he had in fact done the same thing in this very campaign. Back in early July, when the factory towns of Roswell and New Manchester had been captured by Union cavalry, Sherman ordered—and then reconfirmed his order, so there could be no misunderstanding of his intentions—that some four hundred mill workers, most of them women, be arrested and sent northward. "Being exempt from conscription, they are as much governed by the rules of war as if in the ranks," he said. "The women can find employment in Indiana." This act, the still-notorious "removal of the Roswell mill women," drew widespread criticism, even in some Northern newspapers. "Only think of it!" the *Cincinnati Commercial* had written. "Four hundred weeping and terrified Ellens, Susans and Maggies transported, in springless and seatless army wagons, away from their lovers and brothers of the sunny South, and all for the offense of weaving tent-cloth and stocking-yarn!" The *New York Commercial Advertiser* agreed, finding it "hardly conceivable that an officer bearing a United States commission of Major General should have so far forgotten the commonest dictates of decency and humanity (Christianity apart), as to drive four hundred penniless girls hundreds of miles away from their homes and friends to seek their livelihood against strange and hostile people." But Sherman had done just that, and was about to do something like it again, but on a grander scale.[4]

He informed General Hood of his intentions in a fairly stiff letter dated September 7, proposing a two-day truce to effectuate the removal of Atlanta's civilians. "I have deemed it to the interest of the United States that the citizens now residing in Atlanta should remove, those who prefer it to go south and the rest north," he wrote, with the assurance that he would provide transportation by railcar or wagon "so that their removal may be made with as little discomfort as possible."

"Atlanta is no place for families or non-combatants," he added, "and I have no desire to send them north if you will assist in conveying them South."[5]

Hood had no alternative but to agree to the requested truce, though he would not let the expulsion order pass without objection. "Quite an angry correspondence grew up between us," Sherman later recalled—

indeed, a series of increasingly venomous letters that one observer would consider "one of the most interesting exchanges between two opposing generals . . . in the annals of military history." The Southern commander responded to Sherman on September 9, first agreeing to the truce and discussing various details like guards and transportation. But Hood closed his letter with a stinger: "And now, sir, permit me to say that the unprecedented measure you propose transcends, in studied and ingenious cruelty, all acts ever before brought to my attention in the dark history of war," he wrote. "In the name of God and humanity, I protest, believing that you will find that you are expelling from their homes and firesides the wives and children of a brave people."[6]

Sherman, of course, was hardly of a temperament to let such a swipe go unanswered, and he fired off a blistering response the next day. It was unnecessary for Hood to appeal to the "dark history of war, when recent and modern examples are so handy," he said. "You yourself burned dwelling houses along your parapet, and I have seen to-day fifty houses that you have rendered uninhabitable because they stood in the way of your forts and men." He went on to charge Hood with situating his lines "so close to town that every cannon shot and many musket shots from our line of investment, that overshot their mark, went into the habitations of women and children"—quite as if the relentless five-week bombardment of Atlanta had been entirely accidental. "I say that it is kindness to these families of Atlanta to remove them now, at once, from scenes that women and children should not be exposed to," he continued, chiding Hood for appealing to "a just God in such a sacrilegious manner."

"If we must be enemies, let us be men, and fight it out as we propose to do, and not deal in such hypocritical appeals to God and humanity," the Northern general closed. "God will judge us in due time, and he will pronounce whether it be more humane to fight with a town full of women and families of a brave people at our back, or to remove them in time to places of safety among their own friends and people."[7]

Hood, reading Sherman's letter, apparently considered it further provocation, and he fired another volley in response, this one more than twice the length of Sherman's argument. In the heart of the letter, the tawny-bearded general wrote:

> You came into our country with your Army, avowedly for the purpose of subjugating free white men, women, and children, and not only intend to rule over them, but you make negroes your allies, and desire to place over us an inferior race, which we have raised from barbarism to its present position, which is the highest ever attained by that race, in any country, in all time. I must, therefore, decline to accept your statements in reference to your kindness to the people of Atlanta, and your willingness to sacrifice everything for the peace and honor of the South, and refuse to be governed by your decision in regard to matters between myself, my country, and my God.
>
> You say, "Let us fight it out like men." To this my reply is—for myself, and I believe for all the true men, ay, and women and children in my country—we will fight you to the death! Better die a thousand deaths than submit to live under you or your Government and your negro allies!

Hood ended by "humbly and reverently" invoking notwithstanding Sherman's charge of sacrilege—"his Almighty aid in defence of justice and right."[8]

Sherman was a prolific correspondent, said by a biographer to write on some occasions as many as fifty letters or dispatches per day, but he was apparently tiring of the now weeklong and increasingly long-winded debate with Hood. His response this time, in the final missive of the exchange, was very brief, addressing only two points of Hood's 1,665-word letter. First, he wrote: "We have no 'negro allies' in this Army; not a single negro soldier left Chattanooga with this Army, or is with it now. There are a few guarding Chattanooga"—the 14th U.S. Colored Troops—"which General Stedmen sent at one time to drive Wheeler out of Dalton." Second, Sherman addressed the subject of the bombardment. "I was not bound by the laws of war to give notice of the shelling of Atlanta, a 'fortified town, with magazines, arsenals, foundries, and public stores;' you were bound to take notice. See the books."

Then he dismissed Hood and his arguments, almost contemptuously. "This is the conclusion of our correspondence, which I did not begin, and terminate with satisfaction," he wrote.[9]

Readers of this remarkable series of letters, then and later, would almost universally judge that Sherman got the best of the exchange. Having defeated Hood with the sword, as it were, it now appeared that Sherman had whipped him with the pen as well. "How his wrath swells and grows till it bursts,'" Boston editor Charles Eliot Norton wrote, one of millions across the North chortling with delight over Sherman's fiery letters. "He writes as well as he fights." Northern newspapers crowned their new darling Sherman not only the victor in the debate but "one of the great men of the time."

Still, Hood's arguments, however misguided and detestable when viewed through the lens of history, were impassioned and articulate, again giving the lie to the common perception that he was nothing more than a hard-charging simpleton. What was more, just as he had in the battles around Atlanta, Hood got in his shots; for example, in needling Sherman about his disingenuous claims of an unintentional bombardment. "I made no complaint of your firing into Atlanta in any way you thought proper," Hood wrote. "I make none now, but there are a hundred thousand witnesses that you fired into the habitations of women and children for weeks, firing far above and miles beyond my line of defense. I have too good an opinion, founded both upon observation and experience, of the skill of your artillerists, to credit the insinuation that they for several weeks unintentionally fired too high for my modest-field works, and slaughtered women and children by accident and want of skill."[10]

Around the same time, a second and in the end more famous exchange of correspondence occurred between Sherman and the mayor of Atlanta, James M. Calhoun. In a September 11 letter signed by Calhoun and two city councilmen, E. E. Rawson and E. C. Wells, the town fathers did not so much argue with Sherman as to beg him for mercy—though their pleadings were no more successful than Hood's recent protestations. The measure, Calhoun warned, would cause "extraordinary hardship and loss," and he went on to illuminate some particular circumstances. "Many poor women are in advanced state of pregnancy, others having young children, and whose husbands, for the greater part, are either in the Army, prisoners, or dead," Calhoun wrote, and then asked, "how is it possible for the people still here (mostly women and children) to find any shelter? And how can they live through the winter in the woods—no shelter or subsistence, in the midst of strangers who know them not, and without the power to assist them much, if they were willing to do so?" With that (and much more) said, the mayor and councilmen solemnly implored General Sherman to modify his expulsion order, "and suffer this unfortunate people to remain at home, and enjoy what little means they have."[11]

Sherman was a prolific corresondent who wrote as quickly as he talked, often composing dozens of orders and letters a day. (*L. M. Strayer Collection*)

Sherman responded promptly on September 12, fully acknowledging what the mayor called the "consequences appalling and heart-rending" of his order, but refusing to modify the order nonetheless. Of the thousands of pieces of correspondence that the prolific general wrote in the course of his life and career, it would be this letter that would become the most famous, and to some, the most telling about his philosophy and personal character. "You cannot qualify war in harsher terms than I will," Sherman wrote in dismissing Calhoun's effort to paint a picture of the woes that would result from the coming deportation. "War is cruelty, and you cannot refine it; and those who brought war into our country deserve all the curses and maledictions a people can pour out. I know I had no hand in making this war, and I know I will make more sacrifices today than any of you to secure peace. But you cannot have peace and a division of our country."

Back in April, before his campaign began, he had likened war to a thunderbolt, which "turns not aside even if the beautiful, virtuous and charitable stand in its path." Now he returned to the same metaphor:

> You might as well appeal against the thunder-storm as against these terrible hardships of war. They are inevitable, and the only way the people of Atlanta can hope once more to live in peace and quiet at home, is to stop the war, which can only be done

by admitting that it began in error and is perpetuated in pride. We don't want your negroes, or your horses, or your houses, or your lands, or any thing you have, but we do want and will have a just obedience to the laws of the United States. That we will have, and, if it involves the destruction of your improvements, we cannot help it.

I want peace, and believe it can only be reached through union and war, and I will ever conduct war with a view to perfect and early success.

But, my dear sirs, when peace does come, you may call on me for any thing. Then will I share with you the last cracker, and watch with you to shield your homes and families against danger from every quarter.

Now you must go, and take with you the old and feeble, feed and nurse them, and build for them, in more quiet places, proper habitations to shield them against the weather until the mad passions of men cool down, and allow the Union and peace once more to settle over your old homes in Atlanta.

Yours in haste,

W. T. Sherman, Major-General commanding.[12]

The official order of explusion was issued on September 5 by Colonel William Cogswell of the 2nd Massachusetts Regiment, headquartered at City Hall and detailed as the city's provost guard. "All families living in Atlanta, the male representatives of which are in the service of the Confederate States, or who have gone south, will leave the city within five days," Cogswell wrote. "They will be passed through the lines and will go South. All citizens from the North, not connected with the army, and who have not authority from Major-General Sherman or Major-General Thomas to remain in the city, will leave within the time above mentioned. If found within the city after that date they will be arrested."[13]

Hood was far from the only one outraged by these "infamous and inhuman orders"—Southern newspapers, too, were horrified at the mass deportation, which the *Richmond Sentinel* called "an event unparalleled in the American war, and without an example in modern times." As for General Sherman, the paper said, he was nothing less than "the chief among savages, the captain among pirates, the leader among highwaymen, prince among scoundrels and brutes, the foremost villain of the world." Sherman was as always untroubled by such caterwauling in the press—"it did no good," one of his soldiers said, "to call 'Uncle Billy' names." He was prepared to stand by his order and endure whatever criticism came his way, and he believed that time would prove him right. "I am not willing to have Atlanta encumbered by the families of our enemies," he told Halleck. "I want it a pure Gibraltar, and will have it so by the 1st of October."[14]

Just as some among his army had frowned to themselves over the bombardment, so, too, did certain officers register quiet, unofficial protests of the expulsion order. The 20th Corps' quartermaster Colonel William Le Duc, who had known Sherman in the days before the war, asked a member of the general's staff to pass along to the Union commander a message to the effect that his action "wouldn't read well in history." Sherman bristled at the criticism. "You tell Bill Duc I care not a damn how others read it," he said, "I am *making* history, and the citizens of this rebel town shan't eat the rations I need for my army. Tell him to turn them out." Still, Le Duc went about his work somewhat grudgingly, with a twinge of conscience as he "turned them out." After all, he wrote in a letter to his wife, if every man in their hometown of Mount Vernon, Ohio, had been required to leave within ten or twenty days, "you can imagine the consternation it would produce. When will we go? What will we do for a home? How shall we live? Can we take our property with us?"[15]

News of the order had come hard to the remaining residents of Atlanta, many of them with no place to go, others having bravely ridden out the storm of battle, bombardment, and occupation only now to be unceremoniously thrown out of their homes. "We are all in so much trouble," Carrie Berry wrote in her diary on September 9, and a day later gave a glimpse of her feelings and those of her parents. "Every one I see seems sad," she said. "The citizens all think that it is the most cruel thing to drive us from our home but I think it would be so funny to move. Mama seems so troubled and she can't do any thing. Papa says he don't know where on earth to go." Sherman's original deadlines for Atlantans to clear out—"leave the city within five days"—proved to be overly ambitious. The registration of citizens and preparations for the exchange took almost twice that long, and a ten-day rather than a two-day truce was agreed upon to facilitate the evacuation. A few residents would be permitted to stay—including certain avowed Unionists, a few woeful and persuasive petitioners to General Sherman (who found him "very patient, gentlemanly, and obliging"), and those with essential or at least potentially useful occupations. (Carrie's father, Maxwell Berry, a contractor, found work and was permitted to stay.) Mayor Calhoun, too, would remain in the city for now, departing a few weeks hence to join his family in Thomaston.[16]

Residents were warned not to wait until the last minute, with officials on both sides concerned about a lack of transportation, but of course most of them did just that. On September 21, the day the agreed-upon cease-fire was scheduled to expire, the station in Atlanta was thronged with families going north, many of them wealthy citizens with enormous amounts of baggage, furniture, trunks, pets, even pianos. Mary Rawson made her way to the Car Shed with her family—the last time she would stand under its broad arch, as it turned out—and boarded a boxcar with another family and their dog, "sixteen refugees in box," she said, with baggage piled high around them and cobwebs draping the roof of the car above. Samuel Richards, departing with his wife, Sallie, to stay with relatives in New York City, even succeeded in removing much of the stock of his bookstore, loading the volumes onto a boxcar for shipment north. A number of families had their servants with them, though the station was also mobbed with former slaves and freedmen, hopeful for a chance to escape from Georgia to brighter lands somewhere to the north.

The scene at the departure point for those headed south was similar, though more pitiful and tragicomical. The southbound wagon train was "crowded with a heterogeneous medley of poodle dogs, tabby cats, asthmatic pianos, houschold furniture, cross old maids, squalling, wondering children, all of which, huddled together, made anything but a pleasant traveling party," an accompanying correspondent wrote. Their initial destination was the neutral ground twelve miles out the Macon &

Federal troops supervising the forced evacuation of civilians from Atlanta. (*New York Public Library*)

Western at Rough and Ready—which one officer said "as completely answers to the first part of its name as one could imagine, and perhaps to its latter half; for it appears to have been getting ready to be a town since its foundation, and is likely to remain in that condition for an indefinite length of time." The station, such as it was, amounted to little more than "two miserable shanties, the respective quarters of the Rebel and Federal guards, separated for a distance of about 200 yards." In the fields and railyards around the ramshackle depot was presented "a sight enough to make the blood of humanity boil," as one Southern soldier remembered. "We saw men an women old and feeble all carrying what they could. Older boys and girls rolling barrels and push carts. Little 2 years old children all had somthing to carry. The young women some of them with heavy loads. Yet a man like Sherman has a place in the Hall of Fame. And I believe in a place spelled with an H- too thats no ice house."[17]

The civilians were by all accounts treated well by their Union escorts, though a few ladies were unable to hold their tongues. "Some of them are very Saucy and indipendent and it hurts their feelings to be hauled out in a wagon with a Yankee driver," an Indiana colonel wrote in his diary. A Federal aide-de-camp visiting the railside shantytown at Rough and Ready struggled to have polite conversation with a group of ladies sitting amid trunks and baskets and waiting for transport further south. The youngest, "a lady of refinement," the aide recalled, described the hardships attendant to leaving home under these circumstances but also gave her view of the broader national situation and the enmity between North and South. "There are no two peoples in the world who hate each other more," she asserted.

The staff officer, made uncomfortable by the exchange and doing his best to be cordial, gently protested the notion. He ventured an opinion that no such animosity existed generally in the North; and after all, he, for one, did not hate the Southern people.

"Well, sir," the young lady replied, "we hate you."[18]

By September 26, Sherman had removed from Atlanta—which he had claimed back in July was already deserted—to the south 446 families, including 705 adults—the overwhelming majority of them women—867 children, and 79 servants. (The Yankees were, at least, generous in their allowance of baggage—each family carried with them, on average, 1,654 pounds of furniture and household goods.) Colonel Le Duc prepared a detailed list of those removed, which would find its way into the National Archives under the title "The Book of Exodus." A comparable number left the city to go north, bringing the estimated total of citizens removed from Atlanta at Sherman's direction to around 3,500. On the Fourth of July, just before Sherman crossed the Chattahoochee River, more than 20,000 residents called Atlanta home. Now only fifty civilian families remained.[19]

In the meantime, Sherman and Hood also agreed upon an exchange of prisoners. Hood had proposed a general exchange of all prisoners captured during the campaign, but Sherman would only agree to a swap of 2,000 men, to be taken only from those recently captured and "still on hand." Despite his concern for the plight of the poor, emaciated Northern boys suffering under the cruelest of conditions at Andersonville, Sherman wanted only able-bodied men who could return to active service immediately. Hood had "raised the question of humanity," Sherman wrote in a wire to Grant, "but I am not to be moved by such tricks of the enemy." Notable in the exchange was a trade of unfortunate generals—Dan Govan, captured at Jonesboro, and George Stoneman, who had come to grief on his cavalry raid near Macon.

Govan would be back in command of his brigade of Arkansans by the end of October, while Stoneman left the state to command Union cavalry forces in East Tennessee. As for those left wasting at Andersonville, "their condition is hard," Sherman acknowledged, yet he told Halleck: "I have sent word to our prisoners to be of good cheer, for the day of their deliverance and revenge is fast approaching."[20]

Indeed, it seemed to many that the day of revenge, at least, had already arrived. Sherman had been making his presence felt in the state of Georgia for months now, but his actions during his first days inside the city of Atlanta made clear that he intended to bear down even more, leaving marks and scars that would last for decades and perhaps for generations. The Rebel papers howled and the Northern papers marveled, wondering what audacity or atrocity the general next had in mind. As the *Cincinnati Commercial* put it, "Grant walked *into* Vicksburg, McClellan walked *around* Richmond, but Sherman is walking *upon* Atlanta."[21]

"*The Blue Jackets rule the day,*" a triumphant Union soldier wrote to his mother from his new posting inside Atlanta. "The streets are crowded with them from morn to night . . . truly it is a Yankee town now." The three Federal armies now were camped from East Point to Marietta to Decatur and all points in between, with the bulk of the army setting up shop in and around Atlanta. The streets and squares and houses and stores were now thronged with Union blue, and for the most part they were well behaved. "Never has an enemy's town been taken possession of so quietly," a *New York Herald* correspondent wrote, "and life and property in Atlanta to-day is as secure as in the city of New York."[22]

The great market city and warehouse of Atlanta had seen its trade dwindle over the summer, the once-constant flow of business not so much dried up as strangled by the chokehold on the railroad lines coming into the city. Coffee had gotten as high as twenty dollars a pound; eggs twelve dollars a dozen; flour three hundred dollars a barrel. "No butter, however," a reporter wrote, "no chickens, no vegetables, and, in fact, nothing that would tempt an epicure." But within hours of Mayor

Calhoun's surrender, the floodgates of commerce reopened, as a swarm of "sutlers, artisans and news-dealers" descended upon the city, creaking into town with mule-drawn wagons piled high with all manner of luxuries and necessities. Newsboys roamed the streets hocking Northern papers, crying "Here's your *New York Herald*!" "Get your *Harper's Weekly*!" Prices of goods, so recently exorbitant, yielded promptly to the principles of supply and demand, and before long a hungry soldier could wander down to the Car Shed and buy himself a hot meal of pork, beans, cornbread and coffee for fifty cents. Most welcome to the Yankees were the abundant quantities of tobacco, which had been a precious commodity indeed in the Federal camps throughout the campaign. Soldiers who had paid fifteen cents for a single cigar before the city fell now could buy them twenty-five cents for a hundred, while the price for a plug of tobacco had dropped from a dollar to a nickel. Sutlers and merchants accepted both U.S. dollars and Confederate scrip, though they clearly preferred the former to the already deflating Southern "shinplasters."[23]

At his headquarters on Washington Street, Sherman spent most of his time working on his official report of his campaign for Atlanta, from Dalton to Jonesboro, May to September—which he completed and submitted to Halleck on September 15. Even as the papers reviled him as an infernal brute, the red-bearded commander charmed many who came across him in person—including an old woman he had engaged as a housekeeper, who two days before "had been denouncing him as a savage, for whom even the worst fate was too good." Within a week, the lady was telling her friends that the general was "the nicest man in the world, and had been shamefully slandered."[24]

With his report completed, Sherman spent his days writing dispatches and letters—to Ellen, to Lincoln, to Grant, to Hood, and dozens of others—and his nights receiving visitors, smoking cigars on the broad veranda of his handsome brick headquarters as the regimental bands played in the City Hall square across the way. A staff officer sent by Grant found him thus, sitting on the porch tilted back in a large armchair and leafing through a newspaper—"his coat was unbuttoned, his black felt hat slouched over his brow, and on his feet were a pair of slippers very much down at the heels," the aide recalled. The general was "exceedingly cordial" and as always extremely talkative, "uttering crisp words and epigrammatic phrases which fell from his lips as rapidly as shots from a magazine-gun," and by the end of the interview his visitor considered him "one of the most dramatic and picturesque characters of the war." With his "large frame, tall, gaunt form, restless hazel eyes, aquiline nose, bronzed face, and crisp beard, he looked the picture of 'grim-visaged war.'" Grim-visaged war, chatting and listening to "The Blue Juniata" in a pair of threadbare carpet slippers.[25]

His subordinates, meanwhile, were likewise settling in and making themselves at home—officers taking their pick of hotel suites and grand colonnaded mansions and private soldiers constructing their own cozy abodes, tearing down and building up. "General Sherman has given us permission to use deserted buildings in our vicinity as we see fit," an Illinois sergeant wrote. "Wagons and men, loaded with boards, windows and doors, hurry by from sunrise to sunset. Thousands of hatchets hammering thousands of nails are heard in every direction. Thousands of neat, comfortable cabins are springing up in straight rows here, there and everywhere." Departing civilians left a plethora of unguarded homes for use in this fashion, and the bluecoats seemed to take for granted their rights of possession and demolition—after all, they had fought for and won the place and reckoned they could do with it as they pleased. "A house is vacated by a family, some soldier steps inside with a chunk of rail and bursts off a board, and it's goodbye house," an Ohio major wrote, "for you'll soon see a hundred soldiers carrying away windows, flooring, weatherboarding, studding, etc., etc., *ad infinitum*. . . . So you can see we are comfortable."[26]

More comfortable than they could have imagined a few short weeks before. "Isn't a soldier's life a queer one?" a Massachusetts colonel wrote home in a letter. "One month ago, we were lying on the ground in a shelter tent, with nothing but pork and hard bread to eat; now we are in an elegant house, take our dinner at half-past five, and feel disposed to growl if we don't have good soup and roast meat with dessert; after that, we smoke good cigars on the piazza and have a band play for us."[27]

Neatly aligned tent cities appeared in open spaces from City Hall square to the park outside the railroad depot, with most of the shelters more little houses than tents, boasting wood walls and handsome chimneys made of brick or stacked stone. "I have my tent nicely 'fixed up,'" an Ohio captain told his aunt, with a door, two windows, board sides, and a tentcloth roof, and furniture including a rocking chair, an armchair, a chest with three drawers, and a spring seat lounge for a bed. "I have white dishes to eat off and china cup and saucer," he continued. "I procured some of my things with coffee, some with Secesh money and some I 'went for.'"[28]

Other buildings were likewise appropriated and converted for military uses: downtown shops occupied by quartermasters or army sutlers, homes or schools used as headquarters or hospitals, and even local churches confiscated for what a local historian would call "unreligious purposes." A portion of the Immaculate Conception Catholic Church was employed as a hospital; the basement of Central Presbyterian Church converted to a slaughterhouse; and St. Philip's, if one witness is to be believed, was used partly to stable horses and partly as a bowling alley. (The bluecoats called their improvised bowling pins "Rebels," and at times used cannonballs to bowl with.) Other structures resumed their former functions—the Athenaeum theater on Decatur Street, closed earlier in the year by Mayor Calhoun, was reopened with a variety of entertainments, some of them rather coarse and some refined. Amateurs and even soldiers took the stage to reveal hidden talents—though "actresses were conspicuous by their absence," as a patron remembered. "The 'strongman nightly tossed the cannon balls, catching them on the back of his neck, and allowed a rock to be broken on his breast by a sledge in the hands of 't'other strong feller,' and with the help of the soloist, the clog-dancer, the impromptu comedy, and the inevitable minstrels, the time was filled, and a not over-critical audience was delighted." Shortly after the civilian exodus was accomplished, a concert was staged for the benefit of a local widow, pianist and amateur chanteuse named Rebecca Welch, who performed various songs with the "Celebrated Brass Band of the 33d Mass. Vols." The program included Verdi's "Anvil Chorus" from *Il Trovatore*, violin, drum, and piano solos, and a closing medley of national airs, and the standing-room-only crowd was said to include in its numbers the commanding general himself.[29]

These entertainments, along with other balls and parties, drew the ire and scorn of Southern newspapers and spawned dubious stories of not

Top: The Trout House hotel and the Masonic Hall, with Federal encampment. The hotel would be destroyed but the Masonic Hall spared in the burning of the city. Bottom: Atlanta City Hall with camp of the 2nd Massachusetts infantry on the grounds. (*Library of Congress*)

only collusion but also unseemly fraternization with the Yankee conquerors. In mid-September, the *Daily Intelligencer*, now printing in Macon, gave a detailed report of a "grand ball and blow out" thrown by the Yankees at the Trout House hotel and attended by a number of prominent Atlantans—including many who had been "loudest in their boastful protestations to the South"—along with, supposedly, a dancing and gallivanting General Sherman and his staff. Several women were present, "not a decent lady amongst them," and "oh, how they mingled, black and brown, white and gray," the paper said. "Mayor Jim Calhoun was present, toasting and congratulating the Yankees on their handsome trickery and success of their arms," the tale continued.

The Rebel newspapers characterized the event as "a crude parody of a Southern ball," as one historian put it, "as though Northerners longed to emulate Southern traditions, but failed to comprehend the rituals, like a pretender to Christianity gluttonously guzzling the communion wine." Although the story was plainly inaccurate and probably totally false, it nonetheless was widely circulated and reprinted in other newspapers, north and south. Mayor Calhoun—who would later claim Union allegiance but for now was keeping up at least an appearance of steadfast Southern leadership—was understandably outraged by the charge and demanded to know the source, though the *Intelligencer* never revealed it and never retracted its story.[30]

With the resumption of uninterrupted rail traffic down from Chattanooga, Nashville, and parts north, the mail became more reliable, and soldiers enjoyed a consistent flow of letters and packages from home—socks, writing paper, candy, cinnamon sticks. Federal paymasters, too, arrived in the camps in and around Atlanta, charged with seeing that all were happy with the present government as the November election approached. "Uncle Sam owes me over 220 dollars now & it keeps gaining 22 ever month," one soldier had written home just before the city fell. "I ain't afraid to trust him either."[31] And a particularly notable arrival during the occupation was George N. Barnard, a New York photographer. Captain Orlando Poe, who was himself a great aficionado of both military and portrait photography and a collector of autographed *cartes de visite*, had summoned Barnard down from Nashville, where he had spent most of the summer taking portraits and photo-duplicating maps. Barnard arrived in Atlanta in mid-September, along with all his photographic apparatus, including a tent that served as a portable darkroom.

Barnard would spend the next several weeks touring sites in and around the city and taking photographs in various formats, including stereographs and two larger formats, using a twelve-by-fifteen-inch camera. First on his wish list of famous locations was the spot in the woods east of Atlanta where General McPherson had been killed. Arriving there, Barnard found that there was in fact little to see—so he enhanced the scene a bit by adding some battlefield debris, a wagon wheel, and a horse's skull, rendering the image not only more interesting but also causing it to be widely reproduced—including as an engraving in a February 1865 issue of *Harper's Weekly*. Barnard preserved other iconic scenes for history as well, including the shell-torn house of Ephraim Ponder; the ruins of the ordnance train and the rolling mill; and Federal regiments encamped on the grounds of the Atlanta City Hall. He also took a number of views of the abandoned but still-bristling Confederate fortifications outside Atlanta, as well as images of Sherman, both mounted and afoot, visiting Federal forts on the outskirts of the city. Presently, Theodore R. Davis, the accomplished sketch artist and illustrator for *Harper's Weekly*, would also join the Union host at Atlanta, and between them the two men would provide a striking visual record of the campaign just past and the one to come.[32]

There were departures as well. Generals Logan and Blair, both former congressmen, went north for electioneering duty in their respective home states; and in late September, Sherman sent General Thomas northward with portions of the 4th and 14th Corps from his Army of the Cumberland, preparing to defend against an anticipated Rebel strike on middle Tennessee. Others of less exalted rank also left—men whose enlistment furloughs had expired, for example, and soldiers from states like Indiana that did not allow absentee voting, given furloughs and transportation home to cast their ballots. Some absences proved costly in unexpected ways: the 83rd Indiana Regiment lost its chaplain, leaving every man to govern his conduct by "simply doing what was right in his own eyes." The loss of their moral compass was sorely felt by the Hoosier sinners, and now "noble young men of brave hearts, who never uttered an oath at home before tender mother, or sister, or a conscientious father, seem to have lost all sense of that tender regard for the finer feelings of the soul that must preserve us all from great evil," one member of the regiment wrote. "They will (many of them) surprise their friends when they get home in this respect."[33]

Yet despite the departures and distractions, for the most part all was quiet for the thousands of Northern soldiers now living in Atlanta. "It is said that in a cyclone there is a space of quiet and calm in the centre," a young New Yorker reflected, "and similarly our position was now central in the cyclone of war," while another told his parents, "Golley, it is most like a ferlow." Not quite like that, however, as the schedule recorded by an Illinois soldier showed a full day: reveille at sunrise, breakfast at seven, sick call thereafter, with roll call and dinner at noon, another roll call and supper at five, and taps at half past eight—while in between were hours upon hours of drills, marches, parades, and inspections, at which "every man is expected to have his gun shine like a new dollar." The bluecoats passed their days grumbling through the army routine and enjoying their rest and recently acquired luxuries like soft bread and sweet potatoes and fresh tobacco, though the unseasonably warm days made them long for the cool autumns they knew back home. "I am quite home-sick, and I am getting tired of what is called the 'Sunny South,'" John Geary wrote to his wife. "Give me the dear *Old North* in preference yet."[34]

In the meantime, there were growing rumors in the streets and camps and hotel lobbies of a grand movement in the works—a march to Mobile, perhaps, or Charleston, or Savannah. "We must maul the wedge another bit and the log will split in time," Sherman told a friend, with a winking reference to "Old Abe the Rail Splitter." Despite his success thus far, he moved deliberately. "I got my wedge pretty deep," he said, "and must look out that I don't get my fingers pinched." Then, finally, in late October came orders to pack and prepare for a new campaign—Uncle Billy was back on the move. "We are preparing for a huge campaign, and all are right glad of it; 50 days' rations is the word," an Illinois soldier wrote in his diary. "Don't know when we start. Montgomery or Augusta are probably the points."

"We are going to shake up the bones of the rebellion," he continued, scarcely able to contain his excitement. "I would not miss this campaign for anything."[35]

At midafternoon on September 25, 1864, a rainy Sunday, a regiment of Tennesseans stood waiting to greet a distinguished guest at the depot at Palmetto, Georgia—or what was left of it, the town having been burned by Federal cavalry the month before. The soggy honor guard, standing shoetop-deep in a loblolly of mud, watched silently as a train chuffed and squealed to a stop on the glistening rails. The crew set the tender brake, the door of a boxcar was opened—no passenger coaches had been available—and off onto the platform stepped Jefferson Davis, President of the Confederate States of America.

"The first effect of disaster is always to spread a deeper gloom than is due to the occasion," the president had written to a friend the week before, and now he had come south in an effort not only to diffuse that gloom and bolster morale both inside and out of the army, but also to discuss strategy and attempt to resolve the ugly squabbling among the senior commanders of the Army of Tennessee. He had been on the road for six days now, traveling southwest from Richmond through Greensboro, Charlotte, and Augusta, then detouring to Macon and northwest to Palmetto, a muddy trackside village without a single palmetto tree, having been named some years before by members of a South Carolina regiment that had stopped there en route to the Mexican War.[36]

Now fifty-six years old, Davis was "straight and spare, sallow of hue, graceful in movement, quiet, courteous, dignified in manner," a Rebel cannoneer observed. "A sweet smile on a benevolent and thoughtful rather than stern or strong face, with sunken cheeks and rather delicate features. One eye was gone, which however did not show except that 'the light was out' and the lid drooped over it a little." He wore a "quiet suit of gray, with a black velvet collar to the coat," and carried with him an old-fashioned carpet bag, not a modern grip or valise. "He has nothing striking in his appearance," observed a witness who had seen Davis en route, "he would never be selected from a crowd as the founder of a Republic but would more likely to be taken for an intelligent, quiet gentleman of fortune and ease. But when he speaks, no one can mistake the character of the man. . . . The chief peculiarity that was exhibited in his countenance was fierceness and determination." The Mississippi statesman exuded not only resolve but reassurance, an air of calm acceptance of whatever may come—quite as if he were equal parts political leader, steering the nation through the present crisis, and undertaker, able to gravely carry on and see to the arrangements if things didn't work out.[37]

In Macon two days before, Davis had given a soon-to-be-famous speech to a throng of listeners gathered at a Baptist church, many of them refugees lately removed from Atlanta. In his brief remarks, he offered strong if implicit criticism of the Army of Tennessee's former commander General Johnston and a much-needed word of defense for Hood. "I know the deep disgrace felt by Georgia at our army falling back from Dalton to the interior of the State, but I was not of those who considered Atlanta lost when our army crossed the Chattahoochee," he said. "I resolved that it should not, and I then put a man in command who I knew would strike an honest and manly blow for the city, and many a Yankee's blood was made to nourish the soil before the prize was won."

That was all in the past, of course—"Let the dead bury the dead," Davis suggested—and then went on to offer a cheering prediction for the future. "Sherman cannot long keep up his line of communications, and retreat sooner or later, he must," Davis asserted. "And when that day comes, the fate that befell the army of the French Empire and its retreat from Moscow will be re-enacted." (General Grant, reading the speech in a newspaper some days hence, snorted at the notion—"Mr. Davis has not made it quite plain who is to furnish the snow for this Moscow retreat," he remarked.) Davis closed with a call for persistence and optimism. "Let no one despond," he said. "Let no one distrust. And remember that if genius is the beau ideal, hope is the reality."[38]

Davis's speech at Macon—along with other remarks delivered at Salisbury, Greensboro, Charlotte, and Augusta—would be widely reported and blasted in the press, with many observers north and south considering the oratory foolish and rash in the extreme—"so damaging to the Rebel cause," the *Philadelphia Inquirer* concluded, "that attempts are being made to raise doubts as to its authenticity." Other papers agreed, thinking it the height of folly for the Confederate president to give public speeches announcing his army's military plans in advance—outlining the Rebel force's strength, its lines of march, and its objective. "Old Abe will chuckle over this Macon speech as something more refreshing than a joke," the *New York Herald* wrote, "and Grant and Sherman will find in it more useful information than could be gathered by all the scouts of the Union armies in a month." Sherman was particularly amused by Davis's preview of Hood's plans—and in fact within five days dispatched Thomas to Chattanooga to begin preparations to defend his communications there. "To be forewarned was to be forearmed," Sherman later wrote, "and I think we took full advantage of the occasion."[39]

But Davis had more work to do and more speeches to give, beginning at Palmetto. The Army of Tennessee had a few days earlier shifted its headquarters from its former position at Lovejoy's Station to this stop along the Atlanta & West Point Railroad. The new base would serve not only to better protect the Andersonville prison camp, ninety miles to the south—thereby addressing fears that liberation of the 30,000 Union captives there would, as Shelby Foote wrote, "create as if by a sowing of dragon teeth, a ferocious new blue army deep in the Confederate rear"—but also would provide better routes to move west and north for the army's next campaign, which would be waged against Sherman's supply lines or perhaps directed even farther north.[40]

Hood was fast becoming what he would be in the years after the war—a man with few friends and even fewer admirers. Southern newspapers said he had been outgeneraled, and so he had. Hood had not only "miscalculated the enemy's designs," the *Richmond Examiner* observed, he was nothing more than an experienced division commander, "notoriously incapable of managing anything larger than a division." The Northern press derided Hood even as they exalted Sherman for beating him, some editors noting that the gray commander had been not only whipped but fooled entirely, others going so far as to tweak him for his appearance. "A man whose want of beauty is furthermore embellished by a wooden leg and a wilted arm," one Northern paper said of the young general. "Lackluster eyes. Sad, weary, baleful eyes. He can only smile by a facial revolution—a face that speaks of wakeful nights and nerves strung to their utmost tension by anxiety." Still, whatever opprobrium was heaped upon the bearded, battle-scarred Texan, Davis seemed prepared to stand by him. Hood had, after all, done just what Davis had asked and expected of him. Davis had not considered the fall of Atlanta inevitable and, as he told a friend, "was not willing that it should be yielded before manly blows had been struck for its preservation." Hood had done exactly that—manly blows had been struck, indeed, no one could question that—and Davis was unwilling to rebuke Hood for failing to accomplish what Joe Johnston had refused even to attempt. Besides, to relieve Hood at this stage would be to acknowledge that he had been mistaken in elevating the young general in the first place.[41]

For his part, Hood in the days after the fall of Atlanta made what was in many ways his greatest sin of the campaign, or at least the one most difficult to understand. "It's all my fault," General Lee had famously said after his army's failure on the third day at Gettysburg, noting that he had asked of his veterans more than they were able to give. Hood, to his discredit, would never say such a thing. A self-pronounced student if not a graduate of "the Lee and Jackson school," he had asked the same impossibilities of his outnumbered soldiers, but rather than praise them for their valor and take responsibility for the failure to destroy Sherman, he blamed everyone but himself. He criticized his officers, questioned the aggressive spirit of his men, and viewed low casualty figures as evidence of a lack of effort in battle. "According to all human calculations we should have saved Atlanta had the officers and men of the army done what was expected of them," he had written in a letter to Davis just after abandoning the city. "It had been God's will for it to be otherwise. I am of good heart and feel that we shall yet succeed."[42]

The first requirement for success, he asserted, was that General Hardee, his most experienced corps commander, had to be relieved and replaced immediately. "In the battle of July 20 we failed on account of General Hardee," he wrote on September 13. "Our success on July 22 was not what it would have been, owing to this officer. Our failure on August 31 I am now convinced was greatly owing to him. . . . It is of the utmost importance that Hardee should be relieved at once." He made this request not once but three times.[43]

There was much that was unfair in this, of course. Hardee had been late in launching the attack in all three battles and had certainly made tactical errors along the way, but the fault was never entirely his; and though he perhaps should be held responsible for the halfhearted assault on the first day at Jonesboro, he also deserved credit for a stalwart if not impenetrable line of defense against superior numbers on the second day. Still, like Hood, Hardee unquestionably failed in the struggle to save Atlanta. Hardee was no less strident in his denunciations of his chief. Hood was not only incompetent, Hardee asserted, but his conduct in the recent campaign had been "unjust, ungenerous and unmanly." Hardee was not only stung but astounded by Hood's criticism of him. After all, he noted, Hood had not only given him responsibility for two-thirds of the army, but had trusted the most important operations—the attack at Peachtree Creek, the flank march at Bald Hill, and the defense of Jonesboro—to his care. "That in the operations about Atlanta, I failed to accomplish all that General Hood thinks might have been accomplished, is a matter of regret," he would write the following spring in justifying his conduct, "that I committed errors, is very possible; but that I failed in any instance to carry out, in good faith, his orders, I utterly deny." Meeting individually with the two generals at Palmetto, the president heard them out, each arguably displaying more fire and venom toward the other than either had for their blue adversaries, but he rendered no immediate judgments. Davis would also spend hours closeted with Stephen D. Lee and Alexander Stewart—but already his caucuses with Hood and Hardee made abundantly clear that the two could never work together again.[44]

In between these contentious interviews, Davis spent much of his time delivering heartening speeches and reviewing the troops, and while accounts differ in the particulars of how warmly the president was received, there is no question but that a large number of soldiers took the opportunity to voice their dissatisfaction. Indeed, they had much to complain about. In addition to the hardships and losses of the recent campaign, they were still poorly supplied, in need of food and clothing, and many had not been paid in ten months. All through September, they read newspaper reports deriding them for their failures at Atlanta and making comparisons "not only unfavorable, but often insulting," with R. E. Lee's glorious Army of Northern Virginia. Their present misfortune made them hearken back to better days. Called on to give three cheers and a Rebel yell for their president, Davis and Hood instead heard cries of "Johnston! Give us Johnston! Give us our old commander!" Officers scowled and barked at the offenders and even threatened them with arrest, but the insubordinate shouts continued from time to time and point to point along the gray formations. "All looked uneasy and apprehensive," the Carolina brigadier Arthur Manigault wrote of the grand review. "I never remember taking part in an affair of the kind so cheerless and unsatisfactory as this one was, where everyone seemed anxious to have it over."[45]

Nevertheless, for all the grousing about Hood and the longing for the battle-free days of "Old Joe," the speeches and the grand reviews did seem to buck up the army's morale, though a rise in Rebel spirits were also the natural result of three weeks of rest, first at Lovejoy's Station and now at Palmetto. Not only Davis but also a swarm of other Confederate dignitaries—Tennessee Governor Isham G. Harris, Howell Cobb, and Robert Toombs—gave stirring speeches and made the rounds visiting the troops, offering encouraging words and shaking hands until their arms were sore. "It was all hands round, swing the corner, and balance your partner," a Tennessee private wrote. "I shook hand with Hon. Jeff Davis, and he said howdy, Captain; I shook hands with Toombs, and he said howdy, Major; and every big bug that I shook hands with put another star on my collar and chicken guts on my sleeve."[46]

There were other amusing scenes along the ranks of the plucky Confederates. Francis R. Lubbock, a former governor of Texas now serving as President Davis's aide-de-camp, rode along the line in search of the Texas Brigade, thinking they would receive him warmly and give him a hearty cheer—but, as one of the Texans wrote, he "made a serious mistake and so spoiled the whole thing." Reining in his horse too early, he stopped in front of an Irish Brigade that wanted nothing to do with the Lone Star politician. He removed his hat and announced proudly, "I am Governor Lubbock of Texas." The Sons of Erin were unimpressed. "An' who the bloody hell is Gov'ner Lubbock?" an Irishman snarled. The governor wilted at the question, turned without a word, and galloped past the Texas Brigade to catch up with the president.[47]

In the end, Davis resolved the command dilemma to the satisfaction of each of the generals involved in it, though perhaps to the ultimate detriment of the Army of Tennessee. Hardee was relieved of command and given a new post in charge of the Department of South Carolina, Georgia, and Florida—formerly under the direction of General P. G. T.

Beauregard. Beauregard, in turn, was brought west from Charleston to command the Military Division of the West, with Hood as his ostensible subordinate, though the Creole general apparently would lack the power to give direct orders to the armies in the field. Whether Beauregard's new post amounted to an overall theater command or a mere advisory role was unclear, and the arrangement, though it resolved the chafing of egos and tempers in the Army of Tennessee, promised confusion and dissatisfaction in the days to come.

Davis departed Palmetto on September 27, having endorsed Hood's proposal to launch a strike against Sherman's line of communications. Two days later, the gray army, numbering around 40,000 men of all arms, crossed the Chattahoochee River and headed north. "This has been a funny campaign," a Federal officer wrote, "the rebels have been using our breastworks of last Summer, and we have been using theirs." Hood would succeed in making temporary disruptions in Sherman's rail supply line and cause some little concern that he had escaped and was on the loose in north Georgia. But the bluecoats on the spot in Atlanta weren't the least bit worried about Old Pegleg. "It tickles us to see that you home folks are uneasy about us because Hood has got into our rear," an Illinois officer wrote home. "I tell you I have not seen a man uneasy for a minute, on that subject, and that Hood has to run like a hound to get away from us."[48]

Sherman felt much the same way about it. He gave pursuit for a time but considered the effort not only a waste of time, but also an exercise in futility. Now that Hood's army was out of its entrenchments and loose in the Cherokee forest of north Georgia, it would be almost impossible to catch him, especially given his unpredictability. Hood, Sherman charged in early October, "is eccentric, and I cannot guess his movements as I could those of Johnston, who was a sensible man and only did sensible things." There were minor clashes at various points along the Western & Atlantic Railroad—first at Allatoona Pass, a small but vicious fight that Sherman would pronounce, for the numbers engaged, the bloodiest battle ever fought on the American continent—and then at Resaca, where an impudent Union colonel named Clark Wever rebuffed Hood's demand for surrender. "In my opinion I can hold this post," Wever wrote. "If you want it, come and take it." Hood decided against an assault, and departed to break the railroad elsewhere. Still, he presently tired of railroad raids in north Georgia, and Sherman grew weary of chasing after him. "Damn him, if he will go to the Ohio River, I will give him rations," Sherman fumed. "Let him go north. My business is down south."[49]

By late October, Hood and Sherman had basically decided to ignore each other. Having spent most of the year locked in mortal combat, the two armies would now go marching off in opposite directions. Federal track gangs had repaired breaks in the rails so quickly in recent weeks that further attacks at the Western & Atlantic Railroad seemed a profitless exercise for the Confederates, and even the hyperaggressive Hood had no plans to attack Sherman's massive force entrenched at Atlanta. Instead, he conceived a plan to strike north through northern Alabama and on to middle Tennessee. With President Davis and the new department commander General Beauregard having approved the plan, off the Rebels marched, back toward the old Volunteer State, from whence the army took its name. Davis had predicted as much upon his arrival at Palmetto, bucking up the spirits of the rain-sodden soldiers who greeted him at the depot by assuring them, "Be of good cheer, for in a short while your faces will be turned homeward and your feet pressing the soil of Tennessee." But the threads of cynicism are woven thick in the mind of the soldier, and one among the listeners detected in this presidential promise a more doleful invitation, expressed in the old funeral hymn: "Sinner, come and view the ground where you shall shortly lie."[50]

The first Tuesday after the first Monday in November—Election Day—fell on November 8, and the outcome was hardly a surprise. Abraham Lincoln was confident and relaxed as he waited on the returns, having come a long way since the end of August, when he had despondently predicted his own defeat. He spent Election Night in the telegraph office in Washington, eating fried oysters, swapping jokes and reading funny columns penned by his favorite humorist, Petroleum V. Nasby. The early evening returns were slow to arrive due to storms across the East, but by midnight, his friends and advisers were congratulating him on his reelection. "It is no pleasure to me to triumph over any one," he told a group of serenaders gathered outside the White House, "but I give thanks to the Almighty for this evidence of the people's resolution to stand by free government and the rights of humanity."

The results of the presidential election were reported in all the papers, of course, but also in the journal of Henry Wadsworth Longfellow. "Lincoln re-elected beyond a doubt," the poet wrote. "We breathe freer. The country will be saved." For a local pastor in Middletown, Connecticut, the election returns brought to mind the book of Genesis, twenty-second chapter, and he posted the applicable verse during a torchlight vigil: "The angel of the Lord called unto Abraham out of heaven a second time." And so he had. Abraham Lincoln was reelected President of the United States by a half-million vote majority and an electoral landslide, 212 electoral votes to just 21 for McClellan, who carried only Delaware, Kentucky, and New Jersey. "I am pretty sure-footed," the president told his friends. The election was his, and fairly won.[51]

Like many presidential elections in our peculiar American system, however, the contest was closer than it may have seemed at first glance. He had carried New York and its 33 electoral votes, for example, by less than 7,000 votes; New Hampshire by 3,529; Connecticut by only 2,406. As historian Albert Castel has noted, "McClellan lost in seven states—Connecticut, Illinois, Indiana, New Hampshire, New York, Pennsylvania, and Oregon—by such narrow margins that almost surely he would have carried them had the Confederate flag still been flying over Atlanta when the voters of those states went to the polls." The loss of these states would have swung 102 electoral votes over to the Democratic column and thrown the election to McClellan.[52]

In the end, two things catapulted Lincoln to a second term. First was the soldier vote, which had gone decisively for Lincoln despite the popularity in the ranks of the charismatic former Union general who ran against him. Judging by the breakdown of the military votes that were tabulated separately, Lincoln won around 78 percent, compared to the 55 percent of the electorate overall, and the soldier vote broke even stronger for the president in Sherman's army around Atlanta. "Nine-tenths of the soldiers in this Army will vote for Lincoln," John Geary had predicted before the election, and he was nearly correct. An astonishing 87 percent of soldier ballots in the Army of the Cumberland were cast for Lincoln. Official counts and straw polls in individual regiments told the story: the tally in the 75th Indiana, for example, was 310 votes for Lincoln, seven for McClellan, and fourteen who refused to vote. The 22nd Wisconsin counted 372 ballots for Lincoln, and ten for Little Mac. In the 20th Illinois, the count was ninety-seven to one. "From the returns I have seen this morning," Illinois Major James Connolly wrote, "I think Jeff Davis would have received as many votes in these camps as McClellan did."[53]

Second, and most important, was the capture of Atlanta, which had caused not merely a shift but a seismic jolt to the national mood and the electoral landscape. The "disaster at Atlanta," as the *Richmond Examiner* wrote, "came in the very nick of time when a victory alone could save the party of Lincoln from irretrievable ruin."[54]

In the eyes of Southerners, the importance of Lincoln's reelection was unmistakable: the end of any chance for negotiated peace, an endorsement of emancipation and eventual abolition of slavery, a steadfast determination to subjugate the South. The people of the North, the *London Daily News* observed, "are in earnest in a way the like of which the world never saw before, silently, calmly, but desperately in earnest, too."[55]

Sherman was in earnest as well, though perhaps less calmly so. "The rebels are very mad because we reelected Lincoln president and ask us if we think we can conquer the Southerners," the Ohio surgeon S. B. Crew wrote. "Sherman tells them if we can't conquer them, we will *kill* them."[56]

CHAPTER TWELVE

The Whole World on Fire

The Burning of Atlanta

The burning of Atlanta was a long time coming—not only in light of the four-month campaign and two-month Union occupation that preceded it, but also because of a spark that had been struck more than three months before and some 550 miles away, in the south-central Pennsylvania town of Chambersburg. With a wartime population approaching 5,000, Chambersburg was nearly twice the size of its neighbor Gettysburg, two dozen miles to the east. Once the western terminus of the Cumberland Valley Railroad and during the war an active stop on the Underground Railroad, Chambersburg had no major battle to its name, though the town had changed hands repeatedly during the conflict. In June 1863, as the Confederate Army of Northern Virginia began the invasion that would culminate in the Battle of Gettysburg, General Robert E. Lee had made his headquarters in Chambersburg, and from that point had issued an order establishing a policy of respect and protection for civilian homes and property. "It must be remembered that we make war only upon armed men, and that we cannot take vengeance for the wrongs our people have suffered without lowering ourselves in the eyes of all whose abhorrence has been excited by the atrocities of our enemies," Lee had written as he exhorted his troops to abstain from any "unnecessary and wanton injury to private property."[1]

That was then, however, and not only had the war become considerably harsher on both sides in the twelve months since, but the Rebel general who would return to Chambersburg a year later was about as different from R. E. Lee as one could get. In June 1864, even as Sherman and Johnston fought and maneuvered north of Atlanta, Confederate Major General Jubal Early had been dispatched to the Shenandoah Valley to deal with a Union force under General David Hunter and, if possible, to make a push toward Washington. Early was an arthritic, tobacco-chewing fifty-seven-year-old Virginian and a man who seemed to detest just about everyone, even the members of his own staff, who, it was said, he hated "like blazes." Cantankerous and antisocial, a vicious, avowed racist, Early had never married and led the life of a recluse back home in Virginia. He was the only man who was ever known to swear in the presence of General Lee, though Lee liked him nonetheless, and called him "my bad old man."[2]

Riding into northern Pennsylvania in early July, Early was considerably outraged by reports of depredations committed by Hunter's plundering bluecoats, including the burning of the Virginia Military Institute and the homes of three prominent Virginians. Early, or "Old Jube," as the men called him, soon devised a plan for retaliation. He ordered Brigadier General John McCausland to march with two brigades of cavalry and a battery of artillery on Chambersburg, where he was to demand a ransom payment of $100,000 in gold or $500,000 in greenbacks as compensation for the homes Hunter's men had burned. "In default of the payment of this money," Early ordered, the town of Chambersburg was to be "laid in ashes."

Arriving at Chambersburg on July 30, 1864, McCausland had the town fathers brought before him, made his outrageous ransom demand, and gave them six hours to comply. Meanwhile, his troops began looting shops and homes and robbing citizens on the street of their purses and watches. In time—and there is some dispute whether the unlucky borough was given the promised six hours or not—it became clear that no ransom would be paid, and McCausland gave the order to burn the town. Up it went—first the town hall and courthouse, then the shops and warehouses, and finally private homes, most of which were plundered first. A few of the Confederates refused to participate in the destruction—including Colonel William E. Peters, who was relieved of command for insubordination when he told McCausland he would break and discard his sword before he would obey such an order. Other Rebel soldiers helped to fight fires their comrades had set, but there was little they could do. Most of the borough's residents gathered what they could and fled, huddling in fields as they watched nearly two-thirds of the town go up in flames. With their demand for a gold ransom and his men plundering the town, McCausland and his men seemed to the inhabitants of Chambersburg a far cry from the Southern gentlemen they had encountered earlier in the war and more like dastardly pirates of old.[3]

The burning of Chambersburg was widely reported and roundly condemned in the Northern press. Certainly Sherman's men around Atlanta were well aware of the destruction, as the months of August and September and October were short on battles and long on newspaper-reading. "Remember Chambersburg!" became a rallying cry for Union soldiers in both the Eastern and Western Theaters of the war, and provided both motivation and justification for some burning of their own. (General Early, for his part, took full responsibility for the burning of Chambersburg and never felt sorry about it, then or later. "Notwithstanding the lapse of time which has occurred, and the result of the war," he wrote in his postbellum memoirs, "I am perfectly satisfied with my conduct on this occasion, and see no reason to regret it.")[4]

Sherman gave no indication of any desire for vengeance for such past Rebel transgressions; rather, his plans for Atlanta in November of 1864 arose from practical considerations. It had taken several weeks and a barrage of correspondence for Sherman to convince his friend and superior U. S. Grant to approve his plan for what would become the famous March to the Sea. He had had such a movement in mind before the campaign for Atlanta even began—asked by an aide back in the spring about his plans after he captured Atlanta, he flicked the ashes from his cigar and gave a two-word reply. "Salt water," he said. Now, with Hood marching around north Georgia and threatening Tennessee, Sherman inquired of Grant on October 1, "why would it not do for me to leave

Tennessee to the force which Thomas has and the reserves soon to come to Nashville, and for me to destroy Atlanta, and then march across Georgia to Savannah or Charleston, breaking roads and doing irreparable damage? We cannot remain on the defensive." But Grant was concerned, and President Lincoln plainly worried, about the prospect of Sherman marching off to parts unknown while Hood's army remained loose in his rear.[5]

But Sherman, then headquartered at Kingston, sixty railroad miles northwest of Atlanta, insisted that to allow himself to be drawn off farther northward after Hood would merely play into the Confederates' hands and forfeit everything that had been achieved over the past seven months. "If I turn back, the whole effect of my campaign will be lost," he told Grant. "Until we can repopulate Georgia, it is useless to occupy it, but the utter destruction of its roads, houses, and people will cripple their military resources," he added in another dispatch arguing for his plan. "By attempting to hold the roads we will lose 1,000 men monthly, and will gain no result. I can make the march, and make Georgia howl." What Sherman was proposing was not just a long march but a swath of devastation torn across the heart of the state—not for purposes of revenge or retribution per se, but the destruction of military resources, and perhaps some message-sending along the way. "By this," he explained to General Thomas, "I propose to demonstrate the vulnerability of the South, and make its inhabitants feel that war & individual Ruin are synonimous terms."[6]

Grant finally approved Sherman's plan of operations on November 2. "I do not really see that you can withdraw from where you are to follow Hood, without giving up all we have gained in territory," he wrote. "I say, then, go as you propose." That was all Sherman needed to hear. He began his preparations: sending surplus men and matériel to Chattanooga and on to Thomas at Nashville; concentrating his forces, then scattered up and down the railroad line from Kingston to Jonesboro, at Atlanta to prepare for the departure south; getting his army "stripped for the work"; and then wrecking the railroad behind him from Atlanta to Chattanooga. He spent the following week waiting for a round of early November storms to pass, and in the meantime formulated orders for the destruction of the city of Atlanta.[7]

Despite the harsh and oft-repeated expressions of his intentions—to "destroy Atlanta," to achieve the "utter destruction of roads, houses, and people," to bring "individual ruin" to the people of Georgia—Sherman in fact did not give specific orders that Atlanta was to be burned. He charged his capable chief engineer Captain Orlando M. Poe with the task of rendering the Gate City useless for military purposes, and though Sherman and Poe expected the work to be carried out with some degree of precision, both clearly contemplated the use of fire in bringing about the town's ruin. "I want you to take special charge of the destruction in Atlanta of all depots, car-houses, shops, factories, foundries, &c.," Sherman wrote to Poe on November 7, noting that "fire will do most of the work." Four days later, he told Poe, "You may commence the work of destruction at once, but don't use fire until toward the last moment."[8]

Sherman's plan to abandon and destroy the city his men had fought for months to capture may have seemed to some to be counterintuitive and unnecessary, even illogical. Atlanta had always been regarded as a critical strategic point and valuable manufacturing center, and so presumably would be worth holding onto. There was no real, or at least no immediate, possibility of a Confederate military reoccupation of the city—there was no substantial Rebel force within a hundred miles of the place. Other Southern cities had been occupied and held for months (New Orleans), even years (Nashville) by Union forces with no significant displacement of the townspeople and little destruction to the cities themselves. But Sherman hated sitting still—"I'm too red-haired to be patient," he once said—and he thought it useless to stay in Atlanta. With the Rebel army gone, its arsenals and warehouses dismantled, and its railroads a thing of the past, the city wasn't worth the division of soldiers it would take to garrison it. Once a trophy, Atlanta was now an anchor, fixing his army in place and dragging him down.

The plan for leaving Atlanta behind, rather than continuing to occupy it, was not unlike the course of action Sherman had taken the summer before following his capture of Jackson, Mississippi. After Vicksburg fell to Grant's forces on the Fourth of July, 1863, Sherman, then in command of the Army of the Tennessee, marched eastward toward the state capital of Jackson. After a weeklong standoff, the Confederate forces under Joseph E. Johnston had abandoned the city and retreated to the east, and Sherman's men moved in, destroying the town's railroads, warehouses, and much else. Indeed, between blazes ignited by artillery fire, further destruction by the withdrawing Confederates, and new fires set by Sherman's troops, Jackson was soon "one mass of charred ruins," as Sherman described it to Grant. "The inhabitants are subjugated," he wrote. "They cry aloud for mercy. The land is devastated for 30 miles around."[9]

Sherman had seen no point in remaining in Jackson—after all, with its buildings burned and its railroad track torn and twisted, it had essentially ceased to exist as a strategic point, and an occupation would merely tie up his battalions when they could be of service elsewhere. Grant agreed, and just ten days after the city's capture, withdrew Sherman back to Vicksburg, leaving Jackson in ashes behind him. "The wholesale destruction to which this country is now being subjected is terrible to contemplate," he had written on the march through central Mississippi, "but it is the scourge of war, to which ambitions men have appealed, rather than the judgment of the learned and pure tribunals which our forefathers had provided for supposed wrongs and injuries." One thing was certain, as Sherman proudly reported: "Jackson will no longer be a point of danger."

Sherman's soldiers thought so too, and they had their own name for what was left of the Mississippi capital. They called the place "Chimneyville."[10]

The destruction that culminated in the burning of Atlanta was indeed like a terrible storm, one that not only ravaged Atlanta but also rolled across much of northwest Georgia over a period of several days in early November 1864. One of the first places to be laid to waste was Cassville, a village about fifty miles north-northwest of Atlanta charged with the sin of supposedly harboring Southern guerrillas who had attacked the railroad and a Union wagon train nearby. Also weighing in favor of its demise was the unfortunate fact that the town had voted early in the war to change its name to "Manassas," in honor of the 1861 Confederate victory up in Virginia—an act of municipal hubris that didn't sit too well with the occupying Federals. On the afternoon of November 5, the Fifth Ohio Volunteer Cavalry under Colonel Thomas T. Heath arrived with direct and specific orders to "burn the town," giving the residents only twenty minutes to move their things out. The townsfolk pleaded for mercy, or at least for more time, but were flatly refused. "All our tears and prayers availed us nothing," a resident named Frances Elizabeth "Lizzie" Gaines wrote in her diary. "We begged to hearts of stone." In minutes, "the Public Square was one vast sheet of flames. It soon spread all over town, and in a short time nothing was left but the smoky ruins and chimneys." The women and children took cover in the cemetery, huddling among the tombstones as they watched their houses burn. Only the local churches survived the inferno, and the citizens of Cassville never rebuilt, the once-important north Georgia community reduced to a backwoods ghost town.[11]

Next to go was the town of Rome, on the Oostanaula River in northwest Georgia, which Sherman ordered burned on November 10. As Brigadier General John M. Corse prepared to carry out the order, a Federal colonel protested the destruction on the grounds that families were still present in the town. Sherman angrily rejected the appeal. "You have known for ten days that Rome was to be evacuated," he wrote, "and have no right to appeal to my humanity." Then followed a scene of "wantonness and misery," a local historian wrote. "Dry goods boxes and trash were piled high in stores and set off, and the crackling of the timbers furnished a melancholy echo to the wails of women and children. Soldiers ran from place to place with firebrands in their hands, setting the places designated here, and perfectly harmless places there." Corse's men fired two flour mills, two tanneries, one salt mill, one foundry, machine shops, depots, storehouses, and bridges, along with a number of private dwellings and a thousand bales of cotton. A livery stable caught, and the air was filled with the awful plaintive cries of terrified animals and the smell of burning horseflesh. "Only isolated structures escaped," an observer wrote, "until there was no place to do business, and less business to do than places." Sherman, still at Kingston, sent word of his progress to General Thomas in middle Tennessee. "Last night we burned Rome," he wired, "and in two or more days will burn Atlanta."[12]

With these two points off the main railroad line thus disposed of, the Federals prepared to wreck the Western & Atlantic Railroad and its stations as they made their way south toward Atlanta. For days, trains had run on the W&A in one direction, dozens going northward and none passing south, as excess supplies were carried to Chattanooga and beyond and departing soldiers and refugees sought space on the flatcars and boxcars—some even braving the November chill to ride among parcels stacked on the rooftops of the cars. Rumors of Sherman's plans to abandon the city had been widely circulated for several days now, sparking yet another flight by the few remaining noncombatants in Atlanta, including a number of slaves and free blacks worried over the impending loss of Federal protection. "Every boddie seems to be in confusion," diarist Carrie Berry had written on November 7. "The black wimmen are running around trying to get up north for fear that the Rebels will come in and take them." The final train northward, heavy-laden with surplus stores and convalescents, made its way out of Atlanta on November 12.

With the engine and its cars rattling off into the mountains, hundreds of soldiers swarmed onto the tracks behind, sledges and crowbars in hand. Telegraph poles were felled, rails torn and twisted, depots burned, water tanks and woodyards destroyed. The destruction ran for dozens of miles north and south, and the curtain of smoke made it seem that the winding state-owned railroad line itself, referred to by its superintendent as "the crookedest road under the sun," had somehow combusted. "For miles back of Atlanta after the business began, the track of destruction was marked by day by a line of curling smoke, and by night by a broad streak of light that seemed like the Aurora Borealis," one Federal witness wrote. The irony was not lost on the soldiers charged with the road's demolition—for months, they had held the precious supply line, protected it from assault, and diligently repaired it—now they would tear it up themselves. "Not many men know how to build a railroad," Illinois Brigadier General William Carlin wrote, "but almost any ignoramus can destroy one after a little reflection with the aid of a sledge-hammer and a few matches." Severing their only remaining line of communication to the north, a number of Sherman's men were put in mind of the Spanish conquistador Hernando Cortés burning his ships behind him before marching against the Aztecs—while another soldier thought, somewhat less gloriously, that the army was "going into the hole, and pulling the hole in after us." Either way, it was clear that henceforth, for Sherman's army, there would be no going backward.[13]

Observing the progress of the destruction east from Rome and Kingston and then south toward Atlanta was a newly arrived witness, a thirty-five-year-old lawyer from St. Louis named Henry Hitchcock. Initially dissuaded from military service by his uncle, General Ethan Allan Hitchcock, Henry decided in the summer of 1864 that he wanted to see something of the war and applied in person to Secretary of War Edwin Stanton for an officer's commission and a place on General Sherman's staff. His request was granted by both Stanton and Sherman, and he arrived at the latter's headquarters in north Georgia just in time to join the famous general on his storied march.

On Sunday, November 13, Major Hitchcock found Sherman in the town square in Marietta, twenty miles north of Atlanta, and the young officer was shocked to see the destruction going on in the handsome community, right under the commander's nose. A large steam mill had been burned on Sherman's orders, but now other "sundry places" in and around the square were set alight—shops, houses, the courthouse. For a time, a group of soldiers pumped a small engine furiously, trying to tamp down the latter blaze, but it was a losing battle, and the structure was soon a blackened, crackling shell.

"'Twill burn down, sir," Hitchcock said, stating the obvious.

"Yes," Sherman said. "Can't be stopped."

"Was it your intention?"

Sherman dodged the question. "Can't save it," he said, telling his inexperienced aide, "I've seen more of this than you." Besides, whatever the commander's intention, the blaze could hardly be said to be his fault. "There are the men who do this," he remarked, pointing out a band of passing soldiers. "Set as many guards as you please, they will slip in and set fire. . . . Dare say the whole town will burn, at least the business part. I never ordered burning of any dwelling—didn't order this, but it can't be helped. *I say Jeff. Davis burnt them.*"

Hitchcock, having lodged his gentle protest, worried that he had gone too far. He begged the general's pardon, explaining that he had only spoken up because he was "anxious that you not be blamed for what you did not order."

General Sherman was hardly troubled by the thought. He shrugged as he sat his horse and watched the courthouse burn. "Well," he said, "I suppose I'll have to bear it."[14]

With that, the "once beautiful and delightsome" town of Marietta, so recently "noted for the beauty of its situation among the wooden hills, the salubrity of its climate, and the wealth, taste, and refinement of its people," was transformed into what one visitor would call "a ghastly ruin."[15]

"Every house was in flames, it was as light as day," Marietta resident Minerva McClatchey wrote the next day. "Kinesaw mountain was in flames and as far as they eye could see the railroad was burning too and looked like a feiry serpent stretched through the darkness." Mrs. McClatchy confronted some of the Yankee "wretches" and was shocked at their youth—"mere lads" they were, ranging about like rowdy schoolboys, except that they had torches in their hands. She chided the young soldiers and demanded angrily if they liked to burn houses. "No matter whether we like it or not," one replied, "we have to obey orders." The center of town was burned, as was the Georgia Military Institute, a mile to the west, and acres of surrounding woods also were set alight, apparently for no reason at all. "Thank God for his mercy in our preservation," Mrs. McClatchy said, and though she was relieved to have the Yankees gone, she feared for those in their path. "Oh how my heart goes after Sherman's host of unfeeling soldiers," she wrote. "I know terror and dismay and destruction will follow and accompany their march—and I pity the luckless citizens they meet and pass on their route. They have made great threats of what they will do and their hands seldom hesitate to execute the wicked thoughts of their hearts."[16]

The Fifteenth Corps marched out of Marietta to the strains of "Hail Columbia," and Sherman's tenderfoot aide Major Hitchcock found the scene splendid—a "fine show," he wrote in his journal, glad to see that *Harper's Weekly* artist Theodore Davis was hard at work with his sketchpad. But looking over his shoulder, Hitchcock saw "heavy columns of black smoke and lurid flame" rising up from Marietta—a "terrible commentary on this display and its real meaning," he observed. "Thought of Xerxes, etc."[17]

Marching southward, the bluecoats passed through a country made desolate by the recent campaign. The Indian summer was gone and a frosty gray November had taken its place. "A cold & windy day," a Federal adjutant recorded in his diary as his regiment moved down from Allatoona Pass, past Kennesaw Mountain, and on south toward the Chattahoochee River. "No houses—no fences and the road side strewn with dead mules & broken wagons." The fields around them, another soldier wrote, were "filled with women and children, half-naked refugees from their burning homes." The whistle stop at Big Shanty was destroyed, its two-story trackside hotel given over to the flames, and the railroad yard wrecked completely. Approaching the Chattahoochee, the marchers saw dark columns of smoke rising from along its banks as various bridges and riverside structures burned. "I say, Charley," one soldier said to a companion as he hitched his musket up on his shoulder. "I believe Sherman has set the river on fire."

"Reckon not," his friend replied. "But if he has, it's all right."[18]

By November 15, the concentration of Sherman's forces about Atlanta was nearly complete, and there was, as an Illinois soldier wrote, "not a Federal soldier between Atlanta and Chattanooga," the hills and plains behind them "as still and desolate as if a demon of destruction had passed over." The north Georgia towns of Rome, Cassville, Cartersville, Kingston, Acworth, Big Shanty, and Marietta had been substantially if not completely destroyed, and forty-three miles of railroad—from the Etowah River all the way down to Atlanta—had essentially ceased to exist, nothing left but ruined railyards and depots, charred crossties, and thousands of twisted iron rails. Looking south, the soldiers saw "vast clouds of smoke ascending," one remembered, "as if the whole world was on fire," and as darkness fell, a bright glow sifted through the few remaining trees, an angry brushstroke across the southern sky in the direction of Atlanta.[19]

Orlando Poe's "special task of destruction," as Sherman called it, had started out smoothly enough. Poe, with two regiments of Michigan and Missouri engineers, set to work on November 12, the day the railroad was broken, dismantling the city of Atlanta not with torches but with tools, "battering down the walls, throwing down smokestacks, breaking up furnace arches, knocking steam machinery to pieces, and punching all boilers full of holes." Most impressive were the engineers' methodical demolitions of the massive locomotive roundhouse, the stone-walled freight warehouse, and the three-hundred-foot-long Car Shed, which was knocked down arch by arch from end to end. "A Battering Ram was improvised out of a heavy iron rail slung by the middle from a high horse," a watching soldier wrote. "With this a half-a-dozen men knocked away pier after pier while the roof came down a part at a time." It was expertly and for the most part carefully done, the officers in charge of the engineer detachments having been instructed to be "careful not to use fire in doing the work, since it would endanger buildings which it is not intended to destroy."[20]

Poe's engineers were not the problem—as he said, they used fire only to dispose of the wrecks and "heaps of rubbish" left by their various demolition projects, and Poe supervised "to see that the work was done in a proper and orderly manner." But the behavior of other soldiers would be neither proper nor orderly as they ranged about the city in the days to come. Some measures had been taken to guard against plundering and arson—soldiers, for example, were required to walk in the center of the street rather than along the sidewalks where they could easily slip into homes or buildings. The first fires broke out on the night of November 11, when eight buildings went up on Decatur Street and then elsewhere—correspondent David Conyngham was certain that it was the handiwork of "some of the soldiers, who expected to get some booty under cover of the fires." Carrie Berry took note of the fires in her diary. "We were fritened almost to death last night," she wrote. "Some mean soldiers set several houses on fire in different parts of the town. I could not go to sleep for fear that they would set our house on fire. We all dred the next few days to come for they said that they would set the last house on fire if they had to leave this place."[21]

Thc Berry family had done just fine through the month of October, though young Carrie found the days "long and lonesom," especially on Sunday, when she missed attending church and Sunday School. No church services were held in the city, the Yankees having commandeered

The Atlanta railroad depot, the "Car Shed," left, before its destruction. Note boxcars loaded with refugee baggage. The ruins of the Car Shed, right. (*Library of Congress*)

almost all the church buildings, and all the schools had been closed as well—the sole exception being a school for blacks run by a pair of "philanthropic Northmen" with the assistance of free black dentist Roderick Badger. Most of Carrie's friends, as well as her favorite aunt, had departed the city in September after the expulsion order. Carrie stayed busy helping with chores—washing, ironing, hemming dresses, and watching her little sister Zuie. In October, she made herself an apron and a dress for her doll, and cold rains kept her close by the fireside. "Mama and Papa took a walk this evening," she wrote on October 23, "and they say that they never saw a place torn up like Atlanta is." The extent of the family's misfortune was the loss of their last hog, stolen from his pen and led away to slaughter by two Federal soldiers on Zuie's birthday.[22]

But now the fires had begun, and Carrie's diary entries reflected her growing alarm. "The federal soldiers have ben coming to day and burning houses," she wrote on November 13, and the next day recorded, "Mon. Nov. 14. They came burning Atlanta to day. We all dread it because they say that they will burn the last house before they stop. We will dread it." The reporter Conyngham noted increased precautions in town to guard against arson—stepped-up patrols, threats of arrest, even a five-hundred-dollar reward—though none of it seemed to work. What was more, once a fire had started, it was generally allowed to run its course, the soldiers figuring that the town was doomed in any event. "Very little effort had been made to rescue the city from the devouring elements," Conyngham wrote, "for they knew that the fiat had gone forth consigning it to destruction." For his part, engineer Poe attributed the destruction to "lawless persons, who, by sneaking around in blind alleys, succeeded in firing many houses which it was not intended to touch"—though it was clear that those engaged in "the act of incendiarism" were wearing blue uniforms. "It was hard to restrain the soldiers from burning it down," Conyngham wrote matter-of-factly. "With that licentiousness that characterizes an army, they wanted a bonfire."[23]

That they certainly did, and they proceeded under the assumption that their commander wanted one too. "A notion has possessed the army that Atlanta is to be burned," an Indiana chaplain wrote, suggesting that "the wish is father to the thought." An Iowa sergeant agreed. "It seems that everything in sight is being burned," he recorded in his diary. "Every man seems to think he has a free hand to touch the match." Indeed, a sort of circular logic seemed to justify widespread arson. Watching a farmhouse burn, one soldier was heard to exclaim, "Look around boys; I reckon 'Old Billy' has set the world on fire."

"Why, darn it, 'Old Billy' has nothing to do with it; it's ourselves that are making the bonfires," a comrade replied.

"Specks so; guess it's all right, anyhow," shrugged the first.

"Why wouldn't it be right? Old Billy wouldn't have done it otherwise."[24]

Tuesday, November 15 would turn out to be the last day of the Federal occupation of Atlanta, and according to young Carrie, "a dreadful day" it was. "Things have ben burning all around us," she wrote. "We dread to night because we do not know what moment that they will set our house on fire." Sherman returned to the city and reestablished his headquarters in the Neal house near City Hall and spent the day making final preparations for the march to begin early in the morning. His arrival in town did little to tamp down the growing unrest inside the city. Poe's engineers wrapped up their demolition and began firing huge piles of debris, which was done according to plan but may have inspired others in the city to set fires themselves. Near the ruined depot, quartermasters spent the day issuing shoes and uniforms and equipment, though the spreading fires and eye-watering smoke presently caused them to close up shop. "It soon became evident that these fires were but the beginning of a general conflagration which would sweep over the city and blot it out of existence," Illinois Major James Connolly wrote, "so Quartermasters and Commisaries ceased trying to issue clothing or load rations, they told the soldiers to go in and take what they wanted before it burned up." The soldiers did just that, considering themselves unleashed and licensed to plunder. They battered down doors with their muskets, dragging out armfuls of clothes and unearthing caches of tobacco and whiskey, which quickly made the problem worse. As night fell, "drunken soldiers on foot and horseback raced up and down the streets while the buildings on either side were solid sheets of flame," Connolly recalled. "They gathered in crowds before the finest structures and sang 'Rally around the Flag' while the flames enwrapped these costly edifices, and shouted and danced and sang again while pillar and roof and dome sank into one common ruin."[25]

"Fire! Fire!! Fire!!! in every quarter of the city," a twenty-two-year-old Wisconsin commissary clerk and former schoolteacher named Harvey Reid wrote, "but nobody pays any attention to it other than to remark how finely it burns." Sherman watched the flames through the windows of his headquarters on Washington Street with members of his staff fully one-third of the horizon showing immense, raging fires—"a line of fire and smoke," his adjutant Henry Hitchcock remembered, "lurid, angry, dreadful to look upon." Watching the conflagration, the Ohio general made no excuse, but "simply explained the facts," his aide recalled. "This city has done and contributed probably more to carry on and sustain the war than any other, save perhaps Richmond," Sherman said. "We have been fighting *Atlanta* all the time, in the past—have been capturing guns, wagons, etc., etc., marked '*Atlanta*' and made here, all the time—and now since they have been doing so much to destroy us and our Government we have to destroy them, at least enough to prevent any more of that."[26]

"The streets were now in one fierce sheet of flame; houses were falling on all sides, and fiery flakes of cinders were whirled about," the reporter Conyngham wrote. "Occasionally shells exploded, and excited men rushed from the choking atmosphere, and hurried away from the city of ruins. At a distance the city seemed overshadowed by a cloud of black smoke, through which, now and then, darted a gushing flame of fire, or projectiles hurled from the burning ruin. The sun looked, through the hazy cloud, like a blood-red ball of fire; and the air, for miles around, felt impressive and intolerable. The Tyre of the South was laid in ashes, and the 'Gate City' was a thing of the past."[27]

Unoccupied homes, of which there were hundreds, fared the worst; the few citizens who remained in the city, like the Berry family, often were not disturbed. "We all set up all night," Carrie wrote. "If we had not set up our house would have ben burnt up for the fire was very near and the soldiers were going around setting houses on fire where they were not watched. They behaved very badly." A few hard-hearted Yankee soldiers found grim amusement in the terror the spreading blaze caused among the handful of civilians still in town. "Some few families remained in the city regardless of Sherman's order until it was too late to get away, and to witness them getting away from the fire was decidedly rich," an Ohio captain wrote. "They remained long enough to see the folly of their ways but too late to repent and save their furniture."[28]

Indeed, some Federal soldiers expelled residents from their homes before setting them alight. "Most of the people left their houses without saying a word for they heard the cry of 'Chambersburg' and they knew it would be useless to contend with the soldiers," a Michigan sergeant named Allen Campbell remembered. But others lodged protests no less forceful for being meekly stated. By his own admission, Sergeant Campbell was about to fire one house when a little girl, perhaps ten years old, stepped into the torchlight. "Mr. Soldier," she said quietly, "you would not burn our house, would you? If you do, where are we going to live?" The child's question halted the veteran sergeant in his tracks. "She looked into my face with such a pleading look that I could not have the heart to fire the place," he later wrote, "so I dropped the torch and walked away. But Chambersburg is dearly paid for."[29]

Other more prominent citizens of the town resisted the wanton destruction. Father Thomas O'Reilly, the young pastor of the Church of Immaculate Conception, had spent the past several months assisting both soldiers and citizens in their time of trial. An altar boy would recall Father O'Reilly at times working twenty hours a day ministering to the wounded, Catholic and Protestant alike, in the city's wards and hospitals. With his church and parsonage in an adjacent block to City Hall, he had come to know the provost guardsmen of the 2nd Massachusetts Regiment, encamped in the square, and they likewise knew O'Reilly and his works. As the Yankee destruction moved from carefully orchestrated to chaotic, the clergyman ranged about his neighborhood working to protect the heart and perhaps the soul of the city of Atlanta.

Exactly how Father O'Reilly went about saving threatened churches and houses downtown is not entirely clear, though he would in time be celebrated as "the Priest Who Stood Up to Sherman." It appears that he hadn't done that, exactly, but instead lobbied General Slocum and other officers nearby to post guards before the churches and to exempt the City Hall from destruction as well. In approaching Slocum, the reverend unquestionably selected a more sympathetic ear than he would have found with General Sherman. "I wish for humanity's sake that this sad war could be brought to a close," Slocum had written to his wife the week before. "While laboring to make it successful, I shall do all in my power to mitigate its horrors." And so he did that evening. Father O'Reilly's protests saved the Atlanta City Hall and five neighboring churches—his own, as well as St. Philip's Episcopal, Trinity Methodist Church, the Second Baptist Church, and Central Presbyterian. (The fact that Sherman spent that night in the Neal House, directly across from City Hall and within two blocks of all five of the spared churches, may well have helped the parson's case—presumably, no soldier would want to set a fire that might spread to the commanding general's headquarters.)[30]

Nearby, another well-known Atlantan resorted to subterfuge to outsmart the arsonists. Dr. P. P. Noel D'Alvigny was a Paris-born pioneer physician and a veteran of both the French and Confederate armies, and though a brave and brilliant man, he was not above resorting to bribery and trickery. The Atlanta Medical College on Butler Street had been used throughout the past few months as a crowded hospital, though its patients had long since been evacuated. When word came that the place was to be burned, Dr. D'Alvigny gathered his hospital attendants and plied them with whiskey to secure their cooperation in his scheme. An officer in charge arrived at the hospital and stiffly informed the doctor that the place would be burned immediately—soldiers had already spread straw on the floor and splintered cots and beds for kindling. D'Alvigny was incensed. He had served in two armies, he said, and he had never seen sick and wounded men burned without any chance for escape. The puzzled officer was then conducted upstairs and, sure enough, there found a ward crowded with convalescents—the tipsy hospital attendants lying abed and groaning pitifully for assistance. Persuaded of the need for time to evacuate these "patients," the officer gave D'Alvigny until daylight to have the men removed—but just as the good doctor had hoped, the hospital was overlooked as the army stepped off before dawn on its great march.[31]

Unfortunately, that was about the extent of the firefighting activity in Atlanta that night. The volunteer fire companies, modest though they had been, were nowhere to be found, the members either in the Confederate service or long since departed with their families (the chief, for example, had "refugeed" to Baltimore). No matter—the pumps were broken and the cisterns nearly dry in any event, and the absent firemen would have had no engines or equipment to speak of even had they been there. The Federals had sent the one remaining hook and ladder truck to Chattanooga, wrecked Company No. 2's hand engine by rolling it down a steep embankment, and knocked to pieces the wheels and pistons of Company No. 1's engine "Blue Dick." Hooks, axes, and other equipment, along with all the fire hoses, were thrown in a pile, doused with coal oil, and set afire. In short, firefighting during the grand inferno was nonexistent. Although later accounts would suggest that Sherman had "personally supervised efforts to contain the flames," it appears he did so in much the same way that a boy lights the fuse on a firecracker and then "supervises" the bang.

By all accounts, the burning of Atlanta on the night of November 15–16 was a spectacular, unforgettable sight, the fire spreading across the landscape as if in a brightly lit amphitheater. Officers and men posted in camps far outside the city reported being able to plainly read their watches or write letters or peruse newspapers by the bright light of the towering flames. "In the solemn starlight we could see the billows of

View north across the railroad tracks on Whitehall Street, left, before the burning of Atlanta and after the destruction, right. Note the top floor of the Concert Hall on the west side of the street has collapsed and the shell of the Georgia Railroad Bank on the east side. (*Library of Congress*)

smoke rolling up from the city of Atlanta," Captain George Pepper wrote. "Such clouds of smoke, and vast sheets of flame, mortal eye has seldom seen. The whole region for miles was lighted up with a strange and indescribable glare." No bugler sounded "Taps" that night, and many got no sleep as all, staying up through the night to watch the city burn. "Sixty thousand of us witnessed the destruction of Atlanta, while our post band and that of the 33rd Massachusetts played martial airs and operatic selections," a Massachusetts captain recalled. This Nero-like fiddling was accompanied by the periodic rumbling crash of exploding shells, either overlooked in small caches or deliberately placed to disrupt the foundations of certain structures.[32]

Those recording the campaign in diaries and letters struggled to find words to describe the massive inferno. "Such a picture as now presented itself to my gaze, I had never seen before," Indiana chaplain John Hight remembered. "The fires in our cities at home sink into insignificance. Atlanta seemed a very pandemonium. In all hues of glory and terribleness, in all forms and fashions conceivable, the flames and smoke surged among the burning buildings, like ocean waves, and struggled upward like a thousand banners in the sky. How many years of toil and frugality

were, this night, reduced to ashes. How many loved homes no longer exist, save in memory. The sun set upon a man wealthy; it rose, and found him a beggar. The beautiful city has become a desolation." And though he mourned the loss of wealth and toil and property, the Hoosier parson saw in this not only military necessity but divine punishment. "How terrible are the retributions of rebellion," he wrote. "How wondrous the judgments of an avenging God against the crime of slavery."[33]

A Massachusetts colonel was amazed at the fiery spectacle as well. "No darkness—in place of it a great glare of light from acres of burning buildings," he wrote. "This strange light, and the roaring of the flames that licked up everything habitable, the intermittent explosions of powder, stored ammo, and projectiles, streams of fire that shot up here and there from heaps of cotton bales and oil factories, the crash of falling buildings, and the change, as if by a turn of the kaleidoscope, of strong walls and proud structures into heaps of desolation; all this made a dreadful picture of the havoc of war, and of its unrelenting horrors." The precise, controlled demolition Captain Poe had contemplated was a thing of the past. "The city all on fire," Private W. C. Johnson of the 89th Ohio wrote in his diary on November 15. "The writer can never

Sherman's troops leaving Atlanta in flames, November 16, 1864. (*Harper's Weekly*)

forget the awfully grand sight witnessed here to-night, of the burning of the city. It appears as an ocean of fire as we look down on the great columns of fire and smoke, the ruinous flares leaping from building to building, and leaving nothing but the smouldering ruins of this once beautiful city."[34]

A number of soldiers were made to think of the fate of ancient Babylon, while others would compare the scene to the fiery underworld. "All the pictures and verbal descriptions of hell I have ever seen never gave me half so vivid an idea of it, as did this flame wrapped city to-night," Major James Connolly wrote. "The night, for miles around was bright as mid-day; the city of Atlanta was one mass of flame, and the morrow must find it a mass of ruins," though he went on to offer his own excuse for the devastation, one that may have reflected the reasoning of his chief. "Well, the soldiers fought for it, and the soldiers won it, now let the soldiers enjoy it," he said, "and so I suppose Gen. Sherman thinks, for he is somewhere near by, now, looking on at all this, and saying not one word to prevent it."[35]

On the morning of November 16, with the fires still crackling and smoking in the streets of the city, thousands of Union soldiers moved in long, winding columns out of Atlanta. Sherman had divided his force into two wings: the Right Wing consisting of the Army of the Tennessee, 15th and 17th Corps, under O. O. Howard; and the Left Wing, the 14th and 20th Corps, led by Henry W. Slocum, which would now be called the Army of Georgia. The men were in high spirits, laughing and singing as they marched. "Started early this morning for the Southern coast, somewhere, and we don't care, as long as Sherman is leading us," read one soldier's diary entry. "Many conjectures as to our destination," another wrote, "all founded on Tecumseh's remark that he was going to 'feed his boys on oysters this winter.' The romance of seeing 'Old Ocean' and picking up shells on the shore makes the trip rather desirable; anything for a change from this wooden country." Riding out with the 14th Corps east of the city, Sherman reined in his horse near the stand of trees where his friend McPherson had been shot from his horse, four months before. "Behind us lay Atlanta," he would recall, "smoldering and in ruins, the black smoke rising high in the air, and hanging like a pall over the ruined city." A band began playing "John Brown's Body," and the light-hearted marchers began to sing—"never before or since have I heard the chorus of 'Glory, Glory, hallelujah!' done with more spirit, or in better harmony of time or place," Sherman recalled.

"Then we turned our horses' heads to the east," he continued, "Atlanta was soon lost behind the screen of trees, and became a thing of the past. Around it clings many a thought of desperate battle, of hope and fear, that now seem like the memory of a dream. I have never seen the place since."[36]

The extent of the destruction the Federals left behind them that morning is somewhat unclear, though there is no question but that the fires of the previous three days and nights laid waste to an immense area of the city. Captain Poe's staff estimated that, by seven A.M. on the morning of the 16th, 37 percent of the town had been destroyed, and though later commentators would assert that the burning of Atlanta was overstated and that "only" one-third of the city had been burned, a closer examination reveals that the destruction was appalling. Most of the business portion of the town—shops, depots, mills, warehouses, theaters, hotels—was reduced to ashes; this comprised eleven-twelfths of the downtown area, according to one estimate. Applying his own ratios to the destruction, a correspondent returning to the city a few weeks later would report that "About three fourths of the buildings have been torn down or burned, and about nine-tenths of the property value destroyed." These estimates are impossible to validate, but whatever the exact percentages and the street-by-street tallies of the ruins, the departing bluecoats had a straightforward view of the dying town behind them. As an Indiana soldier put it in his diary: "We have utterly destroyed Atlanta."[37]

So, was Sherman responsible? History would lay the blame for the destruction of Atlanta at the feet of General Sherman, something members of his staff worried would happen—"Gen S. will be charged with indiscriminate burning, which is not true," Henry Hitchcock wrote on the night of November 15. Nevertheless, Sherman, despite his thirty-six-year military career and his impressive roster of battles and campaigns, is without question best known for two things: the March to the Sea, and the burning of Atlanta. Ask anyone who burned Atlanta during the Civil War, and the response, if forthcoming, will not be that "lawless persons" or soldiers acting contrary to orders fired the town, but that General Sherman did it. And though *Gone with the Wind*, the most popular depiction of the burning of Atlanta, re-creates the explosive though limited conflagration set by the evacuating Confederates in September 1864, that cinematic spectacle is commonly mistaken for the fire set by Sherman. (Biographer John Marszalek asserts that the idea that Sherman callously burned Atlanta was "fanned by the fiery scenes in *Gone with the Wind*.") In fact, for all its fictionalized silver-screen glory, Hood's deliberately set fire was restricted to the rolling mill and ammunition train, with incidental damage to immediately adjacent buildings, whereas the Federal burning two months later would consume, according to one eyewitness estimate, more than two hundred acres of the city—an inferno perhaps ten times as large as the September blaze—and one not limited to military stores and manufacturing capability. Major Hitchcock would insist that much of the damage was unintentional and that Sherman had directed his troops "to destroy only such buildings as are used for war purposes . . . all others are to be spared and *no dwelling* touched."[38]

Although the commanding general's written orders said nothing about burning innocent structures such as homes, hotels, hospitals, and churches, there remained the danger of more widespread destruction, for several reasons. First was some ambiguity in the orders themselves, which allowed for burning not only military, industrial, and railroad buildings but also "shops of all kinds and descriptions," "lumber and timber," and the catchall "&c." One vague and apparently "over-applied" one-sentence order from Sherman issued on November 7 merely provided that "All houses used for storage along the railroad will be destroyed"—essentially a permit for burning private dwellings, as almost any house could be considered "used for storage" at one time or another.[39]

Second, and probably most significant, was the lack of enforcement among the Federal officers and the want of discipline among the men, many of whom were allowed to do as they pleased. Indeed, a number of prominent historians have suggested that Sherman's orders were written for the record, while wink-and-a-nod verbal orders allowed for considerably rougher handling of Georgia's civilians and their property. "The belief in the army," General Jeff C. Davis told Major Hitchcock during the subsequent march, "is that General Sherman favors and desires it, and one man when arrested told his officer so." Hitchcock, who had so recently defended his chief against charges of indiscriminate destruction, had evolved in his views. "I am bound to say," he recorded in his journal, "I think Sherman lacking in enforcing discipline. Brilliant and daring, fertile, rapid and terrible, he does not seem to me *to carry things out* in this respect."[40]

There are certainly those who defend Sherman against charges that his soldiers went too far, many of them the authors of portraits conceived in hagiography and dedicated to the proposition that the burning of Atlanta and the March to the Sea really weren't so bad. One recent history asserted that the burning of Atlanta was a "myth," a story "depicted in southern lore" and made worse by Hood's destruction of the ammunition train back in September and "some ancillary looting." Another accomplished scholar pointed out, in making his case that the devastation in Atlanta was overblown, that "four hundred buildings stood undamaged" in the city—omitting any mention of the thousands that had been destroyed. Other historians correctly point out that the destruction was contrary to Sherman's orders, chapter and verse—Federal soldiers had merely "torched some vacant homes on their own," one scholar wrote. This plainly minimizes what happened, of course—without question, the fires involved more than a handful of wayward bluecoats setting fire to a few abandoned houses. And to the farmer who lost not only his crops and his fences and his barn but also his house and his furniture, or the young mother who saw her only milk cow slaughtered, or the pastor who watched his church burn, there was little comfort in knowing that the firing and pillage of civilian property was contrary to the Northern commander's direction. "Sherman's general order, prescribing the conduct of the troops in their march, was precise and considerate," the New York editor Horace Greeley later asserted, "though its execution would naturally seem harsh to those it despoiled."[41]

Although Sherman seemed largely indifferent to the destruction going on around him at the time—it was beyond the scope of his orders, perhaps, but that hardly seemed to trouble him—after the war, he wrote letters correcting and chiding those who claimed that his troops had burned Atlanta. "Atlanta was not destroyed by the army of the United States commanded by General Sherman," he wrote in one such letter in 1880. "No private dwelling was destroyed by the United States army, but some were by that commanded by General Hood along his line of defense. The Court House still stands; all the buildings on that side of the railroad and all those along Peachtree street, the best street in the city, still remain. Nothing was destroyed by my orders but the depots, workshops, foundries, etc., close by the depots, and two blocks of mercantile stores also close to the depot took fire from the burning storehouse or foundry." Shortly thereafter, he would tell *Atlanta Constitution* editor Henry W. Grady that "The city of Atlanta was never burned as a city," insisting that his orders only contemplated the burning of "four buildings, as I recollect; not over five or six. . . . As far as burning the city in the sense of wanton destruction, I never thought of such a thing. I shirked no responsibility that war imposed, but I never went beyond my duty."[42]

But his duty, as he saw it, was one of destruction. "Our duty is not to build up, it is rather to destroy both the Rebel Army and whatever of wealth or property it has founded its boasted strength upon," he had written to a group of Mississippi citizens petitioning him for mercy in 1863. As for Atlanta, there is no question that some accounts exaggerate the extent of the damage there—Jefferson Davis, for example, would falsely assert that "Not a single house was spared, not even a church"—but Sherman's postwar assertions overstate his case. Whatever Sherman's orders or his personal intentions, it cannot be disputed that the burning in Atlanta was widespread, and that in addition to military and industrial facilities, hundreds of distinctly nonmilitary structures were consumed as well—not just depots, factories, arsenals, and warehouses, but homes, churches, schools, and hospitals.[43]

Fortunately for the record, the particulars of the Federal destruction in Atlanta were carefully documented by a Georgia militia colonel named W. P. Howard, who had been dispatched to the city by Georgia governor Joseph E. Brown two weeks after the Federals departed. Howard arrived in early December and prepared a detailed report, along with a "pencilled map of the city, showing the position of every house left unburned."[44] (It is telling, perhaps, that he considered it easier to note the houses that had *not* been burned than to indicate those that had.) He began by detailing the destruction of state-owned and public property, already with an eye toward eventual recovery: "a vast deal of valuable material remains in the ruins," he wrote. "Three-fourths of the bricks are good and will be suitable for rebuilding if placed under shelter before freezing weather." Railroad buildings and equipment had been reduced to little more than scrap and debris. "The car shed, the depots, machine shops, foundries, rolling mills, merchant mills, arsenals, laboratory, armory, etc., were all burned," Howard wrote, noting that "every species of machinery that was not destroyed by fire was most ingeniously broken and made worthless in its original form—the large steam boilers, the switches, the frogs, etc. Nothing has escaped." Then he moved on to civilian structures. St. Luke's Episcopal Church, the Protestant Methodist Church, the Christian Church, and the African Church had all been burned to the ground. The Trout House, Washington Hall, and the Atlanta Hotel—every hotel in town, in fact, except the Gate City—were destroyed. The Athenaeum Theater and the Concert Hall were destroyed. Every school and institute of learning was destroyed. Finally, the burning of private dwellings was far from sporadic and certainly not accidental—estimates of the number of houses burned range from 3,200 to 5,000; only 400 houses were left standing.

The city's dead had suffered along with the quick, it seemed. "Horses were turned loose in the cemetery to graze upon the grass and shrubbery," Colonel Howard reported. "The ornaments of graves, such as marble lambs, miniature statuary, souvenirs of departed little ones are broke and scattered abroad. The crowning act of all their wickedness and villiany was committed by our ungodly for in removing the dead from the vaults in the cemetery, and robbing the coffins of the silver name plates and tipping, and depositing their own dead in the vaults."[45]

If this devastation could be said to have been his doing, at least indirectly, Sherman believed that it nonetheless was not his fault. To his way of thinking, the destruction was both inevitable and richly deserved; indeed, the people of the South had brought this on themselves. He echoed these points in the early days of his March to the Sea, after refusing a widow's pleas to post a guard to protect her home. "I'll have to harden my heart to these things," he told his aide Hitchcock. "That poor woman today how could I help her? There's no help for it—the soldiers will take all she has. Jeff Davis is responsible for all this." An Illinois soldier agreed that the state of Georgia had simply gotten what was coming to it, writing that Atlanta and "every other southern city deserve nothing better than general destruction from Yankees."[46]

Yet other Northern soldiers believed otherwise and expressed disapproval, even disgust, at the ruining of Atlanta. "I know not what others may think, but I believe this destruction of private property in Atlanta was entirely unnecessary and therefore a disgraceful piece of business," young Harvey Reid wrote from the camp of the 22nd Wisconsin. "The cruelties practiced in this campaign towards citizens have been enough to blast a more sacred cause than ours. We hardly deserve success." Discussing the want of discipline and the uselessness of posting guards, he added:

> It is not that indiscriminate destruction of property is ordered—quite the contrary. A guard is placed at every house

> we pass with orders to admit no soldier, but he only remains while his division is passing—then come the trains accompanied by a thousand 'bummers'—stragglers under nobody's charge—and they ransack the house, taking every knife and fork, spoon, or any thing else they take a fancy to, break open trunks and bureaus, taking women or children's clothing, or tearing them to pieces, trampling upon them and so forth besides taking everything eatable that can be found. I have never heard of personal violence being offered to any citizen, but they are insulted in every other way possible.[47]

In the end, all of this destruction, though some of it was not done at his orders and may not have been specifically or maliciously intended, was nonetheless a part of the general's plan. Sherman "evidently purposes to make the South feel the horrors of war as much as he legitimately can, and if the men trespass beyond the strict limits of his orders he does not inquire into their cases too curiously," a Northern witness who met the general in Savannah wrote. "He told with evident delight how on his march he could look forty miles in each direction and see the smoke rolling up as from one great bonfire."[48]

In late November, as Sherman's army marched through Georgia toward a destination as yet unknown to most, John Bell Hood led the Confederate Army of Tennessee—now with three divisions, 38,000 men, and 108 pieces of artillery in all—northward from Alabama into middle Tennessee. Having failed to lure Sherman away from Atlanta, Hood had consulted with his new superior, P. G. T. Beauregard, who permitted Hood to "prosecute with vigor" a planned campaign into Tennessee, in the hope that "by defeating Thomas's army and such other forces as might be hastily sent against him, he would compel Sherman, should he reach the coast of Georgia or South Carolina, to repair at once to the defense of Kentucky and, perhaps, Ohio, and thus prevent him from reinforcing Grant." It was a desperate, long-odds venture, and Hood's campaign was plagued with problems from the start, from scattered cavalry to increasingly harsh weather to scarce supplies. More than a quarter of his men were barefoot.[49]

The Confederates finally crossed the Tennessee River and were soon presented with a familiar if elusive opportunity—to crush an isolated segment of the Federal army. Near Columbia, Tennessee, Hood overtook two Union corps, about 20,000 of all arms, under Major General John M. Schofield. Leaving a portion of his army to hold the Federals in place, Hood executed a brilliant flanking maneuver and placed the bulk of his force between Schofield and the remainder of the Union army consolidating under Major General George H. Thomas at Nashville. On November 29, 1864, after what Hood had called "the best move of my career as a soldier," the Confederates were in position near Spring Hill, Tennessee, to crush Schofield's outnumbered, cut-off force at first light. Operating on the assumption that his army had blocked the critical Nashville Turnpike, Schofield's sole escape route northward, Hood ate a hearty dinner and went to bed, exhausted but confident, eager for the fight in the morning.[50]

But morning showed the Federals gone. Within a few yards of the Rebel encampment, two entire Union corps had crept past the sleeping Southerners in the darkness and made their escape up the road toward Nashville. "We were in such close proximity to the Confederates," an Illinois captain in the tiptoeing blue column later wrote, "that we could see their long line of campfires as they burned brightly; could hear the rattle of their canteens; see the officers and men standing around the fires; while the rumbling of our wagon train on the pike, and the beating of our own hearts were the only sounds we could hear on our side." Hood was enraged and outraged at Schofield's escape, "wrathy as a rattlesnake this morning," an aide remarked, "striking at everything." He lashed out at his subordinates, especially Generals Cheatham and Cleburne, and he made it perfectly clear that the army was not to pass up any future opportunity to assault the foe, no matter the circumstances. "If you have a brigade in front as advance guard, order its commander to attack the enemy as soon as he comes up with him," Hood said. "If you have a regiment in advance, and it comes up with the enemy, give the colonel orders to attack him; if there is but a company in advance, and if it overtakes the entire Yankee army, order the captain to attack it forthwith."[51]

The Rebels caught up to the retreating Federals the next day, November 30, in a strong position just south of the town of Franklin, Tennessee, nestled in a bend in the Harpeth River. Schofield's two divisions, along with elements of the 4th Corps, held hastily but stoutly constructed semicircular works, the flanks anchored on the river behind. Hood quickly decided he would rather attack Schofield's 20,000 soldiers here at Franklin, where they had been for just a few hours, than face twice that many in the well-established defenses outside Nashville. Echoing his orders to Hardee at Jonesboro three months earlier, he gave orders to Generals Cheatham and Stewart to "drive the enemy from his position into the river *at all hazards.*" Peering through field glasses and telescopes at the formidable lines, with nearly a mile and a half of flat, open ground before them, Hood's subordinate commanders had no illusions about what was being asked of them and their men. "Well, General," Brigadier General Daniel Govan said to Patrick Cleburne, "few of us will ever return to Arkansas to tell the story of this battle."

"Well, Govan," Cleburne replied, "if we are to die, let us die like men."

Die like men they did. At around four o'clock, with the early-setting November sun casting a crimson light across the field before them, the Confederates launched a hopeless frontal assault, suffering 6,500 casualties, more than 1,700 of those killed—more casualties than Hood had suffered in the Battle of Atlanta. Union casualties were roughly one-third of the Rebel total—1,033 wounded, 1,104 missing, and only 189 killed. Among the Southern dead (or mortally wounded) were six generals: John Adams, John C. Carter, Otho Strahl, States Rights Gist, Hiram Granbury, and the Irish hero Pat Cleburne—shot through the heart as he led his division against the enemy works. (Cleburne's friend Dan Govan actually survived the battle and returned to Arkansas to tell the tale.) "The death-angel was there to gather its last harvest," Tennessee Private Sam Watkins wrote of the Battle of Franklin. "It was the grand coronation of death." Early the following morning, a soldier watched Hood as he looked out over the bloody field. "His sturdy visage assumed a melancholy appearance," the soldier remembered, "and for a considerable time he sat on his horse and wept like a child."[52]

The Federals withdrew to Nashville, with Hood limping behind in pursuit with his depleted army, determined to make, as he later said, a "last and manful effort to lift up the sinking fortunes of the Confederacy." He established a defensive line south of the Tennessee capital, his exhausted men scratching inadequate trenches in the frozen ground, though with recent casualties and cavalry subtractions, his army was down to under 23,000 effectives. In the Federal works across the way, George Thomas waited with nearly 55,000 men. Indeed, the Union-loyal Virginian nearly waited too long, making methodical preparations for his assault in early December and then postponing the attack due to an ice storm. Frustrated at what he perceived as a lack of aggressiveness against a severely outnumbered opponent, General Grant considered relieving Thomas and was on his way to visit the army himself on the day the Rock of Chickamauga finally struck. On December 15 and 16, Thomas executed a masterful tactical plan and routed the frostbitten Confederates in the Battle of Nashville, though a remnant of the gray army managed to escape southward. Hood had lost another 1,500 men killed and wounded, and some 4,500 captured. Returns compiled on the last day of the year showed the once-great Army of Tennessee down to just 18,708 officers and men present for duty—less than half the army's September total. "This thing what they call chargin brest works," one of the late General Granbury's Texans wrote, "is not the thing it is cracked up to be."[53]

On January 23, 1865, at Tupelo, Mississippi, John Bell Hood resigned his command and turned his army, or what was left of it, over to General Beauregard. (In the coming spring, his soldiers would embark on their last campaign under their beloved old chief Joseph E. Johnston, who would finally fight a battle against Sherman at Bentonville, North Carolina, on March 19-21, 1865.) The war had finally defeated the Gallant Hood, and his fruitless battles around Atlanta and especially his losses in middle Tennessee destroyed forever his military reputation. Despite the slings and arrows he would endure, Hood's failing was not that he was stupid, or bloodthirsty, or drug-addicted; instead, he was mistaken in his philosophy and therefore in his priorities. He thought that all that was required for the South to win her independence was for his soldiers to fight harder, to want it badly enough, and he therefore judged their success by how hard they were fighting—how many guns and colors they captured, how many casualties they inflicted and suffered, how willing they were to charge against prepared positions, no matter the odds. With such a strong focus on intangibles like courage and fortitude, he paid comparatively little attention to the hard facts like logistics and supply and comparative strength. As a result, like his idol Robert E. Lee at Gettysburg, he asked more of his men than flesh and blood could give.[54]

John Hood arrived in Columbia, South Carolina, in early February for a brief stay with the family of his hot-and-cold fiancée Sally Buchanan Campbell Preston, known to all as "Buck," a hopeless flirt a dozen years younger than Hood. He had greeted his hosts warmly enough, "a heart-full greeting," one said; but he soon withdrew from the social chatter and the amusing anecdotes of the young ladies of the house. "Maybe you attempted the impossible," the Prestons' friend Isabella Martin offered as a word of comfort, and then launched into one of her funniest stories. But the battered Southern knight did not hear a word she said. He stared into the fire with a gloss of perspiration on his forehead, an agony in his face as he went through in his mind "the torture of the damned."

The visit would mark the end of the tentative romance—"I would not marry him if he had a thousand legs instead of just having lost one," Miss Preston had told a friend—but the lost love seemed to fit with Hood's deteriorating circumstances. He had been shot to pieces and defeated on fields across Georgia and Tennessee, but he was never fully broken until now. Coaxed into reluctant conversation, the young general spoke plainly if painfully of his losses, his "defeat and discomforture," the destruction of his army. He had in the past censured others for these failures, and would do so again in the future—but for now, with the panic at Nashville and the stiffening gray corpses at Franklin weighing on his conscience, he said he had nobody to blame but himself.[55]

Early on Christmas Eve, 1864, a telegram from Georgia, delayed two days by routing problems, arrived at the Telegraph Office in Washington. "To His Excellency President Lincoln, Washington, D.C.," the dispatch read. "I beg to present you as a Christmas-gift the city of

Savannah, with one hundred and fifty heavy guns and plenty of ammunition, also about twenty-five thousand bales of cotton. W. T. SHERMAN, Major General." On Christmas morning, the famous message was reprinted in all the newspapers, and "made many a household unusually happy on that festive day," Sherman would write in his memoirs.

The yuletide capture of Savannah was the culmination of the soon-to-be-legendary March to the Sea, whereby Sherman led an army of 62,000 soldiers on a three-hundred-mile march across the heart of Georgia. Sherman's forces met little opposition and were well-supplied throughout the five-week movement—indeed, compared to the bloody campaign in north Georgia, the grand march seemed quite literally like a picnic; in the words of an Illinois soldier, "probably the most gigantic pleasure excursion ever planned." Sherman made good on his promise to "cut a swath through to the sea" and divide the Confederacy in two, leaving "a black streak behind us about 50 miles wide," as a Minnesota soldier recalled. There was almost no murder and rape and pillage in the barbarian sense—the violence, though widespread, was primarily directed against property. "We had a gay old campaign," a New Yorker wrote to a friend. "Destroyed all we could not eat, stole their negroes, burned their cotton & gins, spilled their Sorgum, burned & twisted their R Roads and raised Hell generally as you know an army can when 'turned loose.'"[56]

Sherman, reporting the details of his successful march to Grant on New Year's Day, 1865, estimated the "damage done to the State of Georgia and her military resources at $100,000,000." Twenty million of that, he said, "inured to our advantage," while "the remainder is simple waste and destruction." He added, "This may seem a hard species of warfare, but it brings the sad realities of war home to those who have been directly or indirectly instrumental in involving us in its attendant calamities." He candidly admitted that his army was "a little loose in foraging" and "did some things they ought not to have done." Still, as he had reminded General Halleck on Christmas Eve, "We are not only fighting hostile armies but a hostile people, and must make young and old, rich and poor, feel the hard hand of war, as well as their organized armies. I know that this recent movement of mine through Georgia has had a wonderful effect in this respect." That it certainly did. "It would be an impossibility for me to give you a detailed account of our operations," a Wisconsin soldier wrote home. "But one thing I can say is that we made a clean sweep of everything that came in our way."[57]

The prize at the end was Savannah, the Queen City of the South, occupied by the Federals without any significant loss of life—though the pattern was again re-created, as at Jackson and Atlanta, whereby Sherman captured the place while the Confederate forces, this time under General Hardee, made their escape. Safely stowed in the beautiful coastal city, and finding himself made considerably more welcome than in Atlanta, Sherman hosted a lavish Christmas dinner for senior commanders and members of his staff. The gathering was, in a sense, "a family dinner-party," with fine china, four robust turkeys, and some very good wine, as a staffer remembered, "as quiet and pleasant a Christmas dinner as one could wish away from home." The artist Theodore Davis would render the scene for the pages of *Harper's Weekly*, as Sherman stood to raise a glass in celebration and give a "patriotic, modest, and pointed" speech.[58]

The accolades rolled in for General Sherman, including a note of personal thanks from the president. "When you were about leaving Atlanta for the Atlantic coast, I was *anxious*, if not fearful," Lincoln admitted, "but feeling you were the better judge, and remembering that 'nothing risked, nothing gained,' I did not interfere. Now, the undertaking being a success, the honor is all yours." Again presidential aspirations were mentioned for the Ohio general, and again Sherman demurred. "I would rather be an engineer of a railroad, than President of the U. S., or any political office," he wrote to his senator brother John. "I have commanded one hundred thousand men in battle, and on the march, successfully and without confusion, and that is enough for reputation. Next I want rest & Peace and they can only be had through war."[59]

Visitors came to express their appreciation, especially crowds of what Hitchcock called "the General's new-found colored friends," who flocked to his headquarters by the hundreds. "For several days there was a constant stream of them," Hitchcock recorded, "old and young, men, women and children, black, yellow and cream-colored, uncouth and well-bred, bashful and talkative—but always respectful and well-behaved—all day long, anxious to pay their respects and to see the man

Christmas dinner in Savannah, Georgia, hosted by Sherman to celebrate the successful campaign through Georgia, December 25, 1864. (*Harper's Weekly*)

they had heard so much of, and whom—as more than one of them told him—God had sent to answer their prayers." Sherman was courteous but understandably amazed at the scene, writing to Ellen, "It would amuse you to See the negroes; they flock to me old & young they pray & shout—and mix up my name with that of Moses, & Simon and other scriptural ones as well as Abram Linkum the Great Messiah of 'Dis Jubilee.'"[60]

These scenes—triumphal dinners and dress parades and hero-worshipping callers—again gave occasion to reflect on the change in the mercurial wartime fortunes of Tecumseh Sherman. "Failure or success determines a man's right to be remembered," an Illinois regimental surgeon wrote the day after Christmas. "Three years ago General Sherman was believed by some to be insane when he expressed it as his opinion that to take Kentucky and keep it would require two hundred thousand men. To-day he is the successful conqueror of Georgia, and a million tongues are speaking his praises. Sycophants write adulatory puff and wonderful descriptions of his personnel, while those who once doubted his sanity, now always knew that he was the greatest and most remarkable general of the age."[61]

Not that all was wine and roses in Savannah—for one thing, the victorious general had sad news from home. His youngest child, Charles, born in June, the son he had never seen, had fallen ill and died on December 4. Sherman admitted to his wife, Ellen, that he was unable to grieve for little Charley the way he had for his precious son Willy—"amid the Scenes of death and desolation through which I daily pass I cannot but become callous to death," he wrote. "I should have liked to have seen the baby of which all spoke of so well, but I seem doomed to pass my life away so that all my children will be strangers."[62]

Other diversions during the occupation were considerably less melancholy, such as the rough treatment received by the pious and usually kindhearted Major General Oliver O. Howard, who always seemed to come up against the feisty Rebels rather than the pliable, accommodating Unionists. On one occasion, a rather insolent Savannah woman stepped off the sidewalk and into the muddy street to avoid passing under the Stars and Stripes in front of Howard's headquarters. Seeing this act of defiance, a guard had the lady brought before General Howard.

"Madam, I understand that you refused to pass under my flag," the general said.

"I did," the lady replied. "Am I not at liberty to walk in the sand if I prefer it to the sidewalk?"

"Yes, but you intentionally avoided my flag," Howard said, standing his ground. "I'll make you walk under it."

"You cannot make me," she insisted. "You may have me carried under it, but then it will be your act, not mine."

"I'll send you to prison."

"Send me if you will," the woman replied. "I know you have the power."

Finally, Howard thought he had the answer. "I'll have the flag hung in front of your door, so that you can't go out without walking under it."

"Then I'll stay home and send the servants. They won't mind."

With that, General Howard acquiesced—outflanked, as it were—and the woman left, stepping carefully around the Union flag out front.

Another confrontation with a young Southern lady came during a Christmastime visit with the family of Confederate Captain William Washington Gordon II. There at the Gordon home at the corner of Bull and South Broad streets, General Howard encountered the absent officer's four-year-old daughter Daisy, who was understandably curious about the blue commander's empty sleeve. "What happened to your arm?" the girl inquired solicitously as she scrambled into the general's lap.

"It was shot off in battle," Howard replied.

"Oh, did the Yankees shoot it off?" Daisy asked.

"No, my dear, the Rebels shot it off."

"Did they?" Daisy said. "Well, I shouldn't wonder if my Papa did it. He's shot lots of Yankees!" (No one knew it at the time, but both individuals were destined for great things. After the war, Howard would head the Freedman's Bureau, fight a famous Western campaign against the Nez Perce Indians and accept the surrender of Chief Joseph, and found Howard University; while little Daisy, whose given name was Juliette Magill Kinzie Gordon, would grow and marry and become Juliette Gordon Low, founder of the Girl Scouts of America.)[63]

In Atlanta, the holiday was much different than the Champagne toasts and oyster bisque enjoyed by the Federal officers in Savannah. Southerners would remember it as "the Last Confederate Christmas," and a threadbare, hardscrabble one it was. "Christmas!" Marietta diarist Louisa Warren Fletcher wrote. "How inappropriate to the sad scenes going on around us. Our Savior came to bring peace! Were it not for hope, my heart would sink within me." But the churches in Atlanta reopened that day—at the First Baptist Church, Rev. H. C. Hornady preached a prophetic sermon, expressing a vision for rebirth and rebuilding that his congregation would see realized in the months and years to come. Still, the persistence of the war and the darkening of Confederate fortunes were difficult to abide—there were few merry gentlemen and much dismay; little comfort and no joy. "This Christmas has been any thing but merry to us; a gloom has hung over all that, do what we will, we cannot dispel," nurse Kate Cumming wrote. "Alas! When will this strife and bloodshed cease? When will we have peace? 'Sweet peace is in her grave!'"[64]

The fall of Savannah was yet another terrible blow to Southern hopes, and for some, an indication of divine will in the present conflict. Samuel Richards, hearing the news from his refugee home in New York City—or "Yankee Gotham," as he called it—wrote in his diary: "Verily it would seem true as Napoleon is reported to have said that 'Providence is on the side of the heaviest battalions.' But 'the Judge of the whole earth will do right' and if it is not right in His sight for the South to be free, we ought certainly not to desire it, and I am willing to abide by His decision." Others closer to the conflict at hand expressed a similar sentiment, if a bit more darkly. "The hand of the Almighty is laid in sore judgment upon us—we are a desolated & smitten people," Mary Mallard wrote from her home near Savannah. "We see not, we know not, but we cling to the hope, that when our Heavenly Father hath sufficiently chastened & humbled us as individuals & as a nation, in wrath he will remember mercy & that we shall be purged & purified in this furnace of affliction and brought out a wiser & a better people to His honor & His glory."[65]

The more secular sentiments of many Southerners, military and civilian, who had been roughly handled by Sherman in recent months, were embodied in a found letter written by a Rebel soldier known only as Jim:

> deer sister libby,
> i hev conkludid that the dam fulishnes uv tryin to lick Shurmin
> Had better be stoped. we hav bin getting nuthin but hell & lots
> uv it ever sinse we saw the dam yankys & i am tirde uv it.[66]

CHAPTER THIRTEEN

RESURGENS

Atlanta Rebuilds

The great storm had passed them now, and for the citizens of Atlanta, an eerie quiet rested over the once-noisy city—"the stillness of the grave," as one reporter called it. "No whistle from railroad engines, no braying of mules, no lowing of cows, no whirring of machinery, no sound of hammer and saw, nothing but the howling of dogs was heard in our midst. The human voice was hushed in our streets, no drays, no wagons, no glorious sound of the Gospel in the churches; the theater was hushed in the silence of death. Ruin, universal ruin, was the exclamation of all. It is true that the same sun shines over our heads, the same healthful breeze sweeps over our hills, the same refreshing draughts of water flow from under the ground, but all else has changed."[1]

Returning citizens and curious travelers heading toward Atlanta stared wide-eyed at the passing desolation. One such traveler, a Rebel telegraph operator making his way into the city by way of Jonesboro, described the torn countryside.

> As you approach Atlanta from the south, at every mile you strike first the Confederate breastworks and rifle pits, then the similar defenses of the Yankees: the torn shrubbery, the scarred oaks, the hastily constructed grave with its pine head-board, giving the name and regiment of the men of both armies, scat-

> tered here and there in twos and threes along the road, all tell the tale, if the burned houses, the desolate chimney stacks, and deserted dwellings, once the scene of peaceful domestic happiness, failed to bring the horrors of war before one's mind. But Atlanta caps the climax. Huge fortifications of red dirt wind snakelike around its whole extent; dead mules and horses and fragments of slaughtered beeves lie around; the absence of all life in the town itself, with its smouldering walls, tall naked chimney shafts, with only an occasional glimpse, as I rode along, of a solitary individual slowly picking his way over the masses of brick and debris in the streets, leaves an impression on the mind not easily described. It is appalling: Atlanta now stands like a grinning skull on the wayside; a fragmentary memento of a former life and greatness.[2]

The scenery was much the same, if not worse, approaching Atlanta from the north. Cincinnati journalist Whitelaw Reid, one of a number of well-known journalists who traveled across the South describing the ruined landscape and gathering first-hand experiences, observed: "Down to Dalton"—the starting point of the 1864 campaign—"the damage from the war has not been so very great, but for the rest of the route, solitary chimneys and the debris of burnt buildings everywhere tell the old, old story. If the country did not reveal it so plainly, it might still be read in the faces of our passengers. Every one of them was a record of some phase of the contest, of its squalor and misery, of its demoralization, of its barbarism, or of its ennoblement." Indeed, it appeared that what one Rebel colonel wryly called "the Shermanizing process" had wrung out the people as effectively as it had scoured the land. "Between Chattanooga and Atlanta," English visitor John H. Kennaway wrote, "I do not remember to have seen a smile upon a single human face." At a supper stop in north Georgia, Kennaway was disappointed when his request for milk for his coffee was politely but matter-of-factly refused. "Sherman has taken all the cows," he was told.[3]

"The entire route to Atlanta is a scene of conflict and desolation," another southbound witness wrote. "Earthworks, like the footprints of Titan on the march; rifle-pits extending for miles along the railroad track; hills all dug up into forts and entrenchments; the town of Marietta in

The ruins of Atlanta. (*Harper's Weekly*)

ruins; farms swept clean of their fences and buildings; everywhere, along the blackened war-path, solitary standing chimneys left, 'like exclamation points,' to emphasize the silent story of destruction." The ruined city, no longer screened by oaks and pines, was visible from miles away in any direction, like a smoldering trash heap in the distance.[4]

Inside Atlanta itself, all was "ruins and rubbish, mud and mortar and misery." James R. Crew, the general ticket agent for the Macon & Western and Georgia Railroads, whose home near City Hall had escaped the fire, had trouble putting the scene in words. "It would be impossible for me to give you a description of matters in that once flourishing city," he wrote to his wife. "I should judge that at least two thirds have been destroyed." The *Atlanta Intelligencer*, recently returned and now printing from a ramshackle shoe factory on Alabama Street, pronounced the streets of Atlanta a "disgusting and heart-sickening scene. . . . Ruin, death and devastation met the eye on every hand." The dirt streets were filled with garbage and debris, broken wheels and axels, nails, charred boards, shards of glass, cannonballs. Landmarks were few, and visitors who were once familiar with the city at times wandered lost, seeing nothing but a jumble of burnt walls and chimneys in every direction. "The city always had a mushroom character, and the fire-king must have laughed with glee when it was given over to his keeping," Northern journalist Sidney Andrews wrote. "There is yet abundant evidence of his energy—not so much in crumbling walls and solitary chimneys, as in thousands of masses of brick and mortar, thousands of pieces of charred timber, thousands of half-burned boards, thousands of scraps of tin roofing, thousands of car and engine bolts and bars, thousands of ruined articles of hardware, thousands of tons of debris of all sorts and shapes."[5]

Sherman's mark, as *Cincinnati Gazette* reporter Whitelaw Reid observed, was "written too plainly to be soon effaced, in gaping windows and roofless houses, heaps of ruins on the principal corners and traces of unsparing destruction everywhere." The buildings in the downtown business district and along the major streets were devastated, as the *Atlanta Intelligencer* documented on December 22: Peachtree Street "all a heap of ruins;" Whitehall Street likewise "an entire ruin"; and on Marietta Street, "nothing but charred ruins are left to mark the spots of business houses, private residences, the sword and button factories, and the grist mill." The lengthy article continued in its detailed block-by-block post mortem: "On the street in rear of the Trout House every house was burned"; "Every house between McDonough and Fair Streets destroyed except L. P. Grant's, Pettus, and one in rear of Williams"; "On Walton Street nearly every house destroyed."[6]

The railroad, once the pride of the city, was a muddy wasteland north and south, as far as the eye could see. "As you stand on the crossing at Whitehall and look up the Western & Atlantic railroad," the *Intelligencer* reporter wrote, "the piles of crossties are so numerous and spread out to such an extent as to remind one of the ocean when its waves are raised by a brisk wind. It is an ocean of ruins." Observers were amazed at the piled remains of the warehouses and freight depots, and especially the battered-down walls of the "extensive and elegant" Car Shed, but most remarkable were the iron rails, "fantastically twisted and bent" as if by an angry god and strewn for miles along the railroad bed. Boasting at the extent of the destruction of the railroad in Atlanta in a letter home, an Ohio sergeant quipped, "I do not think the cars will run for a fieu days yet."[7]

Even the birds had gone from Atlanta. Above were circling buzzards and an occasional ragged murder of crows—but the sparrows and thrushes, the robins and cardinals and doves, were absent from the trees and gardens of the city and would remain so, even in the spring. Stray cats roamed the blackened ruins, and packs of dogs, abandoned by their owners, prowled the streets at night. For a time, an upright horse was a notable sight, as almost all the mounts were either killed or taken by the departing Yankees. Added to their countless other burdens, the residents of the city would for weeks suffer under the oppressive stench of rotting flesh from the thousands of corpses of horses and mules strewn along the roads leading out of Atlanta.[8]

Human scavengers picked their way through the ruins as well. "The legions of carrion crows and vultures," a reporter noted, "were surpassed by Georgia's own sons, who might otherwise have been styled our brothers, congregated here from a distance of fifty miles, in every direction, to steal and haul away the effects of their absent and unfortunate countrymen." The Georgia militia colonel W. P. Howard was shocked at the "exportation of stolen property" from the city, which he chalked up to "bushwackers, robbers and deserters, and citizens from the surrounding country." Arriving in town, he found some 250 wagons "loaded with pilfered plunder; pianoes, mirrors, furniture of all kinds, iron, hides without number, and an incalculable amount of other things, very valuable at the present time." Thieves carried trunks and sofas from houses in broad daylight, or took their pick from the cache of furniture stored by refugee families in Trinity Church—the plunderers having discovered that "all they had to do was to go to church and get a choice load of furniture and haul it home." Carrie Berry observed that "the town is full of country people seeing what they can find," though the few remaining residents, young and old, soon joined in the treasure hunt. "We children have ben plundering about seeing what we could find," Carrie wrote. There were dangers for wandering children, however—open wells, exposed nails and scrap metal, fetid water, tottering brick walls, the occasional unexploded shell.[9]

Yet there was life to be found in the ruins, too, and many Atlanta women fed their families by scouring what they called the "lead mines" collecting spent bullets to sell or barter for food. For hours on end, they picked through the ruins of the city's arsenals and ranged over frost-covered battlefields on the outskirts of town, digging up lead pellets and fragments as if they were gold nuggets until their hands were cramped and bleeding. "Innumerable bullets, minie balls, and pieces of lead seemed to have been left by the irony of fate to supply sustenance for hungry ones, and employment for the poor," Mary Gay recalled. "I felt that I had literally rubbed against Aladdin's lamp when I saw much needed food, good and palatable, given in exchange for minie balls, and for any kind of metal convertible into destructive missiles," though in time the commissary with which she bartered closed and left her back in desperate straits. "The Lord is my shepherd," Miss Mary reminded herself. "I shall not want."[10]

Some of the transients Carrie Berry called the "country people" did not limit themselves to scavenging and stealing, but rather settled in. "Many of the finest houses in the city," Colonel Howard wrote, "are filled with the finest furniture, carpets, pianoes, mirrors, etc., and occupied by parties who six months ago lived in humble style." Most refugees and returning residents had no such lavish accommodations, however, and found shelter from the elements as best they could. Displaced families moved in with neighbors, or made their homes in abandoned army tents, boxcars, or burned-out buildings. Some huddled in bombproofs or camped in the remains of the Confederate fortifications. For months the predominant structures in and around Atlanta would be shacks and shanties, many along the torn-up railroad tracks, constructed of "old boards, with roofs of huge, warped, slouching shreds of tin, kept from blowing away by stones placed on top." Even months later, a Northern visitor would find the place rapidly rebuilding but reported that "hundreds of the inhabitants, white and black, rendered homeless by the destruction of the city, were living in wretched hovels, which made the suburbs look like a fantastic encampment of gypsies or Indians."[11]

Personal property, too, revealed the hardship. Clothing ranged from homespun to threadbare, and here and there children could be seen "clad only in tow sacks with openings at the corners for armholes." Gray uniform coats were a common sight, as returning soldiers had nothing else to wear. Clocks were stopped, with no one to repair them; furniture was broken-down. Many windows were without glass and almost all without curtains, which had been taken down to be used for blankets or sewn into clothing. Silverware was scarce, dishes almost always mismatched. Atlantans made do, but the cold, gray months ahead would be hard. "The destitution consequent upon the scarcity of provisions and fuel, and the utter worthlessness of Confederate currency during the winter months of 1864 and 1865, produced an amount of suffering beyond the comprehension of most persons who did not witness the facts," a local reporter wrote.[12]

"Let no one despond as to the future of our city!" the defiant *Intelligencer* told its handful of forlorn readers in December, though there was much to regret and lament. Indeed, rebuilding and reconciliation must have seemed a long way off as one looked out over the wreckage of the once-thriving junction town. "How can we forget or forgive," one Georgian asked, "with those ruins staring us in the face?" Another resident summed up the devastation to a visiting reporter for the *New York Tribune*. "Hell has laid her egg," he said, "and right here it hatched."[13]

When Sherman departed, folks said, he left north Georgia under the command of "General Starvation." As bad as things were in Atlanta, the poverty and attendant desperation were even worse in the surrounding countryside, especially in the region the natives called the "Burnt Country." On May 31, 1865, Union cavalry commander Colonel E. F. Winslow sent a dispatch from Atlanta to call attention to "the helpless condition of very many people in this and neighboring counties." Winslow estimated that 5,000 to 8,000 families—or between 25,000 and 50,000 people—were "utterly destitute of bread or any kind of food." Passing these numbers up the chain of command to General Thomas, Brigadier General James H. Wilson added, "Women and children walk from ten to forty miles for food and then obtain only a moiety, frequently nothing." The Federal authorities responded as best they could, and in early June provided 45,000 pounds of meat, 45,000 pounds of meal, and 10,000 pounds of flour to Atlanta's poor, though even these quantities failed to provide for even one-quarter of those in need. The previous fall, Sherman had removed Atlanta's civilians in part so he would not have to care for them or listen to their complaints. Now, with the fighting ended and the land stripped, Union officers found themselves burdened with an even greater number of hungry Southern mouths to feed.[14]

And the ranks of the needy continued to grow. The war had come to an end in April, with Lee's capitulation at Appomattox and Johnston's surrender to Sherman in North Carolina—and Georgia soldiers scattered across the South began to make their way homeward. Most of these veterans were poor, many of them wounded, and all worn down by the war and demoralized by the outcome. Though most of these native sons would presently return to work on farms or plantations, others would load up their families and move to neighboring states or strike out west in search of greener pastures, while some would seek their fortune in Southern cities like Atlanta, adding their number to the thousands of residents and refugees already crowding its streets.

What was more, half a million slaves lived in Georgia before and during the war. All were now free, and thousands flocked from farms and plantations to cities and towns in search of work and a new life and community. The newly established Freedmen's Bureau offered assistance in securing at least the bare essentials of life, distributing 95,000 pounds of food in its first month in Atlanta, and the city provided a haven for free blacks from both former masters and acts of violence in rural areas. In the short term, life was hard for these freedmen, but many would benefit in the long run from the clean slate, as they did their part to fill the commercial and cultural vacuum the Yankees left behind them. "The burning of Atlanta," as one scholar noted, "accelerated the transformation from slavery to freedom, from Old to New South." Free blacks often found work as unskilled day laborers, in time some would move into skilled trades, taking advantage of the burgeoning building industry and Atlanta's centerpiece, the fast-rebuilding railroad. Others invested a few precious dollars of capital and opened grocery stores, barbershops, or boardinghouses. In 1860, there were twenty-five free blacks in Atlanta; by 1870, there would be 10,000.[15]

The depth of want in Atlanta gave rise to desperation, and with the jail burned down and organized law enforcement nonexistent, crime became a considerable problem, as some resorted to burglary or robbery or worse. The city's provisional mayor tried to address the problem by naming every able-bodied man a police officer, but this effort to deputize the entire community had no real effect. "A great many rough-looking fellows hand about the numerous shops and the shanties among the ruins where liquor is sold, and a knot of them cluster at each street corner," a somewhat uneasy visitor wrote, while another voiced his concerns to reporter Whitelaw Reid. "I have spent years among the Blackfeet, and have been pretty much all over the world, but I never saw such demoralized faces," he said. "The war has destroyed their moral character. There isn't one man in a score here I would trust with my carpet-bag." Horse thieves became a problem, as did brick thieves, who were known to pull down chimneys and cart off the remains to take advantage of the strong demand for building materials.[16]

All across north Georgia, despite the scarcity and the danger of starvation, residents were coming back to begin the task of rebuilding. "Every body that can is returning as fast as transportation and the roads will permit," one resident wrote. Among the first to return to Atlanta was Mayor James Calhoun, who was said to have covered the last thirty miles of the journey back into town on foot, valise in hand and an overcoat draped over his arm. "What Atlanta now first needs is energetic, good government," the *Intelligencer* wrote in late December. "This, combined with devoted loyalty and enterprise on the part of her citizens, and she will soon rise from the ashes." Mayor Calhoun, reelected to a fourth term by a severely depleted electorate on December 7, was determined to provide the necessary leadership, though obstacles abounded. In addition to the charred condition of most of the city's public and many private structures, the mayor found the city's organization and its services were in a shambles. The city was dark, the gaslights still out and the superintendent, poor shell-torn Mr. Warren, now three months in his grave. Nor was there any money to pay for projects or salaries—the treasurer reported $1.64 in the city treasury.[17]

"Survival required action," a local historian wrote of the period, noting that "gentlemen of the old regime, unaccustomed, for many years at least, to manual labor, set to work knocking the dead mortar off bricks in the debris of their property preparatory to rebuilding." Commercial instincts were strong, and makeshift shops were improvised to begin trading—indeed, "anything with a roof and four sides answered for a shelter and a place to do business." By the spring much of the trash had been cleared, and in their place, as a visitor wrote, "scaffolding, mortar-beds, and lime-barrels, piles of lumber and bricks and mounds of sand, choke every street, and the whole place on working days resounds with the noise of carpenters and masons." Even as streets were repaired and improved—for now, "put in a fair condition," though all would be macadamized by 1867—other projects moved forward as well. The Broad Street bridge across the railroad tracks was repaired, and the City Cemetery enlarged and fenced. Schools were established and reopened over the winter, and the Medical College would resume instruction in the fall of 1865. The city limits were extended a half-mile outward, now encompassing a circle three miles in diameter—still with its center at the railroad station, or what was left of it.[18]

Private enterprise resumed and proceeded at a surprising pace, and many lived in makeshift homes as they focused their efforts on rebuilding their stores and businesses. The free black barber and entrepreneur Robert Webster was one of the first back in operation, reopening his shaving emporium on Decatur Street in early December, when there was little else open but a small grocery, a barroom, and the post office. When Webster's destitute former master Benjamin Yancey wrote to him seeking assistance, Webster loaned him one hundred dollars in gold and one hundred dollars in silver, and told him there was more where that came from if he needed it. Years later, Webster would file a claim with the federal government's Southern Claims Commission, seeking compensation for around ten thousand dollars in tobacco and other goods lost during the Yankee occupation of Atlanta. Although the commissioners were convinced of Webster's loyalty, they denied his claim, apparently because of a lack of evidence and documentation.[19]

Other businesses soon followed: T. Kile & Co., Wholesale Grocers; Clark Howell's flour mill on Peachtree Creek; J. M. and J. C. Alexander's Variety Store, "Consisting of Notions, Dry Goods, Shoes, Boots, Hardware and Groceries"; and George Sharp, Jr.'s "first class Drinking and Billiard Saloon." Law offices reopened, advertising legal services including new specialties like claims against the government and applications for special pardons. Manufacturing had a long way to go, as the English visitor John Kennaway observed: "A few battered brick walls, and an occasional chimney looking grim and gaunt, and ashamed of such prominence, were all that remained to attest the former existence of the great mills and foundries." Bookseller S. P. Richards arrived back in Atlanta from New York on August 10, eager to reestablish his shop with his brother Jabez, and even ten months after the great destruction was startled at what he saw—"a dirty, dusty ruin it is," he said of Atlanta, "but still, busy life is resuming its sway over its desolate streets and any number of stores of all kinds are springing up as if by magic in every part of the burnt district." The place was filthy and fast on its way to being overcrowded, accommodations were primitive, money scarce, and rents exorbitant (as high as forty dollars a foot for frontage on Peachtree or Whitehall streets). But no one seemed dissuaded—in the latter half of 1865, the city council would license 338 business firms of various trades.[20]

"Trade of all kinds is extremely active; the city is full of goods; and though the number of traders seems inordinately great, new ones are pushing into business," one observer wrote. "To a stranger it appears as if the feverish activity of the mercantile community must eventually bring on a crash, but the citizens indulge in glowing anticipations of the future prosperity and growth of their town." Indeed, the city seemed almost northern, as if the departed bluecoats had left the town possessed of a Yankee spirit. "These people were taking lessons from Chicago," Whitelaw Reid wrote, observing that despite its proximity to the Northern states and its abundant capital, Richmond "was not half so far rebuilt as Atlanta." Some considered such comparisons to Northern cities anything but a compliment: "Atlanta is a devil of a place. . . . The men rush about like mad, and keep up such a bustle, worry and chatter that it runs me crazy," one Southerner wrote, while a lifelong Georgian mourned for his beloved state "because her 'gentlemen' had all been ruined, and she must hereafter be the home of 'greasy workingmen.'" Another called Atlanta "the antithesis of Savannah," denouncing the city as "eminently modern and unromantic." That may be—but in 1868, the state legislature would vote to relocate the capital from Milledgeville to Atlanta, as the Old South began to give way, however slowly, to the New.[21]

Most important for the city's future, of course, was the reconnection and resumption of operation of the city's commercial lifelines and its reason for being, the railroads. The rail lines themselves had been heavily damaged by Sherman's army—especially the Western & Atlantic and the Macon & Western, which for scores of miles had simply ceased to be—and what little rolling stock had survived the conflict was scattered across the region. But the state of Georgia and the railroad companies worked quickly to re-lay ties and tracks and refurbish damaged cars and engines, with Atlanta railroad agent James R. Crew overseeing the repair project of the first road to open, the Atlanta & West Point running southwest toward Montgomery. On Friday, March 3, 1865, the *Intelligencer* reported, "the shrill whistle of a steam engine announced the *first* arrival of a train of cars within the corporate limits of Atlanta since its abandonment by the enemy." The reappearance of loaded cars and whistling locomotives in less than four months was incredible. There was no depot, no roundhouse, no freight warehouse, and no platform to speak of, but the opening of the rails themselves was a hopeful sign, at the same time signifying a return to normalcy and a way forward. "Upon hearing it, men, women and boys shouted with joy. The old, familiar and inspiring sound was grateful to all." Not that the place was much to look at—the former bustling railyard at the heart of the city was now, as a Northern traveler wrote, "a great open space of irregular shape, a wilderness of mud, with a confused jumble of railway sheds, and traversed by numberless rails, rusted and splashed, where strings of dirty cars are standing, and engines constantly puff and whistle." The *Intelligencer* predicted, "Soon the other railroads will form a connection with our city and then, from her ashes, Phoenix-like, Atlanta will rise to resume her former importance in Georgia and the South." Three months later, not only the A&WP but all four of the railroads intersecting in Atlanta had been repaired and were in operation.[22]

The city of Atlanta was mostly burnt and almost completely broke—but it was also back in business, reclaiming for good its status as the central transportation hub of the South. "Get to Atlanta," a visiting Yankee told a fellow traveler shortly after the war, "and then you can get anywhere else on God's airth."[23]

"I have never seen the place since," Sherman had said of Atlanta in his memoirs in 1875, but four years later, he took the opportunity to make a tour of the South and along the way to visit the reborn Gate City. Shortly after noon on January 29, 1879, General Sherman returned to Atlanta, his train rolling into the magnificent Union Depot, completed in 1871 on the site of the former Car Shed that had been crumpled on his orders back in '64. The city had a short memory, it seemed, and unlike last time welcomed him with open arms. "Wm. T. 'Come, Sir!'" an *Atlanta Constitution* headline read. Sidewalks were crowded and the depot "comfortably filled" to receive the famous general, and a reporter noted that a "sort of light, good-humor pervaded the crowd, spiced up with curiosity to see the man who burned Atlanta." One wit proposed that the general be greeted with a procession of mourning widows with bundles of kindling in their hands, while another cried, "Ring the fire-bells! The town will be gone in forty minutes!" The general, his once-auburn beard now losing its battle with gray, stepped down onto the platform and "raised his hat with a quick but not ungraceful motion." Trailing behind him were an aide, two of his daughters, Lizzie and Ellie, and the quartermaster general of the army, General Stewart Van Vliet, and his wife.

Sherman had been appointed Commanding General of the United States Army in 1869 by his friend, then President Ulysses S. Grant, and most of his time over the past decade had been spent dealing with Indian problems out on the plains, where he favored an even harder policy than the one he had employed toward Southern civilians in the late war—acting with what he called "vindictive earnestness" against the Sioux and other tribes, even to their extermination. "We are not going to let a few thieving, ragged Indians check and stop the progress of [the railroads], a work of national and world-wide importance," he had told Grant. Just as restless in postwar years as he had been when campaigning, he avoided Washington as much as he could and traveled extensively, attending official functions, reunions, and banquets, in constant demand as a public speaker. The last twenty-five years of his life would be, according to biographer Lloyd Lewis, "one long chicken dinner."[24]

Sherman and his party checked into the Kimball House hotel at Pryor and Decatur streets—the former site of the Atlanta Hotel, which his soldiers had burned—where he "expressed wonder at the magnitude of the hotel and the fineness of its appointments." After a grand dinner, "served in an inimitable style," the distinguished party was taken on a carriage ride around the city. "The general expressed great admiration at the pluck and energy shown by Atlanta, and the marvelous recuperations evidenced by her growth. He was astonished to find in the South the brightness and thrift of the Northern cities." Later that evening, Sherman attended a grand ball in his honor at McPherson Barracks, an infantry post on the southwest corner of town established in 1867 and named in honor of Sherman's friend and protégé, the fallen Union hero James B. McPherson.

The citizens took considerable pride in showing the town off to their former nemesis, delighting in his compliments like a child fawned over by a flattering parent. "Yesterday General Sherman returned to the scene of destruction and disaster, and looked upon the answer that our poor people had made to his torch," the *Atlanta Constitution* wrote. "A proud city, prosperous almost beyond compare, throbbing with vigor and strength, and rapturous with the thrill of growth and expansion, stands before him. A people brave enough to bury their hatreds in the ruins his hands have made, and wise enough to turn their passion towards recuperation rather than revenge, bade him decorous greeting."

The city had come a long way, no question, since what the papers euphemistically called "Sherman's Last Visit." The forthcoming 1880 census would put the population of Atlanta at 37,409, nearly quadruple its prewar tally, a remarkable total given the forced evacuation and destruction of the place just sixteen years before. By the turn of the century, the city's population would be nearly ten times what it had been in 1860. A visiting reporter, marveling at the growth and recovery, observed that "by mutual help and enterprise, together with a vast amount of personal labor, the ruins were replaced by substantial business edifices, new hotels of magnificent proportions were erected, churches more lofty in gable and spire arose upon the sites of those destroyed, and the vacant streets were filled with people." The pace of rebuilding had been almost frenetic: in 1871, for example, the year of the Great Chicago Fire—which one Northern newspaper suggested was "divine retribution for the burning of Atlanta by Sherman's troops"—more than four hundred new buildings were erected in Atlanta.

Peachtree Street in 1875. (*Atlanta Journal-Constitution*)

In addition to the grand railroad depot, also completed in 1871—a commodious iron structure adorned with what a critic called "Second Empire clothing of the so-called 'General Grant style'"—and the South's largest hotel, the town boasted a new state capitol building, a rebuilt commercial district along Peachtree and Whitehall streets, a street railway company, and even a telephone line running between the Western & Atlantic freight depot and the Union Passenger Station. At the corner of Loyd and Hunter streets was the magnificent Shrine of the Immaculate Conception, completed in 1872 to replace the former church of Father O'Reilly, whose health had failed even as the shrine was being constructed. He died that autumn at age forty-one and was laid to rest in a vault under the new church. Also notable, but apparently not included on the general's tour, was the community of Shermantown, established by freed slaves and migrant workers after the war.

(Shermantown would fade in the memory of most residents, but would later become the famous Auburn Avenue district of east Atlanta.)[25]

Despite the remarkable life and livelihood now apparent in Atlanta, the scars of the war were still plainly visible. Sherman looked out over the Peachtree Creek battlefield from the porch of the home of a local judge, and made his way out Marietta Street and past the remains of the old fortifications. "Everywhere as you ride out of Atlanta, you cross cordon after cordon of earth-works, pass through woods torn with round shot, where shells cut long pathways, and wander across fields sown with the leaden seed," a reporter wrote for *Harper's Monthly* that year, though he predicted that these "marks of Mars" were soon to fade: "Gradually the city is extending itself beyond these red lines of embankments, and in twenty years their scant remains will become curiosities to the traveler."[26]

Sherman met with various local dignitaries, including wartime Georgia governor Joseph E. Brown and newly elected Atlanta mayor and former Confederate colonel William Lowndes Calhoun, son of the late Mayor James M. Calhoun, who had passed away in 1875. The garrulous general impressed all who heard him with his detailed recall of names and locations and tactical details of the campaign, and he doled out generous praise for the resuscitated city. "I see the streets are the same," he said, "but the city is wonderfully changed, and has an appearance of enterprise and thrift that is admirable." A young reporter dared to ask the legendary commander why he had burned Atlanta, and Sherman took him by the hand. "Young man, when I got to Atlanta what was left of the Confederacy could roughly be compared to your hand," he said. "Atlanta was the palm and by destroying it, I spared myself much further fighting." Then he added: "But remember, the same reason which caused me to destroy Atlanta will make it a great city in the future."[27]

In the course of his visit, Sherman passed unknowing by glimpses of that future. The *Daily Intelligencer* had given way to the *Atlanta Constitution*, and there a young writer named Joel Chandler Harris would have a story published later that same year—"The Story of Mr. Rabbit and Mr. Fox as told by Uncle Remus." At No. 11 Marietta Street, not far from where Mayor Calhoun had surrendered the city to Colonel Coburn fifteen years before, a pharmacist and former Confederate colonel named John Stith Pemberton had finally paid off his bankruptcy debts and was hard at work on new products like Globe Flower Cough Syrup, Pemberton's Indian Queen Hair Dye, and a dubious rheumatic remedy known as "Prescription 47-11." None of these witches' brews lit the world on fire, but Dr. Pemberton would keep at it, stirring his bubbling cauldron for seven years yet before he would invent the "ideal brain tonic"—a concoction he would call Coca-Cola.

Sherman was pleased with the warm reception he had received in the course of his visit. "Though I was personally regarded the bête-noir of the late war in your region, the author of all your woes," he wrote to E. P. Howell of the *Atlanta Constitution* just after leaving the city, "yet I admit that I have just passed over the very ground desolated by the Civil War, and have everywhere received nothing but kind and courteous treatment from highest to lowest, and I heard of no violence to others for opinions' sake." He had been courteously received, indeed, though the papers pushed back gently on some of the general's statements. "General Sherman says he never burnt any dwellings in Atlanta; he only burnt store-houses," the *Constitution* wrote. "According to this, the city was composed mainly of store-houses when he first visited it."

This time around, Atlantans seemed both glad to have hosted General Sherman and glad to see him go. "The general is doubtless a fine man in his way," the *Constitution* closed its report of the visit, "but whenever he feels his bump of destructiveness feeling tender again, we trust he will find it convenient to dodge Atlanta. One visit of that sort is about all a town can stand."[28]

Even as Lost Cause sentiment swelled across the South, Atlanta quickly accepted the reestablishment of the Federal Union and moved to "enthusiastically embrace the spirit of Yankee capitalism," and in fact almost moved too far and too fast in that direction. In 1867, hoping to attract Northern businessmen to the town, the city council had passed a resolution to consider the construction of a memorial to Abraham Lincoln—a 145-foot tower of Georgia marble on ten acres of municipal property. Citizens opposed the measure, however, and the monument was never built. Nevertheless, a spirit of recovery and reconciliation prevailed in Atlanta after the war, even among many hard-boiled "Southrons." "I'm much calmer and sereener than I was a few months ago," columnist Bill Arp wrote. "I begin to feel kindly towards all people, except some. I'm now endeaverin to be a great national man. I've taken up a motto of no North, no South, no East, no West; but let me tell you, my friend, I'll bet on Dixie as long as I've got a dollar. . . . I'm a good Union reb, and my battle cry is Dixie and the Union."[29]

This sentiment would be most eloquently expressed by renowned orator and *Atlanta Constitution* editor Henry W. Grady on December 22, 1886, at an after-dinner speech to the New England Society at Delmonico's in New York City. Asked by a reporter what he would say to the distinguished Yankee audience, the thirty-six-year-old Grady replied, "The Lord only knows. I have thought of a thousand things to say, five hundred of which if I say they will murder me when I get back home, and if I say the other five hundred they will murder me at the banquet." Rising to speak after General Sherman—always a tough act to follow—with the band playing "Marching Through Georgia," Grady spoke of what he called the New South, a South whose "soul is stirred with the breath of a new life"; a region with "a hundred farms for every plantation, fifty homes for every palace, and a diversified industry that meets the complex needs of this complex age"; a place where cheerfulness and frankness prevail over any bitterness. He described the resilient spirit of a Rebel soldier returning to Georgia: "You may leave the South if you want to," the young man said, "but I'm going to Sandersville, kiss my wife and raise a crop, and if the Yankees fool with me any more I'll whip 'em again." Then Grady gestured over to Sherman, addressing the recently retired Union hero directly. "I want to say to General Sherman," he said, "who is considered an able man in our parts—though some people think he is a kind of careless man about fire—that from the ashes he left us in 1864 we have raised a brave and beautiful city, that somehow or other we have caught the sunshine in the bricks and mortar of our homes, and have builded therein not one ignoble prejudice or memory."

"I am glad," he continued, "that the omniscient God held the balance of battle in His almighty hand and that Human slavery was swept from American soil, the American union saved from the wreck of war."

And he closed his speech by referring back to the city of Atlanta:

> This message comes to you from consecrated ground. Every foot of soil about the city in which I live is as sacred a battleground of the republic. Every hill that invests it is hallowed to you by the blood of your brothers who died for your victory; and doubly hallowed to us by the blood of those who died helpless but undaunted in defeat—sacred soil to all of us—rich in memories that make us purer and stronger and better—silent but staunch witness to the red desolation of the matchless valor of American hearts and the deathless glory of American arms—speaking an eloquent witness in its peace and prosperity to the indissoluble union of American States and the imperishable brotherhood of American people.[30]

The following year, the city of Atlanta adopted a new official seal, one that would bear two dates: 1847, the year of its incorporation, and 1865, the year of its rebirth. The image on the old seal, that of a locomotive, was discarded in favor of a new one: the mythical phoenix, rising from the ashes.

The battle of Franklin, Tennessee, depicted in an 1891 Kurz & Allison print. Here, the Army of Tennessee that had fought hard throughout the long Atlanta campaign suffered a disastrous defeat. "If we are to die," Major General Patrick Cleburne remarked grimly, "let us die like men." (*Library of Congress*)

AFTERWORD

War is Hell

General Sherman never said "War is hell." Not exactly, at least—or not according to any official record or firsthand transcription of a conversation or speech. He had certainly expressed similar sentiments in the course of his military career—"War is war, and not popularity-seeking," he had said; and "War is cruelty and you cannot refine it." "War is violence," he once observed; war is "the Storm" (with a capital S), or is "like the thunderbolt." Never wanting for an evocative metaphor, he had written to Ellen back in 1861, "War like a growing monster demands its victims, and must have them— How few realize the stern fact I too well know." But despite all these statements, and all his years of speeches and letters and memoirs and rapid-fire conversation, it appears that his most famous observation was the result of careless quotation or improper attribution. The closest he came to uttering those exact words was during an address to a veterans' gathering at the fairgrounds in Columbus, Ohio, on August 11, 1880. "There is many a boy here who looks upon war as all glory," he said, giving the youngsters in the audience a stern talking-to, "but, boys, it is all hell. You can bear this warning voice to generations yet to come."[1]

The important thing, however, is not the precise quotation itself, but the sentiment expressed. For Sherman, the statement "War is hell" was, according to one scholar, not description but doctrine—"a moral argument and an attempt at self-justification." There was in the three-word maxim an echo of the sense of inevitability that Sherman had preached to the people of Georgia—the war was indeed cruel, but nothing could be done about that; and they should in a way be thankful, for "the crueler it is, the sooner it will be over"; and in any event, the Southern people had brought this on themselves. The wages of sin is death, and the South's reward for secession, as it turned out, was Sherman.

And though Sherman will ever be deservedly prominent in the annals of military history, his hard-handed approach, though both terrible and undeniably effective, is not unique—foreshadowed by ancient example and emulated by latter-day commanders from Pershing to Patton to Petraeus. During the Gulf War, General H. Norman Schwarzkopf kept on his desk a quote snipped from Sherman's memoirs. "War is the remedy our enemies have chosen," it read. "And I say let us give them all they want."[2]

Even as he got on in years, General Sherman was still a fast talker, and not just while delivering his much sought-after speeches, for which he never prepared. "He always ought to have been accompanied by a stenographer," prominent attorney and fellow orator Chauncey M. Depew wrote. "Once I was with him from ten o'clock in the morning until six in the afternoon and he talked without cessation for the whole period." Sherman was at the same time exceedingly particular with respect to certain things and entirely indifferent as to others. He insisted that household and hotel arrangements be correct to the finest detail—to suit Mrs. Sherman, he said—yet he could sleep anywhere and anytime, even sitting up, and his family recalled that he would drink down a cup of coffee without caring whether it contained one spoonful of sugar or ten.

In the after-years, the prickly old soldier seemed at times as stormy and irritable as in the old days—cramming his hands in his pockets when pressed by well-wishers for a handshake, for example, as he scurried back to the sanctuary of his hotel. ("I'll hire a man to shake hands for me," he said.) He craved fame and recognition and at the same time detested it. He regularly complained about the incessant playing of the jaunty tune "Marching Through Georgia" at his public appearances, yet somehow seemed pleased at the remembrance. On one occasion, Sherman received in the mail a polite request for an autograph and a lock of his famous red hair. He responded promptly with a handwritten letter: "The man who had been writing my autographs has been discharged," it read, "and, as my orderly is bald, I cannot reply to the second of your requests." The letter was, of course, unsigned.[3]

Still, for all his tough talk and hard edges, he also displayed a surprising gentleness, especially toward old soldiers from his army. "Let him in," he invariably responded when a veteran came knocking. He purchased train tickets for them, gave them food and drink, even kept standing accounts at clothiers and general stores to satisfy their needs.[4]

His kindness extended to a number of former adversaries, to whom he was as companionable as he had been ruthless during the war. First was his warm friendship with Joseph E. Johnston, who along with his wife was a regular guest at Sherman's home at 15th and H Streets in Washington. "Well, General," Mrs. Johnston told Sherman during one of their frequent visits, "during the war I spent all my time running away from you; but now it seems I am spending all my time running after you." That was fine with Sherman, who considered their differences dead and buried. "You and I became reconciled in April, 1865," he said in a letter to Johnston, and "have remained so ever since with no apologies or concealments." (Johnston, at age eighty-two, would serve as an honorary pallbearer at Sherman's funeral, and would die himself five weeks later—not of a cold or pneumonia contracted at Sherman's service, as the apocryphal story goes, but of heart failure.)[5]

Indeed, Johnston—"the little precise Scotch-dominie of a general," as the poet Stephen Vincent Benét described him—devoted his energies to warring with his former enemies in gray, especially Jefferson Davis and his former lieutenant John Bell Hood, over blame for the failures of days gone by. "Stubborn as flint," the poet continued, "in advance not so lucky, in retreat more dangerous than a running wolf, he could make men cheer him after six weeks retreating." After the war, his former soldiers, many fellow Southerners, and eventually historians would often cheer him as well, his reputation at times as bright and resilient as it had been during the conflict. Old veterans spoke reverently of Johnston in their postwar reminiscences. "If heaven had no other attraction," a Tennessean wrote, "I should want to go there just to feast my eyes on looking at 'Old Joe.'" Historian Bruce Catton, for one, would consider his firing on the eve of the battles for Atlanta a critical turning point. As a result of Davis's replacement of Johnston with Hood, Catton wrote, "the South lost 20,000 good soldiers, Atlanta, the presidential election, and most of what remained of the war." The United Daughters of the Confederacy, perhaps hearkening back to a moment when the future and the prospects for a winning campaign seemed bright, erected a statue of General Johnston at Dalton, Georgia—the starting point of his long retreat toward Atlanta.[6]

Sherman was also warmly disposed toward John Bell Hood. Shortly after the war, the beleaguered young general's fortunes had taken a much-needed turn for the better, and in 1868 he married Anna Marie Hennen, the lovely, Paris-educated daughter of a New Orleans attorney. Together the couple had eleven children in eleven years, including three sets of twins—"Hood's Brigade," bemused onlookers called them as they filed through hotel lobbies and along depot platforms behind their famous father. Echoing the pattern of his military career, Hood enjoyed initial success as a cotton trader and life insurance broker before failing at both and facing financial ruin. He reached out to Sherman and sought his assistance in selling his wartime papers to the government, and the former enemies at one point had dinner together in St. Louis. Then in 1879, shortly after Sherman's tour through the South, a yellow fever epidemic swept through New Orleans, claiming the life of Hood's beloved wife and then his eldest daughter. Two days later, on August 30, 1879, the disease struck down John Bell Hood at the age of forty-eight.[7]

Sherman, too, found himself fighting battles with former comrades after the war. Although he remained a favorite of foot soldiers, artillerists, and other frontline veterans, his fellow generals and other subordinates in the officers' corps were increasingly harsh in their criticism of him. Some of this rancor Sherman brought on himself with the publication in 1875 of his *Memoirs*—a "monument to his own success," as a biographer noted, in which he claimed too much credit and spoke all too plainly of the shortcomings of others while glossing over his own. Longtime enemies like Joseph Hooker and John McClernand were predictably incensed, and former Atlanta Campaign subordinates like Frank Blair and John Logan, both criticized unfairly for their political activities, were wounded as well. Some enemies went so far as to resurface the charges of mental instability. Joe Hooker, who had hated Sherman before and still hated him now, continued to tell anyone who would listen that his former chief was unstable and overrated. "Sherman has a streak of insanity very near the surface," he insisted. There was also, no doubt, predictable envy and personal animosity involved. "A man who wins victories is apt to become a fair foil for criticism from those who lose them," one historian of the war wrote in reference to Ulysses S. Grant, and the same could be said of Sherman.[8]

In the South, the view of General Sherman, which had perhaps softened for a time given the general's national prominence—or at least was suppressed under a veneer of Southern politeness during his travels—turned ever more sour as the years passed. The loudest critic was Jefferson Davis, who in his 1881 two-volume account *The Rise and Fall of the Confederate Government* as well as in numerous public statements, cast Sherman as a primary, perhaps even the foremost, villain of the war. In an interview given after Sherman's visit to Atlanta, Davis accused Sherman of "waging war with more ferocity than any soldier since Attila," before making his attacks more personal. "The truth is that Sherman is a vain man," he said, "who has been raised by success and flattery, and is possessed of a chronic hallucination that he is a great General. He is really a man of very mediocre talents, either civil or military, and owed his success entirely to superior numbers and the lack of enterprise on the part of his antagonist. . . . Had Stonewall Jackson confronted Sherman in 1864, instead of Joe Johnston, a different tale would have been told in my book."[9]

Southern perceptions would be hardened as well in the 1930s by Margaret Mitchell's wartime saga *Gone with the Wind.* Although Sherman does not appear as a full-fledged character in the novel, he is mentioned several dozen times, almost always as a fearful presence bearing down on Atlanta or tearing his way through Georgia. He is similarly depicted in the famous motion picture, an ominous figure standing in the shadows just offstage, with occasional references to his heartlessness and malice—"Panic hit the city with the first of Sherman's shells," one title card reads, while Scarlett O'Hara later frets that "Sherman will burn the house over our heads if we stay."[10]

Whether Davis's outspoken criticism or Margaret Mitchell's fiction truly changed the tide of Southern opinion is uncertain—the fact is that after 1864, one never had to look very far to find folks in Dixie who hated William Tecumseh Sherman. One Southerner described Sherman to Northern journalist Sidney Andrews as "a child of hell," asserting that the general "couldn't be a gentleman if he would, and I'm damned if I believe he would if he could." Others in the course of Andrews's travels called Sherman infernal, atrocious, cowardly, devilish. "Whatever else Southern mothers may forget," Andrews concluded, "they do not seem likely in this generation to forget to teach their children to hate Sherman." As for the Southern press, the *Macon Telegraph*, by way of example, had called the Northern hero "Judas Iscariot, a betrayer, a creature of depravity, a demon of a thousand fiends." Such newsprint sticks and stones, apart from worsening his hatred of reporters, had never much troubled Old Sherman—"This is somewhat on the order of the school bully who if he cant whip you can call you hard names or make insults at your sister," he once wrote to a friend.[11]

Nor was the bitterness in the South lessened by Sherman's passing in February 1891. A proposed resolution in the Tennessee state legislature eulogizing the late commanding general, for example, met with unexpected and vehement opposition. "Since General Sherman is dead, it would be indelicate to speak against him," one lawmaker said on the floor of the state senate, but he insisted that his constituents were "not sorrowing" over the general's passing. "They would perhaps have been glad if he had died several years ago." Southern newspapers published letters from correspondents attesting to (or, rather, sullying) Sherman's character. One such, published in the *Atlanta Constitution* before the funeral was yet complete, called Sherman "a fierce barbarian" and "a heart untouched by chivalry." The letter continued: "All that General Sherman's friends ought in decency to claim for him is that he was a brave and brilliant soldier, devoted to his party and his section—not to his country or its whole people; a strong, yet erratic, unbalanced mind not controlled at all times by the sense of consistency or truth, for even his friends have had to apologize time and again for his reckless statements. He knew that he was the idol of a few in the north, and he did not care a whiff—'a damn,' as he expressed it—for the rest of the world."[12]

Others took cold comfort in the knowledge that Sherman would at last be called to answer for past deeds. "We looked upon Sherman as a monster in human shape," a Nashville woman wrote shortly after his death, "and now that the grave has closed over him he will have a big account to settle for his treatment of the South in her last struggles." Another displaced by Sherman's wrath felt much the same way. "If the devil don't get old Sherman, there a'n't no use having a devil," he said.[13]

And so there will always be competing images of William Tecumseh Sherman—that of the great general, fearless and resolute, leading a Union host in a righteous crusade across the wayward South; and that of the wild-eyed avenger, heartless and angry, waging war not against opposing armies but on defenseless civilians. Historians sorting through these divergent views to pass judgment on General Sherman are, in the end, both too hard on him, and not hard enough. Distinguished scholars have thrown bombs at Sherman for a variety of military and nonmilitary sins. He "never won a battle," they claim (a curious statement, as he fought four battles at the gates of Atlanta, and didn't lose a one); he failed to destroy Hood's army; he should have listened more to General Thomas; he made miniscule errors in his wartime orders and his memoirs and got times and dates and military titles wrong. Albert Castel, perhaps the preeminent chronicler of the Atlanta Campaign, is by his own admission extremely hard on Sherman, portraying him as an overrated liar who "missed opportunities," "wasted time in operations that either were obviously futile or patently unnecessary," and "suffered from serious flaws as a commander." Despite these criticisms, if we evaluate a military leader the same way we judge a football coach or a politician or a corporate executive; that is, if we apply Albert Sidney Johnston's definition of a successful general—one who wins—then Sherman was a great commander. He was almost vicious, often angry, and certainly made his share of tactical mistakes—but he captured Atlanta, helped to secure Abraham Lincoln's reelection, and by his resolve and his actions, coupled with those of his friend Grant, won the Civil War.

At the same time, even as they nitpick his every fumble or oversight, most historians give Sherman a pass on a number of intentional and egregious transgressions for which he deserves reproach: the callous five-week bombardment of Atlanta; the expulsion of Atlanta's civilians from their homes; the lackadaisical enforcement of orders against arson and house-burning. Sherman's campaigns are still studied today in military academies and war colleges for their mastery of supply lines and logistics, their relentless motion, their flanking maneuvers—but perhaps they also contain lessons on how modern wars should *not* be fought, as well as how they should. War is hell, indeed—but as one scholar observed in discussing Sherman, "even in hell, it is possible to be more or less humane, to fight with or without restraint."[14]

Either way, some might consider such a debate centered around Sherman and his conduct during and after the fight for Atlanta to be a useless exercise, bound up as such opinions are in historical memory, wartime personalities, regional bias, and long-settled views. "Whether the destruction of Atlanta was justifiable as an act of war or not, no good will be accomplished by holding its authors and abettors up to public reprobation," the *Macon Telegraph* argued in 1881. "There is no act of that unhappy period on which the two sections will agree, and the part of wisdom is to avoid controversy. There never was yet a fight which satisfied both parties, and when blows have settled it any other or further controversy is not only useless but mischievous." Indeed, the editors seemed to believe that any effort to knock Sherman down would in fact only serve to lift him up. "The North and West idolize Sherman for his work of rapine," the paper continued. "Why should we practically join in the business of hero-worship by groaning over his inflictions or cursing his cruelty? The more we writhe the more they will bless, and nothing desirable will come of it."

In other words, folks North and South will never agree on General Sherman, and it is just as well to let bygones be bygones. "One can't put down history as it really happened—people don't want it—it would shock them," Union General James H. Wilson told an artist while sitting for a portrait in 1906. "People have formed their own ideas in regard to history and they do not want them dismembered." He then proceeded to share a story about the time a young officer went to Sherman's headquarters late one night to deliver certain important dispatches. The aide was shown down a shadowy hallway and knocked at the general's door. Sherman soon appeared, vacant-eyed and clad only in his nightshirt, holding a lighted candle.

"Did you ever see the devil?" the general asked, earnestly and without preamble.

"No," the puzzled courier replied.

"I did," Sherman said. And he turned and marched off into the darkness.[15]

AUTHOR'S NOTE

Atlanta's Lost Battlefields

Readers hoping to visit the battlegrounds described in this book will find themselves facing considerable challenges. Battlefield stomping in modern-day metropolitan Atlanta is in many ways an exercise in imagination and urban archaeology, if not in futility. The state of Georgia boasts a number of preserved Civil War sites—Kennesaw Mountain National Battlefield Park, Chickamauga National Military Park, the Jefferson Davis capture state historic site near Irwinville, and the Andersonville prison camp National Historic Site outside Americus, for example—but none in Atlanta. Thanks somewhat to Sherman, though mostly to Atlanta's postwar progress, every one of the city's antebellum structures mentioned in this book—from stores and stations to houses and churches—is a thing of the past.

The battlefield of **Peachtree Creek** is covered by the neighborhoods of Peachtree Hills, Collier Hills, and Brookwood Hills (the deceptively named neighborhood called Peachtree Battle, with its pretty homes, shopping center, and elementary school, is actually nearly a mile north of the Union lines). The site of Stewart's headquarters is near the Atlanta Water Works on Howell Mill Road. The best place to visit is Tanyard Creek Park along Collier Road, where the Rebel attack struck Coburn and Harrison's front near Collier's Mill—though visitors should take care to avoid the babbling waters of Tanyard Branch itself, which is subject to occasional overflows from Atlanta's notorious sewage system. To explore the winding banks and waters of Peachtree Creek itself while avoiding private property and all manner of urban dangers, the curious should consult David Kaufman's fine book *Peachtree Creek*—which explores the watershed in maps, narrative, and beautiful historic images and modern-day photographs.

The once-bloody field of the Battle of **Atlanta** is almost entirely paved over. The site of Bald or Leggett's Hill, east of the city, is roughly at the interchange of Interstate 20 and Moreland Avenue, though the hill itself is all but gone, lowered perhaps thirty or forty feet when the right of way was graded in the 1950s. Sherman's headquarters at the Hurt (or Howard) House was located at what is now the parking lot of the Jimmy Carter Presidential Library; nothing remains except a historical marker. No heroic statues stand at the places where William H. T. Walker and James B. McPherson were killed. Their death sites are each marked by cannon-barrel monuments, McPherson's (erected 1877) at the intersection of McPherson and Monument Avenue, and Walker's (erected 1902 and relocated 1936) adjacent to the parking lot of a convenience store on Glenwood Avenue, just off I-20. Of course, the battle is dramatically depicted in the magnificent Atlanta Cyclorama, one of the largest oil paintings in the world, some forty-two feet high and 358 feet in circumference. The painting features a heroic General John A. "Black Jack" Logan, who commissioned it to aid him in his presidential aspirations—though he died a few months before it was completed.

Atlanta's Oakland Cemetery is home to a number of the city's dearly departed, including Carrie Berry Crumley, Dr. P. P. Noel D'Alvigny, Mayor James M. Calhoun ("A true and honorable public servant," his epitaph reads), and Margaret Mitchell Marsh. Approximately 6,900 Confederate soldiers are also buried there—3,000 of them unknown—their dust guarded by a magnificent sculpture, the Lion of the Confederacy. (Sixteen Union soldiers who died in local hospitals are also interred nearby.) A historical marker in the cemetery stands at the site of the two-story house where General Hood watched the progress of the Battle of Atlanta.

The field of the Battle of **Ezra Church** is likewise cut to pieces, bisected by Interstate 20 west of downtown Atlanta and covered over with houses, convenience stores, and fast-food places. No trace of the church or the poor house remains. The open portions of the field are at Mozley Park—where a handful of historical markers briefly describe the battle—and in nearby Westview Cemetery, where the Rebel attack pushed off northward toward the Union center. In the cemetery, a memorial statue of a Confederate soldier stands facing north, as if keeping watch over the fallen. The inscription on the monument is taken from the Book of Isaiah: "Nation shall not rise up against nation. They shall beat their swords into plough shares and their spears into pruning hooks. Neither shall they learn war anymore."

The town of **Jonesboro**, once a trackside village and now an off-the-interstate suburban city, both reveres and disregards its Civil War past. Famous as the fictional (the locals prefer "legendary") setting of *Gone with the Wind*, Jonesboro is home to streets like Rhett Butler Drive and Scarlett Drive, though again little remains of its true-life battlefield. State historical markers just north and west of downtown Jonesboro show the progress of the battle. The Warren House, used as a headquarters and hospital, still stands on Jonesboro Road (Georgia Hwy. 54). Also worth a visit on McDonough Street is the Patrick Cleburne Cemetery—named in honor of the Irish commander, though he is buried in Helena, Arkansas—the final resting place of "several hundred unknown Confederate soldiers" who "gave their lives to parry the final thrust at the heart of the Southern Confederacy."

And don't bother driving up and down Tara Boulevard in Jonesboro looking for Tara. It's not there, and never was.

APPENDIX A

ORDER OF BATTLE

to division level, as of July 20, 1864
(Complete order of battle at www.warlikethethunderbolt.com)

UNION

Military Division of the Mississippi
Maj. Gen. William T. Sherman, Commanding

Army of the Cumberland
Maj. Gen. George H. Thomas

IV Army Corps
Maj. Gen. Oliver Otis Howard
First Division
Maj. Gen. David S. Stanley
Second Division
Brig. Gen. John Newton
Third Division
Brig. Gen. Thomas J. Wood

XIV Army Corps
Maj. Gen. John M. Palmer
First Division
Brig. Gen. Richard W. Johnson
Second Division
Brig. Gen. Jefferson C. Davis
Third Division
Brig. Gen. Absalom Baird

XX Army Corps
Maj. Gen. Joseph Hooker
First Division
Brig. Gen. Alpheus S. Williams
Second Division
Brig. Gen. John W. Geary
Third Division
Brig. Gen. William T. Ward

Cavalry Corps
Brig. Gen. Washington Elliott
First Division
Brig. Gen. Edward M. McCook
Second Division
Brig. Gen. Kenner Garrard

(*Union continued*)

Third Division
Brig. Gen. Judson Kilpatrick

ARMY OF THE TENNESSEE
Maj. Gen. James B. McPherson

XV Army Corps
Maj. Gen. John A. Logan
First Division
Brig. Gen. Peter J. Osterhaus
Second Division
Brig. Gen. Morgan L. Smith
Third Division
Brig. Gen. John E. Smith
Fourth Division
Brig. Gen. William Harrow

XVI Army Corps
Maj. Gen. Grenville M. Dodge
Second Division
Brig. Gen. Thomas M. Sweeny
Fourth Division
Brig. Gen. James C. Veatch

XVII Army Corps
Maj. Gen. Frank P. Blair, Jr.
Third Division
Brig. Gen. Mortimer D. Leggett
Fourth Division
Brig. Gen. Walter Q. Gresham

ARMY OF THE OHIO
Maj. Gen. John M. Schofield
First Division
Brig. Gen. Alvin P. Hovey
Second Division
Brig. Gen. Milo S. Hascall
Third Division
Brig. Gen. Jacob D. Cox
Cavalry Division
Maj. Gen. George Stoneman

CONFEDERATE

Army of Tennessee
Gen. John Bell Hood, Commanding

Hardee's Corps
Lieut. Gen. William J. Hardee

Cheatham's Division
Brig. Gen. George Maney

Cleburne's Division
Maj. Gen. Patrick R. Cleburne

Walker's Division
Maj. Gen. William H. T. Walker

Bate's Division
Maj. Gen. William B. Bate

Hood's Corps
Maj. Gen. Benjamin F. Cheatham

Hindman's Division
Brig. Gen. John C. Brown

Stevenson's Division
Maj. Gen. Carter L. Stevenson

Clayton's Division
Maj. Gen. Henry D. Clayton

Stewart's Corps
Lieut. Gen. Alexander P. Stewart

Loring's Division
Maj. Gen. William W. Loring

French's Division
Maj. Gen. Samuel G. French

Walthall's Division
Maj. Gen. Edward C. Walthall

Cavalry Corps
Maj. Gen. Joseph Wheeler

Martin's Division
Maj. Gen. William T. Martin

Kelly's Division
Brig. Gen. John H. Kelly

Humes' Division
Brig. Gen. William Y. C. Humes

Jackson's Division
Brig. Gen. William H. "Red" Jackson

First Division: Georgia State Militia
Maj. Gen. Gustavus W. Smith

APPENDIX B

Report by Colonel W. P. Howard to Georgia Governor Joseph E. Brown on the Destruction of Atlanta

Atlanta, Ga., Dec. 7th, 1864

To His Excellency Joseph E. Brown, Governor of Georgia:

In obedience to orders of Nov. 25, to inspect the State property in Atlanta, and the city itself, and protect the same, I have the honor to make the following report. With it I beg leave to present your Excellency with a pencilled map of the city, showing the position of every house left unburned.*

The property of the State was destroyed by fire, yet a vast deal of valuable material remains in the ruins. Three-fourths of the bricks are good and will be suitable for rebuilding if placed under shelter before freezing weather. There is a quantity of brass in the journals of burned cars and in the ruins of the various machinery of the extensive railroad shops; also, a valuable amount of copper from the guttering of the State depot, the flue pipes of destroyed engines, stop cocks of machinery, etc. The car wheels that were uninjured by fire were rendered useless by breaking the flanges. In short, every species of machinery that was not destroyed by fire was most ingeniously broken and made worthless in its original form—the large steam boilers, the switches, the frogs, etc. Nothing has escaped. The fire engines, except Tallulah No. 3, were sent North. Tallulah has been overhauled and a new fire company organized. Nos. 1 and 2 fire engine houses were saved. All the city pumps were destroyed, except one on Marietta Street. The car shed, the depots, machine shops, foundries, rolling mills, merchant mills, arsenals, laboratory, armory, etc., were all burned.

In the angle between Hunter Street, commencing at the City hall, running east, and McDonough Street, running southern, all houses were destroyed. The jail and calaboose were burned. All business houses, except those on Alabama Street, commencing with the Gate City Hotel, running east to Loyd Street, were burned. All the hotels, except the Gate City were burned. By referring to my map, you will find about 400 houses standing. The scale of the map is 400 feet to one inch. Taking the car-shed for the center, describe a circle, the diameter of which is twelve inches, and you will perceive that the circle contains about 300 squares. Then, at a low estimate, allow three houses to every 400 feet, and we will have 3600 houses in the circle. Subtract the number of houses indicated on the map, as standing, and you will see by this estimate, the enemy have

*The map referred to by Colonel Howard cannot be found.

destroyed 3200 houses. Refer to the exterior of the circle, and you will discover that it is more than half a mile to the city limits, in every direction, which was thickly populated, say nothing of the houses beyond, and you will see that the enemy have destroyed from four to five thousand houses. Two-thirds of the shade trees in the Park and city, and of the timber in the suburbs have been destroyed. The suburbs present to the eye one vast, naked, ruined, deserted camp. The Masonic Hall is not burned, though the corner-stone is badly scarred by some thief, who would have robbed it of its treasure, but for the timely interference of some mystic brother.

The City Hall is damaged but not burned. The Second Baptist, Second [Central] Presbyterian, Trinity and Catholic churches and all the residences adjacent between Mitchell and Peters streets, running south of east, and Loyd and Washington streets running south of west, are safe, all attributable to Father O'Reilly, who refused to give up his parsonage to Yankee officers, who were looking out for fine houses for quarters, and there being a large number of Catholics in the Yankee army, who volunteered to protect their Church and Parsonage, and would not allow any homes adjacent to be fired that would endanger them. As a proof of their attachment to their Church and love for Father O'Reilly, a soldier who attempted to fire Col. Calhoun's house, the burning of which would have endangered the whole block was shot and killed, and his grave is now marked. So to Father O'Reilly the country is indebted for the protection of the City Hall, Churches, etc.

Dr. Quintard's, Protestant Methodist, the Christian, and African churches were destroyed. All other churches were saved. The Medical College was saved by Dr. D'Alvigny who was left in charge of our wounded. The Female College was torn down for the purpose of obtaining the brick with which to construct winter quarters. All institutions of learning were destroyed. The African church was used as an academy for educating negroes. Roderick Badger, a negro Dentist, and his brother, Bob Badger, a train-hand on the West Point and La Grange Railroad, both well known to the citizens of Atlanta, were assistant professors to three philanthropic Northmen in this institution. Very few negroes remained in the city. Thirteen 32-pound rifle cannon, with cascabels and trunnions broken off and jammed in the muzzles, remain near the Ga. R.R. shop. One well reported to be filled with ammunition. Fragments of wagons, wheels, axles, bodies, etc., are strewn over the city. Could I have arrived ten days earlier, with a guard of 100 men, I could have saved the State and city a million dollars.

There are about 250 wagons in the city on my arrival, loading with pilfered plunder; pianoes, mirrors, furniture of all kinds, iron, hides without number, and an incalculable amount of other things, very valuable at the present time.

This exportation of stolen property had been going on ever since the place had been abandoned by the enemy. Bushwhackers, robbers and deserters, and citizens from the surrounding country for a distance of fifty miles have been engaged in this dirty work.

Many of the finest houses, mysteriously left unburned, are filled with the finest furniture, carpets, pianoes, mirrors, etc., and occupied by parties who six months ago lived in humble style. About fifty families remained during the occupancy of the city by the enemy, and about the same number have returned since its abandonment. From two to three thousand dead carcasses of animals remain in the city limits.

Horses were turned loose in the cemetery to graze upon the grass and shrubbery. The ornaments of graves, such as marble lambs, miniature statuary, souvenirs of departed little ones are broke and scattered abroad. The crowning act of all their wickedness and villiany was committed by our ungodly foe in removing the dead from the vaults in the cemetery, and robbing the coffins of the silver name plates and tipping, and depositing their own dead in the vaults.

I have the honor to be, Respectfully,
Your obedient Servant,
W. P. Howard

NOTES

Preface: "The Greatest Event of the War"

1 Otto Friedrich, *City of Nets: A Portrait of Hollywood in the 1940s* (Berkeley: University of California Press, 1997), p. 17 (Thalberg quote).

2 The negotiations surrounding the acquisition of the film rights to Mitchell's novel are documented in the David O. Selznick Collection at the University of Texas at Austin. See online reference at http://www.hrc.utexas.edu/exhibitions/online/gwtw/book/. See also "Miscellany," *Time*, March 6, 1939 (Gallup poll results); David O. Selznick to George Cukor, Dec. 8, 1938, in *Memo from David O. Selznick: The Creation of "Gone with the Wind" and Other Motion Picture Classics, as Revealed in the Producer's Private Letters, Telegrams, Memorandums, and Autobiographical Remarks* (New York: Modern Library, 2000), p. 197.

3 For descriptions of the filming of the burning of Atlanta scene, see Aljean Harmetz, *On the Road to Tara: The Making of Gone with the Wind* (New York: Abrams, 1996), pp. 97–109, and Gavin Lambert, *GWTW: The Making of Gone with the Wind* (Boston: Little, Brown, 1973), pp. 51–55; Friedrich, *City of Nets*, pp. 20–21 ("arsonist's dream"). Selznick to John Hay Whitney, Dec. 10, 1938, in *Memo from David O. Selznick*, p. 197.

4 "Hotfoot Man," *Time*, Sept. 4, 1939 (Myron Selznick). Ms. Leigh's arrival on the set is described in Alexander Walker, *Vivien: The Life of Vivien Leigh* (New York: Weidenfeld & Nicolson, 1987), pp. 103–4, Harmetz, *On the Road to Tara*, pp. 107–8, and Lambert, *GWTW*, pp. 55–56. There is widespread speculation among film historians and Hollywood cynics that Leigh's dramatic appearance—and the entire "search" for Scarlett O'Hara, for that matter—was staged by Selznick as a publicity stunt.

5 Indeed, Mitchell's research included many key sources listed in the bibliography of this book, including not only the 128-volume *Official Records of the War of the Rebellion*, but also Sherman's *Memoirs*, Hood's *Advance and Retreat*, Johnston's *Narrative of Military Operations*, Cox's *Atlanta*, and Watkins's *Co. Aytch*. See "Frankly, Margaret Mitchell Did Give a Damn," in James Lee McDonough and James Pickett Jones, *War So Terrible: Sherman and Atlanta* (New York: W. W. Norton, 1987), p. 335. W. E. B. Du Bois, quoted in Thomas Cripps, *Slow Fade to Black: The Negro in American Film, 1900–1942* (New York: Oxford University Press, 1977), p. 364. Prominent historian Albert Castel concludes that "Most of the inaccuracies in *Gone with the Wind* are either excusable on grounds of literary need or explainable as the consequences of the author's sources and of the time and place she lived." Castel, "'I Didn't Want to Get Caught Out'; or Gone with the Wind as History," in *Winning and Losing in the Civil War: Essays and Stories* (Columbia: University of South Carolina Press, 1996), pp. 79–88; see also Tom Wicker, "Why, Miss Scarlett, How Well You've Aged," *New York Times Book Review*, May 25, 1986.

6 See generally Herb Bridges, *Gone with the Wind: The Three-Day Premiere in Atlanta* (Macon, Ga.: Mercer University Press, 1999); Matthew Bernstein, "Selznick's March: The Atlanta Premiere of *Gone with the Wind*," *Atlanta History* 43, no. 2 (Summer 1999),

pp. 7–33. "In the South," President Carter further noted, "we date life either before 'Gone with the Wind' or after 'Gone with the Wind,' as you know." Jimmy Carter, *American Film Institute Remarks on the 10th Anniversary of the Institute,* Nov. 17, 1977.

7 Gary W. Gallagher, *Causes Won, Lost and Forgotten: How Hollywood and Popular Art Shape What We Know about the Civil War* (Chapel Hill: University of North Carolina Press, 2008), pp. 9–10, 45. Castel, in the preface to his history of the Atlanta Campaign, credits *Gone with the Wind* with sparking his interest in the war. Castel, *Decision in the West,* xi. Frank S. Nugent, "Recalling Civil War and Plantation Days of the South," *New York Times,* Dec. 28, 1939 (*Times* review of *Gone with the Wind*); Bruce Catton, "The Battle of Atlanta," *Georgia Review* 10 (1956), p. 258. Like me, Noah Andre Trudeau, in his recent book on the Savannah campaign, was struck by Sherman's use of this metaphor. See Noah Andre Trudeau, *Southern Storm: Sherman's March to the Sea* (New York: HarperCollins, 2008), p. 31 ("A recurring metaphor in Sherman's writings likens war to a great storm, and while he may have had the skill and knowledge to generate the tempest, his mastery of it was far from complete").

8 Stephen Davis calls Castel's *Decision in the West* "the definitive classic on the subject." Davis, "Coming to Terms with General Sherman—At Last," *Georgia Historical Quarterly* 77, no. 2 (Summer 1993), p. 331. For other recent works on the Atlanta Campaign, see Davis's *Atlanta Will Fall: Sherman, Joe Johnston, and the Yankee Heavy Battalions* (Wilmington, Del.: SR Books, 2001), and Richard McMurry, *Atlanta 1864: Last Chance for the Confederacy* (Lincoln, Neb.: Bison Books, 2000). For musical references, see, e.g., Jenny Whitely, "Burning of Atlanta" (2003) ("A fire ran through my heart/like the burning of Atlanta"); Whiplash, "The Burning of Atlanta" (1987); The Boys from Indiana, "Atlanta Is Burning" (1975); and Claude King "The Burning of Atlanta" (1962). For one of countless unfortunate references by sportswriters, see Rick Bragg, "Atlantans Smugly Enjoy Braves' Domination of Yankees," *New York Times,* Oct. 23, 1996 ("few people really see this World Series as atonement for the burning of Atlanta").

9 Castel, *Decision in the West,* p. xii; George Templeton Strong, *Diary of the Civil War 1860–1865,* Allan Nevins, ed. (New York: Macmillan, 1962), p. 481; David P. Conyngham, *Sherman's March Through the South with Sketches and Incidents of the Campaign* (New York: Sheldon and Co., 1865), p. 218. Historian Craig L. Symonds wrote that the campaign for Atlanta "outstripped even the Gettysburg Campaign for strategic importance." Symonds, "Johnston's Toughest Fight," *MHQ: Quarterly Journal of Military History* 16 (Winter 2004), p. 56. The reference to a clash of civilizations was first made by historian Henry Steele Commager in his review of *Gone with the Wind* in the *New York Herald Tribune Books,* July 5, 1936 ("For this is a story of a conflict of civilizations, and those civilizations are not necessarily the civilizations of the North and the South, but rather of the old South and the new. And though the material fabric of the old South is gone with the wind, something remains at the end that is shining and imperishable").

Chapter 1: Crazy Bill

1 Accounts of Sherman's swim in the Chattahoochee are after-the-fact and in almost every instance secondhand. See, e.g., Corydon Edward Foote, *With Sherman to the Sea*

(New York: John Day, 1960), pp. 189–90 ("I'd follow Sherman to hell"); Edwin W. Payne, *History of the Thirty-Fourth Regiment of Illinois Volunteer Infantry* (Clinton, Iowa: Allen Printing Co,, 1903), p. 179 (quoting diary of Regimental Surgeon John L. Hostetter, Dec. 26, 1864: "Water is cold, eh?" "Not very, sir"). The scene therefore looks suspiciously like campsite hearsay, passed on from soldier to soldier to be recorded later in memoirs and regimental histories and then recounted by historians and biographers. See, e.g., Lloyd Lewis, *Sherman: Fighting Prophet* (New York: Harcourt, Brace, 1932), p. 381; Albert Castel, *Decision in the West: The Atlanta Campaign of 1864* (Lawrence: University Press of Kansas, 1992), p. 351; David Evans, *Sherman's Horsemen* (Bloomington: Indiana University Press, 1996), p. 67; John F. Marszalek, *Sherman: A Soldier's Passion for Order* (New York: Free Press, 1993), p. 276. Sherman himself made no mention of his soak in the river in correspondence or his memoirs.

Shelby Foote, for one, was extremely fond of the anecdote, though he doubted its authenticity, to say the least, in a letter to his friend Walker Percy. "Red headed Sherman," Foote wrote. "I have a scene of him taking a bath in the Chattahoochee, talking with a teamster on bank; beard bristly and grizzled, face freckled, liver spots on back of hands, pubic hair pink in sunlight. Cant use any of it; I made it up. Wait, sweet Christ, till I get back to novels!" Foote to Percy, Jan. 19, 1970, in Jay Tolson, ed., *The Correspondence of Shelby Foote and Walker Percy* (New York, W. W. Norton, 1997), p. 139. Foote included the scene in his narrative anyway—as I choose to do here. Foote, *The Civil War: A Narrative, Volume III – Red River to Appomattox* (New York: Vintage, 1974), pp. 406–7.

References to informal truces called between the blue and gray antagonists along the Chattahoochee are widespread in soldier's letters, diaries, and memoirs. See, e.g., Alpheus S. Williams to My Dear Daughters, July 15, 1864, in *From the Cannon's Mouth* (Detroit: Wayne State University Press, 1959), p. 330 ("our boys have got up an armistice and they bathe on the opposite banks of the river and meet on a neutral log in the center of the stream and joke one another like old friends"). W. J. Worsham, *The Old Nineteenth Tennessee Regiment, C.S.A.* (Knoxville: Paragon Printing Co., 1902), pp. 124–25 ("Our videttes and those of the enemy sat upon opposite banks of the Chattahoochee and chatted with each other. Now and then they would swim across to each other's post, while some would keep a look-out for the officers of their respective commands. They had been fighting so long on the picket line, now they seemed glad for a change and for a time when they could hold a friendly chat as they had done before. They exchanged pocket knives, combs and anything they had, so long as the river divided the videttes"). S. A. McNeil, *Personal Recollections of Service in the Army of the Cumberland* (Richwood, Ohio: 1910), p. 43 ("the Alabama boys . . . were jolly good fellows and we had carried on quite a business in trading coffee for tobacco"). Stephen F. Fleharty, *Jottings from Dixie: The Civil War Dispatches of Sergeant Major Stephen F. Fleharty, U.S.A.*, Philip J. Rayburn and Terry Wilson, eds. (Baton Rouge: Louisiana State University Press, 1999), pp. 238–39 ("How are you, Johnny?" "How are you, Jimmy? And by the way, why do you call us 'Johnnies'?"). See also Charles Wills, *Army Life of an Illinois Soldier* (Washington: Globe Printing Co., 1906), pp. 274–77 ("everything that ever was eaten by anti-cannibals").

2 George W. Pepper, *Personal Recollections of Sherman's Campaigns in Georgia and the Carolinas* (Zanesville, Ohio: Hugh Dunne, 1866), p. 91 (Chattahoochee description).

3 The definitive study of the entire Atlanta campaign from Dalton on down is Castel, *Decision in the West*; *Memphis Daily Appeal*, May 9, 1864 ("ball has opened").

4 William D. Bickham, *Rosecrans' Campaign with the Fourteenth Army Corps, or the Army of the Cumberland* (Cincinnati: Moore, Wilsatch, Keys & Co., 1863), p. 32 (Thomas "gradually expands upon you"); Lewis, *Sherman: Fighting Prophet*, p. 387 ("I expected something to happen to Grant and me"); Victor Davis Hanson, *The Soul of Battle: From Ancient Times to Present Day, How Three Great Liberators Vanquished Tyranny* (New York: Anchor Books, 2001), p. 8 ("most impressive and deadly body"); Bruce Catton, *This Hallowed Ground: The Story of the Union Side of the Civil War* (New York: Doubleday, 1956), p. 206 ("noisiest crowd").

5 Lee Kennett, *Marching Through Georgia: The Story of Soldiers and Civilians During Sherman's Campaign* (New York: HarperCollins, 1996), p. 9 ("I think God Almighty might have made the world in four days").

6 James A. Connolly, *Three Years in the Army of the Cumberland* (Bloomington: Indiana University Press, 1959), p. 209; Williams, *From the Cannon's Mouth*, p. 334; Sherman to John Sherman, June 9, 1864, in *Sherman's Civil War*, Brooks D. Simpson and Jean V. Berlin, eds. (Chapel Hill: University of North Carolina Press, 1999), p. 645 (hereinafter *SCW*) ("big Indian war").

7 J. Cutler Andrews, *The South Reports the Civil War* (Princeton: Princeton University Press, 1970), p. 438.

8 *Mobile Register and Advertiser*, June 2, 1864 ("midnight corner of Georgia"); Foote, *The Civil War: A Narrative*, vol. 3, p. 518 ("red clay minuet"); Sherman to Ellen, June 30, 1864, in *SCW*, p. 660 ("death and mangling . . . a kind of morning dash"). This apparent disregard of human suffering, even among his own army, was not a recent development. He had earlier in the war shown his grim recognition of what Abraham Lincoln called "the arithmetic," and elsewhere had displayed his willingness to make the necessary investment in blood that was required in order to secure the fruits of victory. "We will lose 5,000 men before we take Vicksburg," Sherman said after suffering 1,700 casualties in a bloody repulse at Chickasaw Bayou, "and we may as well lose them here as anywhere else."

9 Wills, *Army Life*, p. 272 ("muscle and nerve"); Connolly to wife, July 12, 1864, in *Three Years in the Army of the Cumberland*, p. 234 ("promised land"); John W. Geary to My Dearest Mary, July 8, 1864, in *A Politician Goes to War: The Civil War Letters of John White Geary*, William Alan Blair, ed. (University Park: Pennsylvania State University Press, 1995), p. 186; Conyngham, *Sherman's March Through the South*, p. 155 (Jerusalem). The bird's-eye view reminded Ohio Major Thomas Taylor of Jerusalem as well. Taylor wrote to his wife: "It is a glorious scene and most forcibly reminded me of Christ's beholding Jerusalem from the mount and his most fearful curse: 'Oh Jerusalem, Jerusalem, thou that killest the prophets and stoned them which are sent unto thee, how often I would have gathered thy children together, even as a hen gathereth her chickens

under her wings and ye would not! Behold, your house is left with you desolate.'" Albert Castel, ed., *Tom Taylor's Civil War* (Lawrence: University Press of Kansas, 2000), p. 136.

10 Foote, *The Civil War*, vol. 3, p. 491; Joseph E. Brown to Jefferson Davis, June 28, 1864, in *The War of the Rebellion: A Compilation of the Official Records of the Union and Confederate Armies* (Washington, D.C.: Government Printing Office 1880–1901) (hereinafter *OR*), vol. 52, pt. 2, p. 680 ("as the heart is to the human body"). Unless otherwise noted, all citations to the *Official Records* refer to Series 1.

11 Marszalek, *Sherman*, p. 366 ("its glory is all moonshine"); Schofield to Sherman, July 7, 1864, *OR*, vol. 38, pt. 5, p. 78 ("a pretty good crossing").

12 Sherman, "The Grand Strategy of the Last Year of the War," in *Battles and Leaders of the Civil War*. Robert U. Johnson and Clarence C. Buel, eds. (New York: Century Co., 1887), vol. 4, p. 253 ("best line"); Sherman, *Memoirs*, p. 443 ("Johnston neglected his opportunity"), F. A. Shoup, "Dalton Campaign—Works at Chattahoochee River—Interesting History," *Confederate Veteran*, 3, no. 9 (Sept. 1895), p. 262. Shoup's article includes diagrams and sketches of his "Shoupades," ibid. at 63. The earthen remains of nine of the original thirty-six Shoupades are identifiable today. See Georgia Battlefields Association, http://www.georgiabattlefields.org/endangered04.htm.

13 Sherman to Halleck, July 6, 1864, in *SCW*, p. 668; Connolly to wife, July 12, 1864, in *Three Years in the Army of the Cumberland*, p. 255.

14 Leander E. Davis to wife, June 12, 1864, in "'The Consequence of Grandeur': A Union Soldier Writes of the Atlanta Campaign," William C. Nielsen, ed., *Atlanta History* 33, no. 3 (Fall 1989), p. 5 ("a hard fite at Atlanty").

15 Foote, *The Civil War*, vol. 1, p. 321 (Lazarus); Adam Badeau, *Military History of Ulysses S. Grant* (New York: D. Appleton, 1885), vol. 2, p. 19 ("superabundant energy"); Sherman to Ellen, April 15, 1859 ("dead cock in the pit"); Sherman to John Sherman, Nov. 21, 1861, in *SCW*.

16 *Cincinnati Commercial*, Dec. 11, 1861 ("Sherman Insane"); Alexander K. McClure, *Recollections of Half a Century* (Salem: Salem Press, 1902), pp. 332–33. The best recent analysis of Sherman's 1861 breakdown is in Lee Kennett, *Sherman: A Soldier's Life*, pp. 141–49; see also John F. Marszalek, "The Insane General," in *Sherman's Other War: The General and the Civil War Press* (Kent, Ohio: Kent State University Press, 1981), pp. 63–100. Sherman's biographer Michael Fellman calls his life story a "primarily psychological rags-to-riches tale." Fellman, Introduction to Sherman's *Memoirs* (New York: Penguin, 2000), p. viii.

17 Sherman to John Sherman, Jan. 4, 1862, in *SCW*, p. 174; Sherman to Thomas Ewing, Dec. 12, 1861, in *SCW*, p. 161.

18 Michael Fellman, *Citizen Sherman: A Life of William Tecumseh Sherman* (New York: Random House, 1995), p. 114 ("suicidal element"); Albert D. Richardson, *A Personal History of Ulysses S. Grant* (Boston: D. L. Guernsey, 1885), p. 242.

19 Sherman's performance at Shiloh is recounted and evaluated in a number of sources, including Marszalek, *Sherman*, pp. 171–87; Larry J. Daniel, *Shiloh: The Battle that Changed the Civil War* (New York: Simon and Schuster, 1997), pp. 310–11. Sherman to

Ellen, June 6, 1862, in *SCW*, p. 237 ("Scrap book"); Halleck to E. M. Stanton, April 13, 1862, *OR*, vol. 10, pt. 1, p. 98; Sherman, *Memoirs*, p. 236.

20 Sherman to Ellen, Oct. 6, 1863, in *SCW*, pp. 552–53.

21 Pepper, *Personal Recollections*, p. 515; see Shakespeare, *Hamlet*, Act II, Scene 2; see also W. F. G. Shanks, *Personal Recollections of Distinguished Generals* (New York: Harper & Bros., 1866), p. 34 ("Sherman may have been at one time crazy, but his madness, like Hamlet's, certainly had marvelous method in it").

22 Kennett, *Sherman*, pp. 101, 146–49 (diagnoses of Sherman); Stephen Ambrose, "Sherman: A Reappraisal," *American History Illustrated* 1, no. 9 (January 1967), p. 6.

23 John Chipman Gray to John C. Ropes, Dec. 14, 1864 in *War Letters, 1862–1865, of John Chipman Gray and John Codman Ropes, with Portraits* (Boston: Houghton Mifflin, 1927), p. 427 (description of Sherman); Chesley A. Mosman, *The Rough Side of War: The Civil War Journal of Chesley A. Mosman, 1st Lieutenant, Company D, 59th Illinois volunteer Infantry Regiment* (Garden City, N.Y.: Basin Publishing, 1987), p. 266 ("certainly don't look like one").

24 Evans, *Sherman's Horsemen*, p. xxiii ("steam engine in britches"); Shanks, *Personal Recollections*, p. 53 (smoking); Corydon Foote, *With Sherman to the Sea*, p. 183 ("pacing, pacing, pacing").

25 James F. Rusling, *Men and Things I Saw in Civil War Days* (New York: Eaton & Mains, 1899), p. 111 ("eat your mules up!"); Shanks, "Recollections of General Sherman," *Harper's New Monthly Magazine* 30, issue 179 (April 1865), p. 643 ("his temper is uncommonly bad"); *Cincinnati Commercial*, Oct. 25, 1861 (Pawnee Indian).

26 Walt Whitman, *Walt Whitman's Civil War* (New York: Knopf, 1961), p. 247; Lyman, *Meade's Headquarters*, p. 327 ("quintessence of Yankeedom"). John Chipman Gray's characterization of Sherman as "the most American looking man I ever saw" perhaps explains the casting of John Wayne to play General Sherman in John Ford's *How the West Was Won* (1963).

27 *Augusta Daily Constitutionalist*, August 28, 1864 (Southern view of Sherman); *Daily Intelligencer*, July 4, 1864, quoted in Hoehling, *Last Train from Atlanta*, p. 36.

28 Michael Fellman, Introduction to Sherman's *Memoirs*, p. xii ("quirky conquering genius"); Robert Bence to wife, Sept. 11, 1864, quoted in Joseph Glatthaar, *The March to the Sea and Beyond* (New York: NYU Press, 1985), p. 16; George F. Cram, *Soldiering with Sherman* (DeKalb: Northern Illinois University Press, 2000) p. 154 ("method in his madness"); J. Powell Young to Friend Ellen, March 27, 1865, quoted in Mark L. Bradley, *This Astounding Close: The Road to Bennett Place* (Chapel Hill: University of North Carolina Press, 2006), p. 4 ("never such a man as Sherman or as they call him Crazy Bill"); *see also* Young [Powell] to Ellen, March 27, 1865, Duke University, quoted in Glatthaar, *March to the Sea*, p. 175 ("the boys say it is hard to tell which way Crazy Bill will go for he goes wherever he wants and the rebs cant help themselves"); Mosman, *Rough Side of War*, p. 264 ("This 'crazy Sherman' and the 'Bull dog Grant' go at it like a man at a day's work, as long as there is anything in sight to do they are up and doing as though hired 'by the job.' They don't seem to care for clean clothes but require clean guns").

29 Sherman to Ellen, July 29, 1864, in *SCW*, p. 677 ("John Barleycorn"), Sherman to Hugh Ewing, July 13, 1864, in *SCW*, p. 665 ("I should not thus be kept uneasy").

30 Sherman to Philemon B. Ewing, July 13, 1864, in *SCW*, pp. 666–67.

31 Sherman to Ellen, June 30, 1864 ("Shallow People . . . worst of the war has not yet begun"), in *SCW*, p. 660.

32 The 1860 Census counted 7,615 whites, 1,914 slaves, and only 25 free blacks in Atlanta. Thomas W. Dyer, *Secret Yankees: The Union Circle in Confederate Atlanta* (Baltimore: Johns Hopkins University Press, 1999), p. 334 n.7 (citing census). Robert Gibbons, "Life at the Crossroads of the Confederacy: Atlanta, 1861–1865," *Atlanta Historical Journal* 23, no. 2 (Summer 1979), p. 11 ("Gibraltar of the Rebellion"); Margaret Ketcham Ward, "Testimony of Margaret Ketcham Ward on Civil War Times in Georgia," *Georgia Historical Quarterly* 39 (1955), p. 389 ("narrowed down"); *Atlanta Daily Intelligencer*, July 7, 1864 (quoted in Wallace Reed, *History of Atlanta, Georgia* [Syracuse: D. Mason & Co., 1889], p. 171) (second Richmond); T. M. Eddy, *The Patriotism of Illinois* (Chicago: Clarke & Co., 1866) (quoting Southern newspaper on the consequences of the fall of Atlanta). The latter quote has been incorrectly attributed to Jefferson Davis. See Hochling, *Last Train to Atlanta*, p. 17.

33 The definitive history of Atlanta is Franklin Garrett's *Atlanta and Environs: A Chronicle of Its People and Events*, 4 vols. (New York, 1954); *Mobile Advertiser and Register*, Sept. 24, 1863, p. 2 ("invest in dust, heat and noise"). Margaret Mitchell described wartime Atlanta, through the eyes of Scarlett O'Hara, as "a mixture of the old and new in Georgia, in which the old often came off second best in its conflicts with the self-willed and vigorous new." *Gone with the Wind*, p. 143. See also William Stanley Hoole, *Lawley Covers the Confederacy* (Tuscaloosa: Confederate Pub. Co., 1964), pp. 44–45 ("no one goes anywhere without passing through Atlanta"). A variation on the theme is that Atlanta has no natives: "it was said that no one was ever born in Atlanta, but everyone moved there from somewhere else." Lucy Hull Baldwin, Autobiography, MSS 849, Southern Historical Collection, University of North Carolina at Chapel Hill.

34 John W. Geary to My Dearest Mary, in *A Politician Goes to War: The Civil War Letters of John White Geary*, William Alan Blair, ed. (University Park: Pennsylvania State University Press, 1995), p. 206 (noting that "22 years ago, [Atlanta] was a howling wilderness"); Kennett, *Marching Through Georgia*, p. 112 (surveyor rod).

35 Lt. Charles C. Jones, Jr., to Rev. C. C. Jones, July 25, 1862, in *The Children of Pride: A True Story of Georgia and the Civil War* (New Haven: Yale University Press, 1972), p. 284 (description of Atlanta); see also Gibbons, "Life at the Crossroads of the Confederacy: Atlanta, 1861–1865," *Atlanta Historical Journal*, pp. 11–72.

36 James M. Merrill, ed., "Personne Goes to Georgia: Five Civil War Letters," *Georgia Historical Quarterly* 43 (1959), p. 209 (view from the Trout House), Robert Gibbons, "Life at the Crossroads of the Confederacy, 1861–1865," pp. 28–29, 42 (Athenaeum).

37 Sherman to Ellen, June 26, 1864, in *SCW*, p. 657 ("We have devoured the land"); Connolly, *Three Years in the Army of the Cumberland*, p. 238 ("mocking bird"); Blanton Fortson to mother, June 3, 1864, in *"Dear Mother: Don't grieve about me: If I Get Killed,*

I'll only be Dead": Letters from Georgia Soldiers in the Civil War, Mills Lane, ed. (Savannah: Beehive Press, 1977), pp. 295–96.

38 Bill Arp, *Augusta Daily Constitutionalist*, June 15, 1864; *Memphis Daily Appeal*, July 3, 1864 ("The Executive Aid Association has fitted up the city park for the reception of sick and wounded soldiers. The park is filled with tents"); Ward, "Testimony," *Georgia Historical Quarterly*, p. 389 ("sardines"); *Mobile Register and Advertiser*, July 12, 1864 (Confederate *Les Misérables*).

39 For an excellent look at the city's hospitals during the war, see Steve Davis, "Another Look at Civil War Medical Care: Atlanta's Confederate Hospitals," *Journal of the Medical Association of Georgia* 88, no. 2 (April 1999), pp. 9–23; Kennett, *Marching Through Georgia*, p. 116 (quoting R. J. Massey, "Memories of Brown Hospital," *Sunny South*, Oct. 21, 1901) ("Anybody about to die?").

40 Sarah Conley Clayton, *Requiem for a Lost City: A Memoir of Civil War Atlanta and the Old South*, Robert Davis, Jr., ed. (Macon, Ga.: Mercer University Press, 1999), pp. 88 ff. (Gussie Clayton).

41 Kate Cumming, *The Journal of Kate Cumming: A Confederate Nurse, 1862–1865*, Richard Barksdale Harwell, ed. (Savannah: Beehive Press, 1975), pp. 181–84. Cumming lived and worked in Newnan, Georgia, but visited Atlanta twice in 1864.

42 Garrett, *Atlanta and Environs*, pp. 572–73 (Atlanta newspapers); Reed, *History of Atlanta*, pp. 184–86 (same); *Daily Intelligencer*, July 6 and 7, 1864.

43 *Mobile Daily Advertiser and Register*, July 14, 1864; *Southern Confederacy*, n.d., quoted in *Montgomery Daily Mail*, July 16, 1864; see *The Moving Appeal*, p. 309.

44 Sherman, *Memoirs*, p. 439 (capture of Frank Sherman); see also Emerson Opdycke, *To Battle for God and the Right: The Civil War Letterbooks of Emerson Opdycke*, Glenn V. Longacre and John E. Haas, eds. (Urbana: University of Illinois Press, 2003), p. 196 ("Col Sherman has not been heard from since, in *our* Army . . . but he was a right good fellow, and we all feel sorry for him, for we think it a greater misfortune to be captured, than to receive a severe wound").

45 Mary S. Mallard to Laura E. Buttolph, July 18, 1864, in Myers, *Children of Pride*, p. 480; Samuel P. Richards Diary, July 10, 1864 AHC MSS 176.

46 Kennett, *Marching Through Georgia*, pp. 120–21 ("The battle field is a mear Trifal"); Castel, *Decision in the West*, p. 72 ("greybeards"); *Daily Intelligencer*, January 14, 1864 ("any one who desired to get murdered"), quoted in Paul D. Lack, "Law and Disorder in Confederate Atlanta," *Georgia Historical Quarterly* 66 (1982), pp. 179–80; Gussie Clayton to Mary Lou Yancey, June 10, 1864, quoted in Hoehling, *Last Train from Atlanta*, pp. 24, 75 ("happen what may"); Richards Diary, July 10, 1864, AHC.

47 For an excellent study of slaves and free blacks in Georgia, see Clarence L. Mohr, *On the Threshold of Freedom: Masters and Slaves in Civil War Georgia* (Athens: University of Georgia Press, 1986). Mohr notes, for example, that from April to August 1864, 73 percent of workers in the receiving hospital at the Atlanta Fair Grounds were hired black attendants, performing cooking, laundry, and nursing duties. Ibid. at 133 (15 white civilians, 15 detailed soldiers, 80 blacks).

48 Garrett, *Atlanta and Environs*, p. 553; *Daily Intelligencer*, Feb. 13, 1863, quoted in Garrett, p. 553; *Daily Intelligencer*, May 11, 1864, quoted in Garrett, p. 586; General Order No. 1, May 14, 1862, printed in *Intelligencer*, May 23, 1862 (curfew); Jethro W. Manning, *The Code of the City of Atlanta* (Atlanta 1863), p. 40, sections 286, 288, 292.

49 For excellent detective work on free black barber Robert Webster, see Thomas G. Dyer's *Secret Yankees*, pp. 87–90, and his essay "Half Slave, Half Free: Unionist Robert Webster in Confederate Atlanta," in *Inside the Confederate Nation: Essays in Honor of Emory M. Thomas* (Baton Rouge: LSU Press, 1995), pp. 295–314. At least one biographer of Daniel Webster concludes that Robert Webster was "quite possibly" the son of Daniel Webster and "a mulatto of rare beauty" named Charlotte Goodbrick. Robert Vincent Remini, *Daniel Webster: The Man and His Time* (New York: W. W. Norton, 1997), p. 307. Garrett, *Atlanta and Environs*, pp. 453–54; Reed, *History of Atlanta*, p. 81; Garrett, p. 453 (Solomon Luckie). *Williams' Atlanta Directory* for 1859–60 listed seven free blacks in Atlanta: Erasmus Cobb, G. Ezzard, Dougherty Hutchins, Albert Scott, Robert Yancey (Webster), Roderick Badger, and Solomon Luckie. *Atlanta Historical Bulletin*, 1971, p. 76.

50 Patrick H. Calhoun, "Reminiscences of Patrick H. Calhoun," *Atlanta Historical Bulletin*, 1 (1932), pp. 41–47; see generally George Clower, "Mayor James M. Calhoun (1811–1875)," *Atlanta Historical Bulletin* 10, no. 3 (Dec. 1965), pp. 7–11.

51 *Mobile Advertiser and Register*, May 28, 1864 ("utterly demoralized"); *Montgomery Daily Advertiser*, May 29, 1864 ("weak kneed" and of "little faith").

52 W. P. Reed, *Atlanta*, pp. 281–83, and John M. Harrison, "The Volunteer Firemen of Atlanta," *Atlanta Historical Bulletin* 6, no. 26 (Oct. 1941), pp. 239–50 (Atlanta's fire companies); Elise Reid Boylston, *Atlanta: Its Lore, Legends and Laughter* (Doraville, Ga.: Foote & Davis, 1968), p. 52 (fire department uniforms); *Atlanta Fire Department Commemorative Yearbook* (Atlanta: Turner Publishing, 2001), pp. 11–15. The fire companies adopted slogans like "Prompt to Action" (Atlanta Fire Company No. 1) and "We Strive to Save" (Tallulah Fire Company No. 3). Ibid. See also Atlanta City Council Minutes, July 18, 1864, AHC.

CHAPTER 2: THE GAMECOCK

1 References to General Johnston as a "gamecock" abound in the literature, though usually not in soldiers' letters and diaries. See, e.g., John Esten Cooke, *A Life of Robert E. Lee* (New York: D. Appleton & Company, 1876), p. 56 ("a gamecock, ready for battle at any moment"); Wm. Henry Morgan, *Personal Reminiscences of the War of 1861–5* (Lynchburg, Va.: J. P. Bell Company, 1911), p. 99 ("General Johnston was often seen riding along the lines, sitting his horse very erect, and presenting a soldierly appearance. He always reminded me of a gamecock trimmed and gaffed ready for the main"); Douglas Southall Freeman, *Lee's Lieutenants,* Stephen Sears, ed. (New York: Konecky & Konecky, 2005), p. 93 ("A difficult and touchy subordinate he is, though a generous and kindly superior—in sum, a military contradiction and a tempermental enigma. In appearance he is small, soldierly, and graying, with a certain gamecock jauntiness").

The reference to Johnston as a portrait is taken from Sam Watkins, *Co. Aytch, First Tennessee Regiment, or A Side Show of the Big Show*, Ruth Hill Fulton McAllister, ed.

(Franklin, Tenn.: Providence House, 2007), p. 163 ("He looked like the pictures you see hanging upon the walls"). For Watkins's own widely quoted word portrait of Johnston, see ibid., p. 138 ("Fancy, if you please, a man about fifty years old, rather small of stature, but firmly and compactly built"). In contrast, a number of sources recount the anecdote of a napping Sherman being mistaken for a drunk. See, e.g., Conyngham, *Sherman's March*, pp. 48–49. See also Thomas L. Connelly, *The Marble Man: Robert E. Lee and His Image in American Society* (Baton Rouge: Louisiana State University Press, 1977) p. 22 ("pedantic, quarrelsome, bitter and even paranoiac"); Robert Underwood Johnson, *Remembered Yesterdays* (Boston: Little, Brown, 1923), p. 199 ("tempermentally an aristocrat . . . dry as the remainder biscuit"); see also Shakespeare, *As You Like It*, act 2, scene 7 ("as dry as the remainder biscuit").

2 For Johnston's early life and Civil War background, see generally Craig Symonds, *Joseph E. Johnston: A Civil War Biography* (New York: W. W. Norton, 1992), p. 97 (highest ranking general officer to resign); Gilbert E. Govan and James W. Livingood, *A Different Valor: The Story of General Joseph E. Johnston, C.S.A.* (Indianapolis: Bobbs-Merrill, 1956). For more on Johnston's spat with Jefferson Davis in 1861, see Robert K. Krick, "'Snarl and Sneer and Quarrel': General Joseph E. Johnston and an Obsession with Rank," in *Leaders of the Lost Cause: New Perspectives on the Confederate High Command*, Gary W. Gallagher and Joseph T. Glatthaar, eds. (Mechanicsburg, Pa.: Stackpole Books, 2004), pp. 165–203.

3 Dabney H. Maury, "Interesting Reminiscences of General Johnston," *Southern Historical Society Papers* 18 (1890), p. 181 ("the shot that struck me down").

4 Josiah Gorgas, *The Journals of Josiah Gorgas, 1857–1878*, Sarah Woolfolk Wiggins, ed. (Tuscaloosa: University of Alabama Press, 1995), p. 74 ("general outside who wouldn't fight"); J. Longstreet to J. A. Seddon, Sept. 26, 1863, *OR*, vol. 30, pt. 4, p. 706.

5 Watkins, *Co. Aytch*, pp. 138–39, 141.

6 See generally Nathaniel C. Hughes, Jr., *General William J. Hardee: Old Reliable* (Baton Rouge: Louisiana State University Press, 1965); Arthur J. L. Fremantle, *Three Months in the Southern States: April–June 1863* (Mobile: S. H. Goetzel, 1864), p. 139. "And although he is supposed to have converted many of the ladies to the Southern cause," Col. Fremantle said of the amorous General Hardee and his kisses, "yet in many instances their male relatives remain neutral or undecided." Ibid.

7 J.H.L., "Hood 'Feeling the Enemy,'" *Battles and Leaders of the Civil War*, Robert U. Johnson and Clarence C. Buel, eds. (New York: Century Co., 1887), vol. 2, p. 276.

8 "Confederates overused such terms as gallant, chivalrous, and knightly in describing each other," Hood's biographer Richard McMurry wrote. "Yet wartime Southerners seem to have regarded these adjectives as especially appropriate for Hood." McMurry, *John Bell Hood and the War for Southern Independence* (Lincoln: University of Nebraska Press, 1992), p. 191; see also William J. Wood, *Civil War Generalship: The Art of Command* (New York: Da Capo Press, 2000), p. 240 ("John Bell Hood was a name rarely referred to in the South without the appellation 'the gallant Hood' being used"). Mary Chesnut, *Mary Chesnut's Civil War*, C. Vann Woodward, ed. (New Haven: Yale University Press, 1981), p. 625 ("shot to pieces").

9 See generally Sam Davis Elliott, *Soldier of Tennessee: General Alexander P. Stewart and the Civil War in the West* (Baton Rouge: Louisiana State University Press, 2004); Clement Anselm Evans, *Confederate Military History* (Atlanta: Confederate Publishing Co., 1899), vol. 1, p. 693 ("straightforward simplicity"). For more on the death of Bishop Polk, see Russell S. Bonds, "Pawn Takes Bishop: The Death of Lieutenant General Leonidas Polk," *Civil War Times* (May 2006). The bishop-general Polk was not mourned by all in the Confederate ranks. "I thank the Lord Jesus Christ," one Rebel solider was overheard saying, "that that Goddamned good-for-nothing Polk was killed the other day." Pepper, *Personal Recollections*, p. 93.

10 John W. Hagan to Dear Wife, July 4 and July 11, 1864, in "The Confederate Letters of John W. Hagan," Bell Irvin Wiley, ed., *Georgia Historical Quarterly* 38 (1954), pp. 281, 285; *Richmond Whig*, July 9, 1864 (quoted in Govan and Livingood, *A Different Valor*, p. 309); *Memphis Daily Appeal*, July 4, 1864, quoted in *The Moving Appeal*, p. 308.

11 William Adams to sister, quoted in Russell K. Brown, *To the Manner Born: The Life of General William H. T. Walker* (Macon, Ga.: Mercer University Press, 2005), p. 251; Robert Patrick, *Reluctant Rebel: The Secret Diary of Robert Patrick, 1861–1865*, F. Jay Taylor, ed. (Baton Rouge: Louisiana State University Press, 1959), pp. 188, 191–92.

12 Celathiel Helms to Dear wife, July 6, 1864, in Georgia Division of the United Daughters of the Confederacy, *Confederate Reminiscences and Letters, 1861–1865*, 22 vols. to date (Atlanta: Georgia Division of the UDC, 1995–2007), vol. 22, p. 187 (hereinafter UDC *Reminiscences*). Desertions from the ranks of the Army of Tennessee, while not insignificant, should not be overstated, and suggestions that Rebels were "going to the Yankees by . . . hundreds a most every night" are almost certainly exaggerated. Sherman would later list the total number of Confederate deserters as about 2,400 in the course of the entire campaign from May through the end of August. *OR*, vol. 38, pt. 1, p. 85. Moreover, it must be said that Private Helms may not be the best barometer of Southern morale, as he was an observer who never seemed to view the Confederate glass as half full. Almost a year earlier, outside Savannah, he had written to his wife, "I believe that nearly all the people here think that we are whipped and I think that we are whipped and I think the Yankees can take this place when they please." Helms to My dear Companion, Aug. 31, 1863, in UDC *Reminiscences*, p. 166. Charles Fessenden Morse, *Letters Written During the Civil War, 1861–1865* (Boston: Privately Printed, 1898), p. 177 ("How are you, Johnny?"); F. B. Carpenter, *Six Months at the White House with Abraham Lincoln* (New York: Hurd & Houghton, 1866), p. 253 ("General Sherman never makes but one speech").

13 Andrew Jackson Neal to Emma, May 15 and July 17, 1864, Papers, Special Collections, Robert W. Woodruff Library, Emory University, quoted in Richard McMurry, "Confederate Morale in the Atlanta Campaign," *Georgia Historical Quarterly* 54 (1970), pp. 233–34. For detailed analyses of Confederate morale under Johnston, see ibid., pp. 226–43, and William J. McNeill, "A Survey of Confederate Soldier Morale During Sherman's Campaign Through Georgia and the Carolinas," *Georgia Historical Quarterly* 55 (1971), pp. 1–25; see also Larry J. Daniel, *Soldiering in the Army of Tennessee* (Chapel Hill: University of North Carolina Press, 1991), pp. 141–47.

[14] Benedict J. Semmes to Wife, July 7, 1864, Southern Historical Collection, University of North Carolina, Chapel Hill (quoted in Andrew Haughton, *Training, Tactics and Leadership in the Confederate Army of Tennessee* [2000], p. 161); Robert M. Gill to wife, July 14, 1864, quoted in Bell I. Wiley, "A Story of 3 Southern Officers," *Civil War Times Illustrated* 3, no. 1 (April 1964), p. 33; Anonymous Rebel letter, July 4, 1864, in Kennett, *Marching Through Georgia*, p. 78.

[15] Royal Cortissoz, *The Life of Whitelaw Reid* (New York: Charles Scribner's Sons, 1921), vol. 2, p. 336 ("never acknowledged an error"); see also Whitelaw Reid, *Ohio in the War: Her Statesmen, Generals and Soldiers* (Cincinnati: Moore, Wilstach & Baldwin, 1868), vol. 1, p. 454 ("it was characteristic of this gifted commander's mind to be unwilling ever to acknowledge an error"); Sherman to Halleck, July 6, 1864, *OR*, vol. 38, pt. 5, p. 66 ("Instead of attacking Atlanta direct"); Sherman to Halleck, April 10, 1864, *SCW*, p. 618 ("Should Johnston fall behind Chattahoochee"); Sherman to Thomas and McPherson, July 16, 1864, *OR*, Vol 38, Part V, p. 151 ("it behooves us . . . to hurry").

[16] Peach Tree Creek is now known as Peachtree Creek, and Buck Head tavern is today the Buckhead community of Atlanta. The respective terms—Peachtree/Peach Tree, Buckhead/Buck Head—are used interchangeably herein.

[17] Sherman to Halleck, July 11, 1864, *OR*, vol. 38, pt. 5, p. 114 ("real game for Atlanta"); Sherman, *Memoirs*, p. 444 ("general right wheel"); Special Field Orders no. 35, *OR*, vol. 38, pt. 5, p. 142 (warning order). Buck Head (today Atlanta's thriving Buckhead community) was founded by pioneer settler Henry Irby, who opened a general store and tavern along the Roswell Road near Pace's Ferry in 1837. The surrounding community was initially known as "Irbyville," but residents and travelers gave the crossroads a new name when Irby shot a huge deer and mounted its head and antlers on the wall to mark his tavern. Garrett, *Atlanta and Environs*, vol. 1, p. 160.

[18] John A. Logan to Col. W. T. Clark, July 18, 1864, *OR*, vol. 38, pt. 5, p. 177.

[19] Sherman to Thomas, July 18, 1864, *OR*, vol. 38, pt. 5, p. 174.

[20] Sherman to Grant, July 12, 1864, *OR*, vol. 38, pt. 5, pp. 123–24.

[21] David Herbert Donald, *Lincoln* (New York: Simon and Schuster, 1995), p. 517 ("quite paralyzed and wilted down"); Noah Brooks, *Washington in Lincoln's Time* (New York: Century Co., 1895), p. 172.

[22] James Ford Rhodes, *History of the United States from the Compromise of 1850 to the Final Restoration of Home Rule at the South in 1877* (New York: Macmillan, 1913), vol. 4, p. 508 ("worthy of the Hebrews"); *Abraham Lincoln Complete Works, Comprising His Speeches, Letters, State Writings, and Miscellaneous Papers*, John G. Nicolay and John Hay, eds. (New York: Century Co., 1907), vol. 2, p. 544 (resolution for national day of humiliation and prayer).

[23] *New York World*, June 9, 1864 ("backwoods lawyers"). Prominent historians often describe the 1864 election as a referendum on the war. See James M. McPherson, *Ordeal by Fire* (New York: Knopf, 1982), p. 456 ("a referendum on the war and emancipation"); James A. Rawley, *The Politics of Union* (Lincoln: University of Nebraska Press, 1980) pp.

154–55 ("a referendum: on Lincoln himself, on party unity, on peace or war, and on emancipation. On these issues hung American nationality—the continuing life of a nation that could be reunited only by war"); J. Tracy Power, "'In for Four Years More': The Army of Northern Virginia and the United States Presidential Election of 1864," in *The Lincoln Forum: Rediscovering Abraham Lincoln*, John Y. Simon and Harold Holzer, eds. (New York: Fordham University Press, 2002), p. 100 ("a referendum not only on Lincoln and his administration but on the war itself and whether the Union and emancipation had been, or ever would be, worth the sacrifices made so far or likely to be made in the foreseeable future"). See also John C. Waugh, *Reelecting Lincoln: The Battle for the 1864 Presidency* (New York: Crown, 1998), p. 18 ("Running again").

24 *New York Herald*, June 10, 1864 ("Presidential pigmy"); *New York World*, quoted in Carl Sandburg, *Abraham Lincoln: The War Years* (New York: Harcourt, Brace, 1939), p. 100 ("buffoon and a gawk"); William E. Woodward, *Years of Madness* (New York: G. P. Putnam's Sons, 1951), p. 163 ("soul of leather"); Greeley to Lincoln, July 7, 1864, quoted in James M. McPherson, *Battle Cry of Freedom: The Civil War Era* (New York: Oxford University Press, 1988), p. 762.

25 Waugh, *Reelecting Lincoln*, p. 23 ("rarely would a fired employee"). Waugh's book is a thorough analysis of the politics and personalities of the 1864 presidential campaign.

26 McPherson, *Battle Cry*, p. 717; George R. Agassiz, ed., *Meade's Headquarters, 1863–1865: Letters of Colonel Theodore Lyman from the Wilderness to Appomattox* (Boston: Massachusetts Historical Society, 1922), p. 147 (quoting General Gouverneur K. Warren: "For thirty days now, it has been one funeral procession, past me; and it is too much!"); Lincoln, *CW*, vol. 2, p. 534 ("carried mourning to almost every home"); Lincoln, "Proclamation Calling for 500,000 Volunteers," ibid., p. 550.

27 Gorgas, *Journal*, pp. 111, 115.

28 Johnston, *Narrative*, p. 318 ("I thought it our policy"); see Haughton, *Training, Tactics and Leadership*, p. 163 (noting that while Sherman "enjoyed success with his tactic of advancing and entrenching open-order lines, putting Confederate entrenchments under pressure while he put his army past Johnston's flanks—Johnston was left with nothing to fall back on save help from other quarters"). The best discussions of Johnston's creative manipulation of comparative troop strengths—"effectives" vs. "present for duty" vs. "aggregate present—are in Richard McMurry, "A Policy So Disastrous: Joseph E. Johnston's Atlanta Campaign," in *The Campaign for Atlanta and Sherman's March to the Sea: Essays on the American Civil War in Georgia, 1864* (Campbell, Calif.: Savas Woodbury, 1994), pp. 223–48 (demonstrating that "in truth, Johnston's army was considerably larger than he ever admitted and that most historians have acknowledged"); and Thomas Lawrence Connelly, *Autumn of Glory: The Army of Tennessee, 1862–65* (Baton Rouge: Louisiana State University Press, 1971), pp. 385–86. Connelly concludes that Johnston's method of reporting his strength "seemed to create distrust in Richmond and smacked of an attempt to underestimate the strength of the army." Ibid., 385. See also Symonds, *Joseph E. Johnston*, p. 311 (cavalry figures); *OR*, vol. 38, pt. 3, pp. 676–77; E. C. Dawes, "The Confederate Strength in the Atlanta Campaign," *Battles and Leaders*, vol. 4, pp. 281–83.

29 Johnston to Bragg, July 11, 1864, *OR*, vol. 38, pt. 5, p. 876 (recommendation to evacuate Andersonville).

30 Bragg to Davis, July 13, 1864, *OR*, vol. 38, pt. 5, p. 878; Bragg to Davis, July 15, 1864, ibid., p. 881; Davis to Johnston, July 16, 1864, ibid., p. 882; Johnston to Davis, July 16, 1864, p. 883.

31 McMurry, *Atlanta 1864*, p. 138; Watkins, *Co. Aytch*, p. 217; see generally William R. Scaife and William Harris Bragg, *Joe Brown's Pets: The Georgia Militia in the Civil War* (Macon: Mercer University Press, 2004). On July 10, Governor Brown had written to Davis: "If you will order 5,000 more muskets to Atlanta, I will try to furnish that number of old men and boys of the State to use them for the emergency." *OR*, vol. 52, pt. 2, p. 691.

32 Nine years too late, Johnston outlined his plan to defend Atlanta in his memoir, *Narrative of Military Operations During the Late War Between the States* (New York: D. Appleton & Co., 1874), p. 350. He wrote: "I intended to man the works of Atlanta on the side of Peach Tree Creek with [the Georgia militia], and leisurely fall back with the Confederate troops into the town, and, when the Federal army approached, march out with the three corps against one of its flanks." Even if this failed, Johnston asserted that "the Confederate army had a near and secure place of refuge in *Atlanta, which it could hold forever*, and so win the campaign, of which that place was the object" (emphasis added). See also Connelly, *The Army of Tennessee*, p. 399 (noting Senator Louis Wigfall's speech that "depicted Johnston has having his sword figuratively torn from his grasp"); Foote, *The Civil War*, vol. 3, p. 419 ("Johnston would later maintain that just as he was about to deliver the blow that would 'win the campaign,' and which he had had in mind all along, his sword was wrenched from his grasp by the Richmond authorities"). Gorgas, *Journals*, p. 121 ("far enough").

33 Sarah Huff, *My Eighty Years in Atlanta* (Atlanta: n.p., 1937), p. 11; Wilbur G. Kurtz, "At the Dexter Niles House," *Atlanta Constitution Magazine*, Sept. 28, 1930; Th. J. Wood to J. S. Fullerton, July 11, 1864, *OR*, vol. 38, pt. 5, pp. 116–17 ("jollification").

34 Sarah Huff, "I Saw the Battle of Atlanta" (recollection of July 17, 1864); Charles W. Hubner, "Some Recollections of Atlanta During 1864," *Atlanta Historical Bulletin* 1, no. 2 (Jan. 1928), pp. 5–7.

35 *OR*, vol. 38, pt, 5, p. 885 (order relieving Johnston); General Orders, No. 4, ibid., 887 (Johnston's farewell); ibid., 888 (Johnston's reply to Cooper). Lost Cause historian E.A. Pollard called the order for Johnston's removal "the sentence that murdered tens of thousands of brave soldiers, the message of greatest joy and encouragement to the enemy, the death-warrant of the Southern Confederacy." Edward Alfred Pollard, *Life of Jefferson Davis with a Secret History of the Southern Confederacy Gathered Behind the Scenes in Richmond* (Philadelphia: National Publishing Co., 1869), p. 375.

36 John I. Kendall, "Recollections of a Confederate Officer" (John Smith Kendall, ed.), *Louisiana Historical Quarterly*, 29, no. 4 (Oct. 1946), pp. 1175–76 (rumors of Johnston's removal); William Josiah McMurray, *History of the Twentieth Tennessee Regiment Volunteer Infantry, C.S.A.* (Nashville: By the author, 1904), p. 319.

37 James Cooper Nisbet, *Four Years on the Firing Line*, Bell Irvin Wiley, ed. (Jackson, Tenn.: McCowat-Mercer Press, 1963), p. 206; Samuel T. Foster, *One of Cleburne's Command*, Norman D. Brown, ed. (Austin: University of Texas Press, 1980), pp. 106–7; Symonds, *Johnston*, p. 331; Lt. Hamilton Branch to mother, July 19, 1864, quoted in Scott Walker, *Hell's Broke Loose in Georgia: Survival in a Civil War Regiment* (Athens: University of Georgia Press, 2005), p. 148 ("Genl. Hood . . . is a fighting man"); see also Robert Banks to Father, July 25, 1864, in "Civil War Letters of Robert W. Banks: Atlanta Campaign." George C. Osborn, ed., *Georgia Historical Quarterly* 27 (1943), pp. 215–16 ("Army in good spirits—and confidence in General Hood unabated. The grief for the loss of General Johnston was painfully borne by the troops in silence. His removal fell upon us so unexpectedly that it made all feel sad—but we do not [lack] confidence in our present commander").

38 John Bell Hood, *Advance and Retreat: Personal Experiences in the United States and Confederate States Armies* (New Orleans: Beauregard, 1880; reprint, Lincoln: University of Nebraska Press, 1996), p. 126; Philip L. Secrist, "Jefferson Davis and the Atlanta Campaign: A Study in Confederate Command," *Atlanta Historical Bulletin* 17 (Fall–Winter 1972), p. 17 ("classic of military intrigue"); Hood to Bragg, July 14, 1864, *OR*, vol. 38, pt. 5, pp. 879–80; Seddon to Hood, July 17, 1864, *OR*, vol. 38, pt. 5, p. 885; Davis to Hood, Hardee and Stewart, ibid., p. 888.

39 Evans, *Sherman's Horsemen*, p. 85, quoting Thomas Robson Hay, "The Davis-Hood-Johnston Controversy of 1864," *Mississippi Valley Historical Review* 11 (June 1924), pp. 66 n. 39 ("Gentlemen, I am a soldier"); Hood, *Advance and Retreat*, p. 128; Foote, *The Civil War*, vol. 3, p. 421 (Johnston "was off the hook and intended to stay off"). Johnston's sympathetic biographers argue that he was justified in his abrupt, broken-promise departure from Atlanta, first suggesting that Hood's memory was faulty, and arguing that in any event "Johnston would have been less than wise to remain long and thus become a convenient target for responsibility for Hood's failure." Govan and Livingood, *A Different Valor*, p. 318. Of course, the opposite interpretation is possible as well—that Johnston retreated until the fall of Atlanta was all but inevitable, and then left Hood holding the bag. See Chesnut, *Mary Chesnut's Civil War*, p. 622 ("Poor Sam!").

40 Fremantle, *Three Months*, p. 146 ("stout, rather rough-looking man . . . all the necessary swearing"); Christopher Losson, *Tennessee's Forgotten Warriors: Frank Cheatham and His Confederate Division* (Knoxville: University of Tennessee Press, 1989), p. 30 ("one of the wickedest men I ever heard speak").

41 W. H. T. Walker to wife, July 18, 1864, quoted in Brown, *To the Manner Born*, p. 257; Patrick, *Reluctant Rebel*, p. 197 ("Hood is a fighting man"); R. M. Gill to wife, July 18, 1864, quoted in McMurry, "Confederate Morale," *Georgia Historical Quarterly* 54, p. 235..

42 Hagan to Dear Wife, July 19, 1864, in "Confederate Letters," *Georgia Historical Quarterly* 38, p. 286.

CHAPTER 3: OLD WOODENHEAD

1 Samuel G. French diary, July 17, 1864, in *Two Wars: An Autobiography of Gen. Samuel*

G. French (Nashville: Confederate Veteran, 1901), p. 216; R. M. Collins, *Chapters from the Unwritten History of the War Between the States* (St. Louis: Nixon-Jones Printing Co., 1893), p. 226; see also Shakespeare, *King Lear*, act 4, scene 6 ("Through tatter'd clothes small vices do appear").

2 Richards diary, July 17, 1864, AHC.

3 For Hood's background, see generally McMurry, *John Bell Hood and the War for Southern Independence*; and John Percy Dyer, *The Gallant Hood* (New York: Bobbs-Merrill, 1950). For a brief but nonetheless excellent portrait, see Keith Bohannon, "'A Bold Fighter' Promoted Beyond His Abilities: General John Bell Hood," in *Leaders of the Lost Cause: New Perspectives on the Confederate High Command*, Gary W. Gallagher and Joseph T. Glatthaar, eds. (Mechanicsburg, Pa.: Stackpole Books, 2004), pp. 249–87. On Hood's West Point record and infractions, *see* Dyer, p. 31 ("segar in his hat").

4 Jackson to S. Cooper, Sept. 27, 1862, quoted in Hood, *Advance and Retreat*, pp. 45–46; James I. Robertson, *Stonewall Jackson: The Man, the Soldier, the Legend* (New York: Macmillan, 1997), p. 617 ("Oh! He is a soldier!"); *Richmond Enquirer*, Sept. 13, 1862, quoted in McMurry, *John Bell Hood*, p. 61; J. Longstreet to S. Cooper, Sept. 24, 1863, quoted in Hood, *Advance and Retreat*, pp. 65–66; Thomas W. Cutrer, ed., *Longstreet's Aide: The Civil War Letters of Major Thomas J. Goree* (Charlottesville: University of Virginia Press, 1995), p. 100 ("one of the finest young officers I ever saw").

5 Fremantle, *Three Months*, p. 122; Chesnut, *Mary Chesnut's Civil War*, p. 441 (describing Hood's "sad Quixote face, the face of an old Crusader, who believed in his cause, his cross, and his crown"). For an excellent exploration of the rumors of Hood's addiction to drugs, see Steven Davis, "John Bell Hood's 'Addictions' in Civil War Literature." *Blue & Gray* 16, no. 1 (Oct. 1998), pp. 28–31. Examining the dearth of evidence, Davis concludes: "Really, y'all—this talk must stop!"

6 Statistics as to the mortality rate for Hood's surgery vary, and some have suggested that Hood was one of only five men to survive a leg amputation at the hip during the entire war. See *Medical and Surgical History of the War of the Rebellion* (Washington, D.C.: Government Printing Office, 1888), part III, vol. 1, p. 165 (in sixty-six cases treated by exarticulation at the hip, the fatality rate was 83.3 percent); Davis, "Hood's Addictions," p. 30 (noting instead statistics for amputation at the upper third of the femur, where the fatality rate was in excess of 50 percent). Hood letter to friend in *Memphis Appeal*, March 14, 1864, quoted in Davis, ibid. ("I have been riding all over the country"); Bohannon, "John Bell Hood," p. 261 ("I will fight those Yankees").

7 Gerald Linderman, *Embattled Courage: The Experience of Combat in the American Civil War* (New York: Free Press, 1989), p. 162; Lyman, *Meade's Headquarters*, p. 139. Lyman continued: "Very few officers would hold back when they get an order; but the ordeal is so awful, that it requires a peculiar disposition to 'go in gaily.'" Ibid.

8 There are few if any references to Hood as "Old Woodenhead" in contemporaneous diaries and letters, suggesting that this was indeed a postwar label, retroactively applied. Memoirs that make such a reference occur long after the war and almost certainly are based on E. A. Pollard's unflattering portrait of Hood. See, e.g., Nisbet, *Four Years on the Firing Line*, p. 206 ("It has been said of Hood, 'He was a man with a lion's heart, but a

wooden head'"). See Pollard, *Life of Jefferson Davis*, p. 379 ("a lion's heart and a wooden head"). Interestingly, the extremely intelligent Union General Henry W. Halleck was called both "Old Brains" and "Old Woodenhead." I am indebted to Dr. Stephen Davis for identifying Pollard as the likely source of the Woodenhead name.

9 Catton, "Battle of Atlanta," p. 257; R. E. Lee to Davis, July 12, 1864, in *Wartime Papers of R. E. Lee*, Clifford Dowdey, ed. (New York: Little, Brown, 1961), p. 821. Lee is often quoted as having described Hood as "all lion, none of the fox," e.g., McPherson, *Battle Cry*, p. 761, but it appears to be an attempt by some historians (and poets) to encapsulate Lee's views rather than a true and direct quotation. *See* Stephen Vincent Benét, *John Brown's Body* (1927), p. 193: "Yellow-haired Hood with his wounds and his empty sleeve, / Leading his Texans, a Viking shape of a man, / With the thrust and lack of craft of a berserk sword, / All lion, none of the fox." Cf. David Crockett, *A Narrative of the Life of David Crockett of the State of Tennessee*, 6th ed. (Philadelphia: E. L. Carey and A. Hurt, 1834), p. 135 ("This was a hard business on me, for I could just barely write my own name; but to do this, and write the warrants too, was at least a huckleberry over my persimmon").

10 Gorgas, *Journals*, p. 123 (entry for July 22, 1864); Chesnut, *A Diary from Dixie*, p. 633 ("brave as Caesar"; "dash and fire").

11 Chesnut, *Mary Chesnut's Civil War*, p. 268 (Johnston's bird hunt); Johnson, *Remembered Yesterdays*, p. 199 (Johnston "could solve on paper any military problem"); F. Y. Hedley, *Marching Through Georgia: Pen-pictures of Every-day Life in General Sherman's Army, from the Beginning of the Atlanta Campaign Until the Close of the War* (Chicago: R. R. Donnelly & Sons Co., 1885), p. 140 (Hood's poker game).

12 John M. Schofield, *Forty-six Years in the Army* (New York: Century Co., 1897), pp. 231–32 ("He'll hit you like hell"); O. O. Howard to wife, July 23, 1864, quoted in Donald B. Connelly, *John M. Schofield and the Politics of Generalship* (Chapel Hill: University of North Carolina Press, 2006), p. 104; Evans, *Sherman's Horsemen*, p. 86 ("Dodge! Dodge!").

13 Sherman, *Memoirs*, p. 444 ("I inferred that the change of commanders meant 'fight'"); Special Field Orders No. 39, July 19, 1864, *OR*, vol. 38, pt. 5, p. 193.

14 *OR*, vol. 38, pt. 5, p. 889; Hood, *Advance and Retreat*, p. 162 ("Lee and Jackson school").

15 *OR*, vol. 38, pt. 3, p. 630 (Hood's report on Peachtree Creek); Hood, *Advance and Retreat*, p. 168. There is some uncertainty in the literature as to whether Hood's council of war was held the night of the 19th or not until the morning of the 20th. Compare Connelly, *Autumn of Glory*, p. 440 ("Hood, though he had known of the situation since the previous night, had delayed calling a council of war until the morning of July 20"); Castel, *Decision in the West*, p. 368 ("Around midnight [July 19–20], Hood . . . meets with the corps commanders and Smith to explain to them their roles in his plan"); Davis, *Atlanta Will Fall*, p. 133 ("That night at his headquarters Hood discussed his plans for the next day with all three corps commanders"). Hood himself asserts that the meeting was held on the 19th. Hood, *Advance and Retreat*, p. 166.

16 For favorable assessments of Hood's plan for Peachtree Creek, see McMurry, *John Bell Hood*, p. 128 ("Hood's plan was good; its execution would test his worthiness to command an army"); Stephen Davis, "A Reappraisal of the Generalship of General John Bell Hood in the Battles for Atlanta," in *The Campaign for Atlanta*, p. 73 ("Hood's plan was so good—oblique assaults from the right, by division—that Joe Johnston subsequently claimed credit for it"); see Johnston, *Narrative of Military Operations*, pp. 350–51.

17 Benjamin F. Taylor, *Pictures of Life in Camp and Field* (Chicago: S. C. Griggs & Co., 1875), p. 193 (Thomas "hewn out of a large square block"). Thomas's stoicism extended to the everyday hardships of war, as when a despairing private came to him seeking a furlough. "I ain't seen my old woman, General, for four months," the soldier explained. Thomas retorted that he had not seen his own wife in two years, and said, "If a general can submit to such privation, surely a private can." The disappointed soldier was unconvinced. "I don't know about that, General," he said. "Me and my wife aint made that way." Foote, *Civil War*, vol. 3, p. 867.

18 Special Field Orders No. 39, July 19, 1864, *OR*, vol. 38, pt. 5, p. 193; Thomas Maguire journal, quoted in Garrett, *Atlanta and Environs*, vol. 1, p. 609; Mary A. H. Gay, *Life in Dixie During the War 1861–1862–1863–1864–1865*, 4th ed. (Atlanta: Foote & Davies Co., 1901), pp. 125–26. A gentleman arrived at the Gay home some time after in the form of an apologetic major from Schofield's staff, who was angered by the looting by his outriders and sent as "a token of regard and respectful sympathy" a heavy-laden and much-needed tray of food. Ibid., pp. 132–37.

19 Steven E. Woodworth, *Nothing But Victory: The Army of the Tennessee, 1861–65* (New York: Knopf, 2005), p. 531 (Star-Spangled Banner); Felix G. De Fontaine, "Severe Fighting Around Atlanta," *Savannah Republican*, July 24, 1864, reprinted in *Mobile Advertiser and Register*, July 31, 1864.

20 Hooker to Salmon P. Chase, Dec. 28, 1863, *OR*, vol. 31, pt. 2, p. 340 (Sherman "will never be successful"); Hooker to L. L. Crounse, Feb. 2, 1864, quoted in J. Cutler Andrews, *The North Reports the Civil War* (Pittsburgh: University of Pittsburgh Press, 1955), pp. 253–54 ("You must know that I am regarded with more jealousy"). Joseph Hooker is an intriguing character who merits more discussion than is possible here—in fact, he deserves a new biography, the only thorough treatment being Walter H. Hebert's *Fighting Joe Hooker* (Indianapolis: Bobbs-Merrill, 1944).

Despite Hooker's fondness for whiskey and women, there is no truth to the often-repeated assertion that the use of the word "hooker" as a slang term for prostitute derives from the general's name and his alleged frequent presence in the red-light districts of New Orleans and Washington. It appears that the term was in use long before the Civil War and Hooker's rise to prominence. See Thomas P. Lowry, *The Story the Soldiers Wouldn't Tell: Sex in the Civil War* (Mechanicsburg, Pa.: Stackpole Books, 1994, pp. 146–48.

21 *New York Times*, July 27, 1864 ("a small but difficult stream"); see also John W. Geary, *OR*, vol. 38, pt. 2, p. 137 (describing Peachtree Creek as "about twenty feet wide, and deep, with marshy banks and muddy bottom. The hills on both sides were steep, irregular, and heavily timbered"). For the naming and history of Peachtree Creek, see David R. Kaufman, *Peachtree Creek: A Natural and Unnatural History of Atlanta's*

Watershed (Athens: University of Georgia Press, 2007), p. 170; Garrett, *Atlanta and Environs*, vol. 1, pp. 8–11 (history of Standing Peachtree); see also Castel, *Decision in the West*, p. 365 ("There are no peach trees along Peachtree Creek"). For more on Tanyard Branch, *see* Kaufman, *Peachtree Creek*, pp. 116–21.

22 Rice C. Bull, *Soldiering: The Civil War Diary of Rice C. Bull, 123rd New York Volunteer Infantry*. K. Jack Bauer, ed. (San Rafael, Calif.: Presidio Press, 1978), p. 145; Lew Wallace, *Life of Gen. Ben Harrison* (Hartford: S. S. Scranton & Co., 1888), p. 237 ("fight, and fight at once, and all the time"). Blackberries were highly coveted by blue and gray soldiers alike. See, e.g., Rufus Mead, Jr. to "Dear Folks at Home," July 13, 1864, in "With Sherman Through Georgia and the Carolinas: Letters of a Federal Soldier," James A. Padgett, ed., *Georgia Historical Quarterly* 32 (1948), p. 300 ("Blackberries & blueberries are in their glory, but the pickets are too plenty for me to get many. I get red ones and stew them, make a nice sauce of them"); Foote, *With Sherman to the Sea*, p. 122 ("The blackberries are so thick in the abandoned fields that one can pick a ten quart pail full in a few minutes. The boys make pudding, pies and evry thing they can think of").

23 A number of historians assert that the delay in shifting the Rebel line gave the Federals time to dig in and therefore doomed Hood's plan to failure. See, e.g., Connelly, *Autumn of Glory*, p. 440 ff.; McPherson, *Battle Cry*, p. 754; Horn, *Army of Tennessee*, p. 352. Albert Castel argues that such criticism is unfair, and that "only two of Newton's and one of Geary's brigades were behind defensive works when assaulted. . . . All the rest of the Federal units east of the Howell's Mill Road were in the open, exactly as Hood hoped they would be." Castel, "Battle of Peachtree Creek," p. 43. Stephen Davis agrees, concluding: "The two hours lost by the rightward shift were probably not as critical as some scholars have suggested." Davis, "An Assessment of Hood's First Attack—The Battle of Peachtree Creek," *Blue & Gray*, 6, no. 6 (Aug. 1989), p. 17.

24 Howard, "The Battles About Atlanta," *Atlantic Monthly*, p. 389; John T. Raper, "General Thomas at Peach Tree Creek," *Ohio Soldier*, 14, no. 11 (Dec. 31, 1898) ("Here they come, boys!").

Chapter 4: Hood's First Sortie

1 Stephen Pierson, "From Chattanooga to Atlanta in 1864 . . . A Personal Reminiscence," in *The Atlanta Papers*, Sydney C. Kerksis, ed. (Dayton, Ohio: Press of the Morningside Bookshop, 1980), p. 289; Report of Brig. Gen. John W. Geary, Sept. 15, 1864, *OR*, vol. 38, pt. 2, p. 140.

2 Charles H. Olmstead, "The Memoirs of Charles H. Olmstead," *Georgia Historical Quarterly* 45, no. 1 (1961), p. 44.

3 Nisbet, *Four Years on the Firing Line*, p. 169 (description of Stevens, including his "splendid physique"); *OR*, vol. 30, pt. 2, p. 246 (praising the "iron-nerved" Stevens); see also Russell K. Brown, *Our Connection with Savannah: A History of the 1st Battalion Georgia Sharpshooters* (Macon: Mercer University Press, 2004), p. 81.

4 Report of Brig. Gen. Nathan Kimball, Aug. 4, 1864, *OR*, vol. 38, pt. 1, p. 306 ("charging with great confidence"); Castel, *Decision in the West*, p. 376 ("something like

the heavens and earth had suddenly come together"); Howard, "The Battles About Atlanta," *Atlantic Monthly*, p. 389 (Rebel yell); O. O. Howard, *Autobiography of Oliver Otis Howard* (New York: Baker & Taylor, 1907), vol. 1, p. 615 ("grass before the scythe"). The high ground where Newton's men stood is today best known as "Heartbreak Hill," the most challenging incline in Atlanta's annual Peachtree Road Race.

5 Raper, "General Thomas at Peach Tree Creek," *The Ohio Soldier*, Dec. 31, 1898; see also Henry Stone, "The Siege and Capture of Atlanta, July 9 to September 8, 1864," in *The Atlanta Papers*, p. 112 (noting that Thomas "personally directed the placing of some of the guns; and, with blows of his hand, urged on the horses as they dashed by him into position"). Newton later confirmed Thomas's participation in his official report. Report of Brig. Gen. John Newton, July 21, 1864, *OR*, vol. 38, pt. 1, p. 298 ("Spencer's battery of four guns had arrived and was in position, besides the section of Goodspeed's in the rear, and a battery of the Twentieth Corps . . . had gone into position, as I understood, under the immediate supervision of General Thomas").

6 The half-hearted attack of Maney's Tennesseans is a mystery. Cheatham's former division had fought fiercely in a number of battles, most recently at Kennesaw Mountain, and would fight fiercely again two days later. One historian suggests that they balked at attacking the Union fortifications. See Castel, *Decision in the West*, p. 376 ("Too often in past battles—Fort Donelson, Shiloh, Perryville, Murfreesboro, Chickamauga [above all, Chickamauga]—they have rushed headlong against the Yankees, only to be slaughtered to no avail, even at Chickamauga where, supposedly, they won. For that reason they consider . . . 'storming works as belonging to an early part of the War and played out now'").

As usual, Confederate recordkeeping as to number of men is questionable—the most recent reports (July 10) number Cheatham's (Maney's) Division as having 4,733 "aggregate present" and 3,174 "effectives." *Abstract from Returns of the Army of Tennessee*, July 10, 1864, *OR*, vol. 38, pt. 3, p. 679.

7 Report of Brigadier General Winfield S. Featherston, Major Martin A. Oatis, Sept. 12, 1864, *OR*, vol. 38, pt. 3, p. 886 ("Owing to the rough and broken ground"); see also ibid., pp. 880–84 (Featherston's report); ibid., pp. 894–95 (Scott's report).

8 Charlie Cox to "Dear Frank!" May 10, 1864, in "The Civil War Letters of Charles Harding Cox," Lorna Lutes Sylvester, ed., *Indiana Magazine of History* 68 (1972), p. 198 ("poorest excuse for a Genl"); *Soldiering with Sherman: Civil War Letters of George F. Cram*, Jennifer Cain Bohrnstedt, ed. (DeKalb: Northern Illinois University Press, 2000), p. 89 ("regular old Falstaff"); Benjamin Harrison to wife, March 7, 1864, quoted in Harry J. Sievers, *Benjamin Harrison: Hoosier Warrior* (New York: University Publishers, 1960), p. 238 ("road was so crooked it had made him drunk"); Cram to Mother, July 4, 1864, in *Soldiering with Sherman*, pp. 123–24 (mistaken identity of the 23rd Corps). Harrison's letters home contain repeated references to Brig. Gen. Ward's drinking and bumbling.

9 For more on John Coburn, see generally Frank J. Welcher and Larry G. Ligget, *Coburn's Brigade: 85th Indiana, 33rd Indiana, 19th Michigan, and 22nd Wisconsin in the Western Civil War* (Carmel: Guild Press of Indiana, 1999).

10 William Allen White, *Masks in a Pageant* (New York: Macmillan, 1928), p. 69. For stories of Harrison's many virtues—though they should be taken with a *post facto*, hagiographic grain of salt—see soldiers quoted in Wallace, *Life of Gen. Ben Harrison*, pp. 227–28, 233, 242. On his improvisation as a surgeon at Gilgal Church, see Sievers, *Benjamin Harrison: Hoosier Warrior*, p. 255; Harrison to wife, June 18, 1864, quoted in ibid. ("Our surgeons got separated from us, and putting our wounded in a deserted house, I stripped my arms to dress their wounds myself. Poor Fellows! I was but an awkward surgeon, of course, but I hope I gave them some relief").

11 Interview with L. T. Miller, *Indianapolis Daily Journal*, July 1, 1888, quoted in Sievers, *Hoosier Warrior*, pp. 260–61.

12 James M. Perry, *Touched with Fire: Five Presidents and the Civil War Battles That Made Them* (New York: Public Affairs, 2003), p. 251 (quoting Harrison's "unlikely words"); see also Sievers, *Hoosier Warrior*, p. 261; *OR*, vol. 38, pt. 2, p. 345 ("Our advance . . . was steady and unfaltering"). Ward would claim in his official report that he had ordered his division forward to the ridge, and suggested that Harrison and Coburn had merely followed his orders. Report of Brig. Gen. William T. Ward, Sept. 7, 1864, *OR*, vol. 38, pt. 2, pp. 327 ("I immediately dispatched staff officers to order the brigade commanders to move their commands rapidly to the high ground our front") and 328 ("To my brigade commanders . . . I am indebted for their prompt obedience of orders"). Sergeant Major Stephen Fleharty of the 102nd Illinois paid tribute to Harrison, noting that he seemed to possess the spirit of "Old Tippecanoe" as he ranged along the line, "utterly reckless of flying bullets." Fleharty, *Jottings from Dixie*, p. 242.

13 Samuel Merrill, *The Seventieth Indiana Volunteer Infantry in the War of the Rebellion* (Indianapolis. Bowen-Merrill, 1900), pp. 140, 143; George Cram to Dear Mother, July 24, 1864, in *Soldiering with Sherman*, p. 127 ("See my brigade!"); *OR*, vol. 38, pt. 2, p. 328 ("Meeting my line of battle seemed to completely addle their brains").

14 Castel, *Decision in the West*, p. 377; Pierson, "From Chattanooga to Atlanta," in *The Atlanta Papers*, p. 290; Bull, *Soldiering*, p. 149.

15 Bull, *Soldiering*, p. 149.

16 Report of Brig. Gen. John W. Geary, Sept. 15, 1864, *OR*, vol. 38, pt. 2, pp. 138–40; Geary to wife, Aug. 15, 1861, in *A Politician Goes to War*, p. 9 ("stern realities of war"). Geary described the battle (perhaps embellishing his role a bit) in a letter to his wife on July 24, 1864, in *A Politician Goes to War*, pp. 188–89.

17 Merrill, *Seventieth Indiana*, p. 144; Bull, *Soldiering*, p. 150; Ralsa C. Rice, *Yankee Tigers: Through the Civil War with the 125th Ohio*, Richard A. Baumgartner, ed. (Huntington, W.Va.: Blue Acorn Press, 1992), p. 128; W. H. Conner to Dunbar Rowland, Oct. 20, 1927, Mississippi Department of Archives and History, RG 9, Folder 35; Charley to My dear Sister!, July 23, 1864, in "The Civil War Letters of Charles Harding Cox," *Indiana Magazine of History*, p. 211 ("My captures"); see also Kaufman, *Peachtree Creek*, p. 136 ("Whether the description that 'the creek ran red with blood' that July day was hyperbole or fact lies forever with the spirits of the dead"); David T. Thackery, *A Light and Uncertain Hold: A History of the Sixty-Sixth Ohio Volunteer*

Infantry (Kent, Ohio: Kent State University Press, 1999), p. 205 (mass graves); see also Mitchell, *Gone with the Wind*, p. 260 ("Peach-tree Creek was crimson, so they said, after the Yankees crossed it").

An Ohio boy named Frank Miser was severely wounded near the crossings of Peachtree Creek, and when his comrades returned for him, he was dead. They found in his hand a piece of paper, on which he had scrawled in pencil: "Dear father and mother: I am mortally wounded. I die like a soldier, and hope to meet you all in heaven. B.F. Miser." Nixon B. Stewart, *Dan McCook's Regiment, 52nd O.V.I., A History of the Regiment, Its Campaigns and Battles* (By the author, 1900), p. 132.

18 E. B. Fenton, "From the Rapidan to Atlanta," in *The Atlanta Papers*, p. 232; Rufus Mead, Jr., in "With Sherman Through Georgia and the Carolinas: Letters of a Federal Soldier," *Georgia Historical Quarterly* 32 (1948), p. 302; Collins, *Chapters from the Unwritten History*, pp. 230–31.

19 Nisbet, *Four Years on the Firing Line*, p. 210 ("Valhalla"); Angus McDermid, "Letters from a Confederate Soldier," Benjamin Rountree, ed., *Georgia Review* 18 (1964), p. 290. For discussions of casualties at Peachtree Creek, see Castel, "Peachtree Creek," pp. 41–43 (tabulating the losses at 1,900 Federals and 2,500 Confederates, "not counting (as is Confederate practice) lightly wounded men who remain with their units"); McMurry, *Atlanta 1864*, p. 152 (estimating losses of 2,500 Confederates versus 2,000 Federals); but compare William T. Sherman, "Grand Strategy," in *Battles and Leaders*, vol. 4, p. 253 (claiming Confederate loss of 4,796); David J. Eicher, *The Longest Night: A Military History of the Civil War* (New York: Simon & Schuster, 2001), p. 708 (crediting Sherman's figure); Phillip L. Secrist, *Sherman's 1864 Trail of Battle to Atlanta* (Macon, Ga.: Mercer University Press, 2006), p. 143 (asserting that "the battle at Peachtree Creek cost the Confederates more than 5,000 casualties"). Stephen Davis notes that "both sides, literally, were decimated." *Atlanta Will Fall*, p. 135.

20 Castel, *Decision in the West*, p. 381; *OR*, vol. 38, pt. 3, p. 883 (Featherston's casualties); Report of Thomas J. Pulliam, July 23, 1864, ibid. pp. 888–89 (31st Mississippi). The 31st lost its lieutenant colonel, who was injured severely and carried from the field; its major and staff adjutant, both mortally wounded; and "every captain on the field was either killed or wounded." Ibid.

21 *New York Times*, July 24, 1864 (the full headline read: "BEFORE ATLANTA—Partial Occupation of the City—The Desperate Battle of Wednesday—Terrible Repulse of the Enemy by Gen. Hooker"); Mathew Brady photograph, "Hero-Trio at Peach Tree Creek," in *Benjamin Harrison: Hoosier Warrior*, following p. 226; Harrison to wife, Aug. 20, 1864, quoted in *Hoosier Warrior*, p. 264; Foote, *Civil War*, vol. III, p. 475, vol. I, p. 178 (Thomas incapable of surprise).

22 L. D. Young, *Reminiscences of a Soldier of the Orphan Brigade* (Louisville: Courier-Journal Job Printing Co., 1918), p. 90 ("hide and seek affair"); Geary, *OR*, vol. 38, pt. 2, p. 140; Castel, "Peachtree Creek," p. 44. Larry Daniel notes that Confederate artillery at Peachtree Creek was "minimally utilized in tactical execution." Larry J. Daniel, *Cannoneers in Gray: The Field Artillery of the Army of Tennessee* (Tuscaloosa: University of Alabama Press, 1984), p. 169.

23 Olmstead, "Memoirs," *Georgia Historical Quarterly*, p. 43 ("A man of only modest intellectual power").

24 Emory M. Thomas, *Robert E. Lee: A Biography* (New York: W. W. Norton, 1995), p. 246; see also Fremantle, *Three Months*, p. 131 ("It is evidently [Lee's] system to arrange the plan thoroughly with the three corps commanders, and then leave to them the duty of modifying and carrying it out to the best of their abilities").

25 Hood, "The Defense of Atlanta," in *Battles and Leaders*, vol. IV, p. 337. There are contemporaneous suggestions that Hood was right in his subsequent criticism of Hardee. The reporter Felix De Fontaine's account, written on the night of July 20, would identify an affirmative order from Hardee as the reason for the comparative lack of aggressiveness from his troops. Hardee's men "fighting bravely, had overcome every obstacle thus far and were prepared to dash yet further on and drive the enemy into the creek," De Fontaine wrote. "But here, the judgment of the commander and the gallantry of the troops were at variance. Gen. Hardee deemed imprudent to risk the lives of his men in achieving an object which threatened to cost so much. A halt was ordered, and in brief, no further efforts were made to accomplish the end of the expedition." *Savannah Republican*, July 24, 1864.

Many historians are skeptical of Hood's efforts to blame Hardee and yet are willing to blame Hardee themselves. See, e.g., Hughes, *Old Reliable*, p. 225 (describing Peachtree Creek as "one of Hardee's poorest performances"); Connelly, *Autumn of Glory*, p. 443 ("While Hood bore the responsibility for his lack of presence on the field, Hardee handled the attack badly").

26 Report of Capt. Augustus L. Milligan, July 24, 1864, *OR*, vol. 38, pt. 3, p. 897; Report of Maj. Gen. William W. Loring, Sept. 15, 1864, *OR*, vol. 38, pt. 3, p. 877; William J. Oliphant, *Only a Private: A Texan Remembers the Civil War*, James M. McCaffrey, ed. (Houston: Halcyon Press, 2004), p. 68 ("We fought hard . . . and accomplished nothing").

27 Perry, *Touched with Fire*, p. 252 ("By God, Harrison"); Hooker to Stanton, Oct. 31, 1864, quoted in Wallace, *Life of Gen. Ben Harrison*, p. 222. Little Ben's friend and fellow townsman Colonel John Coburn echoed this praise, describing Harrison as "the personification of fiery valor." Wallace, *Life of Gen. Ben Harrison*, p. 237.

28 President Harrison's visit to Atlanta in 1891 and his tour of the wrong creek and mill is reported in the *Atlanta Constitution*, April 16, 1891.

Other effects from the fighting on July 20 would be even more enduring, more painful and more personal. First Lieutenant George Young, 143rd New York Volunteers, was riding near the Collier Road on the morning of July 20 when a Confederate minié ball tore through his horse, killing the animal, and then struck and splintered the courier's leg a few inches below the knee. In and of itself, Young's wounding was sadly not remarkable—forty-seven others from his regiment were killed or wounded that day. The young lieutenant was treated at the regimental hospital, where the ball was extracted and the wound dressed, and would spend the next three weeks in Tennessee hospitals. Though he was fortunate enough to keep his leg, Young received a medical discharge in October 1864.

After the war, George Young made his home in Ellenville, New York, where he would open a paper mill and marry his sweetheart. Well known and respected in the community, he was elected sheriff of Ulster County in 1885. But Young was plagued with chronic pain and repeated infections in his wounded leg, enduring over the years a number of surgeries on his diseased shin bone. After the turn of the century, the pain and the discharge from his wound grew steadily worse, until he went down with an infection and could not recover. George Young died on April Fools' Day, 1909, at his home in Ellenville—as the crow flies, 775 miles from Atlanta. On the death certificate, the attending physician recorded the cause of death as: "Gunshot wound, right tibia, chronic septic infection, many years"—a gunshot wound Young had suffered forty-five years earlier, along the banks of Peachtree Creek. Seward Osborne, Jr., "George Young: Forgotten Hero of Peach Tree Creek," *North South Trader* 7, no. 3 (March–April 1980), pp. 28–32. George Young's uniform, with a bullet hole in the trousers, is on display at the Atlanta History Center.

Chapter 5: Night March

1 *OR*, vol. 38, pt. 5, pp. 196–97. Despite his absence from the field, Sherman would receive his share of accolades for the victory nonetheless, and the name of Peachtree Creek would adorn the postwar roster of his many conquests in gilded lettering on monuments throughout the North—which was probably fair enough, since he certainly would have been tarred with the blame had a disaster occurred.

2 Conyngham, *Sherman's March Through the South*, pp. 40–41 ("Thomastown"); Bruce Catton, *Grant Takes Command*, (Boston, Little Brown, 1969), p. 69 ("It's the God of Mighty's truth"); Christopher J. Einolf, *George Thomas: Virginian for the Union* (Norman: University of Oklahoma Press, 2007), p. 352 (same). A new biography of Thomas strenuously argues that he was *not* slow. Benson Bobrick, *Master of War: The Life of General George H. Thomas* (New York: Simon & Schuster, 2009); compare John F. Marzalek, "Sherman Called It the Way He Saw It," *Civil War History* 40, no. 1 (March 1994), p. 75 ("Thomas was indeed slow moving in personality and cautious in military action. This attribute was neither good nor bad; it simply was"). *OR*, vol. 38, pt. 5, p. 197.

3 J. P. Austin, *The Blue and the Gray: Sketches of a Portion of the Unwritten History of the Great American Civil War* (Atlanta: Franklin Printing & Publishing Co., 1899), p. 131 ("We found the city in a wild state of excitement").

The story of the first federal shell killing a little girl was first reported in 1889 in Reed, *History of Atlanta*, p. 175, before being picked up and repeated in numerous sources. See, e.g., Garrett, *Atlanta and Environs*, p. 626 (the shot "resulted in one of the saddest fatalities of which war is capable—the death of a little child"); Hoehling, *Last Train from Atlanta*, p. 113; Celestine Sibley, *Peachtree Street, U.S.A.: An Affectionate Portrait of Atlanta* (New York: Doubleday, 1963), p. 51; Castel, *Decision in the West*, p. 378. Some accounts went one step further, including the detail that the poor girl had "wandered into the street with her puppy." Boylston, *Atlanta: Its Lore, Legends and Laughter*, p. 88. Although the story fits perfectly into the Southern view of the devil Sherman, either it appears to be entirely untrue, or the incident happened at a later date and location in the city. (There is no question that children were killed by the Union bombardment in the weeks to come.) For a thorough discussion, see Stephen Davis, "How Many Civilians Died in Sherman's Bombardment of Atlanta?" *Atlanta History* 45, no. 4 (2003), pp. 4–23.

4 M. D. Leggett, *The Battle of Atlanta: A paper read by General M.D. Leggett, before the Society of the Army of the Tennessee, October 18th, 1883, at Cleveland* (Cleveland: J. A. Davies, 1883), p. 3.

5 McPherson to Sherman, July 20, 1864, 8:45 P.M., *OR*, vol. 38, pt. 5, p. 208; ibid., pt. 3, p. 952 (Wheeler's report).

6 On McPherson at Snake Creek Gap, see Castel, pp. 141–51; Lewis, *Sherman: Fighting Prophet*, p. 357. Sherman's word-for-word quote varies slightly in the literature. Compare Rowland Cox, "Snake Creek Gap and Atlanta," in Sydney C. Kerksis, ed. *The Atlanta Papers* (Dayton: Press of the Morningside Bookshop, 1980), p. 341 (noting that Sherman said "in substance, and not ungraciously": "Well, Mac, you have missed the opportunity of a lifetime"); Lewis, *Sherman: Fighting Prophet*, p. 357 ("opportunity of your life"); B. H. Liddell Hart, *Sherman: Soldier, Realist, American* (New York: Da Capo Press, 1993), p. 246 ("the great opportunity of your life").

7 Castel, *Decision in the West*, p. 141 (McPherson at Snake Creek Gap); *Tom Taylor's Civil War*, pp. 140–41 ("The precious time passed swiftly away"). For a detailed explanation of McPherson's operations on July 20–21 and the "skirmishing" at Bald/Leggett's Hill, see Woodworth, *Nothing but Victory*, pp. 531–39.Woodworth excuses McPherson for stopping short, dismissing criticism of him by noting that "it was easier to know what the commanding general should do when one was not the commanding general." Ibid., 533; see also Liddell Hart, *Sherman: Soldier, Realist, American*, p. 280 (likewise excusing McPherson and noting that allowance "must be made for the difficult, densely wooded and little-known ground over which they were advancing—rather, groping forward in the fog of war").

8 Sherman to McPherson, 8 P.M., July 20, 1864, *OR*, vol. 38, pt. 5, p. 208.

9 *Charleston Mercury*, Nov. 7, 1864 (Cleburne "as Irish as Sir Patrick O'Penipo"); Cleburne to brother Robert, May 7, 1861, quoted in Irving A. Buck, *Cleburne and His Command* (New York: Neale Publishing Co., 1908), p. 21; see generally Craig L. Symonds, *Stonewall of the West: Patrick Cleburne and the Civil War* (Lawrence: University Press of Kansas, 1998).

10 Conyngham, *Sherman's March*, p. 136 ("the fit type of a lean Cassius"); Buck, *Cleburne and His Command*, p. 107 (bullet "emerging through his mouth"); Rowena Webster, *Memoirs of a Southern Girl*, Tennessee State Library, Nashville, quoted in Mauriel Phillips Joslyn, "A Moral and Upright Man: The Character and Personality of Pat Cleburne," in *A Meteor Shining Brightly: Essays on the Life and Career of Major General Patrick R. Cleburne* (Macon, Ga.: Mercer University Press, 2000), pp. 119–20.

11 Joslyn, "A Moral and Upright Man," in *Meteor Shining Brightly*, pp. 113–14 (stories of Cleburne's marksmanship).

12 Buck, *Cleburne and His Command*, p. 232 ("Five minutes more would have been too late"); Foster, *One of Cleburne's Command*, pp. 108–9 ("killing our men very fast");

Report of Brig. Gen. J. A. Smith, Aug. 5, 1864, *OR*, vol. 38, pt. 3, p. 746 ("I have never before witnessed").

13 Henry Otis Dwight Papers, Ohio Historical Society, Columbus, Ohio, quoted in David Mowery, "Manning Ferguson Force—A Tribute," Cincinnati Civil War Round Table, www.cincinnaticwrt.org ("a spare grave man"; "made every man feel"); Gilbert D. Munson, "The Battle of Atlanta," in *Sketches of War History, 1861–1865, Papers read before the Ohio Commandry of the Military Order of the Loyal Legion of the United States* (Cincinnati: Robert Clarke and Co., 1890), vol. 3, pp. 215–17.

14 James Turner, "Jim Turner Co. G, 6th Texas Infantry, C.S.A., from 1861–1865," *Texana*, no. 2 (1974), quoted in Strayer and Baumgartner, eds., *Echoes of Battle*, pp. 220–21.

15 Report of Brig. Gen. Giles A. Smith, July 28, 1864, *OR*, vol. 38, pt. 3, p. 580.

16 Ibid.; Turner, *Echoes of Battle*, p. 221.

17 Buck, *Cleburne and His Command*, p. 234 ("modern Joshua"); Woodworth, *Nothing but Victory*, p. 537 (afternoon weather); Leggett, *Battle of Atlanta*, p. 7 (noting extreme heat and sunstroke among the officers and men).

18 Hood to J. A. Seddon, July 21, 1864, *OR*, vol. 38, pt. 5, p. 898 ("handsomely repulsed"); J. C. Van Duzer to Thomas T. Eckert, July 21, 1864, ibid., p. 222 ("Skirmishing sharp and lively"); Report of Brig. Gen. Frank P. Blair, Jr., *OR*, vol. 38, pt. 3, p. 544 (XVII Corps casualty report for July 21); William J. Hardee to S. Cooper, April 5, 1865, *OR*, vol. 38, pt. 3, p. 699 (noting "the fight made by Cleburne on the 21st, which he described as the 'bitterest of his life'").

19 W. W. Royall, quoted in *Reminiscences of the Boys in Gray, 1861–1865,* Mamie Yeary, ed. (Dallas: Smith & Lamar, 1912), p. 656. General Cleburne's own report for July 20–21 is missing from the record.

20 Hood, *Advance and Retreat*, p. 175 (recalling that McPherson's flank was "standing out in air, near the Georgia Railroad between Decatur and Atlanta, and a large number of the enemy's wagons had been parked in and around Decatur").

21 William E. Strong, "The Death of General James B. McPherson," in *Military Essays and Recollections, MOLLUS—Illinois* (Chicago: A. C. McClurg & Co., 1891), vol. 1, pp. 319–20 ("McPherson was confident").

22 McPherson to Sherman, July 21, 1864, 3 p.m., *OR*, vol. 38, pt. 5, p. 219. Garrard's raid to Covington is explained in detail in Evans, *Sherman's Horsemen*, pp. 89–91, 175–94.

23 Hood, *Advance and Retreat*, pp. 173, 177.

24 Hood and Hardee would later vehemently disagree as to the specifics of Hardee's instructions. Hood maintained that Hardee "was given clear and positive orders to detach his corps, to swing away from the main body of the army, and to march entirely around and to the rear of McPherson's left flank, even if he was forced to go to and beyond Decatur"—which the Texan disingenuously noted was "only" six miles from Atlanta. This reported distance was accurate enough, as the crow flies, but Hardee's infantry could only reach Decatur by a roundabout march of eighteen miles.

Hardee would contend that he took exception to what he called this "detour to Decatur," noting that his troops had been "marching, fighting and working the night and day previous," and that Hood's original plan had therefore been abandoned in favor of a shorter march that would place Hardee's corps in position to strike the enemy on its flank, instead of directly in its rear. Hood said he agreed to no such modification, though Frank Cheatham would later side with Hardee's version, writing that Hood "finally consented that Genl Hardee should have discretion to make the assault on the flank and rear of McPherson." Wherever the truth lies in this he-said/he-said debate, the result was an apparent disconnect among the senior Confederate commanders as to precisely how the attack was to be conducted. This, combined with what one observer called the "growing coolness between Hardee and Hood," did not bode well for the ultimate success of the enterprise. *OR*, vol. 38, pt. 3, p. 699 (Hardee's report, April 5, 1865); Cheatham to T. B. Roy, quoted in Hughes, *Old Reliable*, p. 226; Wilbur G. Kurtz, "Civil War Days in Georgia: Major-General W. H. T. Walker," *Atlanta Constitution*, July 27, 1930, p. 6 ("growing coolness"). Stephen Davis notes that historians are "perplexed" by the modification of the flank march plan. Davis, *Atlanta Will Fall*, p. 140.

25 Stanley Horn, *The Army of Tennessee* (Indianapolis: Bobbs-Merrill, 1941), p. 304 ("brilliant"); Davis, *Atlanta Will Fall*, p. 137 ("Lee-like in its boldness and sweep"); Castel, *Decision in the West*, p. 379 ("a plan worthy of Lee"). Others are more muted in their praise. See Walker, *Hell's Broke Loose in Georgia*, p. 158 (saying of Hood's plan, "It was a gamble but it was Hood's best option"), Steven E. Woodworth, *Jefferson Davis and His Generals: The Failure of Confederate Command in the West* (Lawrence: University Press of Kansas, 1990), p. 287 ("It was, Hood felt, just what his hero Lee would have done, and in reality, it was not a bad plan at all"); Thomas B. Buell, *The Warrior Generals: Combat Leadership in the Civil War* (New York: Crown, 1997), p. 372 ("Hood's plan was conceptually bold, and it represented the kind of Confederate assault that had broken Federal armies in the past"); Dyer, *The Gallant Hood*, p. 258 (calling the movement "admirably if not brilliantly planned").

26 Hood, *Advance and Retreat*, pp. 174–75.

27 Bate and Walker began the march near the modern-day intersection of Peachtree and Spring Streets in midtown Atlanta. Patrick, *Reluctant Rebel*, pp. 199–200. In 1930, Atlanta historian Wilbur G. Kurtz, accompanied by a veteran of the 42nd Georgia named J. W. McWilliams, measured the distance of the march at 13.7 miles, but noted that the distance "was doubless more than 15 miles for Bate's and Walker's troops, who were to the eastward, and who penetrated points farther to the north, in their attack." Wilbur G. Kurtz, "Major-General W. H. T. Walker," *Atlanta Constitution*, July 27, 1930, p. 6.

28 Philip Daingerfield Stephenson, *The Civil War Memoir of Philip Daingerfield Stephenson, D.D.*, Nathaniel Cheairs Hughes, Jr., ed. (Conway: University of Central Arkansas Press, 1995), p. 215.

29 W. L. Trask Diary, Kennesaw Mountain Battlefield Park Archives (KNMBP), pp. 35–36.

30 Stephenson, *Memoir*, p. 216 ("glorious night," singing); Woodworth, *Nothing but*

Victory, p. 539, quoting Leggett, *National Tribune*, May 6, 1886 ("considerable noise").

31 Stephenson, *Memoir*, p. 217 ("bent forward silently"); Kurtz, "W. H. T. Walker," *Atlanta Constitution*, p. 6 ("a confused mass of milling men").

32 Hardee's Report, April 5, 1865, *OR*, vol. 38, pt. 3, p. 698 ("Walker's beaten troops"); Stephenson, *Memoir*, p. 217 ("Halts came").

33 T. B. Roy, quoted in Castel, *Decision in the West*, p. 391 ("The most tedious . . ."); Young, *Reminiscences of a Soldier of the Orphan Brigade*, p. 90 ("we looked like the imaginary Adam 'of the earth earthy'" and "the most ill-conceived and unsatisfactory executed plan").

34 Kurtz, "William H. T. Walker," *Atlanta Constitution*, July 27, 1930 (describing in detail the encounters with guides William Cobb and Case Turner).

35 Report of Brig. Gen. Mark P. Lowrey, July 29, 1864, *OR*, vol. 38, pt. 3, p. 731.

36 Richard S. Tuthill, "An Artilleryman's Recollections of the Battle of Atlanta," *Military Essays and Recollections. Papers Read before the Commandery of the State of Illinois, Military Order of the Loyal Legion of the United States.* (Chicago: A. C. McClurg and Co. 1891) vol. I, pp. 296–97.

37 For a fine biography of "Shot Pouch," see Brown, *To the Manner Born*; briefer articles include Stephen Davis, "A Georgia Firebrand: Major General W. H. T. Walker, C.S.A." *Georgia Historical Quarterly* (1979), pp. 447–60; and Wilbur G. Kurtz, "The Death of Major-General W.H.T. Walker, July 22, 1864," *Civil War History* 6 (1960), pp. 174–79. Walker's record as a West Point "Immortal" and his grievous wounds are discussed in James S. Robbins, *Last in Their Class: Custer, Pickett and the Goats of West Point* (New York: Encounter Books, 2006), pp. 46, 107–15.

38 Walter A. Clark, *Under the Stars and Bars, or Memories of Four Years Service with the Oglethorpes, of Augusta, Georgia* (Augusta: Chronicle Print. Co., 1900), p. 109 ("bravest man he had ever known"); Richard Taylor, *Destruction and Reconstruction: Personal Experiences of the Late War* (New York: D. Appleton & Co., 1879), p. 23 ("I have dwelt somewhat on his character, because it was one of the strangest I have met"); George Cary Eggleston, *A Rebel's Recollections* (New York: G. P. Putnam's Sons, 1905), p. 161 ("queerest").

39 Walker to daughter Molly, July 2, 1865, quoted in Brown, *To the Manner Born*, p. 253; Davis, "A Georgia Firebrand," p. 452 (quoting letters to wife and children).

40 Stephenson, *Memoir*, p. 217.

41 Report of Brig. Gen. Mark Lowrey, July 29, 1864, *OR*, vol. 38, pt. 3, p. 731; Hardee, quoted in T. B. Roy, "General Hardee and Military Operations About Atlanta," *Southern Historical Society Papers*, 8, p. 360 ("I marched in line for two miles through a dense forest . . .").

42 "Address of Joseph B. Cumming at the Unveiling of the Monument to Maj. Gen'l William Henry Talbot Walker on the Battle Field of Atlanta, July 22, 1902," Chronicle Job Office, 1902.

43 Kurtz, "William H. T. Walker," *Atlanta Constitution*, July 27, 1930 ("anywhere on the other side"); Young, *Reminiscences*, p. 91 ("Out of dust ankle deep").

44 "Address of Joseph B. Cumming"; Stephenson, *Memoir*, p. 221 (eyewitness description of "Fighting Billy"). A sword presented to General Walker by the state of Georgia in 1850 in honor of his service in the Mexican War is on display at the Atlanta History Center.

45 Kurtz, "Death of W. H. T. Walker," *Civil War History*, p. 181 ("began the battle of Atlanta"); Clark, *Under the Stars and Bars*, p. 109 ("no battle soil on God's green earth"); see also Davis, "A Georgia Firebrand," p. 447 (noting garbled initials). Among the accounts who jumble Walker's initials are Hood, *Advance and Retreat*, p. 181 ("W. H. S. Walker"); Johnston, *Narrative*, p. 254 ("W. H. S. Walker"); French, *Two Wars*, p. 209 ("W. A. T. Walker"). Sherman avoids any possibility of such an error, referring in his memoirs to "the rebel General Walker." Sherman, *Memoirs*, p. 516. Walker perhaps proves Sherman's definition of military fame: "to be killed on the field of battle and have our names spelled wrong in the newspapers." Lewis, *Sherman: Fighting Prophet*, p. 635.

CHAPTER 6: "AN ILIAD OF WOES"

1 *OR*, vol. 38, pt. 5, pp. 224 ("The enemy has evacuated his works in front of General Stanley"), 225 ("the enemy have left my front"), 227 "The enemy has evacuated Atlanta and his works around that place"), 228 ("The enemy has evacuated his works around Atlanta"; "The enemy has evacuated Atlanta").

2 McPherson to Logan, July 22, 1864, 6 A.M., *OR*, vol. 38, pt. 5, p. 231; J. C. Van Duzer to Thomas T. Eckert, July 22, 1864, 9 P.M., ibid., p. 232. The erroneous reports of the Rebel "evacuation" of Atlanta did not result in widespread newspaper articles incorrectly reporting that Atlanta had fallen, though certain papers, including the influential *New York Herald*, did carry the false news. Marszalek, *Sherman's Other War*, pp. 184–85; *New York Herald*, July 23, 1864.

3 Wilbur G. Kurtz, "The Augustus F. Hurt House," *Atlanta Constitution Magazine*, June 22, 1930; Sherman, *Memoirs*, pp. 447–48; Sherman to Thomas, July 28 [22], 1864, *OR*, vol. 38, pt. 5, p. 223 ("we were mistaken").

4 Strong, "Death of General McPherson," *MOLLUS—Illinois*, vol. 1, p. 318 ("without the aid of a field-glass"; "severest battle of the campaign"); Sherman to McPherson, July 22, 1864, quoted in ibid., p. 319 ("Instead of sending Dodge to your left").

5 Sherman, *Memoirs*, p. 448.

6 "General John A. Logan," *Lippincott's Monthly Magazine*, August 1887, p. 510.

7 McPherson to Dodge, July 22, 1864, 12m., in Strong, "Death of McPherson," *MOLLUS—Illinois*, vol. 1, p. 321.

8 Zack C. Waters, ed., "The Partial Atlanta Reports of Confederate Maj. Gen. William B. Bate," in *The Campaign for Atlanta*, p. 218; Walker, *Hell's Broke Loose in Georgia*, p. 162 (describing Bate's confusion).

9 On General Dodge, see generally Stanley P. Hirshon, *Grenville M. Dodge, Soldier, Politician, Railroad Pioneer* (Bloomington: Indiana University Press, 1967).

10 Woodworth, *Nothing but Victory*, p. 549 (praising "McPherson's foresight"), quoting Robert M. Adams, "The Battle and Capture of Atlanta," in *Glimpses of the Nation's*

Struggle—MOLLUS Minnesota (St. Paul: H. L. Collins Co., 1898), p. 150 ("The Lord put Dodge in the right place to-day").

11 William H. Chamberlin, "Hood's Second Sortie at Atlanta," in *Battles and Leaders*, vol. 4, p. 326; Report of Brig. Gen. Elliott W. Rice, Aug. 4, 1864, *OR*, vol. 38, pt. 3, pp. 418–19.

12 Chamberlin, "Hood's Second Sortie," *Battles and Leaders*, vol. 4, p. 326; Strong, "Death of General McPherson," *MOLLUS—Illinois*, vol. 1, p. 323 ("mowed great swaths"; "showed great steadiness"); Joseph G. Bilby, *Civil War Firearms: Their Historical Background and Tactical Use* (New York: Da Capo Press, 2005), p. 189 ("fastest shooting firearm used in the Civil War"); Prosper Bowe, quoted in Joseph G. Bilby, *A Revolution in Arms: A History of the First Repeating Rifles* (Yardley, Pa.: Westholme Publishing, 2006), p. 170.

13 Report of Col. William Barkuloo, Sept. 22, 1864, *OR*, vol. 38, pt. 3, p. Brigadier General Mercer, incidentally, was the great-grandfather of composer and lyricist Johnny Mercer.

14 Chamberlin, "Hood's Second Sortie," *Battles and Leaders*, vol. 4, p. 326 ("one of the fiercest of the war"). Castel notes the futility and short duration of Bate's and Walker's attack, as well as the six vs. three brigades, *Decision in the West*, p. 398 ("Nowhere did they get within a hundred yards of the Union line").

15 Castel, *Decision in the West*, p. 394 ("Blackberry Charge"); Report of Brig. Gen. Daniel C. Govan, July 30, 1864, *OR*, vol. 38, pt. 3, p. 738 (describing the attack, surrender, and redemption of the 2nd and 24th Arkansas Regiments); Symonds, *Stonewall of the West*, pp. 226–27; Kennett, *Marching Through Georgia*, p. 193 ("I'll be damned if I know").

16 Report of Brig. Gen. James A. Smith, Aug. 5, 1864, *OR*, vol. 38, pt. 3, p. 747; Foster, *One of Cleburne's Command*, p. 111. Adding to the challenge of understanding the Battle of Atlanta for students down the years was the presence on the field and the active participation of no fewer than four generals (some blue, some gray) named Smith: Morgan L. Smith (Federal XV Corps), Giles A. Smith (Federal XVII Corps), James A. Smith (Confederate Texas Brigade), and G. W. Smith (Georgia militia).

17 Sherman, *Memoirs*, p. 449 ("in his prime"; "very handsome man"); *Richmond Daily Dispatch*, June 15, 1864 ("If some enterprising Confederate sharpshooter had shot a bullet through McPherson's head, and knocked out Sherman's brains"); Bruce Catton, *This Hallowed Ground*, p. 344 (McPherson's serenades at Vicksburg); Hirshon, *Grenville M. Dodge*, p. 96 (noting McPherson's smile and thoughtfulness). Slights of Hood's intelligence are generally overstated, but the comparison between his West Point record and McPherson's in various subjects is striking. McPherson ranked first in engineering, first in artillery, second in infantry, and third in ethics; while Hood's rankings were 45th in engineering, 45th in artillery, 47th in infantry, and 52nd in ethics. United States Military Academy Class Standings, Class of 1853, USMA Archives, quoted in Connolly, *John M. Schofield*, p. 348 n. 34.

18 Lewis, *Sherman: Fighting Prophet*, p. 346 ("Mac, it wrings my heart").

19 Strong, "Death of General McPherson," *MOLLUS—Illinois*, vol. 1, p. 323. Sherman would recall McPherson's departure differently. He would remember conferring with his young lieutenant in the yard of the Hurt/Howard House when they heard a "brisk" clatter of musketry somewhere in the trees to the southeast, along with the boom of "an occasional gun back toward Decatur." Sherman consulted his compass and concluded that the sound of battle "was too far to our left rear to be explained by known facts." McPherson immediately called for his horse and rode away to investigate. *Memoirs*, pp. 448–49.

20 The 3rd Confederate Regiment was so named because it was raised by the Confederate government rather than from a particular state, sometimes in an effort to consolidate depleted regiments into a full complement. The regiment was organized in early 1862 by redesignating the 18th Arkansas Infantry and thus contained mostly Arkansans—eight companies from Arkansas and two from Mississippi.

21 "Gen. M'Pherson's Death—The Detailed Story Told by His Orderly," *New York Times*, Aug. 15, 1881; Richard Beard, "An Incident of the Battle of Atlanta, July 26 [*sic*], 1864," in *Battles and Sketches of the Army of Tennessee*, Bromfield L. Ridley, ed. (Mexico: Missouri Printing & Publishing Co., 1906), pp. 324–27. Although the most widely accepted account holds that McPherson was alone with his orderly when he was shot, others claim to have witnessed the scene or to have come upon McPherson, still alive, sometime afterward. These include Colonel R. K. Scott, who was lightly wounded and claimed he came upon McPherson; Lt. William Sherfy, the signal corps officer; and George J. Reynolds, an Iowa private who was later awarded a medal for tending to General McPherson until he died. These accounts are collected in Strong's "The Death of General McPherson." Both the orderly Thompson and Sherman himself asserted that Reynolds was not and could not have been there when McPherson died. See W. T. Sherman, *Some Facts Relating to Maj. Gen. James B. McPherson and Events Attending His Death* (Washington, D.C.: n.p., 1878), pp. 8–9. There is some confusion as to who was actually present at the moment McPherson died, and who (Scott or Thompson) said to Beard, "You have killed the best man in our army." See, e.g., Thomson, quoted in "Gen. M'Pherson's Death," ("Owing to the fact that I was rather confused by the blow I received on the head, I cannot remember whether Capt. Beard asked me this or not. If he did, I must have made him the answer nearly as he gives it"). Steven Woodworth does an admirable job of attempting to reconcile the various eyewitness accounts in his *Nothing but Victory*, pp. 550–52.

On the Confederate side, the conflicting accounts would lead to a somewhat unseemly argument as to who should get the credit for shooting a fleeing officer in the back. Capt. Beard wrote that the shot was fired by Corporal Robert F. Coleman, though another account gives the honor to Private Robert D. Compton of the 24th Texas Cavalry. For a discussion of the issue, see editor Norman Brown's comments in Foster, *One of Cleburne's Command*, p. 112 n. 49 (noting that "since a volley was fired, several men may each have thought it was his bullet that struck the general").

22 Sherman, *Memoirs*, p. 449 ("the firing was too far to our left rear to be explained by known facts"); Castel, *Decision in the West*, p. 400 ("McPherson dead! Can it be?").

23 Strong, "Death of General McPherson," *MOLLUS—Illinois*, vol. 1, p. 334 (surgeon's examination); Sherman, *Memoirs*, vol. 2, p. 542 ("still and beautiful in death"); Evans, *Sherman's Horsemen*, p. 95 (describing transportation of McPherson's body; "Better start at once"); Schofield, *Forty-six Years*, p. 146.

24 Rowland Cox, "Snake Creek Gap, and Atlanta," in *Personal Recollections of the War of the Rebellion*, A. Noel Blakeman, ed. (New York: G. P. Putnam's Sons, 1897), p. 25 ("Fight 'em!").

25 Evans, *Sherman's Horsemen*, p. 95.

26 Myron B. Loop, "Sounding the Alarm: The 68th Ohio's Trying Time at the Battle of Atlanta," *National Tribune*, Dec. 1, 1898, quoted in *Echoes of Battle*, p. 243 ("I don't care which side"). For a similar story involving a Wisconsin colonel, see Woodworth, *Nothing but Victory*, pp. 555–56. Hardee to S. Cooper, April 5, 1865, *OR*, vol. 38, pt. 3, p. 699 ("one of the most desperate and bloody"); Henry O. Dwight, "How We Fight at Atlanta," *Harper's New Monthly Magazine*. 29 (Oct. 1864), p. 666.

27 Tuthill, "Artilleryman's Recollections," *MOLLUS—Illinois*, vol. 1, pp. 305–6; cf. Laurence Sterne, *The Life and Opinions of Tristam Shandy, Gentleman* (London: George Routledge & Sons, 3d ed. 1887), p. 210 ("dropped a tear upon the word, and blotted it out forever").

28 Smith's Report, Aug. 5, 1864, *OR*, vol. 38, pt. 3, p. 747 ("much worn and exhausted").

29 Capt. Alfred Fielder Diary, Tennessee State Library and Archives, quoted in Castel, *Decision in the West*, p. 404 ("we mowed them down with awful havoc").

30 Watkins, *Co. Aytch*, p. 202.

31 Tuthill, "An Artilleryman's Recollections," p. 305; Dwight, "How We Fight at Atlanta," *Harper's Magazine*, p. 665; Henry O. Dwight, "The Battle of July 22, 1864," *New York Times*, Aug. 12, 1864 ("toy-monkeys"). A number of witnesses would comment on the extraordinary degree of chaos and confusion at the Battle of Atlanta. "The narrative of the 22d of July will never be written, and even the most authentic accounts we have are not likely to be credited." Cox, "Snake Creek Gap, and Atlanta," p. 24.

32 W. E. Mathews Preston, "The 33rd Alabama Regiment in the Civil War," L. B. Williams, ed. (typescript), Alabama Department of Archives and History, p. 36; for a similar story, see also Munson, "Battle of Atlanta," p. 222 (noting "one poor fellow, with a bullet sticking square in his forehead, dazed and lost"); Edmund E. Nutt, "The 20th Ohio at Atlanta," *Ohio Soldier* 7, no. 21, July 28, 1894, quoted in *Echoes of Battle*, p. 239 (Bob and Matt Elliott); see also D. W. Wood, ed., *History of the 20th OVVI Regiment* (Columbus: Paul & Thrall, 1876).

33 Adams, "Battle and Capture of Atlanta," *MOLLUS—Minnesota*, p. 154; cf. Job 38:11 (KJV) ("And I said, 'Hitherto shalt thou come, but no further; and here shall your proud waves be stayed'").

34 Gay, *Life in Dixie*, p. 137, Adams, "Battle and Capture of Atlanta," *MOLLUS—Minnesota*, p. 149 ("That's Wheeler after our hard tack").

35 John P. Dyer, *From Shiloh to San Juan: The Life of "Fighting Joe" Wheeler*, rev. ed.

(Baton Rouge: Louisiana State University Press, 1992), pp. 4–5, 13 (descriptions of Wheeler).

36 Ibid. Interestingly, after the war, Wheeler would return to the U.S. Army, serving in both the Spanish-American and Philippine-American wars, and would become the only man to attain the rank of general and serve as a corps commander in both the Confederate and the United States Armies. This return to the U.S. Army would prompt an acidic comment in 1898 from a former Rebel colleague: "Wheeler, I hope I die and go to hell before you do because I want to see Beauregard rake you over the coals for having on that damned Yankee uniform." Ibid., 4.

37 Report of Maj. Gen. Joseph Wheeler, Oct. 9, 1864, *OR*, vol. 38, pt. 3, pp. 952–53.

38 Gay, *Life in Dixie*, pp. 139–40.

39 Ibid. For a detailed account of the Battle of Decatur, see Evans, *Sherman's Horsemen*, pp. 91–94.

40 Report of Maj. Gen. Joseph Wheeler, Oct. 9, 1864, *OR*, vol. 38, pt. 3, pp. 952–53.

41 Reed, *History of Atlanta*, p. 180.

42 Clayton, *Requiem for a Lost City*, pp. 125–26; Reed, *History of Atlanta*, p. 192 ("a bad time for funerals").

43 Hood, *Advance and Retreat*, p. 180.

44 The Troup Hurt house and the unidentified "white house" nearby are discussed in detail in Wilbur G. Kurtz, "At the Troup Hurt House," *Atlanta Constitution*, Jan. 25, 1931. The white house is sometimes referred to as the Pope House, though this may be a misnomer—a historical marker on the site even seems to hedge a bit, stating that the house was "said to have been the residence of the Widow Pope." For a discussion of the rejected proposal to tear down these houses and barricade the railroad cut, see Woodworth, *Nothing but Victory*, pp. 541–42, and Castel, *Decision in the West*, p. 406; see also Castel, ed., *Tom Taylor's Civil War*, p. 147 ("open and unoccupied by works or troops").

45 Castel, ed., *Tom Taylor's Civil War*, p. 146.

46 Arthur Middleton Manigault, *A Carolinian Goes to War: The Civil War Narrative of Arthur Middleton Manigault, Brigadier General, C.S.A.*, R. Lockwood Tower, ed. (Columbia: University of South Carolina Press, 1983), p. 227.

47 Castel, *Decision in the West*, p. 406 ("suddenly and spectacularly, the course of the fighting changes"); William Bakhaus, "The Battle of Atlanta," *Ohio Soldier* 2, no. 29 (April 27, 1889), quoted in *Echoes of Battle*, p. 249 ("such 'gitting' you never saw before"); Wiley, "A Story of Three Southern Officers," *Civil War Times Illustrated* 3, no. 1 (April 1964), p. 33 ("Are you going to kill all of us?").

48 Report of Brig. Gen. Joseph A. J. Lightburn, July 23, 1864, *OR*, vol. 38, pt. 3, p. 180.

49 Robert M. Gill to wife Bettie, July 23, 1864, in Wiley, "Three Southern Officers," p. 33; Charles D. Miller, *The Struggle for the Life of the Republic: A Civil War Narrative by Brevet Major Charles Dana Miller, 76th Ohio Infantry*, Stewart Bennett and Barbara

Tillery, eds. (Kent, Ohio: Kent State University Press, 2004), p. 186 ("a great stream of grey").

50 Woodworth, *Nothing but Victory*, p. 565.

51 Sherman, *Memoirs*, p. 453 ("the Army of the Tennessee would be jealous"), Howard, *Autobiography*, vol. II, p. 14 ("Let the Army of the Tennessee fight it out"); Schofield, *Forty-six Years*, p. 148 (stating that "I cannot but believe, as I then thought, that we were losing a great opportunity that day"). Civil War historians are prone to criticize Sherman for, as he put it, "purposely allow[ing] the Army of the Tennessee to fight this battle almost unaided." See, e.g., Castel, *Decision in the West*, p. 414 (calling Sherman's statement about jealousy "sheer nonsense," and suggesting that instead of just a defensive victory for the Federals, the battle could have been "a decisive triumph, producing the fall of Atlanta and the virtual destruction of Hood's army"); Alfred Higgins Burne, *Lee, Grant and Sherman: A Study in Leadership in the 1864–65 Campaign* (New York: Charles Scribner's Sons, 1939), p. 108 (criticizing Sherman's "extraordinary failure to utilise five-eighths of his army").

52 Howard, *Autobiography*, vol. 2, p. 13 ("I had never till then seen Sherman with such a look on his face"); Manigault, *A Carolinian Goes to War*, p. 228 ("The artillery practice of the enemy was splendid"); Schofield, *Forty-six Years*, p. 147.

53 Lucien B. Crooker, et al., *The Story of the Fifty-fifth Regiment Illinois Volunteer Infantry in the Civil War, 1861–1865* (Clinton, Mass.: W. J. Coulter, 1887), p. 341 ("human hurricane"); George Francis Dawson, *Life and Services of John A. Logan as Soldier and Statesman* (Chicago: Belford, Clarke & Co., 1887), p. 69; see generally Gary Ecelbarger, *Black Jack Logan* (Guilford, Conn.: Lyons Press, 2005), p. 179.

54 Manigault, *A Carolinian Goes to War*, p. 229; Miller, *Struggle for the Life of the Republic*, p. 188. Sherman specifically wrote of the loss and recapture of DeGress's battery in his memoirs. "Poor Captain de Gress came to me in tears, lamenting the loss of his favorite guns; when they were regained he had only a few men left, and not a single horse." Sherman, *Memoirs*, p. 453.

55 Report of Maj. Gen. Frank P. Blair, Jr., July 22, 1864, 4:30 P.M., *OR*, vol. 38, pt. 3, pp. 542, 547. Blair reported the ground in his front "literally strewn with the enemy's dead, but as the enemy held the ground up to our lines until nearly daylight the next morning, he was able to remove all of his wounded and the dead bodies of many officers." He also noted: "I believe that the killed exceeded the usual proportion of wounded on such occasions, not only on account of the closeness and desperate character of the fighting, but as the enemy charged repeatedly over the same ground upon which they had left their wounded it is altogether probable that many of them were slain by the tremendous fire which swept the ground on which they lay after being wounded." Ibid., 547–48.

56 Tuthill, "An Artilleryman's Recollections," p. 309.

57 Sherman, *Memoirs*, vol. 2, p. 82 ("marks of a bloody conflict"); Report of Lt. George Echte, Sept. 6, 1864, *OR*, vol. 38, pt. 3, p. 262 ("55 horses"); Report of Capt. Francis DeGress, Sept. 1, 1864, *OR*, vol. 38, pt. 3, p. 265 ("My losses on that day were very heavy—14 men, 39 horses, 1 limber, ambulance, and harness").

58 A. W. Reese, "Personal Recollections of the Late Civil War in the United States," photocopy of manuscript, Western Historical Manuscript Collection, University of Missouri–Columbia, pp. 531, 532–35, quoted in Dyer, *Secret Yankees*, pp. 182–83.

59 Dwight, "How We Fight at Atlanta," *Harper's Magazine*, p. 665. Dwight's sketch, now in the collection of the Ohio Historical Society, is reproduced in Castel, *Decision in the West*, p. 415.

60 Foster, *One of Cleburne's Command*, p. 115 (diary entry for July 23, 1864); Yeary, *Reminiscences of the Boys in Gray*, p. 809.

61 Report of Maj. Gen. John A. Logan, July 10 and Sept. 10, 1864, *OR*, vol. 38, pt. 3, pp. 21, 28 (casualty reports); Report of Maj. Gen. W. T. Sherman, Sept. 15, 1864, *OR*, vol. 38, pt. 1, p. 75 ("I entertain no doubt that in the battle of July 22 the enemy sustained an aggregate loss of full 8,000 men"). Logan's losses were precisely tabulated as 430 killed, 1,559 wounded, and 1,733 missing. Ibid. The deans of Atlanta Campaign history—Stephen Davis, Albert Castel, and Richard McMurry—all agree that Confederate casualties were likely around 5,500. Davis, "Atlanta Campaign," *Blue and Gray*, p. 25 (placing Hood's losses at "well over 5,000—but not nearly as high as the 8,000 Rebel casualties estimated by General Sherman"); Castel, *Decision in the West*, p. 412 (5,500); McMurry, *Atlanta 1864*, p. 165 (same).

62 Hood to Seddon, July 22, 1864, *OR*, vol. 38, pt. 5, p. 900.

63 Lurton Dunham Ingersoll, *Iowa and the Rebellion* (Philadelphia: J. B. Lippincott & Co., 1867), p. 261 ("warfare of giants"). This quote is often mistakenly attributed to Maj. Gen. Giles A. Smith. See, e.g., Buck, *Cleburne and His Command*, p. 244; Carter, *Siege of Atlanta*, p. 222.

64 Frank Blair to J. E. Austin, February 1875, quoted in *Advance and Retreat*, p. 190; Chamberlin, "Hood's Second Sortie at Atlanta," p. 326; Report of Lieut. Gen. John B. Hood, Feb. 15, 1865, *OR*, vol. 38, pt. 3, p. 631 ("the grand results desired were not accomplished").

65 Hood, *Advance and Retreat*, p. 173 ("endeavor to bring the entire Confederate Army into united action"); Sherman, *OR*, vol. 38, pt. 1, p. 73 ("fortunately . . . not simultaneous"); Stephenson, *Memoir*, pp. 220–21 ("infantry fight"; "Another fiasco"). For a discussion of the limited role played by the Rebel artillery, see Daniel, *Cannoneers in Gray*, pp. 170–71.

66 Hood, "The Defense of Atlanta," *Battles and Leaders*, vol. 4, p. 341; Buck, *Cleburne and His Command*, p. 229 ("an Iliad of woes"), John Hill Ferguson, *On to Atlanta: The Civil War Diaries of John Hill Ferguson, Illinois Tenth Regiment of Volunteers*, Janet Correll Ellison, ed. (Lincoln: University of Nebraska Press, 2001), p. 67 (diary entry for July 23).

67 Hedley, *Pen-Pictures*, p. 154.

68 Herman Melville, "A Dirge for McPherson," in *Battle-Pieces and Aspects of the War* (New York: Harper & Bros., 1866), pp. 46–47; Sherman to L. Thomas, July [23], 1864, in *Sherman's Civil War*, p. 671; Conyngham, *Sherman's March*, p. 170 ("Strong men, who unmoved saw their comrades fall around them, wept like children"); J. T. Headley, *The Life of Ulysses S. Grant* (New York: E. B. Treat & Co., 1868) ("I have lost my best

friend"); Hood, *Advance and Retreat*, p. 182; see also Grant, *Personal Memoirs*, p. 169 ("In his death the army lost one of its ablest, purest and best generals").

69 Sherman to Miss Emily Hoffman, Aug. 5, 1864, in *Sherman's Civil War*, pp. 682–83. Sherman added, "The lives of a thousand men such as Davis and Yancey and Toombs and Floyd, and Buckner, and Greeley, and Lovejoy would not atone for that of McPherson. But so it is in this world. Some men by falsehood and agitation raise the Storm which falls upon the honorable and young." Ibid.

70 Lewis, *Fighting Prophet*, p. 387; Walter Lord, "General Sherman and the Baltimore Belle," *American Heritage*, 9, no. 3 (April 1958).

Chapter 7. The Battle of the Poor House

1 *Richmond Enquirer*, July 25, 1864; *Savannah Republican*, July 26, 1864, quoted in Walker, *Hell's Broke Loose in Georgia*, p. 170; other Southern newspaper headlines quoted in Davis, *Atlanta Will Fall*, p. 147.

2 R. E. Lee to Jefferson Davis, July 23, 1864, *OR*, vol. 38, pt. 5, p. 903; Bragg to Davis, July 25, 1864, ibid., p. 908.

3 Hood, General Field Orders No. 7, July 25, 1864, *OR*, vol. 38, pt. 5, p. 909.

4 Stephenson, *Memoir*, p. 223 ("sick at heart").

5 Major Thos. C. Fitzgibbon to Emma Jane Kennon, Aug. 8, 1864, quoted in Kennett, *Marching Through Georgia*, p. 197.

6 Clark, *Under the Stars and Bars*, p. 136 (first roll call after a battle); Walker, *Hell's Broke Loose in Georgia*, p. 172 (noting Cleburne's losses). The dispersal of the brigades of Walker's Division probably made sense. Not only was Walker dead, but all three brigade commanders were gone, too—Rock Stevens died from his Peachtree Creek head wound on July 25, States Rights Gist was wounded, and Hugh Mercer's "age and physical inability unfit him for active service." Bragg to John B. Sale, July 24, 1864, *OR*, vol. 38, pt. 5, p. 907.

7 Geary, *A Politician Goes to War*, p. 193 ("quietness"); William C. Davis, *The Orphan Brigade: The Kentucky Confederates Who Couldn't Go Home* (New York: Doubleday, 1980), p. 230; Wiley, "A Story of Three Southern Officers," *Civil War Times Illustrated* (April 1964), p. 33.

8 Connolly to wife, July 23, 1864, in *Three Years*, pp. 238–40; A. J. Neal to Mother, July 23, 1864, Special Collections, Emory.

9 Dyer, *Secret Yankees*, pp. 184–85.

10 Richards Diary, July 23, 1864.

11 Sherman to Halleck, Aug. 16, 1864, *OR*, vol. 38, pt. 5, p. 522 ("a delicate and difficult task"); Hebert, *Fighting Joe Hooker*, p. 284 ("fightingest corps").

12 *Cincinnati Enquirer*, Dec. 31, 1886, quoted in Dawson, *Life and Services*, p. 517 ("You cannot do better than put Howard in command of that army. . . . He is tractable"). Sherman, tellingly, referred to his nonprofessional generals like Logan, Frank Blair, and Dodge as "civilians." Ibid.

13 John L. Collins, "When Stonewall Jackson Turned Our Right," in *Battles and*

Leaders, vol. 3, p. 184.

14 Howard to Thomas, May 27, 1864, *OR*, vol. 38, pt. 4, p. 324 ("I . . . am now turning the enemy's right flank, *I think*") (emphasis added); see also Ambrose Bierce, "The Crime at Pickett's Mill." For more on Howard, see his *Autobiography of Oliver Otis Howard*, and John A. Carpenter, *Sword and Olive Branch: Oliver Otis Howard* (New York: Fordham University Press, 1999). Historians, too, disagree starkly on O. O. Howard. Compare Stephen W. Sears, *Chancellorsville* (New York: Houghton Mifflin, 1996), p. 263 (calling Howard "unimaginitive, unenterprising, uninspiring . . . the wrong general in the wrong place with the wrong troops"); and Woodworth, *Nothing but Victory*, p. 570 (asserting that at Chancellorsville and Gettysburg, "his superiors' misjudgments and the tides of battle had handed him impossible situations, leading to disasters that Howard could do little to prevent"). See also Margaret S. Creighton, *The Colors of Courage: Gettysburg's Forgotten History* (New York: Basic Books, 2006), p. 178 ("Opinion on Oliver Otis Howard was always divided between those who viewed him as a decent, competent, God-honoring general and those who dismissed him as 'Uh Oh Howard,' a man who commanded two of the most famous routs in the Civil War").

15 *OR*, vol. 38, pt. 5, p. 273 (Hooker's request to be relieved); Sherman to Ellen Sherman, July 29 and Aug. 2, 1864 ("envious"); Hebert, *Fighting Joe Hooker*, p. 287 ("his sun had set"). After leaving the Army of the Cumberland, Hooker publicly criticized Sherman and predicted that he would fail. Ibid.; see also *OR*, vol. 38, pt. 5, p. 857 and vol. 45, pt. 2, p. 111 (asserting that "Sherman is crazy; he has no more judgment than a child"); Gamaliel Bradford, "Joseph Hooker," *Atlantic Monthly*, July 1914, p. 30.

A couple of early sources suggest that Lincoln directed Sherman to appoint Hooker but that Sherman held fast, going so far as to offer his resignation should Lincoln insist. There is no correspondence to support this story (which was possibly circulated by Hooker's supporters); and in fact, it seems unlikely. Lincoln didn't much care for Hooker either. See Hebert, *Fighting Joe Hooker*, p. 285; Shanks, *Personal Recollections*, pp. 186–87.

Although they were often of one mind, in this case, General U. S. Grant disagreed with Sherman's decision to bypass John Logan. Grant, *Memoirs*, vol. 2, pp. 353–54 (noting that Sherman had made his appointment "for the good of the service," but adding: "I doubt whether [Sherman] had an officer with him who could have filled that place as Logan would have done"). Sherman did attempt to soothe Logan by sending to him a personal note expressing his appreciation for "the responsibility that devolved on you so unexpectedly and the noble manner in which you met it." Sherman to Logan, July 27, 1864, quoted in John A. Logan, *The Volunteer Soldier in America* (Chicago: R. S. Peale, 1887), p. 58.

16 See Leslie Anders, "Fisticuffs at Headquarters: Sweeny vs. Dodge," *Civil War Times Illustrated*, 15, no. 10 (Feb. 1977), pp. 8–9, 25; see also Jack Morgan, *Through American and Irish Wars: The Life and Times of Thomas W. Sweeny, 1820–1892* (Dublin: Irish Academic Press, 2005), p. 103. Interestingly, Sherman himself came to Sweeny's defense: "I beg you to see that no injustice is done to General Sweeny," he wrote to Logan. See Sherman to Logan, July 25, 1864, *OR*, vol. 38, pt. 5, p. 252.

17 Conyngham, *Sherman's March*, p. 201 ("great game of chess").

18 Sherman to Halleck, July 24 and 26, 1864, *OR*, vol. 38, pt. 5, pp. 240, 260; Howard, General Field Orders No. 5, July 27, 1864, ibid., p. 277.

19 Harold Adams Small, ed., *The Road to Richmond: The Civil War Letters of Major Abner R. Small of the 16th Maine Volunteers* (New York: Fordham University Press, 2000), p. 9 ("profusion of flowing moustache"; "Ten Commandments"); Widney, *Campaigning with Uncle Billy*, p. 270 ("The promotion of General Howard suits the rank and file . . . 'Thank God for one Christian soldier'").

20 "Gen. Sherman's Army–Conflagration in Atlanta—Full Details of the Battle of July 28" (*Cincinnati Gazette* report), reprinted in *New York Times*, Aug. 7, 1864; Miller, *Struggle for the Life of the Republic*, p. 190 ("Look!"; "We could see forty thousand men").

21 Castel, *Decision in the West*, p. 424; Evans, *Sherman's Horsemen*, p. 207 ("I don't think Hood will trouble you"); Howard, *Autobiography*, vol. II, pp. 17–18 ("meager headquarters" . . . "Sherman said he did not think that Hood would trouble me").

22 See generally Herman Hattaway, *General Stephen D. Lee* (1976; reprint, Oxford: University Press of Mississippi, 1989); Braxton Bragg to John D. Sale, July 26, 1864, *OR*, vol. 38, pt. 5, p. 911 ("Lieutenant-General Lee arrived and goes on duty today. He is most favorably received"). Lee's biographer suggests a distant connection between the Lees of Virginia and the Lees of South Carolina, but Stephen D. Lee himself always told inquirers that he was not related to Robert E. Lee, but that he would "consider it quite an honor to be." Hattaway, *General Stephen D. Lee*, p. 3.

23 L. S. Ross to Jackson, July 26, 1864, 10:45 A.M., *OR*, vol. 38, pt. 5, p. 911; Jno. S. Smith to Wheeler, July 27, 1864, 4:15 A.M., ibid., p. 913. For a good explanation of the orders leading up to the Battle of Ezra Church, see Davis, *Atlanta Will Fall*, pp. 150–51. See also Horn, *Army of Tennessee*, p. 360 (Hood "still dreaming of Stonewall Jackson").

24 Cox, *Atlanta*, p. 182 ("cacophonous name of Lickskillet"); see generally Henry M. Hope, *The Poor Houses* (Xulon Press, 2008), p. 43ff. The village of Lick Skillet changed its name to Adamsville in 1861, and is now a community in southwest Atlanta. Lickskillet Road is today known as Martin Luther King, Jr. Drive. See also Howard, "The Struggle for Atlanta," *Battles and Leaders*, vol. 4, p. 319 ("indomitable").

25 Hood to Hardee, July 28, 1864, *OR*, vol. 38, pt. 5, p. 919 ("General Lee is directed to prevent the enemy from gaining the Lick Skillet road, and not to attack unless the enemy exposes himself in attacking us"); Hood to Lee, ibid. ("General Hood directs that you hold the enemy in check."); Report of Brig. Gen. John C. Brown, ibid., p. 767 ("attack and drive the enemy to Ezra Church"); O. O. Howard, "The Struggle for Atlanta," *Battles and Leaders*, vol. 4, p. 319.

26 Howard, *Autobiography*, vol. 2, p. 22.

27 Connolly, *Three Years*, p. 248.

28 Report of Brig. Gen. John C. Brown, July 31, 1864, *OR*, vol. 38, pt. 3, p. 768; Manigault, *A Carolinian Goes to War*, p. 234.

29 Report of Brig. Gen. H. D. Clayton, Sept. 16, 1864, *OR*, vol. 38, pt. 3, p. 821 ("driven back with great loss" and "in strong works"); Crooker, *Fifty-Fifth Regiment*, pp.

346–47; Thomas M. Coleman to Sister, July 29, 1864, Thomas M. Coleman Papers, AHC MSS 655f; *Frank Leslie's Illustrated Weekly*, quoted in Hoehling, *Last Train From Atlanta*, p. 182.

30 Report of Lt. Gen. Stephen D. Lee, Jan. 30, 1865, *OR*, vol. 38, pt. 3, p. 763; Manigault, *A Carolinian Goes to War*, p. 235; Report of Maj. Gen. Edward C. Walthall, Jan. 14, 1865, *OR*, vol. 38, pt. 3, p. 927 (reporting loss of 152 officers and 1,000 men).

31 Charles E. Smith, *The Civil War Diaries of Corporal Charles E. Smith* (Delaware, Ohio: Delaware County Historical Society, 1999), p. 422 ("murderous volley"); William Worth Belknap, *History of the Fifteenth Regiment, Iowa Veteran Volunteer Infantry* (Keokuk: R. B. Ogden & Son, 1887), p. 380. Another Federal marksman also shot at Walthall, "singling him out," taking "deliberate aim" and firing "until I got disgusted"—but "it was no go; like Banquo's ghost he would not go down." Private Edwin W. Smith, "Battle of Ezra Church: A Coffee-Cooler's Experience," *National Tribune*, July 5, 1888, quoted in *Echoes of Battle*, p. 262.

32 Allen L. Fahnestock, *Diary of Colonel Allen L. Fahnestock, 86th Regiment, Illinois Infantry Volunteers* (typescript), KMNBP, p. 50 ("They done the charging and our men the shooting"); Albert B. Crummel, "Ezra Chapel," *National Tribune*, April 26, 1888.

33 Joseph Grecian, *History of the Eighty-Third Regiment, Indiana Volunteer Infantry* (Cincinnati, 1865), p. 55 ("terrific affair"); Dale Greenwell, *The Third Mississippi Regiment, C.S.A.* (Pascagoula, Miss.: Lewis Print. Services, 1972), p. 95 ("sittin' ducks"). The exact nature of Major General W. W. Loring's wound is uncertain. Some sources report him as "severely wounded," though Hood described him as "slightly wounded." He returned to duty September 10. See Hood, *Advance and Retreat*, p. 194; Jack D. Welsh, *Medical Histories of Confederate Generals* (Kent, Ohio: Kent State University Press, 1999), p. 144.

34 Walthall's Report, *OR*, vol. 38, pt. 3, p. 927.

35 *OR*, vol. 38, pt. 3, p. 699.

36 Hood to James A. Seddon, July 28, 1864, *OR*, vol. 38, pt. 5, p. 917; Davis, *Atlanta Will Fall*, p. 154 ("shameful insensitivity to the truth"); Patrick, *Reluctant Rebel*, p. 202 ("perfect slaughter"). Hood would maintain the fiction of a "draw" at Ezra Church in his writings after the war. See Hood, "The Defense of Atlanta," in *Battles and Leaders*, vol. 4, p. 341 ("The contest lasted till near sunset without any material advantage having been gained by either opponent"). For various pronounced judgments on Ezra Church, see Davis, *Atlanta Will Fall*, p. 152 ("S. D. Lee's botched attack"); Symonds, *Stonewall of the West*, p. 232 ("a series of fruitless frontal assaults"); Woodworth, *Nothing but Victory*, p. 576 ("an easy victory though a hard fight").

37 Herman Melville, *Battle-Pieces and Aspects of the War*, p. 91, n. 13; Stephenson, *Memoir*, p. 225 ("It occurred on the 28th and was always known to us as the Battle of the 28th").

38 Hardee, *OR*, vol. 38, pt. 3, p. 699 ("So great was the loss in men"); John W. Lavender, *They Never Came Back: The War Memoirs of Captain John W. Lavender, C.S.A.* (Pine Bluff, Ark.: Southern Press, 1956), quoted in *Echoes of Battle*, p. 264.

39 *Cincinnati Commercial*, Aug. 5, 1864, quoted in Andrews, *The North Reports the Civil War*, p. 565; Pepper, *Personal Recollections*, p. 132.

40 W. P. Archer, "History of the Siege and Battles of Atlanta," n.p., n.d., p. 16.

41 Lyman S. Widney, *Campaigning with Uncle Billy: The Civil War Memoirs of Sgt. Lyman S. Widney, 34th Illinois Volunteer Infantry*. Robert I. Girardi, ed. (Bloomington, Ind.: Trafford Publishing, 2008), p. 271 ("This pays for Kennesaw"); Howard to Mrs. Howard, July 29, 1864, quoted in Carpenter, *Sword and Olive Branch*, p. 71.

42 Connolly, *Three Years*, p. 247. The apocryphal tale of the exchange between blue and gray pickets after Ezra Church is memorialized in countless sources, and its sporadic appearance in contemporaneous accounts suggests that it was another "campfire story" that made the rounds in the Federal bivouacs at the time. The exact wording of the Yankee question and the Rebel answer varies slightly, depending on the source. See, e.g., Jacob D. Cox, *Atlanta* (New York: Charles Scribner's Sons, 1882), p. 186 ("Well, Johnny"); Foote, *The Civil War*, vol. 3, p. 490 (same); B. F. McGee, *History of the 72d Indiana Volunteer Infantry of the Mounted Lightning Brigade* (Lafayette, Ind.: S. Vater & Co., 1882), p. 360 ("Well, about enough for two more killings if you don't make them too large"); see also Horn, *Army of Tennessee*, p. 362 (calling the anecdote an "old army story").

43 Stoneman to Sherman and Sherman to Stoneman, July 26, 1864, *OR*, vol. 38, pt. 5, pp. 264–65; see also Sherman to Halleck, ibid., p. 260 ("This is probably more than [Stoneman] can accomplish, but it is worthy of a determined effort").

44 Granville C. West, "McCook's Raid in the Rear of Atlanta and Hood's Army," in Kerksis, ed., *The Atlanta Papers*, p. 550; McGee, *History of the 72d Indiana*, p. 356 ("Bub, where does this road go?"); Evans, *Sherman's Horsemen*, p. 210 ("like schoolboys in a game of baseball").

45 Evans, *Sherman's Horsemen*, pp. 242 (Wheeler in 600 battles and skirmishes), 213 ("Tell your general"). Detailed tactical accounts of the various cavalry battles from July 27 to August 4 are beyond the scope of this narrative. By far the best account is David Evans's excellent *Sherman's Horsemen*, pp. 195–354, wherein the (mis)adventures and various fates of Garrard's, Stoneman's, and McCook's columns are recounted in detail. See also William R. Scaife, *The Campaign for Atlanta* (Saline, Mich.: McNaughton & Gunn, 1993), pp. 99–107. Scaife's two maps comparing the three-pronged cavalry raid as Sherman conceived it and the raid as it actually took place are particularly telling. Ibid., maps following p. 108.

46 *Augusta Chronicle and Sentinel*, Aug. 4, 1864, and *Macon Telegraph*, Aug. 4, 1864, both quoted in Anne J. Bailey, *War and Ruin: William T. Sherman and the Savannah Campaign* (Wilmington, Del.: SR Books, 2002), p. 71; Foote, *The Civil War*, vol. III, p. 488; Sherman to Halleck, Sept. 15, 1864, *OR*, vol. 38, pt. 1, p. 77 ("on the whole"). Albert Castel notes that in the aftermath of the failed raid, Sherman "did something he rarely ever did, to wit, admit that he had committed a military error in sanctioning any attempt at all by Stoneman to liberate the prisoners." Castel, "Quest of Glory: George Stoneman's Attempt to Free the Andersonville Prisoners," in *Articles of War: Winners,*

Losers, and Some Who Were Both During the Civil War (Mechanicsburg, Pa.: Stackpole Books, 2001), p. 124; see also Sherman to Thos. Ewing, Aug. 11, 1864, in *Sherman's Civil War*, p. 190 ("I have made no professional mistakes but one, in consening that Stoneman should make the premature attempt to reach our prisoners of war. . . . Stoneman begged for it & I consented, my judgment being warped by our Feelings for 20,000 poor men penned up like cattle"). Castel calls Stoneman's Raid the "greatest cavalry fiasco of the Civil War." Castel, "Stoneman's Raid," in David S. and Jeanne T. Heidler, eds., *Encyclopedia of the American Civil War: A Political, Social and Military History* (New York: W. W. Norton, 2000), p. 1872.

47 Palmer to Sherman, *OR*, vol. 38, pt. 5, p. 355 ("I am General Schofield's senior"); Palmer to Schofield, ibid. ("I will not obey either General Sherman's order or yours"); Sherman to Palmer, Aug. 4, 1864, 10:45 p.m., ibid. p. 356 (Schofield "ranks you"). For the multitude of dispatches regarding the Palmer-Schofield controversy over rank, see ibid., pp. 354–64. See also J. C. Van Duzer to Thomas Eckert, Aug. 4, 1864, 11 p.m., ibid., p. 364.

48 Sherman to Thomas, Aug. 5, 1864, ibid., p. 371; Bentley, William Garrigues Bentley, *"Burning Rails as We Pleased": The Civil War Letters of William Garrigues Bentley, 104th Ohio Volunteer Infantry* (Jefferson, N.C.: McFarland & Co., 2004), p. 107 ("Our brave old General cried like a child when he was refused reinforcements, with which there seems to be no doubt but we could have taken the works in the evening"); see generally Albert Castel, "Union Fizzle at Atlanta: The Battle of Utoy Creek," *Civil War Times Illustrated* 16, no. 10 (Feb. 1978), pp. 26–31.

49 Sherman to Halleck, Aug. 7, 1864, ibid., p. 408.

CHAPTER 8. "A USED-UP COMMUNITY"

1 Sherman to Halleck, July 21, 1864, *OR*, vol. 38, pt. 5, p. 211; Report of Francis DeGress, ibid., pt. 3, p. 265 ("three shells into Atlanta"); Thomas to Sherman, July 21, 1864, ibid., pt. 5, p. 213 ("Prisoners say that our shells yesterday fell into Atlanta, producing great consternation"); see also Garrett, *Atlanta and Environs*, p. 626 (noting "light shelling" from July 20 to August 9; "hell on earth").

2 P. G. T. Beauregard to Q. A. Gillmore, Aug. 22, 1863, *OR*, vol. 28, pt. 2, p. 59; Foote, *The Civil War*, vol. II, p. 28; James Longstreet, "The Battle of Fredericksburg," *Battles and Leaders*, vol. 3, p. 75. Historian Mark Grimsley asserts that the shelling of Fredericksburg "fully accorded with the laws and usages of war: The Federals informed the Confederates of their intentions well ahead of time, and gave ample opportunity for the town's residents to find safety elsewhere. Moreover, it had a distinct military purpose, for it sought to neutralize Confederate sharpshooters." Mark Grimsley, *The Hard Hand of War: Union Military Policy Toward Southern Civilians, 1861–65* (Cambridge: Cambridge University Press, 1995), p. 108. Sherman gave no such warning or opportunity to the residents of Atlanta before opening fire—nor was there any allegation that sharpshooters were taking refuge in downtown Atlanta's homes and buildings. Grimsley does not address the bombardment of Atlanta in his study of Union "hard war" policy.

3 Henry C. Lay, "Sherman in Georgia," *Atlantic Monthly*, 149, no. 2 (Feb. 1932), pp.

166–72. An excellent, incisive analysis of the bombardment of Atlanta is found in two articles by Stephen Davis: "A Very Barbarous Mode of Carrying on War: Sherman's Artillery Bombardment of Atlanta, July 20–August 24, 1864," *Georgia Historical Quarterly* 79 (1995), pp. 57–90; and "How Many Civilians Died in Sherman's Bombardment of Atlanta?" *Atlanta History* 45, no. 4 (2003), pp. 4–23. Davis notes four major bombardments of towns or cities in the Civil War: Charleston, Fredericksburg, Petersburg,, and Atlanta. (For what it is worth, all four involve shelling by Federal troops of Southern civilians.)

For Sherman's assertions that civilians had left Atlanta, *see* Sherman to Ellen, Aug. 2, 1864, *SCW*, p. 681 ("Most of the People are gone"); Sherman to Thomas, Aug. 10, 1864, *OR*, vol. 38, pt. 5, p. 448 ("The inhabitants have, of course, got out"). But see "From Sherman," *New York Times*, Aug. 15, 1864 (reporting many noncombatants remaining in Atlanta, "including ladies, but that most of them lived in cellars or large caves"); *Richmond*; Castel, *Decision in the West*, p. 489 (noting that Sherman "assuredly" knew that many civilians remained in Atlanta); Martin, *Atlanta and Its Builders*, p. 498 ("Sherman was well aware that the inhabitants had not got out"); Castel, *Decision in the West*, p. 464 (noting that at least 2,000 and perhaps as many as 5,000 citizens remained in the city).

Finally, the bombardment lasted either thirty-six or thirty-seven days, depending on whether August 25 is interpreted as the last day of the bombardment of the first day of quiet. Compare Davis, "A Very Barbarous Mode of Carrying on War," p. 57 ("thirty-six day bombardment") with Davis, "How Many Civilians Died," p. 5 ("thirty-seven day artillery bombardment").

4 Sherman's bombardment orders, Aug. 1864, *OR*, vol. 38, pt. 5, pp. 324, 412, 428, 429, 436, 452 (emphasis added). "There are many who do not believe that Sherman bombarded Atlanta in the sense of training his guns on the buildings of the city with the intention of reducing the city to ruins," an early Atlanta historian wrote. "It is needless to say that these skeptics were not in Atlanta at the time, and that most of them reside above Mason and Dixon's line." Thomas H. Martin, *Atlanta and Its Builders: A Comprehensive History of the Gate City of the South* (Atlanta: Century Memorial Publishing Co., 1902), vol. I, p. 491. Martin goes on to point out that "A remarkably large number of shells fell in all parts of Atlanta, to have been unintentionally fired there." Ibid.; see also Davis, "A Very Barbarous Mode of Carrying on War," p. 67 ("The Union commander evidenced no pangs of regret for the systematic shelling; in fact, he seemed to take a personal interest in the destruction of the city"). As Davis notes, the total number of guns that participated in the bombardment of Atlanta cannot be exactly determined, though it is reasonable to conclude that during some days in August, well over a hundred cannon—10- and 20-pounder Parrotts, 4 1/2-inch rifled cannon, and 3-inch ordnance rifles—were firing on Atlanta. Ibid., p. 69, n. 16; see also Davis, *Cannoneers in Gray*, p. 173 (noting that on August 16, the Federals counted 216 guns).

5 Kennett, *Marching Through Georgia*, p. 127 (shell at St. Luke's). See Castel, *Decision in the West*, p. 489 (stating that "Under the rules and practices of war, Atlanta (since it was the headquarters of an army, was a railroad and supply center, and was fortified and

garrisoned) was a legitimate target for bombardment"); see also Edward Caudill and Paul Ashdown, *Sherman's March in Myth and Memory* (Lanham, Md.: Rowman & Littlefield, 2008), pp. 21–22 (asserting, by way of excuse for Sherman: "Military targets were scattered about Atlanta, so the bombardment of the city inevitably and unintentionally found civilian targets"). For analysis under the laws of war, see David J. Barron and Martin S. Lederman, "The Commander in Chief at the Lowest Ebb: A Constitutional History," 121 *Harvard Law Review* 4 (Feb. 2008), pp. 995–96 n.199: ("Even to this day, heated debate continues as to whether at least one major Union initiative—Sherman's unannounced bombarding of Atlanta and (especially) his subsequent evacuation and burning of the city in the autumn of 1864—complied with the laws of war"); James G. Garner, "General Order No. 100 Revisited," *Military Law Review* 27 (1965), pp. 35–36 (noting that Sherman's shelling of the city without warning "cannot be reconciled with Article 19 of the Lieber Code"). For shell damage to the city, including specific homes that were struck by shells, see Reed, *History of Atlanta*, pp. 177–79; Martin, *Atlanta and Its Builders*, pp. 501–3.

6 Rice, *Yankee Tigers*, p. 135.

7 W. W. Hopkins to A. Williams, Aug. 24, 1864, *OR*, vol. 38, pt. 5, p. 651 ("I have the honor to report that at least three houses . . . were destroyed"); Thomas to Sherman, ibid., p. 448 ("burst beautifully"); ibid., pt. 1, p. 504 (reporting erection of temporary furnace and heating of "hot shot"). Thomas's comment that shells from the 4 1/2-inch guns "burst beautifully" has been misquoted or misparaphrased and then attributed to Sherman as a comment that the bombardment of Atlanta and the corpses of women and children were "a beautiful sight." Thomas DiLorenzo, *The Real Lincoln*, p. 186. There is no indication that Sherman ever said any such thing.

On the efforts of Atlanta volunteer firemen, see Garrett, *Atlanta and Environs*, p. 628; Reed, *History of Atlanta*, p. 192; Davis, "A Very Barbarous Mode of Carrying on War," p. 82; see also *Augusta Daily Constitutionalist*, Aug. 28, 1864 (noting that "The fire brigade works manfully under a raking cannonade" and "During these conflagrations the Yankee batteries played vigorously among the fire battalion").

8 Carrie Berry's original diary is at the Atlanta History Center, though portions have been published as a book for young readers, *A Confederate Girl: The Diary of Carrie Berry, 1864*, Christy Steele and Anne Todd, eds. (Mankato, Minn.: Blue Earth Books, 2000). Additional information, and a great deal of novel-like speculation, is found in A. A. Hoehling's *Last Train from Atlanta*.

9 Sherman to Thomas, August 8, 1864, *OR*, vol. 38, pt. 5, p. 431 ("Orders for to-morrow, August 9"); Reed, *History of Atlanta*, pp. 191–92 ("that red day in August"); Berry Diary, Aug. 9, 1864, AHC. Stephen Davis notes that the 4 1/2-inch siege guns arrived shortly thereafter, and during the course of the bombardment would fire a total of 4,256 33-pound shells into the city—nearly 75 tons. Davis, "A Very Barbarous Mode of Carrying on War," p. 68.

10 "From Atlanta: A Glimpse, Picturesque and Critical at the Situation and the City," *Augusta Daily Constitutionalist*, Aug. 10, 1864 ("The old burgh has fared roughly").

11 Noble C. Williams, *Echoes from the Battlefield; or, Southern Life During the War*

(Atlanta: Franklin Printing Co., 1902), p. 38 (describing bombproofs); Hood, *Advance and Retreat*, pp. 202–3.

12 Huff, *My 80 Years in Atlanta*, p. 25; Martin, *Atlanta and Its Builders*, p. 504 ("dignified and courageous men").

13 Jackman, *Diary of a Confederate Soldier*, p. 132 (Rebel artillery "not worth a damn"); Mosman, *Rough Side of War*, pp. 250–51.

14 Report of John Corse, *OR*, vol. 38, pt. 3, p. 411 ("There was no safety or security"); S. B. Crew to Brother & Sister, July 11, 1864, Collection of Mary Louise Dunn Fleming; John O. Holzheuter, ed., "William Wallace's Civil War Letters: The Atlanta Campaign," *Wisconsin Magazine of History* 57, no. 2 (Winter 1973–74), p. 103 ("Try it again, Johnny").

15 Victims of the bombardment are described in Garrett, *Atlanta and Environs*, and other sources. On J. F. Warner and his daughter, see Reed, *History of Atlanta*, p. 191; Davis, "How Many Civilians Died," pp. 15, 22 n. 34; Emily E. Molineaux, *Lifetime Recollections: An interesting Narrative of Life in the Southern States before and during the Civil War, with incidents of the bombardment of Atlanta by the Union forces, the author being then a resident of that City* (San Francisco: C. W. Gordon, 1902), pp. 33–34. As Davis notes, the newspapers carried gruesome descriptions of the deaths of Warner and his daughter. See "Death of Mr. Warner and Daughter," *Augusta Daily Constitutionalist*, Aug. 10, 1864; "Sherman's Murders," *Mobile Advertiser and Register*, Aug. 13, 1864. On Solomon Luckie, see Garrett, *Atlanta and Environs*, p. 628; see also Mary Davis, "Shell-Scarred Lamp Post Relic of Atlanta Civil War Days," *Atlanta Constitution*, Oct. 8, 1919. Atlanta's Luckie Street is not named for Solomon Luckie, but for Atlanta pioneer citizen Alexander F. Luckie (1798–1854).

16 *Mobile Advertiser and Register*, Sept. 3, 1864; Richards Diary, Aug. 21, 1864; Davis, "How Many Civilians Died," pp. 8, 19; Watterson, *Augusta Daily Constitutionalist*, Aug. 24, 1864, quoted in Davis, ibid., p. 17. Most historians and biographers minimize, excuse or entirely ignore the five-week bombardment of Atlanta, and Sherman escapes censure even from those who criticize him for other acts. An article analyzing Sherman's "ethics" makes no mention of the shelling of Atlanta. John W. Brinsfield, "The Military Ethics of General William T. Sherman: A Reassessment," *Parameters* 12 (1983), pp. 36–48.

17 "Wallace's Civil War Letters," *Wisconsin Magazine of History*, p. 102; see also James Comfort Patten, "An Indiana Doctor Marches with Sherman: The Diary of James Comfort Patten," *Indiana Magazine of History* (Robert G. Athearn, ed.) 49 (1953), p. 411 ("Truly the Spade wins more Battles than the sword").

18 Stephens Mitchell, "Colonel L. P. Grant and the Defenses of Atlanta," *Atlanta Historical Bulletin* 1, no. 6 (1932), pp. 32–34; Garrett, *Atlanta and Environs*, pp. 567–69. On March 12, 1864, Grant had been summoned to headquarters for an early spring meeting with General Johnston, who had just arrived to inspect the city's defenses. This was certainly prudent but perhaps should have been alarming—more than two months before the campaign for Atlanta even opened, the commander of the Army of Tennessee had traveled from his present position to take a look at the fortifications one

hundred miles in his rear. Just in case. Davis, *Atlanta Will Fall*, p. 34 (pointing out Johnston's somewhat disturbing visit to inspect the Atlanta fortifications in March 1864); see also Colonel Grant's sketch of the Atlanta fortifications which appears in the *Atlas to Accompany the Official Records of the Union and Confederate Armies* (Washington, D.C.: Government Printing Office, 1891–95), Plate LI.

19 "Wallace's Civil War Letters," *Wisconsin Magazine of History*, p. 102 (Rebel skirmisher blowing his nose); Elias Smith, *New York Tribune*, Aug. 19, 1864; Stephenson, *Memoir*, pp. 228–29.

20 Alfred Ringgold Gibbons, *Recollections of an Old Confederate Soldier* (Shelbyville, Mo.: Herald Print, 1931), p. 5 ("common saying among the boys"); *The Memoirs of Brigadier General William Passmore Carlin, U.S.A.* Robert Girardi and Nathaniel C. Hughes, eds. (Lincoln: University of Nebraska Press, 1999), p. 132 ("Mein Gott, Sheneral").

21 Mosman, *Rough Side of War*, pp. 212–13 ("We go right along"); Erastus Winters, *In the 50th Ohio Serving Uncle Sam: Memoirs of One Who Wore Blue* (1905), quoted in *EOB*, p. 287 (story of Henry Shepherd).

22 S. B. Crew to Brother & Sister, Aug. 8, 1864, Collection of Mary Louise Dunn Fleming.

23 Mary Clark, *Under the Stars and Bars*, p. 141 ("Picket firing is . . . legalized murder"). Another Southern soldier agreed, writing near Kennesaw the month before: "This picket firing is beneath the dignity of civilized warfare, as it accomplishes nothing but murder and has nothing to recommend it. No Nation does it but ours and the Indian tribes that we got it from that I know of. It is real 'bushwhacking' and nothing else." William Norrell Diary, May 30, 1864, KMNBP, quoted in Daniel, *Soldiering in the Army of Tennessee*, p. 156.

24 McDaniel, "Letters from a Confederate Soldier," *Georgia Review*, p. 291 ("a heep hearder hearted"); Mosman, *Rough Side of War*, p. 248; Wills, *Army Life*, pp. 278–79 ("good burying facilities").

25 Hedley, *Marching Through Georgia*, p. 117.

26 Sherman to Ellen Ewing Sherman, Aug. 9, 1864, in *Sherman's Civil War*, p. 685; Rusling, *Men and Things I Saw in Civil War Days*, p. 112 ("cool as a cucumber"; "like a ripe apple"); Sherman to Grant, Aug. 7, 1864, in *Sherman's Civil War*, p. 684.

27 Sherman to Palmer, Aug. 5, 1864, *OR*, vol. 38, pt. 5, p. 384 (the campaign "having settled down into a quasi siege"); *Augusta Daily Constitutionalist*, Aug. 10, 1864 ("It is Hood"). Stephen Davis explains how the erroneous story developed that Hood had sent a white-flag protest through the lines to Sherman during the bombardment. Davis, "A Very Barbarous Mode of Carrying on War," pp. 86–88 n. 42 (noting that "postbellum Atlanta writers seem to have confused the dates of the Hood-Sherman correspondence, and constructed it to have occurred during the siege"). For a few among many sources repeating this error, see Reed, *History of Atlanta*, p. 193 (noting a "vigorous protest by General Hood"); Carter, *Siege of Atlanta*, pp. 287–88; Peggy Robbins, "Hood vs. Sherman: A Duel of Words," *Civil War Times Illustrated* 17 (July 1978), p. 25. On the

contrary, Hood would later point out to Sherman that he had *not* lodged any protest during the shelling of the city. Hood to Sherman, Sept. 12, 1864, in *Advance and Retreat*, p. 283 ("I made no complaint of your firing into Atlanta in any way you thought proper. I make none now, but there are a hundred thousand witnesses that you fired into the habitations of women and children for weeks, firing above and miles beyond my line of defence").

28 Hood to Davis, Aug. 2, 1864, *Advance and Retreat*, p. 940; Davis to Hood, Aug. 5, 1864, ibid., p. 946.

29 B. Laiboldt to Jos. Wheeler, Aug. 14, 1864, *OR*, vol. 38, pt. 1, p. 324.

30 Sherman to Halleck, Sept. 4, 1864, in *SCW*, p. 700. On the 14th Regiment USCT at Dalton, see Noah Andre Trudeau, *Like Men of War: Black Troops in the Civil War, 1862–1865* (New York: Little, Brown, 1998), pp. 275–77; Thomas J. Morgan, quoted in Joseph Thomas Wilson, *The Black Phalanx: A History of the Negro Soldiers of the United States in the Wars of 1775–1812; 1861–'65* (Hartford: American Publishing Co., 1890), p. 297. Several hearsay accounts contain stories that surrounded Confederate cavalrymen refused to give themselves up and had to be killed, or (alternatively) that they did surrender and that the black soldiers bayoneted them nonetheless, crying "Remember Fort Pillow!" See, e.g., "Wheeler's Raid: Slight Damage Done to the Roads," *Cincinnati Commercial*, Aug. 19, 1864, quoted in *New York Times*, Aug. 26, 1864; William R. Hartpence, *History of the Fifty-First Indiana Veteran Volunteer Infantry* (Cincinnati: Robert Clarke Co., 1894), p. 219. Relative casualties suffered in the engagement are uncertain and disputed. Compare Report of Maj. Gen. James B. Steedman, Sept. 11, 1864, *OR*, vol. 38, pt. 2, pp. 495–96 ("The enemy's loss at Dalton could not have been less than 200. . . . My loss was 1 officers and 8 men killed, 1 officer and 29 men wounded, 1 officer and 23 men missing; total, 63"); Wheeler's Report, ibid., pt. 3, p. 958 ("I was attacked by a strong force of infantry and cavalry under Major General Steedman. My loss was trifling, that of the enemy more severe").

31 Sherman to Halleck, Aug. 17, 1864, *OR*, vol. 38, pt. 5, p. 547 ("East Tennessee is a good place for him to break down his horses"). Historians are virtually unanimous in agreeing with Sherman that Hood made a grave error in sending Wheeler into north Georgia—an error compounded by Wheeler extending the raid all the way to Knoxville and Nashville. See, e.g., Connelly, *Autumn of Glory*, p. 457 (calling Wheeler's raid "a particularly serious error" by Hood); Govan, *A Different Valor*, p. 328 (a "glaring mistake"); Dyer, *The Gallant Hood*, p. 267 ("This raid of Wheeler's was Hood's first major blunder"); but see Davis, *Atlanta Will Fall*, p. 172 (acknowledging the raid's failure but noting that in deploying Wheeler, Hood was complying with the wishes of the Confederate government and the Southern people).

32 Connolly, *Three Years*, p. 238 ("popinjay"); Charles S. Wainwright, *A Diary of Battle: The Personal Journals of Colonel Charles S. Wainwright*, Allan Nevins, ed. (New York: Harcourt, 1962), p. 326 ("frothy braggart"); James H. Wilson, *Under the Old Flag: Recollections of Military Operations in the War for the Union, The Spanish War, the Boxer Rebellion, Etc.* (New York: D. Appleton & Co., 1912), vol. 2, p. 13 ("hell of a damned fool"); Lyman, *Meade's Headquarters*, p. 76 ("usual combination of Gypsy and Don Cossack"). Lyman is also the source of the widely quoted remark that it was hard to look

at Kilpatrick without laughing. Ibid. See also John P. Rea, "Kilpatrick's Raid Around Atlanta," in *The Atlanta Papers*, p. 647.

33 For a detailed study of Kilpatrick's raid to Jonesboro (and back), see Evans, *Sherman's Horsemen*, pp. 404–67; for specific details of the pillage and burning of Jonesboro, see ibid., pp. 428–29. See also *Ninety-Second Illinois Volunteers* (Freeport, Ill.: Journal Steam Publishing House, 1875), p. 150 (quoted in Evans, p. 429) ("sea of fire"). A Northern newspaper report, blaming a "brisk wind," noted that "over two-thirds of the town was burned to the ground, together with considerable public property and effects of the citizens." *New York Times*, Sept. 4, 1864.

34 Evans, *Sherman's Horsemen*, p. 461 (lost hats); Rea, "Kilpatrick's Raid Around Atlanta," in *The Atlanta Papers*, p. 661 (87 hours, circuit of Atlanta, 140 miles); "Kilpatrick's Raid Around Atlanta," *Cincinnati Commercial*, n.d., reprinted in *New York Times*, Sept. 4, 1864. In describing Kilpatrick's raid, Evans invokes a maxim of George Washington: "An army of asses led by a lion is vastly superior to an army of lions led by an ass." *Sherman's Horsemen*, p. 418.

35 Thomas to Sherman, Aug. 28, 1864, *OR*, vol. 38, pt. 5, p. 629; Wainwright, *A Diary of Battle*, p. 265 (Kilpatrick's reports); Connolly, *Three Years*, p. 335 (cavalry "good for nothing").

36 Sherman, *Memoirs*, p. 473 (cavalry "could not or would not").

37 *Augusta Daily Constitutionalist*, Aug. 10, 1864.

38 *Chicago Tribune*, Aug. 4, 1864; Worsham, *Old Nineteenth Tennessee*, p. 127 ("one armed one legged fighting devil"); W. H. Russell, *London Gazette*, Sept. 3, 1864, quoted in Ephraim Douglas Adams, *Great Britain and the Civil War*, vol. 2, p. 353.

39 *London Index*, Aug. 18, 1864, quoted in *Great Britain and the Civil War*, n. 1222; *Richmond Whig*, Aug. 16, 1864.

40 On the impact of the Atlanta Campaign on the election, see Albert Castel, "The Atlanta Campaign and the Presidential Election of 1864: How the South Almost Won by Not Losing," in *Winning and Losing in the Civil War: Essays and Stories* (Columbia: University of South Carolina Press, 1996), pp. 15–32; see also Waugh, *Reelecting Lincoln*, pp. 295–97; Opdycke, *To Battle for God and the Right*, p. 217; Weed to Seward, August 22, 1864, quoted in John G. Nicolay and John Hay, "Abraham Lincoln: A History," *Century Magazine*, 38 (1889), p. 548.

41 Abraham Lincoln, "Memorandum Concerning His Probable Failure of Re-Election," *The Collected Works of Abraham Lincoln*, Roy P. Basler et al., eds. (Springfield, Ill.: Abraham Lincoln Association, 1953), vol. 7, pp. 514–15; Donald, *Lincoln*, p. 529.

42 Waugh, *Reelecting Lincoln*, p. 290 (the band played "Dixie"); Sherman, *Memoirs*, p. 477.

43 Brooks, *Washington in Lincoln's Time*, p. 181.

CHAPTER 9: "I HAVE ATLANTA IN MY HAND"

1 *Augusta Daily Constitutionalist*, Aug. 28, 1864 (report dated Aug. 23).

2 Davis, "The Consequence of Grandeur," *Atlanta History* 33, no. 3 (Fall 1989), p. 15.

3 Carrie Berry Diary, Aug. 15, 16, 20, and 24, AHC.

4 *Augusta Daily Constitutionalist*, Sept. 1, 1864 (report dated Aug. 28); Thomas Key Diary, Aug. 25, quoted in Wirt Armistead Cate, *Two Soldiers: The Campaign Diaries of Thomas J. Key, C.S.A. and Robert J. Campbell, U.S.A.* (Chapel Hill: University of North Carolina Press, 1938), p. 120.

5 George Mercer Diary, quoted in Walker, *Hell's Broke Loose in Georgia*, p. 173 ("badly policed and very filthy"); *Augusta Daily Constitutionalist*, Sept. 1, 1864 ("The boys had a merry time"); Foster, *One of Cleburne's Command*, p. 125 (notes left behind); Olmstead, "Memoirs," *Georgia Historical Quarterly*, p. 47 (same, "we'll see you later"). General Samuel French noted that the Union works were "horribly filthy, and alive with 'dog' flies to such an extent that our horses could not be managed." He added, "There are no flies or vermin in our camp—strange but true." French, *Two Wars*, p. 221. An Alabama soldier wrote home of finding a lone Yankee asleep in a ditch—"said he went out to get some apples and when he returned his command was gone and he knew not where." Joel Dyer Murphree, "Autobiography and Civil War Letters of Joel Dyer Murphree," *Alabama Historical Quarterly* 19, no. 1 (Spring 1957), p. 193 (calling Sherman's move "a mistery to all outsiders").

6 *Memphis* (Atlanta) *Appeal*, Aug. 27, 1864; Mollie Smith, "Dodging Shells in Atlanta," *Atlanta Journal Magazine*, March 24, 1929 ("nary a Yank did I find").

7 Reed, *History of Atlanta*, p. 183 (the siege liar); H. T. Howard to My dear Wife, Aug. 22, 1864, in *"Dear Mother: Don't grieve about me: If I Get Killed, I'll only be Dead,"* p. 331 (rumors of armistice, Longstreet); Trask Diary, KMNBP, p. 38 ("Ten thousand rumors").

8 Stephenson, *Memoir*, p. 231 ("rather contrary to common sense"); Key Diary, Aug. 26, in *Two Soldiers*, p. 121; Richards Diary, Aug. 27, 1864.

9 French, *Two Wars*, pp. 221–22.

10 William Pitt Chambers, *Blood and Sacrifice: The Civil War Journal of a Confederate Soldier*, Richard Baumgartner, ed. (Huntington, W.Va.: Blue Acorn Press, 1994), pp. 163–64 (Aug. 28 sermon); Stephenson, *Memoir*, p. 230 (Rev. Markham).

11 Mosman, *Rough Side of War*, p. 266.

12 Sherman to Grant, Aug. 10, 1864, *OR*, vol. 38, pt. 5, p. 447; Sherman to Thomas and Sherman to Howard, Aug. 23, 1864, ibid., pp. 641–43 (inquiring as to readiness to execute "the former plan").

13 Sherman to Halleck, Aug. 13, 1864, ibid., p. 482 ("60,000 men, reduced to fighting trim"); Report of Captain Orlando M. Poe, ibid., pt. 1, p. 135 ("August 23, under instructions from the major-general commanding, I went to the Chattahoochee railroad bridge and selected a line to be occupied by the corps (Twentieth), which was to be left behind during our movement to the rear of Atlanta"); Special Field Orders No. 91, Aug. 23, 1864, ibid., pt. 5, p. 649 ("Every effort must be made to preserve secrecy relative to the proposed movement. Conversation between pickets is strictly prohibited").

14 Sherman to Halleck, Aug. 24, 1864, *OR*, vol. 38, pt. 5, pp. 649 ("movement round Atlanta"), 669 ("I have moved the Twentieth Corps").

15 F. M. McAdams, *Every-Day Soldier Life, or, A History of the One Hundred and Thirteenth Ohio Volunteer Infantry* (Columbus: C. M. Cott & Co., 1884), p. 98 ("several good looking women"); Lewis W. Day, *Story of the One Hundred and First Ohio Infantry* (Cleveland: W. M. Bayne Printing Co., 1894), pp. 251–52, 255 ("stripped"; "unlimited ammunition"; "Every man seemed to know"); Frank Moore, ed., *The Rebellion Record: A Diary of American Events* (New York: D. Van Nostrand, 1868), vol. 11, p. 274 ("tinkerish aspect").

16 Connolly, *Three Years*, pp. 224–25.

17 McAdams, *Every-Day Soldier Life*, p. 99 ("Our men are living high"); O. M. Poe to wife, Aug. 30, 1864, Poe Letters, Library of Congress. General Howard issued an order on August 29 attempting to stop these offenses against civilians. "It is not the good soldiers who do these things, but the vilest miscreants," he wrote. See Special Field Orders No. 113, Aug. 29, 1864, *OR*, vol. 38, pt. 5, p. 709.

18 Mosman, *Rough Side of War*, p. 266.

19 Moore, ed., *The Rebellion Record*, vol. 11, pp. 274–75.

20 Sherman, *Memoirs*, p. 474 ("hot but otherwise very pleasant"); Sherman to Thomas, Aug. 28, 1864, *OR*, vol. 38, pt. 5, p. 688 (instructions on destroying the railroad).

21 Day, *Story of the One Hundred and First Ohio*, pp. 257–58; Fahnestock diary, Aug. 30, p. 54, KMNBP ("fight or a foot race"). For criticism of Sherman's supposedly wasteful destruction of the Atlanta & West Point Railroad, see Larry J. Daniel, *Days of Glory: The Army of the Cumberland, 1861–1865* (Baton Rouge: Louisiana State University Press, 2004), p. 421 (calling the destruction "a waste of time"); Castel, *Decision in the West*, p. 489 (noting that Sherman either "does not know or does not care that the West Point railroad . . . has been carrying little traffic"); McMurry, *Atlanta 1864*, p. 170 (arguing that Sherman "wasted a day"); Davis, *Atlanta Will Fall*, p. 178 (commenting on Sherman's "virtual fetish about the wrecking of rail"). Such criticism is arguably akin to a baseball writer complaining about pitch selection after a three-hit shutout.

22 Howard, *Autobiography*, pp. 34–36 (describing the march from Fairburn to Jonesboro); O. M. Poe to wife, Aug. 30, 1864, Poe Letters, Library of Congress; Lay, "Sherman in Georgia," *Atlantic Monthly*, p. 169 ("I have Atlanta as certainly as if it were in my hand"). A few historians have criticized the allegedly hapless Howard for not attacking immediately upon his arrival at Jonesboro on the evening of August 30, pointing out that only 2,500 Confederates manned the works before the town. Again, this is an unfair point based upon retroactive omniscience. Howard had no way of knowing the strength of the Rebels in his front; his men had just completed a fourteen-mile march in the August heat ("a fearfully hot march," one remembered); only the 15th Corps was "up" and across the river at dusk; and it would have been well after dark before he could have deployed for an attack. See Castel, *Decision in the West*, p. 495 (likening Howard's halt to McPherson's hesitation at Resaca); Miller, *Struggle for the Life of the Republic*, p. 201 ("fearfully hot").

23 See Fletcher Pratt, *Ordeal by Fire: An Informal History of the Civil War* (New York: H. Smith and R. Hass, 1935), p. 375 ("Sherman is starved out!"). Hood's elation at the sup-

posed "full retreat" of the Federals is often repeated, but never with firsthand witnesses. Somewhat preposterously, some accounts claim that Hood "leaped to his feet" at the news—something he surely never did in his stiff, one-footed condition. Ibid.; see also Carter, *Siege of Atlanta*, p. 307 (claiming that the amputee Hood "paced the floor nervously"). The only contemporaneous primary source suggesting that Hood thought Sherman was retreating is W. L. Trask's diary, noting that "General Hood and his Chief of Staff Shoup are in high glee at the flattering prospect (to them) of Sherman's speedy destruction. They think that he is now preparing to retreat." Trask diary, KMNBP, p. 43. But Trask was an adjutant to General Hardee, who despised Hood by that time, and chief of staff Shoup's own contemporaneous journal reflects no such misimpression or elation. See Shoup Journal, Aug. 27, 1864, *OR*, vol. 38, pt. 3, p. 693 ("The exact intention of the enemy has not yet been ascertained. In consequence of the enemy's late movements, the general commanding has disposed of his troops so as to be prepared for any emergency"). The primary critic of Hood's actions during this time was General Hardee, who later wrote that Hood believed that Sherman was retreating, and as a result that the "opportunity to strike the flank of the enemy exposed during the five days occupied in the movement from Atlanta to Jonesborough was lost." Ibid., p. 700. But Hardee did not have any more an idea of the strength or intentions than did Hood, and he never urged Hood to such an attack on "the flank of the enemy."

In recent years, a number of prominent historians have rejected or discredited Hardee's assertions and come to Hood's defense. See, e.g., Castel, *Decision in the West*, p. 487 ("Far from being deluded by the Union withdrawals into thinking that Sherman is retreating, as contemporaneous critics and critical historians will subsequently charge, Hood realizes that Sherman is most likely launching, or is about to launch, another large-scale flanking movement to the south"); Connelly, *Autumn of Glory*, pp. 460–61. Stephen Davis compares Hood's reaction to Sherman's movement before Jonesboro to Robert E. Lee's cautious response to Grant's march toward Petersburg in June 1864, though he concludes: "just as Lee was outgeneraled at the James [River], so was Hood at Jonesboro." Davis, *Atlanta Will Fall*, pp. 187–90.

24 Hood to Jackson, Aug. 26, 1864, *OR*, vol. 38, pt. 3, p. 992; Hood to Cleburne, quoted in Davis, *Atlanta Will Fall*, p. 176; Hood to Bragg, Sept. 4, 1864, *OR*, vol. 52, pt. 2, p. 729; Davis, *Atlanta Will Fall*, p. 179 ("There is a vast difference").

25 Shoup Journal, Aug. 29, 1864, *OR*, vol. 38, pt. 3, p. 694.

26 Hood, *Advance and Retreat*, p. 204.

27 Hardee to Davis, Aug. 3, 1864, *OR*, vol. 38, pt. 5, p. 987; Davis to Hardee, Aug. 4 and 7, ibid., p. 988.

28 Report of Maj. Gen. Henry D. Clayton, *OR*, vol. 38, pt. 3, p. 821 ("exceedingly fatiguing march"); Manigault, *A Carolinian Goes to War*, p. 244.

29 Report of Maj. Gen. Patton Anderson, Feb. 9, 1865, *OR*, vol. 38, pt. 3, pp. 772–73; John Kendall, "Recollections of a Confederate Officer," *Louisiana Historical Quarterly*, 29, no. 4, p. 1197.

30 Patten, "An Indiana Doctor Marches with Sherman," *Indiana Magazine of History*, p.

408 ("It has been a very pretty town"); see also John Hill Ferguson, *On to Atlanta: The Civil War Diaries of John Hill Ferguson, Illinois Tenth Regiment of Volunteers*, Janet Correll Ellison, ed. (Lincoln: University of Nebraska Press, 2001), p. 83 ("Jonesboro has been a comfortable town of about 2,000 inhabitance, but nearly all has gon and lef the place destitude"); see Mitchell, *Gone with the Wind*, p. 320 ("And even if you reached Jonesboro safely, there'd be a five-mile ride over a rough road before you ever reached Tara").

31 Howard to Sherman, Aug. 31, 1864, 9:10 A.M., *OR*, vol. 38, pt. 5, p. 726 ("The enemy is shoving troops down here").

32 Hood, *Advance and Retreat*, p. 205; Hood/Shoup to Hardee, August 31, 1864, 3:00 A.M., 3:10 A.M., 3:20 A.M., 10:00 A.M., *OR*, vol. 38, pt. 5, pp. 1006–7. A number of historians have remarked on this stream of dispatches from Hood to Hardee. See, e.g., Connelly, *Autumn of Glory*, p. 463 n. 79; Castel, *Decision in the West*, p. 496; McMurry, *John Bell Hood*, p. 148.

33 Olmstead, "Memoirs," *Georgia Historical Quarterly*, p. 47; Manigault, *A Carolinian Goes to War*, p. 245.

34 Jacob A. Gilberg, "Battle of Jonesboro: A Day's History by One of Gen. J. A. Logan's Bodyguard," *National Tribune*, May 6, 1909, quoted in Strayer, *Echoes of Battle*, pp. 294–95 ("Shovels was the order of the night"; "I vill make 'em hell schmell").

35 Foster, *One of Cleburne's Command*, p. 125 ("breeck loaders and SixShooters"); Connolly, *Three Years*, pp. 83, 127 ("any two Rebs in Dixie"; "heathen do their idols").

36 For a discussion of Maney's halt and relief from command, see Losson, *Tennessee's Forgotten Warriors*, pp. 189–90.

37 Ephraim A. Wilson, *Memoirs of the War* (Cleveland: W. M. Bayne Printing Co., 1893), pp. 358–59 ("colors flying"); Taylor, *Tom Taylor's Civil War*, p. 178 ("fierce monsoon"); Pepper, *Personal Recollections*, p. 168 ("ball hurled against a rock"). Pepper further described the Rebel charge as "unfruitful of success—fruitful of carnage." Ibid.

38 Snell, *Illinois in the Civil War*, p. 271 (describing laughing at the charging Rebels).

39 Report of P. Jos. Osterhaus, *OR*, vol. 38, pt. 3, p. 136; Gilberg, "Battle of Jonesboro," quoted in *Echoes of Battle*, p. 295 ("woodchopper at work"; "river steamboat").

40 Report of John A. Logan, *OR*, vol. 38, pt. 3, p. 109.

41 Castel, *Decision in the West*, p. 504 (Logan under the influence?); Kendall, "Recollections of a Confederate Officer," *Louisiana Historical Quarterly*, p. 1198; Peter J. Meaney, "Valiant Chaplain of the Bloody Tenth," *Tennessee Historical Quarterly*, 41, no. 1 (Spring 1982), pp. 37–47 (Father Bliemel); Wiley, "A Story of 3 Southern Officers," *Civil War Times Illustrated* 3, no. 1 (April 1964), p. 34 (death of Lt. Gill).

42 S. D. Lee, Jan. 30, 1865, *OR*, vol. 38, pt. 3, p. 764. "The attack was not made by the troops with the spirit and inflexible determination that would insure success," Lee further reported. "Several brigades behaved with great gallantry, and in each brigade many instances of gallant conduct were exhibited by regiments and individuals; but generally the troops halted in the charge when they were much exposed, and within easy range of the enemy's musketry, and when they could do but little damage to the enemy

behind his works, instead of moving directly and promptly forward against the temporary and informidable works in their front." Ibid. Hood to Bragg, Sept. 5, 1864, ibid., p. 1021 ("To let you know what a disgraceful effort was made by our men in the engagement of August 31, I give you the wounded in the two corps: Hardee's corps, 539; Lee's, 946; killed, a very small number"); Castel, *Tom Taylor's Civil War,* p. 178; Bushrod Jones (*OR* vol. 38, pt. 3, p. 835); Patton Anderson, ibid., 3, 774; Wills, *Army Life*, p. 295.

43 Trask Diary, KMNBP, Aug. 31 (Hardee in vacant lot at Jonesboro); Hardee report, *OR*, vol. 38, pt. 3, p. 702.

44 Kendall, "Recollections of a Confederate Officer," *Louisiana Historical Quarterly*, pp. 1199–1200 (St. Helena Rifles); see also A. P. Richards, *The St. Helena Rifles*, Randall Shoemaker, ed. (Houston: n.p., 1968); Castel, *Tom Taylor's Civil War*, p. 179 ("perhaps the most one-sided slaughter").

Federal casualties on August 31 were precisely reported by Howard as 172 killed and wounded, *OR*, vol. 38, pt. 3, p. 45 (154 in Logan's 15th Corps plus 18 in Corse's Division of the 16th Corps); while Confederate estimates (due to a paucity of official numbers) vary. *See* McMurry, *Atlanta 1864*, p. 173 ("at least 2,000"); Davis, *Atlanta Will Fall*, p. 185 ("some 2,200"); Woodworth, *Nothing But Victory*, p. 581 ("approximately 2,200").

45 Hiram Smith Williams, *This War So Horrible: The Civil War Diary of Hiram Smith Williams*, Lewis N. Wynne and Robert A. Taylor, eds. (Tuscaloosa: University of Alabama Press, 1993), p. 110 ("Our boys have been repulsed"); John Williams Green, *Johnny Green of the Orphan Brigade: The Journal of a Confederate Soldier*, A. D. Kirwan, ed. (Lexington: University of Kentucky Press, 2002), p. 161.

46 Hood, *Advance and Retreat*, p. 205; F.A. Shoup, Aug. 31, 1864, *OR*, vol. 38, pt. 5, p. 1008 ("Enemy at Rough and Ready in considerable force").

47 Report of W. J. Hardee, Apr. 5, 1865, *OR*, vol. 38, pt. 3, p. 701 (noting recall of Lee's corps "to protect Atlanta from an apprehended attack by Sherman's army, which General Hood, with a marvelous want of information, evidently still believed to be in front of Atlanta"); Shoup to Hardee, Aug. 31, 1864, 6 p.m., ibid., pt. 5, p. 1007.

48 Trask Diary, KMNBP ("My God! It cannot be possible!"); see also Castel, *Decision in the West*, p. 509; Hood, *Advance and Retreat*, p. 206.

49 Sherman to Schofield, Aug. 31, 1864, *OR*, vol. 38, pt. 5, p. 733 ("I have your dispatch and am rejoiced"); Sherman to Thomas, Aug. 31, 1864, ibid., p. 724 ("dilly-dally").

50 Wills, *Army Life*, p. 295 (diary entry for September 1); Hardee at Jonesboro, Calhoun Benham, "Major-Gen. P. R. Cleburne, A Biography," *Kennesaw Gazette*, Nov. 1, 1889, quoted in Symonds, *Stonewall of the West*, p. 240 ("Our position was a sorry one" "not quite touching elbows").

51 See generally Nathaniel C. Hughes and Gordon D. Whitney, *Jefferson Davis in Blue: The Life of Sherman's Relentless Warrior* (Baton Rouge: Louisiana State University Press, 2002); Joseph P. Fried, "How One Union General Murdered Another," *Civil War Times Illustrated* (June 1962), pp. 14–16; Carl Schurz, "The Battle of Missionary Ridge,"

McClure's Magazine (Sept. 1907), p. 491 ("mastered the vocabulary of the 'Army in Flanders'").

52 George Ward Nichols, *The Story of the Great March, from the Diary of a Staff Officer* (New York: Harper & Brothers, 1865), p. 46 ("one of the most elegant officers"); William Bluffton Miller, *Fighting for Liberty and Right: The Civil War Diary of William Bluffton Miller, First Sergeant, Company K, Seventy-fifth Indiana Volunteer Infantry* (Knoxville: University of Tennessee Press, 2004), p. 249; Green, *Johnny Green of the Orphan Brigade*, p. 158 ("We cut & piled some logs & dug for dear life").

53 Miller, *Fighting for Liberty and Right*, p. 248 ("Double quick with fixed Bayonetts"); Letter of George E. Sloat, Surg. 14th Ohio, *Daily Toledo Blade*, Sept. 17, 1864; John McElroy, *Andersonville: A Story of Rebel Military Prisons* (Toledo: D. R. Locke, 1879), p. 442 (10th Kentucky vs. 9th Kentucky). Private Henry B. Mattingly of the 10th Kentucky—one of seven Mattinglys in Company B of that regiment—would be awarded the Medal of Honor for his gallantry in capturing the colors of the 6th/7th Arkansas. Strayer and Baumgartner, *Echoes of Battle*, p. 314.

54 Gervis D. Grainger, *Four Years with the Boys in Gray* (Franklin, Ky., 1902), quoted in Strayer, *Echoes of Battle*, p. 309 ("like an avalanche"); Stan C. Harvey to *Little Rock Gazette*, quoted in Evans, *Confederate Military History*, vol. 10, p. 372 ("like a drove of Texas beeves"); Buck, *Cleburne and His Command*, p. 256 ("seemed to be in the center of a circle").

55 William E. Bevens, *Reminscences of a Private: William E. Bevens of the First Arkansas Infantry, C.S.A.*, Daniel E. Sutherland, ed. (Fayetteville: University of Arkansas Press, 1992), p. 191; Foster, *One of Cleburne's Command*, p. 128.

56 Miller, *Struggle for the Life of the Republic*, p. 202 ("grand sight"); Crooker, *Fifty-Fifth Regiment*, p. 369 (quoting Sherman: "They're rolling them up like sheet of paper"). Davis's charge at Jonesboro was, as one historian noted, "the only successful large-scale frontal assault of the Atlanta campaign." Walker, *Hell's Broke Loose in Georgia*, p. 178.

A few of Govan's men escaped, including one Private Hammett, who felt the sickening thud of a bullet and the wet seep of blood trickling into his boots—but then found that the liquid was only water. "The bullet has pierced his canteen and torn through his clothing and let the water in upon him," the story goes. "Beyond a grazing of the skin he is not hurt at all. Up he jumps and exultingly continues his flight for safety." Stephenson, *Memoir*, pp. 239–40.

57 Sherman, *Memoirs*, p. 476 ("and that is the only time during the campaign I can recall seeing General Thomas urge his horse into a gallop"). Castel suggests that Sherman fabricated this anecdote to make Thomas look bad, but O. O. Howard appears to corroborate the incident. See Castel, *Decision in the West*, pp. 570–71; Howard, "The Battles About Atlanta," *Atlantic Monthly* (Oct.–Nov. 1876), p. 565 ("This was the time, just before sun-down, when General Thomas was said for the first time to have set his horse into a gallop, so anxious was he to push forward the fourth corps to the east of Jonesboro'. (Thomas was fleshy and very heavy, and it took a pretty good-sized horse to carry him, even at a walk or trot)"); see also Daniel, *Days of Glory*, p. 424 n. 25.

58 Wills, *Army Life*, p. 297; Connolly, *Three Years*, p. 258.

59 Gilberg, "Battle of Jonesboro," quoted in Strayer, *Echoes of Battle*, p. 208 ("cries, groans, prayers, even cursings"); Miller, *Struggle for the Life of the Republic*, p. 203 (the well).

60 Foster, *One of Cleburne's Command*, p. 129 ("Our movements are very quiet . . . He is in a bad fix"). Again, Union casualties are fairly well established at 1,274, while Confederate losses are unclear, again because only one of Hardee's three divisions reported their casualties—Cleburne, who counted 911 men killed, wounded or missing, most of them captured. See Report of Mark Lowrey, commanding Cleburne's Division, Sept. 10, 1864, *OR*, vol. 38, pt. 3, p. 729 (reporting losses of 55 killed, 197 wounded, and 659 missing). Stephen Davis estimates Rebel casualties in the second day of the Battle of Jonesboro at about 1,400, more than half of them prisoners. Davis, "Atlanta Campaign," *Blue & Gray Magazine* 6, no. 6 (Aug. 1989), p. 60.

61 Patrick, *Reluctant Rebel*, p. 209 ("'ood's played 'ell, 'asn't 'e?"), quoted in McMurry, *John Bell Hood*, p. 147. Notably, of all the battles of the Atlanta Campaign—including Rocky Face Ridge, Resaca, Adairsville, New Hope Church, Pickett's Mill, Dallas, Gilgal Church, Kolb's Farm, Kennesaw Mountain, Peachtree Creek, Ezra Church and Utoy Creek—the Battle of Jonesboro on September 1 is the only instance in which the *attacking* force succeeded (with the exception of the temporary breakthrough achieved by Cheatham in the Battle of Atlanta).

Castel asserts that because Hardee was heavily outnumbered and threatened with destruction, by partially repelling the Federal attack and then escaping he "achieved a tactical and strategical victory." Castel, *Decision in the West*, p. 525. I cannot agree. Hardee failed to dislodge the Union force on the first day of the battle, suffering ten times the number of casualties as his opponent, and then suffered a crushed flank on the second day, about which the best thing that can be said is that his corps sealed off the break and survived the onslaught. But escape alone does not convert a defeat into a victory. At Jonesboro, the Rebels lost the battle, lost the railroad, lost their position, and lost the city of Atlanta.

Chapter 10. "A Day of Terror and a Night of Dread"

1 Hood to Bragg, Sept. 3, 1864, *OR*, vol. 38, pt. 5, p. 1016 (reporting abandonment of Atlanta); Reed, *History of Atlanta*, pp. 192–93; Richards Diary, Sept. 1, 1864; Berry Diary, Sept. 1, 1864; Richards Diary, Sept. 1, 1864; Manigault, *Carolinian Goes to War*, p. 249.

2 *OR*, vol. 38, pt. 3, p. 765 (withdrawal at 5 P.M.); *Augusta (Ga.) Sentinel*, n.d., reprinted in *New York Herald*, Sept. 17, 1864.

3 Reed, *History of Atlanta*, p. 194; French, *Two Wars*, p. 222; *OR*, vol. 38, pt. 3, p. 906.

4 Reed, *History of Atlanta*, p. 194; Mary Rawson Diary, AHC; Patrick, *Reluctant Rebel*, pp. 204–5 ("perfectly deafening"). Other candidates for the distinction of the greatest explosion of the war would include the Crater (July 30, 1864), the sabotage at City Point, Virginia (Aug. 9, 1864), and the destruction of the ordnance warehouse at Mobile, Alabama (May 25, 1865).

5 For official tabulations from the destruction of the ordnance train, see Reports of Chas. Swett and W. D. Humphries and "Approximate statement of ordnance stores destroyed in the evacuation of Atlanta September 1, 1864," *OR*, vol. 38, pt. 3, pp. 684–86. Humphries noted that his report did not include all the stores destroyed but "only the leading items." A large quantity of other matériel and implements were destroyed "of which no estimate can be given." Ibid. See also "Findings of the Court of Inquiry upon the loss of Confederate stores at Atlanta," *OR*, vol. 38, pt. 3, pp. 991–92; *Richmond Whig*, Sept. 12, 1864 ("Enfield or Tower muskets," etc.); Key, *Two Soldiers*, p. 129 ("one million dollars worth of ordnance which we so much needed. The explosions of our magazines were heard thirty miles, and the flashes of powder lit up the whole country").

The five locomotives included the *Etowah*, the *E. Y. Hill*, the *Missouri*, and the famous engine *General*, stolen by a party of Union raiders back in April 1862 to start the Great Locomotive Chase up the Western & Atlantic Railroad. See generally Russell S. Bonds, *Stealing the General* (Yardley, Pa.: Westholme Publishing, 2006). The fifth engine was probably the *N. C. Munroe*, the locomotive that had transported Generals Hardee and Lee up to Atlanta for Hood's final council of war there on the night of August 30. For details of the destruction of the ordnance trains and rolling mills, see Edison H. Thomas, "The Night They Burned the Train," *L&N Magazine* (Sept. 1964), pp. 18–19, James G. Bogle, "The Locomotive *General*," *The Landmarker* (Fall 1980), p. 7.

Although Hood believed that the ordnance train was lost because it was not moved out of the city early on August 31, in fact it probably could not have escaped down the Macon & Western at that point in any event. By that time, Howard's Army of the Tennessee was within easy cannon range of the M&W at Jonesboro, and its gunners surely would have enjoyed firing at a passing train heavy-laden with ammunition. Moreover, there are some indications that the ordnance train was actually summoned back up to Atlanta *by General Hood* when East Point and Rough and Ready were threatened. See Hood to J. T. Morgan at East Point, Aug. 31, 1864, *OR*, vol. 38, pt. 3, p. 1008 ("Move the ordnance train to this place at once").

6 Patrick, *Reluctant Rebel*, pp. 204–5.

7 John R. Green, in *The Tennessee Civil War Veterans Questionnaires*, Gustavus W. Dyer et al., eds. (Easley, S.C.: Southern Historical Press, 1985), vol. 3, p. —.

8 B. W. Frobel, "The Georgia Campaign, or, a South-Side View of Sherman's March to the Sea." *Scott's Monthly Magazine* 7 (Jan. 1869), p. 7.

9 Berry Diary, Sept. 2, 1864; Richards Diary, Sept. 2, 1864.

10 Reed, *History of Atlanta*, pp. 194–95.

11 "Civil War Letters of Charles Harding Cox," *Indiana Magazine of History*, p. 218 ("a soft thing"); Oliver A. Rea, Letter of Aug. 29, 1864, *National Tribune*, Jan. 27, 1898, quoted in *Echoes of Battle*, p. 293; "Wallace's Civil War Letters," *Wisconsin Magazine of History*, p. 107.

12 Davis, "The Consequence of Grandeur," *Atlanta History* (Fall 1989), p. 18 ("ground trembled under us").

[13] Both Mayor Calhoun and Colonel Coburn provided firsthand accounts of the surrender meeting, which occurred at the present-day intersection of Marietta Street and Northside Drive. Report of Col. John Coburn, *OR*, vol. 38, pt. 2, pp. 392–93; see also Report of Capt. Henry M. Scott, ibid., pp. 332–33; James M. Calhoun, "Affidavit of James M. Calhoun, Mayor of Atlanta as to the Facts in Regard to the Surrender of Atlanta, September 2, 1864," Calhoun Family Papers, AHC MSS 50 ("I will always regret my failure to give Gen Sherman notice of his promise of protection"); see also William B. Hartsfield, "Document in Handwriting of Atlanta's War-Time Mayor Describes Formal Surrender of the City to Federal Army," *Atlanta Constitution*, May 31, 1931. The scene is recorded in numerous histories, many of whom suggest that a written surrender document was prepared at the time, rather than reduced to writing later, as Calhoun makes clear in his affidavit. Garrett, *Atlanta and Environs*, vol. 1, pp. 634–36; Kennett, *Marching Through Georgia*, p. 200; Dyer, *Secret Yankees*, pp. 190–91; Evans, *Sherman's Horsemen*, pp. 470–71. Mayor Calhoun's written surrender is found in the Official Records at vol. 38, pt. 2, p. 333. As for Coburn's promise, scholar Mark Grimsley asserts that "the colonel spoke honestly, for he did not know that Sherman had very different plans for Atlanta." Grimsley, *The Hard Hand of War*, p. 187.

[14] Richards Diary, Sept. 2, 1864; *Echoes of Battle*, pp. 316–19 (discussing controversy between the 70th Indiana and the 111th Pennsylvania).

[15] Williams, *Echoes from the Battlefield*, pp. 41–42 (account of frightened young boys in Atlanta); L.C. Butler, "Reminiscences of Old Atlanta by Newsboy of the Sixties," *Atlanta Constitution*, Nov. 7, 1937 ("they had neither hoofs nor horns").

[16] Edwin Weller, *A Civil War Courtship: The Letters of Edwin Weller from Antietam to Atlanta*, William Walton, ed. (Garden City, N.Y.: Doubleday, 1980), p. 104, quoted in *Echoes of Battle*, p. 320; *Cincinnati Gazette*, Sept. 13, 1864; Adin B. Underwood, *The Three Years' Service of the Thirty-Third Massachusetts Infantry Regiment* (Boston: A. Williams & Co., 1881), p. 233, quoted in *Echoes of Battle*, pp. 319–20.

[17] "William Wallace's Civil War Letters," *Wisconsin Magazine of History*, p. 108; Bull, *Soldiering*, p. 167 ("We'll hang Jeff Davis on a sour apple tree").

[18] Richards Diary, Sept. 3, 1864; Berry Diary, Sept. 2, 1864.

[19] Sherman, *Memoirs*, pp. 476–77; Girardi, ed., *Memoirs of Brigadier General Carlin*, p. 136 ("At times the roar would rise").

[20] Stanley to Brig. Gen. Whipple, Sept. 2, 1864, 7:30 P.M., *OR*, vol. 38, pt. 5, p. 765; Sherman to Howard, Sept. 2, 1864, ibid., p. 771.

[21] Schofield to Sherman, Sept. 2, 1864, 8 A.M. and 10:25 A.M., ibid., pp. 772–73 ("Very large fires"; "A negro has just come in from Atlanta").

[22] Sherman to Howard, Sept. 2, 1864, 8 p.m. ("General Garrard reports General Slocum in possession of Atlanta"); Lewis M. Hosea, "Some Side Lights on the War for the Union," in *Sketches of War History, 1861–1865. MOLLUS–Ohio* (Cincinnati: Robert Clarke and Co., 1912–1916), vol. 9, pp. 42–43 (Garrard's staff officer, describing the exultation of Sherman and Thomas). Sherman, too, would recall in his memoirs the celebration at the news that Atlanta had fallen, noting that Thomas "snapped his fingers,

whistled, and almost danced." Thomas fans insist that this story is untrue and that Sherman was trying to make Old Tom look silly. Sherman, *Memoirs*, p. 477.

23 J. T. Headley, *Grant and Sherman; Their Campaigns and Generals* (New York: E. B. Treat & Co., 1866), p. 396 (Slocum "is certainly one of the most persevering and indefatigable men I ever knew, and was always esteemed lucky"); Sherman to Halleck, Sept. 4, 1864, *OR*, vol. 38, pt. 5, p. 793 ("Hooker was a fool").

24 H. W. Slocum to E. M. Stanton, Sept. 2, 1864, received 10:05 P.M., *OR*, vol. 38, pt. 5, p. 763 ("General Sherman has taken Atlanta").

25 Sherman to Halleck, Sept. 3, 1864, 6 a.m., ibid. p. 777. Historians and newspapers, almost without exception, quote only the meat of Sherman's report—"Atlanta is ours, and fairly won"—without any mention of the longer dispatch. See, e.g., *Baltimore American*, Sept. 8, 1864 (praising Sherman for his "words of pith and conciseness, that have already become historic"); P. C. Headley, *Life and Military Career of Major-General William Tecumseh Sherman* (New York: W. H. Appleton, 1865), p. 217 ("'Atlanta is ours, and fairly won,' was the sublimely simple message of General Sherman"); Doris Kearns Goodwin, *Team of Rivals* (New York: Simon & Schuster, 2005), p. 654 ("'Atlanta is ours, and fairly won,' Sherman wired Washington on September 3"); Charles Bracelan Flood, *Grant and Sherman: The Friendship That Won the Civil War* (New York: Macmillan, 2005), p. 258 ("Sherman sent Halleck these electrifying words: 'Atlanta is ours, and fairly won'").

26 Archer Jones, *Civil War Command and Strategy: The Process of Victory and Defeat* (New York: Free Press, 1992), p. 207 ("All Yankeedoodledom"); Rusling, *Men and Things I Saw in Civil War Days*, p. 333; J. W. Gaskill, *Footprints Through Dixie: Everyday Life of the Man Under a Musket: On the Firing Line and In the Trenches 1862–1865* (Alliance, Ohio: Bradshaw Printing Co., 1919), p. 121 ("Atlanta, the heart of the Confederacy, has been pierced, and Grant is pounding away at its head"); Sherman to Halleck, Sept. 4, 1864, in *Sherman's Civil War*, p. 700 ("Grant has the perseverance of a scotch terrier").

27 *New York Herald*, Sept. 3, 1864; "The New and Great Victory," *New York Times*, Sept. 3, 1864.

28 *London Gazette*, Sept. 24, 1864; *Jersey City Standard*, Sept. 3, 1864, quoted in William Gillette, *Jersey Blue: Civil War Politics in New Jersey, 1864–1865* (New Brunswick, N.J.: Rutgers University Press, 1995), p. 275.

29 Strong, *Diary*, pp. 480–81 ("Glorious news this morning"); *New York Times*, Sept. 3, 1864 ("Thunderbolt for Copperheads"); *Cleveland Leader*, Sept. 6, 1864 ("sunlight is again shining").

30 Abraham Lincoln Executive Order, Sept. 3, 1864, and Grant to Sherman, Sept. 4, 1864, both *OR*, vol. 38, pt. 1, p. 87; Halleck to Sherman, Sept. 4, 1864, ibid., pt. 5, p. 856; see also Grant to Sherman, Sept. 12, 1864, ibid., pt. 2, pp. 364–65.

31 Sherman to Halleck, Sept. 4, 1864, in *Sherman's Civil War*, p. 701.

32 Sherman to Dearest Ellen, Sept. 17, 1864, *Sherman's Civil War*, p. 717.

33 Sherman to Halleck, Sept. 4, 1864, *Sherman's Civil War*, p. 699 (Atlanta "was the prize I fought for"). See generally Errol MacGregor Clauss, "Sherman's Failure at Atlanta," *Georgia Historical Quarterly* 53 (1969), pp. 321–29.

34 Girardi, ed., *Memoirs of Brigadier General Carlin*, p. 136.

35 *Richmond Dispatch*, Sept. 5, 1864.

36 *Richmond Whig*, Sept. 12, 1864; *Columbus Times*, Sept. 9, 1864.

37 Jefferson Davis to Confederate Congress, Nov. 7, 1864, *OR*, ser. 4, vol. 3, p. 792.

38 Hood, *Advance and Retreat*, p. 206; *Mobile Advertiser and Register*, Sept. 12, 1864, quoted in Andrews, *The South Reports the Civil War*; Chesnut, *Mary Chesnut's Civil War*, p. 642.

39 Trask Diary, Sept. 4, 1864, KMNBP.

40 Stephenson, *Memoir*, pp. 244–45 ("hot and vicious"); Hood to Bragg, Sept. 3, 1864, *OR*, vol. 38, pt. 5, p. 1016 (request for reinforcements); Hardee to J. Davis, Sept. 4, 1864, ibid., p. 1018 (same).

41 Hood to Bragg, Sept. 3, 1864, *OR*, vol. 38, pt. 5, p. 1016 (request for reinforcements); Davis to Hardee, Sept. 5, 1864, ibid., p. 1021 ("No other resource remains").

42 Foster, *One of Cleburne's Command*, p. 130.

43 Hood, *Advance and Retreat*, pp. 209–10.

44 Stephenson, *Civil War Memoir*, pp. 241–42.

45 Chambers, *Blood and Sacrifice*, p. 167.

46 Special Orders No. 62, Sept, 3, 1864, *OR*, vol. 38, pt. 5, p. 789; Jackson, *The Colonel's Diary*, p. 151.

47 Geary, *A Politician Goes to War*, p. 199 ("The city is a very pretty place"); Joseph Franklin Culver, *"Your Affectionate Husband, J. F. Culver": Letters Written During the Civil War*, Leslie W. Dunlap et al., eds. (Friends of the University of Iowa Libraries, 1978), p. 359 ("half as large as Nashville"); Patten, "An Indiana Doctor Marches with Sherman," p. 410 ("about the size of Evansville"); O. M. Poe to wife, Sept. 7, 1864, Poe Letters, Library of Congress.

48 Connolly, *Three Years*, pp. 259–60 ("Atlanta looks more like a new, thriving Western city"); Leander Davis, in "The Consequence of Grandeur," *Atlanta History*, p. 18 (describing the ladies).

49 Davis, in "The Consequence of Grandeur," *Atlanta History*, p. 18.

50 Mead, "With Sherman Through Georgia and the Carolinas," p. 309.

51 Geary to My Dearest Mary, Oct. 1, 1864, in *A Politician Goes to War*, p. 207; Benjamin T. Smith, *Private Smith's Journal*, Clyde C. Walton, ed. (Chicago: R. R. Donnelly & Sons, 1963) p. 177 ("the ravages of war illustrated"); Mead, "With Sherman Through Georgia and the Carolinas," pp. 310–11 ("I know our batteries threw over enormous quantity of shells").

52 Patten, "An Indiana Doctor Marches with Sherman," p. 410.

53 Poe to wife, Poe Papers, Library of Congress, Sept. 7. Northern newspaper correspondents likewise provided eyewitness accounts of the damage from shot and shell. See, e.g., Hugenot, "Inside View of Atlanta," *New York Times*, Sept. 16, 1864 ("Almost every house in the centre and on the north and west ends of the town bear testimony to the

skill and execution of our gunnery. The central portion of the city, located on Whitehall street, and about the depot, is very much destroyed by shells").

54 "Wallace's Civil War Letters," *Wisconsin Magazine of History*, pp. 108–9 (describing destruction of the ordnance train); Harvey Reid, *The View from Headquarters: Civil War Letters of Harvey Reid*, Frank L. Burns, ed. (Madison: State Historical Society of Wisconsin, 1965), pp. 183–84 ("unexploded shell, solid shot").

55 Geary to My Dearest Mary, Sept. 3, 1864, in *A Politician Goes to War*, p. 199.

56 Report of Brig. Gen. John W. Geary, Sept. 15, 1864, *OR*, vol. 38, pt. 2 p. 147; Geary to My Dearest Mary, Sept. 18, 1864, in *A Politician Goes to War*, p. 201; Widney, *Campaigning with Uncle Billy*, p. 285 (sixty miles of trenches); Report of Capt. Thomas G. Baylor, Ordnance Corps, Sept. 18, 1864, *OR*, vol. 38, pt. 1, p. 124–26 (expenditures of artillery and small-arms ammunition). Attesting to Sherman's logistical prowess in the campaign, Captain Baylor noted: "The expenditures of ammunition were quite large, still at no time during the campaign, notwithstanding the several interruptions of our railroad communications, were we without a good supply." Ibid., p. 124.

57 For casualty figures, I relied upon Richard McMurry's excellent analysis in "Appendix Two: Numbers and Losses," in his *Atlanta 1864*, pp. 195–97. Other sources vary wild ly, placing Confederate losses as low as 21,995 and as high as 50,000. Hood claimed in his memoirs that between July 18 and September 20 he suffered total losses of only 9,124, an implausibly low number. *Advance and Retreat*, pp. 225–26. See also Young, *Reminiscences of a Soldier of the Orphan Brigade*, p. 200.

CHAPTER 11: YANKEE TOWN

1 Conyngham, *Sherman's March Through the South,* p. 216 (Sherman's entry into Atlanta); George Pepper, *Personal Recollections of Sherman's Campaigns in Georgia and the Carolinas* , p. 171 ("Lord, massa, is dat General Sherman?"). Sources differ on the exact date of Sherman's ride into the city. Sherman himself recalls September 8 (in his *Memoirs*, vol. 2, p. 111), though contemporaneous correspondence suggests his entry occurred on September 7. See Castel, *Decision in the West*, p. 626 n.1.

2 Sherman to Halleck, Sept. 4, 1864, *OR*, vol. 38, pt. 5, p. 794. The home where Sherman made his headquarters is sometimes referred to as "the house of Judge Lyons"—that is, Judge Richard F. Lyon of the Georgia Supreme Court. Lyon bought the house from John Neal in early 1864 but never lived there, and Neal later repurchased it. Garrett, *Atlanta and Environs*, vol. 1, pp. 638–30. "To General Sherman's credit," Garrett wrote, "it must be said that he left the house in excellent condition, and the Neal furniture, stored in the parlor, was disturbed but little." Ibid.

3 Davis, *Atlanta Will Fall*, p. 158 (1,500 rations); John G. Winter to Andrew Johnson, Oct. 8, 1864, quoted in Marszalek, *Sherman*, p. 286 ("nothing more than a clever ruse to provide 15,000 Missionaries"); Sherman, *Memoirs*, p. 479.

4 Kennett, *Marching Through Georgia*, p. 211 ("an act virtually without precedent in the war"); Sherman to Halleck, July 7, 1864, *OR*, vol. 38, pt. 5, p. 73 ("Being exempt from conscription"); see also Sherman to Garrard, July 7, 1864, ibid., p. 76 ("I repeat my orders that you arrest all people, male and female, connected with those factories, no

matter what the clamor, and let them foot it under guard to Marietta, whence I will send them by cars to the North"); *Cincinnati Commercial*, July 20, 1864; *New York Commercial Advertiser*, quoted in Hartwell T. Bynum, "Sherman's Expulsion of the Roswell Mill Women in 1864," *Georgia Historical Quarterly* 54 (1970), pp. 169–81.

The story of the Roswell mill women is explored in detail in Mary Deborah Petite, *The Women Will Howl: The Union Capture of Roswell and New Manchester, Georgia, and the Forced Relocation of Mill Workers* (Jefferson, N.C.: McFarland, 2008). General Sherman made no mention of the incident in his memoirs. See also Tammy Harden Galloway, *Dear Old Roswell: The Civil War Letters of the King Family of Roswell, Georgia* (Macon, Ga.: Mercer University Press, 2003), p. 9; Sarah Blackwell Gober Temple, *The First Hundred Years: A Short History of Cobb County, in Georgia*, 7th printing (Marietta, Ga.: Cobb Landmarks and Historical Society, 1997), pp. 332–35.

5 Sherman to Hood, Sept. 7, 1864, *OR*, vol. 38, pt. 5, p. 822.

6 Hood to Sherman, Sept. 9, 1864, in Hood, *Advance and Retreat*, p. 230. The exchange of letters between Hood and Sherman is well worth reading in its entirety, and is presented in full in both their memoirs. See Hood, ibid., pp. 229–36; Sherman, *Memoirs*, pp. 485–96; see also David Woodbury, *Of Battlefields and Bibliophiles* (Dec. 14, 2006) ("Sherman initiated one of the most interesting exchanges between two opposing generals . . . in the annals of military history").

7 Sherman to Hood, Sept. 10, 1864, *OR*, vol. 39, pt. 2, p. 416.

8 Hood to Sherman, Sept. 12, 1864, in Hood, *Advance and Retreat*, pp. 232–35.

9 Sherman to Hood, Sept. 14, 1864, *OR*, vol. 39, pt. 2, p. 422.

10 Charles Eliot Norton to G. W. Curtis, Sept. 25, 1864, in *Letters of Charles Eliot Norton* (Boston: Houghton Mifflin, 1913), pp. 279–80 ("How his wrath swells and grows . . . He writes as well as he fights"); *New York Herald*, Sept. 25, 1864 ("one of the great men of the time"); Hood, *Advance and Retreat*, p. 233.

11 James M. Calhoun, E. E. Rawson, and S. C. Wells to W. T. Sherman, Sept. 11, 1864, quoted in Sherman, *Memoirs*, vol. 2, pp. 124–25.

12 Sherman to Calhoun et al., Sept. 12, 1864, in *SCW*, pp. 707–9. Mark Grimsley has noted that "Sherman's response [to Mayor Calhoun] has since become a classic, consistently quoted as an example of the 'realist' approach to war." Grimsley, *The Hard Hand of War*, p. 188. For evidence this is perhaps Sherman's most famous letter, note its inclusion in the collection edited by Andrew Carroll, *Letters of a Nation: A Collection of Extraordinary American Letters* (New York: Random House, 1999).

13 William Cogswell, Gen. Order No. 3, Sept. 5, 1864, quoted in Bradley, *The Star Corps*, p. 166.

14 Key, *Two Soldiers*, p. 132 ("infamous and inhuman orders"); *Richmond Sentinel*, Sept. 12, 1864, quoted in *New York Herald*, Sept. 16, 1864; Sherman to Halleck, Sept. 9, 1864, *OR*, ser. 2, vol. 7, p. 791 ("pure Gibraltar").

15 William G. Le Duc, *This Business of War: Recollections of a Civil War Quartermaster* (St. Paul: Minnesota Historical Society Press, 2003), pp. 128–29 ("You tell Bill Duc I care not a damn").

16 Carrie Berry Diary, Sept. 9–10, 1864, AHC; "Atlanta: A Rebel Exile on General Sherman," *New York Times*, Dec. 1, 1864 ("The lady from whom these facts were obtained says that Sherman had a vast number of applications from ladies and others in reference to their moving, and that so far as she could learn he was patient, gentlemanly and obliging, as much so as he could be to them, consistent with his prescribed policy"); see also Wilbur G. Kurtz, "Leave Atlanta Within Five Days," *Atlanta Journal Magazine*, Oct. 12, 1941.

17 Mary Rawson Diary, AHC; Conyngham, *Sherman's March Through the South*, pp. 225–26; Nichols, *Story of the Great March*, p. 20.

18 Miller, *Fighting for Liberty and Right*, p. 253; Washburn, *Reminiscences*, pp. 76–77 ("a sight enough to make the blood of humanity boil"); Nichols, *Story of the Great March*, pp. 20–23 ("Well, sir, we hate you"); see also Kennett, *Marching Through Georgia*, p. 209 (same). For detailed discussions of the departure of Atlanta's civilians, see ibid., pp. 207–11; Dyer, *Secret Yankees*, pp. 202–4.

19 Dyer, *Secret Yankees*, p. 360 n. 65 (citing and describing the "Book of Exodus"), p. 204 (fifty families remained); Wilbur G. Kurtz, ed., "Persons Sent from Atlanta by General Sherman," *Atlanta Historical Bulletin* 1 (1932), p. 32; W. P. Howard to Joseph E. Brown, Dec. 7, 1864 (noting that "about fifty families remained") quoted in Martin, *Atlanta and Its Builders*, vol. 1, p. 633.

20 On the prisoner exchange, see Sherman to Halleck, Sept. 20, 1864, *OR*, ser. 2, vol. 7, pp. 846–47 ("still on hand"; "I have sent word to our prisoners to be of good cheer"); Sherman to Grant, Sept. 19, 1864, *OR*, ser. 1, vol. 39, pt. 2, p. 404 ("He raised the question of humanity").

21 *Cincinnati Commercial*, Oct. 13, 1864 ("Sherman is walking upon Atlanta"). The hard news from Atlanta led to considerable distress across the South. "The end has come. No doubt of the fact," diarist Mary Chesnut wrote on September 21, the day the refugee truce expired in Atlanta. "We are going to be wiped off the face of the earth." *Mary Chesnut's Civil War*, p. 645.

22 Kennett, *Marching Through Georgia*, p. 214 ("Blue Jackets rule the day"), "D. P. Conyngham's Dispatch," *New York Herald*, Sept. 20, 1864 ("Never has an enemy's town been taken possession of so quietly").

23 Reed, *History of Atlanta*, p. 181 (prices of goods); Bailey, *War and Ruin*, p. 19 (same); Hirshon, *The White Tecumseh*, p. 242 (tobacco prices).

24 Sherman to Halleck, Sept. 15, 1864, *OR*, vol. 38, pt. 1, pp. 61–85 (Sherman's official report of "the whole campaign which has resulted in the capture and occupation of the city of Atlanta"); Reed, *History of Atlanta*, p. 198 (Sherman's housekeeper), see also Wallace Reed, "Why Mrs. Melton Changed Her Opinion of Sherman," *Atlanta Constitution*, July 30, 1900 ("I must admit that he is a very different man from the brutal soldier I believed him to be. He is a perfect gentleman, kind-hearted and considerate").

25 Porter, *Campaigning with Grant*, pp. 289–90; see also Shakespeare, *Richard III*, act I, scene 1 ("Grim-visaged war hath smoothed his wrinkled front").

26 Widney, *Campaigning with Uncle Billy*, p. 287; James Taylor Holmes to My Dear Parents, Sept. 14, 1864, in *Echoes of Battle*, p. 333 ("it's goodbye house").

27 Morse, *Letters Written During the Civil War*, p. 193.

28 Ira Beaman Read, "The Campaign from Chattanooga to Atlanta as Seen by a Federal Soldier," Richard B. Harwell, ed. *Georgia Historical Quarterly* 25, no. 3 (Sept. 1941), p. 277 ("I have my tent nicely 'fixed up'"). Not all were made comfortable by their new quarters in Atlanta. General Alpheus Williams, sleeping in a house for the first time in four months, found the air oppressive and the bedbugs fierce. He tossed and turned all night, stumbled from bed in the morning and resolved "to have my tent pitched and go back to the luxury of my cot and blankets." Williams, *From the Cannon's Mouth*, p. 342.

29 Benton, *As Seen From the Ranks*, p. 207 (describing the strongman and other entertainments at the Athenaeum); Garrett, *Atlanta and Environs*, vol. 1, pp. 645–46 (describing and reproducing the program of the Sept. 24 "Vocal and Instrumental Concert" at the Athenaeum featuring the 33rd Massachusetts band).

30 "The Federal Festivities in Atlanta," *New York Herald*, Sept. 20, 1864, reprinting story from the *Richmond Examiner*, Sept. 16; Dyer, *Secret Yankees*, p. 199 (describing the newspaper account and pronouncing it "clearly false"); Caudill and Ashdown, *Sherman's March in Myth and Memory*, p. 44 ("crude parody of a Southern ball").

31 Mead, "With Sherman Through Georgia and the Carolinas," pp. 309, 314.

32 For more on George Barnard, see Bob Zeller, *The Blue and Gray in Black and White: A History of Civil War Photography* (Westport, Conn.: Praeger, 2005), pp. 147–51; Walter F. Rowe, "The Case of the Lying Photographs: The Civil War Photography of George N. Barnard," *Journal of Forensic Sciences* 28, no. 3 (July 1983), pp. 735–55; see also *Harper's Weekly*, Feb. 18, 1865, p. 101 (engraving of "The Spot Where General James B. McPherson Fell"). George Barnard's campaign photographs are collected in *Barnard's Photographic Views of Sherman's Campaign* (New York: Press of Wynkoop & Hallenbeck, 1866). The original 1866 edition is extremely rare, though numerous inexpensive reprint editions are available.

33 Grecian, *83rd Indiana*, pp. 89–90.

34 Benton, *As Seen From the Ranks*, p. 204 (cyclone); Kennett, *Marching Through Georgia*, p. 205 ("most like a ferlow"); Cram, *Soldiering with Sherman*, p. 140 (camp routine); Geary, *A Politician Goes to War*, p. 209 ("home-sick").

35 Sherman to Silas Miller, Sept. 22, 1864, in Andrew Carroll, ed., *War Letters* (New York: Scribner's, 2002), p. 106 ("We must maul the wedge another bit"). Miller had given Sherman his horse Duke, which he rode into Atlanta on September 7. Ibid. Wills, *Army Life*, p. 318 ("We are preparing for a huge campaign").

36 Davis to Herschel V. Johnson, Sept. 18, 1864, in *Papers of Jefferson Davis*, vol. 2, p. 53.

37 Stephenson, *Memoir* ("straight and spare, sallow of hue"); *Papers of Jefferson Davis*, vol. 2, p. 68 ("quiet suit of gray"), p. 60 ("nothing striking in his appearance").

38 "Speech at Macon," in *Papers of Jefferson Davis*, vol. 2, pp. 60–64; Porter, *Campaigning with Grant*, p. 313 (Grant's remark on snow for the Moscow retreat).

39 *Philadelphia Inquirer*, Oct. 10, 1864; *New York Herald*, Oct. 8, 1864. Southern critics of Davis were also furious at the speech. Georgia Governor Joseph Brown charged that it gave the enemy "delight, hope and encouragement," and Confederate Congressman Henry S. Foote called it "the most disgusting spectacle of fustian and billingsgate oratory that has ever been uttered outside of an insane asylum." Ibid., p. 66 n.24 (quoting various reactions to the speech). Sherman, *Memoirs*, vol. 2, p. 141 (noting that Davis "made no concealment of these vainglorious boasts, and thus gave us the full key to his future designs").

40 Foote, *The Civil War*, vol. 3, p. 417.

41 *Richmond Examiner*, Sept. 5, 1864; *Mary Chesnut's Civil War*, p. 662 (quoting Northern newspaper on Hood's appearance); Davis to Herschel V. Johnson, Sept. 18, 1864, in *Papers of Jefferson Davis*, vol. 2, p. 53.

42 Hood to Davis, Sept. 6, 1864, *OR*, vol. 38, pt. 5, p. 1023 ("According to all human calculations we should have saved Atlanta").

43 Hood to Davis, Sept. 13, 1864, *OR*, vol. 39, pt. 2, p. 832 ("In the battle of July 20 we failed on account of General Hardee"). Hood's other two requests to relieve Hardee are at *OR*, vol. 38, pt. 5, p.1030 (Hood to Bragg, Sept. 8), and *OR*, vol. 39, pt. 2, p. 842 (Hood to Davis, Sept. 17).

44 For Hardee's criticisms of Hood, see "Conversation with William J. Hardee," Sept. 26, 1864, in *Papers of Jefferson Davis*, vol. 2, pp. 67–68 ("unjust, ungenerous and unmanly"); *OR*, vol. 38, pt. 3, p. 697 (Hardee's April 5, 1865 report).

President Davis, for his part, seemed to blame neither Hood nor Hardee, and certainly not the rank and file of the Army of Tennessee, but rather his old nemesis Joe Johnston. After all, he pointed out to a correspondent that "it was my opinion then, as clearly as now, that Atlanta could best be defended by holding some of the strong positions to the North of it." Noting that everything possible had been done to give Johnston the resources he needed to stop Sherman: "Charleston, Savannah, Mobile, Mississippi, and north Alabama were stripped to give him a force which would ensure success so speedily, that the troops could return to those places in time to prevent disaster. The resolution did not bring success, but bitter results have followed." Davis to Herschel V. Johnson, Sept. 18, 1864, *Papers of Jefferson Davis*, vol. 2, p. 50.

45 Davis's visit to the army at Palmetto and his mixed reception by the troops is widely discussed in soldier diaries and reminiscences. Even Hood acknowledged in his memoirs that some brigades "were seemingly dissatisfied and inclined to cry out 'Give us General Johnston.'" Hood continued: "I regretted that I should have been the cause of this uncourteous reception to His Excellency; at the same time, I could recall no offence save that of having insisted that they should fight for and hold Atlanta forty-six days, whereas they had previously retreated one hundred miles within sixty-six days." Hood, *Advance and Retreat*, p. 253; Manigault, *A Carolinian Goes to War*, pp. 254–57; see also Chambers, *Blood and Sacrifice*, p. 170 (noting that Davis's reception was "much less cordial than usual").

46 Watkins, *Co. Aytch*, p. 238. Watkins's reference to "chicken guts on my sleeve" is sol-

diers' slang for the gold-braided insignia that appeared on the uniform sleeves of Confederate officers.

47 Foster, *One of Cleburne's Command*, p. 133.

48 Connolly, *Three Years*, p. 274 ("This has been a funny campaign"); Wills, *Army Life*, p. 315 ("It tickles us that you home folks are uneasy").

49 Sherman to Corse, Oct. 7, 1864, *OR*, vol. 39, pt. 3, p. 135 (calling Hood "eccentric"); Wever to J. B. Hood, Oct. 12, 1864, vol. 39, pt. 1, p. 753. The tales of Resaca and Allatoona Pass, great stories both, are sadly beyond the scope of this narrative. For more, see William R. Scaife, *Allatoona Pass: A Needless Effusion of Blood* (Etowah Valley Historical Society, 1995). Perhaps not surprisingly, Colonel Wever's name is frequently misspelled as "Weaver."

50 Watkins, *Co. Aytch*, p. 238 ("Sinner, come view the ground"). Watkins refers to Isaac Watts's profoundly grim 1719 hymn "Hark! From the Tombs a Doleful Sound."

51 Waugh, *Reelecting Lincoln*, pp. 352–55 (Lincoln on election night); Donald, *Lincoln*, p. 544–45 (same); Longfellow's journal, Nov. 10, in Samuel Longfellow, ed., *Life of Henry Wadsworth Longfellow, with Extracts from His Journals and Correspondence* (Boston: Houghton Mifflin, 1891), vol. 3, p. 47; Francis Bicknell Carpenter, *Six Months at the White House*, p. 231; Genesis 22:15.

52 Hanson, *The Soul of Battle*, p. 242 ("Sherman's capture of Atlanta saved Lincoln the election"); Castel, "The Atlanta Campaign and the Presidential Election of 1864: How the South Almost Won by Not Losing," in *Winning and Losing in the Civil War: Essays and Stories* (Columbia: University of South Carolina Press, 1996), p. 29 (stating that "the fall of Atlanta, taking place when it did, turned what Republicans and Democrats alike had perceived as certain victory for McClellan in the upcoming presidential election into foregone defeat").

53 Geary, *A Politician Goes to War*, p. 210; Miller, *Fighting for Liberty and Right*, p. 271 (75th Indiana results); Bradley, *The Star Corps* (22nd Wisconsin results); Woodworth, *Nothing but Victory*, p. 587 (20th Illinois results); Connolly, *Three Years*, p. 293. William Wallace reported to his family that "The election was conducted with as good regularity as if we were at the old school house. Our tent served as a school house and cigar box for a ballot box." "William Wallace's Civil War Letters," *Wisconsin Magazine of History*, p. 113.

54 *Richmond Examiner*, Sept. 5, 1864.

55 *London Daily News*, Sept. 27, 1864, quoted in McPherson, *Battle Cry of Freedom*, p. 806.

56 S. B. Crew to Dear Brother & Sister, Dec. 15, 1864, Collection of Mary Louise Dunn Fleming.

Chapter 12. The Whole World on Fire

1 General Orders No. 73, Chambersburg, Pa., June 27, 1863, *OR*, vol. 27, pt. 3, pp. 942–43.

2 Mark Leepson, *Desperate Engagement* (New York: Macmillan, 2007) (description of Early, "hates his staff like blazes").

3 Jubal Early's burning of Chambersburg, Pennsylvania, is described in numerous sources. For an excellent recent account, see Scott Patchan, *Shenandoah Summer: The 1864 Valley Campaign* (Lincoln: University of Nebraska Press, 2007), pp. 273–82; see also Liva Baker, "The Burning of Chambersburg," *American Heritage* 24, no. 5 (Aug. 1974); Grimsley, *Hard Hand of War*, pp. 179–81.

4 Pennsylvania editor Alexander McClure, whose home was destroyed by McCausland's men, later called the burning of Chambersburg an act of "unexampled barbarity," one that "accomplished nothing in the war beyond making hundreds of homeless families in the South . . . where the people learned to associate the cry of Chambersburg with sweeping destruction. Every drunken Union soldier in Southern cities applied the torch as did the drunken soldiers of McCausland in Chambersburg, always preceding it with the cry of 'Remember Chambersburg!'" A. K. McClure, *Abraham Lincoln and Men of War-Times*, 2nd ed. (Philadelphia: Times Publishing, 1892), p. 421; see also Jubal A. Early, *A Memoir of the Last Year of the War for Independence in the Confederate States of America* (Lynchburg: Charles W. Button, 1867), p. 70 ("I am perfectly satisfied with my conduct").

Sherman made no particular mention of Chambersburg in his wartime correspondence, but cited it years later. "The rebels were notoriously more cruel than our men," he contended in an 1881 letter to a friend. "We never could work up our men to the terrible earnestness of the Southern forces. Their murdering of Union fugitives, burning of Lawrence, Chambersburg, Paducah, etc., were all right in their eyes; and if we burned an old cotton gin or shed it was barbarism. I am tired of such perversion, and will resist it always." Sherman to T. H. Lee, June 14, 1881, in *Southern Historical Society Papers*, vol. 9, p. 380.

5 Willard Warner to Mrs. General W. T. Sherman, Feb. 22, 1876, in Sherman, *Memoirs*, vol. 2, p. 538 ("Salt water"); Sherman to Grant, Oct. 1, 1864, *OR*, vol. 39, pt. 3, p. 3.

6 Sherman to Grant, Nov. 2, 1864, *OR*, vol. 39, pt. 3, p. 595 ("the whole effect of my campaign will be lost"); Sherman to Grant, Oct. 9, 1864, ibid., p. 162 ("make Georgia howl"); Sherman to Thomas, Oct. 2, 1864, in *Sherman's Civil War*, p. 730 ("synonimous terms").

7 Grant to Sherman, Nov. 2, 1864, *OR*, vol. 39, pt. 3, p. 594 ("I say, then, go as you propose"); Sherman to Thomas, Oct. 2, 1864, in *Sherman's Civil War*, p. 730 ("stripped for the work"). Grant's November 2 approval of Sherman's plan is often quoted as "go on as you propose." See, e.g., Sherman, *Memoirs*, vol. 2, p. 166.

8 Sherman to Poe, Nov. 7, 1864, *OR*, vol. 39, pt. 3, p. 680 ("fire will do most of the work"); Sherman to Poe, Nov. 11, 1864, ibid., p. 741.

9 Sherman to Grant, July 18, 1863, *OR*, vol. 24, pt. 2, p. 529 ("The inhabitants are subjugated"), ibid. p. 528 ("one mass of charred ruins").

10 Sherman to Grant, July 18, 1863, *OR*, vol. 24, pt. 2, p. 526 ("The wholesale destruction," etc.). For more on the burning of Jackson, see Michael B. Ballard, *Vicksburg: The Campaign that Opened the Mississippi* (Chapel Hill: University of North Carolina Press, 2003), pp. 409–11; William L. Shea and Terrence J. Winschel, *Vicksburg Is the Key: The*

Struggle for the Mississippi (Lincoln: University of Nebraska Press, 2003), pp. 184–86. Sherman blamed most of the burned buildings in Jackson on the Confederates. "The enemy burned nearly all the handsome dwellings round about the town because they gave us shelter or to light up the ground to prevent night attacks," he told Admiral David Dixon Porter. "He also set fire to a chief block of stores in which were commissary supplies, and our men, in spite of guards, have widened the circle of fire, so that Jackson, once the pride and boast of Mississippi, is now a ruined town." Sherman to Porter, July 19, 1863, *OR*, vol. 24, pt. 3, p. 531. Another precursor to the destruction in Georgia was Sherman's Meridian Campaign of February 1864. See generally Kennett, *Sherman*, p. 237 (describing the Meridian raid as "an overture of sorts" to the campaign in Georgia).

11 S. M. Budlong to T. T. Heath, Oct. 30, 1864, *OR*, vol. 39, pt. 3, p. 513 (orders for the destruction of Canton and Cassville: "You will permit the citizens to remove what they desire, and burn the town"); Frances Elizabeth Gaines, "We Begged to Hearts of Stone," Frances Josephine Black, ed., *Northwest Georgia Historical and Genealogical Quarterly* 20 (Winter 1988), pp. 1–6; see also Lucy Josephine Cunyus, *The History of Bartow County, Formerly Cass* (Bartow County, Ga.: Tribune Publishing, 1933), p. 244; see also Connolly, *Three Years*, p. 296 ("As we were marching through Cass Station, we could see the one solitary church spire of Cassville, the rest of the village having been burned yesterday by our soldiers, on account of its being a guerilla haunt"). Old Cassville was never rebuilt—most of its residents moved to nearby Cartersville.

12 Sherman to Corse, Nov. 10, 1864, *OR*, vol. 39, pt. 3, p. 729 (order to burn Rome); Sherman to Spencer, Nov. 10, 1864, ibid., p. 730 ("You have known for ten days"); George Magruder Battey, *A History of Rome and Floyd County, State of Georgia* (Atlanta: Webb and Vary Co., 1922), p. 178; see also Andrew J. Boies, *Record of the Thirty-Third Massachusetts Volunteer Infantry from Aug. 1862 to Aug. 1865* (Fitchburg, Mass.: Sentinel Printing Co., 1880), p. 100 (describing "an awful scene: the burning of Rome").

13 Berry Diary, Nov. 7, 1864, AHC; Underwood, *Three Years' Service*, p. 240 ("Aurora Borealis"); Girardi, ed., *Memoirs of Brigadier General Carlin*, p. 142. For thoughts of Cortés, *see* Connolly, *Three Years*, p. 292 ("Nothing in military history compares with it except the invasion of Mexico by Cortez"); Nichols, *Story of the Great March*, p. 37 ("The history of war bears no similar example, except that of Cortés burning his ships. It is a bold, hazardous undertaking"); Castel, *Decision in the West*, p. 554. See also Hanson, *The Soul of Battle*, p. 150 ("going into the hole and pulling the hole in after us").

14 Henry Hitchcock, *Marching with Sherman: Passages from the Letters and Campaign Diaries of Henry Hitchcock, Major and Assistant Adjutant General of Volunteers, November 1864–May 1865*, M. A. DeWolfe Howe, ed. (Lincoln: University of Nebraska Press, 1995), pp. 52–53. Hitchcock's account of Sherman at Marietta was corroborated by a Federal colonel. See Michael H. Fitch, *Echoes of the Civil War as I Hear Them* (New York: R. F. Fenno, 1905), p. 232 ("All the principal buildings around the public square in this town were burning as we passed. General Sherman was standing looking on").

15 Benson J. Lossing, *Pictorial History of the Civil War in the United States of America* (Hartford: T. Belknap, 1868), vol. 3, p. 403 (description of Marietta; "a ghastly ruin").

16 Minerva Leah Rowles McClatchey, "A Georgia Woman's Civil War Diary: The Journal of Minerva Leah Rowles McClatchey," *Georgia Historical Quarterly* 51 (1967), pp. 210–11 ("Every house was in flames"); see also Louisa Warren Fletcher, *Journal of a Landlady*, H. Higgins and C. Cox, eds. (Chapel Hill: Professional Press, 1995), p. 151 ("Nearly all the public buildings & some twenty or more private residences have been destroyed. . . . These were days of terror—everyone in dread for fear their turn would come next").

17 Hitchcock, *Marching with Sherman*, p. 54.

18 Cornelius C. Platter, Diary, Nov. 12, 1864, Hargrett Rare Book and Manuscript Library, University of Georgia ("No houses—no fences"); Nichols, *Story of the Great March*, pp. 37–38 ("I say, Charley").

19 Hedley, *Marching Through Georgia*, p. 256 ("not a Federal soldier . . . demon of destruction"); Sgt. Jerome Carpenter, *Rochester Chronicle*, Jan. 12, 1865, quoted in Jack K. Overmyer, *A Stupendous Effort: The 87th Indiana in the War of the Rebellion* (Bloomington: Indiana University Press, 1997), p. 155 ("vast clouds of smoke ascending").

20 Sherman, *Memoirs*, vol. 2, p. 177 (Poe's "special task of destruction"); Poe's report, Oct. 8, 1865, *OR*, vol. 44, pt. 1, p. 60 ("battering down the walls"); Trudeau, *Southern Storm*, p. 67 ("Battering Ram").

21 Conyngham, *Sherman's March*, p. 236; Berry Diary, Nov. 12, 1864, AHC.

22 Berry Diary, Oct. 23, 1864, AHC.

23 Berry Diary, Nov. 13–14, 1864, AHC; Conyngham, *Sherman's March*, p. 236.

24 John J. Hight, *History of the Fifty-eighth Regiment of Indiana Volunteer Infantry* (Princeton, Ind.: Press of the Clarion, 1895), p. 409 ("A notion has possessed the army that Atlanta is to be burned"); Alexander G. Downing, *Downing's Civil War Diary*, Olynthus B. Clark, ed. (Des Moines: Historical Department of Iowa, 1916), p. 228 ("Every man seems to think he has a free hand to touch the match"); Conyngham, *Sherman's March*, p. 241 ("Look around boys; I reckon 'Old Billy' has set the world on fire").

25 Berry Diary, Nov. 15, 1864, AHC; Connolly, *Three Years*, p. 301.

26 Reid, *The View from Headquarters*, p. 202; Hitchcock, *Marching with Sherman*, pp. 57–58.

27 Conyngham, *Sherman's March*, p. 238.

28 Berry Diary, Nov. 16, 1864, AHC; James Royal Ladd Diary, Nov. 15, 1864, "From Atlanta to the Sea," *American Heritage* 30, no. 1 (Dec. 1978).

29 Sgt. Allen Campbell to father, Dec. 21, 1864, quoted in Mark Hoffman, *"My Brave Mechanics": The First Michigan Engineers and Their Civil War* (Detroit: Wayne State University Press, 2007), pp. 242–43. Interestingly, Campbell was a member of the 1st Michigan Engineers and Mechanics, one of the regiments assigned to Poe to carry out the destruction. Campbell's clearly voluntary and open participation in house burning may suggest that Poe's engineers were not quite as scrupulous as his official report suggests.

30 For more on Father O'Reilly, see generally "In Memoriam: Father Thomas O'Reilly," *Atlanta Historical Bulletin* 30 (Oct. 1945); Garrett, *Atlanta and Environs*, vol. 1, p. 652; and John Wesley Brinsfield, Jr., *The Spirit Divided: Memoirs of Civil War Chaplains—The Confederacy* (Macon, Ga.: Mercer University Press, 2006), p. 225. Gen. Slocum to wife Clara, Nov. 7, 1864, quoted in Brian C. Melton, *Sherman's Forgotten General: Henry W. Slocum* (Columbia: University of Missouri Press, 2007), p. 184. Some accounts of Father O'Reilly's story suggest that he confronted Sherman directly, warning that Catholic soldiers would mutiny if their church were burned, or would face excommunication if they participated in the destruction. A monument to Father O'Reilly was dedicated in 1945 and stands at the corner of Mitchell and Courtland streets in downtown Atlanta. The city's Irish Catholics conduct an annual wreath-laying in the heroic priest's honor.

31 Garrett, *Atlanta and Environs*, vol. 1, pp. 651–52. Dr. D'Alvigny was reportedly the model for the character of brave Dr. Meade in *Gone with the Wind.*

32 *Atlanta Fire Department Commemorative Yearbook* (Atlanta: Turner Publishing Co., 2001), p. 15; Grimsley, *Hard Hand of War*, p. 191 ("personally supervised efforts to contain the flames"); Pepper, *Personal Recollections*, p. 239; Patten, "An Indiana Doctor Marches with Sherman," *Indiana Magazine of History*, p. 417 ("We could see Atlanta burning. I looked at my watch and could see the time very plainly at a distance of ten miles"); Joseph T. Glatthaar, "Sherman's Army and Total War: Attitudes on Destruction in the Savannah and Carolinas Campaign," *Atlanta Historical Journal* 29, no. 1 (Spring 1985), p. 47 (in Atlanta, "the fire was so bright a soldier a mile and a half away noted, 'We could see to read newspapers at midnight at our camp from the light of the burning buildings'"); Daniel Oakey, "Marching Through Georgia and the Carolinas," *Battles and Leaders*, vol. 4, p. 672 ("Sixty thousand of us witnessed the destruction of Atlanta").

33 Hight, *History of the Fifty-eighth Regiment*, pp. 410–11.

34 Underwood, *The Three Years' Service*, p. 240 ("No darkness"); W. C. Johnson, "The March to the Sea," *GAR War Papers* (Cincinnati: Fred C. Jones Post, 1891), pp. 314–15.

35 Connolly, *Three Years*, pp. 301–2 ("All the pictures and verbal descriptions of hell"). For comparisons to ancient Babylon, see, e.g., Sgt. Jerome Carpenter, quoted in Overmyer, *A Stupendous Effort*, p. 155 ("by the time we left . . . it might have been very appropriately said, as of ancient Babylon, 'Atlanta, that great city, has fallen and has become the habitation of moles and bats'"); Miller, *Fighting for Liberty and Right*, p. 278 ("It reminds me of the distruction of the city of Babalon as spoken of in the bible whis was destroyed because of the wickedness of her people and that is the case with Atlanta. I feel Sorry for some of the people but a Soldier is not supposed to have any concience and must lay aside all scruples he may have").

36 Downing, *Downing's Civil War Diary*, p. 229 ("Started early this morning for the Southern coast"); Albion W. Tourgee, *The Story of a Thousand* (Buffalo: S. McGerald & Son, 1896), p. 334 ("Many conjectures"); Sherman, *Memoirs*, vol. 2, pp. 178–79.

37 Lewis, *Sherman, Fighting Prophet*, p. 435 ("approximately 37 per cent of the city's area was in ashes when at 7 a.m. Sherman departed"); Miles, *To the Sea*, p. 25 ("Poe estimat-

ed that thirty-seven percent of the city had been destroyed, but that was a charitable estimate"); Evans, *Confederate Military History*, vol. 7, p. 360 ("More than 4,000 houses, including dwellings, shops, stores, mills and depots were burned, about eleven-twelfths of the city"); *Augusta Chronicle and Sentinel*, Dec. 15, 1864, quoted in "Atlanta as Sherman Left It: Atlanta Then and Now," *Atlanta Historical Bulletin* 1, no. 3 (May 1930), p. 15 (three-fourths burned; nine-tenths destroyed). See also Theodore F. Upson, *With Sherman to the Sea*, O. O. Winther, ed. (Bloomington: Indiana University Press, 1958), p. 133 ("We have utterly destroyed Atlanta").

38 Hitchcock, *Marching with Sherman*, pp. 57–58; Marszalek, *Sherman*, p. 299; *New York Evening Post*, n.d., quoted in W. Fletcher Johnson, *Life of Wm. Tecumseh Sherman, Late Retired General, U.S.A.* ([Philadelphia]: Edgewood Publishing Co., 1891), p. 371 ("buildings covering over two hundred acres are in ruins or in flames").

39 Orders for burning Rome, *OR*, vol. 39, pt. 3, pp. 628–29 ("shops of all kinds and descriptions"; "lumber or timber"); orders for the special destruction of Atlanta, ibid., p. 680 ("&c."); Sherman to Slocum, Nov. 7, 1864, ibid., p. 681 ("All houses used for storage along the railroad will be destroyed"); Kennett, *Marching Through Georgia*, pp. 233–34 (noting that "The rather generalized practice of burning homes may have been an 'over-application' of an order Sherman issued for the destruction of all structures that had been used to store army supplies—a number of houses in each town had been used for this purpose").

40 Hitchcock, *Marching with Sherman*, pp. 86-87. Historian John Bennett Walters, a sharp critic of Sherman and his methods, wrote of Sherman's orders for limited destruction: "It is difficult to escape the conviction that these orders were issued by Sherman more for the record than for the governing of his troops' actions." John B. Walters, *Merchant of Terror: General Sherman and Total War* (Indianapolis: Bobbs-Merrill, 1973), p. 154. Historian Mark Grimsley, who largely defends Sherman against Walters's attacks, nonetheless writes: "Sherman clearly knew that those instructions would be imperfectly carried out—that some soldiers would pillage and plunder and vandalize. And many people, then and later, have suspected that Sherman secretly (or not so secretly) wanted that to happen. His comments about 'desolating the land as we progress' and 'making Georgia howl' suggest as much. So too does the grim relish with which he greeted the destruction of Atlanta's war resources, a task that got out of hand and resulted in considerable destruction to the city's residential quarter." Grimsley, *Hard Hand of War*, p. 191. See also Michael Fellman, *Citizen Sherman: A Life of William Tecumseh Sherman* (New York: Random House, 1995), p. 214 ("Sherman's ever-increasing keenness to destroy shone through even his field orders, which were official documents almost certain to be more law-affirming than any practical limits he or his subordinates might set on actual behavior while in the heat of action. Certainly his men acted on their general's covert intentions rather than on his published orders").

41 Connelly, *John M. Schofield and the Politics of Generalship*, pp. 111–12 (the "myth of the burning of Atlanta"); Marszalek, *Sherman*, p. 300 ("at least four-hundred buildings stood undamaged"); Horace Greeley, *The American Conflict: A History of the Great Rebellion in the United States of America, 1860–'65* (Chicago: O. D. Case, 1866), Vol. 2, p. 703.

42 Sherman to Captain Burke, March 1880, quoted in Johnson, *Life of Wm. Tecumseh Sherman,* pp. 553–54; Sherman conversation with Hon. Henry W. Grady, quoted in ibid., pp. 554–55.

43 Sherman to H. W. Hill, Chairman of Meeting of Citizens of Warren County, Miss., Sept. 7, 1863, in *Sherman's Civil War,* p. 538; Jefferson Davis, *Rise and Fall,* vol. 2, p. 564.

44 Colonel Howard's report is quoted in full as Appendix B.

45 W. P. Howard to Joseph E. Brown, Dec. 7, 1864, *Macon Telegraph,* Dec. 12, 1864. Much of Howard's description is corroborated by a similar street-by-street account in a letter from railroad agent James R. Crew to his wife, Dec. 1, 1864, AHC, and in the *Daily Intelligencer,* Dec. 22, 1864.

46 Hitchcock, *Marching with Sherman,* p. 77; Lysander Wheeler to Dear Parents, Bro and Sister, Nov. 2, 1864, in Robert E. Bonner, ed., *The Soldier's Pen: Firsthand Impressions of the Civil War* (New York: Hill and Wang, 2006), pp. 107–8.

47 Reid, *The View from Headquarters,* p. 203.

48 John Chipman Gray to John C. Ropes, Dec. 14, 1864, in *War Letters, 1862–1865,* p. 428.

49 Beauregard to Davis, Dec. 6, 1864, quoted in Hood, *Advance and Retreat,* p. 280.

50 Hood, *Advance and Retreat,* p. 290 ("The best move in my career as a soldier, I was thus destined to behold come to naught").

51 James A. Sexton, quoted in Walker, *Hell's Broke Loose in Georgia,* p. 196; J. P. Young, "Hood's Failure at Spring Hill," *Confederate Veteran* 17 (Jan. 1908), p. 36 ("wrathy as a rattlesnake"); Henry Martyn Field, *Bright Skies and Dark Shadows* (New York: Charles Scribner's Sons, 1890), p. 219 (hearsay account of Hood's insistence on attack).

52 J. B. Hood, "The Invasion of Tennessee," *Battles and Leaders,* vol. 4, p. 433 ("drive the enemy"); Walker, *Hell's Broke Loose in Georgia,* p. 199; Watkins, *Co. Aytch,* p. 260 ("The death-angel was there"); Wiley Sword, *The Confederacy's Last Hurrah: Spring Hill, Franklin, and Nashville* (Lawrence: University Press of Kansas, 1993), p. 278 (Hood wept like a child); see also Hood, *Advance and Retreat,* pp. 295–96 ("I rode over the scene of action the next morning, and could not but indulge in sad and painful thought, as I beheld so many brave soldiers stricken down by the enemy whom, a few hours previous, at Spring Hill, we had held within the palm of our hands"). Sam Watkins asserts that Cleburne's body was pierced by forty-nine bullets. *Co. Aytch,* p. 263.

53 Hood, *Advance and Retreat,* p. 300 ("a last and manful effort"); McMurry, *John Bell Hood and the War for Southern Independence,* p. 182 (returns of Dec. 31). Albert Castel notes that sources on Hood's Tennessee campaign are "enormous in quantity and horrendous in controversy." Castel, *Decision in the West,* p. 627. See generally Sword, *The Confederacy's Last Hurrah*; Walker, *Hell's Broke Loose in Georgia,* pp. 202–8; Anne Bailey, *The Chessboard of War: Sherman and Hood in the Autumn Campaign of 1864* (Lincoln: University of Nebraska Press, 2000), pp. 151–68. Bailey analyzes Hood's casualties and asserts that his year-end strength returns are probably inflated. Ibid., p. 167–68 ("This thing what they call chargin brest works").

54 Yet unlike Lee, who always took the responsibility for his army's failures, Hood blamed his setbacks and losses on his subordinate officers, and worse, on his men. "Military operations, however well conceived, are not always successful, and I have had my share of failures and disappointments," General Frank Cheatham wrote years after the war, chiding his former chief for this unbecoming tendency. "But I never found it necessary to seek a scape-goat for my transgressions, nor to maintain my own reputation by aspersions of my subordinates. No chieftain since the world began ever commanded an army of men more confident in themselves, more ready to endure and to dare whatever might be required of them, or more capable of exalted heroism than that which obeyed the will of their General from Peach-Tree creek to Nashville." Benjamin Franklin Cheatham, "The Lost Opportunity at Spring Hill, Tenn.—General Cheatham's Reply to General Hood," *Southern Historical Society Papers* 9 (1881), p. 533.

55 *Mary Chesnut's Civil War*, p. 708 (Hood at the Prestons).

56 Sherman to Lincoln, Dec. 22, 1864, *OR*, vol. 44, pt. 1, p. 783; Sherman, *Memoirs*, vol. 2, p. 231; Wills, *Army Life*, p. 330 ("the most gigantic pleasure excursion ever planned"); C. S. Brown to family, Dec. 16, 1864, Charles S. Brown Papers, Duke University Library, quoted in Lawrence, *A Present for Mr. Lincoln*, p. 163 ("black streak behind us"); Bruce Catton, *Never Call Retreat* (New York: Doubleday, 1961), p. 415 ("We had a gay old campaign").

57 Sherman to Grant, Jan. 1, 1865, *OR*, vol. 44, pt. 1, pp. 13–14; Sherman to Halleck, Dec. 24, 1864, in *Sherman's Civil War*, p. 776; Wallace, "William Wallace's Civil War Letters," *Wisconsin Magazine of History*, p. 113.

58 Hitchcock, *Marching with Sherman*, pp. 201–2 (Christmas dinner in Savannah). see also *Harper's Weekly*, Jan. 28, 1865, p. 53 (Theodore Davis sketch of "Christmas-Day in Savannah—General Sherman's Christmas Dinner at Mr. Green's").

59 Lincoln to Sherman, Dec. 26, 1864, *OR*, vol. 44, p. 809; Sherman to John Sherman, Jan. 22, 1865, in *SCW*, pp. 808–9.

60 Hitchcock, *Marching with Sherman*, pp. 201–2 (Sherman's visitors); Sherman to Ellen, Dec. 25, 1864, in *Sherman's Civil War*, p. 778.

61 Hostetter Diary, Dec. 26, 1864, quoted in Payne, *History of the Thirty-fourth Illinois*, p. 179.

62 Sherman to Ellen, Dec. 31, 1864, in *Sherman's Civil War*, p. 785.

63 Katharine M. Jones, *When Sherman Came: Southern Women and the "Great March"* (Indianapolis: Bobbs-Merrill, 1964), pp. 91–92, 99 (Howard's encounter over the flag and with Daisy Gordon); see also Burke Davis, *Sherman's March* (New York: Random House, 1985), pp. 125–26 (same).

64 Fletcher, *Journal of a Landlady*, p. 155 ("Christmas! How inappropriate"); Cumming, *Journal of Kate Cumming*, p. 229 ("This one has been any thing but merry"). Some stalwart Rebel optimists attempted to downplay Sherman's latest exploit, including the humorist Bill Arp. "Spose Sherman did walk rite thru the State. Spose he did," Arp wrote defiantly. "Was eny body whipped? Didn't the rebellyun just klose rite up behind him, like shettin a pair of waful irons? He parted the atmosphere as he went along, and

it kollapsed agin in his reer immegitly. He'll have to go over that old ground sevrul times yet, and then sell out and move away." The Georgia columnist insisted, "we ain't whipped yet—not by three or four jug fulls." "Bill Arp Filosofizes on the War, Etc.," in *Bill Arp's Peace Papers* (New York: G. W. Carleton, 1873), p. 105; see also Charles C. Jones, Jr., *General Sherman's March from Atlanta to the Coast. An Address Delivered before the Confederate Survivor's Association, in Augusta, Georgia, at its Sixth Annual Meeting, on Memorial Day, April 26, 1884* (Augusta, Ga.: Chronicle, 1884), pp. 9–10 (deriding Sherman's march as a campaign waged against "unprotected women, fatherless children, and old men" and calling it "a holiday excursion . . . not a martial enterprise involving exposures, dangers and uncertainties").

65 Richards Diary, Dec. 26, 1864, AHC; Mary Mallard Diary, in Mary Sharpe Jones and Mary Jones Mallard, *Yankees A'Coming: One Month's Experience During the Invasion of Liberty County, Georgia 1864–1865*, Haskell Monroe, ed. (Tuscaloosa: Confederate Pub. Co., 1959), p. 76.

66 Letter from " jim" to "libby," quoted in Edmund N. Hatcher, *The Last Four Weeks of the War* (Columbus: By the author, 1891), p. 224.

Chapter 13. Resurgens

1 *Atlanta Daily Intelligencer*, Dec. 22, 1864.

2 William R. Plum, *The Military Telegraph During the Civil War in the United States* (Chicago: Jansen, McClurg & Co., 1882), vol. 2, p. 242.

3 Whitelaw Reid, *After the War: A Southern Tour* (London: Sampson Low, Son, & Marson, 1866), p. 360; Sir John Henry Kennaway, *On Sherman's Track; or, The South After the War* (London: Seeley, Jackson and Halliday, 1867), p. 106.

4 J. T. Trowbridge, *The South: A Tour of Its Battle-Fields and Ruined Cities, A Journey Through the Desolated States and Talks with the People* (Hartford: L. Stebbins, 1866), p. 270.

5 Trowbridge, *The South*, p. 453 ("ruins and rubbish"); James R. Crew to wife Jane, Dec. 1, 1864, Crew Papers, AHC; see also T. D. Killian, "James R. Crew," *Atlanta Historical Bulletin* 1, no. 6 (Jan. 1932), pp. 5–15; *Atlanta Intelligencer*, quoted in Martin, *Atlanta and Its Builders*, vol. 2, p. 9; Gibbons, "Life at the Crossroads of the Confederacy, 1861–1865," p. 58 (quoting lost Kentucky refugee: "Turn which way I would nothing met my eyes but a confused mass of chimneys").

6 Reid, *After the War*, p. 355 (Sherman's mark); *Atlanta Intelligencer*, Dec. 22, 1864, quoted in Garrett, *Atlanta and Environs*, pp. 655–59; cf. "Atlanta as Sherman Left It—Atlanta Then and Now,"*Atlanta Historical Bulletin* 1, no. 3 (May 1930), pp. 15–20.

7 *Atlanta Intelligencer*, Dec. 22, 1864, quoted in Garrett, *Atlanta and Environs*, pp. 655–59;G.W. Hanger, "With Sherman in Georgia: A Letter from the Coast," *Georgia Historical Quarterly* 42, p. 441 ("I do not think the cars will run for a fieu days yet").

8 Huff, *My 80 Years in Atlanta*, pp. 33–34 (noting that "no doves or other birds were heard, even when the springtime came. The bluebirds were missed for three years"); W. P. Howard to Joseph E. Brown, Dec. 7, 1864 ("From two to three thousand dead carcasses of animals remain in the city limits").

9 *Atlanta Intelligencer*, quoted in Martin, *Atlanta and Its Builders*, vol. 2, p. 9; W. P. Howard to Joseph E. Brown, Dec. 7, 1864; Berry Diary, Nov. 17–18, 1864, AHC.

10 Gibbons, "Life at the Crossroads of the Confederacy," pp. 57–58 ("lead mines"). Decatur resident Mary A. H. Gay describes in detail the work of her little "lead digging company" in Gay, *Life in Dixie During the War*, pp. 255–67.

11 Trowbridge, *The South*, p. 453 (describing huts and shanties).

12 Garrett, *Atlanta and Environs*, vol. 1, p. 662 (children "clad only in tow sacks"); Martin, *Atlanta and Its Builders*, vol. 2, p. 9.

13 *Atlanta Daily Intelligencer*, Dec. 22, 1864; Kennaway, *The South After the War*, p. 106 ("How can we forget or forgive"); *New York Tribune*, July 25, 1865, in Oberholtzer, *History of the United States Since the Civil War*, p. 57 n. 3 ("Hell has laid her egg").

14 E. F.Winslow to Captain Griffin, May 31, 1865, *OR*, vol. 49, pt. 2, p. 939 (5,000 to 8,000 families, 25,000 to 50,000 persons); J. H. Wilson to George H. Thomas, ibid., p. 949 ("Women and children walk from ten to forty miles"). For a description and reaction to the "Burnt Country," see Eliza Frances Andrews, *The War-Time Journal of a Georgia Girl, 1864–1865* (New York: D. Appleton and Co., 1908), pp. 32–33.

15 Allison G. Dorsey, *To Build Our Lives Together: Community Formation in Black Atlanta, 1875–1906* (Athens: University of Georgia Press, 2004), pp. 29–30, 34. Garrett, *Atlanta and Environs*, vol. 1, p. 690–91 (Freedmen's Bureau).

16 John Richard Dennett, *The South as It Is, 1865–1866*, Henry M. Christman, ed. (New York: Viking Press, 1965), p. 266 ("rough-looking fellows"); Reid, *After the War*, p. 356.

17 O. S. Hammond to Mrs. Adair, Feb. 10, 1865, quoted in Garrett, *Atlanta and Environs*, vol. 1, p. 670, ("Every body that can is returning"); Kennett, *Marching Through Georgia*, p. 314 (describing Calhoun's return); *Atlanta Intelligencer*, Dec. 22, 1864; Garrett, *Atlanta and Environs*, vol. 1, p. 669, 675 ($1.64 in the city treasury).

18 Garrett, *Atlanta and Environs*, vol. 1, p. 669, 675 ("Survival required action"); Dennett, *The South As It Is*, p. 268 (scaffolding, etc.); V. T. Barnwell, *Barnwell's Atlanta City Directory and Strangers' Guide* (Atlanta: Intelligencer Book and Job Office, 1867), p. 33 (describing municipal improvements and noting streets "have been put in a fair condition").

19 Dyer, "Half Slave Half Free," pp. 303–4 (Robert Webster's loan to his former master).

20 Garrett, *Atlanta and Environs*, pp. 661, 686–88 (describing opened businesses and advertising in 1864–65); Kennaway, *The South After the War*, pp. 115–16 (remains of manufacturing; frontage $40 a foot); S. P. Richards Diary, Aug. 10, 1864, AHC; *Barnwell's City Directory*, p. 33 (338 businesses licensed in the last six months of 1865).

21 Dennett, *The South As It Is*, p. 268; Reid, *After the War*, p. 355 ("These people were taking lessons from Chicago"); James Michael Russell, *Atlanta 1847–1890: City Building in the Old South and the New* (Baton Rouge: Louisiana State University Press, 1988), p. 126 ("Atlanta is a devil of a place"); Edward King, *The Great South* (Hartford: American Publishing Co., 1875), p. 350 ("antithesis of Savannah").

22 Andrews, *The South Since the War*, p. 375 ("gentlemen"/"greasy workingmen"); *Atlanta Intelligencer*, March 3, 1865, quoted in Franklin Garrett, "The Phoenix Begins to Rise: The Atlanta Daily Intelligencer Announces the Return of the Railroads," *Atlanta History* 37, no. 4 (Winter 1994), pp. 5–8; Dennett, *The South As It Is*, p. 267 ("a wilderness of mud").

23 George Rose [Arthur Sketchley], *The Great Country; of Impressions of America* (London: Tinsley Brothers, 1868), p. 175.

24 *Atlanta Constitution*, Jan. 30, 1879; ibid., Jan. 31, 1879 ("Wm. T., Come, Sir!"); Sherman to Grant, May 27, 1867, quoted in Fellman, *Citizen Sherman*, p. 264; Lewis, *Sherman: Fighting Prophet*, p. 631 ("one long chicken dinner"). On Sherman's visit to Atlanta, see also John M. Marszalek, "Celebrity in Dixie: Sherman Tours the South, 1879," *Georgia Historical Quarterly* 66 (1982), pp. 366–83.

25 The best overview of Atlanta's recovery and postwar progress is James Michael Russell's *Atlanta, 1847–1890: City Building in the Old South and the New*; see also Don H. Doyle, *New Men, New Cities, New South: Atlanta, Nashville, Charleston, Mobile, 1860–1910* (Chapel Hill: University of North Carolina Press, 1990), pp. 31–38 For an eyewitness picture of the street life and culture around the time of Sherman's visit, see Ernest Ingersoll, "The City of Atlanta,"*Harper's New Monthly Magazine* 60, no. 355 (Dec. 1879), pp. 30–44; Wilber W. Caldwell, *The Courthouse and the Depot: The Architecture of Hope in an Age of Despair* (Macon, Ga.: Mercer University Press, 2001), pp. 278–79 (400 buildings built in 1871; new Atlanta depot; "Second Empire clothing of the so-called 'General Grant style'").

26 Ingersoll, "The City of Atlanta," *Harper's Monthly*, p. 36.

27 *Atlanta Constitution*, Jan. 30, 1879; Gary M. Pomerantz, *Where Peachtree Meets Sweet Auburn: The Saga of Two Families and the Making of Atlanta* (New York: Scribner, 1996), p. 54 (story of Sherman and the hand); Margaret Mitchell to Lutie Marshall Bradfield, March 16, 1937, in Richard Harwell, ed., *Margaret Mitchell's Gone with the Wind Letters, 1936–1949* (New York: Macmillan, 1976), pp. 132–33 (version of same story).

28 *Atlanta Constitution*, July 20, 1879 (Uncle Remus); Mark Pendergrast, *For God, Country and Coca-Cola: The Definitive History of the Great American Soft Drink and the Company that Makes It* (New York: Basic Books, 2000), p. 20; see also John Stainback Wilson, *Atlanta As It Is* (New York: Little, Rennie & Co., 1871), pp. 90–92 (providing an early description of the drug and chemical house of Pemberton, Taylor & Co.). The famous Dr. Pemberton, by the way, is no relation to the Pennsylvania-born Confederate General John C. Pemberton, who surrendered the garrison at Vicksburg on July 4, 1863. Sherman to E. P. Howell, quoted in "The New South: Letter from General Sherman," *Atlanta Constitution*, Feb. 11, 1879. Samuel P. Richards noted the occasion in his diary: "Gen. Sherman has just honored our city by a visit to see how nicely we have builded it up after his burning it." S. P. Richards Diary, Jan. 31, 1879, quoted in Garrett, *Atlanta and Environs*, vol. 1, p. 953. Sherman's visit and the subsequent publication of his letter inspired a different reaction from Bill Arp, writing in the *Constitution*: "I thought about prarie fires and Mississippi hurricanes and avalanches and the pestilence that walketh at noonday. I thought about women and children made homeless and desolate, and driv-

en away to wander in search of food and shelter and a hiding place. I don't think about these things often, for the old sore has got well, but, then, the scar is there, and theres a weak spot in the bone underneath, and it takes the rumatics whenever anything happens that freshens up the horrors of that march to the sea." Arp, "Fifteen Years Back, With Tecumseh Sherman," *Atlanta Constitution*, Feb. 16, 1879.

29 James Michael Russell, "The Phoenix City After the Civil War: Atlanta's Economic Miracle," *Atlanta History* 33, no. 4 (Winter 1990), p. 21 ("spirit of Yankee capitalism," proposed Lincoln monument); see also Russell, *Atlanta 1847–1890*, p. 149 (same); Arp, "Bill Arp on the State of the Country," in *Bill Arp's Peace Papers*, p. 116.

30 *New York Times*, Dec. 26, 1886 ("The Lord only knows"); Henry W. Grady, "The New South," speech at the New England Society, New York City, Dec. 21, 1886, in *The Complete Orations and Speeches of Henry W. Grady*, Edwin DuBois Shurter, ed. (Norwood, Mass.: Norwood Press, 1910), pp. 7–22. The *New York Times* wrote the next day: "No postprandial oration of any recent occasion has aroused such enthusiasm in this city as the speech of Henry W. Grady, editor of the *Atlanta Constitution*. . . . His expression of the Southern feeling of thankfulness at the death of slavery, and at the better condition of the South now that the bondmen were free, his fervent declaration of the existence of a brotherly feeling in the South and an unswerving loyalty, aroused boundless enthusiasm, bringing every man in the room to his feet with waving handkerchief and sonorous cheers." "Boasting of Puritan Sires," *New York Times*, Dec. 23, 1886.

Afterword: War Is Hell

1 Marszalek, *Sherman*, p. 477; Kennett, *Sherman*, p. 328 ("Nowhere in the surviving texts of Sherman's speeches does the term 'War is Hell' appear"); "War Is Hell," *New York Times*, Sept. 8, 1914 ("In view of the constant and tiresome iteration of the saying 'War is hell' and its ascription to Gen. Sherman, it is somewhat of a relief to learn that this is a misquotation"). Relatives and acquaintances offered their own stories of how the famous quote originated—some arguing that it was a distortion of his statement to Mayor Calhoun ("War is cruelty") that then made its way into the record; others claiming they were present when the fiery Ohioan said it, or at least confirmed that he had said it. One story appeared in the *New York Times* more than two decades after Sherman's death: "Many years ago I sat as one of a good many guests at the same table with Gen. Sherman at a semi-public dinner, men only being present, and heard his reply to a somewhat inquisitive participant—it was after the table had been cleared and punch and cigars added to the wine—who had asked him . . . whether he had ever really used the expression 'war is hell.' Gen. Sherman's reply was substantially that, ever since the Mexican war of 1847, he had many times expressed the opinion upon men friends, especially during and since the conflict of 1861–5, that war is hell." A.J.B., Letter to the Editor, *New York Times*, Sept. 12, 1914. For more on Sherman's 1880 speech, see Lewis, *Sherman: Fighting Prophet*, p. 637.

2 "General Sherman and the Burning of Atlanta," in Michael Walzer, *Just and Unjust Wars: A Moral Argument with Historical Illustrations,* 4th ed. (New York: Basic Books, 2006), pp. 32–33 ("The sentence 'War is hell' is doctrine, not description: it is a moral argument, an attempt at self-justification"). On Sherman as a military example, see gen-

erally Hanson, *The Soul of Battle*; George F. Will, "The Relevance of General Sherman" (Dec. 27, 2001) in *With a Happy Eye, But . . . America and the World, 1997–2002* (New York: Simon & Schuster, 2003), pp. 71–72; H. Norman Schwarzkopf with Peter Petre, *It Doesn't Take a Hero: The Autobiography* (New York: Bantam, 1992), p. 430 (Sherman quote); Kennett, *Sherman: A Soldier's Life*, p. 353 (noting Patton and Pershing, and the quote on Schwarzkopf's desk).

3 Lewis, *Sherman, Fighting Prophet*, pp. 632–33 ("I'll hire a man to shake hands for me"; "Marching Through Georgia"; Chauncey Depew quote).

4 *Frank Leslie's Pleasant Hours* (New York: Frank Leslie's Publishing House, 1884), vol. 36, p. 319 (request for Sherman's autograph and lock of hair); Charles Dickens, ed., *Household Words* (London: Charles Dickens & Evans, 1883), p. 420 (same).

5 Hirshon, *The White Tecumseh*, p. 369 (Mrs. Johnston quote); Sherman to Johnston, Jan. 5, 1891, quoted in Fellman, *Citizen Sherman*, p. 402 ("You and I became reconciled in April, 1865"); Welsh, *Medical Histories of Confederate Generals*, p. 121 (Johnston's cause of death).

6 Benét, *John Brown's Body*, p. 83; Bruce Catton, *The Centennial History of the Civil War: Never Call Retreat* (New York: Doubleday, 1961), p. 383. Sherman was also friendly in postwar years with other Confederate generals, including Joe Wheeler and James Longstreet. The statue at Dalton is the only statue of General Johnston anywhere. Symonds, *Joseph E. Johnston*, p. 4 (noting that "there is but one statue of Joe Johnston in the Old South. It is on the main street of Dalton, Georgia").

7 On Hood's postwar years, see McMurry, *John Bell Hood*, pp. 192–203; Dyer, *The Gallant Hood*, pp. 304–21; on his relationship with Sherman, see Hirshon, *The White Tecumseh*, p. 355. The war of words between Hood and Johnston, though it began in official reports during the war, was continued and broadened in their respective memoirs: Johnston's *Narrative of Military Operations* (1874), followed by Hood's *Advance and Retreat* (1880). Although his memoirs contain a number of errors and he died before they were published, Hood got the best of the exchange. According to Richard McMurry, Hood "successfully demolished one after another of his antagonist's assertions and demonstrated that Johnston's account was inaccurate if not deliberately distorted." McMurry, *John Bell Hood*, p. 200. As for who was truly responsible for the fall of Atlanta, Stephen Davis notes with approval General Pickett's comment on the reason the Confederates lost at Gettysburg: "I've always thought the Yankees had something to do with it." Davis, "A Reappraisal of the Generalship of John Bell Hood in the Battles for Atlanta," p. 95.

8 Marszalek, "Sherman Called It the Way He Saw It," p. 78 ("monument to his own success"); Joseph Hooker, quoted in William Styple, ed., *Generals in Bronze: Interviewing the Commanders of the Civil War* (Kearny, N.J.: Belle Grove Publishing, 2005), p. 42; Charles Morris, *The History and Triumphs of the Nineteenth Century* (Philadelphia: John C. Winston Co., 1899), p. 451 ("A man who wins victories").

9 Jefferson Davis, *The Rise and Fall of the Confederate Government* (New York: D. Appleton & Co., 1881), vol. 2, p. 564 (noting the "barbarous cruelty" of Sherman's "inhuman" expulsion order at Atlanta); "Jefferson Davis on Sherman's Speech,"

Indianapolis Sentinel, n.d., reprinted in *Dublin* (Ga.) *Post*, June 22, 1881.

10 Margaret Mitchell defended her depiction of Sherman's burning of Atlanta in a letter written in 1940: "it was one of *general* destruction"—not *total*, she acknowledged, though she told her correspondent: "If your impression is that the burning of Atlanta was a neatly and precisely controlled conflagration in which no churches and no residences were burned, I can only say that the facts of history disagree with you." Margaret Mitchell to Arthur H. Morse, June 24, 1940, in Harwell, ed., *Margaret Mitchell's Gone with the Wind Letters*, pp. 307–10.

11 Andrews, *The South Since the War*, pp. 31–32 (Southern insults of Sherman); *Macon Telegraph*, quoted in Carl Sandburg, *Abraham Lincoln: The War Years* (New York: Harcourt, Brace, 1939), p. 619; Sherman to H. V. Casserly, circa Sept. 1864, quoted in Fellman, *Citizen Sherman*, p. 183 ("This is somewhat on the order of the school bully"). Southerners would have been even more incensed had they seen the general's private home letters, in which he complained to his wife about how difficult the ordeal was on *him*. "It is pretty hard on me," he wrote to Ellen shortly after the March to the Sea, "that I am compelled to make these blows which are necessarily trying to *me*, but it seems devolved on me and can not be avoided." Sherman to Ellen, Jan. 5, 1865, in *Sherman's Civil War*, p. 791.

12 "Not Weeping over Sherman: Resolution in Tennessee Legislature Is Amended," *Atlanta Constitution*, Feb. 19, 1891 (describing the debate over the resolution, which was amended to simply note the passing of a famous general and to offer sympathy for Sherman's family); "Sherman's Character Discussed," *Atlanta Constitution*, Feb. 20, 1891.

13 Julia Morgan, *How It Was: Four Years Among the Rebels* (Nashville: Publishing House Methodist Episcopal Church South, 1891), p. 140 ("monster in human shape"); Trowbridge, *The South*, p. 576.

14 Hughes, *Old Reliable*, p. 302 (General A. S. Johnston's definition of a successful general). Could all these criticisms of Sherman possibly be true? Could Sherman be such a great commander, so successful in his campaigns, so widely studied and admired by modern commanders, and yet be so overrated and incompetent? Or, as Richard McMurry wrote of the Atlanta Campaign, "could it be that historians, with the benefit of hindsight, are expecting too much of men who had to act on the basis of uncertain information and to bear the responsibility for the success or failure of nations?" Richard M. McMurry, "The Atlanta Campaign: A New Look," *Civil War History* 22 (March 1976), p. 15; Walzer, *Just and Unjust Wars*, p. 33 ("Even in hell, it is possible to be more or less humane, to fight with or without restraint").

15 For a glimpse of the contrasting views of General Sherman, compare W. D. Pickett, "Why General Sherman's Name Is Detested," *Confederate Veteran* 14 (1906), pp. 295–98, with Peveral H. Peake, "Why the South Hates Sherman," *American Mercury* (August 1937), pp. 441–48; see also Daniel Pearl, "Pariah in the South, William T. Sherman's Getting a Makeover," *Wall Street Journal*, June 9, 1993, pp. A1, A5. *Macon* (Ga.) *Telegraph*, quoted in *Chicago Tribune*, Dec. 8, 1881 ("Whether the destruction of Atlanta was justifiable or not"); Styple, ed., *Generals in Bronze*, p. 277 (James H. Wilson story of Sherman).

BIBLIOGRAPHY

Correspondence, Diaries, Memoirs, and Personal Papers (Civilian)

Andrews, Eliza Frances. *The War-Time Journal of a Georgia Girl, 1864–1865.* New York: D. Appleton and Co., 1908.

Andrews, Sidney. *The South Since the War: As Shown by Fourteen Weeks of Travel and Observation in Georgia and the Carolinas.* Boston: Ticknor and Fields, 1866.

Arp, Bill [Charles Henry Smith]. *Bill Arp, So Called: A Side Show of the Southern Side of the War.* New York: Metropolitan Record Office, 1866.

———. *Bill Arp's Peace Papers.* New York: G. W. Carleton & Co., 1873.

"Atlanta as Sherman Left It—Atlanta Then and Now." *Atlanta Historical Bulletin* 1, no. 3 (May 1930), pp. 15–20.

Baldwin, Lucy Hull. Autobiography. MS849, Southern Historical Collection, University of North Carolina at Chapel Hill.

Berry, Carrie. *A Confederate Girl: The Diary of Carrie Berry, 1864.* Christy Steele and Anne Todd, eds. Mankato, Minn.: Blue Earth Books, 2000.

———. Diary. Atlanta History Center.

Brooks, Noah. *Lincoln Observed: Civil War Dispatches of Noah Brooks.* Michael Burlingame, ed. Baltimore: Johns Hopkins University Press, 1998.

———. *Washington in Lincoln's Time.* New York: Century Co., 1895.

Calhoun, James M. "Affidavit of James M. Calhoun, Mayor of Atlanta as to the Facts in Regard to the Surrender of Atlanta, September 2, 1864." Calhoun Family Papers, Atlanta History Center MSS 50.

Chesnut, Mary. *Mary Chesnut's Civil War.* C. Vann Woodward, ed. New Haven: Yale University Press, 1981.

Clayton, Sarah Conley. *Requiem for a Lost City: A Memoir of Civil War Atlanta and the Old South.* Robert Scott Davis, Jr., ed. Macon, Ga.: Mercer University Press, 1999.

Confederate Reminiscences and Letters, 1861–1865. Atlanta: United Daughters of the Confederacy, 1995–99.

Crew, James R. Papers. Atlanta History Center.

Cumming, Kate. *The Journal of Kate Cumming: A Confederate Nurse, 1862–1865.* Richard Barksdale Harwell, ed. Savannah: Beehive Press, 1975.

Davis, Jefferson. *Jefferson Davis, Constitutionalist: His Letters, Papers, and Speeches.* Dunbar Rowland, ed. Jackson: Mississippi Department of Archives and History, 1923.

———. *The Papers of Jefferson Davis.* Lynda Lasswell Crist et al., eds. Baton Rouge: Louisiana State University Press, 1971–97.

———. *The Rise and Fall of the Confederate Government.* New York: D. Appleton & Co., 1881.

Dennett, John Richard. *The South as it Is, 1865–1866.* Henry M. Christman, ed. New York: Viking Press, 1965.

Fletcher, Louisa Warren. *Journal of a Landlady.* H. Higgins and C. Cox, eds. Chapel Hill, N.C.: Professional Press, 1995.

Gardiner, William M. "A Yankee Views the Agony of Savannah." Frank Otto Gatell, ed. *Georgia Historical Quarterly* 43 (1959), pp. 428–31.

Gay, Mary A. H. *Life in Dixie During the War 1861–1862–1863–1864–1865.* 4th ed. Atlanta: Foote & Davies, 1901.

Grady, Henry W. "The New South" (speech at the New England Society, New York City, December 21, 1886), in *The Complete Orations and Speeches of Henry W. Grady.* Edwin DuBois Shurter, ed. Norwood, Mass.: Norwood Press, 1910.

Huff, Sarah. *My Eighty Years in Atlanta.* Atlanta: n.p., 1937.

Jones, Mary Sharpe, and Mary Jones Mallard. *Yankees A'Coming: One Month's Experience During the Invasion of Liberty County, Georgia 1864–1865.* Haskell Monroe, ed. Tuscaloosa: Confederate Pub. Co., 1959.

Kennaway, John Henry, Sir. *On Sherman's Track; or, The South After the war.* London: Seeley, Jackson and Halliday, 1867.

King, William. Diary of William King, Cobb County, Georgia. Southern Historical Collection, University of North Carolina, Chapel Hill.

Kurtz, Wilbur G. Wilbur G. Kurtz Collection, Atlanta History Center.

Lay, Henry C. "Sherman in Georgia." *Atlantic Monthly* 149, no. 2 (Feb. 1932), pp. 166–72.

McClatchey, Minerva Leah Rowles. "A Georgia Woman's Civil War Diary: The Journal of Minerva Leah Rowles McClatchey." *Georgia Historical Quarterly* 51 (1967), pp. 197–216.

McClure, Alexander K. *Recollections of Half a Century.* Salem, Mass.: Salem Press Co., 1902.

Molineaux, Emily E. *Lifetime Recollections: An interesting Narrative of Life in the Southern States before and during the Civil War, with incidents of the bombardment of Atlanta by the Union forces, the author being then a resident of that City.* San Francisco: C. W. Gordon, 1902.

Myers, Robert Manson. *The Children of Pride: A True Story of Georgia and the Civil War.* New Haven: Yale University Press, 1972.

Perkerson, Lizzie. "Lizzie's Letter." *Atlanta Journal Magazine*, April 23, 1944.

Quintard, Charles T. *Doctor Quintard: Chaplain, C.S.A. and Second Bishop of Tennessee, Being His Story of the War (1861–1865).* Arthur Howard Noll, ed. Sewanee, Tenn.: University Press of Sewanee, 1905.

Rawson, Mary. Diary. Atlanta History Center.

Reid, Whitelaw. *After the War: A Southern Tour—May 1, 1865 to May 1, 1866.* Cincinnati: Moore, Wilstach & Baldwin, 1866.

———. *A Radical View: The "Agate" Dispatches of Whitelaw Reid, 1861–1865.* Memphis: Memphis State University Press, 1976.

Richards, Samuel P. Diary. S. P. Richards Collection, Atlanta History Center.

Smith, Mollie. "Dodging Shells in Atlanta." *Atlanta Journal Magazine.* March 24, 1929.

Stone, Cyrena Bailey. Diary, 1864. Hargrett Rare Book and Manuscript Library, University of Georgia.

Strong, George Templeton. *Diary of the Civil War 1860–1865.* Allan Nevins, ed. New York: Macmillan, 1962.

Trowbridge, J. T. *The South: A Tour of its Battle-Fields and Ruined Cities, A Journey Through the Desolated States and Talks with the People*. Hartford: L. Stebbins, 1866.

Ward, Margaret Ketcham. "Testimony of Margaret Ketcham Ward on Civil War Times in Georgia." *Georgia Historical Quarterly* 39 (1955), pp. 375–89.

Whitman, Walt. *Walt Whitman's Civil War*. Walter Lowenfels, ed. New York: Alfred A. Knopf, 1961.

Williams, Noble C. *Echoes From the Battlefield*. Atlanta: Franklin Printing Co., 1902.

Wilson, John Stainback. *Atlanta As It Is*. New York: Little, Rennie & Co., 1871.

Correspondence, Diaries, Memoirs and Personal Papers (Military)

Ankeny, Henry G. *Kiss Josey for Me*. Florence Marie Ankeny Cox, ed. Santa Ana, Calif.: Friis-Pioneer Press, 1974.

Badeau, Adam. *Military History of Ulysses S. Grant From April, 1861 to April, 1865*. New York: D. Appleton & Co., 1882.

Banks, Robert W. "Civil War Letters of Robert W. Banks: Atlanta Campaign." George C. Osborn, ed. *Georgia Historical Quarterly* 27 (1943), pp. 208–16.

Bate, William B. "Lines of Battle: The Partial Atlanta Reports of Confederate Maj. Gen. William B. Bate." Zack Waters, ed., in *The Campaign for Atlanta and Sherman's March to the Sea: Essays on the American Civil War in Georgia, 1864*. Campbell, Calif.: Savas Woodbury, 1994, pp. 197–219.

Bennitt, John. *I Hope to Do My Country Service: The Civil War Letters of John Bennitt, M.D., Surgeon, 19th Michigan Infantry*. Robert Beasecker, ed. Detroit: Wayne State University Press, 2005.

Bentley, William Garrigues. *"Burning Rails as We Pleased": The Civil War Letters of William Garrigues Bentley, 104th Ohio Volunteer Infantry*. Jefferson, N.C.: McFarland, 2004.

Benton, Charles Edward. *As Seen from the Ranks: A Boy in the Civil War*. New York: G. P. Putnam's Sons, 1902.

Bevens, William E. *Reminiscences of a Private: William E. Bevens of the First Arkansas Infantry, C.S.A.* Fayetteville: University of Arkansas Press, 1992.

Bradley, G.S. *The Star Corps, or Notes of an Army Chaplain During Sherman's Famous March to the Sea*. Milwaukee, 1865.

Bull, Rice C. *Soldiering: The Civil War Diary of Rice C. Bull, 123rd New York Volunteer Infantry*. K. Jack Bauer, ed. San Rafael, Calif.: Presidio Press, 1978.

Butler, Jay Caldwell. *Letters Home*. Birmingham, N.Y.: n.p., 1930.

Cain, J. Isaiah. "The Battle of Atlanta as Described by a Confederate Soldier." Andrew Forest Muir, contributor. *Georgia Historical Quarterly* 42 (1958), pp. 109–11.

Candler, Allen D. "Watch on the Chattahoochee: A Civil War Letter." Elizabeth Hulsey Marshall, contributor. *Georgia Historical Quarterly* 43 (1959), pp. 427–28.

Carlin, William Passmore. *The Memoirs of Brigadier General William Passmore Carlin, U.S.A.* Robert Girardi and Nathaniel C. Hughes, eds. Lincoln: University of Nebraska Press, 1999.

Chamberlin, William H. "Hood's Second Sortie at Atlanta." *Battles and Leaders of the Civil War*. Robert U. Johnson and Clarence C. Buel, eds. 4 vols. New York: Century Co., 1887. Vol. 4, pp. 326–31.

———. "Recollections of the Battle of Atlanta." *Sketches of War History, 1861–1865.* Papers read before the Ohio Commandry of the Military Order of the Loyal Legion of the United States Monfort and Company, 1908. Vol. 6, pp. 276–86.

———. "The Skirmish Line in the Atlanta Campaign." *Sketches of War History, 1861–1865.* Papers read before the Ohio Commandry of the Military Order of the Loyal Legion of the United States. Cincinnati: Robert Clarke and Company, 1890. Vol. 3, pp. 182–96.

Chambers, William Pitt. *Blood and Sacrifice: The Civil War Journal of a Confederate Soldier.* Richard A. Baumgartner, ed. Huntington, W.Va.: Blue Acorn Press, 1994.

Clark, Walter A. *Under the Stars and Bars, or Memories of Four Years Service with the Oglethorpes, of Augusta, Georgia.* 1900; reprint, Jonesboro, Ga.: Freedom Hill Press, 1987.

Collins, R. M. *Chapters from the Unwritten History of the War Between the States; or, Incidents in the Life of a Confederate Soldier, in Camp, on the March, in the Great Battles, and in Prison.* St. Louis: Nixon-Jones Printing Co., 1893.

Confederate Veteran. 40 vols. Nashville, Tenn., 1893–1932.

Connolly, James A. *Three Years in the Army of the Cumberland: The Letters and Diary of Major James A. Connolly.* Bloomington: Indiana University Press, 1959.

Conyngham, David P. *Sherman's March Through the South, With sketches and incidents of the campaign.* New York: Sheldon & Co., 1865.

Cox, Charles Harding. "The Civil War Letters of Charles Harding Cox." Lorna Lutes Sylvester, ed. *Indiana Magazine of History* 68 (March and Sept. 1972), pp. 24–78, 181–239.

———. Papers 1860–1928. Special Collections Department, Robert W. Woodruff Library, Emory University.

Cox, Jacob D. *Atlanta.* New York: Charles Scribner's Sons, 1882.

———. *Military Reminiscences of the Civil War.* 2 vols. New York: Scribner's, 1900.

Cox, Rowland. "Snake Creek Gap, and Atlanta," in *Personal Recollections of the War of the Rebellion.* A. Noel Blakeman, ed. New York: G. P. Putnam's Sons, 1897, pp. 7–29.

Cram, George F. *Soldiering with Sherman: Civil War Letters of George F. Cram.* Jennifer Cain Bohrnstedt, ed. DeKalb: Northern Illinois University Press, 2000.

Crew, S. B. Letters, 1863–84. Collection of Mary Louise Dunn Fleming.

Culver, Joseph Franklin. *"Your Affectionate Husband, J. F. Culver": Letters Written During the Civil War.* Leslie W. Dunlap et al., eds. Friends of the University of Iowa Libraries, 1978.

Davis, Leander E. "'The Consequence of Grandeur': A Union Soldier Writes of the Atlanta Campaign." William C. Niesen, ed. *Atlanta History* 33, no. 3 (Fall 1989), pp. 5–20.

Dodge, Grenville M. *The Battle of Atlanta and Other Campaigns: Addresses, Etc.* Council Bluffs, Iowa: Monarch, 1911.

———. *Personal Recollections of President Abraham Lincoln, General Ulysses S. Grant and General William T. Sherman.* Council Bluffs, Iowa: Monarch, 1914.

Downing, Alexander G. *Downing's Civil War Diary.* Olynthus B. Clark, ed. Des Moines: Historical Department of Iowa, 1916.

Dwight, Henry O. "How We Fight at Atlanta." *Harper's New Monthly Magazine* 29 (Oct. 1864), pp. 663–66.

Ewing, Charles. "Sherman's March Through Georgia: Letters from Charles Ewing to His Father Thomas Ewing." George C. Osborn, ed. *Georgia Historical Quarterly* 42 (1958), pp. 323–27.

Fahnestock, Allen L. *Diary of Colonel Allen L. Fahnestock, 86th Regiment, Illinois Infantry Volunteers* (typescript). Kennesaw Mountain National Battlefield Park Archives.

Fenton, Ebenezer B. *From the Rapidan to Atlanta: Leaves from the Diary of Companion E. B. Fenton.* Winn & Hammond, 1893.

Ferguson, John Hill. *On to Atlanta: The Civil War Diaries of John Hill Ferguson, Illinois Tenth Regiment of Volunteers.* Janet Correll Ellison, ed. Lincoln: University of Nebraska Press, 2001.

Fleharty, S. F. *Jottings from Dixie: The Civil War Dispatches of Sergeant Major Stephen F. Fleharty, U.S.A.* Philip J. Rayburn and Terry Wilson, eds. Baton Rouge: Louisiana State University Press, 1999.

Foote, Corydon Edward. *With Sherman to the Sea: A Drummer Boy's Story of the Civil War.* Olive Dean Hormel, ed. New York: John Day Co., 1960.

Forry, Michael. "'Enough to Make a Preacher Sware': A Union Mule Driver's Diary of Sherman's March." *Atlanta History* 33, no. 3 (Fall 1989), pp. 21–36.

Foster, Samuel T. *One of Cleburne's Command.* Norman D. Brown, ed. Austin: University of Texas Press, 1980.

Fremantle, Arthur J. L. *Three Months in the Southern States: April–June 1863.* Mobile: S. H. Goetzel, 1864.

French, Samuel G. *Two Wars: An Autobiography of Gen. Samuel G. French.* Nashville: Confederate Veteran, 1901.

Frobel, B. W. "The Georgia Campaign, or, a South-Side View of Sherman's March to the Sea." *Scott's Monthly Magazine* 5–7 (Nov. 1868–March 1869).

Gaskill, J. W. *Footprints Through Dixie: Everyday Life of the Man Under a Musket. On the Firing Line and In the Trenches 1862–1865.* Alliance, Ohio: Bradshaw Printing Co., 1919.

Geary, John W. Letters. Atlanta History Center.

———. *A Politician Goes to War: The Civil War Letters of John White Geary.* William Alan Blair, ed. University Park: Pennsylvania State University Press, 1995.

Gorgas, Josiah. *The Journals of Josiah Gorgas, 1857–1878.* Sarah Woolfolk Wiggins, ed. Tuscaloosa: University of Alabama Press, 1995.

Grant, Ulysses S. *Personal Memoirs.* New York: Penguin, 1999.

Gray, John Chipman. *War Letters, 1862–1865, of John Chipman Gray and John Codman Ropes, with Portraits.* Boston: Houghton Mifflin, 1927.

Gray, R. M. Reminiscences. Southern Historical Collection, University of North Carolina.

Green, John Williams. *Johnny Green of the Orphan Brigade: The Journal of a Confederate Soldier.* A. D. Kirwan, ed. Lexington: University of Kentucky Press, 2002.

Hagan, John W. "The Confederate Letters of John W. Hagan." Bell Irvin Wiley, ed. *Georgia Historical Quarterly* 38 (1954), pp. 268–94.

Hardee, William J. Correspondence. Hardee Family Papers. Alabama Department of Archives and History.

Harrison, Benjamin. Papers. Library of Congress.

Hedley, F. Y. *Marching Through Georgia: Pen-pictures of Every-day Life in General Sherman's Army, from the Beginning of the Atlanta Campaign until the Close of the War*. Chicago: R. R. Donnelly & Sons, 1885.

Helms, Celathiel. Letters. Georgia Department of Archives and History (GDAH).

Hemstreet, William. "Little Things About Big Generals." *MOLLUS—NY* III, pp. 160–61.

Hill, Andrew Malone. "Personal Recollections of Andrew Malone Hill." *Alabama Historical Quarterly* 20, no. 1 (Spring 1958), pp. 85–94.

Hitchcock, Henry. *Marching with Sherman: Passages from the Letters and Campaign Diaries of Henry Hitchcock, Major and Assistant Adjutant General of Volunteers, November 1864–May 1865*. M. A. DeWolfe Howe, ed. Lincoln: University of Nebraska Press, 1995.

Hood, John Bell. *Advance and Retreat: Personal Experiences in the United States and Confederate States Armies*. New Orleans: Beauregard, 1880; reprint, Lincoln: University of Nebraska Press, 1996.

———. "The Defense of Atlanta." *Battles and Leaders*. Vol. 4, pp. 336–44.

Hosea, Lewis M. "Some Side Lights on the War for the Union." In *Sketches of War History, 1861–1865*. Papers read before the Ohio Commandry of the Military Order of the Loyal Legion of the United States. Cincinnati: Robert Clarke and Co., 1912–16.

Hostetter, John L. Diary, 1864–65. Special Collections, Iowa State University Library, MS 662.

Howard, Oliver Otis. *Autobiography of Oliver Otis Howard, Major General, United States Army*. New York: Baker & Taylor, 1907.

———. "Sherman's Advance from Atlanta." *Battles and Leaders*. Vol. 4, pp. 663–66.

———. "The Struggle for Atlanta." *The Century* 34, no. 3 (July 1887), pp. 442–64 (also in *Battles and Leaders*).

Hubner, Charles W. "Some Recollections of Atlanta During 1864." *Atlanta Historical Bulletin* 1, no. 2 (Jan. 1928), pp. 5–7.

Jackman, John S. *Diary of a Confederate Soldier: John S. Jackman of the Orphan Brigade*. William C. Davis, ed. Columbia: University of South Carolina Press, 1990.

———. "From Dalton to Atlanta." *Southern Bivouac* 1, no. 12 (Aug. 1883), pp. 451–59.

Jackson, Oscar L. *The Colonel's Diary: Journal Kept Before and During the Civil War by the Late Colonel Oscar L. Jackson . . . sometime commander of the 63rd regiment O.V.I.* David P. Jackson, ed. Sharon, Pa.: 1922.

Johnson, W. C. "The March to the Sea." *G.A.R. War Papers*. Cincinnati, Fred C. Jones Post, 1891, pp. 309–36.

Johnston, Joseph E. *Narrative of Military Operations During the Late War Between the States*. New York: D. Appleton & Co., 1874.

———. "Opposing Sherman's Advance to Atlanta." *The Century*. 34, no. 4 (Aug. 1887), pp. 585–97 (also in *Battles and Leaders*).

Jones, Charles C., Jr. *General Sherman's March from Atlanta to the Coast. An Address Delivered before the Confederate Survivor's Association, in Augusta, Georgia, at its Sixth Annual Meeting, on Memorial Day, April 26, 1884*. Augusta, Ga.: Chronicle, 1884.

Kendall, John I. "Recollections of a Confederate Officer." John Smith Kendall, ed. *Louisiana Historical Quarterly* 29, no. 4 (Oct. 1946), pp. 1041 ff.

Key, Thomas J. *Two Soldiers: The Campaign Diaries of Thomas J. Key, C.S.A., December 7, 1863–May 17, 1865, and Robert J. Campbell, U.S.A., January 1, 1864–July 21, 1864*. Chapel Hill: University of North Carolina Press, 1938.

Lane, Mills, ed. *"Dear Mother: Don't grieve about me: If I Get Killed, I'll only be Dead." Letters from Georgia Soldiers in the Civil War*. Savannah: Beehive Press, 1977.

Lavender, John W. *They Never Came Back: The War Memoirs of Captain John W. Lavender, C.S.A.* Worley, Ted R., ed. Pine Bluff, Ark.: Southern Press, 1956.

Leggett, M. D. *The Battle of Atlanta: A paper read by General M. D. Leggett, before the Society of the Army of the Tennessee, October 18th, 1883, at Cleveland*. Cleveland: J. A. Davies, 1883.

Lyman, Theodore. *Meade's Headquarters, 1863–1865: Letters of Colonel Theodore Lyman from the Wilderness to Appomattox*. George R. Agassiz, ed. Boston: Atlantic Monthly Press, 1922.

Mackey, Leonidas. Letters. MSS 215f. Atlanta History Center.

Manigault, Arthur Middleton. *A Carolinian Goes to War: The Civil War Narrative of Arthur Middleton Manigault, Brigadier General, C.S.A.* R. Lockwood Tower, ed. Columbia: University of South Carolina Press, 1983.

McDermid, Angus. "Letters from a Confederate Soldier." Benjamin Rountree, ed. *Georgia Review* 18 (1964), pp. 267–97.

McElroy, John. *Andersonville: A Story of Rebel Military Prisons*. Toledo: D. R. Locke, 1879.

McKittrick, Samuel. "A Confederate Officer's Letters on Sherman's March to Atlanta." Donald W. Lewis, ed. *Georgia Historical Quarterly* 51 (1967), pp. 491–94.

McNeil, S.A. *Personal Recollections of Service in the Army of the Cumberland and Sherman's Army: From August 17, 1861 to July 20, 1865*. Richwood, Ohio, 1910.

Mead, Rufus. "With Sherman Through Georgia and the Carolinas: Letters of a Federal Soldier." James A. Padgett, ed. *Georgia Historical Quarterly* 32 (1948), p. 302.

Miller, Alonzo. Letters and Diary. Atlanta History Center.

Miller, Charles D. *The Struggle for the Life of the Republic: A Civil War Narrative by Brevet Major Charles Dana Miller, 76th Ohio Infantry*. Stewart Bennett and Barbara Tillery, eds. Kent, Ohio: Kent State University Press, 2004.

Miller, William Bluffton. *Fighting for Liberty and Right: The Civil War Diary of William Bluffton Miller, First Sergeant, Company K, Seventy-fifth Indiana Volunteer Infantry*. Knoxville: University of Tennessee Press, 2004.

Montgomery, Frank Alexander. *Reminiscences of a Mississippian in Peace and War*. Cincinnati: Robert Clarke Company Press, 1901.

Morse, Charles F. *Letters Written During the Civil War*. Boston: Privately printed, 1898.

Mosman, Chesley A. *The Rough Side of War: The Civil War Journal of Chesley A. Mosman, 1st Lieutenant, Company D, 59th Illinois volunteer Infantry Regiment*. Arnold Gates, ed. Garden City, N.Y.: Basin Publishing Co., 1987.

Munson, Gilbert D. "The Battle of Atlanta." *Sketches of War History, 1861–1865.* Papers read before the Ohio Commandry of the Military Order of the Loyal Legion of the United States. Cincinnati: Robert Clarke and Co., 1890. Vol. 3, pp. 212–230.

Murphree, Joel Dyer. "Autobiography and Civil War Letters of Joel Dyer Murphree." *Alabama Historical Quarterly* 19, no. 1 (Spring 1957), pp. 170–208.

Neal, Andrew Jackson. Papers, 1856–1881. Special Collections, Robert W. Woodruff Library, Emory University.

Nichols, George Ward. Diary, quoted in "Sherman's Great March," *Harper's New Monthly Magazine* 31, no. 185 (Oct. 1865), pp. 571–89.

———. *The Story of the Great March, from the Diary of a Staff Officer*. New York: Harper & Brothers, 1865.

Nisbet, James Cooper. *Four Years on the Firing Line*. Bell Irvin Wiley, ed. Jackson, Tenn.: McCowat-Mercer Press, 1963.

Nutt, E.E. "The 20th Ohio at Atlanta," *The Ohio Soldier* 7, no. 21, July 28, 1894.

Oakey, Daniel. "Marching Through Georgia and the Carolinas." *Battles and Leaders*, Vol. 4, pp. 671–79.

Oliphant, William J. *Only a Private: A Texan Remembers the Civil War*. James M. McCaffrey, ed. Houston: Halcyon Press, 2004.

Olmstead, Charles H. "The Memoirs of Charles H. Olmstead." *Georgia Historical Quarterly*, Dec. 1960.

Opdyke, Emerson. *To Battle for God and the Right: The Civil War Letterbooks of Emerson Opdyke*. Glenn V. Longacre and John E. Haas, eds. Urbana: University of Illinois Press, 2003.

Patrick, Robert. *Reluctant Rebel: The Secret Diary of Robert Patrick, 1861–1865*. F. Jay Taylor, ed. Baton Rouge: Louisiana State University Press, 1959.

Patten, James Comfort. "An Indiana Doctor Marches With Sherman: The Diary of James Comfort Patten." Robert G. Athearn, ed. *Indiana Magazine of History* 49 (1953), pp. 405–22.

Pepper, George W. *Personal Recollections of Sherman's Campaigns in Georgia and the Carolinas*. Zanesville, Ohio: Hugh Dunne, 1866.

Pickett, William D. "Why General Sherman's Name Is Detested." *Confederate Veteran* 14 (1906), pp. 295–98.

Pierson, Stephen. "From Chattanooga to Atlanta in 1864 . . . A Personal Reminiscence." *Proceedings of the New Jersey Historical Society* 16 (1931), pp. 324–56.

Platter, Cornelius C. Diary, 1864–65. Hargrett Rare Book and Manuscript Library, University of Georgia.

Poe, Orlando M. Letters. Library of Congress.

Porter, Alexander Q. Diary (typescript). Robert W. Woodruff Library, Emory University.

Porter, Horace. *Campaigning with Grant*. New York: Century Co., 1897.

Reed, Ira B. "The Campaign from Chattanooga to Atlanta as seen by a Federal Soldier." Richard B. Harwell, ed. *Georgia Historical Quarterly* 25, no. 3 (Sept. 1941), pp. 262–78.

Reid, Harvey. *The View from Headquarters: Civil War Letters of Harvey Reid.* Frank L. Burns, ed. Madison: State Historical Society of Wisconsin, 1965.

Rice, Ralsa C. *Yankee Tigers: Through the Civil War with the 125th Ohio.* Richard A. Baumgartner and Larry A. Strayer, eds. Huntington, W.Va.: Blue Acorn Press, 1992.

Roy, T. B. "General Hardee and Military Operations about Atlanta." *Southern Historical Society Papers* 8, pp. 337–87.

Rusling, James F. *Men and Things I Saw in Civil War Days.* New York: Eaton & Mains, 1899.

Schofield, John M. *Forty-Six Years in the Army.* New York: Century Co., 1897.

Schurz, Carl. *The Reminiscences of Carl Schurz.* 3 vols. New York: McClure Company, 1908.

———. "The Battle of Missionary Ridge." *McClure's* (Sept. 1907), pp. 483–96.

Shanks, W. F. G. *Personal Recollections of Distinguished Generals.* New York: Harper and Brothers, 1866.

Sherman, William Tecumseh. Diaries and Correspondence. William T. Sherman Family Papers, Archives of the University of Notre Dame.

———. "The Grand Strategy of the Last Year of the War," in *Battles and Leaders of the Civil War.* Robert U. Johnson and Clarence C. Buel, eds. 4 vols. New York: Century Co., 1887. Vol. 4, pp. 247–55.

———. *Home Letters of General Sherman.* M. A. DeWolfe Howe, ed. New York: C. Scribner's Sons, 1909.

———. *Memoirs of General W. T. Sherman.* New York: D. Appleton & Co., 1875.

———. Papers. Library of Congress.

———. *Sherman's Civil War: Selected Correspondence of William T. Sherman, 1860–1865.* Brooks D. Simpson and Jean V. Berlin, eds. Chapel Hill: University of North Carolina Press, 1999.

———. *Some Facts Relating to Maj. Gen. James B. McPherson, and Events Attending His Death.* Washington, D.C.: n.p., 1878.

Sherman, William Tecumseh, and John Sherman. *The Sherman Letters: Correspondence Between General and Senator Sherman from 1837 to 1891.* Rachel Sherman Thorndike, ed. New York: Charles Scribner's Sons, 1894.

Smith, Benjamin T. *Private Smith's Journal.* Clyde C. Walton, ed. Chicago: R. R. Donnelly & Sons, 1963.

Smith, Charles E. *A View from the Ranks: The Civil War Diaries of Corporal Charles E. Smith.* George R. Cryder and Stanley R. Miller, eds. Delaware, Ohio: Delaware County Historical Society, 1999.

Smith, Gustavas W. "The Georgia Militia About Atlanta." *Battles and Leaders.* Vol. 4, pp. 331–35.

Spence, Alexander E., and Thomas F. *Getting Used to Being Shot At: The Spence Family Civil War Letters.* Mark K. Christ, ed. Fayetteville: University of Arkansas Press, 2002.

Stephenson, Philip Daingerfield. *The Civil War Memoir of Philip Daingerfield Stephenson, D.D.* Nathaniel Cheairs Hughes, Jr., ed. Conway: University of Central Arkansas Press, 1995.

Stockwell, Elisha. *Private Elisha Stockwell, Jr. Sees the Civil War*. Norman: University of Oklahoma Press, 1985.

Taylor, Thomas Thomson. *Tom Taylor's Civil War*. Albert Castel, ed. Lawrence: University Press of Kansas, 2000.

Trask, W. L. *The Georgia Campaign of 1864, From the war journal of W. L. Trask*. (Typescript.) Kennesaw Mountain National Battlefield Park.

Tuthill, Richard S. "An Artilleryman's Recollections of the Battle of Atlanta." *Military Essays and Recollections*. Papers Read before the Commandery of the State of Illinois, Military Order of the Loyal Legion of the United States. Published by the Commandery. Vol. I. Chicago: A. C. McClurg and Co. 1891, pp. 293–310.

Upson, Theodore F. *With Sherman to the Sea*. O. O. Winther, ed. Bloomington: Indiana University Press, 1958.

Van Duzer, John C. "The John Van Duzer Diary of Sherman's March from Atlanta to Hilton Head." Charles J. Brockman, Jr., ed. *Georgia Historical Quarterly* 53 (1969), pp. 220–40.

Wallace, William. "William Wallace's Civil War Letters: The Atlanta Campaign." John O. Holzheuter, ed. *Wisconsin Magazine of History* 57, no. 2 (Winter 1973–74), pp. 90–116.

Washburn, Wiley A. "Reminiscences of Confederate Service by Wiley A. Washburn." James L. Nichols and Frank Abbott, eds. *Arkansas Historical Quarterly* 35 (Spring 1976), pp. 47–87.

Watkins, Sam. *Co. Aytch: A Confederate Memoir of the Civil War*. New York: Touchstone, 2003.

Widney, Lyman S. *Campaigning with Uncle Billy: The Civil War Memoirs of Sgt. Lyman S. Widney, 34th Illinois Volunteer Infantry*. Robert I. Girardi, ed. Bloomington, Ind.: Trafford Publishing, 2008.

———. Letter (typescript), June 30, 1864. Kennesaw Mountain National Battlefield Park.

Williams, Alpheus S. *From the Cannon's Mouth: The Civil War Letters of General Alpheus S. Williams*. Milo M. Quaife. Detroit: Wayne State University Press, 1959.

Williams, Hiram Smith. *This War So Horrible: The Civil War Diary of Hiram Smith Williams*. Lewis N. Wynne and Robert A. Taylor, eds. Tuscaloosa: University of Alabama Press, 1993.

Wills, Charles W. *Army Life of an Illinois Soldier*. Washington, D.C.: Globe Printing Co., 1906.

Wilson, Ephraim A. *Memoirs of the War*. Cleveland: W. M. Bayne Printing Co., 1893.

Young, L. D. *Reminiscences of a Soldier of the Orphan Brigade*. Louisville: Courier-Journal Job Printing Co., 1918.

Regimental and Unit Histories

Allendorf, Donald. *Long Road to Liberty: The Odyssey of a German Regiment in the Yankee Army*. Kent, Ohio: Kent State University Press, 2006.

Anderson, Ephraim McD. *Memoirs Historical and Personal Including the Campaign of the First Missouri Confederate Brigade*. St. Louis: Times Printing Co., 1868.

Aten, Henry J. *History of the Eighty-Fifth Regiment, Illinois Volunteer Infantry.* Hiawatha, Kan.: The Association, 1901.

Boies, Andrew J. *Record of the Thirty-Third Massachusetts Volunteer Infantry from Aug. 1862 to Aug. 1865.* Fitchburg: Sentinel Printing Co., 1880.

Boyle, John Richards. *Soldiers True: The Story of the One Hundred and Eleventh Regiment Pennsylvania Veteran Volunteers.* New York: Eaton & Mains, 1903.

Brown, Edmund Randolph. *The Twenty-Seventh Indiana Volunteer Infantry in the War of the Rebellion 1861–1865.* N.p., 1899.

Brown, Russell K. *Our Connection With Savannah: A History of the 1st Battalion Georgia Sharpshooters.* Macon, Ga.: Mercer University Press, 2004.

Calkins, William Wirt. *The History of the One Hundred and Fourth Regiment of Illinois Volunteer Infantry.* Chicago: Donohue & Henneberry, 1895.

Cope, Alexis. *The Fifteenth Ohio Volunteers and Its Campaigns.* Columbus, Ohio: By the author, 1916.

Crooker, Lucien B. et al. *The Story of the Fifty-fifth Regiment Illinois Volunteer Infantry in the Civil War, 1861–1865. By a Committee of the Regiment.* Clinton, Mass.: W. J. Coulter, 1887.

Davis, William C. *The Orphan Brigade: The Kentucky Confederates Who Couldn't Go Home.* New York: Doubleday, 1980.

Day, L.W. *Story of the One Hundred and First Ohio Infantry.* Cleveland: W. M. Bayne Printing Co., 1894.

Dodge, William Sumner. *A Waif of the War; or, The History of the Seventy-fifth Illinois Infantry.* Chicago: Church & Goodman, 1866.

Dunkelman, Mark H. and Michael Winey. *The Hardtack Regiment: An Illustrated History of the 154th Regiment, New York State Infantry Volunteers.* Rutherford, N.J.: Fairleigh-Dickinson University Press, 1981.

Grecian, Joseph. *History of the Eighty-Third Regiment, Indiana Volunteer Infantry.* Cincinnati: J. F. Ulhorn, 1865.

Hayes, Philip C. *Journal-History of the Hundred & Third Ohio Volunteer Infantry.* Bryan, Ohio: Toledo Steam Printing House, 1872.

Hight, John J. *History of the Fifty-eighth Regiment of Indiana Volunteer Infantry.* Princeton, Ind.: Press of the Clarion, 1895.

Hughes, Nathaniel Cheairs. *The Pride of the Confederate Artillery: The Washington Artillery in the Army of Tennessee.* Baton Rouge: Louisiana State University Press, 1997.

Hunter, Alfred G. *History of the Eighty-second Indiana Volunteer Infantry.* Indianapolis: William B. Burford, 1893.

Losson, Christopher. *Tennessee's Forgotten Warriors: Frank Cheatham and His Confederate Division.* Knoxville: University of Tennessee Press, 1989.

McAdams, F. M. *Every-Day Soldier Life, or, A History of the One Hundred and Thirteenth Ohio Volunteer Infantry.* Columbus: C. M. Cott & Co., 1884.

McGee, B. F. *History of the 72d Indiana Volunteer Infantry of the Mounted Lightning Brigade.* Lafayette, Ind.: S. Vater & Co., 1882.

McMurray, William Josiah. *History of the Twentieth Tennessee Regiment Volunteer Infantry, C.S.A.* Nashville: By the author, 1904.

Merrill, Samuel. *The Seventieth Indiana Volunteer Infantry in the War of the Rebellion.* Indianapolis: Bowen-Merrill, 1900.

Overmyer, Jack K. *A Stupendous Effort: The 87th Indiana in the War of the Rebellion.* Bloomington: Indiana University Press, 1997.

Payne, Edwin Waters. *History of the Thirty-fourth Regiment of Illinois Volunteer Infantry, Sept. 7, 1861–July 12, 1865.* Clinton, Iowa: Allen Printing Co., 1903.

Stewart, Nixon B. *Dan McCook's Regiment: 52nd O.V.I.: A History of the Regiment, Its Campaigns and Battles from 1862–65.* Huntington, W.Va.: Blue Acorn Press, 1999.

Thackery, David T. *A Light and Uncertain Hold: A History of the Sixty-Sixth Ohio Volunteer Infantry.* Kent, Ohio: Kent State University Press, 1999.

Tourgee, Albion Winegar. *The Story of a Thousand, Being a History of the Service of the 105th Ohio Volunteer Infantry.* Buffalo, Ohio: S. McGerald & Son, 1896.

Underwood, Adin B. *The Three Years' Service of the Thirty-Third Massachusetts Infantry Regiment.* Boston: A. Williams and Co., 1880.

Welcher, Frank J., and Larry G. Ligget. *Coburn's Brigade: 85th Indiana, 33d Indiana, 19th Michigan, and 22nd Wisconsin in the Western Civil War.* Indianapolis: Cardinal Publishers Group, 1999.

Worsham, W.J. *The Old Nineteenth Tennessee Regiment, C.S.A.* Knoxville: Paragon Printing Co., 1902.

Yeary, Mamie, ed. *Reminiscences of the Boys in Gray 1861–1865.* Dallas: Smith & Lamar, 1912.

Books and Compilations

Andrews, J. Cutler. *The North Reports the Civil War.* Pittsburgh: University of Pittsburgh Press, 1955.

———. *The South Reports the Civil War.* Princeton: Princeton University Press, 1970.

Ash, Stephen V. *When the Yankees Came: Conflict and Chaos in the Occupied South, 1861–1865.* Chapel Hill: University of North Carolina Press, 1995.

Atlanta: Voices of the Civil War. New York: Time-Life Books, 1996.

Bailey, Anne J. *The Chessboard of War: Sherman and Hood in the Autumn Campaigns of 1864.* Lincoln: University of Nebraska Press, 2000.

———. *War and Ruin: William T. Sherman and the Savannah Campaign.* Wilmington, Del.: SR Books, 2002.

Barnard, George N. *Photographic Views of Sherman's Campaign, From Negatives Taken in the Field, by . . . Official Photographer of the Military Division of the Mississippi.* New York: Wynkoop & Hallenbeck, 1866.

Barnwell, V. T. *Barnwell's Atlanta City Directory and Stranger's Guide.* Atlanta: Intelligencer Book and Job Office, 1867.

Battles and Leaders of the Civil War. Vol. 4. New York: Yoseloff, 1956.

Benét, Stephen Vincent. *John Brown's Body.* New York: Rinehart and Co., 1927.

Bilby, Joseph G. *A Revolution in Arms: A History of the First Repeating Rifles.* Yardley, Pa.: Westholme Publishing, 2005.

Bobrick, Benson. *Master of War: The Life of General George H. Thomas.* New York: Simon & Schuster, 2009.

Boritt, Gabor, ed. *Jefferson Davis's Generals*. New York: Oxford University Press, 1999.

Boritt, Gabor, and Stephen W. Sears, eds. *Lincoln's Generals*. New York: Oxford University Press, 1994.

Boylston, Elise Reid. *Atlanta: Its Lore, Legends and Laughter*. Doraville, Ga.: Foote & Davis, 1968.

Brinsfield, John Wesley, Jr. *The Spirit Divided: Memoirs of Civil War Chaplains—The Confederacy*. Macon, Ga.: Mercer University Press, 2006.

Brown, Joseph M. *The Great Retreat: Could Johnston Have Defended Atlanta Successfully? The Policy of the Great Southern General Defended and the Field Looked Over in Light of Events. A Review of his Plan of Campaign*. Atlanta: Railroad Record Print, n.d.

———. *Marietta: The Gem City of Georgia* (1887); reprinted by Cobb Landmarks and Historical Society.

———. *The Mountain Campaigns in Georgia, or War Scenes on the W&A*. Buffalo, N.Y.: Matthews, 1886.

Brown, Russell K. *To the Manner Born: The Life of General William H. T. Walker*. Macon, Ga.: Mercer University Press, 2005.

Bryan, Thomas Conn. *Confederate Georgia*. Athens: University of Georgia Press, 1953.

Buck, Irving A. *Cleburne and His Command*. New York: Neale Publishing Co., 1908.

Buell, Thomas B. *The Warrior Generals: Combat Leadership in the Civil War*. New York: Crown, 1997.

Caldwell, Wilber W. *The Courthouse and the Depot: The Architecture of Hope in an Age of Despair*. Macon, Ga.: Mercer University Press, 2001.

Carpenter, John A. *Sword and Olive Branch: Oliver Otis Howard*. New York: Fordham University Press, 1999.

Carr, Caleb. *The Lessons of Terror: A History of Warfare Against Civilians*. New York: Random House, 2003.

Carter, Samuel III. *The Siege of Atlanta*. New York: St. Martin's Press, 1973.

Castel, Albert. *Decision in the West: The Atlanta Campaign of 1864*. Lawrence: University Press of Kansas, 1992.

———. *Winning and Losing the Civil War: Essays and Stories*. Columbia: University of South Carolina Press, 1996.

Catton, Bruce. *Grant Takes Command*. Boston: Little, Brown, 1969.

Cleaves, Freeman. *Rock of Chickamauga: The Life of General George H. Thomas*. Norman: University of Oklahoma Press, 1948; reprint, Westport, Conn.: Greenwood Press, 1974.

Connelly, Donald B. *John M. Schofield and the Politics of Generalship*. Chapel Hill: University of North Carolina Press, 2006.

Connelly, Thomas Lawrence. *Autumn of Glory: The Army of Tennessee, 1862–65*. Baton Rouge: Louisiana State University Press, 1971.

Cunningham, H. H. *Doctors in Gray: The Confederate Medical Service*. Gloucester, Mass.: Peter Smith, 1970.

Daniel, Larry J. *Cannoneers in Gray: The Field Artillery of the Army of Tennessee*. Tuscaloosa: University of Alabama Press, 1984.

———. *Days of Glory: The Army of the Cumberland, 1861–1865*. Baton Rouge: Louisiana State University Press, 2004.

———. *Soldiering in the Army of Tennessee: A Portrait of Life in a Confederate Army*. Chapel Hill: University of North Carolina Press, 2003.

Davis, Burke. *Sherman's March*. New York: Random House, 1985.

Davis, Stephen. *Atlanta Will Fall: Sherman, Joe Johnston and the Yankee Heavy Battalions*. Wilmington, Del.: SR Books, 2001.

Davis, William C. *Jefferson Davis: The Man and His Hour—A Biography*. New York: HarperCollins, 1991.

Dorsey, Allison G. *To Build Our Lives Together: Community Formation in Black Atlanta 1875–1906*. Athens: University of Georgia Press, 2004.

Doyle, Don H. *New Men, New Cities, New South: Atlanta, Nashville, Charleston, Mobile, 1860–1910*. Chapel Hill: University of North Carolina Press, 1990.

Dyer, John Percy. *The Gallant Hood*. New York: Bobbs-Merrill, 1950.

———. *From Shiloh to San Juan: The Life of "Fighting Joe" Wheeler*. Baton Rouge: Louisiana State University Press, 1992.

Dyer, Thomas G. *Secret Yankees: The Union Circle in Confederate Atlanta*. Baltimore: Johns Hopkins University Press, 1999.

Eicher, John H., and David J. Eicher. *Civil War High Commands*. Stanford, Calif.: Stanford University Press, 2001.

Einolf, Christopher J. *George Thomas: Virginian for the Union*. Norman: University of Oklahoma Press, 2007.

Elliott, Sam Davis. *Soldier of Tennessee: General Alexander P. Stewart and the Civil War in the West*. Baton Rouge: Louisiana State University Press, 2004.

Evans, David. *Sherman's Horsemen: Union Cavalry Operations in the Atlanta Campaign*. Bloomington: Indiana University Press, 1996.

Fellman, Michael. *Citizen Sherman: A Life of William Tecumseh Sherman*. New York: Random House, 1995.

Flood, Charles Bracelen. *Grant and Sherman: The Friendship That Won the Civil War*. New York: Farrar, Straus and Giroux, 2005.

Foote, Shelby. *The Civil War: A Narrative*. 3 vols. New York: Random House, 1958.

Gallagher, Gary W. *The Confederate War*. Cambridge, Mass.: Harvard University Press, 1997.

Gallagher, Gary W., and Joseph T. Glatthaar, eds. *Leaders of the Lost Cause: New Perspectives on the Confederate High Command*. Mechanicsburg, Pa.: Stackpole Books, 2004.

Galloway, Tammy Harden. *Dear Old Roswell: The Civil War Letters of the King Family of Roswell, Georgia*. Macon, Ga.: Mercer University Press, 2003.

Gardner, Sarah E. *Blood and Irony: Southern White Women's Narratives of the Civil War, 1861–1937*. Chapel Hill: University of North Carolina Press, 2003.

Garrett, Franklin M. *Atlanta and Environs: A Chronicle of Its People and Events*. 2 vols. New York, 1954.

Glatthaar, Joseph T. *The March to the Sea and Beyond: Sherman's Troops in the Savannah and Carolinas Campaigns*. New York: New York University Press, 1985.

Glover, James Bolan V et al. *Marietta 1833–2000.* Charleston: Arcadia Publishing, 1999.

Gordon, Lesley J., and John C. Inscoe, eds. *Inside the Confederate Nation: Essays in Honor of Emory M. Thomas.* Baton Rouge: Louisiana State University Press, 2005.

Govan, Gilbert E., and James W. Livingood. *A Different Valor: The Story of General Joseph E. Johnston, C.S.A.* Indianapolis: Bobbs-Merrill, 1956.

Grant, Donald L. *The Way It Was in the South: The Black Experience in Georgia.* New York: Birch Lane Press, 1993.

Grimsley, Mark. *The Hard Hand of War: Union Military Policy Toward Southern Civilians, 1861–65.* Cambridge: Cambridge University Press, 1995.

Hanson, Victor Davis. *The Soul of Battle: From Ancient Times to the Present Day, How Three Great Liberators Vanquished Tyranny.* New York: Anchor Books, 2001.

Harmetz, Aljean. *On the Road to Tara: The Making of Gone with the Wind.* Abrams, 1996.

Hart, B. H. Liddell. *Sherman: Soldier, Realist, American.* New York: DaCapo Press, 1993.

Haughton, Andrew. *Training, Tactics and Leadership in the Confederate Army of Tennessee.* Portland, Ore.: Frank Cass, 2000.

Hebert, Walter H. *Fighting Joe Hooker.* Indianapolis: Bobbs-Merrill, 1944; Lincoln: University of Nebraska Press, 1999.

Heidler, David S. and Jeanne T., eds. *Encyclopedia of the American Civil War: A Political, Social and Military History.* New York: W. W. Norton, 2000.

Hicken, Victor. *Illinois in the Civil War.* 2nd ed. Urbana: University of Illinois Press, 1991.

Hirshon, Stanley P. *The White Tecumseh: A Biography of General William T. Sherman.* New York: Wiley, 1997.

History of Service: Atlanta Fire Department Commemorative Yearbook. Atlanta: Turner Publishing, 2001.

Hoehling, A.A. *Last Train from Atlanta.* New York: T. Yoseloff, 1958.

Horn, Stanley F. *The Army of Tennessee.* Norman: University of Oklahoma Press, 1941.

Hornady, John R. *Atlanta, Yesterday, Today and Tomorrow.* [Atlanta]: American Cities Book Company, 1922.

Hughes, Nathaniel C., Jr. *General William J. Hardee: Old Reliable.* Baton Rouge: Louisiana State University Press, 1965.

Hughes, Nathaniel C., and Gordon D. Whitney. *Jefferson Davis in Blue: The Life of Sherman's Relentless Warrior.* Baton Rouge: Louisiana State University Press, 2002.

Johnston, James Houstoun. *Western and Atlantic Railroad of the State of Georgia.* Atlanta: Stein Printing Co., 1932.

Johnson, Mark W. *That Body of Brave Men: The U.S. Regular Infantry and the Civil War in the West.* New York: Da Capo Press, 2003.

Jones, Katharine M. *When Sherman Came: Southern Women and the "Great March."* Indianapolis: Bobbs-Merrill, 1964.

Joslyn, Mauriel Phillips, ed. *A Meteor Shining Brightly: Essays on the Life and Career of Major General Patrick R. Cleburne.* Macon, Ga.: Mercer University Press, 2000.

Kaufman, David R. *Peachtree Creek: A Natural and Unnatural History of Atlanta's Watershed*. Athens: University of Georgia Press, 2007.

Kennett, Lee. *Marching Through Georgia: The Story of Soldiers and Civilians During Sherman's Campaign*. New York: HarperCollins, 1996.

———. *Sherman: A Soldier's Life*. New York: HarperCollins, 2001.

Kerksis, Sydney C., ed. *The Atlanta Papers*. Dayton: Press of the Morningside Bookshop, 1980.

Key, William. *The Battle of Atlanta and the Georgia Campaign*. New York: Twayne, 1958.

Krakow, Kenneth K. *Georgia Place-Names: Their History and Origins*. 3rd ed. Macon, Ga.: Winship Press, 1975.

Kurtz, Wilbur G. *Atlanta and the Old South: Paintings and Drawings*. Atlanta: American Lithography Co., 1969.

Lambert, Gavin. *GWTW: The Making of Gone with the Wind*. Boston: Little, Brown, 1973.

Lewis, Lloyd. *Sherman: Fighting Prophet*. New York: Harcourt, Brace and Company, 1932.

Marszalek, John F. "Abraham Lincoln and William T. Sherman: The Cause Was Union," in *The Lincoln Forum: Rediscovering Abraham Lincoln*. John Y. Simon and Harold Holzer, eds. New York: Fordham University Press, 2002.

———. *Sherman: A Soldier's Passion for Order*. New York: Free Press, 1993.

———. *Sherman's March to the Sea*. Abilene, Tex.: McWhiney Foundation Press, 2005.

———. *Sherman's Other War: The General and the Civil War Press*. 2nd ed. Kent, Ohio: Kent State University Press, 1981.

Martin, Thomas H. *Atlanta and Its Builders: A Comprehensive History of the Gate City of the South*. Atlanta: Century Memorial Publishing Co., 1902.

McMurry, Richard M. *Atlanta 1864: Last Chance for the Confederacy*. Lincoln, Neb.: Bison Books, 2001.

———. *John Bell Hood and the War for Southern Independence*. Lawrence: University Press of Kansas, 1992.

———. *The Road Past Kennesaw: The Atlanta Campaign of 1864*. Washington, D.C.: National Park Service, 1972.

———. *Two Great Rebel Armies: An Essay in Confederate Military History*. Chapel Hill: University of North Carolina Press, 1996.

McPherson, James M. *Battle Cry of Freedom: The Civil War Era*. New York: Oxford University Press, 1988.

———. *For Cause and Comrades: Why Men Fought in the Civil War*. New York: Oxford University Press, 1998.

Melville, Herman. *Battle-Pieces and Aspects of the War*. New York: Harper & Bros., 1866.

Miers, Earl Schenck. *The General Who Marched to Hell: William Tecumseh Sherman and His March to Fame and Infamy*. New York: Knopf, 1951.

Miles, Jim. *Fields of Glory: A History and Tour Guide of the Atlanta Campaign*. 2nd ed. Nashville: Cumberland House, 2002.

———. *To the Sea: A History and Tour Guide of Sherman's March*. Nashville: Rutledge Hill Press, 1989.

Mitchell, Margaret. *Gone with the Wind*. New York: Macmillan, 1936.

Mohr, Clarence L. *On the Threshold of Freedom: Masters and Slaves in Civil War Georgia*. Athens: University of Georgia Press, 1986.

Morris, Roy. *Ambrose Bierce: Alone in Bad Company*. New York: Oxford University Press, 1995.

O'Briant, Don. *Looking for Tara: The Gone with the Wind Guide to Margaret Mitchell's Atlanta*. Atlanta: Longstreet Press, 1994.

Perry, James M. *Touched with Fire: Five Presidents and the Civil War Battles That Made Them*. New York: Public Affairs, 2003.

Pioneer Citizens' History of Atlanta, 1833–1902. Atlanta: Byrd Printing Co., 1902.

Pollard, Edward Alfred. *The Lost Cause: A New Southern History of the War of the Confederates*. New York: E. B. Treat & Co., 1866.

———. *Life of Jefferson Davis with a Secret History of the Southern Confederacy Gathered Behind the Scenes in Richmond*. Philadelphia: National Publishing Co., 1869.

Pyron, Darden Asbury, ed. *Recasting: Gone with the Wind in American Culture*. Miami: University Presses of Florida, 1983.

Reed, Wallace P., ed. *History of Atlanta, Georgia: With Illustrations and Biographical Sketches of Some of its Prominent Men and Pioneers*. Syracuse: D. Mason, 1889.

Reid, Whitelaw. *Ohio in the War: Her Statesmen, Her Generals, and Soldiers*. Cincinnati: Moore, Wilstach and Baldwin, 1868.

Royster, Charles. *The Destructive War: William Tecumseh Sherman, Stonewall Jackson, and the Americans*. New York: Alfred A. Knopf, 1991.

Russell, James Michael. *Atlanta, 1847–1890: City Building in the Old South and the New*. Baton Rouge: Louisiana State University Press, 1980.

Savas, Theodore P., and David A. Woodbury. *The Campaign for Atlanta and Sherman's March to the Sea: Essays on the American Civil War in Georgia, 1864*. Campbell, Calif.: Savas Woodbury, 1994.

Scaife, William R. *The Campaign for Atlanta*. Saline, Mich.: McNaughton & Gunn, 1993.

Scaife, William R., and William Harris Bragg. *Joe Brown's Pets: The Georgia Militia in the Civil War*. Macon, Ga.: Mercer University Press, 2004.

Secrist, Philip L. *Sherman's 1864 Trail of Battle to Atlanta*. Macon, Ga.: Mercer University Press, 2006.

Selznick, David O. *Memo from David O. Selznick: The Creation of "Gone with the Wind" and Other Motion Picture Classics, as Revealed in the Producer's Private Letters, Telegrams, Memorandums, and Autobiographical Remarks*. New York: Modern Library, 2000.

Sievers, Harry J. *Benjamin Harrison: Hoosier Warrior*. Chicago: H. Regnery, 1952.

Strayer, Larry M., and Richard A. Baumgartner. *Echoes of Battle: The Atlanta Campaign: An Illustrated Collection of Union and Confederate Narratives*. Huntington, W.Va.: Blue Acorn Press, 1991.

Styple, William, ed. *Generals in Bronze: Interviewing the Commanders of the Civil War*. Kearny, N.J.: Belle Grove Publishing, 2005.

Sword, Wiley. *The Confederacy's Last Hurrah: Spring Hill, Franklin and Nashville.* Lawrence: University Press of Kansas, 1993.

Symonds, Craig L. *Joseph E. Johnston: A Civil War Biography.* New York: W. W. Norton, 1992.

———. *Stonewall of the West: Patrick Cleburne and the Civil War.* Lawrence: University Press of Kansas, 1998.

Taylor, Paul. *Orlando M. Poe: Civil War General and Great Lakes Engineer.* Kent, Ohio: Kent State University Press, 2009.

Temple, Sarah Blackwell Gober. *The First Hundred Years: A Short History of Cobb County in Georgia.* Atlanta: Walter D. Brown, 1935.

Trudeau, Noah Andre. *Southern Storm: Sherman's March to the Sea.* New York: HarperCollins, 2008.

Walker, Alexander. *Vivien: The Life of Vivien Leigh.* New York: Weidenfeld and Nicolson, 1987.

Walker, Scott. *Hell's Broke Loose in Georgia: Survival in a Civil War Regiment.* Athens: University of Georgia Press, 2005.

Wallace, Lew. *Life of Gen. Ben Harrison.* Philadelphia: Hubbard Bros., 1888.

Walters, John B. *Merchant of Terror: General Sherman and Total War.* Indianapolis: Bobbs-Merrill, 1973.

Walzer, Michael. "General Sherman and the Burning of Atlanta," in *Just and Unjust Wars: A Moral Argument with Historical Illustrations.* New York: Basic Books, 2000.

Waugh, John C. *Reelecting Lincoln: The Battle for the 1864 Presidency.* New York: Crown, 1997.

Wheeler, Richard. *We Knew William Tecumseh Sherman.* New York: Crowell, 1977.

White, William Allen. *Masks in a Pageant.* New York: Macmillan, 1928.

Williams, C. S. *Williams' Atlanta Directory, City Guide and Business Mirror, Vol. 1, 1859–60.* Atlanta: M. Lynch, 1859.

Woodworth, Steven E. *Jefferson Davis and His Generals: The Failure of Confederate Command in the West.* Lawrence: University Press of Kansas, 1990.

———. *Nothing but Victory: The Army of the Tennessee, 1861–65.* New York: Knopf, 2005.

Zeller, Bob. *The Blue and Gray in Black and White.* Westport, Conn.: Praeger, 2005.

Articles and Essays

Adophson, Steven J. "An Incident of Valor in the Battle of Peach Tree Creek, 1864." *Georgia Historical Quarterly* 57 (1973), pp. 406–20.

Ambrose, Stephen. "William T. Sherman: A Reappraisal." *American History Illustrated* 1, no. 9 (Jan. 1967), pp. 5–11, 54–57.

Bernstein, Matthew. "Selznick's March: Atlanta Premiere of Gone with the Wind." *Atlanta History* 43, no. 2 (Summer 1999), pp. 7–33.

Bonds, Russell S. "Sherman's First March Through Georgia." *Civil War Times* (Aug. 2007), pp. 30–37.

———. "Pawn Takes Bishop: The Death of Lieutenant General Leonidas Polk." *Civil War Times* (May 2006), pp. 52–58.

Bower, Stephen E. "The Theology of the Battlefield: William Tecumseh Sherman and the U.S. Civil War." *Journal of Military History* 64, no. 4. (Oct. 2000), pp. 1005–34.

Bussel, Alan. "The Atlanta *Daily Intelligencer* Covers Sherman's March." *Journalism Quarterly* 51 (Autumn 1974), pp. 405–10.

Byrne, Frank J. "Rebellion and Retail: A Tale of Two Merchants in Confederate Atlanta." *Georgia Historical Quarterly* 79 (1995), pp. 30–56.

Byrne, William A. "'Uncle Billy' Sherman Comes to Town: The Free Winter of Black Savannah." *Georgia Historical Quarterly* 79 (1995), pp. 91–116.

Castel, Albert. "The Atlanta Campaign and the Presidential Election of 1864: How the South Almost Won by Not Losing," in *Winning and Losing in the Civil War: Essays and Stories*. Columbia: University of South Carolina Press, 1996, pp. 15–32.

———. "'Don't He Look Savage!': Black Jack Logan," in *Articles of War: Winners, Losers, and Some Who Were Both During the Civil War*. Mechanicsburg, Pa.: Stackpole Books, 2001, pp. 55–67.

———. "The Fall and Rise of William Tecumseh Sherman," in *Articles of War: Winners, Losers, and Some Who Were Both during the Civil War*. Mechanicsburg, Pa.: Stackpole Books, 2001, pp. 195–232.

———. "'The Heavens and Earth had Suddenly Come Together': The Battle of Peachtree Creek," in *The Campaign for Atlanta and Sherman's March to the Sea: Essays on the American Civil War in Georgia, 1864*. Campbell, Calif.: Savas Woodbury, 1994.

———. "'I Didn't Want to Get Caught Out'; or Gone with the Wind as History," in *Winning and Losing in the Civil War: Essays and Stories*. Columbia: University of South Carolina Press, 1996, pp. 79–88.

———. "In Quest of Glory: George Stoneman's Attempt to Free the Andersonville Prisoners," in *Articles of War: Winners, Losers, and Some Who Were Both During the Civil War*. Mechanicsburg, Pa.: Stackpole Books, 2001, pp. 114–24.

———. "Prevaricating Through Georgia: Sherman's Memoirs as a Source on the Atlanta Campaign," in *Winning and Losing in the Civil War: Essays and Stories*. Columbia: University of South Carolina Press, 1996, pp. 23–48.

———. "Union Fizzle at Atlanta: The Battle of Utoy Creek." *Civil War Times Illustrated* 16, no. 10 (Feb. 1978), pp. 26–31.

Catton, Bruce. "The Battle of Atlanta." *Georgia Review* 10 (1956), pp. 256–64.

Clauss, Errol MacGregor. "The Battle of Jonesborough." *Civil War Times Illustrated* (Nov. 1968), pp. 12–23.

———. "Sherman's Failure at Atlanta." *Georgia Historical Quarterly* 53 (1969), pp. 321–29.

Clower, George. "Mayor James M. Calhoun (1811–1875)." *Atlanta Historical Bulletin* 10, no. 3 (Dec. 1965), pp. 7–11.

Daniel, Larry J. "The South Almost Won by Not Losing: A Rebuttal." *North and South* 1, no. 3. (2000).

Davis, Stephen. "Another Look at Civil War Medical Care: Atlanta's Confederate Hospitals." *Journal of the Medical Association of Georgia* 88, no. 2 (April 1999), pp. 9–23.

———."The Death of Bishop Polk." *Blue & Gray* 6 (June 1989), p. 13.

———. "A Georgia Firebrand: Major General W. H. T. Walker, C.S.A." *Georgia Historical Quarterly* (1979), pp. 447–60.

———. "How Many Civilians Died in Sherman's Bombardment of Atlanta?" *Atlanta History* 45, no. 4 (2003), pp. 4–23.

———. "John Bell Hood's 'Addictions' in Civil War Literature." *Blue & Gray* 16, no. 1 (Oct. 1998), pp. 28–31.

———. "A Reappraisal of the Generalship of General John Bell Hood in the Battles for Atlanta," in *The Campaign for Atlanta and Sherman's March to the Sea: Essays on the American Civil War in Georgia, 1864*. Campbell, Calif.: Savas Woodbury, 1994, pp. 49–98.

———. "A Very Barbarous Mode of Carrying on War: Sherman' s Artillery Bombardment of Atlanta, July 20–August 24, 1864." *Georgia Historical Quarterly* 79 (1995), pp. 57–90.

Davis, William C. "The Turning Point that Wasn't: The Confederates and the Election of 1864," in *The Cause Lost: Myths and Realities of the Confederacy*. Lawrence: University Press of Kansas, 2003.

Dolzall, Gary W. "O. O. Howard's Long Road to Redemption." *America's Civil War* 14, no. 5 (Nov. 2001), p. 38ff.

Evans, David. "The Atlanta Campaign." *Civil War Times Illustrated* 28 (Summer 1989).

Ferguson, Ernest B. "Catching Up With 'Old Slow Trot'." *Smithsonian Magazine* (March 2007).

Fried, Joseph P. "How One Union General Murdered Another." *Civil War Times Illustrated* (June 1962), pp. 14–16.

Gannon, B. Anthony. "A Consistent Deist: Sherman and Religion." *Civil War History* 42, no. 4 (Dec. 1996), pp. 307–21.

Garrett, Franklin. "The Phoenix Begins to Rise: The Atlanta Daily Intelligencer Announces the Return of the Railroads." *Atlanta History* 37, no. 4 (Winter 1994), pp. 5–8.

Gibbons, Robert. "Life at the Crossroads of the Confederacy: Atlanta 1861–1865." *Atlanta Historical Journal* 23, no. 2 (Summer 1979), pp. 11–72.

Glatthaar, Joseph. "Sherman's Army and Total War: Attitudes on Destruction in the Savannah and Carolinas Campaigns." *Atlanta Historical Journal* 29, no. 1 (Spring 1985), pp. 41–52.

Harrison, John M. "The Volunteer Firemen of Atlanta." *Atlanta Historical Bulletin* 6, no. 26 (Oct. 1941), pp. 239–74.

Hartsfield, William B. "Document in Handwriting of Atlanta's War-Time Mayor Describes Formal Surrender of the City to Federal Army." *Atlanta Constitution Magazine*, May 31, 1931.

Harwell, Richard, ed. "Technical Adviser: The Making of GWTW: The Hollywood Journals of Wilbur Kurtz." *Atlanta Historical Journal* 22, no. 2 (Summer 1978).

Hess, Earl J. "Civilians at War: The Georgia Militia in the Atlanta Campaign." *Georgia Historical Quarterly* (1982), pp. 332–45.

"In Memoriam: Father Thomas O'Reilly." *Atlanta Historical Bulletin* 30 (Oct. 1945).

Ingersoll, Ernest. "The City of Atlanta." *Harper's New Monthly Magazine* 60, no. 355 (Dec. 1879), pp. 30–44.

Jones, James P. "General Jeff C. Davis, U.S.A., and Sherman's Georgia Campaign." *Georgia Historical Quarterly* (1963), pp. 231–48.

Kelly, Dennis. "Atlanta Campaign: Mountains to Pass, A River to Cross; The Battle of Kennesaw Mountain and Related Actions From June 10 to July 9, 1864." *Blue & Gray* 6 (Jun. 1989).

Killian, T. D. "James R. Crew." *Atlanta Historical Bulletin* 1, no. 6 (1932), pp. 5–14.

Kime, Marlin G. "Sherman's Gordian Knot: Logistical Problems in the Atlanta Campaign." *Georgia Historical Quarterly* 70, no. 1 (Spring 1986), pp. 102–10.

Kurtz, Wilbur G. "The 23rd Corps at Soap Creek." *Atlanta Constitution Magazine*. Oct. 26, 1930.

———. "5000 Killed in Battle of Atlanta." *Atlanta Journal Magazine*. July 27, 1941.

———."The Atlanta Campaign and Gone with the Wind." *The Red Barrel* (The Coca-Cola Company Magazine, Dec. 1939), pp. 2–9.

———. "The Augustus F. Hurt House." *Atlanta Constitution Magazine*. June 22, 1930.

———. "The Death of Major-General W. H. T. Walker, July 22, 1864." *Civil War History* 6 (1960), pp. 174–79.

———. "At the Dexter Niles House." *Atlanta Constitution Magazine*. Sept. 28, 1930.

———. "A Federal Spy in Atlanta." *Atlanta Historical Bulletin* 10 (1957), pp. 13–20.

———. "Last Battle Near Atlanta." *Atlanta Journal Magazine*. Feb. 26, 1933.

———. "Leave Atlanta Within Five Days." *Atlanta Journal Magazine*. Oct. 12, 1941.

———. "St. Luke's Baptized by War." *Atlanta Journal Magazine*. July 3, 1932.

———. "Walter Q. Gresham at Atlanta." *Atlanta Constitution*, Aug. 24, 1930.

Lack, Paul D. "Law and Disorder in Confederate Atlanta." *Georgia Historical Quarterly* 66 (1982), pp. 171–95.

Lambert, Gavin. "The Making of *Gone with the Wind*." *Atlantic Monthly*, 231, no. 2 (Feb. 1973), pp. 37–51.

Leff, Leonard J. "Gone with the Wind and Hollywood's Racial Politics." *Atlantic Monthly* 284, no. 6 (Dec. 1999), pp. 106–14.

Little, Robert D. "General Hardee and the Atlanta Campaign." *Georgia Historical Quarterly* 29 (1945), pp. 1–22.

Logue, Cal M. "Coping with Defeat Rhetorically: Sherman's March Through Georgia." *Southern Communication Journal* 58, 1 (Fall 1992), pp. 55–66.

"Lizzie's Letter." *Atlanta Journal Magazine*. April 23, 1944.

Marszalek, John M. "Sherman Called It the Way He Saw It." *Civil War History* 40, no. 1 (March 1994), pp. 72–78.

———. "Celebrity in Dixie: Sherman Tours the South, 1879." *Georgia Historical Quarterly* 66 (1982), pp. 366–83.

McMurry, Richard M. "The Atlanta Campaign: A New Look." *Civil War History* 22 (March 1976): pp. 5–15.

———. "Confederate Morale in the Atlanta Campaign." *Georgia Historical Quarterly* 54 (1970), pp. 226–43.

———. "The Enemy at Richmond: Joseph E. Johnston and the Confederate Government." *Civil War History* 27 (March 1981), pp. 5–31.

———. "The Mackall Journal and Its Antecedents." *Civil War History* 20 (1974), pp. 311–28.

———. "More on Raw Courage." *Civil War Times Illustrated* (October 1975), pp. 36–38.

———. "A Policy So Disastrous: Joseph E. Johnston's Atlanta Campaign," in *The Campaign for Atlanta & Sherman's March to the Sea: Essays on the American Civil War in Georgia, 1864*. Campbell, Calif.: Savas Woodbury, 1994, pp. 223–48.

McNeill, William J. "A Survey of Confederate Soldier Morale During Sherman's Campaign Through Georgia and the Carolinas." *Georgia Historical Quarterly* 55 (1971), pp. 1–25.

McPherson, James M. "Two Strategies of Victory: William T. Sherman in the Civil War." *Atlanta History* 33, no. 4 (Winter 1990), pp. 5–17.

McWhirter, Cameron. "Sherman Still Burns Atlanta." *Atlanta Journal-Constitution*. May 7, 2004.

Merrill, James M. "Personne Goes to Georgia: Five Civil War Letters." *Georgia Historical Quarterly* 43 (1959), pp. 202–11.

Mitchell, Stephens. "Colonel L. P. Grant and the Defenses of Atlanta." *Atlanta Historical Bulletin* 1, no. 6 (1932), pp. 32–34.

Peake, Peveral H. "Why the South Hates Sherman." *American Mercury* (Aug. 1937), pp. 441–48.

Pearl, Daniel. "Pariah in the South, William T. Sherman's Getting a Makeover." *Wall Street Journal*, June 9, 1993, pp. A1, A5.

Phillips, Jason. "The Grape Vine Telegraph: Rumors and Confederate Persistence." *Journal of Southern History* 72, no. 4 (2006).

Robbins, Peggy. "Hood vs. Sherman: A Duel of Words." *Civil War Times Illustrated* (July 1978), pp. 22–29.

Rowe, Walter F. "The Case of the Lying Photographs: The Civil War Photography of George N. Barnard." *Journal of Forensic Sciences* 28, no. 3 (July 1983), pp. 735–55.

Russell, James Michael. "The Phoenix City After the Civil War: Atlanta's Economic Miracle." *Atlanta History* 33, no. 4 (Winter 1990), pp. 18–28.

Scaife, William. "The Chattahoochee River Line: An American Maginot?" *North and South*. 1, no. 1 (Nov. 1997).

Secrist, Philip L. "Jefferson Davis and the Atlanta Campaign: A Study in Confederate Command." *Atlanta Historical Bulletin* 17 (Fall–Winter 1972).

———. "Prelude to the Atlanta Campaign: The Davis-Bragg-Johnston Controversy." *Atlanta Historical Bulletin* 17 (Spring–Summer 1972).

Shanks, W. F. G. "Fighting Joe Hooker." *Harper's New Monthly Magazine* 31, no. 185 (Oct. 1865), pp. 639–45.

———. "Gossip About Our Generals." *Harper's New Monthly Magazine* 35, no. 206 (July 1867), pp. 210–15.

———. "Recollections of General Sherman." *Harper's New Monthly Magazine* 30, no. 179 (April 1865), pp. 640–46.

———. "Recollections of General Thomas." *Harper's New Monthly Magazine* 30, no. 180 (May 1865), pp. 754–59.

Smalley, E. V. "General Sherman." *Century Magazine* 27, no. 3 (Jan. 1884), pp. 450–62.

Smith, John Robert. "The Day Atlanta Was Occupied." *Atlanta Historical Bulletin* 21 (Fall 1977), pp. 61–70.

Strong, William E. "The Death of General James B. McPherson." *Military Essays and Recollections. MOLLUS–Illinois* (Chicago: A. C. McClurg & Co., 1891), vol. 1, pp. 311–44.

Sweat, Edward. "Free Blacks in Antebellum Atlanta." *Atlanta Historical Bulletin* 21, no. 1 (Spring 1977), pp. 64–71.

Symonds, Craig L. "Johnston's Toughest Fight." *MHQ: Quarterly Journal of Military History* 16 (Winter 2004), pp. 56–61.

Thomas, Edison H. "The Night They Burned the Train." *L&N Railroad Magazine* (Sept. 1964), pp. 18–19.

Thornton, Ella Mae. "Mr. S. P. Richards." *Atlanta Historical Bulletin* 3 (Dec. 1937), pp. 73–79.

Vetter, Charles E. "From Atlanta to Savannah: A Sociological Perspective of William T. Sherman's March Through Georgia," in *The Campaign for Atlanta and Sherman's March to the Sea: Essays on the American Civil War in Georgia, 1864*. Campbell, Calif.: Savas Woodbury, 1994, pp. 375–410.

Wicker, Tom. "Why, Miss Scarlett, How Well You've Aged." *New York Times Book Review* (May 25, 1986).

Wiley, Bell Irvin. "A Story of Three Southern Officers." *Civil War Times Illustrated* 3, no. 1 (April 1964), pp. 6–9, 28–34

Atlases, Maps, and Official Reports

Atlanta, from Vincent's Subdivision Map, published by the City Council, Drawn and printed at Topl. Engr. Office, H.Q. A.C., in the field, July 25th, 1864. Hargrett Rare Map Collection, University of Georgia.

Atlas to Accompany the Official Records of the Union and Confederate Armies. Washington: Government Printing Office, 1891–95.

Birds-eye map of the Western & Atlantic R.R., the great Kennesaw Route from Atlanta to the north and north-west, 1864. New York: Fleming, Brewster & Alley (July 1887). Library of Congress.

Blakeslee, G. H. *Map of the Environs of Pine Mountain, Lost Mountain, Kenesaw Mountain, and Little Kenesaw Mountain*, June 2–22, 1864. Library of Congress.

Civil War Centennial: City of Atlanta: Showing the area of the three major engagements and deployment of Union and Confederate Forces during the summer of 1864. Prepared by State Highway Department of Georgia, Division of Highway Planning (1964). Library of Congress.

Drummond, William J. *3D Battlefield Images from the Siege of Atlanta*. City Planning Department, College of Architecture, Georgia Institute of Technology, Atlanta. http://civilwar.gatech.edu/siege/.

Kurtz, Wilbur G. "Embattled Atlanta." *Atlanta Constitution*. July 20, 1930.

Map of the country embracing the various routes surveyed for the Western & Atlantic Rail Road of Georgia, under the direction of Lieut. Col. S. H. Long, Chief Engineer. U.S. Topographical Bureau (1837). Library of Congress Geography and Map Division, Washington, D.C.

Minutes of Meetings of the Atlanta City Council, 1864. Atlanta History Center.

Poe, Orlando. *Map illustrating the Siege of Atlanta, Ga. by the U.S. Forces, under Command of Maj. Gen. W.T. Sherman from the passage of Peach Tree Creek, July 19th 1864 to the commencement of the movement upon the Enemy's Lines of communication south of Atlanta, August 26, 1864.*

Scaife, William R. *Atlas of Atlanta Area Civil War Battles*. By the author, 1982.

Sneden, Robert Knox. *Atlanta, Georgia and its Rebel Defences*. Library of Congress.

The War of the Rebellion: A Compilation of the Official Records of the Union and Confederate Armies. 128 vols. Washington, D.C.: Government Printing Office 1880–1901.

Newspapers

Atlanta Constitution
Atlanta Daily Intelligencer
Atlanta Journal
(Atlanta) Southern Confederacy
Augusta Daily Chronicle and Sentinel
Augusta Daily Constitutionalist
Cincinnati Commercial
Cincinnati Gazette
Dublin (Ga.) Post
Harper's Weekly
Knoxville Register
Macon Daily Telegraph
Memphis Daily Appeal
Mobile Daily Advertiser and Register
Montgomery Daily Advertiser
New York Herald
New York Times
New York Tribune
New York World
Richmond Daily Dispatch
Richmond Enquirer
Richmond Whig
Savannah Republican
Toledo Blade

INDEX

ACKNOWLEDGMENTS

I owe much to many. First, I acknowledge my debt to the many authors who have gone before, especially the late, great historians of Atlanta, Franklin W. Garrett and Wilbur G. Kurtz, Sr. Among more recent historians, I benefited greatly from the work of Stephen Davis, Albert Castel, Richard McMurry, Lee Kennett, David Evans, and Steven E. Woodworth; the credit I give to them in the notes seems inadequate to acknowledge the extent of their contributions to our understanding of the war in Georgia. Dr. Gordon Jones at the Atlanta History Center offered kind encouragement and helped to steer this project in its early stages; I very much appreciate his friendship and advice. I am also grateful to the staffs of the Kenan Research Center Library at the Atlanta History Center; the Archives at the Robert W. Woodruff Library at Emory University; and the Cobb County Public Library.

My good friend and mentor John H. Fleming shared the previously unpublished letters of his Union ancestor, Ohio surgeon S. B. Crew, who added an insightful voice to the memory of the campaign. Sam Hood answered a number of questions about his ancestor John Bell Hood and helped to shape my perception of Old Pegleg. Paul Taylor, the author of an excellent forthcoming biography on Orlando M. Poe, answered my questions on Sherman's engineer and shared copies of Captain Poe's letters to his wife in August and September 1864. Phil Mooney, archivist and Director of Heritage Communications at The Coca-Cola Company, gave warm encouragement and helped track down a useful article from an old Company magazine. David Wynn Vaughan answered my questions on Civil War photography and provided rare images from his incomparable collection.

Various Civil War scholars gave generous assistance as well. University of West Georgia Professor Keith Bohannon shared elusive newspapers sources as well as a copy of his fall 2008 lecture at Kennesaw Mountain, and answered various questions along the way. Professor William Drummond of Georgia Tech met with me to discuss the lost battlefields of Atlanta, and his GIS technology and views of the urban landscape greatly informed my understanding of what happened where.

At Kennesaw Mountain National Battlefield Park, Rangers W. R. Johnson and Retha Stephens, as well as Mike Stoudemire and Clay Melvin of the Kennesaw Mountain Historical Association, provided helpful guidance and support. Civil War author, blogger, and medical expert James Schmidt answered questions regarding John Bell Hood's amputation. John Fox, Mike Peters, Eric Wittenberg, David Woodbury, and J. D. Petruzzi offered help and encouragement at various points along the way. Thank you, gentlemen.

And a special word of thanks to Charlie Crawford, president of the Georgia Battlefields Association, for his direction as a guide, for his detailed maps that helped me to develop some of the battle maps in this book, and for his answers to my questions about the campaign and the commanders involved. Charlie's suggestions on the manuscript were invaluable.

At Westholme, publisher Bruce H. Franklin was accessible, encouraging, inspiring, and as always a great collaborator. Thanks, Bruce, for the canvas and the paint. Copyeditor Noreen O'Connor did an excellent job and improved the manuscript throughout. Tracy Dungan crafted the maps to help make sense of my tangled tactical talk. John Hubbard created the beautiful and evocative design, again making me hopeful that readers would judge the book by its cover.

Joe Kirby and Jane Thorpe read chapters and offered suggestions that greatly improved the manuscript. I am grateful for their time and most of all for their friendship. My friend and fellow author Michael J. Kline was there all along on this one; thanks, Mike. Other close friends and colleagues encouraged me along the way, including Ann and Tom Curvin, Christine and Ted Scartz, Todd Grice, Livingstone Johnson, Mary Williams, Anthony Cabrera, John Packman, Vail Thorne, Ben Garren, Elizabeth Finn Johnson, and my neighbors on Taylors Court. My manager Joel Neuman was generous and supportive throughout.

My deepest debts, of course, are to my family. My mother, Nancy Bonds, is at the same time my sharpest proofreader, most effective salesperson, and greatest fan—thanks, Mom, for everything. My sister Holly was enthusiastic and supportive as well. To my children, Caroline, Sophie, and Ava, I offer my love and heartfelt thanks—and more of my time and attention, I promise. Finally, and most of all, I am grateful to my wife, Jill, for her amazing support of this demanding project. Her love and encouragement is something that I can never repay, though I will surely try.